PEARSON CUSTOM BUSINESS RESOURCES

Compiled by

DePaul University

FIN 310 FINANCIAL MANAGEMENT

Special Edition

Pearson Learning Solutions

New York   Boston   San Francisco
London   Toronto   Sydney   Tokyo   Singapore   Madrid
Mexico City   Munich   Paris   Cape Town   Hong Kong   Montreal

Senior Vice President, Editorial and Marketing: Patrick F. Boles
Associate Editor: Ana Díaz-Caneja
Development Editor: Abbey Lee Briggs
Marketing Manager: Jack Cooney
Operations Manager: Eric M. Kenney
Production Manager: Jennifer Berry
Rights Manager: Jillian Santos
Art Director: Renée Sartell
Cover Designer: Renée Sartell

Cover Art: Courtesy of EyeWire/Getty Images and PhotoDisc/Getty Images. Photodisc, "Globe surrounded by business people on computer monitors," courtesy of Photodisc/Getty Images. Dave Cutler (Artist), "Man Dropping Coins Into Glass Jar,"courtesy of David Cutler/Images.com. Dave Cutler (Artist), "Three Coins in Glass Jar," courtesy of David Cutler/Images.com. Dean Turner, "Stock Vector: Global Finance" Courtesy of Dean Turner/iStockphoto. Hal Bergman, "Refinery Silhouette" Courtesy of Hal Bergman/iStockphoto. Dan Barnes, "Cargo Container Ship Aerial View" Courtesy of Dan Barnes/iStockphoto. Franc Podgorsek, "Stock Numbers" Courtesy of Franc Podgorsek/iStockphoto. "Customer in Line at Grocery Store" Courtesy of Digital Vision Photography/Veer Inc. Owaki-Kulla, "Pumping Gas" Courtesy of Flirt Photography/Veer Inc. Lynn Johnson, "Yunnan Province, People's Republic of China" Courtesy of Lynn Johnson/Getty Images, Inc. Thomas Bendy, "Student Typing" Courtesy of Thomas Bendy/iStockphoto.

This special edition published in cooperation with Pearson Learning Solutions.

Printed in the United States of America.

Please visit our web site at *www.pearsoncustom.com.*

Attention bookstores: For permission to return any unsold stock, contact us at *pearsonscustomreturns@pearson.com.*

Pearson Learning Solutions, 501 Boylston Street, Suite 900, Boston, MA 02116
A Pearson Education Company
www.pearsoned.com

ISBN 10: 0-558-72612-7
ISBN 13: 978-0-558-72612-6

Editorial Advisory Board

Contents

Chapter 1

Financial Economics

OBJECTIVES

- Define finance.
- Explain why finance is worth studying.
- Introduce two of the main players in the world of finance—households and firms—and the kinds of financial decisions they make.

CONTENTS

From Chapter 1 of *Financial Economics*, 2/e. Zvi Bodie, Robert C. Merton, David L. Cleeton.
Copyright © 2008 by Pearson Prentice Hall. All rights reserved.

3

- You have started to save for the future and all of your savings are in a bank account. Should you invest in mutual funds? What kind of mutual funds?
- You have decided to get a car. Should you buy it or lease it?
- You worked as a waiter during your college years and are thinking about starting your own restaurant when you graduate. Is it worth doing? How much money do you need to start? Where can you get the money?
- You are advising the chief financial officer (CFO) of a major computer manufacturer whether to expand into the telecommunications business. It is expected to cost $3 billion over the next few years to enter the business, and the expected benefits are increased profits of $1 billion per year thereafter. What do you recommend?
- You are part of a team working at the World Bank analyzing an application for a loan to a small country in Latin America to finance a major hydroelectric project. How do you decide what to recommend?

These are all examples of financial decisions. This book will provide you with a way of addressing these and similar questions by exploring the basic principles of finance. In this chapter we define finance and consider why it is worth studying; then we introduce the main players in the world of finance—households and firms—and the kinds of financial decisions they make.

1 Defining Finance

Finance is the study of how people allocate scarce resources *over time*. Two features that distinguish financial decisions from other resource allocation decisions are that the costs and benefits of financial decisions are (1) spread out over time and (2) usually not known with certainty in advance by either the decision makers or anybody else. In deciding whether to start your own restaurant, for example, you must weigh the *costs* (such as the investment in fixing up the place and buying the stoves, tables, chairs, little paper umbrellas for exotic drinks, and other equipment you need) against the uncertain *benefits* (your future profits) that you expect to reap over several years.

In implementing their decisions people make use of the **financial system,** defined as *the set of markets and other institutions used for financial contracting and the exchange of assets and risks.* The financial system includes the markets for stocks, bonds, and other financial instruments; financial intermediaries (such as banks and insurance companies); financial service firms (such as financial advisory firms); and the regulatory bodies that govern all of these institutions. The study of how the financial system evolves over time is an important part of the subject matter of finance.

Finance theory consists of a set of concepts that help you to organize your thinking about how to allocate resources over time and a set of quantitative models to help you evaluate alternatives, make decisions, and implement them. The same basic concepts and quantitative models apply at all levels of decision making, from your decision to lease a car or to start a business, to the decision of the CFO of a major corporation to enter the telecommunications business, to the decision of the World Bank about which development projects to finance.

A basic tenet of finance is that the ultimate function of the system is to satisfy people's *consumption preferences,* including all the basic necessities of life, such as food, clothing, and shelter. Economic organizations such as firms and governments exist in order to facilitate the achievement of that ultimate function.

2 Why Study Finance?

There are at least five good reasons to study finance:

- to manage your personal resources.
- to deal with the world of business.
- to pursue interesting and rewarding career opportunities.
- to make informed public choices as a citizen.
- to expand your mind.

Let us elaborate on each of these reasons one at a time.

First, knowing some finance helps you to manage your own resources. Can you get along without knowing anything about finance? Perhaps. But if you are completely ignorant, then you are at the mercy of others. Remember the old adage: "A fool and his money are soon parted."

In some cases you will seek the help of experts. There are many finance professionals and financial service firms that provide financial advice—bankers, stockbrokers, insurance brokers, and firms selling mutual funds and other financial products and services. Often the advice is "free" if you are a potential customer. But how do you evaluate the advice you are given? The study of finance provides a conceptual framework for doing so.

A second reason to study finance is that a basic understanding of finance is essential in the business world. Even if you do not intend to specialize in finance, you must have a sufficient understanding of the concepts, techniques, and terminology employed by finance specialists to communicate with them and to recognize the limits of what they can do for you.

Box 1 | **Job Opportunities in Financial Engineering**

At the prestigious Ecole Polytechnique in Paris, mathematics professor Nicole El Karoui continues to lead the way in teaching the modeling of derivatives to future quantitative analysts. Professor El Karoui has been instrumental in providing knowledge on derivatives through classes in financial mathematics. Her students are highly sought after by the world's top investment banks for their understanding of these increasingly important financial instruments.

Derivatives—financial contracts that derive their values from the performance of an underlying asset—were once used primarily as a hedge for banks against market risk. In the past, investment banks made most of their profits from underwriting and trading stocks and bonds in addition to providing financial advice. Presently, around 30% of their stock-related revenue comes from derivatives. Professor El Karoui's classes teach the necessary skill for students to become competitive in working in the service-sector firms driven by much of the demand caused by this change in investment structure.

El Karoui first became interested in modeling derivatives during a six-month sabbatical she spent working at a consumer credit bank. She noticed that employees in the derivatives department experienced problems similar to those facing students of stochastic calculus—the study of the impact of random variation over time. When she returned to teaching she implemented a postgraduate mathematical finance program, meeting the growing demand for understanding of derivatives among banks. Professor El Karoui's students are eagerly sought after by recruiters for their technical skills, which enable them to understand the underlying behavior of derivatives. These core quantitative skills have come to constitute an integral part of the work of investment bankers.

Source: "Why Students of Prof. El Karoui Are in Demand," *Wall Street Journal,* March 9, 2006.

> ## Box 2 — Debt Finance in Higher Education, University Bonds
>
> Universities across the country are realizing the financing potential of issuing debt in order to raise money for operations and investment. For many years colleges have entrusted financial planners to manage their endowment funds, and now several wealthier schools have shown an increased eagerness to raise money by issuing bonds. In 2006, an estimated $33 billion was raised in the initial issue market for higher-education debt, and this figure is expected to rise rapidly in the future.
>
> Public and not-for-profit private institutions can issue tax-free debt—due to their nonprofit status—and invest this money in high-yield markets. This strategy has been shown to be extremely profitable, aided by the fact that public and not-for-profit private universities are also exempt from taxes on the investment earnings produced. In turn, universities can use these expanded resources to help build new facilities, such as stadiums, athletic facilities, and theaters—all in high demand by incoming students. It is likely that as students continue to expect top-notch facilities in their universities, schools will continue to finance a significant portion of their operations by issuing more bonds.
>
> *Source:* "An Education in Finance," *The Economist*, May 18, 2006.

Third, you may be interested in a career in finance. There are varied and potentially rewarding career opportunities in the field of finance and many possible paths you can follow as a finance professional. Most finance professionals are employed in the financial services sector of the economy—such as banking, insurance, or investment management. However, many others work as financial managers in nonfinancial firms or in government. Some even pursue academic careers.

Households, businesses, and government agencies often seek the advice of financial consultants. Moreover, a background in finance provides a good foundation for a career in general management. Many of the chief executives of major corporations around the world started in finance.

Fourth, to make informed public choices as a citizen, you should have a basic understanding of how the financial system works. The financial system is an important part of the infrastructure of any market-oriented society. Indeed, a sound set of financial institutions is believed by many to be an essential element in economic growth and development. As citizens we sometimes must make political choices that affect the functioning of the financial system. For example, do you want to vote for a political candidate who favors abolishing government deposit insurance or one who would impose strict controls on stock-market trading?

Fifth, finance can be a fascinating field of study on purely intellectual grounds. It expands your understanding of how the real world works. The scientific study of finance has a long history. Adam Smith's *The Wealth of Nations*, published in 1776, is widely regarded as the beginning of the science of economics. Finance theorists today are generally economists specializing in financial economics. Indeed, in 1990 and again in 1997, the Nobel Prize in economics was awarded to scholars for their scientific contributions in the field of finance (see Box 3).

3 Financial Decisions of Households

Most households are families. Families come in many forms and sizes. At one extreme is the *extended family,* which consists of several generations living together under one roof and sharing their economic resources. At the other extreme is the single person living

Box 3 — Nobel Prize in Economics for Work in Finance

In 1990 the Nobel Prize in economics was awarded to three scholars—Harry Markowitz, Merton Miller, and William Sharpe—for scientific contributions that have had a powerful impact on both the theory and practice of finance. Let us briefly explain their contributions.

Harry Markowitz is the father of modern portfolio theory, the scientific study of how to trade off risk and reward in choosing among risky investments. In his seminal article, "Portfolio Selection," which appeared in the *Journal of Finance* in 1952, he developed a mathematical model showing how investors could achieve the lowest possible risk for any given target rate of return. The Markowitz model has been incorporated into basic finance theory and is widely used by practicing investment managers.

William Sharpe took Markowitz's results as his starting point and developed their implications for asset prices. By adding the assumption that at all times asset prices will adjust to equate demand and supply for each risky asset, he showed that a very specific structure must exist among the expected rates of return on risky assets ("Capital Asset Prices: A Theory of Market Equilibrium under Conditions of Risk," *Journal of Finance,* 1964). The structure suggested by Sharpe's theory is widely used today as the basis for making risk adjustments in many areas of finance theory and practice.

Merton Miller has contributed mainly to the theory of corporate finance. He and Franco Modigliani (an earlier recipient of the Nobel Prize in economics) addressed the dividend and borrowing policies of firms in a series of articles, starting with "The Cost of Capital, Corporation Finance, and the Theory of Investment," which appeared in the *American Economic Review* in 1958. Their fundamental contribution was to focus the attention of theorists and practitioners of finance on how corporate dividend and financing policies affect the total value of a firm. The M&M (Modigliani-Miller) propositions developed in their joint papers are among the basic building blocks of modern corporate finance.

Again in 1997 the Nobel Prize in economics was awarded to financial economists. The laureates were Robert C. Merton (one of the authors of this textbook) and Myron Scholes. The prize committee also mentioned a third scholar, Fischer Black, whose untimely death in 1995 at age 57 made him ineligible to share the prize. These three men discovered a mathematical formula for the pricing of options and other derivative securities that has had an enormous impact on both the theory and practice of finance. It is generally known as the Black-Scholes option pricing formula.

alone, whom most people wouldn't think of as a "family." In finance, however, all are classified as households.

Households face four basic types of financial decisions:

- *Consumption and saving decisions:* How much of their current wealth should they spend on consumption and how much of their current income should they save for the future?
- *Investment decisions:* How should they invest the money they have saved?
- *Financing decisions:* When and how should households use other people's money to implement their consumption and investment plans?
- *Risk-management decisions:* How and on what terms should households seek to reduce the financial uncertainties they face or when should they increase their risks?

As a result of saving part of their income for use in the future, people accumulate a pool of wealth, which can be held in any number of different forms. One form is bank accounts, another might be a piece of real estate or a share in a business venture. All of these are **assets.** *An asset is anything that has economic value.*

When people choose how to hold their pool of accumulated savings, it is called *personal investing* or **asset allocation.** In addition to investing in their own homes, people will often choose to invest in financial assets, such as stocks or bonds.

<table>
<tr><td>Box 4</td><td>New Trends in the Market for College Loans</td></tr>
</table>

Private student loans have become a growing, lucrative segment of consumer finance. Their profitability is derived from the relatively high interest rates they carry and the continually increasing demand generated by a growing number of students financing college tuition. Unlike federal loans, private loans can earn revenue by charging market rates in addition to up-front fees. These fees, which make private loans so rewarding for investors, can constitute 6% to 7% of the total amount of the loan. Furthermore, tuition increases around the country, combining with a growing number of baby boomers' children attending colleges, are the main factors that underlie a strong demand for student loans. Not only do college costs continue to rise, but federal aid in the form of grants and loans has remaining stagnant—and in many cases actually declined. The gap between the higher price of an education and the ability of families to pay is widening; private student loans have come to fill this gap.

Private loans, packaged by lenders such as Sallie Mae, have recently exploded in popularity, currently capturing 22% of the volume of federal student loans, up from 5% in 1994–1995. They are being praised as the fastest-growing and most profitable segment of consumer finance, with a total of $13.8 billion in student loans in the 2004–2005 school year—with the expectation of a further doubling within the following three years. As the number of college students continues to increase along with their tuitions, the private student loan industry is expected to maintain its strong record of growth.

Source: "Thanks to the Banks," *The Economist,* February 16, 2006.

When people borrow, they incur a **liability,** which is just another word for debt. A household's wealth or **net worth** is measured by the value of its assets minus its liabilities. Say you own a house worth $100,000 and have a $20,000 bank account. You also owe $80,000 to the bank on your home mortgage loan (a liability) and have a $5,000 credit card debt outstanding. Your net worth is $35,000: your total assets ($120,000) minus your total liabilities ($85,000). Ultimately, all of society's resources belong to households because they own the firms (either directly or through their ownership of shares of stock, pension plans, or life insurance policies) and pay the taxes spent by governments.

Finance theory treats people's consumption preferences as given. Although preferences may change over time, how and why they change is not addressed by the theory.[1] People's behavior is explained as an attempt to satisfy those preferences. The behavior of firms and governments is viewed from the perspective of how it affects the welfare of people.

Quick Check 1

What are the four basic types of financial decisions households have to make? Give an example of each.

---

4 Financial Decisions of Firms

By definition, business firms—or simply firms—are entities whose primary function is to produce goods and services. Like households, firms come in many different shapes and sizes. At the one extreme are small workshops, retail outlets, and restaurants owned by a

---

[1]Elements of a theory that are not explained by the theory itself are called *exogenous.* In contrast, those elements that are explained by the theory are called *endogenous.* In finance, people's preferences are exogenous to the theory, but the objectives of firms are endogenous.

single individual or family. At the other extreme are giant corporations, such as Mitsubishi or General Motors, with a workforce of hundreds of thousands of people and an even greater number of owners. The branch of finance dealing with financial decisions of firms is called *business finance* or *corporate finance.*

In order to produce goods and services, all firms—small and large—need *capital.* The buildings, machinery, and other intermediate inputs used in the production process are called *physical capital.* The stocks, bonds, and loans used to finance the acquisition of the physical capital are called *financial capital.*

The first decision any firm must make is what businesses it wants to be in. This is called *strategic planning.* Because strategic planning involves the evaluation of costs and benefits spread out over time, it is largely a financial decision-making process.

Often a firm will have a core business defined by its main product line, and it may branch out into related lines of business. For example, a firm that produces computer hardware may also choose to produce the software. It may also choose to service computers.

A firm's strategic goals may change over time, sometimes quite dramatically. Some corporations enter into businesses that are seemingly unrelated to each other. They may even abandon their original core business altogether so that the company's name ceases to have any connection with its current business.

For example, ITT Corporation started out as a telephone company in 1920. Its name stood for International Telephone and Telegraph. In the 1970s ITT became a large multinational conglomerate, operating a diverse set of businesses including insurance, munitions, hotels, bakeries, automobile rentals, mining, forest products, and gardening products in addition to telecommunications. During the 1980s, ITT shed many of its businesses and focused on operating hotels and casinos. By 1996 it had abandoned its original core business of producing telephone equipment and telecommunication services.

Once a firm's managers have decided what businesses they are in, they must prepare a plan for acquiring factories, machinery, research laboratories, showrooms, warehouses, and other such long-lived assets and for training the personnel who will operate them all. This is the *capital budgeting process.*

The basic unit of analysis in capital budgeting is an *investment project.* The process of capital budgeting consists of identifying ideas for new investment projects, evaluating them, deciding which ones to undertake, and then implementing them.

Once a firm has decided what projects it wants to undertake, it must figure out how to finance them. Unlike capital budgeting decisions, the unit of analysis in *capital structure* decisions is *not* the individual investment project but the firm as a whole. The starting point in making capital structure decisions is determining a feasible financing plan for the firm. Once a feasible financing plan has been achieved, the issue of the optimal financing mix can be addressed.

Firms can issue a wide range of financial instruments and claims. Some are standardized securities that can be traded in organized markets, such as common stock, preferred stock, bonds, and convertible securities. Others are nonmarketable claims, such as bank loans, employee stock options, leases, and pension liabilities.

A corporation's capital structure determines who gets what share of its future cash flows. For example, bonds promise fixed cash payments, whereas stocks pay the residual value left over after all other claimants have been paid. Capital structure also partially determines who gets to control the company. In general, shareholders have control through their right to elect the board of directors. But often bonds and other loans include contractual provisions, called *covenants,* restricting the activities of management. These covenant restrictions give the creditors some control over the company's affairs.

Working capital management is extremely important to the success of a firm. The best long-term plans can go away if the firm's management does not attend to the day-to-day

9

financial affairs of the business. Even in a growing, successful firm, cash flows in and out may not match up exactly in time. Managers must worry about collecting from customers, paying bills as they come due, and generally managing the firm's cash flow to ensure that operating cash-flow deficits are financed and that cash-flow surpluses are efficiently invested to earn a good return.

The choices that a firm makes in all areas of financial decision making—investment, financing, and working capital management—depend on its technology and on the specific regulatory, tax, and competitive environment in which it operates. The policy choices are also highly interdependent.

Quick Check 2

What are the basic types of financial decisions firms have to make? Give an example of each.

5 Forms of Business Organization

There are three basic types of organizational form for a firm: a sole proprietorship, a partnership, and a corporation. A **sole proprietorship** is a firm owned by an individual or a family, in which the assets and liabilities of the firm are the personal assets and liabilities of the proprietor. A sole proprietor has *unlimited liability* for the debts and other liabilities of the firm. This means that if the firm cannot pay its debts, the proprietor's other personal assets can be seized to satisfy the demands of the firm's creditors.

Many firms start out as sole proprietorships and then change their organizational form as they become established and expand. But frequently a business such as a restaurant, a real estate agency, or a small workshop will remain a sole proprietorship throughout its existence.

A **partnership** is a firm with two or more owners, called the partners, who share the equity in the business. A partnership agreement usually stipulates how decisions are to be made and how profits and losses are to be shared. Unless otherwise specified, all partners have unlimited liability as in the sole proprietorship.

However, it is possible to limit the liability for some partners called *limited partners.* At least one of the partners, called the general partner, has unlimited liability for the debts of the firm. Limited partners typically do not make the day-to-day business decisions of the partnership; the general partner does.

Unlike a sole proprietorship or a partnership, a **corporation** is a firm that is a legal entity distinct from its owners. Corporations can own property, borrow, and enter into contracts. They can sue and be sued. They are usually taxed according to rules that differ from the rules that apply to the other forms of business organization.

The charter of a corporation sets down the rules that govern it. Shareholders are entitled to a share of any distributions from the corporation (e.g., cash dividends) in proportion to the number of shares they own. The shareholders elect a *board of directors,* which in turn selects managers to run the business. Usually there is one vote per share, but sometimes there are different classes of stocks with different voting rights.

An advantage of the corporate form is that ownership shares can usually be transferred without disrupting the business. Another advantage is *limited liability,* which means that if the corporation fails to pay its debts, the creditors can seize the assets of the corporation but have no recourse to the personal assets of the shareholders. In that sense a corporation serves the same function as a general partner in a partnership, and its shareholders are like limited partners.

Box 5	How to Identify That a Firm Is a Corporation

In the United States, corporations are identified by the letters *Inc.* after their name. It stands for the English word *incorporated*. In France the letters are *SA* (Societé Anonime); in Italy *SpA* (Societa per Azioni); in the Netherlands *NV* (Naamloze Vennootschap); and in Sweden *AB* (Aktiebolag).

In Germany, public corporations are called Aktienge-sellschaften, identifiable by the letters *AG* after the company name, whereas private corporations are Gesellschaften mit beschränkter Haftung, denoted by *GmbH*. The parallel designations in the United Kingdom are *PLC* for public limited company, and *LTD* for private corporations.

The earliest known corporations were formed in Amsterdam and in London in the 1600s and were called *joint stock companies* in English. That term has fallen into disuse.

Around the world, large firms are almost always organized as corporations, although ownership of the corporation may be restricted to a single person or family. In the United States, corporations with broadly dispersed ownership are called *public corporations;* those with concentrated ownership are called *private corporations.*

Laws governing the corporate form of organization differ in their details from country to country, and even within a country they may differ from one jurisdiction to another. In the United States, for example, laws governing corporations are created and administered at the state level (see Box 5).

Quick Check 3

A corporation owned by a single person is not a sole proprietorship. Why?

6 Separation of Ownership and Management

In sole proprietorships and even in many partnerships the owners and the active managers of the business are the same people. But in many firms, especially the large ones, the owners do not themselves manage the business. Instead they delegate that responsibility to professional managers, who may not own any shares in the business. There are at least five reasons for the owners of a firm to turn over the running of the business to others to manage.

First, professional managers may be found who have a superior ability to run the business. This may be because the professional managers have better technological knowledge, more experience, or a more suitable personality to run the business. In a structure in which the owner is also the manager, the owner must have both the talents of a manager and the financial resources necessary to carry out production. In the separated structure, no such coincidence is required.

For example, consider the entertainment industry. The people most qualified to manage a film studio or a television network may not have the financial resources to own the business, and the people with the wealth to own such a business may have no ability to manage it. Therefore, it makes sense for the managerially competent people to produce and distribute the movies and for the wealthy people to simply provide the capital.

Second, to achieve the efficient scale of a business the resources of many households may have to be pooled. For example, the cost of producing a single movie is in the millions of dollars for a low-budget film, and the average feature-length movie costs many millions

11

of dollars to produce. The need to pool resources to achieve an efficient scale of production calls for a structure with many owners, not all of whom can be actively involved in managing the business.

Third, in an uncertain economic environment, owners will want to diversify their risks across many firms. To diversify optimally requires the investor to hold a portfolio of assets, in which each security is but a small part. Such efficient diversification is difficult to achieve without separation of ownership and management.

For example, suppose an investor thinks that firms in the entertainment industry will do well over the next few years and would like to buy a diversified stake in that industry. If the investor had to also manage the firms she invests in, there is no way she could diversify across many firms. The corporate form is especially well suited to facilitating diversification by investor-owners because it allows them to own a relatively small share of each firm.

Fourth, the separated structure allows for savings in the costs of information gathering. Managers can gather the most accurate information available about the firm's production technology, the costs of its inputs, and the demand for its products. The owners of the firm need to know relatively little about the technology of the firm, the intensity at which it is being operated, and the demand for the firm's products.

Again, consider the entertainment industry. The information needed to successfully manage the production and distribution of a movie is substantial. Although information about top actors and directors who might be hired to star in a movie is readily available at low cost, this is not so with respect to other resource inputs to movie production and distribution. Establishing information networks of agents and jobbers is costly and is most efficiently handled by having movie executives specialize in doing it.

Fifth, there is the "learning curve" or "going concern" effect, which favors the separated structure. Suppose the owner wants to sell all or part of his technology either now or at a later date. If the owner must also be the manager, the new owners have to learn the business from the former owner in order to manage it efficiently. However, if the owner does *not* have to be the manager, then when the business is sold, the manager continues in place and works for the new owners. When a company issues shares to the public for the first time, the original owner-managers often continue to manage the business even if they no longer own any shares in the business.

The corporate form is especially well suited to the separation of owners and managers because it allows relatively frequent changes in owners by share transfer without affecting the operations of the firm. Millions of shares in corporations around the world change hands and rarely is there any effect on the management or operations of the business.

Quick Check 4

What are the main reasons for having a separation of management and ownership of firms? How does the corporate form of organization facilitate this separation?

Offsetting all the reasons in favor of a separation of ownership and management, the separated structure creates the potential for a *conflict of interest* between the owners and the managers. Because the owners of a corporation have only incomplete information about whether the managers are serving their interests effectively, managers may neglect their obligations to the shareholders. In extreme cases, managers may even act *contrary* to the interests of their shareholders. Adam Smith, the father of classical economics, summed it up as follows:

The directors of such [joint-stock] companies, however, being the managers rather of other people's money than of their own, it cannot well be expected, that they should watch over it with the same anxious vigilance with which the partners in a private copartnery frequently watch over their own. Like the stewards of a rich man, they are apt to consider attention to small matters as not for their master's honour, and very easily give themselves a dispensation from having it. Negligence and profusion, therefore, must always prevail, more or less, in the management of the affairs of such a company.[2]

In those business environments in which the potential for conflicts of interest between owners and managers can be resolved at a reasonable cost, we would expect to find that the owners of business firms will not be the managers. And we would expect that the ownership of firms is dispersed among many individuals. Furthermore, we would expect to observe that, over time, the changes in the composition of the ownership would be far more common than the changes in the composition of the management.

7 The Goal of Management

Because the managers of corporations are hired by the shareholders (through the board of directors), the managers' primary commitment is to make decisions that are in the best interests of the shareholders. This is not the exclusive goal of management. Like everyone else in society, corporate managers must obey the law. They are also expected to respect ethical norms and to promote desirable social goals when it is possible to do so at a reasonable cost to shareholders.[3]

However, even if we restrict the goal of corporate management exclusively to serving the best interests of the shareholders, it is not obvious how managers can achieve this goal. In principle, managers could review each decision with the owners including the production choices, cost of obtaining capital, and so on and ask them which combination they prefer. But, in that case, the owners would have to have the same knowledge and spend essentially the same amount of time as they would if they were managing the business themselves. There would, therefore, be little point in hiring managers to run the business.

Moreover, although this procedure might be feasible when there are a few owners of the firm, it becomes completely impractical as the number of shareholders becomes large. Indeed, for a large multinational corporation, the number of shareholders can exceed a million, and they may reside in many different countries. Hence, it is essential to find a goal or rule to guide managers of the firm without having to "poll" the owners about most decisions.

To be effective, such a rule should not require the managers to know the risk preferences or opinions of the shareholders because such data are virtually impossible to obtain. And even if the data were available at one point in time, they change over time. Indeed, because shares of stock change hands every day, the owners of the corporation change every day. Thus, to be feasible, the right rule should be independent of who the owners are.

If a feasible rule for the managers to follow were found that would lead them to make the same investment and financing decisions that each of the individual owners would have made had they made the decisions themselves, then such a rule would clearly be the right one. To *maximize the wealth of current stockholders* is just such a rule.[4] Let us explain why.

For example, suppose you are the manager of a corporation trying to decide between two alternative investments. The choice is between a very risky investment project and

---

[2]Adam Smith, *The Wealth of Nations* (Chicago: University of Chicago Press, 1977).
[3]We assume that the goal of maximizing shareholder wealth does not necessarily conflict with other desirable social goals.
[4]This rule, like any all-encompassing dictum, is not always correct. It needs to be qualified in several respects. First, it assumes well-functioning and competitive capital markets. It also assumes that managers do not make decisions that are illegal or unethical.

a very safe one. Some shareholders might want to avoid taking these risks, and others might be pessimistic about the future of the investment. Still other shareholders might be risk lovers or might be optimistic about the outcome of the investment. How then can management make a decision in the best interests of all shareholders?

Suppose that undertaking the risky project would increase the market value of the firm's shares more than would the safe project. Even if some shareholders ultimately want to invest their money in safer assets, it would not be in their best interests for you as the firm's manager to choose the safer project.

This is because in well-functioning capital markets shareholders can adjust the riskiness of their personal portfolios by selling some of the shares in the firm you manage and investing the proceeds in safe assets. By your accepting the riskier project, even these risk-averse shareholders will wind up better off. They will have extra dollars today, which they can invest or consume as they see fit.

Thus, we see that individual owners would want managers to choose the investment project that maximizes the market value of their shares. The only risks relevant to the decision by managers are those of the project that affect the market value of the firm's shares.

The shareholder-wealth-maximization rule depends on the firm's production technology, market interest rates, market risk premiums, and security prices. It leads managers to make the same investment decisions that each of the individual owners would have made had they made the decisions themselves. At the same time, it does not depend upon the *risk aversion* or *wealth* of the owners, and so it can be made without any specific information about the owners. Thus, the shareholder-wealth-maximization rule is the "right" rule for managers to follow in running the firm. They can follow it without polling the owners each time a decision arises.

Scholars and other commentators on corporate behavior sometimes assert that the goal of managers is to maximize the firm's *profits*. Under certain specialized conditions, profit maximization and maximizing shareholder wealth lead to the same decisions. But in general there are two fundamental ambiguities with the profit-maximization criterion:

- If the production process requires many periods, then which period's profit is to be maximized?
- If either future revenues or expenses are uncertain, then what is the meaning of "maximize profits" when profits are described by a probability distribution?

Let us illustrate each of these problems with the profit-maximization criterion. First, the problem of many periods.

Suppose the firm faces a choice between two projects, both of which require an initial outlay of $1 million but last for a different number of years. Project A will return $1.05 million one year from now and then is over. Its profit is, therefore, $50,000 ($1.05 million–$1 million). Project B will last for two years, return nothing in the first year, and then $1.1 million two years from now. How do you apply a profit-maximization criterion in this case?

Now let us illustrate the difficulty of using a profit maximization criterion in an uncertain environment. Suppose you are the manager of a firm trying to choose between two investment projects, both of which require an initial outlay of $1 million and produce all of their returns one period from now. As in the previous example, project A will pay $1.05 million with certainty. We can, therefore, say unambiguously that the profit on project A is $50,000 ($1.05 million–$1 million).

Project C has an uncertain return. It will either pay $1.2 million or $0.9 million, each with probability 0.5. Thus, project C will either produce a profit of $200,000 or a loss of $100,000. What does it mean in this context to say "choose the project that maximizes the firm's profits"?

Unlike profits, it is clear that the current market value of the firm's shareholders' equity is still well defined (e.g., the future cash flows of the IBM corporation are uncertain, but there is a current price for its stock that is not uncertain). Hence, unlike the profit-maximization rule, the shareholder-wealth-maximization rule causes no ambiguities when future cash flows of the firm are uncertain.

Quick Check 5

Why is the shareholder-wealth-maximization rule a better one for corporate managers to follow than the profit-maximization rule?

Of course, management still has the difficult task of estimating the impact of its decision on the value of the firm's shares. Thus, in our preceding illustrations, in order to choose between projects A and B, or between A and C, management would have to determine which of them is likely to increase the value of the firm the most. This is not easy, but the criterion for making the decision is unambiguous.

Thus, the goal of management is to make decisions so as to maximize the firm's value to its shareholders. The main challenge in implementing this criterion is to obtain information about the likely impact of its decisions on the firm's value. Management's task is made much easier when it can observe market prices of its own and other firms' shares.

Indeed, in the absence of such market price information, it is difficult to see how they can implement this criterion at all. Although it is reasonable to assume that good managers will have as much information about their firm's production technology as anyone, such *internal* (to the firm) information is not sufficient to make effective decisions. In the absence of a stock market, managers would require *external* (to the firm) information that is costly if not impossible to obtain: namely, the wealth, preferences, and other investment opportunities of the owners.

Thus, the existence of a stock market allows the manager to substitute one set of external information that is relatively easy to obtain—namely, stock prices—for another set that is virtually impossible to obtain—information about the shareholders' wealth, preferences, and other investment opportunities. The existence of a well-functioning stock market, therefore, facilitates the efficient separation of the ownership and management of firms.

Note that in one respect the corporation's own senior managers and outside stock analysts who follow the corporation face a common task. Both groups are concerned with answering the question: How will the actions taken by management affect the market price of the firm's shares? The big difference is that the managers are the ones who actually make the decisions and have responsibility for implementing them.

One place to look for a statement of the goals of a corporation's top managers is the annual report to shareholders. Often the opening letter from the company's chief executive officer states what management's financial goals are and the general strategic plan for achieving them (see Box 6).

Quick Check 6

How does the existence of a well-functioning stock market facilitate the separation of ownership and management of firms?

Box 6 — Corporate Financial Goals and the Annual Report

Here is an excerpt from Honeywell Corporation's 1994 annual report to shareholders. Honeywell's chairman and chief executive officer, Michael R. Bonsignore, writes in his letter to the shareholders:

> Profitable growth. Delighted customers. Worldwide leadership in control. This is the vision for Honeywell that I and Honeywell people around the world have set for ourselves. It embodies what we want to be. It underpins how we set our goals. And it defines how we will fulfill the purpose of the company—which is to create value for our shareholders. . . .

> The company is now poised to achieve our primary financial objective: first-quartile total shareholder returns among our peers. We define total shareholder returns as share price appreciation plus dividends reinvested in the stock.

> Our management team is steadfast in achieving this objective. It is a key goal in our long-range incentive system. Our short-term executive compensation program rewards economic value added. We have constructed an integrated financial plan that sets aggressive targets in each driver of shareholder value: sales growth, operating margins, working capital, capital expenditures, and taxes.

---

8 Market Discipline: Takeovers

What forces are there to compel managers to act in the best interests of the shareholders? The shareholders could fire the managers by voting them out. But because a major benefit of the separated structure is that the owners can remain relatively uninformed about the operations of the firm, it is not apparent how these owners could know whether their firm is being mismanaged.

The value of voting rights as a means of enforcement is further cast into doubt if ownership of the firm is widely dispersed. If that is the situation, then the holdings of any single owner are likely to be so small that he or she would not incur the expense to become informed and to convey this information to other owners.[5] Thus, voting rights alone can do little to solve this dilemma.

The existence of a competitive stock market offers another important mechanism for aligning the incentives of managers with those of shareholders. It is called the *takeover.*

To see how the threat of a takeover can compel managers to act in the best interests of shareholders, suppose some entity, call it the takeover bidder, has identified a significantly mismanaged firm (i.e., one whose management has chosen an investment plan that leads to a market value that is significantly less than the maximum value that could be achieved from the firm's resources). If the bidder successfully buys enough shares of the undervalued firm to gain control, it replaces the managers with ones who will operate it optimally.

Having announced the change in the firm's investment plans, the bidder now sells the shares of the firm at the new market price for an immediate profit. Note that the bidder did not have to add any tangible resources to the firm to achieve this profit. Hence, the only expenses incurred are the cost of identifying a mismanaged firm and the cost of acquiring the firm's shares.

Although the cost of identifying a mismanaged firm will vary, it can be quite low if the takeover bidder happens to be a supplier, customer, or competitor of the firm because much of the information required may have been gathered for other purposes already. For this

---

[5]This is called the "paradox" of voting. The paradox is that when there are many voters, none of whose individual vote would appreciably affect the final outcome, it does not pay any individual voter to incur the costs of becoming informed and exercising the right to vote.

reason, the takeover mechanism can work even if resources are not spent for the explicit reason of identifying mismanaged firms.

However, if significant mismanagement of firms were widespread, then it would pay to spend resources in search of such firms in much the same way that resources are spent on research of new physical investment projects. There are indeed firms that specialize in making hostile (to the management) takeovers. Therefore, the threat of a takeover is credible and the subsequent replacement of management provides a strong incentive for current managers (acting in their self-interest) to act in the interests of the firm's current shareholders by maximizing market value.

Indeed, even in the absence of any explicit instructions from the shareholders or knowledge of the theory for good management, one might expect managers to move in the direction of value maximization as a matter of self-preservation. Moreover, it should be noted that it does not matter whether the source of the mismanagement is incompetence or the pursuit of different objectives, the takeover mechanism serves equally well to correct either one.

The effectiveness of the takeover mechanism can be reduced by government policies. For example, in an attempt to prevent the formation of monopolies in various product markets, the U.S. Department of Justice will take legal action under the antitrust laws to prevent mergers or acquisitions that might reduce competition. Because it is more likely that a supplier, customer, or competitor will be the takeover bidder who identifies the mismanaged firm, this public policy will tend to reduce the threat of takeover.

Quick Check 7

How does the threat of a takeover serve as a mechanism to deal with the conflict of interest between owners and managers of a corporation?

9 The Role of the Finance Specialist in a Corporation

Virtually all decisions made in a corporation are at least partially financial because they involve making trade-offs between costs and benefits that are spread over time. Therefore, in large corporations virtually all managers from the chief executive at the top down to managers of individual production units, marketing units, research labs, or other departments make use of the services of finance specialists.

The Financial Executives Institute, a voluntary organization of corporate executives who specialize in finance, offers a broad definition of a financial executive as anyone who has authority for one of the functions listed in Table 1.

The organization of the finance function and its relation to other departments vary from company to company, but Figure 1 shows a typical organization chart in a large corporation.

At the top is the firm's chief executive officer (CEO) who often is also the president. The chief financial officer (CFO) is a senior vice president with responsibility for all the financial functions in the firm and reports directly to the CEO. The firm also has senior vice presidents in charge of marketing and operations. In large firms, there is sometimes a chief operating officer (COO), who takes responsibility for implementing the CEO's strategy for the firm.

The CFO has three departments reporting to him or her: financial planning, treasury, and control, each headed by a vice president. The vice president for financial planning has responsibility for analyzing major capital expenditures such as proposals to enter new lines

TABLE 1 Financial Functions in a Corporation

1. PLANNING

Establishment, coordination, and administration, as an integral part of management, of an adequate plan for the control of operations. Such a plan, to the extent required in the business, would provide the following:

a. Long- and short-range financial and corporate planning

b. Budgeting for capital expenditures and/or operations

c. Sales forecasting

d. Performance evaluation

e. Pricing policies

f. Economic appraisal

g. Analysis of acquisitions and divestments

2. PROVISION OF CAPITAL

Establishment and execution of programs for the provision of the capital required by the business.

3. ADMINISTRATION OF FUNDS

a. Management of cash

b. Maintenance of banking arrangements

c. Receipt, custody, and disbursement of the company's monies and securities

d. Credit and collection management

e. Management of pension funds

f. Management of investments

g. Custodial responsibilities

4. ACCOUNTING AND CONTROL

a. Establishment of accounting policies

b. Development and reporting of accounting data

c. Cost standards

d. Internal auditing

e. Systems and procedures (accounting)

f. Government reporting

g. Report and interpretation of results of operations to management

h. Comparison of performance with operating plans and standards

5. PROTECTION OF ASSETS

a. Provision of insurance coverage as required

b. Assure protection of business assets and loss prevention through internal control and internal auditing

c. Real estate management

6. TAX ADMINISTRATION

a. Establishment and administration of tax policies and procedures

b. Relations with taxing agencies

c. Preparation of tax reports

d. Tax planning

TABLE 1   Continued

7. INVESTOR RELATIONS

a. Establishment and maintenance of liaison with the investment community

b. Establishment and maintenance of communications with company stockholders

c. Counseling with analysts—public financial information

8. EVALUATION AND CONSULTING

Consultation with and advice to other corporate executives on company policy, operations, objectives, and the effectiveness thereof

9. MANAGEMENT INFORMATION SYSTEMS

a. Development and use of electronic data processing facilities

b. Development and use of management information systems

c. Development and use of systems and procedures

Source: Financial Executives Institute.

FIGURE 1

Organization Chart for ZYX Corporation

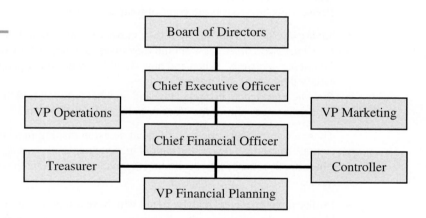

of business or to exit existing businesses. This includes analyzing proposed mergers, acquisitions, and spin-offs.

The treasurer has responsibility for managing the financing activities of the firm and for working capital management. The treasurer's job includes managing relations with the external investor community, managing the firm's exposure to currency and interest rate risks, and managing the tax department.

The controller oversees the accounting and auditing activities of the firm. This includes preparation of internal reports comparing planned and actual costs, revenues, and profits from the corporation's various business units. It also includes preparation of financial statements for use by shareholders, creditors, and regulatory authorities.

Summary

Finance is the study of how to allocate scarce resources over time. The two features that distinguish finance are that the costs and benefits of financial decisions are spread out over time and are usually not known with certainty in advance by either the decision maker or anybody else.

A basic tenet of finance is that the ultimate function of the system is to satisfy people's *consumption preferences*. Economic organizations such as firms and governments exist in order to facilitate the achievement of that ultimate function. Many financial decisions can be made strictly on the basis of improving the trade-offs available to people without knowledge of their consumption preferences.

There are at least five good reasons to study finance:

- To manage your personal resources.
- To deal with the world of business.
- To pursue interesting and rewarding career opportunities.
- To make informed public choices as a citizen.
- To expand your mind.

The players in finance theory are households, business firms, financial intermediaries, and governments. Households occupy a special place in the theory because the ultimate function of the system is to satisfy the preferences of people, and the theory treats those preferences as given. Finance theory explains household behavior as an attempt to satisfy those preferences. The behavior of firms is viewed from the perspective of how it affects the welfare of households.

Households face four basic types of financial decisions:

- *Saving decisions:* How much of their current income should they save for the future?
- *Investment decisions:* How should they invest the money they have saved?
- *Financing decisions:* When and how should they use other people's money to satisfy their wants and needs?
- *Risk-management decisions:* How and on what terms should they seek to reduce the economic uncertainties they face or to take calculated risks?

There are three main areas of financial decision making in a business: capital budgeting, capital structure, and working capital management.

There are five reasons for separating the management from the ownership of a business enterprise:

- Professional managers may be found who have a superior ability to run the business.
- To achieve the efficient scale of a business the resources of many households may have to be pooled.
- In an uncertain economic environment, owners will want to diversify their risks across many firms. Such efficient diversification is difficult to achieve without separation of ownership and management.
- To achieve savings in the costs of gathering information.
- The "learning curve" or "going concern" effect: When the owner is also the manager, the new owner has to learn the business from the former owner in order to manage it efficiently. If the owner is not the manager, then when the business is sold, the manager continues in place and works for the new owner.

The corporate form is especially well suited to the separation of ownership and management of firms because it allows relatively frequent changes in owners by share transfer without affecting the operations of the firm.

The primary goal of corporate management is to maximize shareholder wealth. It leads managers to make the same investment decisions that each of the individual owners would have made had they made the decisions themselves.

A competitive stock market imposes a strong discipline on managers to take actions to maximize the market value of the firm's shares.

Key Terms

- finance
- financial system
- assets
- asset allocation
- liability
- net worth
- sole proprietorship
- partnership
- corporation

Answers to Quick Check Questions

Quick Check 1   What are the four basic types of financial decisions households have to make? Give an example of each.
Answer:
- Consumption/saving decisions, such as how much to save for a child's education or for retirement.
- Investment decisions, such as how much to invest in stocks or bonds.
- Financing decisions, such as what type of loan to take to finance the purchase of a home or a car.
- Risk-management decisions, such as whether to buy disability insurance.

Quick Check 2   What are the basic types of financial decisions firms have to make? Give an example of each.
Answer:
- Capital budgeting decisions, such as whether to build a plant to produce a new product.
- Financing decisions, such as how much debt and how much equity it should have in its capital structure.
- Working capital decisions, such as whether it should extend credit to customers or demand cash on delivery.

Quick Check 3   A corporation owned by a single person is not a sole proprietorship. Why?
Answer: In a corporation the liability of the single shareholder would be limited to the assets of the corporation.

Quick Check 4   What are the main reasons for having a separation of management and ownership of firms? How does the corporate form of organization facilitate this separation?
Answer: Five reasons:
- Professional managers may be found who have a superior ability to run the business.
- To achieve the efficient scale of a business the resources of many households may have to be pooled.
- In an uncertain economic environment, owners will want to diversify their risks across many firms. Such efficient diversification is difficult to achieve without separation of ownership and management.
- To achieve savings in the costs of gathering information.
- The "learning curve" or "going concern" effect: When the owner is also the manager, the new owner has to learn the business from the former owner in order to manage it efficiently. If the owner is not the manager, then when the business is sold, the manager continues in place and works for the new owner.

The corporate form is especially well suited to the separation of ownership and management of firms because it allows relatively frequent changes in owners by share transfer without affecting the operations of the firm.

Quick Check 5   Why is the shareholder-wealth-maximization rule a better one for corporate managers to follow than the profit-maximization rule?

Answer: There are two fundamental ambiguities with the profit-maximization criterion:
- If the production process requires many periods, then which period's profit is to be maximized?
- If either future revenues or expenses are uncertain, then what is the meaning of "maximize profits" when profits are described by a probability distribution?

Quick Check 6   How does the existence of a well-functioning stock market facilitate the separation of ownership and management of firms?

Answer: In the absence of a stock market, managers would require information that is costly if not impossible to obtain: namely, the wealth, preferences, and other investment opportunities of the owners.

Quick Check 7   How does the threat of a takeover serve as a mechanism to deal with the conflict of interest between owners and managers of a corporation?

Answer: Managers know that if they fail to maximize the market value of the firm's shares, the firm will be vulnerable to a takeover in which managers might lose their jobs.

Sources of Information

On the Internet you can complement your understanding of the core structures of financial markets and corporations with the following links:

Survey on Corporate Social Responsibility, *The Economist,* January 20, 2005, http://www.economist.com/surveys/displayStory.cfm?Story_ID=3574392

Financial Market Trends, Organization for Economic Cooperation and Development http://www.oecd.org/document/36/0,2340,en_2649_201185_1962020_1_1_1_1,00.html

Quarterly Review, Bank for International Settlements http://www.bis.org/publ/quarterly.htm

EDGAR Database, U.S. Securities and Exchange Commission http://www.sec.gov/edaux/searches.htm

Questions and Problems

Defining Finance

1. What are your main goals in life? How does finance play a part in achieving those goals? What are the major tradeoffs you face?

Financial Decisions of Households

2. What is your net worth? What have you included among your assets and your liabilities? Would you list the value of your potential lifetime earning power as an asset or liability? How does it compare in value to other assets you have listed?

3. How are the financial decisions faced by a single person living alone different from those faced by the head of a household with responsibility for several children of school age? Are the tradeoffs they have to make different, or will they evaluate the tradeoffs differently?

4. Family A and Family B both consist of a father, mother, and two children of school age. In Family A both spouses have jobs outside the home and earn a combined income of $100,000 per year. In Family B, only one spouse works outside the home and earns $100,000 per year. How do the financial circumstances and decisions faced by the two families differ?

5. Suppose we define financial independence as the ability to engage in the four basic household financial decisions without resort to the use of relatives' resources when making financing decisions. At what age should children be expected to become financially independent?

6. You are thinking of buying a car. Analyze the decision by addressing the following issues:
    a. Are there other ways to satisfy your transportation requirements besides buying a car? Make a list of all the alternatives and write down the pros and cons.
    b. What are the different ways you can finance the purchase of a car?
    c. Obtain information from at least three different providers of automobile financing on the terms they offer.
    d. What criteria should you use in making your decision?

7. Match each of the following examples with one of the four categories of basic types of household financial decisions.
    • At the Safeway paying with your debit card rather than taking the time to write a check
    • Deciding to take the proceeds from your winning lottery ticket and use it to pay for an extended vacation on the Italian Riviera
    • Following Hillary's advice and selling your Microsoft shares to invest in pork belly futures
    • Helping your 15-years-old son learn to drive by putting him behind the wheel on the back road into town
    • Taking up the offer from the pool supply company to pay off your new hot tub with a 15-month loan with zero payments for the first three months

Forms of Business Organization

8. You are thinking of starting your own business, but have no money.
    a. Think of a business that you could start without having to borrow any money.
    b. Now think of a business that you would want to start if you could borrow any amount of money at the going market interest rate.
    c. What are the risks you would face in this business?
    d. Where can you get financing for your new business?

9. Choose an organization that is not a firm, such as a club or church group, and list the most important financial decisions it has to make. What are the key tradeoffs the organization faces? What role do preferences play in choosing among alternatives? Interview the financial manager of the organization and check to see whether he or she agrees with you.

Market Discipline: Takeovers

10. *Challenge Question:* While there are clear advantages to the separation of management from ownership of business enterprises, there is also a fundamental disadvantage in that it may be costly to align the goals of management with those of the owners. Suggest at

least two methods, other than the takeover market, by which the conflict can be reduced, albeit at some cost.

11. *Challenge Question:* Consider a poorly run local coffee shop with its prime location featuring a steady stream of potential clients passing by on their way to and from campus. How does the longtime disgruntled, sloppy, and inefficient owner-manager of Cup-a-Joe survive and avoid disciplining from the takeover market?

The Role of the Finance Specialist in a Corporation

12. Which of the following tasks undertaken within a corporate office are likely to fall under the supervision of the treasurer? The controller?
- Arranging to extend a line of credit from a bank
- Arranging with an investment bank for a foreign exchange transaction
- Producing a detailed analysis of the cost structure of the company's alternative product lines
- Taking cash payments for company sales and purchasing U.S. Treasury Bills
- Filing quarterly statements with the Securities and Exchange Commission

Chapter 2

Overview of the Financial System

Preview

Suppose that you want to start a business that manufactures a recently invented low-cost robot that cleans the house (even does windows), mows the lawn, and washes the car, but you have no funds to put this wonderful invention into production. Walter has plenty of savings that he has inherited. If you and Walter could get together so that he could provide you with the funds, your company's robot would see the light of day, and you, Walter, and the economy would all be better off: Walter could earn a high return on his investment, you would get rich from producing the robot, and we would have cleaner houses, shinier cars, and more beautiful lawns.

Financial markets (bond and stock markets) and financial intermediaries (banks, insurance companies, pension funds) have the basic function of getting people such as you and Walter together by moving funds from those who have a surplus of funds (Walter) to those who have a shortage of funds (you). More realistically, when Apple invents a better iPod, it may need funds to bring it to market. Similarly, when a local government needs to build a road or a school, it may need more funds than local property taxes provide. Well-functioning financial markets and financial intermediaries are crucial to our economic health.

To study the effects of financial markets and financial intermediaries on the economy, we need to acquire an understanding of their general structure and operation. In this chapter we learn about the major financial intermediaries and the instruments that are traded in financial markets.

This chapter offers a preliminary overview of the fascinating study of financial markets and institutions.

From Chapter 2 of *Financial Markets & Institutions*, 6/e. Frederic S. Mishkin. Stanley G. Eakins. Copyright © 2008 by Pearson Prentice Hall. All rights reserved.

Function of Financial Markets

Financial markets perform the essential economic function of channeling funds from households, firms, and governments that have saved surplus funds by spending less than their income to those that have a shortage of funds because they wish to spend more than their income. This function is shown schematically in Figure 1. Those who have saved and are lending funds, the lender-savers, are at the left, and those who must borrow funds to finance their spending, the borrower-spenders, are at the right. The principal lender-savers are households, but business enterprises and the government (particularly state and local government), as well as foreigners and their governments, sometimes also find themselves with excess funds and so lend them out. The most important borrower-spenders are businesses and the government (particularly the federal government), but households and foreigners also borrow to finance their purchases of cars, furniture, and houses. The arrows show that funds flow from lender-savers to borrower-spenders via two routes.

In *direct finance* (the route at the bottom of Figure 1), borrowers borrow funds directly from lenders in financial markets by selling them *securities* (also called *financial instruments*), which are claims on the borrower's future income or assets. Securities are assets for the person who buys them but they are **liabilities** (IOUs or debts) for the individual or firm that sells (issues) them. For example, if General Motors needs to borrow funds to pay for a new factory to manufacture electric

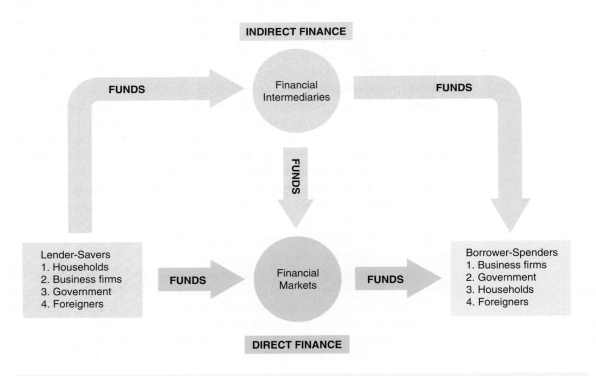

Figure 1 Flows of Funds Through the Financial System

cars, it might borrow the funds from savers by selling them a *bond*, a debt security that promises to make payments periodically for a specified period of time, or a *stock*, a security that entitles the owner to a share of the company's profits and assets.

Why is this channeling of funds from savers to spenders so important to the economy? The answer is that the people who save are frequently not the same people who have profitable investment opportunities available to them, the entrepreneurs. Let's first think about this on a personal level. Suppose that you have saved $1,000 this year, but no borrowing or lending is possible because there are no financial markets. If you do not have an investment opportunity that will permit you to earn income with your savings, you will just hold on to the $1,000 and will earn no interest. However, Carl the Carpenter has a productive use for your $1,000: He can use it to purchase a new tool that will shorten the time it takes him to build a house, thereby earning an extra $200 per year. If you could get in touch with Carl, you could lend him the $1,000 at a rental fee (interest) of $100 per year, and both of you would be better off. You would earn $100 per year on your $1,000, instead of the zero amount that you would earn otherwise, while Carl would earn $100 more income per year (the $200 extra earnings per year minus the $100 rental fee for the use of the funds).

In the absence of financial markets, you and Carl the Carpenter might never get together. You would both be stuck with the status quo, and both of you would be worse off. Without financial markets, it is hard to transfer funds from a person who has no investment opportunities to one who has them. Financial markets are thus essential to promoting economic efficiency.

The existence of financial markets is beneficial even if someone borrows for a purpose other than increasing production in a business. Say that you are recently married, have a good job, and want to buy a house. You earn a good salary, but because you have just started to work, you have not saved much. Over time, you would have no problem saving enough to buy the house of your dreams, but by then you would be too old to get full enjoyment from it. Without financial markets, you are stuck; you cannot buy the house and must continue to live in your tiny apartment.

If a financial market were set up so that people who had built up savings could lend you the funds to buy the house, you would be more than happy to pay them some interest so that you could own a home while you are still young enough to enjoy it. Then, over time, you would pay back your loan. If this loan could occur, you would be better off, as would the persons who made you the loan. They would now earn some interest, whereas they would not if the financial market did not exist.

Now we can see why financial markets have such an important function in the economy. They allow funds to move from people who lack productive investment opportunities to people who have such opportunities. Financial markets are critical for producing an efficient allocation of **capital** (wealth, either financial or physical, that is employed to produce more wealth), which contributes to higher production and efficiency for the overall economy. Indeed, when financial markets break down during financial crises, as they have in Mexico, East Asia, and Argentina in recent years, severe economic hardship results, which can even lead to dangerous political instability.

Well-functioning financial markets also directly improve the well-being of consumers by allowing them to time their purchases better. They provide funds to young people to buy what they need and can eventually afford without forcing them to wait until they have saved up the entire purchase price. Financial markets that are operating efficiently improve the economic welfare of everyone in the society.

Structure of Financial Markets

Now that we understand the basic function of financial markets, let's look at their structure. The following descriptions of several categorizations of financial markets illustrate essential features of these markets.

Debt and Equity Markets

A firm or an individual can obtain funds in a financial market in two ways. The most common method is to issue a debt instrument, such as a bond or a mortgage, which is a contractual agreement by the borrower to pay the holder of the instrument fixed dollar amounts at regular intervals (interest and principal payments) until a specified date (the maturity date), when a final payment is made. The **maturity** of a debt instrument is the number of years (term) until that instrument's expiration date. A debt instrument is **short-term** if its maturity is less than a year and **long-term** if its maturity is ten years or longer. Debt instruments with a maturity between one and ten years are said to be **intermediate-term.**

The second method of raising funds is by issuing **equities,** such as common stock, which are claims to share in the net income (income after expenses and taxes) and the assets of a business. If you own one share of common stock in a company that has issued one million shares, you are entitled to 1 one-millionth of the firm's net income and 1 one-millionth of the firm's assets. Equities often make periodic payments (**dividends**) to their holders and are considered long-term securities because they have no maturity date. In addition, owning stock means that you own a portion of the firm and thus have the right to vote on issues important to the firm and to elect its directors.

The main disadvantage of owning a corporation's equities rather than its debt is that an equity holder is a *residual claimant*; that is, the corporation must pay all its debt holders before it pays its equity holders. The advantage of holding equities is that equity holders benefit directly from any increases in the corporation's profitability or asset value because equities confer ownership rights on the equity holders. Debt holders do not share in this benefit, because their dollar payments are fixed.

The total value of equities in the United States has typically fluctuated between $4 trillion and $20 trillion since the early 1990s, depending on the prices of shares. Although the average person is more aware of the stock market than any other financial market, the size of the debt market is often substantially larger than the size of the equities market: The value of debt instruments was $43.4 trillion at the end of 2006, while the value of equities was $19.3 trillion at the end of 2006.

Primary and Secondary Markets

go online

www.nyse.com
New York Stock Exchange. Find listed companies, quotes, company historical data, real-time market indices, and more.

A **primary market** is a financial market in which new issues of a security, such as a bond or a stock, are sold to initial buyers by the corporation or government agency borrowing the funds. A **secondary market** is a financial market in which securities that have been previously issued can be resold.

The primary markets for securities are not well known to the public because the selling of securities to initial buyers often takes place behind closed doors. An important financial institution that assists in the initial sale of securities in the primary market is the **investment bank.** It does this by **underwriting** securities: It guarantees a price for a corporation's securities and then sells them to the public.

The New York Stock Exchange and NASDAQ (National Association of Securities Dealers Automated Quotation System), in which previously issued stocks are traded, are the best-known examples of secondary markets, although the bond markets, in which previously issued bonds of major corporations and the U.S. government are bought and sold, actually have a larger trading volume. Other examples of secondary markets are foreign exchange markets, futures markets, and options markets. Securities brokers and dealers are crucial to a well-functioning secondary market. **Brokers** are agents of investors who match buyers with sellers of securities; **dealers** link buyers and sellers by buying and selling securities at stated prices.

When an individual buys a security in the secondary market, the person who has sold the security receives money in exchange for the security, but the corporation that issued the security acquires no new funds. A corporation acquires new funds only when its securities are first sold in the primary market. Nonetheless, secondary markets serve two important functions. First, they make it easier and quicker to sell these financial instruments to raise cash; that is, they make the financial instruments more **liquid.** The increased liquidity of these instruments then makes them more desirable and thus easier for the issuing firm to sell in the primary market. Second, they determine the price of the security that the issuing firm sells in the primary market. The investors who buy securities in the primary market will pay the issuing corporation no more than the price they think the secondary market will set for this security. The higher the security's price in the secondary market, the higher the price that the issuing firm will receive for a new security in the primary market, and hence the greater the amount of financial capital it can raise. Conditions in the secondary market are therefore the most relevant to corporations issuing securities. It is for this reason that books like this one, which deal with financial markets, focus on the behavior of secondary markets rather than primary markets.

Exchanges and Over-the-Counter Markets

go online

www.nasdaq.com
Detailed market and security information for the Nasdaq OTC stock exchange.

Secondary markets can be organized in two ways. One method is to organize **exchanges,** where buyers and sellers of securities (or their agents or brokers) meet in one central location to conduct trades. The New York and American Stock Exchanges for stocks and the Chicago Board of Trade for commodities (wheat, corn, silver, and other raw materials) are examples of organized exchanges.

The other method of organizing a secondary market is to have an **over-the-counter (OTC) market,** in which dealers at different locations who have an inventory of securities stand ready to buy and sell securities "over the counter" to anyone who comes to them and is willing to accept their prices. Because over-the-counter dealers are in computer contact and know the prices set by one another, the OTC market is very competitive and not very different from a market with an organized exchange.

Many common stocks are traded over-the-counter, although a majority of the largest corporations have their shares traded at organized stock exchanges. The U.S. government bond market, with a larger trading volume than the New York Stock Exchange, by contrast, is set up as an over-the-counter market. Forty or so dealers establish a "market" in these securities by standing ready to buy and sell U.S.

government bonds. Other over-the-counter markets include those that trade other types of financial instruments such as negotiable certificates of deposit, federal funds, banker's acceptances, and foreign exchange.

Money and Capital Markets

Another way of distinguishing between markets is on the basis of the maturity of the securities traded in each market. The **money market** is a financial market in which only short-term debt instruments (generally those with original maturity of less than one year) are traded; the **capital market** is the market in which longer-term debt (generally with original maturity of one year or greater) and equity instruments are traded. Money market securities are usually more widely traded than longer-term securities and so tend to be more liquid. In addition, short-term securities have smaller fluctuations in prices than long-term securities, making them safer investments. As a result, corporations and banks actively use the money market to earn interest on surplus funds that they expect to have only temporarily. Capital market securities, such as stocks and long-term bonds, are often held by financial intermediaries such as insurance companies and pension funds, which have little uncertainty about the amount of funds they will have available in the future.

Internationalization of Financial Markets

The growing internationalization of financial markets has become an important trend. Before the 1980s, U.S. financial markets were much larger than financial markets outside the United States, but in recent years the dominance of U.S. markets has been disappearing. (See the Global box, "Are U.S. Capital Markets Losing Their Edge?") The extraordinary growth of foreign financial markets has been the result of both large increases in the pool of savings in foreign countries such as Japan and the deregulation of foreign financial markets, which has enabled foreign markets to expand their activities. American corporations and banks are now more likely to tap international capital markets to raise needed funds, and American investors often seek investment opportunities abroad. Similarly, foreign corporations and banks raise funds from Americans, and foreigners have become important investors in the United States. A look at international bond markets and world stock markets will give us a picture of how this globalization of financial markets is taking place.

International Bond Market, Eurobonds, and Eurocurrencies

The traditional instruments in the international bond market are known as **foreign bonds.** Foreign bonds are sold in a foreign country and are denominated in that country's currency. For example, if the German automaker Porsche sells a bond in the United States denominated in U.S. dollars, it is classified as a foreign bond. Foreign bonds have been an important instrument in the international capital market for centuries. In fact, a large percentage of U.S. railroads built in the nineteenth century were financed by sales of foreign bonds in Britain.

A more recent innovation in the international bond market is the **Eurobond,** a bond denominated in a currency other than that of the country in which it is

global

Are U.S. Capital Markets Losing Their Edge?

Over the past few decades the United States lost its international dominance in a number of manufacturing industries, including automobiles and consumer electronics, as other countries became more competitive in global markets. Recent evidence suggests that financial markets now are undergoing a similar trend: Just as Ford and General Motors have lost global market share to Toyota and Honda, U.S. stock and bond markets recently have seen their share of sales of newly issued corporate securities slip. In 2006 the London and Hong Kong stock exchanges each handled a larger share of initial public offerings (IPO) of stock than did the New York Stock Exchange, which had been by far the dominant exchange in terms of IPO value just three years before. Likewise, the portion of new corporate bonds issued worldwide that are initially sold in U.S. capital markets has fallen below the share sold in European debt markets in each of the past two years.*

Why do corporations that issue new securities to raise capital now conduct more of this business in financial markets in Europe and Asia? Among the factors contributing to this trend are quicker adoption of technological innovation by foreign financial markets, tighter immigration controls in the United States following the terrorist attacks in 2001, and perceptions that listing on American exchanges will expose foreign securities issuers to greater risks of lawsuits.

Many people see burdensome financial regulation as the main cause, however, and point specifically to the Sarbanes-Oxley Act of 2002. Congress passed this act after a number of accounting scandals involving U.S. corporations and the accounting firms that audited them came to light. Sarbanes-Oxley aims to strengthen the integrity of the auditing process and the quality of information provided in corporate financial statements. The costs to corporations of complying with the new rules and procedures are high, especially for smaller firms, but largely avoidable if firms choose to issue their securities in financial markets outside the United States. For this reason, there is much support for revising Sarbanes-Oxley to lessen its alleged harmful effects and induce more securities issuers back to United States financial markets. However, there is not conclusive evidence to support the view that Sarbanes-Oxley is the main cause of the relative decline of U.S. financial markets and therefore in need of reform.

Discussion of the relative decline of U.S. financial markets and debate about the factors that are contributing to it likely will continue.

*Down on the Street," *The Economist*, November 25, 2006, pp. 69–71.

sold—for example, a bond denominated in U.S. dollars sold in London. Currently, over 80% of the new issues in the international bond market are Eurobonds, and the market for these securities has grown very rapidly. As a result, the Eurobond market is now larger than the U.S. corporate bond market.

A variant of the Eurobond is **Eurocurrencies,** which are foreign currencies deposited in banks outside the home country. The most important of the Eurocurrencies are **Eurodollars,** which are U.S. dollars deposited in foreign banks outside the United States or in foreign branches of U.S. banks. Because these short-term deposits earn interest, they are similar to short-term Eurobonds. American banks borrow Eurodollar deposits from other banks or from their own foreign branches, and Eurodollars are now an important source of funds for American banks (over $190 billion outstanding).

Note that the euro, the currency used by countries in the European Monetary System, can create some confusion about the terms Eurobond, Eurocurrencies, and

Eurodollars. A bond denominated in euros is called a Eurobond only *if it is sold outside the countries that have adopted the euro.* In fact, most Eurobonds are not denominated in euros but are instead denominated in U.S. dollars. Similarly, Eurodollars have nothing to do with euros, but are instead U.S. dollars deposited in banks outside the United States.

World Stock Markets

go online

http://stockcharts.com/
def/servlet/Favorites
.CServlet?obj=msummary
&cmd=show&disp=SXA
This site contains historical
stock market index charts
for many countries around
the world.

go online

http://quote.yahoo
.com/m2?u
Major world stock indexes,
with charts, news, and
components.

Until recently, the U.S. stock market was by far the largest in the world, but foreign stock markets have been growing in importance, with the United States not always being number one. The increased interest in foreign stocks has prompted the development in the United States of mutual funds that specialize in trading in foreign stock markets. American investors now pay attention not only to the Dow Jones Industrial Average but also to stock price indexes for foreign stock markets such as the Nikkei 300 Average (Tokyo) and the Financial Times Stock Exchange (FTSE) 100-Share Index (London).

The internationalization of financial markets is having profound effects on the United States. Foreigners, particularly Japanese investors, are not only providing funds to corporations in the United States, but are also helping finance the federal government. Without these foreign funds, the U.S. economy would have grown far less rapidly in the last 20 years. The internationalization of financial markets is also leading the way to a more integrated world economy in which flows of goods and technology between countries are more commonplace (see the Following the Financial News box).

Function of Financial Intermediaries: Indirect Finance

As shown in Figure 1, funds also can move from lenders to borrowers by a second route called *indirect finance* because it involves a financial intermediary that stands between the lender-savers and the borrower-spenders and helps transfer funds from one to the other. A financial intermediary does this by borrowing funds from the lender-savers and then using these funds to make loans to borrower-spenders. For example, a bank might acquire funds by issuing a liability to the public (an asset for the public) in the form of savings deposits. It might then use the funds to acquire an asset by making a loan to General Motors or by buying a U.S. Treasury bond in the financial market. The ultimate result is that funds have been transferred from the public (the lender-savers) to GM or the U.S. Treasury (the borrower-spender) with the help of the financial intermediary (the bank).

The process of indirect finance using financial intermediaries, called **financial intermediation,** is the primary route for moving funds from lenders to borrowers. Indeed, although the media focus much of their attention on securities markets, particularly the stock market, financial intermediaries are a far more important source of financing for corporations than securities markets are. This is true not only for the United States but for other industrialized countries as well (see the Global box). Why are financial intermediaries and indirect finance so important in financial markets? To answer this question, we need to understand the role of transaction costs, risk sharing, and information costs in financial markets.

following the financial news

Foreign Stock Market Indexes

International Stock Indexes

Region/Country	Index	Close	LATEST Net chg	% chg	YTD % chg
World	DJ World Index	299.53	−0.15	−0.05	7.9
	DJ World ex U.S.	265.12	0.27	0.10	9.1
	MSCI EAFE*	2242.88	2.80	0.12	8.1
Americas	DJ Americas	377.60	−0.97	−0.26	7.4
Brazil	Sao Paulo Bovespa	50510.76	−391.62	−0.77	13.6
Canada	S&P/TSX Comp	13903.28	−100.54	−0.72	7.7
Mexico	IPC-All-Share	29766.33	−292.42	−0.97	12.5
Venezuela	Caracas General	42471.63	−508.40	−1.18	−18.7
Europe	DJ Stoxx 600	388.96	−0.82	−0.21	6.5
Euro zone	DJ Euro Stoxx	428.00	−0.69	−0.16	8.2
Belgium	Bel-20	4658.76	−8.36	−0.18	6.2
France	CAC 40	6026.42	−24.21	−0.40	8.7
Germany	DAX	7459.61	−19.73	−0.26	13.1
Israel	Tel Aviv	1114.25	−2.24	−0.20	20.3
Italy	S&P/MIB	43629	39	0.09	5.3
Netherlands	AEX	529.89	−1.31	−0.25	7.0
Spain	IBEX 35	14686.0	−50.3	−0.34	3.8
Sweden	SX All Share	408.53	2.77	0.68	9.1
Switzerland	Swiss Market	9387.29	−20.96	−0.22	6.8
U.K.	FTSE 100	6555.5	−10.2	−0.16	5.4
Asia-Pacific	DJ Asia-Pacific	155.97	0.81	0.52	6.7
Australia	S&P/ASX 200	6345.1	47.7	0.76	11.9
China	DJ CBN China 600	29951.59	209.38	0.70	92.1
Hong Kong	Hang Seng	20979.24	511.03	2.50	5.1
India	Bombay Sensex	13965.86	169.70	1.23	1.3
Japan	Nikkei Stock Avg	17677.94	124.22	0.71	2.6
Russia	DJ Russia Titans 10	6525.12	31.13	0.48	−2.1
Singapore	Straits Times	3501.10	54.18	1.57	17.3
South Korea	Kospi	1605.77	2.21	0.14	11.9
Taiwan	Weighted	8030.56	−0.98	−0.01	2.6

*Europe, Australia, Far East, U.S.-dollar terms   Sources: Reuters; WSJ Market Data Group

 Foreign stock market indexes are published daily in the *Wall Street Journal* next to the "World Markets" column, which reports developments in foreign stock markets.

The first two columns identify the foreign stock exchange and the market index; for example, the colored entry is for the DAX for the German Stock Exchange. The third column, "CLOSE," gives the closing value of the index, which was 7460 for the DAX on May 15, 2007. The "NET CHG" column indicates the change in the index from the previous trading day, −19.73, and the "% CHG" column indicates the percentage change in the index, −0.26. The next column indicates the year-to-date percentage change of the index (+13.1%).

Transaction Costs

Transaction costs, the time and money spent in carrying out financial transactions, are a major problem for people who have excess funds to lend. As we have seen, Carl the Carpenter needs $1,000 for his new tool, and you know that it is an excellent investment opportunity. You have the cash and would like to lend him the money, but to protect your investment, you have to hire a lawyer to write up the loan contract that specifies how much interest Carl will pay you, when he will make these interest payments, and when he will repay you the $1,000. Obtaining the contract will

global

The Importance of Financial Intermediaries Relative to Securities Markets: An International Comparison

Patterns of financing corporations differ across countries, but one key fact emerges: Studies of the major developed countries, including the United States, Canada, the United Kingdom, Japan, Italy, Germany, and France, show that when businesses go looking for funds to finance their activities, they usually obtain them indirectly through financial intermediaries and not directly from securities markets.* Even in the United States and Canada, which have the most developed securities markets in the world, loans from financial intermediaries are far more important for corporate finance than securities markets are. The countries that have made the least use of securities markets are Germany and Japan; in these two countries, financing from financial intermediaries has been almost 10 times greater than that from securities markets. However, after the deregulation of Japanese

securities markets in recent years, the share of corporate financing by financial intermediaries has been declining relative to the use of securities markets.

Although the dominance of financial intermediaries over securities markets is clear in all countries, the relative importance of bond versus stock markets differs widely across countries. In the United States, the bond market is far more important as a source of corporate finance: On average, the amount of new financing raised using bonds is 10 times the amount raised using stocks. By contrast, countries such as France and Italy make more use of equities markets than of the bond market to raise capital.

*See, for example, Colin Mayer, "Financial Systems, Corporate Finance, and Economic Development," in *Asymmetric Information, Corporate Finance, and Investment,* ed. R. Glenn Hubbard (Chicago: University of Chicago Press, 1990), pp. 307–332.

cost you $500. When you figure in this transaction cost for making the loan, you realize that you can't earn enough from the deal (you spend $500 to make perhaps $100) and reluctantly tell Carl that he will have to look elsewhere.

This example illustrates that small savers like you or potential borrowers like Carl might be frozen out of financial markets and thus be unable to benefit from them. Can anyone come to the rescue? Financial intermediaries can.

Financial intermediaries can substantially reduce transaction costs because they have developed expertise in lowering them, and because their large size allows them to take advantage of **economies of scale,** the reduction in transaction costs per dollar of transactions as the size (scale) of transactions increases. For example, a bank knows how to find a good lawyer to produce an airtight loan contract, and this contract can be used over and over again in its loan transactions, thus lowering the legal cost per transaction. Instead of a loan contract (which may not be all that well written) costing $500, a bank can hire a topflight lawyer for $5,000 to draw up an airtight loan contract that can be used for 2,000 loans at a cost of $2.50 per loan. At a cost of $2.50 per loan, it now becomes profitable for the financial intermediary to lend Carl the $1,000.

Because financial intermediaries are able to reduce transaction costs substantially, they make it possible for you to provide funds indirectly to people like Carl with productive investment opportunities. In addition, a financial intermediary's low transaction costs mean that it can provide its customers with **liquidity services,** services that make it easier for customers to conduct transactions. For example, banks provide depositors with checking accounts that enable them to pay their bills easily. In addition, depositors can earn interest on checking and savings accounts and yet still convert them into goods and services whenever necessary.

Risk Sharing

Another benefit made possible by the low transaction costs of financial institutions is that they can help reduce the exposure of investors to **risk**—that is, uncertainty about the returns investors will earn on assets. Financial intermediaries do this through the process known as **risk sharing:** They create and sell assets with risk characteristics that people are comfortable with, and the intermediaries then use the funds they acquire by selling these assets to purchase other assets that may have far more risk. Low transaction costs allow financial intermediaries to share risk at low cost, enabling them to earn a profit on the spread between the returns they earn on risky assets and the payments they make on the assets they have sold. This process of risk sharing is also sometimes referred to as **asset transformation,** because in a sense, risky assets are turned into safer assets for investors.

Financial intermediaries also promote risk sharing by helping individuals to diversify and thereby lower the amount of risk to which they are exposed. **Diversification** entails investing in a collection (**portfolio**) of assets whose returns do not always move together, with the result that overall risk is lower than for individual assets. (Diversification is just another name for the old adage, "You shouldn't put all your eggs in one basket.") Low transaction costs allow financial intermediaries to do this by pooling a collection of assets into a new asset and then selling it to individuals.

Asymmetric Information: Adverse Selection and Moral Hazard

The presence of transaction costs in financial markets explains, in part, why financial intermediaries and indirect finance play such an important role in financial markets. An additional reason is that in financial markets, one party often does not know enough about the other party to make accurate decisions. This inequality is called **asymmetric information.** For example, a borrower who takes out a loan usually has better information about the potential returns and risks associated with the investment projects for which the funds are earmarked than the lender does. Lack of information creates problems in the financial system on two fronts: before the transaction is entered into and after.[1]

Adverse selection is the problem created by asymmetric information *before* the transaction occurs. Adverse selection in financial markets occurs when the potential borrowers who are the most likely to produce an undesirable (*adverse*) outcome—the bad credit risks—are the ones who most actively seek out a loan and are thus most likely to be selected. Because adverse selection makes it more likely that loans might be made to bad credit risks, lenders may decide not to make any loans even though there are good credit risks in the marketplace.

To understand why adverse selection occurs, suppose that you have two aunts to whom you might make a loan—Aunt Louise and Aunt Sheila. Aunt Louise is a conservative type who borrows only when she has an investment she is quite sure will pay off. Aunt Sheila, by contrast, is an inveterate gambler who has just come across a get-rich-quick scheme that will make her a millionaire if she can just borrow $1,000 to invest in it. Unfortunately, as with most get-rich-quick schemes, there is a high probability that the investment won't pay off and that Aunt Sheila will lose the $1,000.

---

[1]Asymmetric information and the adverse selection and moral hazard concepts are also crucial problems for the insurance industry.

Which of your aunts is more likely to call you to ask for a loan? Aunt Sheila, of course, because she has so much to gain if the investment pays off. You, however, would not want to make a loan to her because there is a high probability that her investment will turn sour and she will be unable to pay you back.

If you knew both your aunts very well—that is, if your information were not asymmetric—you wouldn't have a problem, because you would know that Aunt Sheila is a bad risk and so you would not lend to her. Suppose, though, that you don't know your aunts well. You are more likely to lend to Aunt Sheila than to Aunt Louise because Aunt Sheila would be hounding you for the loan. Because of the possibility of adverse selection, you might decide not to lend to either of your aunts, even though there are times when Aunt Louise, who is an excellent credit risk, might need a loan for a worthwhile investment.

Moral hazard is the problem created by asymmetric information *after* the transaction occurs. Moral hazard in financial markets is the risk (*hazard*) that the borrower might engage in activities that are undesirable (*immoral*) from the lender's point of view, because they make it less likely that the loan will be paid back. Because moral hazard lowers the probability that the loan will be repaid, lenders may decide that they would rather not make a loan.

As an example of moral hazard, suppose that you made a $1,000 loan to another relative, Uncle Melvin, who needs the money to purchase a computer so he can set up a business typing students' term papers. Once you have made the loan, however, Uncle Melvin is more likely to slip off to the track and play the horses. If he bets on a 20-to-1 long shot and wins with your money, he is able to pay you back your $1,000 and live high off the hog with the remaining $19,000. But if he loses, as is likely, you don't get paid back, and all he has lost is his reputation as a reliable, upstanding uncle. Uncle Melvin therefore has an incentive to go to the track because his gains ($19,000) if he bets correctly are much greater than the cost to him (his reputation) if he bets incorrectly. If you knew what Uncle Melvin was up to, you would prevent him from going to the track, and he would not be able to increase the moral hazard. However, because it is hard for you to keep informed about his whereabouts—that is, because information is asymmetric—there is a good chance that Uncle Melvin will go to the track and you will not get paid back. The risk of moral hazard might therefore discourage you from making the $1,000 loan to Uncle Melvin, even if you were sure that you would be paid back if he used it to set up his business.

Another way of describing the moral hazard problem is that it leads to **conflicts of interest,** in which one party in a financial contract has incentives to act in its own interest rather than in the interests of the other party. Indeed, this is exactly what happens if your Uncle Melvin is tempted to go to the track and gamble at your expense.

study guide

Because the concepts of adverse selection and moral hazard are extremely useful in understanding the behavior we examine in this and many of the later chapters (and in life in general), you must understand them fully. One way to distinguish between them is to remember that adverse selection is a problem of asymmetric information *before* entering into a transaction, whereas moral hazard is a problem of asymmetric information *after* the transaction has occurred. A helpful way to nail down these concepts is to think of other examples, for financial or other types of transactions, in which adverse selection or moral hazard plays a role. Several problems at the end of the chapter provide additional examples of situations involving adverse selection and moral hazard.

The problems created by adverse selection and moral hazard are an important impediment to well-functioning financial markets. Again, financial intermediaries can alleviate these problems.

With financial intermediaries in the economy, small savers can provide their funds to the financial markets by lending these funds to a trustworthy intermediary—say, the Honest John Bank—which in turn lends the funds out either by making loans or by buying securities such as stocks or bonds. Successful financial intermediaries have higher earnings on their investments than small savers, because they are better equipped than individuals to screen out bad credit risks from good ones, thereby reducing losses due to adverse selection. In addition, financial intermediaries have high earnings because they develop expertise in monitoring the parties they lend to, thus reducing losses due to moral hazard. The result is that financial intermediaries can afford to pay lender-savers interest or provide substantial services and still earn a profit.

As we have seen, financial intermediaries play an important role in the economy because they provide liquidity services, promote risk sharing, and solve information problems, thereby allowing small savers and borrowers to benefit from the existence of financial markets. The success of financial intermediaries in performing this role is evidenced by the fact that most Americans invest their savings with them and obtain loans from them. Financial intermediaries play a key role in improving economic efficiency because they help financial markets channel funds from lender-savers to people with productive investment opportunities. Without a well-functioning set of financial intermediaries, it is very hard for an economy to reach its full potential.

Types of Financial Intermediaries

We have seen why financial intermediaries play such an important role in the economy. Now we look at the principal financial intermediaries themselves and how they perform the intermediation function. They fall into three categories: depository institutions (banks), contractual savings institutions, and investment intermediaries. Table 1 provides a guide to the discussion of the financial intermediaries that fit into these three categories by describing their primary liabilities (sources of funds) and assets (uses of funds). The relative size of these intermediaries in the United States is indicated in Table 2, which lists the amount of their assets at the end of 1980, 1990, 2000, and 2007.

Depository Institutions

Depository institutions (for simplicity, we refer to these as *banks* throughout this text) are financial intermediaries that accept deposits from individuals and institutions and make loans. These institutions include commercial banks and the so-called **thrift institutions (thrifts):** savings and loan associations, mutual savings banks, and credit unions.

Commercial Banks These financial intermediaries raise funds primarily by issuing checkable deposits (deposits on which checks can be written), savings deposits (deposits that are payable on demand but do not allow their owner to write checks), and time deposits (deposits with fixed terms to maturity). They then use these funds

TABLE 1 Primary Assets and Liabilities of Financial Intermediaries

Type of Intermediary	Primary Liabilities (Sources of Funds)	Primary Assets (Uses of Funds)
Depository institutions (banks)		
Commercial banks	Deposits	Business and consumer loans, mortgages, U.S. government securities and municipal bonds
Savings and loan associations	Deposits	Mortgages
Mutual savings banks	Deposits	Mortgages
Credit unions	Deposits	Consumer loans
Contractual savings institutions		
Life insurance companies	Premiums from policies	Corporate bonds and mortgages
Fire and casualty insurance companies	Premiums from policies	Municipal bonds, corporate bonds and stock, U.S. government securities
Pension funds, government retirement funds	Employer and employee contributions	Corporate bonds and stock
Investment intermediaries		
Finance companies	Commercial paper, stocks, bonds	Consumer and business loans
Mutual funds	Shares	Stocks, bonds
Money market mutual funds	Shares	Money market instruments

Source: Federal Reserve Flow of Funds Accounts: www.federalreserve.gov/releases/Z1/.

to make commercial, consumer, and mortgage loans and to buy U.S. government securities and municipal bonds. There are slightly fewer than 7,500 commercial banks in the United States, and as a group, they are the largest financial intermediary and have the most diversified portfolios (collections) of assets.

Savings and Loan Associations (S&Ls) and Mutual Savings Banks These depository institutions, of which there are approximately 1,300, obtain funds primarily through savings deposits (often called *shares*) and time and checkable deposits. In the past, these institutions were constrained in their activities and mostly made mortgage loans for residential housing. Over time, these restrictions have been loosened so that the distinction between these depository institutions and commercial banks has blurred. These intermediaries have become more alike and are now more competitive with each other.

Credit Unions These financial institutions, numbering about 9,500, are typically very small cooperative lending institutions organized around a particular group: union members, employees of a particular firm, and so forth. They acquire funds from deposits called *shares* and primarily make consumer loans.

Contractual Savings Institutions

Contractual savings institutions, such as insurance companies and pension funds, are financial intermediaries that acquire funds at periodic intervals on a contractual basis. Because they can predict with reasonable accuracy how much they will have to pay

TABLE 2 Principal Financial Intermediaries and Value of Their Assets

	Value of Assets ($ billions, end of year)			
Type of Intermediary	1980	1990	2000	2006
Depository institutions (banks)				
Commercial banks	1,481	3,334	6,469	7,613
Savings and loan associations and mutual savings banks	792	1,365	1,218	1,715
Credit unions	67	215	441	719
Contractual savings institutions				
Life insurance companies	464	1,367	3,136	4,709
Fire and casualty insurance companies	182	533	862	1,365
Pension funds (private)	504	1,629	4,355	5,558
State and local government retirement funds	197	737	2,293	2,979
Investment intermediaries				
Finance companies	205	610	1,140	1,889
Mutual funds	70	654	4,435	7,093
Money market mutual funds	76	498	1,812	2,313

Source: Federal Reserve Flow of Funds Accounts: www.federalreserve.gov/releases/Z1/.

out in benefits in the coming years, they do not have to worry as much as depository institutions about losing funds quickly. As a result, the liquidity of assets is not as important a consideration for them as it is for depository institutions, and they tend to invest their funds primarily in long-term securities such as corporate bonds, stocks, and mortgages.

Life Insurance Companies Life insurance companies insure people against financial hazards following a death and sell annuities (annual income payments upon retirement). They acquire funds from the premiums that people pay to keep their policies in force and use them mainly to buy corporate bonds and mortgages. They also purchase stocks, but are restricted in the amount that they can hold. Currently, with $4.7 trillion in assets, they are among the largest of the contractual savings institutions.

Fire and Casualty Insurance Companies These companies insure their policyholders against loss from theft, fire, and accidents. They are very much like life insurance companies, receiving funds through premiums for their policies, but they have a greater possibility of loss of funds if major disasters occur. For this reason, they use their funds to buy more liquid assets than life insurance companies do. Their largest holding of assets is municipal bonds; they also hold corporate bonds and stocks and U.S. government securities.

Pension Funds and Government Retirement Funds Private pension funds and state and local retirement funds provide retirement income in the form of annuities to employees who are covered by a pension plan. Funds are acquired by contributions from employers and from employees, who either have a contribution automatically deducted from their paychecks or contribute voluntarily. The largest asset holdings of pension funds are corporate bonds and stocks. The establishment of pension funds has been actively encouraged by the federal government, both through legislation requiring pension plans and through tax incentives to encourage contributions.

Investment Intermediaries

This category of financial intermediaries includes finance companies, mutual funds, and money market mutual funds.

Finance Companies Finance companies raise funds by selling commercial paper (a short-term debt instrument) and by issuing stocks and bonds. They lend these funds to consumers, who make purchases of such items as furniture, automobiles, and home improvements, and to small businesses. Some finance companies are organized by a parent corporation to help sell its product. For example, Ford Motor Credit Company makes loans to consumers who purchase Ford automobiles.

Mutual Funds These financial intermediaries acquire funds by selling shares to many individuals and use the proceeds to purchase diversified portfolios of stocks and bonds. Mutual funds allow shareholders to pool their resources so that they can take advantage of lower transaction costs when buying large blocks of stocks or bonds. In addition, mutual funds allow shareholders to hold more diversified portfolios than they otherwise would. Shareholders can sell (redeem) shares at any time, but the value of these shares will be determined by the value of the mutual fund's holdings of securities. Because these fluctuate greatly, the value of mutual fund shares will, too; therefore, investments in mutual funds can be risky.

Money Market Mutual Funds These financial institutions have the characteristics of a mutual fund but also function to some extent as a depository institution because they offer deposit-type accounts. Like most mutual funds, they sell shares to acquire funds that are then used to buy money market instruments that are both safe and very liquid. The interest on these assets is paid out to the shareholders.

A key feature of these funds is that shareholders can write checks against the value of their shareholdings. In effect, shares in a money market mutual fund function like checking account deposits that pay interest. Money market mutual funds have experienced extraordinary growth since 1971, when they first appeared. By 2006, their assets had climbed to nearly $2.3 trillion.

Investment Banks Despite its name, an investment bank is not a bank or a financial intermediary in the ordinary sense; that is, it does not take in deposits and then lend them out. Instead, an investment bank is a different type of intermediary that helps a corporation issue securities. First it advises the corporation on which type of securities to issue (stocks or bonds); then it helps sell (underwrite) the securities by purchasing them from the corporation at a predetermined price and reselling them in the market. Investment banks also act as deal makers and earn enormous fees by helping corporations acquire other companies through mergers or acquisitions.

Regulation of the Financial System

go online

www.sec.gov
The United States Securities and Exchange Commission home page. It contains vast SEC resources, laws and regulations, investor information, and litigation.

The financial system is among the most heavily regulated sectors of the American economy. The government regulates financial markets for two main reasons: to increase the information available to investors and to ensure the soundness of the financial system. We will examine how these two reasons have led to the present regulatory environment. As a study aid, the principal regulatory agencies of the U.S. financial system are listed in Table 3.

Increasing Information Available to Investors

Asymmetric information in financial markets means that investors may be subject to adverse selection and moral hazard problems that may hinder the efficient operation of financial markets. Risky firms or outright crooks may be the most eager to sell securities to unwary investors, and the resulting adverse selection problem may keep investors out of financial markets. Furthermore, once an investor has bought a security, thereby lending money to a firm, the borrower may have incentives to engage in risky activities or to commit outright fraud. The presence of this moral hazard problem may also keep investors away from financial markets. Government regulation can reduce adverse selection and moral hazard problems in financial

TABLE 3 Principal Regulatory Agencies of the U.S. Financial System

Regulatory Agency	Subject of Regulation	Nature of Regulations
Securities and Exchange Commission (SEC)	Organized exchanges and financial markets	Requires disclosure of information, restricts insider trading
Commodities Futures Trading Commission (CFTC)	Futures market exchanges	Regulates procedures for trading in futures markets
Office of the Comptroller of the Currency	Federally chartered commercial banks	Charters and examines the books of federally chartered commercial banks and imposes restrictions on assets they can hold
National Credit Union Administration (NCUA)	Federally chartered credit unions	Charters and examines the books of federally chartered credit unions and imposes restrictions on assets they can hold
State banking and insurance commissions	State-chartered depository institutions	Charter and examine the books of state-chartered banks and insurance companies, impose restrictions on assets they can hold, and impose restrictions on branching
Federal Deposit Insurance Corporation (FDIC)	Commercial banks, mutual savings banks, savings and loan associations	Provides insurance of up to $100,000 for each depositor at a bank, examines the books of insured banks, and imposes restrictions on assets they can hold
Federal Reserve System	All depository institutions	Examines the books of commercial banks that are members of the system, sets reserve requirements for all banks
Office of Thrift Supervision	Savings and loan associations	Examines the books of savings and loan associations, imposes restrictions on assets they can hold

markets and increase their efficiency by increasing the amount of information available to investors.

As a result of the stock market crash in 1929 and revelations of widespread fraud in the aftermath, political demands for regulation culminated in the Securities Act of 1933 and the establishment of the Securities and Exchange Commission (SEC). The SEC requires corporations issuing securities to disclose certain information about their sales, assets, and earnings to the public and restricts trading by the largest stockholders (known as *insiders*) in the corporation. By requiring disclosure of this information and by discouraging insider trading, which could be used to manipulate security prices, the SEC hopes that investors will be better informed and protected from some of the abuses in financial markets that occurred before 1933. Indeed, in recent years, the SEC has been particularly active in prosecuting people involved in insider trading.

Ensuring the Soundness of Financial Intermediaries

Asymmetric information can lead to the widespread collapse of financial intermediaries, referred to as a **financial panic.** Because providers of funds to financial intermediaries may not be able to assess whether the institutions holding their funds are sound, if they have doubts about the overall health of financial intermediaries, they may want to pull their funds out of both sound and unsound institutions. The possible outcome is a financial panic that produces large losses for the public and causes serious damage to the economy. To protect the public and the economy from financial panics, the government has implemented six types of regulations.

Restrictions on Entry State banking and insurance commissions, as well as the Office of the Comptroller of the Currency (an agency of the federal government), have created tight regulations governing who is allowed to set up a financial intermediary. Individuals or groups that want to establish a financial intermediary, such as a bank or an insurance company, must obtain a charter from the state or the federal government. Only if they are upstanding citizens with impeccable credentials and a large amount of initial funds will they be given a charter.

Disclosure There are stringent reporting requirements for financial intermediaries. Their bookkeeping must follow certain strict principles, their books are subject to periodic inspection, and they must make certain information available to the public.

Restrictions on Assets and Activities There are restrictions on what financial intermediaries are allowed to do and what assets they can hold. Before you put your funds into a bank or some other such institution, you would want to know that your funds are safe and that the bank or other financial intermediary will be able to meet its obligations to you. One way of doing this is to restrict the financial intermediary from engaging in certain risky activities. Legislation passed in 1933 (repealed in 1999) separated commercial banking from the securities industry so that banks could not engage in risky ventures associated with this industry. Another way to limit a financial intermediary's risky behavior is to restrict it from holding certain risky assets, or at least from holding a greater quantity of these risky assets than is prudent. For example, commercial banks and other depository institutions are not allowed to hold common stock because stock prices experience substantial fluctuations. Insurance companies are allowed to hold common stock, but their holdings cannot exceed a certain fraction of their total assets.

Deposit Insurance The government can insure people's deposits so that they do not suffer great financial loss if the financial intermediary that holds these deposits should fail. The most important government agency that provides this type of insurance is the Federal Deposit Insurance Corporation (FDIC), which insures each depositor at a commercial bank, savings and loan association, or mutual savings bank up to a loss of $100,000 per account ($250,000 for individual retirement accounts). Premiums paid by these financial intermediaries go into the FDIC's Deposit Insurance Fund, which is used to pay off depositors if an institution fails. The FDIC was created in 1934 after the massive bank failures of 1930–33, in which the savings of many depositors at commercial banks were wiped out. The National Credit Union Share Insurance Fund (NCUSIF) provides similar insurance protection for deposits (shares) at credit unions.

Limits on Competition Politicians have often declared that unbridled competition among financial intermediaries promotes failures that will harm the public. Although the evidence that competition has this effect is extremely weak, state and federal governments at times have imposed restrictions on the opening of additional locations (branches). In the past, banks were not allowed to open up branches in other states, and in some states, banks were restricted from opening branches in additional locations.

Restrictions on Interest Rates Competition has also been inhibited by regulations that impose restrictions on interest rates that can be paid on deposits. For decades after 1933, banks were prohibited from paying interest on checking accounts. In addition, until 1986, the Federal Reserve System had the power under *Regulation Q* to set maximum interest rates that banks could pay on savings deposits. These regulations were instituted because of the widespread belief that unrestricted interest-rate competition helped encourage bank failures during the Great Depression. Later evidence does not seem to support this view, and Regulation Q has been abolished (although there are still restrictions on paying interest on checking accounts held by businesses).

Financial Regulation Abroad

Not surprisingly, given the similarity of the economic system here and in Japan, Canada, and the nations of western Europe, financial regulation in these countries is similar to financial regulation in the United States. The provision of information is improved by requiring corporations issuing securities to report details about assets and liabilities, earnings, and sales of stock, and by prohibiting insider trading. The soundness of intermediaries is ensured by licensing, periodic inspection of financial intermediaries' books, and the provision of deposit insurance (although its coverage is smaller than in the United States and its existence is often intentionally not advertised).

The major differences between financial regulation in the United States and abroad relate to bank regulation. In the past, the United States was the only industrialized country to subject banks to restrictions on branching, which limited banks' size and restricted them to certain geographic regions. (These restrictions were abolished by legislation in 1994.) U.S. banks are also the most restricted in the range of assets they may hold. Banks abroad frequently hold shares in commercial firms; in Japan and Germany, those stakes can be sizable.

SUMMARY

1. The basic function of financial markets is to channel funds from savers who have an excess of funds to spenders who have a shortage of funds. Financial markets can do this either through direct finance, in which borrowers borrow funds directly from lenders by selling them securities, or through indirect finance, which involves a financial intermediary that stands between the lender-savers and the borrower-spenders and helps transfer funds from one to the other. This channeling of funds improves the economic welfare of everyone in the society. Because they allow funds to move from people who have no productive investment opportunities to those who have such opportunities, financial markets contribute to economic efficiency. In addition, channeling of funds directly benefits consumers by allowing them to make purchases when they need them most.

2. Financial markets can be classified as debt and equity markets, primary and secondary markets, exchanges and over-the-counter markets, and money and capital markets.

3. An important trend in recent years is the growing internationalization of financial markets. Eurobonds, which are denominated in a currency other than that of the country in which they are sold, are now the dominant security in the international bond market and have surpassed U.S. corporate bonds as a source of new funds. Eurodollars, which are U.S. dollars deposited in foreign banks, are an important source of funds for American banks.

4. Financial intermediaries are financial institutions that acquire funds by issuing liabilities and, in turn, use those funds to acquire assets by purchasing securities or making loans. Financial intermediaries play an important role in the financial system because they reduce transaction costs, allow risk sharing, and solve problems created by adverse selection and moral hazard. As a result, financial intermediaries allow small savers and borrowers to benefit from the existence of financial markets, thereby increasing the efficiency of the economy.

5. The principal financial intermediaries fall into three categories: (a) banks—commercial banks, savings and loan associations, mutual savings banks, and credit unions; (b) contractual savings institutions—life insurance companies, fire and casualty insurance companies, and pension funds; and (c) investment intermediaries—finance companies, mutual funds, and money market mutual funds.

6. The government regulates financial markets and financial intermediaries for two main reasons: to increase the information available to investors and to ensure the soundness of the financial system. Regulations include requiring disclosure of information to the public, restrictions on who can set up a financial intermediary, restrictions on the assets financial intermediaries can hold, the provision of deposit insurance, limits on competition, and restrictions on interest rates.

KEY TERMS

adverse selection
asset transformation
asymmetric information
brokers
capital
capital market
conflicts of interest
dealers
diversification
dividends
economies of scale
equities
Eurobond
Eurocurrencies
Eurodollars
exchanges

financial intermediation
financial panic
foreign bonds
intermediate-term
investment bank
liabilities
liquid
liquidity services
long-term
maturity
money market
moral hazard
over-the-counter (OTC) market
portfolio
primary market
risk

risk sharing
secondary market
short-term

thrift institutions (thrifts)
transaction costs
underwriting

QUESTIONS

1. Why is a share of Microsoft common stock an asset for its owner and a liability for Microsoft?

2. If I can buy a car today for $5,000 and it is worth $10,000 in extra income next year to me because it enables me to get a job as a traveling anvil seller, should I take out a loan from Larry the Loan Shark at a 90% interest rate if no one else will give me a loan? Will I be better or worse off as a result of taking out this loan? Can you make a case for legalizing loan-sharking?

3. Some economists suspect that one of the reasons that economies in developing countries grow so slowly is that they do not have well-developed financial markets. Does this argument make sense?

4. The U.S. economy borrowed heavily from the British in the nineteenth century to build a railroad system. What was the principal debt instrument used? Why did this make both countries better off?

5. "Because corporations do not actually raise any funds in secondary markets, they are less important to the economy than primary markets." Comment.

6. If you suspect that a company will go bankrupt next year, which would you rather hold, bonds issued by the company or equities issued by the company? Why?

7. How can the adverse selection problem explain why you are more likely to make a loan to a family member than to a stranger?

8. Think of one example in which you have had to deal with the adverse selection problem.

9. Why do loan sharks worry less about moral hazard in connection with their borrowers than some other lenders do?

10. If you are an employer, what kinds of moral hazard problems might you worry about with your employees?

11. If there were no asymmetry in the information that a borrower and a lender had, could there still be a moral hazard problem?

12. "In a world without information and transaction costs, financial intermediaries would not exist." Is this statement true, false, or uncertain? Explain your answer.

13. Why might you be willing to make a loan to your neighbor by putting funds in a savings account earning a 5% interest rate at the bank and having the bank lend her the funds at a 10% interest rate rather than lend her the funds yourself?

14. How does risk sharing benefit both financial intermediaries and private investors?

15. Discuss some of the manifestations of the globalization of world capital markets.

WEB EXERCISES

The Financial System

1. One of the single best sources of information about financial institutions is the U.S. Flow of Funds report produced by the Federal Reserve. This document contains data on most financial intermediaries. Go to **www.federalreserve.gov/releases/Z1/**. Go to the most current release. You may have to load Acrobat Reader if your computer does not already have it; the site has a link for a free patch. Go to the Level Tables and answer the following questions.

a. What percentage of assets do commercial banks hold in loans? What percentage of assets are held in mortgage loans?

b. What percentage of assets do savings and loans hold in mortgage loans?

c. What percentage of assets do credit unions hold in mortgage loans and in consumer loans?

2. The most famous financial market in the world is the New York Stock Exchange. Go to **www.nyse.com**.

a. What is the mission of the NYSE?

b. Firms must pay a fee to list their shares for sale on the NYSE. What would be the fee for a firm with five million common shares outstanding?

Chapter 3

The Valuation Principle: The Foundation of Financial Decision Making

From Chapter 3 of *Fundamentals of Corporate Finance*, 1/e. Jonathan Berk, Peter DeMarzo, Jarrad Harford. Copyright © 2009 by Pearson Prentice Hall. All rights reserved.

The Valuation Principle: The Foundation of Financial Decision Making

LEARNING OBJECTIVES

▶ Identify the role of financial managers in decision making

▶ Recognize the role competitive markets play in determining the value of a good

▶ Understand the Valuation Principle, and how it can be used to identify decisions that increase the value of the firm

▶ Assess the effect of interest rates on today's value of future cash flows

▶ Use the Net Present Value Rule to make investment decisions

▶ Understand the Law of One Price

notation

r	interest rate	PV	present value
NPV	net present value		

INTERVIEW WITH — Matt Herriot, Oxford & Hill Home Products

What do mothballs and finance have in common? Both are important to entrepreneur Matt Herriot, executive vice president of Oxford & Hill Home Products. The company's innovative products, such as Moth Avoid, protect clothing, linens, collectibles and other natural fiber valuables from damage caused by moths, moisture, and mildew. "My finance courses at the University of Georgia's Terry School of Business provided the background I need for my responsibilities, including pricing and sales forecasting. They also help me to communicate with partners and investors in the language of business."

Terry School of Business, University of Georgia, 2005

"We weighed the high cost of getting EPA registration now against its future benefits and decided the revenues and earnings potential made it a good investment."

Matt received his MBA in 2005 and immediately put his finance background to work at the newly launched Oxford & Hill. Based on his experience at other clothing care companies, he saw an untapped opportunity in the moth-prevention market. A major hurdle for companies making chemically based products is the Environmental Protection Agency (EPA) regulatory process. "We weighed the high cost of getting EPA registration now against its future benefits—entrance to a big market with significant barriers to entry and a slower moving competitor—and decided the revenues and earnings potential made it a good investment and the basis for a good business." He worked with prospective investors to find the right financing options for the company and with his management team to allocate resources effectively, to increase the value of the business.

Prior to joining Oxford & Hill and before his formal course work in finance, Matt had a successful career in sales management. However, his limited knowledge of finance was a major disadvantage. When the sales brokerage and importing company he started ran out of cash to service its substantial debt, Matt closed the business and worked in sales management for a consumer products company. "Not having a formal business education kept me from advancing, so I decided to get my MBA while continuing to work full time. The analytical course work was fascinating to me, and I could apply what I learned to the real world." The cost of Matt's decision to return to school has certainly been outweighed by the benefits of his experience at Oxford & Hill.

In mid 2007, Microsoft decided to enter a bidding war with competitors Google and Yahoo! for a stake in the fast-growing social networking site, Facebook. How did Microsoft's managers decide that this was a good decision?

Every decision has future consequences that will affect the value of the firm. These consequences will generally include both benefits and costs. For example, after raising its offer, Microsoft ultimately succeeded in buying a 1.6% stake in Facebook, along with the exclusive right to place ads on the Facebook Web site, for $240 million. In addition to the upfront cost of $240 million for the deal, Microsoft will also incur ongoing costs associated with software development for the platform, network infrastructure, and international marketing efforts to attract advertisers. The benefits of the deal to Microsoft include the revenues associated with the advertising sales, together with the potential appreciation of its 1.6% stake in Facebook should it be sold or it sells shares to the public. This decision will increase Microsoft's value if these benefits outweigh the costs.

More generally, a decision is good for the firm's investors if it increases the firm's value by providing benefits whose value exceeds the costs. But comparing costs and benefits is often complicated because they occur at different points in time, or are in different currencies, or have different risks associated with them. To make a valid comparison, we must use the tools of finance to express all costs and benefits in common terms. In this chapter, we introduce the central concept of finance, and the unifying theme of this book, the *Valuation Principle.* The Valuation Principle states that we can use current market prices to determine the value today of the different costs and benefits associated with a decision. The Valuation Principle allows us to apply the concept of *net present value (NPV)* to compare the costs and benefits of a project in terms of a common unit—namely, dollars today. We will then be able to evaluate a decision by answering this question: *Does the cash value today of its benefits exceed the cash value today of its costs?* In addition, we will see that the difference between the cash values of the benefits and costs indicates the net amount by which the decision will increase the value of the firm and therefore the wealth of its investors. The Valuation Principle also leads to the important concept of the *Law of One Price,* which will prove to be a key tool in understanding the value of stocks, bonds, and other securities that are traded in the market.

 # Managerial Decision Making

A financial manager's job is to make decisions on behalf of the firm's investors. For example, a manager of a manufacturing company has to decide how much to produce. By increasing production more units can be sold, but the price per unit will likely be lower. Does it make sense to increase production? A manager of another company might expect an increase in demand for her products. Should she raise prices or increase production? If the decision is to increase production and a new facility is required, is it better to rent or purchase the facility? When should managers give their workers a pay increase? These are a few examples of the kinds of choices managers face every day.

Our objective in this book is to explain how to make decisions that increase the value of the firm to its investors. In principal, the idea is simple and intuitive: For good decisions, the benefits exceed the costs. Of course, real-world opportunities are usually complex and so the costs and benefits are often difficult to quantify. Quantifying them often involves using skills from other management disciplines, as in the following examples:

Marketing: to determine the increase in revenues resulting from an advertising campaign

Economics: to determine the increase in demand from lowering the price of a product

Organizational Behavior: to determine the effect of changes in management structure on productivity

Strategy: to determine a competitor's response to a price increase

Operations: to determine production costs after the modernization of a manufacturing plant

For the remainder of this text, we will assume that we can rely on experts in these different areas to provide this information so that the costs and benefits associated with a decision have already been identified. With that task done, the financial manager's job is to compare the costs and benefits and determine the best decision to make for the value of the firm.

1. What defines a good decision?

2. What is the financial manager's role in decision making for the firm?

2 Cost-Benefit Analysis

As we have already seen, the first step in decision making is to identify the costs and benefits of a decision. The next step is quantifying the costs and benefits. Any decision in which the value of the benefits exceeds the costs will increase the value of the firm. To evaluate the costs and benefits of a decision, we must value the options in the same terms—cash today. Let's make this concrete with a simple example.

Suppose a jewelry manufacturer has the opportunity to trade 200 ounces of silver for 10 ounces of gold today. An ounce of silver differs in value from an ounce of gold. Consequently, it is incorrect to compare 200 ounces to 10 ounces and conclude that the larger quantity is better. Instead, to compare the costs of the silver and benefit of the gold, we first need to quantify their values in equivalent terms—cash today.

Consider the silver. What is its cash value today? Suppose silver can be bought and sold for a current market price of $10 per ounce. Then the 200 ounces of silver we give up has a cash value of:[1]

$$(200 \text{ ounces of silver}) \times (\$10/\text{ounce of silver}) = \$2000$$

If the current market price for gold is $500 per ounce, then the 10 ounces of gold we receive has a cash value of

$$(10 \text{ ounces of gold}) \times (\$500/\text{ounce of gold}) = \$5000$$

We have now quantified the decision. The jeweler's opportunity has a benefit of $5000 and a cost of $2000. The net benefit of the decision is $5000 − $2000 = $3000 today. The net value of the decision is positive, so by accepting the trade, the jewelry firm will be richer by $3000.

EXAMPLE 1

Comparing Costs and Benefits

Problem

Suppose you work as a customer account manager for an importer of frozen seafood. A customer is willing to purchase 300 pounds of frozen shrimp today for a total price of $1500, including delivery. You can buy frozen shrimp on the wholesale market for $3 per pound today, and arrange for delivery at a cost of $100 today. Will taking this opportunity increase the value of the firm?

Solution

▶ **Plan**

To determine whether this opportunity will increase the value of the firm, we need to value the benefits and the costs using market prices. We have market prices for our costs:

Wholesale price of shrimp: $3/pound   Delivery cost: $100

We have a customer offering the following market price for 300 pounds of shrimp delivered: $1500. All that is left is to compare them.

▶ **Execute**

The benefit of the transaction is $1500 today. The costs are (300 lbs.) × $3/lbs. = $900 today for the shrimp, and $100 today for delivery, for a total cost of $1000 today. If you are certain about these costs and benefits, the right decision is obvious: You should seize this opportunity because the firm will gain $1500 − $1000 = $500.

▶ **Evaluate**

Thus, taking this opportunity contributes $500 to the value of the firm, in the form of cash that can be paid out immediately to the firm's investors.

Concept Check

3. How do we determine whether a decision increases the value of the firm?

4. When costs and benefits are in different units or goods, how can we compare them?

---

[1]You might worry about commissions or other transactions costs that are incurred when buying or selling silver, in addition to the market price. For now, we will ignore transactions costs, and discuss their effect later.

3 Valuation Principle

In the previous examples, the right decisions for the firms were clear because the costs and benefits were easy to evaluate and compare. They were easy to evaluate because we were able to use current market prices to convert them into equivalent cash values. Once we can express costs and benefits in terms of "cash today," it is a straightforward process to compare them and determine whether the decision will increase the firm's value.

Note that in both the examples, we used market prices to assess the values of the different commodities involved. What about the firm's other possible uses for those commodities? For example, consider the jewelry manufacturer with the opportunity to trade silver for gold. When evaluating the trade, we did not concern ourselves with whether the jeweler thought that the price was fair or whether the jeweler would actually have a use for the silver or gold. Suppose, for example, that the jeweler thinks the current price of silver is too high. Does this matter—would he value the silver at less than $2000? The answer is no—he can always sell the silver at the current market price and receive $2000 right now, so he would never place a lower value on the silver. Similarly, he also will not pay more than $2000 for the silver. Even if he really needs silver or for some reason thinks the price of silver is too low, he can always buy 200 ounces of silver for $2000 and so would not pay more than that amount. Thus, independent of his own views or preferences, the value of the silver to the jeweler is $2000.

competitive market A market in which the good can be bought *and* sold at the same price.

Note that the jeweler can both buy and sell silver at its current market price. His personal preferences or use for the silver and his opinion of the fair price are therefore irrelevant in evaluating the value of this opportunity. This observation highlights an important general principle related to goods trading in a **competitive market**, a market in which a good can be bought *and* sold at the same price. Whenever a good trades in a competitive market, that price determines the value of the good. This point is one of the central and most powerful ideas in finance. It will underlie almost every concept that we develop throughout the text.

EXAMPLE 2

Competitive Market Prices Determine Value

Problem

You have just won a radio contest and are disappointed to find out that the prize is four tickets to the Def Leppard reunion tour (face value $40 each). Not being a fan of 1980s power rock, you have no intention of going to the show. However, it turns out that there is a second choice: two tickets to your favorite band's sold-out show (face value $45 each). You notice that on eBay, tickets to the Def Leppard show are being bought and sold for $30 apiece and tickets to your favorite band's show are being bought and sold at $50 each. What should you do?

Solution

▸ **Plan**

Market prices, not your personal preferences (nor the face value of the tickets), are relevant here:

    4 Def Leppard tickets at $30 apiece
    2 of your favorite band's tickets at $50 apiece

You need to compare the market value of each option and choose the one with the highest market value.

> ▶ **Execute**
>
> The Def Leppard tickets have a total value of $120 (4 × $30) versus the $100 total value of the other 2 tickets (2 × $50). Instead of taking the tickets to your favorite band, you should accept the Def Leppard tickets, sell them on eBay, and use the proceeds to buy 2 tickets to your favorite band's show. You'll even have $20 left over to buy a T-shirt.

> ▶ **Evaluate**
>
> Even though you prefer your favorite band, you should still take the opportunity to get the Def Leppard tickets instead. As we emphasized earlier, whether this opportunity is attractive depends on its net value using market prices. Because the value of Def Leppard tickets is $20 more than the value of your favorite band's tickets, the opportunity is appealing.

Once we use market prices to evaluate the costs and benefits of a decision in terms of cash today, it is then a simple matter to determine the best decision for the firm. The best decision makes the firm and its investors wealthier, because the value of its benefits exceeds the value of its costs. We call this idea the Valuation Principle:

The Valuation Principle:

The value of a commodity or an asset to the firm or its investors is determined by its competitive market price. The benefits and costs of a decision should be evaluated using those market prices. When the value of the benefits exceeds the value of the costs, the decision will increase the market value of the firm.

The Valuation Principle provides the basis for decision making throughout this text. In the remainder of this chapter, we first apply it to decisions whose costs and benefits occur at different points in time and develop the main tool of project evaluation, the *Net Present Value Rule*. We then consider its consequences for the prices of assets in the market and develop the concept of the *Law of One Price*.

When Competitive Market Prices Are Not Available

Competitive market prices allow us to calculate the value of a decision without worrying about the tastes or opinions of the decision maker. When competitive prices are not available, we can no longer do this. Prices at retail stores, for example, are one-sided: You can buy at the posted price, but you cannot sell the good to the store at that same price. We cannot use these one-sided prices to determine an exact cash value. They determine the maximum value of the good (since it can always be purchased at that price), but an individual may value it for much less depending on his or her preferences for the good.

Let's consider an example. It has long been common for banks to try to entice people to open accounts by offering them something for free in exchange (it used to be a toaster). In 2007 Key Bank offered college students a free iPod nano if they would open a new checking account and make two deposits. At the time, the retail price of that model of nano was $199. Because there is no competitive market to trade iPods, the value of the nano depends on whether you were going to buy one or not.

If you planned to buy a nano anyway, then the value to you of the nano is $199, the price you would otherwise pay for it. In this case, the value of the bank's offer is $199. But suppose you do not want or need a nano. If you were to get it from the bank and then sell it, the value of taking the deal would be whatever price you could get for the nano. For example, if you could sell the nano for $150 to your friend, then the bank's offer is worth $150 to you. Thus, depending on your desire to own a new nano, the bank's offer is worth somewhere between $150 (you don't want a nano) and $199 (you definitely want one).

EXAMPLE 3

Applying the Valuation Principle

Problem

You are the operations manager at your firm. Due to a pre-existing contract, you have the opportunity to acquire 200 barrels of oil and 3000 pounds of copper for a total of $25,000. The current market price of oil is $90 per barrel and for copper is $3.50 per pound. You are not sure that you need all of the oil and copper, so you are wondering if you should take this opportunity. How valuable is it? Would your decision change if you believed the value of oil or copper would plummet over the next month?

Solution

▶ **Plan**

We need to quantify the costs and benefits using market prices. We are comparing $25,000 with:

> 200 barrels of oil at $90 per barrel
> 3000 pounds of copper at $3.50 per pound

▶ **Execute**

Using the competitive market prices we have:

$$(200 \text{ barrels}) \times (\$90/\text{barrel today}) = \$18{,}000 \text{ today}$$
$$(3000 \text{ pounds of copper}) \times (\$3.50/\text{pound today}) = \$10{,}500 \text{ today}$$

The value of the opportunity is the value of the oil plus the value of the copper less the cost of the opportunity, or $18,000 + $10,500 − $25,000 = $3500 today. Because the value is positive, we should take it. This value depends only on the *current* market prices for oil and copper. If we do not need all of the oil and copper, we can sell the excess at current market prices. Even if we thought the value of oil or copper was about to plummet, the value of this investment would be unchanged. (We can always exchange them for dollars immediately at the current market prices.)

▶ **Evaluate**

Since we are transacting today, only the current prices in a competitive market matter. Our own use for or opinion about the future prospects of oil or copper do not alter the value of the decision today. This decision is good for the firm, and will increase its value by $3500.

Concept Check

5. How should we determine the value of a good?

6. If crude oil trades in a competitive market, would an oil refiner that has a use for the oil value it differently than another investor would?

4 The Time Value of Money and Interest Rates

For most financial decisions, unlike in the examples presented so far, costs and benefits occur at different points in time. For example, typical investment projects incur costs upfront and provide benefits in the future. In this section, we show how to account for this time difference when using the Valuation Principle to make a decision.

The Time Value of Money

Consider a firm's investment opportunity with the following cash flows:

> Cost: $100,000 today
> Benefit: $105,000 in one year

Because both are expressed in dollar terms, are the cost and benefit directly comparable? Calculating the project's net value as $105,000 − $100,000 = $5000 is incorrect because it ignores the *timing* of the costs and benefits. That is, it treats money today as equivalent to money in one year. In general, a dollar today is worth *more* than a dollar in one year. To see why, note that if you have $1 today, you can invest it. For example, if you deposit it in a bank account paying 7% interest, you will have $1.07 at the end of one year. We call the difference in value between money today and money in the future the **time value of money**. We now develop the tools needed to value our $100,000 investment opportunity correctly.

time value of money The difference in value between money today and money in the future; also, the observation that two cash flows at two different points in time have different values.

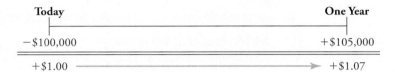

The Interest Rate: Converting Cash Across Time

By depositing money into a savings account, we can convert money today into money in the future with no risk. Similarly, by borrowing money from the bank, we can exchange money in the future for money today. The rate at which we can exchange money today for money in the future is determined by the current interest rate. In the same way that an exchange rate allows us to convert money from one currency to another, the interest rate allows us to convert money from one point in time to another. In essence, an interest rate is like an exchange rate across time. It tells us the market price today of money in the future.

Suppose the current annual interest rate is 7%. By investing $1 today we can convert this $1 into $1.07 in one year. Similarly, by borrowing at this rate, we can exchange $1.07 in one year for $1 today. More generally, we define the **interest rate**, r, for a given period as the interest rate at which money can be borrowed or lent over that period. In our example, the interest rate is 7% and we can exchange 1 dollar today for $(1 + .07)$ dollars in the future. In general, we can exchange 1 dollar today for $(1 + r)$ dollars in the future, and vice versa. We refer to $(1 + r)$ as the **interest rate factor** for cash flows; it defines how we convert cash flows across time, and has units of "$ in one year/$ today."

interest rate The rate at which money can be borrowed or lent over a given period.

interest rate factor One plus the interest rate, it is the rate of exchange between dollars today and dollars in the future. It has units of "$ in one year/$ today."

As with other market prices, the interest rate ultimately depends on supply and demand. In particular, at the interest rate the supply of savings equals the demand for borrowing. But regardless of how it is determined, once we know the interest rate, we can apply the Valuation Principle and use it to evaluate other decisions in which costs and benefits are separated in time.

Value of $100,000 Investment in One Year. Let's reevaluate the investment we considered earlier, this time taking into account the time value of money. If the interest rate is 7%, then we can express the cost of the investment as:

$$\text{Cost} = (\$100,000 \text{ today}) \times (1.07 \text{ \$ in one year/\$ today})$$
$$= \$107,000 \text{ in one year}$$

Think of this amount as the opportunity cost of spending $100,000 today: The firm gives up the $107,000 it would have had in one year if it had left the money in the bank.

Alternatively, by borrowing the $100,000 from the same bank, the firm would owe $107,000 in one year.

	Today		One Year
Investment	−$100,000		+$105,000
Bank	−$100,000		+$107,000

We have used a market price, the interest rate, to put both the costs and benefits in terms of "dollars in one year," so now we can use the Valuation Principle to compare them and compute the investment's net value by subtracting the cost of the investment from the benefit in one year:

$$\$105,000 - \$107,000 = -\$2000 \text{ in one year}$$

In other words, the firm could earn $2000 more in one year by putting the $100,000 in the bank rather than making this investment. Because the net value is negative, we should reject the investment: If we took it, the firm would be $2000 poorer in one year than if we didn't.

Value of $100,000 Investment Today.   The previous calculation expressed the value of the costs and benefits in terms of dollars in one year. Alternatively, we can use the interest rate factor to convert to dollars today. Consider the benefit of $105,000 in one year. What is the equivalent amount in terms of dollars today? That is, how much would we need to have in the bank today so that we would end up with $105,000 in the bank in one year? We find this amount by dividing by the interest rate factor:

$$\text{Benefit} = (\$105,000 \text{ in one year}) \div (1.07 \text{ \$ in one year/\$ today})$$
$$= \$98,130.84 \text{ today}$$

This is also the amount the bank would lend to us today if we promised to repay $105,000 in one year.[2] Thus, it is the competitive market price at which we can "buy" or "sell" $105,000 in one year.

	Today		One Year
Value of Cost Today	−$100,000		+$105,000
Value of Benefit Today	+$ 98,130.84	$\dfrac{105,000}{1.07}$	

Now we are ready to compute the net value of the investment by subtracting the cost from the benefit:

$$\$98,130.84 - \$100,000 = -\$1869.16 \text{ today}$$

Once again, the negative result indicates that we should reject the investment. Taking the investment would make the firm $1869.16 poorer today because it gave up $100,000 for something worth only $98,130.84.

---

[2]We are assuming the bank is willing to lend at the same 7% interest rate, which would be the case if there were no risk associated with the cash flow.

present value (PV) The value of a cost or benefit computed in terms of cash today.

future value The value of a cash flow that is moved forward in time.

discount factor The value today of a dollar received in the future.

discount rate The appropriate rate to discount a stream of cash flows to determine their value at an earlier time.

Present Versus Future Value. This calculation demonstrates that our decision is the same whether we express the value of the investment in terms of dollars in one year or dollars today: We should reject the investment. Indeed, if we convert from dollars today to dollars in one year,

$$(-\$1869.16 \text{ today}) \times (1.07 \text{ \$ in one year/\$ today}) = -\$2000 \text{ in one year}$$

we see that the two results are equivalent, but expressed as values at different points in time. When we express the value in terms of dollars today, we call it the **present value (PV)** of the investment. If we express it in terms of dollars in the future, we call it the **future value** of the investment.

Discount Factors and Rates. In the preceding calculation, we can interpret

$$\frac{1}{1+r} = \frac{1}{1.07} = 0.93458$$

as the *price* today of \$1 in one year. In other words, for just under 93.5 cents, you can "buy" \$1 to be delivered in one year. Note that the value is less than \$1—money in the future is worth less today, and so its price reflects a discount. Because it provides the discount at which we can purchase money in the future, the amount $\frac{1}{1+r}$ is called the one-year **discount factor**. The interest rate is also referred to as the **discount rate** for an investment.

EXAMPLE 4

Comparing Revenues at Different Points in Time

Problem

The launch of Sony's PlayStation 3 was delayed until November 2006, giving Microsoft's Xbox 360 a full year on the market without competition. Imagine that it is November 2005 and you are the marketing manager for the PlayStation. You estimate that if PlayStation 3 were ready to be launched immediately, you could sell \$2 billion worth of the console in its first year. However, if your launch is delayed a year, you believe that Microsoft's head start will reduce your first-year sales by 20%. If the interest rate is 8%, what is the cost of a delay of the first year's revenues in terms of dollars in 2005?

Solution

▶ **Plan**

Revenues if released today: \$2 billion   Revenue decrease if delayed: 20%   Interest rate: 8%

We need to compute the revenues if the launch is delayed and compare them to the revenues from launching today. However, in order to make a fair comparison, we need to convert the future revenues of the PlayStation if they are delayed into an equivalent present value of those revenues today.

▶ **Execute**

If the launch is delayed to 2006, revenues will drop by 20% of \$2 billion, or \$400 million, to \$1.6 billion. To compare this amount to revenues of \$2 billion if launched in 2005, we must convert it using the interest rate of 8%:

$$\$1.6 \text{ billion in 2006} \div (\$1.08 \text{ in 2006/\$1 in 2005}) = \$1.481 \text{ billion in 2005}$$

Therefore, the cost of a delay of one year is

$$\$2 \text{ billion} - \$1.481 \text{ billion} = \$0.519 \text{ billion } (\$519 \text{ million}).$$

▶ **Evaluate**

Delaying the project for one year was equivalent to giving up $519 million in cash. In this example, we focused only on the effect on the first year's revenues. However, delaying the launch delays the entire revenue stream by one year, so the total cost would be calculated in the same way by summing the cost of delay for each year of revenues.

We can use the interest rate to determine values in the same way we used competitive market prices. Figure 1 illustrates how we use competitive market prices and interest rates to convert between dollars today and other goods, or dollars in the future. Once we quantify all the costs and benefits of an investment in terms of dollars today, we can rely on the Valuation Principle to determine whether the investment will increase the firm's value.

FIGURE 1   Converting Between Dollars Today and Gold or Dollars in the Future

We can convert dollars today to different goods or points in time by using the competitive market price or interest rate. Once values are in equivalent terms, we can use the Valuation Principle to make a decision.

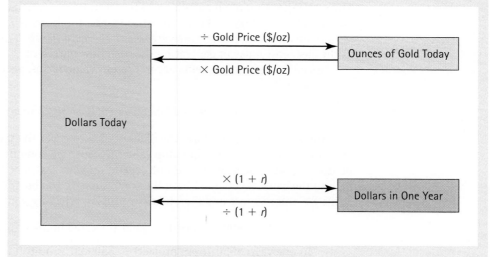

  Concept Check

7. How do you compare costs at different points in time?

8. Is the value today of money to be received in one year higher when interest rates are high or when interest rates are low?

5 The NPV Decision Rule

In Section 4, we converted between cash today and cash in the future using the interest rate. As long as we convert costs and benefits to the same point in time, we can use the Valuation Principle to make a decision. In practice, however, most corporations prefer to measure values in terms of their present value—that is, in terms of cash today. In this section, we apply the Valuation Principle to derive the concept of the *net present value* or *NPV*, which we can use to define the "golden rule" of financial decision making, the *NPV Rule*.

Net Present Value

When the value of a cost or benefit is computed in terms of cash today, we refer to it as the present value (PV). Similarly, we define the **net present value (NPV)** of a project or investment as the difference between the present value of its benefits and the present value of its costs:

net present value (NPV)
The difference between the present value of a project or investment's benefits and the present value of its costs.

Net Present Value

$$NPV = PV(\text{Benefits}) - PV(\text{Costs}) \qquad (1)$$

Let's consider a simple example. Suppose your firm is offered the following investment opportunity: In exchange for $500 today, you will receive $550 in one year. If the interest rate is 8% per year then:

$$PV(\text{Benefit}) = (\$550 \text{ in one year}) \div (1.08 \, \$ \text{ in one year/\$ today})$$
$$= \$509.26 \text{ today}$$

This PV is the amount you would need to put in the bank today to generate $550 in one year ($509.26 \times 1.08 = \$550$). In other words, *the present value is the amount you need to invest at the current interest rate to recreate the cash flow.* We can think of this as the cash cost today of generating the cash flow ourselves.

Once the costs and benefits are in present value terms, we can compute the investment's NPV:

$$NPV = \$509.26 - \$500 = \$9.26 \text{ today}$$

But what if you don't have the $500 needed to cover the initial cost of the project? Does the project still have the same value? Because we computed the value using competitive market prices, it should not depend on your tastes or the amount of cash you have in the bank. If you don't have the $500, suppose you borrow $509.26 from the bank at the 8% interest rate and then take the project. What are your cash flows in this case?

Today: $509.26 (loan) − $500 (invested in the project) = $9.26

In one year: $550 (from project) − $509.26 × 1.08 (loan balance) = $0

This transaction leaves you with exactly $9.26 extra cash in your pocket today and no future net obligations. So taking the project is similar to having an extra $9.26 in cash up front. Thus, the NPV expresses the value of an investment decision as an amount of cash received today. *As long as the NPV is positive, the decision increases the value of the firm and is a good decision regardless of your current cash needs or preferences regarding when to spend the money.*

The NPV Decision Rule

As shown in the last example, the Valuation Principle implies that we should undertake projects with a positive NPV. That is, good projects are those for which the present value of the benefits exceeds the present value of the costs. As a result, the value of the firm increases and investors are wealthier. Projects with negative NPVs have costs that exceed their benefits. Accepting them is equivalent to losing money today.

We capture this logic in the **NPV Decision Rule**:

NPV Decision Rule When choosing among investment alternatives, take the alternative with the highest NPV. Choosing this alternative is equivalent to receiving its NPV in cash today.

> *When making an investment decision, take the alternative with the highest NPV. Choosing this alternative is equivalent to receiving its NPV in cash today.*

Because NPV is expressed in terms of cash today, using the NPV decision rule is a simple way to apply the Valuation Principle. Decisions that increase wealth are superior to those that decrease wealth. We don't need to know anything about the investor's preferences to reach this conclusion. As long as we have correctly captured all of the cash flows of a project, being wealthier increases our options and makes us better off, whatever our preferences are.

We now look at some common ways the NPV rule is applied in practice.

Accepting or Rejecting a Project.   A common financial decision is whether to accept or reject a project. Because rejecting the project generally has $NPV = 0$ (there are no new costs or benefits from not doing the project), the NPV decision rule implies that we should

▶ Accept positive-NPV projects; accepting them is equivalent to receiving their NPV in cash today, and

▶ Reject negative-NPV projects; accepting them would reduce the value of the firm, whereas rejecting them has no cost (NPV = 0).

If the NPV is exactly zero, then you will neither gain nor lose by accepting the project instead of rejecting it, which also has an NPV of zero. It is not a bad project because it does not reduce the firm's value, but it does not add value to the firm either.

EXAMPLE 5

The NPV Is Equivalent to Cash Today

Problem

After saving $1500 waiting tables, you are about to buy a 42-inch plasma TV. You notice that the store is offering a "one-year same as cash" deal. You can take the TV home today and pay nothing until one year from now, when you will owe the store the $1500 purchase price. If your savings account earns 5% per year, what is the NPV of this offer? Show that its NPV represents cash in your pocket.

Solution

▶ **Plan**

You are getting something (the TV) worth $1500 today and in exchange will need to pay $1500 in one year. Think of it as getting back the $1500 you thought you would have to spend today to get the TV. We treat it as a positive cash flow.

Cash flows:

Today	In one year
+$1500	−$1500

The discount rate for calculating the present value of the payment in one year is your interest rate of 5%. You need to compare the present value of the cost ($1500 in one year) to the benefit today (a $1500 TV).

▶ **Execute**

$$NPV = +1500 - \frac{1500}{(1.05)} = 1500 - 1,428.57 = \$71.43$$

You could take $1428.57 of the $1500 you had saved for the TV and put it in your savings account. With interest, in one year it would grow to $1428.57 × (1.05) = $1500, enough to pay the store. The extra $71.43 is money in your pocket to spend as you like (or put toward the speaker system for your new media room).

▶ **Evaluate**

By taking the delayed payment offer, we have extra net cash flows of $71.43 today. If we put $1428.57 in the bank, it will be just enough to offset our $1500 obligation in the future. Therefore, this offer is equivalent to receiving $71.43 today, without any future net obligations.

Choosing Among Alternatives. Managers also use the NPV decision rule to choose among projects. Suppose you own a coffee stand across from campus and you hire someone to operate it for you. You will be graduating next year and have started to consider selling it. An investor has offered to buy the business from you for $20,000 whenever you are ready. Your interest rate is 10% and you are considering three alternatives:

1. Sell the business now.
2. Operate normally for one more year and then sell the business (requiring you to spend $5000 on supplies and labor now, but earn $10,000 at the end of the year).
3. Be open only in the mornings for one more year and then sell the business (requiring you to spend $3000 on supplies and labor now, but earn $6000 at the end of the year).

The cash flows and NPVs are given in Table 1.

TABLE 1		Now	One Year	NPV	
Cash Flows and NPVs for Coffee Stand Alternatives	Sell	+$20,000	0	$20,000	
	Operate Normally	−$5,000	+$10,000 +$20,000	$-\$5,000 + \dfrac{\$30,000}{1.10}$	$= \$22,273$
	Mornings Only	−$3,000	+$6,000 +$20,000	$-\$3,000 + \dfrac{\$26,000}{1.10}$	$= \$20,636$

Among these three alternatives, you would choose the one with the highest NPV: operate normally for one year and then sell.

NPV and Cash Needs

When we compare projects with different patterns of present and future cash flows, we may have preferences regarding when to receive the cash. Some may need cash today; others may prefer to save for the future. In our coffee stand example, operating normally for one more year and then selling has the highest NPV. However, this option does require an initial outlay for supplies (as opposed to selling the coffee stand and receiving

TABLE 2		Cash Flow Today	Cash Flow in One Year
	Operate Normally	−$5,000	$30,000
Cash Flows from Combining One More Year of Operating with Borrowing	Borrow	$25,000	−$25,000 × (1.10) = −$27,500
	Total	$20,000	$2,500
	Sell Today	$20,000	0

$20,000 today). Suppose we would prefer to avoid the negative cash flow today. Would selling the business be a better choice in that case?

As was true for the jeweler considering trading silver for gold in Section 2, the answer is again no. As long as we are able to borrow and lend at the interest rate, operating for one more year is superior, whatever our preferences regarding the timing of the cash flows. To see why, suppose we borrow $25,000 at the rate of 10% (in one year, we will owe $25,000 × (1.10) = $27,500) and operate the stand normally for one more year. Our total cash flows are shown in Table 2. Compare these cash flows to those for selling. The combination of borrowing and operating for a year generates the same initial cash flow as selling. Notice, however, that there is a higher final cash flow ($2500 versus $0). Thus, we are better off operating for a year and borrowing $25,000 today than we would be selling immediately.

This example illustrates the following general principle:

Regardless of our preferences for cash today versus cash in the future, we should always maximize NPV first. We can then borrow or lend to shift cash flows through time and find our most preferred pattern of cash flows.

9. What is the NPV decision rule? How is it related to the Valuation Principle?

10. Why doesn't the NPV decision rule depend on the investor's preferences?

 ## The Law of One Price

Up to this point, we have emphasized the importance of using competitive market prices to compute the NPV. But is there always only one such price? What if the same good trades for different prices in different markets? Consider gold. Gold trades in many different markets, with the largest markets in New York and London. Gold can trade easily in many markets because investors are not literally transacting in the gold bars themselves (which are quite heavy!), but are trading ownership rights to gold that is stored securely elsewhere. To value an ounce of gold, we could look up the competitive price in either of these markets. But suppose gold is trading for $850 per ounce in New York and $900 per ounce in London. Which price should we use?

In fact, situations such as this one, where the same asset is trading with different prices, should not occur in a competitive market. Let's see why. Recall that these are competitive market prices, at which you can both buy *and* sell. Thus, you can make money in this situation simply by buying gold for $850 per ounce in New York and then immediately selling it for $900 per ounce in London. You will make $900 − $850 = $50 per ounce for each ounce you buy and sell. Trading 1 million ounces at these prices, you would make $50 million with no risk or investment! This is a case where that old adage, "Buy low, sell high," can be followed perfectly.

Of course, you will not be the only one making these trades. Everyone who sees these prices will want to trade as many ounces as possible. Within seconds, the market in New York would be flooded with buy orders, and the market in London would be flooded with sell orders. Although a few ounces (traded by the lucky individuals who spotted this opportunity first) might be exchanged at these prices, the price of gold in New York would quickly rise in response to all the orders, and the price in London would rapidly fall. Prices would continue to change until they were equalized somewhere in the middle, such as $875 per ounce. This example illustrates an *arbitrage opportunity*, the focus of this section.

arbitrage The practice of buying and selling equivalent goods or portfolios to take advantage of a price difference.

arbitrage opportunity Any situation in which it is possible to make a profit without taking any risk or making any investment.

Arbitrage

The practice of buying and selling equivalent goods in different markets to take advantage of a price difference is known as **arbitrage**. More generally, we refer to any situation in which it is possible to make a profit without taking any risk or making any investment as an **arbitrage opportunity**. Because an arbitrage opportunity has positive NPV, whenever an arbitrage opportunity appears in financial markets, the Valuation Principle indicates that investors will race to take advantage of it. Those investors who spot the opportunity first and who can trade quickly will have the ability to exploit it. Once they place their trades, prices will respond, causing the arbitrage opportunity to evaporate.

Arbitrage

Retail Prices From Around the World

CITY	CURRENCY	US$
Tokyo	9,800 yen	$80
Hong Kong	HK$4,695	83
NY		85
Frankfurt	€79	102
Rome	€79	102
London	£55	108
Brussels	€89	115
Paris	€89	115

iPod shuffle 1GB

Prices, including taxes, as provided by retailers in each city, averaged and converted to U.S. dollars

The *Wall Street Journal* occasionally reports on "arbitrage opportunities" by noting price differences for the same item in different countries. In this installment from January 2007, the *Journal* compares prices for the iPod shuffle. The price in the local currency and converted to U.S. dollars is listed. If shipping were free, you would buy as many shuffles as you could get your hands on in Tokyo and sell them in Paris and Brussels. If you could buy and sell at retail prices, you would have a profit of $115 − $80 = $35 on each shuffle!

Source: Wall Street Journal, Jan 31, 2007.

Arbitrage opportunities are like money lying in the street; once spotted, they will quickly disappear. Thus, the normal state of affairs in markets should be that no arbitrage opportunities exist.

Law of One Price

Law of One Price In competitive markets, securities or portfolios with the same cash flows must have the same price.

In a competitive market, the price of gold at any point in time will be the same in London and New York. The same logic applies more generally whenever equivalent investment opportunities trade in two different competitive markets. If the prices in the two markets differ, investors will profit immediately by buying in the market where it is cheap and selling in the market where it is expensive. In doing so, they will equalize the prices. As a result, prices will not differ (at least not for long). This important property is the **Law of One Price**:

An Old Joke

There is an old joke that many finance professors enjoy telling their students. It goes like this:

A finance professor and a student are walking down a street. The student notices a $100 bill lying on the pavement and leans down to pick it up. The finance professor immediately intervenes and says, "Don't bother; there is no free lunch. If that were a real $100 bill lying there, somebody would already have picked it up!"

This joke makes fun of the principle of no arbitrage in competitive markets. But have you ever *actually* found a real $100 bill lying on the pavement? Herein lies the real lesson behind the joke.

This joke sums up the point of focusing on markets in which no arbitrage opportunities exist. Free $100 bills lying on the pavement, like arbitrage opportunities, are extremely rare for two reasons: (1) Because $100 is a large amount of money, people are especially careful not to lose it, and (2) in the rare event when someone does inadvertently drop $100, the likelihood of your finding it before someone else does is extremely small.

If equivalent investment opportunities trade simultaneously in different competitive markets, then they must trade for the same price in both markets.

The Law of One Price will prove to be a powerful tool later in the text when we value securities such as stocks or bonds. We will show that any financial security can be thought of as a claim to future cash flows. The Law of One Price implies that if there is another way to recreate the future cash flows of the financial security, then the price of the financial security and the cost of recreating it must be the same. Recall that earlier we defined the present value of a cash flow to be the cost of recreating it in a competitive market. Thus, we have the following key implication of the Law of One Price for financial securities:

The price of a security should equal the present value of the future cash flows obtained from owning that security.

EXAMPLE 6

Pricing a Security using the Law of One Price

Problem

You are considering purchasing a security, a "bond," that pays $1000 without risk in one year, and has no other cash flows. If the interest rate is 5%, what should its price be?

Solution

▶ **Plan**

The security produces a single cash flow in one-year:

The Law of One Price tells you that the value of a security that pays $1000 in one year is the present value of that $1000 cash flow, calculated as the cash flow discounted at the interest rate. The 5% interest rate implies that $1.05 in one year is worth $1 today.

▶ **Execute**

The present value of the $1000 cash flow is

$$\$1000 \text{ in one year} \div \frac{1.05 \text{ \$ in one year}}{\$ \text{ today}} = \$952.38 \text{ today}$$

So the price must be $952.38.

> ▶ **Evaluate**
>
> Because we can receive $1000 in one year for a "price" of $952.38 by simply investing at the interest rate (i.e., $952.38 × 1.05 = $1000), the Law of One Price tells you that the price of the security must equal this "do it yourself" price, which is the present value of its cash flow evaluated using market interest rates. To see why this must be so, consider what would happen if the price were different. If the price were $950, you could borrow $950 at 5% interest and buy the bond. In one year, you would collect the $1000 from the bond and pay off your loan ($950 × 1.05 = $997.50), pocketing the difference. In fact, you would try to do the same thing for as many bonds as possible. But everyone else would also want to take advantage of this arbitrage by buying the bond, and so its price would quickly rise. Similarly, if the price were above $952.38, everyone would sell the bond, invest the proceeds at 5%, and in one year would have more than the $1000 needed to pay the buyer of the security. The selling would cause the price of the bond to drop until this arbitrage was no longer possible—when it reaches $952.38. This powerful application of the Law of One Price shows that the price you pay for a security's cash flows cannot be different from their present value.

transactions costs
Expenses such as broker commission and the bid-ask spread investors must pay in most markets in order to trade securities.

Transactions Costs

In our examples up to this point, we have ignored the costs of buying and selling goods or securities. In most markets, there are additional costs that you will incur when trading assets, called **transactions costs**. When you trade securities in markets such as the NYSE and NASDAQ, you must pay two types of transactions costs. First, you must pay your broker a commission on the trade. Second, because you will generally pay a slightly higher price when you buy a security (the ask price) than you will receive when you sell (the bid price) it, you will also pay the bid-ask spread. For example, a share of Dell Inc. stock (ticker symbol DELL) might be quoted as follows:

Bid: $40.50   Ask: $40.70

We can interpret these quotes as if the competitive price for DELL is $40.60, but there is a transaction cost of $0.10 per share when buying or selling.

What consequence do these transaction costs have for no-arbitrage prices and the Law of One Price? Earlier we stated that the price of gold in New York and London must be identical in competitive markets. Suppose, however, that total transactions costs of $5 per ounce are associated with buying gold in one market and selling it in the other. Then, if the price of gold is $850 per ounce in New York and $852 per ounce in London, the "Buy low, sell high" strategy no longer works:

Cost: $850 per ounce (buy gold in New York) + $5 (transactions costs)

Benefit: $852 per ounce (sell gold in London)

NPV: $852 − $850 − $5 = −$3 per ounce

Indeed, there is no arbitrage opportunity in this case until the prices diverge by more than $5, the amount of the transactions costs.

In general, we need to modify our previous conclusions about prices and values by appending the phrase "up to transactions costs." In this example, there is only one competitive price for gold—up to a discrepancy of the $5 transactions cost.

Fortunately, for most financial markets, these costs are small. For example, in 2007 typical bid-ask spreads for large NYSE stocks were between 2 and 5 cents per share. As a first approximation, we can ignore these spreads in our analysis. Only in situations in which the NPV is small (relative to the transactions costs) will any discrepancy matter. In that case, we will need to carefully account for all transaction costs to decide whether the NPV is positive or negative.

To summarize, when there are transactions costs, arbitrage keeps prices of equivalent goods and securities close to each other. Prices can deviate, but not by more than the amount of the transactions costs.

In the rest of the text, we will explore the details of implementing the Law of One Price to value securities. Specifically, we will determine the cash flows associated with stocks, bonds and other securities, and learn how to compute the present value of these cash flows by taking into account their timing and risk.

Concept Check

11. If the Law of One Price were violated, how could investors profit?

12. What implication does the Law of One Price have for the price of a financial security?

---

myfinancelab

Here is what you should know after reading this chapter. MyFinanceLab will help you identify what you know, and where to go when you need to practice.

Key Points and Equations	Terms	Online Practice Opportunities
1 Managerial Decision Making ▶ To evaluate a decision, we must value the incremental costs and benefits associated with that decision. A good decision is one for which the value of the benefits exceeds the value of the costs.		MyFinanceLab Study Plan 3.1
2 Cost-Benefit Analysis ▶ To compare costs and benefits that occur at different points in time we must put all costs and benefits in common terms. Typically, we convert costs and benefits into cash today.		MyFinanceLab Study Plan 3.2
3 Valuation Principle ▶ A competitive market is one in which a good can be bought and sold at the same price. We use prices from competitive markets to determine the cash value of a good. ▶ The Valuation Principle states that the value of a commodity or an asset to the firm or its investors is determined by its competitive market price. The benefits and costs of a decision should be evaluated using those market prices. When the value of the benefits exceeds the value of the costs, the decision will increase the market value of the firm	competitive market Valuation Principle	MyFinanceLab Study Plan 3.3
4 The Time Value of Money ▶ The time value of money is the difference in value between money today and money in the future.	discount factor discount rate	MyFinanceLab Study Plan 3.4

▶ The rate at which we can exchange money today for money in the future by borrowing or investing is the current market interest rate. ▶ The present value (PV) of a cash flow is its value in terms of cash today.	future value interest rate interest rate factor present value (PV) time value of money	
5 The NPV Decision Rule ▶ The net present value (NPV) of a project is PV(Benefits) − PV(Costs) ▶ A good project is one with a positive net present value. ▶ The NPV Decision Rule states that when choosing from among a set of alternatives, choose the one with the highest NPV. The NPV of a project is equivalent to the cash value today of the project. ▶ Regardless of our preferences for cash today versus cash in the future, we should always first maximize NPV. We can then borrow or lend to shift cash flows through time and find our most preferred pattern of cash flows.	Net Present Value (NPV) NPV Decision Rule	MyFinanceLab Study Plan 3.5
6 The Law of One Price ▶ Arbitrage is the process of trading to take advantage of equivalent goods that have different prices in different competitive markets. ▶ The Law of One Price states that if equivalent goods or securities trade simultaneously in different competitive markets, they will trade for the same price in each market. This law is equivalent to saying that no arbitrage opportunities should exist. ▶ The price of a security should equal the present value of the expected future cash flows obtained from owning that security.	arbitrage arbitrage opportunity Law of One Price transactions costs	MyFinanceLab Study Plan 3.6

Review Questions

1. What makes an investment decision a good one?

2. How important are our personal preferences in valuing an investment decision?

3. Why are market prices useful to a financial manager?

4. How does the Valuation Principle help a financial manager make decisions?

5. Can we directly compare dollar amounts received at different points in time?

6. How is the Net Present Value Rule related to cost-benefit analysis?

7. If there is more than one project to take, how should the financial manager choose among them?

8. What is the relation between arbitrage and the Law of One Price?

Problems

A blue box (■) indicates problems available in MyFinanceLab. An asterisk (*) indicates problems with a higher level of difficulty.

Cost-Benefit Analysis

1. Honda Motor Company is considering offering a $2000 rebate on its minivan, lowering the vehicle's price from $30,000 to $28,000. The marketing group estimates that this rebate will increase sales over the next year from 40,000 to 55,000 vehicles. Suppose Honda's profit margin with the rebate is $6000 per vehicle. If the change in sales is the only consequence of this decision, what are its costs and benefits? Is it a good idea?

2. You are an international shrimp trader. A food producer in the Czech Republic offers to pay you 2 million Czech koruna today in exchange for a year's supply of frozen shrimp. Your Thai supplier will provide you with the same supply for 3 million Thai baht today. If the current competitive market exchange rates are 25.50 koruna per dollar and 41.25 baht per dollar, what is the value of this deal?

3. Suppose your employer offers you a choice between a $5000 bonus and 100 shares of the company's stock. Whichever one you choose will be awarded today. The stock is currently trading for $63 per share.
   a. Suppose that if you receive the stock bonus, you are free to trade it. Which form of the bonus should you choose? What is its value?
   b. Suppose that if you receive the stock bonus, you are required to hold it for at least one year. What can you say about the value of the stock bonus now? What will your decision depend on?

Valuation Principle

4. Bubba is a shrimp farmer. In an ironic twist, Bubba is allergic to shellfish, so he cannot eat any shrimp. Each day he has a one-ton supply of shrimp. The market price of shrimp is $10,000 per ton.
   a. What is the value of a ton of shrimp to him?
   b. Would this value change if he were not allergic to shrimp? Why or why not?

5. Brett has almond orchards, but he is sick of almonds and prefers to eat walnuts instead. The owner of the walnut orchard next door has offered to swap this year's crop with him in an even exchange. Assume he produces 1000 tons of almonds and his neighbor produces 800 tons of walnuts. If the market price of almonds is $100 per ton and the market price of walnuts is $1.10 per ton:
   a. Should he make the exchange?
   b. Does it matter whether he prefers almonds or walnuts? Why or why not?

Interest Rates and the Time Value of Money

6. You have $100 and a bank is offering 5% interest on deposits. If you deposit the money in the bank, how much will you have in one year?

7. You expect to have $1000 in one year. A bank is offering loans at 6% interest per year. How much can you borrow today?

 8. A friend asks to borrow $55 from you and in return will pay you $58 in one year. If your bank is offering a 6% interest rate on deposits and loans:
a. How much would you have in one year if you deposited the $55 instead?
b. How much money could you borrow today if you pay the bank $58 in one year?
c. Should you loan the money to your friend or deposit it in the bank?

 9. Suppose the interest rate is 4%.
a. Having $200 today is equivalent to having what amount in one year?
b. Having $200 in one year is equivalent to having what amount today?
c. Which would you prefer, $200 today or $200 in one year? Does your answer depend on when you need the money? Why or why not?

The NPV Decision Rule

10. Your storage firm has been offered $100,000 in one year to store some goods for one year. Assume your costs are $95,000, payable immediately, and the interest rate is 8%. Should you take the contract?

 11. You run a construction firm. You have just won a contract to build a government office building. Building it will require an investment of $10 million today and $5 million in one year. The government will pay you $20 million in one year upon the building's completion. Suppose the interest rate is 10%.
a. What is the NPV of this opportunity?
b. How can your firm turn this NPV into cash today?

12. Your firm has identified three potential investment projects. The projects and their cash flows are shown here:

Project	Cash Flow Today ($)	Cash Flow in One Year ($)
A	−10.00	20.00
B	5.00	5.00
C	20.00	−10.00

Suppose all cash flows are certain and the interest rate is 10%.
a. What is the NPV of each project?
b. If the firm can choose only one of these projects, which should it choose?
c. If the firm can choose any two of these projects, which should it choose?

13. Your computer manufacturing firm must purchase 10,000 keyboards from a supplier. One supplier demands a payment of $100,000 today plus $10 per keyboard payable in one year. Another supplier will charge $21 per keyboard, also payable in one year. The interest rate is 6%.
a. What is the difference in their offers in terms of dollars today? Which offer should your firm take?
b. Suppose your firm does not want to spend cash today. How can it take the first offer and not spend $100,000 of its own cash today?

74

The Law of One Price

14. Suppose Bank One offers an interest rate of 5.5% on both savings and loans, and Bank Enn offers an interest rate of 6% on both savings and loans.
  a. What arbitrage opportunity is available?
  b. Which bank would experience a surge in the demand for loans? Which bank would receive a surge in deposits?
  c. What would you expect to happen to the interest rates the two banks are offering?

15. If the cost of buying a CD and ripping the tracks to your iPod (including your time) is $25, what is the most Apple could charge on iTunes for a whole 15-track CD?

16. Some companies cross-list their shares, meaning that their stock trades on more than one stock exchange. For example, Research in Motion, the maker of Blackberry mobile devices, trades on both the Toronto Stock Exchange and NASDAQ. If its price in Toronto is 100 Canadian dollars per share and anyone can exchange Canadian dollars for U.S. dollars at the rate of US$0.95 per C$1.00, what must RIM's price be on NASDAQ?

*17. Use the concept of arbitrage and the fact that interest rates are positive to prove that time travel will never be possible.

Chapter 4

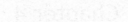

Time Value of Money

From Chapter 4 of *Principles of Managerial Finance*, Brief 5th Edition. Lawrence J. Gitman. Copyright © 2009 by Pearson Prentice Hall. All rights reserved.

Time Value of Money

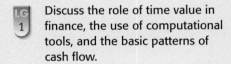

WHY THIS CHAPTER MATTERS TO YOU

In Your Professional Life

Accounting: You need to understand time-value-of-money calculations to account for certain transactions such as loan amortization, lease payments, and bond interest rates.

Information systems: You need to understand time-value-of-money calculations to design systems that accurately measure and value the firm's cash flows.

Management: You need to understand time-value-of-money calculations so that you can manage cash receipts and disbursements in a way that will enable the firm to receive the greatest value from its cash flows.

Marketing: You need to understand time value of money because funding for new programs and products must be justified financially using time-value-of-money techniques.

Operations: You need to understand time value of money because the value of investments in new equipment, in new processes, and in inventory will be affected by the time value of money.

In Your Personal Life

Time value of money techniques are widely used in personal financial planning. You can use them to calculate the value of savings at given future dates and to estimate the amount you need now to accumulate a given amount at a future date. You also can apply them to value lump-sum amounts or streams of periodic cash flows and to the interest rate or amount of time needed to achieve a given financial goal.

LEARNING GOALS

LG 1 Discuss the role of time value in finance, the use of computational tools, and the basic patterns of cash flow.

LG 2 Understand the concepts of future value and present value, their calculation for single amounts, and the relationship between them.

LG 3 Find the future value and the present value of an ordinary annuity, and find the present value of a perpetuity.

LG 4 Calculate both the future value and the present value of a mixed stream of cash flows.

LG 5 Understand the effect that compounding interest more frequently than annually has on future value and on the effective annual rate of interest.

LG 6 Describe the procedures involved in (1) determining deposits needed to accumulate a future sum, (2) loan amortization, (3) finding interest or growth rates, and (4) finding an unknown number of periods.

Because we view the firm as a going concern, we assess the decisions of its financial managers, and ultimately the value of the firm itself, in light of its cash flows. The opportunity to earn interest on the firm's funds makes the timing of its cash flows important, because a dollar received in the future is not the same as a dollar received today. Thus, money has a time value, which affects everyone—individuals, businesses, and government. In this chapter we explore the concepts related to the time value of money.

1 | The Role of Time Value in Finance

> **Hint** The time value of money is one of the most important concepts in finance. Money that the firm has in its possession today is more valuable than money in the future because the money it now has can be invested and earn positive returns.

Financial managers and investors are always confronted with opportunities to earn positive rates of return on their funds, whether through investment in attractive projects or in interest-bearing securities or deposits. Therefore, the timing of cash outflows and inflows has important economic consequences, which financial managers explicitly recognize as the *time value of money*. Time value is based on the belief that a dollar today is worth more than a dollar that will be received at some future date. We begin our study of time value in finance by considering the two views of time value—future value and present value, the computational tools used to streamline time value calculations, and the basic patterns of cash flow.

Future Value versus Present Value

Financial values and decisions can be assessed by using either future value or present value techniques. Although these techniques will result in the same decisions, they view the decision differently. Future value techniques typically measure cash flows at the *end* of a project's life. Present value techniques measure cash flows at the *start* of a project's life (time zero). *Future value* is cash you will receive at a given future date, and *present value* is just like cash in hand today.

> **time line**
> A horizontal line on which time zero appears at the leftmost end and future periods are marked from left to right; can be used to depict investment cash flows.

A **time line** can be used to depict the cash flows associated with a given investment. It is a horizontal line on which time zero appears at the leftmost end and future periods are marked from left to right. A time line covering five periods (in this case, years) is given in Figure 1. The cash flows occurring at time zero and at the end of each year are shown above the line; the negative values represent *cash outflows* ($10,000 at time zero) and the positive values represent *cash inflows* ($3,000 inflow at the end of year 1, $5,000 inflow at the end of year 2, and so on).

Because money has a time value, all of the cash flows associated with an investment, such as those in Figure 1, must be measured at the same point in time. Typically, that point is either the end or the beginning of the investment's

FIGURE 1

Time Line
Time line depicting an investment's cash flows

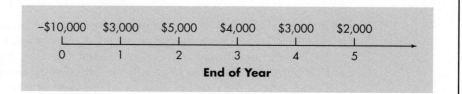

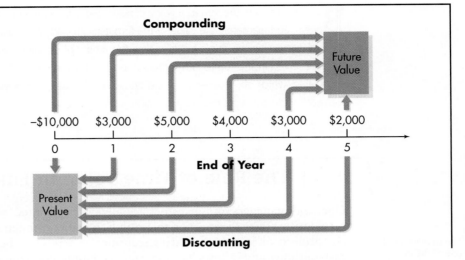

FIGURE 2

Compounding and Discounting
Time line showing compounding to find future value and discounting to find present value

life. The future value technique uses *compounding* to find the *future value* of each cash flow at the end of the investment's life and then sums these values to find the investment's future value. This approach is depicted above the time line in Figure 2. The figure shows that the future value of each cash flow is measured at the end of the investment's 5-year life. Alternatively, the present value technique uses *discounting* to find the *present value* of each cash flow at time zero and then sums these values to find the investment's value today. Application of this approach is depicted below the time line in Figure 2.

The meaning and mechanics of compounding to find future value and of discounting to find present value are covered in this chapter. Although future value and present value result in the same decisions, *financial managers—because they make decisions at time zero—tend to rely primarily on present value techniques.*

Computational Tools

Time-consuming calculations are often involved in finding future and present values. Although you should understand the concepts and mathematics underlying these calculations, the application of time value techniques can be streamlined. We focus on the use of hand-held financial calculators, electronic spreadsheets, and financial tables as aids in computation.

Financial Calculators

Financial calculators can be used to simplify time value computations. Generally, *financial calculators* include numerous preprogrammed financial routines. This chapter and those that follow show the keystrokes for calculating interest factors and making other financial computations. For convenience, we use the important financial keys, labeled in a fashion consistent with most major financial calculators.

We focus primarily on the keys pictured and defined in Figure 3. We typically use four of the first five keys shown in the left column, along with the compute (**CPT**) key. One of the four keys represents the unknown value being calculated.

Calculator Keys
Important financial keys on the typical calculator

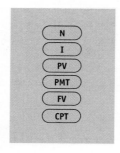

N — Number of periods
I — Interest rate per period
PV — Present value
PMT — Amount of payment (used only for annuities)
FV — Future value
CPT — Compute key used to initiate financial calculation once all values are input

(Occasionally, all five of the keys are used, with one representing the unknown value.) The keystrokes on some of the more sophisticated calculators are menu-driven: After you select the appropriate routine, the calculator prompts you to input each value; on these calculators, a compute key is not needed to obtain a solution. Regardless, any calculator with the basic future and present value functions can be used to simplify time value calculations. See Appendix: Financial Tables for keystrokes for some of the more popular calculators. The keystrokes for other financial calculators are explained in the reference guides that accompany them.

Once you understand the basic underlying concepts, you probably will want to use a calculator to streamline routine financial calculations. With a little practice, you can increase both the speed and the accuracy of your financial computations. Remember that *conceptual understanding of the material is the objective.* An ability to solve problems with the aid of a calculator does not necessarily reflect such an understanding, so don't just settle for answers. Work with the material until you are sure you also understand the concepts.

Electronic Spreadsheets

Hint Anyone familiar with an electronic spreadsheet, such as Excel, realizes that most of the time-value-of-money calculations can be performed expeditiously by using the special functions contained in the spreadsheet.

Like financial calculators, electronic spreadsheets have built-in routines that simplify time value calculations. We provide in the text a number of spreadsheet solutions that identify the cell entries for calculating time values. The value for each variable is entered in a cell in the spreadsheet, and the calculation is programmed using an equation that links the individual cells. If values of the variables are changed, the solution automatically changes as a result of the equation linking the cells. In the spreadsheet solutions in this text, the equation that determines the calculation is shown at the bottom of the spreadsheet.

The ability to use electronic spreadsheets has become a prime skill for today's managers. As the saying goes, "Get aboard the bandwagon, or get run over." The spreadsheet solutions we present in this text will help you climb up onto that bandwagon!

Financial Tables

Financial tables include various future and present value interest factors that simplify time value calculations. The values shown in these tables are easily developed from formulas, with various degrees of rounding. As a result, slight differences are likely to exist between table-based calculations and the more precise values obtained using a financial calculator or spreadsheet.

FIGURE 4

Financial Tables
Layout and use of
a financial table

Period	1%	2%	⋯	10%	⋯	**20%**	⋯	50%
1			⋯		⋯	⋮	⋯	
2			⋯		⋯	⋮	⋯	
3			⋯		⋯	⋮	⋯	
⋮	⋮	⋮	⋯	⋮	⋯	⋮	⋯	⋮
→ 10	⋯	⋯	⋯	⋯	⋯	**X.XXX**	⋯	⋯
⋮	⋮	⋮	⋯	⋮	⋯	⋮	⋯	⋮
20			⋯		⋯		⋯	
⋮	⋮	⋮	⋯	⋮	⋯	⋮	⋯	⋮
50			⋯		⋯		⋯	

Interest Rate ↓

The financial tables are typically indexed by the interest rate (in columns) and the number of periods (in rows). Figure 4 shows this general layout. The interest factor at a 20 percent interest rate for 10 years would be found at the intersection of the 20% column and the 10-period row, as shown by the dark blue box. A full set of the four basic financial tables is included in Appendix: Financial Tables. These tables are described more fully later in the chapter.

Basic Patterns of Cash Flow

The cash flow—both inflows and outflows—of a firm can be described by its general pattern. It can be defined as a single amount, an annuity, or a mixed stream.

Single amount: A lump-sum amount either currently held or expected at some future date. Examples include $1,000 today and $650 to be received at the end of 10 years.

Annuity: A level periodic stream of cash flow. For our purposes, we'll work primarily with *annual* cash flows. Examples include either paying out or receiving $800 at the end of each of the next 7 years.

Mixed stream: A stream of cash flow that is *not* an annuity; a stream of unequal periodic cash flows that reflect no particular pattern. Examples include the following two cash flow streams A and B.

	Mixed cash flow stream	
End of year	A	B
1	$ 100	−$ 50
2	800	100
3	1,200	80
4	1,200	− 60
5	1,400	
6	300	

Note that neither cash flow stream has equal, periodic cash flows and that A is a 6-year mixed stream and B is a 4-year mixed stream.

In the next three sections of this chapter, we develop the concepts and techniques for finding future and present values of single amounts, annuities, and mixed streams, respectively. Detailed demonstrations of these cash flow patterns are included.

REVIEW QUESTIONS

1   What is the difference between *future value* and *present value?* Which approach is generally preferred by financial managers? Why?

2   Define and differentiate among the three basic patterns of cash flow: (1) a single amount, (2) an annuity, and (3) a mixed stream.

2 | Single Amounts

Imagine that at age 25 you began making annual purchases of $2,000 of an investment that earns a guaranteed 5 percent annually. At the end of 40 years, at age 65, you would have invested a total of $80,000 (40 years × $2,000 per year). Assuming that all funds remain invested, how much would you have accumulated at the end of the fortieth year? $100,000? $150,000? $200,000? No, your $80,000 would have grown to $242,000! Why? Because the time value of money allowed your investments to generate returns that built on each other over the 40 years.

Future Value of a Single Amount

The most basic future value and present value concepts and computations concern single amounts, either present or future amounts. We begin by considering the future value of present amounts. Then we will use the underlying concepts to determine the present value of future amounts. You will see that although future value is more intuitively appealing, present value is more useful in financial decision making.

future value
The value at a given future date of a present amount placed on deposit today and earning interest at a specified rate. Found by applying *compound interest* over a specified period of time.

We often need to find the value at some future date of a given amount of money placed on deposit today. For example, if you deposit $500 today into an account that pays 5 percent annual interest, how much would you have in the account at the end of exactly 10 years? **Future value** is the value at a given future date of a present amount placed on deposit today and earning interest at a specified rate. It depends on the rate of interest earned and the length of time a given amount is left on deposit. Here we explore the future value of a single amount.

The Concept of Future Value

compound interest
Interest that is earned on a given deposit and has become part of the *principal* at the end of a specified period.

principal
The amount of money on which interest is paid.

We speak of **compound interest** to indicate that the amount of interest earned on a given deposit has become part of the *principal* at the end of a specified period. The term **principal** refers to the amount of money on which the interest is paid. Annual compounding is the most common type.

The *future value* of a present amount is found by applying *compound interest* over a specified period of time. Savings institutions advertise compound interest returns at a rate of x percent, or x percent interest, compounded annually, semiannually, quarterly, monthly, weekly, daily, or even continuously. The concept of future value with annual compounding can be illustrated by a simple example.

Personal Finance Example   If Fred Moreno places $100 in a savings account paying 8% interest compounded annually, at the end of 1 year he will have $108 in the account—the initial principal of $100 plus 8% ($8) in interest. The future value at the end of the first year is calculated by using Equation 1:

$$\text{Future value at end of year 1} = \$100 \times (1 + 0.08) = \$108 \qquad \text{(1)}$$

If Fred were to leave this money in the account for another year, he would be paid interest at the rate of 8% on the new principal of $108. At the end of this second year there would be $116.64 in the account. This amount would represent the principal at the beginning of year 2 ($108) plus 8% of the $108 ($8.64) in interest. The future value at the end of the second year is calculated by using Equation 2:

$$\text{Future value at end of year 2} = \$108 \times (1 + 0.08) \qquad \text{(2)}$$
$$= \$116.64$$

Substituting the expression between the equals signs in Equation 1 for the $108 figure in Equation 2 gives us Equation 3:

$$\text{Future value at end of year 2} = \$100 \times (1 + 0.08) \times (1 + 0.08) \qquad \text{(3)}$$
$$= \$100 \times (1 + 0.08)^2$$
$$= \$116.64$$

The equations in the preceding example lead to a more general formula for calculating future value.

The Equation for Future Value

The basic relationship in Equation 3 can be generalized to find the future value after any number of periods. We use the following notation for the various inputs:

FV_n = future value at the end of period n

PV = initial principal, or present value

i = annual rate of interest paid. (*Note:* On financial calculators, I is typically used to represent this rate.)

n = number of periods (typically years) that the money is left on deposit

The general equation for the future value at the end of period n is

$$FV_n = PV \times (1 + i)^n \qquad \text{(4)}$$

A simple example will illustrate how to apply Equation 4.

Personal Finance Example   Jane Farber places $800 in a savings account paying 6% interest compounded annually. She wants to know how much money will be in the account at the end of 5 years. Substituting $PV = \$800$, $i = 0.06$, and $n = 5$ into Equation 4 gives the amount at the end of year 5.

$$FV_5 = \$800 \times (1 + 0.06)^5 = \$800 \times (1.338) = \$1{,}070.40$$

Time line for future value of a single amount ($800 initial principal, earning 6%, at the end of 5 years)

This analysis can be depicted on a time line as follows:

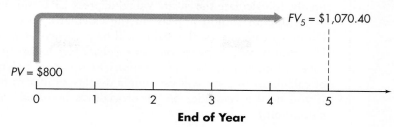

Using Computational Tools to Find Future Value

Solving the equation in the preceding example involves raising 1.06 to the fifth power. Using a financial calculator, an electronic spreadsheet, or a future value interest table greatly simplifies the calculation. A table that provides values for $(1 + i)^n$ in Equation 4 is in Appendix: Financial Tables, Table A-1. The value in each cell of the table is called the **future value interest factor**. This factor is the multiplier used to calculate, at a specified interest rate, the future value of a present amount as of a given time. The future value interest factor for an initial principal of $1 compounded at i percent for n periods is referred to as $FVIF_{i,n}$.

future value interest factor The multiplier used to calculate, at a specified interest rate, the future value of a present amount as of a given time.

$$\text{Future value interest factor} = FVIF_{i,n} = (1 + i)^n \tag{5}$$

By finding the intersection of the annual interest rate, i, and the appropriate periods, n, you will find the future value interest factor that is relevant to a particular problem.[1] Using $FVIF_{i,n}$ as the appropriate factor, we can rewrite the general equation for future value (Equation 4) as follows:

$$FV_n = PV \times (FVIF_{i,n}) \tag{6}$$

This expression indicates that to find the future value at the end of period n of an initial deposit, we have merely to multiply the initial deposit, PV, by the appropriate future value interest factor.[2]

Personal Finance Example In the preceding example, Jane Farber placed $800 in her savings account at 6% interest compounded annually and wishes to find out how much will be in the account at the end of 5 years.

Calculator Use[3] The financial calculator can be used to calculate the future value directly.[4] First punch in $800 and depress **PV**; next punch in 5 and depress

---

1. Although we commonly deal with years rather than periods, financial tables are frequently presented in terms of periods to provide maximum flexibility.

2. Occasionally, you may want to estimate roughly how long a given sum must earn at a given annual rate to double the amount. The *Rule of 72* is used to make this estimate; dividing the annual rate of interest into 72 results in the approximate number of periods it will take to double one's money at the given rate. For example, to double one's money at a 10% annual rate of interest will take about 7.2 years ($72 \div 10 = 7.2$). Looking at Table A–1, we can see that the future value interest factor for 10% and 7 years is slightly less than 2 (1.949); this approximation therefore appears to be reasonably accurate.

3. Many calculators allow the user to set the number of payments per year. Most of these calculators are preset for monthly payments—12 payments per year. Because we work primarily with annual payments—one payment per year—it is important to *be sure that your calculator is set for one payment per year.* And although most calculators are preset to recognize that all payments occur at the end of the period, it is important to *make sure that your calculator is correctly set on the END mode.* Consult the reference guide that accompanies your calculator for instructions for setting these values.

4. To avoid including previous data in current calculations, *always clear all registers of your calculator before inputting values and making each computation.*

Input	Function
800	PV
5	N
6	I
	CPT
	FV

Solution
1,070.58

N; then punch in 6 and depress **I** (which is equivalent to "*i*" in our notation)[5]; finally, to calculate the future value, depress **CPT** and then **FV.** The future value of $1,070.58 should appear on the calculator display as shown at the left. On many calculators, this value will be preceded by a minus sign (−1,070.58). *If a minus sign appears on your calculator, ignore it here as well as in all other "Calculator Use" illustrations in this text.*[6] (*Note:* In future examples of calculator use, we will use only a display similar to that shown on this page. If you need a reminder of the procedures involved, go back and review this paragraph.)

Spreadsheet Use The future value of the single amount also can be calculated as shown on the following Excel spreadsheet.

	A	B
1	FUTURE VALUE OF A SINGLE AMOUNT	
2	Present value	$800
3	Interest rate, pct per year compounded annually	6%
4	Number of years	5
5	Future value	$1,070.58
	Entry in Cell B5 is =FV(B3,B4,0,−B2,0) The minus sign appears before B2 because the present value is an outflow (i.e., a deposit made by Jane Farber).	

Table Use The future value interest factor for an initial principal of $1 on deposit for 5 years at 6% interest compounded annually, $FVIF_{6\%,\ 5yrs}$, found in Appendix: Financial Tables, Table A–1, is 1.338. Using Equation 6, $800 × 1.338 = $1,070.40. Therefore, the future value of Jane's deposit at the end of year 5 will be $1,070.40.

Because both the calculator and the spreadsheet are more accurate than the future value factors, which have been rounded to the nearest 0.001, a slight difference—in this case, $0.18—will frequently exist between the values found by these alternative methods. Clearly, the improved accuracy and ease of calculation tend to favor the use of the calculator.

A Graphical View of Future Value

Remember that we measure future value at the *end* of the given period. Figure 5 illustrates the relationship among various interest rates, the number of periods interest is earned, and the future value of one dollar. The figure shows that (1) the higher the interest rate, the higher the future value, and (2) the longer the period of time, the higher the future value. Note that for an interest rate of 0 percent, the future value always equals the present value ($1.00). But for any interest rate greater than zero, the future value is greater than the present value of $1.00.

---

5. The known values *can be punched into the calculator in any order;* the order specified in this as well as other demonstrations of calculator use included in this text merely reflects convenience and personal preference.

6. The calculator differentiates inflows from outflows by preceding the outflows with a negative sign. For example, in the problem just demonstrated, the $800 present value (PV), because it was keyed as a positive number (800), is considered an inflow or deposit. Therefore, the calculated future value (FV) of −1,070.58 is preceded by a minus sign to show that it is the resulting outflow or withdrawal. Had the $800 present value been keyed in as a negative number (−800), the future value of $1,070.58 would have been displayed as a positive number (1,070.58). Simply stated, *the cash flows—present value* (PV) *and future value* (FV)—*will have opposite signs.*

Future Value Relationship
Interest rates, time periods, and future value of one dollar

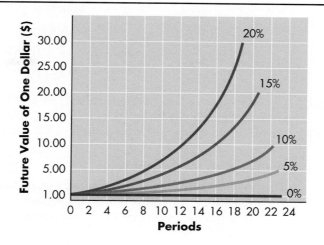

Present Value of a Single Amount

present value
The current dollar value of a future amount—the amount of money that would have to be invested today at a given interest rate over a specified period to equal the future amount.

It is often useful to determine the value today of a future amount of money. For example, how much would I have to deposit today into an account paying 7 percent annual interest to accumulate $3,000 at the end of 5 years? **Present value** is the current dollar value of a future amount—the amount of money that would have to be invested today at a given interest rate over a specified period to equal the future amount. Present value depends largely on the investment opportunities and the point in time at which the amount is to be received. This section explores the present value of a single amount.

The Concept of Present Value

discounting cash flows
The process of finding present values; the inverse of compounding interest.

The process of finding present values is often referred to as **discounting cash flows**. It is concerned with answering the following question: If I can earn i percent on my money, what is the most I would be willing to pay now for an opportunity to receive FV_n dollars n periods from today?

This process is actually the inverse of compounding interest. Instead of finding the future value of present dollars invested at a given rate, discounting determines the present value of a future amount, assuming an opportunity to earn a certain return on the money. This annual rate of return is variously referred to as the *discount rate, required return, cost of capital,* and *opportunity cost*. These terms will be used interchangeably in this text.

Personal Finance Example   Paul Shorter has an opportunity to receive $300 one year from now. If he can earn 6% on his investments in the normal course of events, what is the most he should pay now for this opportunity? To answer this question, Paul must determine how many dollars he would have to invest at 6% today to have $300 one year from now. Letting PV equal this unknown amount and using the same notation as in the future value discussion, we have

$$PV \times (1 + 0.06) = \$300 \qquad \text{(7)}$$

Solving Equation 7 for *PV* gives us Equation 8:

$$PV = \frac{\$300}{(1 + 0.06)} \qquad \text{(8)}$$

$$= \$283.02$$

The value today ("present value") of $300 received one year from today, given an opportunity cost of 6%, is $283.02. That is, investing $283.02 today at the 6% opportunity cost would result in $300 at the end of one year.

The Equation for Present Value

The present value of a future amount can be found mathematically by solving Equation 4 for *PV*. In other words, the present value, *PV*, of some future amount, FV^n, to be received *n* periods from now, assuming an opportunity cost of *i*, is calculated as follows:

$$PV = \frac{FV_n}{(1 + i)^n} = FV_n \times \left[\frac{1}{(1 + i)^n} \right] \qquad \text{(9)}$$

Note the similarity between this general equation for present value and the equation in the preceding example (Equation 8). Let's use this equation in an example.

Personal Finance Example   Pam Valenti wishes to find the present value of $1,700 that will be received 8 years from now. Pam's opportunity cost is 8%. Substituting FV_8 = $1,700, *n* = 8, and *i* = 0.08 into Equation 9 yields Equation 10:

$$PV = \frac{\$1,700}{(1 + 0.08)^8} = \frac{\$1,700}{1.851} = \$918.42 \qquad \text{(10)}$$

The following time line shows this analysis.

Time line for present value of a single amount ($1,700 future amount, discounted at 8%, from the end of 8 years)

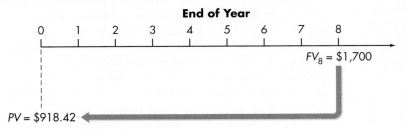

Using Computational Tools to Find Present Value

present value interest factor
The multiplier used to calculate, at a specified discount rate, the present value of an amount to be received in a future period.

The present value calculation can be simplified by using a **present value interest factor**. This factor is the multiplier used to calculate, at a specified discount rate, the present value of an amount to be received in a future period. The present value interest factor for the present value of $1 discounted at *i* percent for *n* periods is referred to as $PVIF_{i,n}$.

$$\text{Present value interest factor} = PVIF_{i,n} = \frac{1}{(1 + i)^n} \qquad \text{(11)}$$

Appendix: Financial Tables, Table A–2 presents present value interest factors for $1. By letting $PVIF_{i,n}$ represent the appropriate factor, we can rewrite the general equation for present value (Equation 9) as follows:

$$PV = FV_n \times (PVIF_{i,n}) \qquad (12)$$

This expression indicates that to find the present value of an amount to be received in a future period, n, we have merely to multiply the future amount, FV_n, by the appropriate present value interest factor.

Personal Finance Example   As noted, Pam Valenti wishes to find the present value of $1,700 to be received 8 years from now, assuming an 8% opportunity cost.

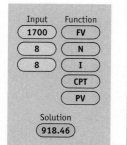

Input   Function
1700   FV
8   N
8   I
    CPT
    PV

Solution
918.46

Calculator Use   Using the calculator's financial functions and the inputs shown at the left, you should find the present value to be $918.46. The value obtained with the calculator is more accurate than the values found using the equation or the table (shown below), although for the purposes of this text, these differences are insignificant.

Spreadsheet Use   The present value of the single future amount also can be calculated as shown on the following Excel spreadsheet.

	A	B
1	PRESENT VALUE OF A SINGLE AMOUNT	
2	Future value	$1,700
3	Interest rate, pct per year compounded annually	8%
4	Number of years	8
5	Present value	$918.46
	Entry in Cell B5 is =–PV(B3,B4,0,B2) The minus sign appears before PV to change the present value to a positive amount.	

Table Use   The present value interest factor for 8% and 8 years, $PVIF_{8\%, 8 \text{ yrs}}$, found in Appendix: Financial Tables, Table A–2, is 0.540. Using Equation 12, $1,700 \times 0.540 = $918. The present value of the $1,700 Pam expects to receive in 8 years is $918.

A Graphical View of Present Value

Remember that present value calculations assume that the future values are measured at the *end* of the given period. The relationships among the factors in a present value calculation are illustrated in Figure 6. The figure clearly shows that, everything else being equal, (1) the higher the discount rate, the lower the present value, and (2) the longer the period of time, the lower the present value. Also note that given a discount rate of 0 percent, the present value always equals the future value ($1.00). But for any discount rate greater than zero, the present value is less than the future value of $1.00.

Comparing Present Value and Future Value

We will close this section with some important observations about present values. One is that the expression for the present value interest factor for i percent and n periods, $1/(1 + i)^n$, is the *inverse* of the future value interest factor for i percent and

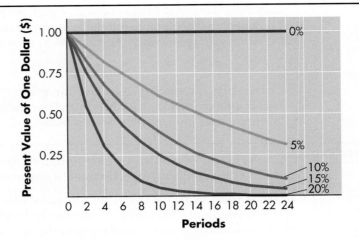

FIGURE 6

Present Value Relationship
Discount rates, time periods, and present value of one dollar

n periods, $(1 + i)^n$. You can confirm this very simply: Divide a present value interest factor for i percent and n periods, $PVIF_{i,n}$, given in Appendix: Financial Tables, Table A–2, into 1.0, and compare the resulting value to the future value interest factor given in Table A–1 for i percent and n periods, $FVIF_{i,n}$. The two values should be equivalent.

Second, because of the relationship between present value interest factors and future value interest factors, we can find the present value interest factors given a table of future value interest factors, and vice versa. For example, the future value interest factor (from Table A–1) for 10 percent and 5 periods is 1.611. Dividing this value into 1.0 yields 0.621, which is the present value interest factor (given in Table A–2) for 10 percent and 5 periods.

REVIEW QUESTIONS

3   How is the *compounding process* related to the payment of interest on savings? What is the general equation for future value?

4   What effect would a *decrease* in the interest rate have on the future value of a deposit? What effect would an *increase* in the holding period have on future value?

5   What is meant by "the present value of a future amount"? What is the general equation for present value?

6   What effect does *increasing* the required return have on the present value of a future amount? Why?

7   How are present value and future value calculations related?

3   # Annuities

How much would you pay today, given that you can earn 7 percent on low-risk investments, to receive a guaranteed $3,000 at the end of *each* of the next 20 years? How much will you have at the end of 5 years if your employer withholds and invests $1,000 of your year-end bonus at the end of *each* of the next 5 years,

annuity
A stream of equal periodic cash flows, over a specified time period. These cash flows can be *inflows* of returns earned on investments or *outflows* of funds invested to earn future returns.

ordinary annuity
An annuity for which the cash flow occurs at the *end* of each period.

annuity due
An annuity for which the cash flow occurs at the *beginning* of each period.

guaranteeing you a 9 percent annual rate of return? To answer these questions, you need to understand the application of the time value of money to *annuities*.

An **annuity** is a stream of equal periodic cash flows, over a specified time period. These cash flows are usually annual but can occur at other intervals, such as monthly (rent, car payments). The cash flows in an annuity can be *inflows* (the $3,000 received at the end of each of the next 20 years) or *outflows* (the $1,000 invested at the end of each of the next 5 years).

Types of Annuities

There are two basic types of annuities. For an **ordinary annuity,** the cash flow occurs at the *end* of each period. For an **annuity due,** the cash flow occurs at the *beginning* of each period.

Personal Finance Example   Fran Abrams is choosing which of two annuities to receive. Both are 5-year, $1,000 annuities; annuity A is an ordinary annuity, and annuity B is an annuity due. To better understand the difference between these annuities, she has listed their cash flows in Table 1. Note that the amount of each annuity totals $5,000. The two annuities differ in the timing of their cash flows: The cash flows are received sooner with the annuity due than with the ordinary annuity.

Although the cash flows of both annuities in Table 1 total $5,000, the annuity due would have a higher future value than the ordinary annuity, because each of its five annual cash flows can earn interest for one year more than each of the ordinary annuity's cash flows. In general, as will be demonstrated later in this chapter, *both the future value and the present value of an annuity due are always greater than the future value and the present value, respectively, of an otherwise identical ordinary annuity.*

Because ordinary annuities are more frequently used in finance, *unless otherwise specified, the term* annuity *is intended throughout this book to refer to ordinary annuities.* Discussions of annuities in this text concentrate on ordinary annuities. For discussion and computation of annuities due, see the text's website.

TABLE 1	Comparison of Ordinary Annuity and Annuity Due Cash Flows ($1,000, 5 Years)	
	Annual cash flows	
End of year[a]	Annuity A (*ordinary*)	Annuity B (*annuity due*)
0	$ 0	$1,000
1	1,000	1,000
2	1,000	1,000
3	1,000	1,000
4	1,000	1,000
5	1,000	0
Totals	$5,000	$5,000

[a]The ends of years 0, 1, 2, 3, and 4 are equivalent to the beginnings of years 1, 2, 3, 4, and 5, respectively.

Finding the Future Value of an Ordinary Annuity

The calculations required to find the future value of an ordinary annuity are illustrated in the following example.

___

Personal Finance Example   Fran Abrams wishes to determine how much money she will have at the end of 5 years if she chooses annuity A, the ordinary annuity. It represents deposits of $1,000 annually, at the *end of each* of the next 5 years, into a savings account paying 7% annual interest. This situation is depicted on the following time line:

Time line for future value of an ordinary annuity ($1,000 end-of-year deposit, earning 7%, at the end of 5 years)

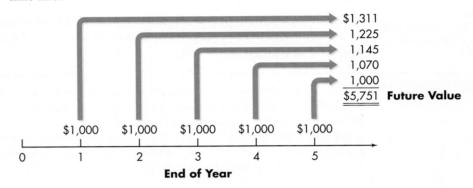

As the figure shows, at the end of year 5, Fran will have $5,751 in her account. Note that because the deposits are made at the end of the year, the first deposit will earn interest for 4 years, the second for 3 years, and so on.

Using Computational Tools to Find the Future Value of an Ordinary Annuity

Annuity calculations can be simplified by using a financial calculator, an electronic spreadsheet, or an interest table. A table for the future value of a $1 *ordinary annuity* is given in Appendix: Financial Tables, Table A–3. The factors in the table are derived by summing the future value interest factors for the appropriate number of years. For example, the factor for the annuity in the preceding example is the sum of the factors for the five years (years 4 through 0): 1.311 + 1.225 + 1.145 + 1.070 + 1.000 = 5.751. Because the deposits occur at the end of each year, they will earn interest from the end of the year in which each occurs to the end of year 5. Therefore, the first deposit earns interest for 4 years (end of year 1 through end of year 5), and the last deposit earns interest for zero years. The future value interest factor for zero years at any interest rate i, $FVIF_{i,0}$, is 1.000, as we have noted. The formula for the **future value interest factor for an ordinary annuity** when interest is compounded annually at i percent for n periods, $FVIFA_{i,n}$, is[7]

future value interest factor for an ordinary annuity The multiplier used to calculate the future value of an *ordinary annuity* at a specified interest rate over a given period of time.

$$FVIFA_{i,n} = \sum_{t=1}^{n} (1+i)^{t-1} \qquad (13)$$

___

7. A mathematical expression that can be applied to calculate the future value interest factor for an ordinary annuity more efficiently is

$$FVIFA_{i,n} = \frac{1}{i} \times [(1+i)^n - 1] \qquad (13a)$$

The use of this expression is especially attractive in the absence of any financial calculator, electronic spreadsheet, or the appropriate financial tables.

This factor is the multiplier used to calculate the future value of an *ordinary annuity* at a specified interest rate over a given period of time.

Using FVA_n for the future value of an *n*-year annuity, *PMT* for the amount to be deposited annually at the *end* of each year, and $FVIFA_{i,n}$ for the appropriate *future value interest factor for a one-dollar ordinary annuity compounded at* i *percent for* n *years*, we can express the relationship among these variables as

$$FVA_n = PMT \times (FVIFA_{i,n}) \tag{14}$$

The following example illustrates this calculation using a calculator, a spreadsheet, and a table.

Personal Finance Example   As noted earlier, Fran Abrams wishes to find the future value (FVA_n) at the end of 5 years (*n*) of an annual *end-of-year deposit* of $1,000 (*PMT*) into an account paying 7% annual interest (*i*) during the next 5 years.

Calculator Use   Using the calculator inputs shown at the left, you will find the future value of the ordinary annuity to be $5,750.74, a slightly more precise answer than that found using the table (shown below).

Spreadsheet Use   The future value of the ordinary annuity also can be calculated as shown on the following Excel spreadsheet.

Input	Function
1000	PMT
5	N
7	I
	CPT
	FV

Solution
5,750.74

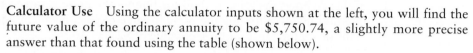

	A	B
1	FUTURE VALUE OF AN ORDINARY ANNUITY	
2	Annual payment	$1,000
3	Annual rate of interest, compounded annually	7%
4	Number of years	5
5	Future value of an ordinary annuity	$5,750.74

Entry in Cell B5 is =FV(B3,B4,–B2)
The minus sign appears before B2 because
the annual payment is a cash outflow.

Table Use   The future value interest factor for an ordinary 5-year annuity at 7% ($FVIFA_{7\%,5yrs}$), found in Appendix: Financial Tables, Table A–3, is 5.751. Using Equation 14, the $1,000 deposit × 5.751 results in a future value for the annuity of $5,751.

Finding the Present Value of an Ordinary Annuity

Quite often in finance, there is a need to find the present value of a *stream* of cash flows to be received in future periods. An annuity is, of course, a stream of equal periodic cash flows. (We'll explore the case of mixed streams of cash flows in a later section.) The method for finding the present value of an ordinary annuity is similar to the method just discussed. There are long and short methods for making this calculation.

Example   Braden Company, a small producer of plastic toys, wants to determine the most it should pay to purchase a particular ordinary annuity. The annuity consists of cash flows of $700 at the end of each year for 5 years. The firm requires the annuity to provide a minimum return of 8%. This situation is depicted on the following time line:

Time line for present value of an ordinary annuity ($700 end-of-year cash flows, discounted at 8%, over 5 years)

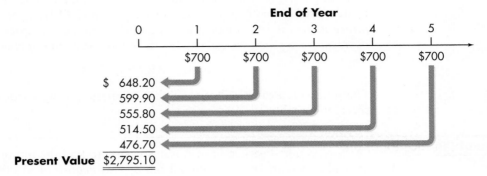

Table 2 shows the long method for finding the present value of the annuity. This method involves finding the present value of each payment and summing them. This procedure yields a present value of $2,795.10.

Using Computational Tools to Find the Present Value of an Ordinary Annuity

present value interest factor for an ordinary annuity
The multiplier used to calculate the present value of an *ordinary annuity* at a specified discount rate over a given period of time.

Annuity calculations can be simplified by using a financial calculator, an electronic spreadsheet, or an interest table for the present value of an annuity. The values for the present value of a $1 ordinary annuity are given in Appendix: Financial Tables, Table A–4. The factors in the table are derived by summing the present value interest factors (in Table A–2) for the appropriate number of years at the given discount rate. The formula for the **present value interest factor for an ordinary annuity** with cash flows that are discounted at i percent for n periods, $PVIFA_{i,n}$, is[8]

$$PVIFA_{i,n} = \sum_{t=1}^{n} \frac{1}{(1 + i)^t} \tag{15}$$

This factor is the multiplier used to calculate the present value of an *ordinary annuity* at a specified discount rate over a given period of time.

By letting PVA_n equal the present value of an n-year *ordinary annuity*, letting PMT equal the amount to be received annually at the *end* of each year, and letting $PVIFA_{i,n}$ represent the appropriate *present value interest factor for a one-dollar ordinary annuity discounted at* i *percent for* n *years,* we can express the relationship among these variables as

$$PVA_n = PMT \times (PVIFA_{i,n}) \tag{16}$$

The following example illustrates this calculation using a calculator, a spreadsheet, and a table.

---

8. A mathematical expression that can be applied to calculate the present value interest factor for an ordinary annuity more efficiently is

$$PVIFA_{i,n} = \frac{1}{i} \times \left[1 - \frac{1}{(1 + i)^n} \right] \tag{15a}$$

The use of this expression is especially attractive in the absence of any financial calculator, electronic spreadsheet, or the appropriate financial tables.

| TABLE 2 | Long Method for Finding the Present Value of an Ordinary Annuity | | |

Year (n)	Cash flow (1)	$PVIF_{8\%,n}{}^a$ (2)	Present value [(1) × (2)] (3)
1	$700	0.926	$ 648.20
2	700	0.857	599.90
3	700	0.794	555.80
4	700	0.735	514.50
5	700	0.681	476.70
		Present value of annuity	$2,795.10

^{a}Present value interest factors at 8% are from Table A–2.

Example

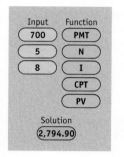

Input	Function
700	PMT
5	N
8	I
	CPT
	PV

Solution
2,794.90

Braden Company, as we have noted, wants to find the present value of a 5-year ordinary annuity of $700, assuming an 8% opportunity cost.

Calculator Use   Using the calculator's inputs shown at the left, you will find the present value of the ordinary annuity to be $2,794.90. The value obtained with the calculator is more accurate than those found using the equation or the table (shown below).

Spreadsheet Use   The present value of the ordinary annuity also can be calculated as shown on the following Excel spreadsheet.

	A	B
1	PRESENT VALUE OF AN ORDINARY ANNUITY	
2	Annual payment	$700
3	Annual rate of interest, compounded annually	8%
4	Number of years	5
5	Present value of an ordinary annuity	$2,794.90
	Entry in Cell B5 is =PV(B3,B4,–B2) The minus sign appears before B2 because the annual payment is a cash outflow.	

Table Use   The present value interest factor for an ordinary annuity at 8% for 5 years ($PVIFA_{8\%,5yrs}$), found in Appendix: Financial Tables, Table A–4, is 3.993. If we use Equation 16, $700 annuity × 3.993 results in a present value of $2,795.10.

Finding the Present Value of a Perpetuity

perpetuity
An annuity with an infinite life, providing continual annual cash flow.

A **perpetuity** is an annuity with an infinite life—in other words, an annuity that never stops providing its holder with a cash flow at the end of each year (for example, the right to receive $500 at the end of each year forever).

It is sometimes necessary to find the present value of a perpetuity. The present value interest factor for a perpetuity discounted at the rate i is

$$PVIFA_{i,\infty} = \frac{1}{i} \qquad (17)$$

As the equation shows, the appropriate factor, $PVIFA_{i,\infty}$, is found simply by dividing the discount rate, i (stated as a decimal), into 1. The validity of this method can be seen by looking at the factors in Appendix: Financial Tables, Table A–4 for 8, 10, 20, and 40 percent: As the number of periods (typically years) approaches 50, these factors approach the values calculated using Equation 17: $1 \div 0.08 = 12.50$; $1 \div 0.10 = 10.00$; $1 \div 0.20 = 5.00$; and $1 \div 0.40 = 2.50$.

Personal Finance Example   Ross Clark wishes to endow a chair in finance at his alma mater. The university indicated that it requires $200,000 per year to support the chair, and the endowment would earn 10% per year. To determine the amount Ross must give the university to fund the chair, we must determine the present value of a $200,000 perpetuity discounted at 10%. The appropriate present value interest factor can be found by dividing 1 by 0.10, as noted in Equation 17. Substituting the resulting factor, $PVIFA_{10\%,\infty} = 10$, and the amount of the perpetuity, $PMT = \$200,000$, into Equation 16 results in a present value of $2,000,000 for the perpetuity. In other words, to generate $200,000 every year for an indefinite period requires $2,000,000 today if Ross Clark's alma mater can earn 10% on its investments. If the university earns 10% interest annually on the $2,000,000, it can withdraw $200,000 per year indefinitely without touching the initial $2,000,000, which would never be drawn upon.

REVIEW QUESTIONS

8   What is the difference between an *ordinary annuity* and an *annuity due*? Which always has greater future value and present value for identical annuities and interest rates? Why?

9   What are the most efficient ways to calculate the present value of an ordinary annuity? What is the relationship between the *PVIF* and *PVIFA* interest factors given in Appendix: Financial Tables, Tables A–2 and A–4, respectively?

10   What is a *perpetuity*? How can the present value interest factor for such a stream of cash flows be determined?

4 | Mixed Streams

mixed stream
A stream of unequal periodic cash flows that reflect no particular pattern.

Two basic types of cash flow streams are possible: the annuity and the mixed stream. Whereas an *annuity* is a pattern of equal periodic cash flows, a **mixed stream** is a stream of unequal periodic cash flows that reflect no particular pattern. Financial managers frequently need to evaluate opportunities that are expected to provide mixed streams of cash flows. Here we consider both the future value and the present value of mixed streams.

Future Value of a Mixed Stream

Determining the future value of a mixed stream of cash flows is straightforward. We determine the future value of each cash flow at the specified future date and then add all the individual future values to find the total future value.

Example   Shrell Industries, a cabinet manufacturer, expects to receive the following mixed stream of cash flows over the next 5 years from one of its small customers.

End of year	Cash flow
1	$11,500
2	14,000
3	12,900
4	16,000
5	18,000

If Shrell expects to earn 8% on its investments, how much will it accumulate by the end of year 5 if it immediately invests these cash flows when they are received? This situation is depicted on the following time line:

Time line for future value of a mixed stream (end-of-year cash flows, compounded at 8% to the end of year 5)

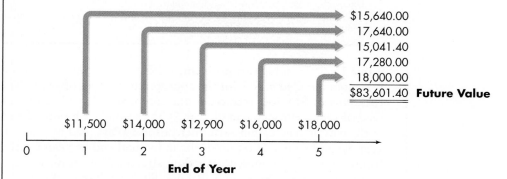

Calculator Use You can use your calculator to find the future value of each individual cash flow, as demonstrated earlier, and then sum the future values, to get the future value of the stream. Unfortunately, unless you can program your calculator, most calculators lack a function that would allow you to input *all of the cash flows,* specify the interest rate, and directly calculate the future value of the entire cash flow stream. Had you used your calculator to find the individual cash flow future values and then summed them, the future value of Shrell Industries' cash flow stream at the end of year 5 would have been $83,608.15.

Spreadsheet Use The future value of the mixed stream also can be calculated as shown on the following Excel spreadsheet.

	A	B
1	FUTURE VALUE OF A MIXED STREAM	
2	Interest rate, pct/year	8%
3	Year	Year-End Cash Flow
4	1	$11,500
5	2	$14,000
6	3	$12,900
7	4	$16,000
8	5	$18,000
9	Future value	$83,608.15

Entry in Cell B9 is
=−FV(B2,A8,0,NPV(B2,B4:B8)).
The minus sign appears before FV to convert the future value to a positive amount.

	Cash flow	Number of years earning interest (n)	$FVIF_{8\%,n}{}^a$	Future value $[(1) \times (3)]$
Year	(1)	(2)	(3)	(4)
1	$11,500	$5-1=4$	1.360	$15,640.00
2	14,000	$5-2=3$	1.260	17,640.00
3	12,900	$5-3=2$	1.166	15,041.40
4	16,000	$5-4=1$	1.080	17,280.00
5	18,000	$5-5=0$	1.000^b	18,000.00
			Future value of mixed stream	$83,601.40

TABLE 3   Future Value of a Mixed Stream of Cash Flows

^{a}Future value interest factors at 8% are from Table A–1.

^{b}The future value of the end-of-year-5 deposit at the end of year 5 is its present value because it earns interest for zero years and $(1+0.08)^0 = 1.000$.

Table Use To solve this problem, we determine the future value of each cash flow compounded at 8% for the appropriate number of years. Note that the first cash flow of $11,500, received at the end of year 1, will earn interest for 4 years (end of year 1 through end of year 5); the second cash flow of $14,000, received at the end of year 2, will earn interest for 3 years (end of year 2 through end of year 5); and so on. The sum of the individual end-of-year-5 future values is the future value of the mixed cash flow stream. The future value interest factors required are those shown in Appendix: Financial Tables, Table A–1. Table 3 presents the calculations needed to find the future value of the cash flow stream, which turns out to be $83,601.40. This value is less precise than the value obtained using a calculator or spreadsheet.

If Shrell Industries invests at 8% interest the cash flows received from its customer over the next 5 years, the company will accumulate about $83,600 by the end of year 5.

Present Value of a Mixed Stream

Finding the present value of a mixed stream of cash flows is similar to finding the future value of a mixed stream. We determine the present value of each future amount and then add all the individual present values together to find the total present value.

Example

Frey Company, a shoe manufacturer, has been offered an opportunity to receive the following mixed stream of cash flows over the next 5 years:

End of year	Cash flow
1	$400
2	800
3	500
4	400
5	300

If the firm must earn at least 9% on its investments, what is the most it should pay for this opportunity? This situation is depicted on the following time line:

Time line for present value of a mixed stream (end-of-year cash flows, discounted at 9% over the corresponding number of years)

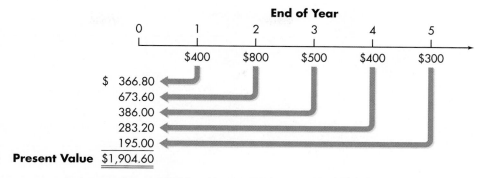

End of Year

	0	1	2	3	4	5
		$400	$800	$500	$400	$300

$ 366.80
673.60
386.00
283.20
195.00

Present Value $1,904.60

Calculator Use You can use a calculator to find the present value of each individual cash flow, as demonstrated earlier, and then sum the present values, to get the present value of the stream. However, most financial calculators have a function that allows you to punch in *all cash flows,* specify the discount rate, and then directly calculate the present value of the entire cash flow stream. Because calculators provide solutions more precise than those based on rounded table factors, the present value of Frey Company's cash flow stream found using a calculator is $1,904.76.

Spreadsheet Use The present value of the mixed stream of future cash flows also can be calculated as shown on the following Excel spreadsheet.

	A	B
1	PRESENT VALUE OF A MIXED STREAM OF CASH FLOWS	
2	Interest rate, pct/year	9%
3	Year	Year-End Cash Flow
4	1	$400
5	2	$800
6	3	$500
7	4	$400
8	5	$300
9	Present value	$1,904.76
	Entry in Cell B9 is =NPV(B2,B4:B8).	

Table Use To solve this problem, determine the present value of each cash flow discounted at 9% for the appropriate number of years. The sum of these individual values is the present value of the total stream. The present value interest factors required are those shown in Appendix: Financial Tables, Table A–2. Table 4 presents the calculations needed to find the present value of the cash flow stream, which turns out to be $1,904.60. This value is close to the more precise value of $1,904.76 found by using a calculator or spreadsheet.

Paying about $1,905 would provide exactly a 9% return. Frey should pay no more than that amount for the opportunity to receive these cash flows.

TABLE 4	Present Value of a Mixed Stream of Cash Flows		
Year (n)	Cash flow (1)	$PVIF_{9\%,n}{}^{a}$ (2)	Present value [(1) × (2)] (3)
1	$400	0.917	$ 366.80
2	800	0.842	673.60
3	500	0.772	386.00
4	400	0.708	283.20
5	300	0.650	195.00
		Present value of mixed stream	$1,904.60

[a]Present value interest factors at 9% are from Table A–2.

REVIEW QUESTION

11 How is the future value of a mixed stream of cash flows calculated? How is the present value of a mixed stream of cash flows calculated?

5 | Compounding Interest More Frequently Than Annually

Interest is often compounded more frequently than once a year. Savings institutions compound interest semiannually, quarterly, monthly, weekly, daily, or even continuously. This section discusses various issues and techniques related to these more frequent compounding intervals.

Semiannual Compounding

semiannual compounding
Compounding of interest over two periods within the year.

Semiannual compounding of interest involves two compounding periods within the year. Instead of the stated interest rate being paid once a year, one-half of the stated interest rate is paid twice a year.

Personal Finance Example Fred Moreno has decided to invest $100 in a savings account paying 8% interest *compounded semiannually*. If he leaves his money in the account for 24 months (2 years), he will be paid 4% interest compounded over four periods, each of which is 6 months long. Table 5 uses interest factors to show that at the end of 12 months (1 year) with 8% semiannual compounding, Fred will have $108.16; at the end of 24 months (2 years), he will have $116.99.

Quarterly Compounding

quarterly compounding
Compounding of interest over four periods within the year.

Quarterly compounding of interest involves four compounding periods within the year. One-fourth of the stated interest rate is paid four times a year.

TABLE 5	Future Value from Investing $100 at 8% Interest Compounded Semiannually over 24 Months (2 Years)		
Period	Beginning principal (1)	Future value interest factor (2)	Future value at end of period [(1) × (2)] (3)
6 months	$100.00	1.04	$104.00
12 months	104.00	1.04	108.16
18 months	108.16	1.04	112.49
24 months	112.49	1.04	116.99

Personal Finance Example   Fred Moreno has found an institution that will pay him 8% interest *compounded quarterly*. If he leaves his money in this account for 24 months (2 years), he will be paid 2% interest compounded over eight periods, each of which is 3 months long. Table 6 uses interest factors to show the amount Fred will have at the end of each period. At the end of 12 months (1 year), with 8% quarterly compounding, Fred will have $108.24; at the end of 24 months (2 years), he will have $117.17.

Table 7 compares values for Fred Moreno's $100 at the end of years 1 and 2 given annual, semiannual, and quarterly compounding periods at the 8 percent rate. As shown, *the more frequently interest is compounded, the greater the amount of money accumulated*. This is true for *any interest rate* for *any period of time*.

A General Equation for Compounding More Frequently Than Annually

The interest-factor formula for annual compounding (Equation 5) can be rewritten for use when compounding takes place more frequently. If m equals the

TABLE 6	Future Value from Investing $100 at 8% Interest Compounded Quarterly over 24 Months (2 Years)		
Period	Beginning principal (1)	Future value interest factor (2)	Future value at end of period [(1) × (2)] (3)
3 months	$100.00	1.02	$102.00
6 months	102.00	1.02	104.04
9 months	104.04	1.02	106.12
12 months	106.12	1.02	108.24
15 months	108.24	1.02	110.41
18 months	110.40	1.02	112.62
21 months	112.61	1.02	114.87
24 months	114.86	1.02	117.17

TABLE 7	Future Value at the End of Years 1 and 2 from Investing $100 at 8% Interest, Given Various Compounding Periods		
		Compounding period	
End of year	Annual	Semiannual	Quarterly
1	$108.00	$108.16	$108.24
2	116.64	116.99	117.17

number of times per year interest is compounded, the interest-factor formula for annual compounding can be rewritten as

$$FVIF_{i,n} = \left(1 + \frac{i}{m}\right)^{m \times n} \tag{18}$$

The basic equation for future value (Equation 4) can now be rewritten as

$$FV_n = PV \times \left(1 + \frac{i}{m}\right)^{m \times n} \tag{19}$$

If $m = 1$, Equation 19 reduces to Equation 4. Thus, if interest is compounded annually (once a year), Equation 19 will provide the same result as Equation 4. The general use of Equation 19 can be illustrated with a simple example.

Personal Finance Example   The preceding examples calculated the amount that Fred Moreno would have at the end of 2 years if he deposited $100 at 8% interest compounded semiannually and compounded quarterly. For semiannual compounding, m would equal 2 in Equation 19; for quarterly compounding, m would equal 4. Substituting the appropriate values for semiannual and quarterly compounding into Equation 19, we find that

1. *For semiannual compounding:*

$$FV_2 = \$100 \times \left(1 + \frac{0.08}{2}\right)^{2 \times 2} = \$100 \times (1 + 0.04)^4 = \$116.99$$

2. *For quarterly compounding:*

$$FV_2 = \$100 \times \left(1 + \frac{0.08}{4}\right)^{4 \times 2} = \$100 \times (1 + 0.02)^8 = \$117.17$$

These results agree with the values for FV_2 in Tables 5 and 6.

If the interest were compounded monthly, weekly, or daily, m would equal 12, 52, or 365, respectively.

Using Computational Tools for Compounding More Frequently Than Annually

We can use the future value interest factors for one dollar, given in Table A–1 of Appendix: Financial Tables, when interest is compounded m times each year. Instead of indexing the table for i percent and n years, as we do when interest is compounded annually, we index it for $(i \div m)$ percent and $(m \times n)$ periods. However, the table is less useful, because it includes only selected rates for a limited number of periods. Instead, a financial calculator or an electronic spreadsheet is typically required.

Personal Finance Example   Fred Moreno wished to find the future value of $100 invested at 8% interest compounded both semiannually and quarterly for 2 years. The number of compounding periods m, the interest rate $(i \div m)$, and the number of periods $(m \times n)$ used, along with the future value interest factor, are as follows:

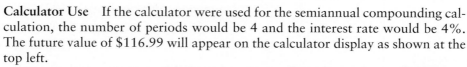

Compounding period	m	Interest rate $(i \div m)$	Periods $(m \times n)$	Future value interest factor from Table A–1
Semiannual	2	8% ÷ 2 = 4%	2 × 2 = 4	1.170
Quarterly	4	8% ÷ 4 = 2%	4 × 2 = 8	1.172

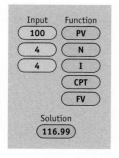

Input	Function
100	PV
4	N
4	I
	CPT
	FV

Solution
116.99

Calculator Use   If the calculator were used for the semiannual compounding calculation, the number of periods would be 4 and the interest rate would be 4%. The future value of $116.99 will appear on the calculator display as shown at the top left.

For the quarterly compounding case, the number of periods would be 8 and the interest rate would be 2%. The future value of $117.17 will appear on the calculator display as shown in the second display at the left.

Input	Function
100	PV
8	N
2	I
	CPT
	FV

Solution
117.17

Spreadsheet Use   The future value of the single amount with semiannual and quarterly compounding also can be calculated as shown on the following Excel spreadsheet.

	A	B
1	FUTURE VALUE OF A SINGLE AMOUNT WITH SEMIANNUAL AND QUARTERLY COMPOUNDING	
2	Present value	$100
3	Interest rate, pct per year compounded semiannually	8%
4	Number of years	2
5	Future value with semiannual compounding	$116.99
6	Present value	$100
7	Interest rate, pct per year compounded quarterly	8%
8	Number of years	2
9	Future value with quarterly compounding	$117.17

Entry in Cell B5 is =FV(B3/2,B4*2,0,−B2,0).
Entry in Cell B9 is =FV(B7/4,B8*4,0,−B2,0).
The minus sign appears before B2 because the present value is a cash outflow (i.e., a deposit made by Fred Moreno).

Table Use   Multiplying each of the future value interest factors by the initial $100 deposit results in a value of $117.00 ($1.170 \times \$100$) for semiannual compounding and a value of $117.20 ($1.172 \times \$100$) for quarterly compounding.

Comparing the calculator, spreadsheet, and table values, we can see that the calculator and spreadsheet values agree with the values in Table 7 but are more precise because the table factors have been rounded.

Continuous Compounding

continuous compounding
Compounding of interest an infinite number of times per year at intervals of microseconds.

In the extreme case, interest can be compounded continuously. **Continuous compounding** involves compounding over every microsecond—the smallest time period imaginable. In this case, m in Equation 18 would approach infinity. Through the use of calculus, we know that as m approaches infinity, the interest-factor equation becomes

$$FVIF_{i,n} \text{ (continuous compounding)} = e^{i \times n} \qquad (20)$$

where e is the exponential function,[9] which has a value of 2.7183. The future value for continuous compounding is therefore

$$FV_n \text{ (continuous compounding)} = PV \times (e^{i \times n}) \qquad (21)$$

Personal Finance Example
To find the value at the end of 2 years ($n = 2$) of Fred Moreno's $100 deposit ($PV = \$100$) in an account paying 8% annual interest ($i = 0.08$) compounded continuously, we can substitute into Equation 21:

$$FV_2 \text{ (continuous compounding)} = \$100 \times e^{0.08 \times 2}$$
$$= \$100 \times 2.7183^{0.16}$$
$$= \$100 \times 1.1735 = \$117.35$$

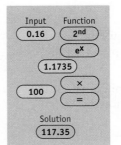

Calculator Use To find this value using the calculator, you need first to find the value of $e^{0.16}$ by punching in 0.16 and then pressing **2nd** and then e^x to get 1.1735. Next multiply this value by $100 to get the future value of $117.35 as shown at the left. (*Note:* On some calculators, you may not have to press **2nd** before pressing e^x.)

Spreadsheet Use The future value of the single amount with continuous compounding of Fred's deposit also can be calculated as shown on the following Excel spreadsheet.

	A	B
1	FUTURE VALUE OF A SINGLE AMOUNT WITH CONTINUOUS COMPOUNDING	
2	Present value	$100
3	Annual rate of interest, compounded continuously	8%
4	Number of years	2
5	Future value with continuous compounding	$117.35
	Entry in Cell B5 is =B2*EXP(B3*B4).	

The future value with continuous compounding therefore equals $117.35. As expected, the continuously compounded value is larger than the future value of interest compounded semiannually ($116.99) or quarterly ($117.17). Contin-

9. Most calculators have the exponential function, typically noted by e^x, built into them. The use of this key is especially helpful in calculating future value when interest is compounded continuously.

uous compounding results in the largest future value that would result from compounding interest more frequently than annually at a given rate over a stated period of time.

Nominal and Effective Annual Rates of Interest

nominal (stated) annual rate
Contractual annual rate of interest charged by a lender or promised by a borrower.

effective (true) annual rate (EAR)
The annual rate of interest actually paid or earned.

Both businesses and investors need to make objective comparisons of loan costs or investment returns over different compounding periods. To put interest rates on a common basis, so as to allow comparison, we distinguish between nominal and effective annual rates. The **nominal, or stated, annual rate** is the contractual annual rate of interest charged by a lender or promised by a borrower. The **effective, or true, annual rate (EAR)** is the annual rate of interest actually paid or earned. The effective annual rate reflects the effects of compounding frequency, whereas the nominal annual rate does not.

Using the notation introduced earlier, we can calculate the effective annual rate, EAR, by substituting values for the nominal annual rate, i, and the compounding frequency, m, into Equation 22:

$$EAR = \left(1 + \frac{i}{m}\right)^m - 1 \tag{22}$$

We can apply this equation using data from preceding examples.

Personal Finance Example   Fred Moreno wishes to find the effective annual rate associated with an 8% nominal annual rate ($i = 0.08$) when interest is compounded (1) annually ($m = 1$); (2) semiannually ($m = 2$); and (3) quarterly ($m = 4$). Substituting these values into Equation 22, we get

1. *For annual compounding:*

$$EAR = \left(1 + \frac{0.08}{1}\right)^1 - 1 = (1 + 0.08)^1 - 1 = 1 + 0.08 - 1 = 0.08 = 8\%$$

2. *For semiannual compounding:*

$$EAR = \left(1 + \frac{0.08}{2}\right)^2 - 1 = (1 + 0.04)^2 - 1 = 1.0816 - 1 = 0.0816 = 8.16\%$$

3. *For quarterly compounding:*

$$EAR = \left(1 + \frac{0.08}{4}\right)^4 - 1 = (1 + 0.02)^4 - 1 = 1.0824 - 1 = 0.0824 = 8.24\%$$

These values demonstrate two important points: The first is that nominal and effective annual rates are equivalent for annual compounding. The second is that the effective annual rate increases with increasing compounding frequency, up to a limit that occurs with *continuous compounding.*[10]

---

10. The effective annual rate for this extreme case can be found by using the following equation:

$$EAR \text{ (continuous compounding)} = e^i - 1 \tag{22a}$$

For the 8% nominal annual rate ($i = 0.08$), substitution into Equation 24a results in an effective annual rate of

$$e^{0.08} - 1 = 1.0833 - 1 = 0.0833 = 8.33\%$$

in the case of continuous compounding. This is the highest effective annual rate attainable with an 8% nominal rate.

annual percentage rate (APR)
The *nominal annual rate* of interest, found by multiplying the periodic rate by the number of periods in one year, that must be disclosed to consumers on credit cards and loans as a result of "truth-in-lending laws."

annual percentage yield (APY)
The *effective annual rate* of interest that must be disclosed to consumers by banks on their savings products as a result of "truth-in-savings laws."

At the consumer level, "truth-in-lending laws" require disclosure on credit card and loan agreements of the **annual percentage rate (APR)**. The APR is the *nominal annual rate* found by multiplying the periodic rate by the number of periods in one year. For example, a bank credit card that charges $1^1/_2$ percent per month (the periodic rate) would have an APR of 18 percent (1.5% per month $\times$ 12 months per year).

"Truth-in-savings laws," on the other hand, require banks to quote the **annual percentage yield (APY)** on their savings products. The APY is the *effective annual rate* a savings product pays. For example, a savings account that pays 0.5 percent per month would have an APY of 6.17 percent $[(1.005)^{12} - 1]$.

Quoting loan interest rates at their lower nominal annual rate (the APR) and savings interest rates at the higher effective annual rate (the APY) offers two advantages: It tends to standardize disclosure to consumers, and it enables financial institutions to quote the most attractive interest rates: low loan rates and high savings rates.

REVIEW QUESTIONS

12 What effect does compounding interest more frequently than annually have on (**a**) future value and (**b**) the *effective annual rate (EAR)?* Why?

13 How does the future value of a deposit subject to continuous compounding compare to the value obtained by annual compounding?

14 Differentiate between a *nominal annual rate* and an *effective annual rate (EAR).* Define *annual percentage rate (APR)* and *annual percentage yield (APY).*

---

6 | Special Applications of Time Value

Future value and present value techniques have a number of important applications in finance. We'll study four of them in this section: (1) determining deposits needed to accumulate a future sum, (2) loan amortization, (3) finding interest or growth rates, and (4) finding an unknown number of periods.

Determining Deposits Needed to Accumulate a Future Sum

Suppose you want to buy a house 5 years from now, and you estimate that an initial down payment of $30,000 will be required at that time. To accumulate the $30,000, you will wish to make equal annual end-of-year deposits into an account paying annual interest of 6 percent. The solution to this problem is closely related to the process of finding the future value of an annuity. You must determine what size annuity will result in a single amount equal to $30,000 at the end of year 5.

Earlier in the chapter we found the future value of an *n*-year ordinary annuity, FVA_n, by multiplying the annual deposit, *PMT*, by the appropriate interest factor, $FVIFA_{i,n}$. The relationship of the three variables was defined by Equation 14, which is repeated here as Equation 23:

$$FVA_n = PMT \times (FVIFA_{i,n}) \tag{23}$$

We can find the annual deposit required to accumulate FVA_n dollars by solving Equation 23 for PMT. Isolating PMT on the left side of the equation gives us

$$PMT = \frac{FVA_n}{FVIFA_{i,n}} \tag{24}$$

Once this is done, we have only to substitute the known values of FVA_n and $FVIFA_{i,n}$ into the right side of the equation to find the annual deposit required.

Personal Finance Example   As just stated, you want to determine the equal annual end-of-year deposits required to accumulate $30,000 at the end of 5 years, given an interest rate of 6%.

Input	Function
30000	FV
5	N
6	I
	CPT
	PMT

Solution
5,321.89

Calculator Use   Using the calculator inputs shown at the left, you will find the annual deposit amount to be $5,321.89. Thus, if $5,321.89 is deposited at the end of each year for 5 years at 6% interest, there will be $30,000 in the account at the end of 5 years.

Spreadsheet Use   The annual deposit needed to accumulate the future sum also can be calculated as shown on the following Excel spreadsheet.

	A	B
1	ANNUAL DEPOSITS NEEDED TO ACCUMULATE A FUTURE SUM	
2	Future value	$30,000
3	Number of years	5
4	Annual rate of interest	6%
5	Annual deposit	$5,321.89

Entry in Cell B5 is =–PMT(B4,B3,0,B2).
The minus sign appears before PMT because the annual deposits are cash outflows.

Table Use   Table A–3, in Appendix: Financial Tables, indicates that the future value interest factor for an ordinary annuity at 6% for 5 years ($FVIFA_{6\%,5yrs}$) is 5.637. Substituting $FVA_5 = \$30,000$ and $FVIFA_{6\%,5yrs} = 5.637$ into Equation 26 yields an annual required deposit, PMT, of $5,321.98. Note that this value, except for a slight rounding difference, agrees with the value found using a calculator and spreadsheet.

loan amortization
The determination of the equal periodic loan payments necessary to provide a lender with a specified interest return and to repay the loan principal over a specified period.

loan amortization schedule
A schedule of equal payments to repay a loan. It shows the allocation of each loan payment to interest and principal.

Loan Amortization

The term **loan amortization** refers to the determination of equal periodic loan payments. These payments provide a lender with a specified interest return and repay the loan principal over a specified period. The loan amortization process involves finding the future payments, over the term of the loan, whose present value at the loan interest rate equals the amount of initial principal borrowed. Lenders use a **loan amortization schedule** to determine these payment amounts and the allocation of each payment to interest and principal. In the case of home mortgages, these tables are used to find the equal *monthly* payments necessary to *amortize*, or pay off, the mortgage at a specified interest rate over a 15- to 30-year period.

Amortizing a loan actually involves creating an annuity out of a present amount. For example, say you borrow $6,000 at 10 percent and agree to make equal annual end-of-year payments over 4 years. To find the size of the payments, the lender determines the amount of a 4-year annuity discounted at 10 percent that has a present value of $6,000. This process is actually the inverse of finding the present value of an annuity.

Earlier in the chapter, we found the present value, PVA_n, of an n-year ordinary annuity by multiplying the annual amount, PMT, by the present value interest factor for an annuity, $PVIFA_{i,n}$. This relationship, which was originally expressed as Equation 16, is repeated here as Equation 25:

$$PVA_n = PMT \times (PVIFA_{i,n})$$ (25)

To find the equal annual payment required to pay off, or amortize, the loan, PVA_n, over a certain number of years at a specified interest rate, we need to solve Equation 25 for PMT. Isolating PMT on the left side of the equation gives us

$$PMT = \frac{PVA_n}{PVIFA_{i,n}}$$ (26)

Once this is done, we have only to substitute the known values into the righthand side of the equation to find the annual payment required.

Personal Finance Example As just stated, you want to determine the equal annual end-of-year payments necessary to amortize fully a $6,000, 10% loan over 4 years.

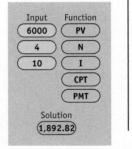

Calculator Use Using the calculator inputs shown at the left, you will find the annual payment amount to be $1,892.82. Thus, to repay the interest and principal on a $6,000, 10%, 4-year loan, equal annual end-of-year payments of $1,892.82 are necessary.

The allocation of each loan payment (based on table use, a payment of $1,892.74) to interest and principal can be seen in columns 3 and 4 of the *loan amortization schedule* in Table 8. The portion of each payment that represents interest (column 3) declines over the repayment period, and the portion going to

TABLE 8	Loan Amortization Schedule ($6,000 Principal, 10% Interest, 4-Year Repayment Period)				

| End of year | Beginning-of-year principal (1) | Loan payment[a] (2) | Payments | | End-of-year principal [(1) − (4)] (5) |
			Interest [0.10 × (1)] (3)	Principal [(2) − (3)] (4)	
1	$6,000.00	$1,892.74	$600.00	$1,292.74	$4,707.26
2	4,707.26	1,892.74	470.73	1,422.01	3,285.25
3	3,285.25	1,892.74	328.53	1,564.21	1,721.04
4	1,721.04	1,892.74	172.10	1,720.64	—[b]

[a]Based on the use of tables.

[b]Because of rounding, a slight difference ($0.40) exists between the beginning-of-year-4 principal (in column 1) and the year-4 principal payment (in column 4).

principal repayment (column 4) increases. This pattern is typical of amortized loans; as the principal is reduced, the interest component declines, leaving a larger portion of each subsequent loan payment to repay principal.

Spreadsheet Use The annual payment to repay the loan also can be calculated as shown on the first Excel spreadsheet below. The amortization schedule allocating each loan payment to interest and principal can be calculated precisely as shown on the second spreadsheet.

	A	B
1	ANNUAL PAYMENT TO REPAY A LOAN	
2	Loan principal (present value)	$6,000
3	Annual rate of interest	10%
4	Number of years	4
5	Annual payment	$1,892.82

Entry in Cell B5 is =–PMT(B3,B4,B2).
The minus sign appears before PMT because
the annual payments are cash outflows.

	A	B	C	D	E
1		LOAN AMORTIZATION SCHEDULE			
2		Data: Loan principal		$6,000	
3		Annual rate of interest		10%	
4		Number of years		4	
5		Annual Payments			
6	Year	Total	To Interest	To Principal	Year-End Principal
7	0				$6,000.00
8	1	$1,892.82	$600.00	$1,292.82	4,707.18
9	2	$1,892.82	$470.72	$1,422.11	3,285.07
10	3	$1,892.82	$328.51	$1,564.32	1,720.75
11	4	$1,892.82	$172.07	$1,720.75	0.00

Key Cell Entries
Cell B8: =–PMT(D3,D4,D2), copy to B9:B11
Cell C8: =–CUMIPMT(D3,D4,D2,A8,A8,0), copy to C9:C11
Cell D8: =–CUMPRINC(D3,D4,D2,A8,A8,0), copy to D9:D11
Cell E8: =E7–D8, copy to E9:E11
The minus signs appear before the entries in Cells B8, C8, and D8
because these are cash outflows.

Table Use Table A–4, in Appendix: Financial Tables, indicates that the present value interest factor for an ordinary annuity corresponding to 10% and 4 years ($PVIFA_{10\%, 4yrs}$) is 3.170. Substituting $PVA_4 = \$6,000$ and $PVIFA_{10\%, 4yrs} = 3.170$ into Equation 28 and solving for PMT yield an annual loan payment of $1,892.74. Except for a slight rounding difference, this agrees with the calculator and spreadsheet value.

To attract buyers who could not immediately afford 15- to 30-year mortgages of equal annual payments, lenders offered mortgages whose interest rates adjusted at certain points. The *Focus on Practice* box discusses how such mortgages have worked out for some "subprime" borrowers.

IN PRACTICE

Focus on Practice New Century Brings Trouble for Subprime Mortgages

As the housing market began to boom at the end of the twentieth century and into the early twenty-first, the market share of subprime mortgages climbed from near 0 percent in 1997 to about 20 percent of mortgage originations in 2006. Several factors combined to fuel the rapid growth of lending to borrowers with tarnished credit, including a low interest rate environment, loose underwriting standards, and innovations in mortgage financing such as "affordability programs" to increase rates of homeownership among lower-income borrowers.

Particularly attractive to new homebuyers was the hybrid adjustable rate mortgage (ARM), which featured a low introductory interest rate that reset upward after a preset period of time. Interest rates began a steady upward trend beginning in late 2004. In 2006, some $300 billion worth of adjustable

ARMs were reset to higher rates. In 2007, that figure will triple. The rise in interest rates will push monthly payments beyond what some homeowners can afford. For those who cannot make their payments, foreclosure and repossession by the lender may be the only way out.

Foreclosure on a nonproductive mortgage is particularly unwelcome and unrewarding for subprime mortgages. With very small equity margins in the original purchase, any drop in housing prices, as is currently happening in some overheated housing markets, exposes the lender to losses. They simply cannot sell the repossessed home for more than the outstanding loan. Typical of such lenders is **New Century Financial Corp.** The company, based in Irvine, California, entered Chapter 11 bankruptcy in April 2007, cutting 3,200 of its 7,200 employees as part of

its reorganization. One of the largest providers of subprime mortgages, New Century made $51.6 billion in subprime loans in 2006.

Problems with subprime loans were not limited to New Century. The Mortgage Bankers Association estimates that subprime loans were used to finance about 17 percent of home purchases in 2006. The mortgage bankers group reported in March 2007 that 13 percent of all subprime loans were in delinquency, more than five times the delinquency rate for home loans to borrowers with the best credit ratings. Like most bubbles, excesses will lead to corrections and the financial fallout from the subprime delinquencies will eventually run its course.

■ As a reaction to problems in the subprime area, lenders are already tightening lending standards. What effect will this have on the housing market?

Finding Interest or Growth Rates

It is often necessary to calculate the compound annual interest or *growth rate* (that is, the annual rate of change in values) of a series of cash flows. Examples include finding the interest rate on a loan, the rate of growth in sales, and the rate of growth in earnings. In doing this, we can use either future value or present value interest factors. The use of present value interest factors is described in this section. The simplest situation is one in which a person wishes to find the rate of interest or growth in a *series of cash flows*.[11]

Personal Finance Example Ray Noble wishes to find the rate of interest or growth reflected in the stream of cash flows he received from a real estate investment over the period 2005 through 2009. The following table lists those cash flows:

---

11. Because the calculations required for finding interest rates and growth rates, given the series of cash flows, are the same, this section refers to the calculations as those required to find interest *or* growth rates.

Year	Cash flow
2009	$1,520 ⎫4
2008	1,440 ⎬3
2007	1,370 ⎬2
2006	1,300 ⎬1
2005	1,250

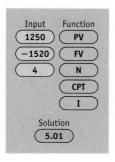

Input — Function
1250 — PV
−1520 — FV
4 — N
— CPT
— I
Solution
5.01

By using the first year (2005) as a base year, we see that interest has been earned (or growth experienced) for 4 years.

Calculator Use Using the calculator to find the interest or growth rate, we treat the earliest value as a present value, PV, and the latest value as a future value, FV_n. (*Note:* Most calculators require *either* the PV or the FV value to be input as a negative number to calculate an unknown interest or growth rate. That approach is used here.) Using the inputs shown at the left, you will find the interest or growth rate to be 5.01%.

Spreadsheet Use The interest or growth rate for the series of cash flows also can be calculated as shown on the following Excel spreadsheet.

	A	B
1	INTEREST OR GROWTH RATE– SERIES OF CASH FLOWS	
2	Year	Cash Flow
3	2009	$1,520
4	2008	$1,440
5	2007	$1,370
6	2006	$1,300
7	2005	$1,250
8	Annual growth rate	5.01%

Entry in Cell B8 is =RATE((A3–A7),0,B7,–B3,0). The expression A3–A7 in the entry calculates the number of years of growth. The minus sign appears before B3 because the investment in 2009 is treated as a cash outflow.

Table Use The first step is to divide the amount received in the earliest year (PV) by the amount received in the latest year (FV_n). Looking back at Equation 12, we see that this results in the present value interest factor for a *single amount* for 4 years, $PVIF_{i,4yrs}$, which is 0.822 ($1,250 ÷ $1,520). The interest rate in Appendix: Financial Tables, Table A–2 associated with the factor closest to 0.822 for 4 years is the interest or growth rate of Ray's cash flows. In the row for year 4 in Table A–2, the factor for 5 percent is 0.823—almost exactly the 0.822 value. Therefore, the interest or growth rate of the given cash flows is approximately (to the nearest whole percent) 5%, which is consistent with the value found using a calculator or spreadsheet.[12]

Another type of interest-rate problem involves finding the interest rate associated with an *annuity,* or equal-payment loan.

---

12. To obtain more precise estimates of interest or growth rates, *interpolation*—a mathematical technique for estimating unknown intermediate values—can be applied. For information on how to interpolate a more precise answer in this example, see the text's home page at **www.prenhall.com/gitman**.

Personal Finance Example

Input / Function
514.14 / PMT
−2000 / PV
5 / N
/ CPT
/ I

Solution
9.00

Jan Jacobs can borrow $2,000 to be repaid in equal annual end-of-year amounts of $514.14 for the next 5 years. She wants to find the interest rate on this loan.

Calculator Use (*Note:* Most calculators require *either* the *PMT* or the *PV* value to be input as a negative number to calculate an unknown interest rate on an equal-payment loan. That approach is used here.) Using the inputs shown at the left, you will find the interest rate to be 9.00%.

Spreadsheet Use The interest or growth rate for the annuity also can be calculated as shown on the following Excel spreadsheet.

	A	B
1	INTEREST OR GROWTH RATE– ANNUITY	
2	Present value (loan principal)	$2,000
3	Number of years	5
4	Annual payments	$514.14
5	Annual interest rate	9.00%

Entry in Cell B5 is =RATE(B3,B4,−B2).
The minus sign appears before B2 because
the loan principal is treated as a cash outflow.

Table Use Substituting $PVA_5 = \$2,000$ and $PMT = \$514.14$ into Equation 25 and rearranging the equation to solve for $PVIFA_{i,5\text{yrs}}$, we get

$$PVIFA_{i,5\text{yrs}} = \frac{PVA_5}{PMT} = \frac{\$2,000}{\$514.14} = 3.890 \qquad \text{(27)}$$

The interest rate for 5 years associated with the annuity factor closest to 3.890 in Table A–4 (in Appendix: Financial Tables) is 9%. Therefore, the interest rate on the loan is approximately (to the nearest whole percent) 9%, which is consistent with the value found using a calculator or spreadsheet.

Finding an Unknown Number of Periods

Sometimes it is necessary to calculate the number of time periods needed to generate a given amount of cash flow from an initial amount. Here we briefly consider this calculation for both single amounts and annuities. This simplest case is when a person wishes to determine the number of periods, n, it will take for an initial deposit, PV, to grow to a specified future amount, FV_n, given a stated interest rate, i.

Personal Finance Example Ann Bates wishes to determine the number of years it will take for her initial $1,000 deposit, earning 8% annual interest, to grow to equal $2,500. Simply stated, at an 8% annual rate of interest, how many years, n, will it take for Ann's $1,000, PV, to grow to $2,500, FV_n?

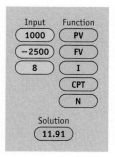

Input Function
1000   PV
−2500   FV
8   I
        CPT
        N

Solution
11.91

Calculator Use   Using the calculator, we treat the initial value as the present value, *PV*, and the latest value as the future value, *FV$_n$*. (*Note:* Most calculators require *either* the *PV* or the *FV* value to be input as a negative number to calculate an unknown number of periods. That approach is used here.) Using the inputs shown at the left, we find the number of periods to be 11.91 years.

Spreadsheet Use   The number of years for the present value to grow to a specified future value also can be calculated as shown on the following Excel spreadsheet.

	A	B
1	YEARS FOR A PRESENT VALUE TO GROW TO A SPECIFIED FUTURE VALUE	
2	Present value (deposit)	$1,000
3	Annual rate of interest, compounded annually	8%
4	Future value	$2,500
5	Number of years	11.91
	Entry in Cell B5 is =NPER(B3,0,B2,−B4). The minus sign appears before B4 because the future value is treated as a cash outflow.	

Table Use   In a manner similar to our approach for finding an unknown interest or growth rate in a series of cash flows, we begin by dividing the amount deposited in the earliest year by the amount received in the latest year. This results in the present value interest factor for 8% and *n* years, *PVIF*$_{8\%,n}$, which is 0.400 ($1,000 ÷ $2,500). The number of years (periods) in Table A–2, Appendix: Financial Tables, associated with the factor closest to 0.400 for an 8% interest rate is the number of years required for $1,000 to grow to $2,500 at 8%. In the 8% column of Table A–2, the factor for 12 years is 0.397—almost exactly the 0.400 value. Therefore, the number of years necessary for the $1,000 to grow to a future value of $2,500 at 8% is approximately (to the nearest year) 12. This number is consistent with, but not as precise as, the value found using a calculator or spreadsheet.

Another type of number-of-periods problem involves finding the number of periods associated with an *annuity*. Occasionally we wish to find the unknown life, *n*, of an annuity, *PMT*, that is intended to achieve a specific objective, such as repaying a loan of a given amount, *PVA$_n$*, with a stated interest rate, *i*.

Personal Finance Example   Bill Smart can borrow $25,000 at an 11% annual interest rate; equal, annual, end-of-year payments of $4,800 are required. He wishes to determine how long it will take to fully repay the loan. In other words, he wishes to determine how many years, *n*, it will take to repay the $25,000, 11% loan, *PVA$_n$*, if the payments of $4,800, *PMT*, are made at the end of each year.

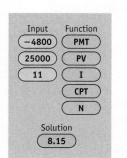

Input Function
−4800   PMT
25000   PV
11   I
        CPT
        N

Solution
8.15

Calculator Use   (*Note:* Most calculators require *either* the *PV* or the *PMT* value to be input as a negative number to calculate an unknown number of periods. That approach is used here.) Using the inputs shown at the left, you will find the number of periods to be 8.15 years.

Spreadsheet Use   The number of years to pay off the loan also can be calculated as shown on the Excel spreadsheet.

	A	B
1	YEARS TO PAY OFF A LOAN	
2	Annual payment	$4,800
3	Annual rate of interest, compounded annually	11%
4	Present value (loan principal)	$25,000
5	Number of years to pay off the loan	8.15
Entry in Cell B5 is =NPER(B3,−B2,B4). The minus sign appears before B2 because the payments are treated as cash outflows.		

Table Use Substituting $PVA_n = \$25,000$ and $PMT = \$4,800$ into Equation 25 and rearranging the equation to solve $PVIFA_{11\%,n}$, we get

$$PVIFA_{11\%,n} = \frac{PVA_n}{PMT} = \frac{\$25,000}{\$4,800} = 5.208 \qquad \text{(28)}$$

The number of periods for an 11% interest rate associated with the annuity factor closest to 5.208 in Appendix: Financial Tables, Table A–4 is 8 years. Therefore, the number of periods necessary to repay the loan fully is approximately (to the nearest year) 8 years. This value is consistent with the number of periods found using a calculator or spreadsheet.

REVIEW QUESTIONS

15 How can you determine the size of the equal, annual, end-of-period deposits necessary to accumulate a certain future sum at the end of a specified future period at a given annual interest rate?

16 Describe the procedure used to amortize a loan into a series of equal periodic payments.

17 Which present value interest factors would be used to find (a) the growth rate associated with a series of cash flows and (b) the interest rate associated with an equal-payment loan?

18 How can you determine the unknown number of periods when you know the present and future values—single amount or annuity—and the applicable rate of interest?

Summary

Focus on Value

Time value of money is an important tool that financial managers and other market participants use to assess the effects of proposed actions. Because firms have long lives and some decisions affect their long-term cash flows, the effective application of time-value-of-money techniques is extremely important. These techniques enable financial managers to evaluate cash flows occurring at different times so as to combine, compare, and evaluate them and link them to the firm's **overall goal of share price maximization.** The application of time value techniques is a key part of the value determination process needed to make intelligent value-creating decisions.

Review of Learning Goals

Key definitions, formulas, and equations for this chapter are summarized in Table 9.

LG 1 **Discuss the role of time value in finance, the use of computational tools, and the basic patterns of cash flow.** Financial managers and investors use time-value-of-money techniques when assessing the value of expected cash flow streams. Alternatives can be assessed by either compounding to find future value or discounting to find present value. Financial managers rely primarily on present value techniques. Financial calculators, electronic spreadsheets, and financial tables can streamline the application of time value techniques. The cash flow of a firm can be described by its pattern—single amount, annuity, or mixed stream.

LG 2 **Understand the concepts of future value and present value, their calculation for single amounts, and the relationship between them.** Future value (FV) relies on compound interest to measure future amounts: The initial principal or deposit in one period, along with the interest earned on it, becomes the beginning principal of the following period.

The present value (PV) of a future amount is the amount of money today that is equivalent to the given future amount, considering the return that can be earned. Present value is the inverse of future value.

LG 3 **Find the future value and the present value of an ordinary annuity, and find the present value of a perpetuity.** An annuity is a pattern of equal periodic cash flows. For an ordinary annuity, the cash flows occur at the end of the period. For an annuity due, cash flows occur at the beginning of the period.

The future value of an ordinary annuity can be found by using the future value interest factor for an annuity. The present value of an ordinary annuity can be found by using the present value interest factor for an annuity. The present value of a perpetuity—an infinite-lived annuity—is found using 1 divided by the discount rate to represent the present value interest factor.

LG 4 **Calculate both the future value and the present value of a mixed stream of cash flows.** A mixed stream of cash flows is a stream of unequal periodic cash flows that reflect no particular pattern. The future value of a mixed stream of cash flows is the sum of the future values of each individual cash flow. Similarly, the present value of a mixed stream of cash flows is the sum of the present values of the individual cash flows.

LG 5 **Understand the effect that compounding interest more frequently than annually has on future value and on the effective annual rate of interest.** Interest can be compounded at intervals ranging from annually to daily, and even continuously. The more often interest is compounded, the larger the future amount that will be accumulated, and the higher the effective, or true, annual rate (EAR).

TABLE 9	**Summary of Key Definitions, Formulas, and Equations for Time Value of Money**

Definitions of variables

e = exponential function = 2.7183
EAR = effective annual rate
FV_n = future value or amount at the end of period n
FVA_n = future value of an n-year annuity
i = annual rate of interest
m = number of times per year interest is compounded
n = number of periods—typically years—over which money earns a return
PMT = amount deposited or received annually at the end of each year
PV = initial principal or present value
PVA_n = present value of an n-year annuity
t = period number index

Interest factor formulas

Future value of a single amount with annual compounding:

$$FVIF_{i,n} = (1 + i)^n$$ [Equation 5; factors in Table A–1]

Present value of a single amount:

$$PVIF_{i,n} = \frac{1}{(1 + i)^n}$$ [Equation 11; factors in Table A–2]

Future value of an ordinary annuity:

$$FVIFA_{i,n} = \sum_{t=1}^{n} (1 + i)^{t-1}$$ [Equation 13; factors in Table A–3]

Present value of an ordinary annuity:

$$PVIFA_{i,n} = \sum_{t=1}^{n} \frac{1}{(1 + i)^t}$$ [Equation 15; factors in Table A–4]

Present value of a perpetuity:

$$PVIFA_{i,\infty} = \frac{1}{i}$$ [Equation 17]

Future value with compounding more frequently than annually:

$$FVIF_{i,n} = \left(1 + \frac{i}{m}\right)^{m \times n}$$ [Equation 18]

For continuous compounding, $m = \infty$:

$$FVIF_{i,n} \text{ (continuous compounding)} = e^{i \times n}$$ [Equation 20]

To find the effective annual rate:

$$EAR = \left(1 + \frac{i}{m}\right)^m - 1$$ [Equation 22]

Basic equations

Future value (single amount):	$FV_n = PV \times (FVIF_{i,n})$	[Equation 6]
Present value (single amount):	$PV = FV_n \times (PVIF_{i,n})$	[Equation 12]
Future value (annuity):	$FVA_n = PMT \times (FVIFA_{i,n})$	[Equation 14]
Present value (annuity):	$PVA_n = PMT \times (PVIFA_{i,n})$	[Equation 16]

The annual percentage rate (APR)—a nominal annual rate—is quoted on credit cards and loans. The annual percentage yield (APY)—an effective annual rate—is quoted on savings products.

 Describe the procedures involved in (1) determining deposits needed to accumulate a future sum, (2) loan amortization, (3) finding interest or growth rates, and (4) finding an unknown number of periods. (1) The periodic deposit to accumulate a given future sum can be found by solving the equation for the future value of an annuity for the annual payment. (2) A loan can be amortized into equal periodic payments by solving the equation for the present value of an annuity for the periodic payment. (3) Interest or growth rates can be estimated by finding the unknown interest rate in the equation for the present value of a single amount or an annuity. (4) An unknown number of periods can be estimated by finding the unknown number of periods in the equation for the present value of a single amount or an annuity.

Self-Test Problems

 ST4–1 Future values for various compounding frequencies Delia Martin has $10,000 that she can deposit in any of three savings accounts for a 3-year period. Bank A compounds interest on an annual basis, bank B compounds interest twice each year, and bank C compounds interest each quarter. All three banks have a stated annual interest rate of 4%.

a. What amount would Ms. Martin have at the end of the third year, leaving all interest paid on deposit, in each bank?
b. What *effective annual rate* (*EAR*) would she earn in each of the banks?
c. On the basis of your findings in parts **a** and **b**, which bank should Ms. Martin deal with? Why?
d. If a fourth bank (bank D), also with a 4% stated interest rate, compounds interest continuously, how much would Ms. Martin have at the end of the third year? Does this alternative change your recommendation in part **c**? Explain why or why not.

ST4–2 Future values of annuities Ramesh Abdul wishes to choose the better of two equally costly cash flow streams: annuity X and annuity Y. Annuity X provides a cash inflow of $9,000 at the end of each of the next 6 years. Annuity Y provides a cash inflow of $10,000 at the end of each of the next 6 years. Assume that Ramesh can earn 11% on annuity X and 15% on annuity Y.

a. On a purely subjective basis, which annuity do you think is more attractive? Why?
b. Find the future value at the end of year 6, FVA_6, for both annuity X and annuity Y.
c. Use your finding in part **b** to indicate which annuity is more attractive. Compare your finding to your subjective response in part **a**.

 ST4–3 Present values of single amounts and streams You have a choice of accepting either of two 5-year cash flow streams or single amounts. One cash flow stream is an ordinary annuity, and the other is a mixed stream. You may accept alternative A or B—either as a cash flow stream or as a single amount. Given the cash flow stream and single amounts associated with each (see the following table), and assuming a

9% opportunity cost, which alternative (A or B) and in which form (cash flow stream or single amount) would you prefer?

	Cash flow stream	
End of year	Alternative A	Alternative B
1	$700	$1,100
2	700	900
3	700	700
4	700	500
5	700	300
	Single amount	
At time zero	$2,825	$2,800

ST4–4 **Deposits needed to accumulate a future sum** Judi Janson wishes to accumulate $8,000 by the end of 5 years by making equal, annual, end-of-year deposits over the next 5 years. If Judi can earn 7% on her investments, how much must she deposit at the *end of each year* to meet this goal?

Warm-Up Exercises A blue box (■) indicates exercises available in .

E4–1 Assume a firm makes a $2,500 deposit into its money market account. If this account is currently paying 0.7%, (yes, that's right, less than 1%!), what will the account balance be after 1 year?

E4–2 If Bob and Judy combine their savings of $1,260 and $975, respectively, and deposit this amount into an account that pays 2% annual interest, compounded monthly, what will the account balance be after 4 years?

E4–3 Gabrielle just won $2.5 million in the state lottery. She is given the option of receiving a total of $1.3 million now or she can elect to be paid $100,000 at the end of each of the next 25 years. If Gabrielle can earn 5% annually on her investments, from a strict economic point of view which option should she take?

E4–4 Your firm has the option of making an investment in new software that will cost $130,000 today and is estimated to provide the savings shown in the following table over its 5-year life:

Year	Savings estimate
1	$35,000
2	50,000
3	45,000
4	25,000
5	15,000

Should the firm make this investment if it requires a minimum annual return of 9% on all investments?

E4–5 Joseph is a friend of yours. He has plenty of money but little financial sense. He received a gift of $12,000 for his recent graduation and is looking for a bank in which to deposit the funds. Partners' Savings Bank offers an account with an annual interest rate of 3% compounded semiannually, while Selwyn's offers an account with a 2.75% annual interest rate compounded continuously. Calculate the value of the two accounts at the end of one year and recommend to Joseph which account he should choose.

 E4–6 Jack and Jill have just had their first child. If college is expected to cost $150,000 per year in 18 years, how much should the couple begin depositing annually at the end of each year to accumulate enough funds to pay the first year's tuition at the beginning of the 19th year? Assume that they can earn a 6% annual rate of return on their investment.

 Go to the text's companion website at **www.prenhall.com/gitman** to find a series of Personal Finance Warm-Up Exercises.

Problems

A blue box (■) indicates problems available in myfinancelab.

 P4–1 **Using a time line** The financial manager at Starbuck Industries is considering an investment that requires an initial outlay of $25,000 and is expected to result in cash inflows of $3,000 at the end of year 1, $6,000 at the end of years 2 and 3, $10,000 at the end of year 4, $8,000 at the end of year 5, and $7,000 at the end of year 6.

    a. Draw and label a time line depicting the cash flows associated with Starbuck Industries' proposed investment.

    b. Use arrows to demonstrate, on the time line in part **a,** how compounding to find future value can be used to measure all cash flows at the end of year 6.

    c. Use arrows to demonstrate, on the time line in part **b,** how discounting to find present value can be used to measure all cash flows at time zero.

    d. Which of the approaches—*future value* or *present value*—do financial managers rely on most often for decision making? Why?

 P4–2 **Future value calculation** *Without referring to the preprogrammed function on your financial calculator or to tables,* use the basic formula for future value along with the given interest rate, i, and the number of periods, n, to calculate the future value interest factor in each of the cases shown in the following table. Compare the calculated value to the value in Appendix: Financial Tables, Table A–1.

Case	Interest rate, i	Number of periods, n
A	12%	2
B	6	3
C	9	2
D	3	4

P4-3 **Future value tables** Use the future value interest factors in Appendix: Financial Tables, Table A–1 in each of the cases shown in the following table to estimate, to the nearest year, how long it would take an initial deposit, assuming no withdrawals,
a. To double.
b. To quadruple.

Case	Interest rate
A	7%
B	40
C	20
D	10

P4-4 **Future values** For each of the cases shown in the following table, calculate the future value of the single cash flow deposited today that will be available at the end of the deposit period if the interest is compounded annually at the rate specified over the given period.

Case	Single cash flow	Interest rate	Deposit period (years)
A	$ 200	5%	20
B	4,500	8	7
C	10,000	9	10
D	25,000	10	12
E	37,000	11	5
F	40,000	12	9

PERSONAL FINANCE PROBLEM

P4-5 **Time value** You have $1,500 to invest today at 7% interest compounded annually.
a. Find how much you will have accumulated in the account at the end of (1) 3 years, (2) 6 years, and (3) 9 years.
b. Use your findings in part **a** to calculate the amount of interest earned in (1) the first 3 years (years 1 to 3), (2) the second 3 years (years 4 to 6), and (3) the third 3 years (years 7 to 9).
c. Compare and contrast your findings in part **b**. Explain why the amount of interest earned increases in each succeeding 3-year period.

PERSONAL FINANCE PROBLEM

P4-6 **Time value** As part of your financial planning, you wish to purchase a new car exactly 5 years from today. The car you wish to purchase costs $14,000 today, and your research indicates that its price will increase by 2% to 4% per year over the next 5 years.
a. Estimate the price of the car at the end of 5 years if inflation is (1) 2% per year and (2) 4% per year.
b. How much more expensive will the car be if the rate of inflation is 4% rather than 2%?

PERSONAL FINANCE PROBLEM

P4–7 **Time value** You can deposit $10,000 into an account paying 9% annual interest either today or exactly 10 years from today. How much better off will you be at the end of 40 years if you decide to make the initial deposit today rather than 10 years from today?

PERSONAL FINANCE PROBLEM

P4–8 **Time value** Misty needs to have $15,000 at the end of 5 years to fulfill her goal of purchasing a small sailboat. She is willing to invest the funds as a single amount today but wonders what sort of investment return she will need to earn. Use your calculator or the time value tables to figure out the approximate annually compounded rate of return needed in each of these cases:
a. Misty can invest $10,200 today.
b. Misty can invest $8,150 today.
c. Misty can invest $7,150 today.

PERSONAL FINANCE PROBLEM

P4–9 **Single-payment loan repayment** A person borrows $200 to be repaid in 8 years with 14% annually compounded interest. The loan may be repaid at the end of any earlier year with no prepayment penalty.
a. What amount will be due if the loan is repaid at the end of year 1? 228
b. What is the repayment at the end of year 4? 337.79
c. What amount is due at the end of the eighth year? 570.51

P4–10 **Present value calculation** *Without referring to the preprogrammed function on your financial calculator or to tables,* use the basic formula for present value, along with the given opportunity cost, *i,* and the number of periods, *n,* to calculate the present value interest factor in each of the cases shown in the following table. Compare the calculated value to the table value.

Case	Opportunity cost, i	Number of periods, n
A	2%	4
B	10	2
C	5	3
D	13	2

P4–11 **Present values** For each of the cases shown in the following table, calculate the present value of the cash flow, discounting at the rate given and assuming that the cash flow is received at the end of the period noted.

Case	Single cash flow	Discount rate	End of period (years)
A	$ 7,000	12%	4
B	28,000	8	20
C	10,000	14	12
D	150,000	11	6
E	45,000	20	8

123

P4–12 **Present value concept**   Answer each of the following questions.
  a. What single investment made today, earning 12% annual interest, will be worth $6,000 at the end of 6 years?
  b. What is the present value of $6,000 to be received at the end of 6 years if the discount rate is 12%?
  c. What is the most you would pay today for a promise to repay you $6,000 at the end of 6 years if your opportunity cost is 12%?
  d. Compare, contrast, and discuss your findings in parts **a** through **c**.

 P4–13 **Time value**   Jim Nance has been offered a future payment of $500 three years from today. If his opportunity cost is 7% compounded annually, what value should he place on this opportunity today? What is the most he should pay to purchase this payment today?

 P4–14 **Time value**   An Iowa state savings bond can be converted to $100 at maturity 6 years from purchase. If the state bonds are to be competitive with U.S. savings bonds, which pay 8% annual interest (compounded annually), at what price must the state sell its bonds? Assume no cash payments on savings bonds prior to redemption.

 P4–15 **Time value and discount rates**   You just won a lottery that promises to pay you $1,000,000 exactly 10 years from today. Because the $1,000,000 payment is guaranteed by the state in which you live, opportunities exist to sell the claim today for an immediate single cash payment.
  a. What is the least you will sell your claim for if you can earn the following rates of return on similar-risk investments during the 10-year period?
    (1) 6%
    (2) 9%
    (3) 12%
  b. Rework part **a** under the assumption that the $1,000,000 payment will be received in 15 rather than 10 years.
  c. On the basis of your findings in parts **a** and **b,** discuss the effect of both the size of the rate of return and the time until receipt of payment on the present value of a future sum.

 P4–16 **Time value comparisons of single amounts**   In exchange for a $20,000 payment today, a well-known company will allow you to choose *one* of the alternatives shown in the following table. Your opportunity cost is 11%.

Alternative	Single amount
A	$28,500 at end of 3 years
B	$54,000 at end of 9 years
C	$160,000 at end of 20 years

  a. Find the value today of each alternative.
  b. Are all the alternatives acceptable—that is, worth $20,000 today?
  c. Which alternative, if any, will you take?

P4–17 **Cash flow investment decision**   Tom Alexander has an opportunity to purchase any of the investments shown in the following table. The purchase price, the amount of the single cash inflow, and its year of receipt are given for each investment. Which purchase recommendations would you make, assuming that Tom can earn 10% on his investments?

Investment	Price	Single cash inflow	Year of receipt
A	$18,000	$30,000	5
B	600	3,000	20
C	3,500	10,000	10
D	1,000	15,000	40

 P4–18 **Future value of an annuity**   For each case in the accompanying table, calculate the future value of the annuity at the end of the deposit period, assuming that the annuity cash flows occur at the end of each year.

Case	Amount of annuity	Interest rate	Deposit period (years)
A	$ 2,500	8%	10
B	500	12	6
C	30,000	20	5
D	11,500	9	8
E	6,000	14	30

P4–19 **Present value of an annuity**   For each case in the following table, calculate the present value of the annuity, assuming that the annuity cash flows occur at the end of each year.

Case	Amount of annuity	Interest rate	Period (years)
A	$ 12,000	7%	3
B	55,000	12	15
C	700	20	9
D	140,000	5	7
E	22,500	10	5

 P4–20 **Retirement planning**   Hal Thomas, a 25-year-old college graduate, wishes to retire at age 65. To supplement other sources of retirement income, he can deposit $2,000 each year into a tax-deferred individual retirement arrangement (IRA). The IRA will be invested to earn an annual return of 10%, which is assumed to be attainable over the next 40 years.

a. If Hal makes annual end-of-year $2,000 deposits into the IRA, how much will he have accumulated by the end of his sixty-fifth year?

b. If Hal decides to wait until age 35 to begin making annual end-of-year $2,000 deposits into the IRA, how much will he have accumulated by the end of his sixty-fifth year?

c. Using your findings in parts **a** and **b,** discuss the impact of delaying making deposits into the IRA for 10 years (age 25 to age 35) on the amount accumulated by the end of Hal's sixty-fifth year.

PERSONAL FINANCE PROBLEM

P4–21 **Value of a retirement annuity** An insurance agent is trying to sell you an immediate-retirement annuity, which for a single amount paid today will provide you with $12,000 at the end of each year for the next 25 years. You currently earn 9% on low-risk investments comparable to the retirement annuity. Ignoring taxes, what is the most you would pay for this annuity?

PERSONAL FINANCE PROBLEM

P4–22 **Funding your retirement** You plan to retire in exactly 20 years. Your goal is to create a fund that will allow you to receive $20,000 at the end of each year for the 30 years between retirement and death (a psychic told you would die exactly 30 years after you retire). You believe that you will be able to earn 11% per year during the 30-year retirement period.

a. How large a fund will you need *when you retire* in 20 years to provide the 30-year, $20,000 retirement annuity?

b. How much will you need *today* as a single amount to provide the fund calculated in part **a** if you earn only 9% per year during the 20 years preceding retirement?

c. What effect would an increase in the rate you can earn both during and prior to retirement have on the values found in parts **a** and **b?** Explain.

PERSONAL FINANCE PROBLEM

P4–23 **Value of an annuity versus a single amount** Assume that you just won the state lottery. Your prize can be taken either in the form of $40,000 at the end of each of the next 25 years (i.e., $1,000,000 over 25 years) or as a single amount of $500,000 paid immediately.

a. If you expect to be able to earn 5% annually on your investments over the next 25 years, ignoring taxes and other considerations, which alternative should you take? Why?

b. Would your decision in part **a** change if you could earn 7% rather than 5% on your investments over the next 25 years? Why?

c. On a strictly economic basis, at approximately what earnings rate would you be indifferent between the two plans?

P4–24 **Perpetuities** Consider the data in the following table.

Perpetuity	Annual amount	Discount rate
A	$ 20,000	8%
B	100,000	10
C	3,000	6
D	60,000	5

Determine, for each of the perpetuities:
a. The appropriate present value interest factor.
b. The present value.

P4–25 **Creating an endowment** Upon completion of her introductory finance course, Marla Lee was so pleased with the amount of useful and interesting knowledge she gained that she convinced her parents, who were wealthy alumni of the university she was attending, to create an endowment. The endowment is to allow three needy students to take the introductory finance course each year in perpetuity. The guaranteed annual cost of tuition and books for the course is $600 per student. The endowment will be created by making a single payment to the university. The university expects to earn exactly 6% per year on these funds.

a. How large an initial single payment must Marla's parents make to the university to fund the endowment?

b. What amount would be needed to fund the endowment if the university could earn 9% rather than 6% per year on the funds?

P4–26 **Value of a mixed stream** For each of the mixed streams of cash flows shown in the following table, determine the future value at the end of the final year if deposits are made at the *beginning of each year* into an account paying annual interest of 12%, assuming that no withdrawals are made during the period.

| | Cash flow stream | | |
Year	A	B	C
1	$ 900	$30,000	$1,200
2	1,000	25,000	1,200
3	1,200	20,000	1,000
4		10,000	1,900
5		5,000	

 P4–27 **Value of a single amount versus a mixed stream** Gina Vitale has just contracted to sell a small parcel of land that she inherited a few years ago. The buyer is willing to pay $24,000 at the closing of the transaction or will pay the amounts shown in the following table at the *beginning* of each of the next 5 years. Because Gina doesn't really need the money today, she plans to let it accumulate in an account that earns 7% annual interest. Given her desire to buy a house at the end of 5 years after closing on the sale of the lot, she decides to choose the payment alternative— $24,000 single amount or the mixed stream of payments in the following table— that provides the higher future value at the end of 5 years.

| Mixed stream | |
Beginning of year	Cash flow
1	$ 2,000
2	4,000
3	6,000
4	8,000
5	10,000

a. What is the future value of the single amount at the end of year 5?

b. What is the future value of the mixed stream at the end of year 5?

c. On the basis of your findings in parts **a** and **b**, which alternative should Gina take?

d. If Gina could earn 10% rather than 7% on the funds, would your recommendation in part **c** change? Explain.

 P4–28 **Value of mixed streams**   Find the present value of the streams of cash flows shown in the following table. Assume that the firm's opportunity cost is 12%.

A		B		C	
Year	Cash flow	Year	Cash flow	Year	Cash flow
1	−$2,000	1	$10,000	1–5	$10,000/yr
2	3,000	2–5	5,000/yr	6–10	8,000/yr
3	4,000	6	7,000		
4	6,000				
5	8,000				

 P4–29 **Present value—Mixed streams**   Consider the mixed streams of cash flows shown in the following table.

	Cash flow stream	
Year	A	B
1	$ 50,000	$ 10,000
2	40,000	20,000
3	30,000	30,000
4	20,000	40,000
5	10,000	50,000
Totals	$150,000	$150,000

a. Find the present value of each stream using a 15% discount rate.

b. Compare the calculated present values and discuss them in light of the fact that the undiscounted cash flows total $150,000 in each case.

  P4–30 **Value of a mixed stream**   Harte Systems, Inc., a maker of electronic surveillance equipment, is considering selling to a well-known hardware chain the rights to market its home security system. The proposed deal calls for the hardware chain to pay Harte $30,000 and $25,000 at the end of years 1 and 2 and to make annual year-end payments of $15,000 in years 3 through 9. A final payment to Harte of $10,000 would be due at the end of year 10.

a. Lay out the cash flows involved in the offer on a time line.

b. If Harte applies a required rate of return of 12% to them, what is the present value of this series of payments?

c. A second company has offered Harte an immediate one-time payment of $100,000 for the rights to market the home security system. Which offer should Harte accept?

PERSONAL FINANCE PROBLEM

P4–31 **Funding budget shortfalls**   As part of your personal budgeting process, you have determined that in each of the next 5 years you will have budget shortfalls. In other words, you will need the amounts shown in the following table at the end of the given year to balance your budget—that is, to make inflows equal outflows. You expect to be able to earn 8% on your investments during the next 5 years and wish to fund the budget shortfalls over the next 5 years with a single amount.

End of year	Budget shortfall
1	$ 5,000 4629.6?
2	4,000 3429.35
3	6,000 4762.99
4	10,000 7350.29
5	3,000 2041.74
	22,214

a. How large must the single deposit today into an account paying 8% annual interest be to provide for full coverage of the anticipated budget shortfalls?
b. What effect would an increase in your earnings rate have on the amount calculated in part **a**? Explain.

P4–32 **Relationship between future value and present value—Mixed stream**   Using *only* the information in the accompanying table, answer the questions that follow.

Year (*t*)	Cash flow	Future value interest factor at 5% ($FVIF_{5\%,n}$)
1	$ 800	1.050
2	900	1.102
3	1,000	1.158
4	1,500	1.216
5	2,000	1.276

a. Determine the *present value* of the mixed stream of cash flows using a 5% discount rate.
b. How much would you be willing to pay for an opportunity to buy this stream, assuming that you can at best earn 5% on your investments?
c. What effect, if any, would a 7% rather than a 5% opportunity cost have on your analysis? (Explain verbally.)

P4–33 **Changing compounding frequency**   Using annual, semiannual, and quarterly compounding periods, for each of the following, (1) calculate the future value if $5,000 is deposited initially, and (2) determine the *effective annual rate* (*EAR*).
a. At 12% annual interest for 5 years.
b. At 16% annual interest for 6 years.
c. At 20% annual interest for 10 years.

P4–34 **Compounding frequency, time value, and effective annual rates**   For each of the cases in the following table:
a. Calculate the future value at the end of the specified deposit period.
b. Determine the *effective annual rate, EAR.*
c. Compare the nominal annual rate, *i*, to the effective annual rate, EAR. What relationship exists between compounding frequency and the nominal and effective annual rates?

Case	Amount of initial deposit	Nominal annual rate, *i*	Compounding frequency, *m* (times/year)	Deposit period (years)
A	$ 2,500	6%	2	5
B	50,000	12	6	3
C	1,000	5	1	10
D	20,000	16	4	6

P4–35 **Continuous compounding**   For each of the cases in the following table, find the future value at the end of the deposit period, assuming that interest is compounded continuously at the given nominal annual rate.

Case	Amount of initial deposit	Nominal annual rate, *i*	Deposit period (years), *n*
A	$1,000	9%	2
B	600	10	10
C	4,000	8	7
D	2,500	12	4

PERSONAL FINANCE PROBLEM

P4–36 **Compounding frequency and time value**   You plan to invest $2,000 in an individual retirement arrangement (IRA) today at a *nominal annual rate* of 8%, which is expected to apply to all future years.
a. How much will you have in the account at the end of 10 years if interest is compounded (1) annually, (2) semiannually, (3) daily (assume a 365-day year), and (4) continuously?
b. What is the *effective annual rate, EAR,* for each compounding period in part **a**?
c. How much greater will your IRA balance be at the end of 10 years if interest is compounded continuously rather than annually?
d. How does the compounding frequency affect the future value and effective annual rate for a given deposit? Explain in terms of your findings in parts **a** through **c**.

PERSONAL FINANCE PROBLEM

P4–37 **Comparing compounding periods**   René Levin wishes to determine the future value at the end of 2 years of a $15,000 deposit made today into an account paying a nominal annual rate of 12%.

a. Find the future value of René's deposit, assuming that interest is compounded (1) annually, (2) quarterly, (3) monthly, and (4) continuously.

b. Compare your findings in part **a**, and use them to demonstrate the relationship between compounding frequency and future value.

c. What is the maximum future value obtainable given the $15,000 deposit, the 2-year time period, and the 12% nominal annual rate? Use your findings in part **a** to explain.

PERSONAL FINANCE PROBLEM

 P4–38 **Annuities and compounding** Janet Boyle intends to deposit $300 per year in a credit union for the next 10 years, and the credit union pays an annual interest rate of 8%.

a. Determine the future value that Janet will have at the end of 10 years, given that end-of-period deposits are made and no interest is withdrawn, if
(1) $300 is deposited annually and the credit union pays interest annually.
(2) $150 is deposited semiannually and the credit union pays interest semiannually.
(3) $75 is deposited quarterly and the credit union pays interest quarterly.

b. Use your finding in part **a** to discuss the effect of more frequent deposits and compounding of interest on the future value of an annuity.

 P4–39 **Deposits to accumulate future sums** For each of the cases shown in the following table, determine the amount of the equal, annual, end-of-year deposits necessary to accumulate the given sum at the end of the specified period, assuming the stated annual interest rate.

Case	Sum to be accumulated	Accumulation period (years)	Interest rate
A	$ 5,000	3	12%
B	100,000	20	7
C	30,000	8	10
D	15,000	12	8

PERSONAL FINANCE PROBLEM

 P4–40 **Creating a retirement fund** To supplement your planned retirement in exactly 42 years, you estimate that you need to accumulate $220,000 by the end of 42 years from today. You plan to make equal, annual, end-of-year deposits into an account paying 8% annual interest.

a. How large must the annual deposits be to create the $220,000 fund by the end of 42 years?

b. If you can afford to deposit only $600 per year into the account, how much will you have accumulated by the end of the forty-second year?

PERSONAL FINANCE PROBLEM

 P4–41 **Accumulating a growing future sum** A retirement home at Deer Trail Estates now costs $185,000. Inflation is expected to cause this price to increase at 6% per year over the 20 years before C. L. Donovan retires. How large an equal, annual, end-of-year deposit must be made each year into an account paying an annual interest rate of 10% for Donovan to have the cash needed to purchase a home at retirement?

P4–42 **Deposits to create a perpetuity**   You have decided to endow your favorite university with a scholarship. It is expected to cost $6,000 per year to attend the university into perpetuity. You expect to give the university the endowment in 10 years and will accumulate it by making equal annual (end-of-year) deposits into an account. The rate of interest is expected to be 10% for all future time periods.
  a. How large must the endowment be?
  b. How much must you deposit at the end of each of the next 10 years to accumulate the required amount?

PERSONAL FINANCE PROBLEM

  P4–43 **Inflation, time value, and annual deposits**   While vacationing in Florida, John Kelley saw the vacation home of his dreams. It was listed with a sale price of $200,000. The only catch is that John is 40 years old and plans to continue working until he is 65. Still, he believes that prices generally increase at the overall rate of inflation. John believes that he can earn 9% annually after taxes on his investments. He is willing to invest a fixed amount at the end of each of the next 25 years to fund the cash purchase of such a house (one that can be purchased today for $200,000) when he retires.
  a. Inflation is expected to average 5% per year for the next 25 years. What will John's dream house cost when he retires?
  b. How much must John invest at the *end* of each of the next 25 years to have the cash purchase price of the house when he retires?

 P4–44 **Loan payment**   Determine the equal, annual, end-of-year payment required each year over the life of the loans shown in the following table to repay them fully during the stated term of the loan.

Loan	Principal	Interest rate	Term of loan (years)
A	$12,000	8%	3
B	60,000	12	10
C	75,000	10	30
D	4,000	15	5

PERSONAL FINANCE PROBLEM

 P4–45 **Loan amortization schedule**   Joan Messineo borrowed $15,000 at a 14% annual rate of interest to be repaid over 3 years. The loan is amortized into three equal, annual, end-of-year payments.
  a. Calculate the annual, end-of-year loan payment.
  b. Prepare a loan amortization schedule showing the interest and principal breakdown of each of the three loan payments.
  c. Explain why the interest portion of each payment declines with the passage of time.

P4–46 **Loan interest deductions**   Liz Rogers just closed a $10,000 business loan that is to be repaid in three equal, annual, end-of-year payments. The interest rate on the loan is 13%. As part of her firm's detailed financial planning, Liz wishes to determine the annual interest deduction attributable to the loan. (Because it is a business loan, the interest portion of each loan payment is tax-deductible to the business.)

a. Determine the firm's annual loan payment.
b. Prepare an amortization schedule for the loan.
c. How much interest expense will Liz's firm have in *each* of the next 3 years as a result of this loan?

PERSONAL FINANCE PROBLEM

LG 6 P4–47 Monthly loan payments   Tim Smith is shopping for a used car. He has found one priced at $4,500. The dealer has told Tim that if he can come up with a down payment of $500, the dealer will finance the balance of the price at a 12% annual rate over 2 years (24 months).

a. Assuming that Tim accepts the dealer's offer, what will his *monthly* (end-of-month) payment amount be?
b. Use a financial calculator or Equation 15a (found in footnote 8) to help you figure out what Tim's *monthly* payment would be if the dealer were willing to finance the balance of the car price at a 9% annual rate.

LG 6 P4–48 Growth rates   You are given the series of cash flows shown in the following table.

	Cash flows		
Year	A	B	C
1	$500	$1,500	$2,500
2	560	1,550	2,600
3	640	1,610	2,650
4	720	1,680	2,650
5	800	1,760	2,800
6		1,850	2,850
7		1,950	2,900
8		2,060	
9		2,170	
10		2,280	

a. Calculate the compound annual growth rate associated with each cash flow stream.
b. If year-1 values represent initial deposits in a savings account paying annual interest, what is the annual rate of interest earned on each account?
c. Compare and discuss the growth rate and interest rate found in parts **a** and **b,** respectively.

PERSONAL FINANCE PROBLEM

LG 6 P4–49 Rate of return   Rishi Singh has $1,500 to invest. His investment counselor suggests an investment that pays no stated interest but will return $2,000 at the end of 3 years.

a. What annual rate of return will Rishi earn with this investment?
b. Rishi is considering another investment, of equal risk, that earns an annual return of 8%. Which investment should he make, and why?

PERSONAL FINANCE PROBLEM

P4–50 **Rate of return and investment choice** Clare Jaccard has $5,000 to invest. Because she is only 25 years old, she is not concerned about the length of the investment's life. What she is sensitive to is the rate of return she will earn on the investment. With the help of her financial advisor, Clare has isolated four equally risky investments, each providing a single amount at the end of its life, as shown in the following table. All of the investments require an initial $5,000 payment.

Investment	Single amount	Investment life (years)
A	$ 8,400	6
B	15,900	15
C	7,600	4
D	13,000	10

a. Calculate, to the nearest 1%, the rate of return on each of the four investments available to Clare.

b. Which investment would you recommend to Clare, given her goal of maximizing the rate of return?

P4–51 **Rate of return—Annuity** What is the rate of return on an investment of $10,606 if the company will receive $2,000 each year for the next 10 years?

PERSONAL FINANCE PROBLEM

P4–52 **Choosing the best annuity** Raina Herzig wishes to choose the best of four immediate-retirement annuities available to her. In each case, in exchange for paying a single premium today, she will receive equal, annual, end-of-year cash benefits for a specified number of years. She considers the annuities to be equally risky and is not concerned about their differing lives. Her decision will be based solely on the rate of return she will earn on each annuity. The key terms of the four annuities are shown in the following table.

Annuity	Premium paid today	Annual benefit	Life (years)
A	$30,000	$3,100	20
B	25,000	3,900	10
C	40,000	4,200	15
D	35,000	4,000	12

a. Calculate to the nearest 1% the rate of return on each of the four annuities Raina is considering.

b. Given Raina's stated decision criterion, which annuity would you recommend?

PERSONAL FINANCE PROBLEM

P4–53 **Interest rate for an annuity** Anna Waldheim was seriously injured in an industrial accident. She sued the responsible parties and was awarded a judgment of $2,000,000. Today, she and her attorney are attending a settlement conference with the defendants. The defendants have made an initial offer of $156,000 per year for

25 years. Anna plans to counteroffer at $255,000 per year for 25 years. Both the offer and the counteroffer have a present value of $2,000,000, the amount of the judgment. Both assume payments at the end of each year.

a. What interest rate assumption have the defendants used in their offer (rounded to the nearest whole percent)?

b. What interest rate assumption have Anna and her lawyer used in their counteroffer (rounded to the nearest whole percent)?

c. Anna is willing to settle for an annuity that carries an interest rate assumption of 9%. What annual payment would be acceptable to her?

PERSONAL FINANCE PROBLEM

P4–54 **Loan rates of interest**   John Flemming has been shopping for a loan to finance the purchase of a used car. He has found three possibilities that seem attractive and wishes to select the one with the lowest interest rate. The information available with respect to each of the three $5,000 loans is shown in the following table.

Loan	Principal	Annual payment	Term (years)
A	$5,000	$1,352.81	5
B	5,000	1,543.21	4
C	5,000	2,010.45	3

a. Determine the interest rate associated with each of the loans.
b. Which loan should John take?

P4–55 **Number of years to equal future amount**   For each of the following cases, determine the number of years it will take for the initial deposit to grow to equal the future amount at the given interest rate.

Case	Initial deposit	Future amount	Interest rate
A	$ 300	$ 1,000	7%
B	12,000	15,000	5
C	9,000	20,000	10
D	100	500	9
E	7,500	30,000	15

PERSONAL FINANCE PROBLEM

P4–56 **Time to accumulate a given sum**   Manuel Rios wishes to determine how long it will take an initial deposit of $10,000 to double.

a. If Manuel earns 10% annual interest on the deposit, how long will it take for him to double his money?

b. How long will it take if he earns only 7% annual interest?

c. How long will it take if he can earn 12% annual interest?

d. Reviewing your findings in parts a, b, and c, indicate what relationship exists between the interest rate and the amount of time it will take Manuel to double his money.

P4-57 **Number of years to provide a given return** In each of the following cases, determine the number of years that the given annual *end-of-year* cash flow must continue to provide the given rate of return on the given initial amount.

Case	Initial amount	Annual cash flow	Rate of return
A	$ 1,000	$ 250	11%
B	150,000	30,000	15
C	80,000	10,000	10
D	600	275	9
E	17,000	3,500	6

PERSONAL FINANCE PROBLEM

P4-58 **Time to repay installment loan** Mia Salto wishes to determine how long it will take to repay a loan with initial proceeds of $14,000 where annual *end-of-year* installment payments of $2,450 are required.

a. If Mia can borrow at a 12% annual rate of interest, how long will it take for her to repay the loan fully?

b. How long will it take if she can borrow at a 9% annual rate?

c. How long will it take if she has to pay 15% annual interest?

d. Reviewing your answers in parts **a, b,** and **c,** describe the general relationship between the interest rate and the amount of time it will take Mia to repay the loan fully.

P4-59 **ETHICS PROBLEM** A manager at a "check into cash" business defends his business practice of charging high percentage fees for cashing checks as simply "charging what the market will bear." "After all," says the manager, "we don't force people to come in the door." How would you respond to this ethical defense of the payday-advance business?

Chapter Case

Funding Jill Moran's Retirement Annuity

Sunrise Industries wishes to accumulate funds to provide a retirement annuity for its vice president of research, Jill Moran. Ms. Moran, by contract, will retire at the end of exactly 12 years. Upon retirement, she is entitled to receive an annual end-of-year payment of $42,000 for exactly 20 years. If she dies prior to the end of the 20-year period, the annual payments will pass to her heirs. During the 12-year "accumulation period," Sunrise wishes to fund the annuity by making equal, annual, end-of-year deposits into an account earning 9% interest. Once the 20-year "distribution period" begins, Sunrise plans to move the accumulated monies into an account earning a guaranteed 12% per year. At the end of the distribution period, the account balance will equal zero. Note that the first deposit will be made at the end of year 1 and that the first distribution payment will be received at the end of year 13.

To Do

a. Draw a time line depicting all of the cash flows associated with Sunrise's view of the retirement annuity.

b. How large a sum must Sunrise accumulate by the end of year 12 to provide the 20-year, $42,000 annuity?

c. How large must Sunrise's equal, annual, end-of-year deposits into the account be over the 12-year accumulation period to fund fully Ms. Moran's retirement annuity?

d. How much would Sunrise have to deposit annually during the accumulation period if it could earn 10% rather than 9% during the accumulation period?

e. How much would Sunrise have to deposit annually during the accumulation period if Ms. Moran's retirement annuity were a perpetuity and all other terms were the same as initially described?

Spreadsheet Exercise

At the end of 2009, Uma Corporation was considering undertaking a major long-term project in an effort to remain competitive in its industry. The production and sales departments determined the potential annual cash flow savings that could accrue to the firm if it acts soon. Specifically, they estimate that a mixed stream of future cash flow savings will occur at the end of the years 2010 through 2015. The years 2016 through 2020 will see consecutive and equal cash flow savings at the end of each year. The firm estimates that its discount rate over the first 6 years will be 7%. The expected discount rate over the years 2016 through 2020 will be 11%.

The project managers will find the project acceptable if it results in present cash flow savings of at least $860,000. The following cash flow savings data are supplied to the finance department for analysis:

End of Year	Cash Flow Savings
2010	$110,000
2011	120,000
2012	130,000
2013	150,000
2014	160,000
2015	150,000
2016	90,000
2017	90,000
2018	90,000
2019	90,000
2020	90,000

To Do

Create spreadsheets similar to Tables 2 and 4 (which can be viewed at www .prenhall.com/gitman as Tables 4.2 and 4.4), and then answer the following questions:

a. Determine the value (at the beginning of 2010) of the future cash flow savings expected to be generated by this project.
b. Based solely on the one criterion set by management, should the firm undertake this specific project? Explain.
c. What is the "interest rate risk," and how might it influence the recommendation made in part **b**? Explain.

Web Exercise

Go to the text's companion website at **www.prenhall.com/gitman** to find the Web Exercise for this chapter.

> Remember to check the text's website at **www.prenhall.com/gitman** to find additional resources, including Web Exercises and a Web Case.

Solutions to Self-Test Problems

ST4–1 a. *Bank A:*

$FV_3 = \$10,000 \times FVIF_{4\%/3yrs} = \$10,000 \times 1.125 = \underline{\underline{\$11,250}}$

(Calculator solution = $11,248.64)

Bank B:

$FV_3 = \$10,000 \times FVIF_{4\%/2,2 \times 3yrs} = \$10,000 \times FVIF_{2\%,6yrs}$
$= \$10,000 \times 1.126 = \underline{\underline{\$11,260}}$

(Calculator solution = $11,261.62)

Bank C:

$FV_3 = \$10,000 \times FVIF_{4\%/4,4 \times 3yrs} = \$10,000 \times FVIF_{1\%,12yrs}$
$= \$10,000 \times 1.127 = \underline{\underline{\$11,270}}$

(Calculator solution = $11,268.25)

b. *Bank A:*

$EAR = (1 + 4\%/1)^1 - 1 = (1 + 0.04)^1 - 1 = 1.04 - 1 = 0.04 = \underline{\underline{4\%}}$

Bank B:

$EAR = (1 + 4\%/2)^2 - 1 = (1 + 0.02)^2 - 1 = 1.0404 - 1 = 0.0404 = \underline{\underline{4.04\%}}$

Bank C:

$EAR = (1 + 4\%/4)^4 - 1 = (1 + 0.01)^4 - 1 = 1.0406 - 1 = 0.0406 = \underline{\underline{4.06\%}}$

c. Ms. Martin should deal with Bank C: The quarterly compounding of interest at the given 4% rate results in the highest future value as a result of the corresponding highest effective annual rate.

d. *Bank D:*

$FV_3 = \$10,000 \times FVIF_{4\%,3yrs}$ (continuous compounding)

$\quad = \$10,000 \times e^{0.04 \times 3} = \$10,000 \times e^{0.12}$

$\quad = \$10,000 \times 1.127497$

$\quad = \underline{\$11,274.97}$

This alternative is better than Bank C; it results in a higher future value because of the use of continuous compounding, which with otherwise identical cash flows always results in the highest future value of any compounding period.

ST4–2   a. On a purely subjective basis, annuity Y looks more attractive than annuity X because it provides $1,000 more each year than does annuity X. Of course, the fact that Ramesh can earn 15% on annuity X and only 11% on annuity Y will impact this decision.

b. *Annuity X:*

$FVA_6 = \$9,000 \times FVIFA_{15\%,6yrs}$

$\quad = \$9,000 \times 8.754 = \underline{\$78,786.00}$

(Calculator solution = $78,783.65)

Annuity Y:

$FVA_6 = \$10,000 \times FVIFA_{11\%,6yrs}$

$\quad = \$10,000 \times 7.913 = \underline{\$79,130.00}$

(Calculator solution = $79,128.60)

c. Annuity Y is more attractive, because its future value at the end of year 6, FVA_6, of $79,130.00 is greater than annuity X's end-of-year-6 future value, FVA_6, of $78,786.00. The subjective assessment in part **a** was correct.

The benefit of receiving annuity Y's $1,000-larger cash inflows every year appears to have outweighed the fact that Ramesh will earn 15% annually on annuity X and only 11% annually on annuity Y.

ST4–3   *Alternative A:*

Cash flow stream:

$PVA_5 = \$700 \times PVIFA_{9\%,5yrs}$

$\quad = \$700 \times 3.890 = \underline{\$2,723}$

(Calculator solution = $2,722.76)

Single amount: $\underline{\$2,825}$

Alternative B:

Cash flow stream:

Year (n)	Cash flow (1)	$PVIF_{9\%,n}$ (2)	Present value $[(1) \times (2)]$ (3)
1	$1,100	0.917	$1,008.70
2	900	0.842	757.80
3	700	0.772	540.40
4	500	0.708	354.00
5	300	0.650	195.00
		Present value	$2,855.90

(Calculator solution = $2,856.41)

Single amount: $2,800

Conclusion: Alternative B in the form of a cash flow stream is preferred because its present value of $2,855.90 is greater than the other three values.

ST4–4 $FVA_5 = \$8,000$; $FVIFA_{7\%,5yrs} = 5.751$; $PMT = ?$

$FVA_n = PMT \times (FVIFA_{i,n})$ [Equation 4.14 or 4.24]

$\$8,000 = PMT \times 5.751$

$PMT = \$8,000/5.751 = \underline{\$1,391.06}$

(Calculator solution = $1,391.13)

Judi should deposit $1,391.06 at the end of each of the 5 years to meet her goal of accumulating $8,000 at the end of the fifth year.

Answers to Selected End-of-Chapter Problems

4–3   C: 3 years $< n <$ 4 years
4–4   A: $530.60
        D: $78.450
4–6   a. (1) $15,456
4–8   a. 8% $< i <$ 9%
4–11   B: $6,020
        D $80,250
4–22   b. $30,950.64
4–24   b. B: $1,000,000
        D: $1,200,000
4–26   a. A: $3,862.50
4–28   b. B: $26,039
4–31   a. $22,215
4–33   b. B: 12.6%
        D: 17.0%
4–33   a.
        (1) Annual: $8,810
            Semiannual: $8,955
            Quarterly: $9,030
4–39   B: $2,439.32

4–42   a. $60,000
        b. $3,764.82
4–44   A: $4,656.58
        B: $10,619.47
        C: $7,955.87
4–48   a. A: 12% $< i <$ 13%
            Calculator solution 12.47%
            C: 2% $< i <$ 3%
            Calculator solution 2.50%
4–50   a. B: 8% $< i <$ 9%
            Calculator solution 8.02%
            D: 10% $< i <$ 11%
            Calculator solution 10.03%
4–55   A: 17 $< n <$ 18
            Calculator solution 17.79
        D: 18 $< n <$ 19
            Calculator solution 18.68

Chapter 5

Interest Rates

From Chapter 5 of *Fundamentals of Corporate Finance*, 1/e. Jonathan Berk, Peter DeMarzo, Jarrad Harford.

Interest Rates

▶ Understand the different ways interest rates are quoted

▶ Use quoted rates to calculate loan payments and balances

▶ Know how inflation, expectations, and risk combine to determine interest rates

▶ See the link between interest rates in the market and a firm's opportunity cost of capital

notation

APR	annual percentage rate	*n*	number of periods
APY	annual percentage yield	*NPV*	net present value
C	cash flow	*PV*	present value
C_n	cash flow that arrives in period *n*	*r*	interest rate or discount rate
EAR	effective annual rate	r_n	interest rate or discount rate for an *n*-year term
FV	future value		

Jason Moore, Bradford & Marzec, LLC

California State University, Long Beach, 2004

Jason Moore graduated in 2004 from the California State University, Long Beach, with a major in Business Finance. As a fixed-income analyst at Bradford & Marzec, LLC, a Los Angeles-based institutional fixed-income manager with over $4 billion in assets, he pays close attention to interest rate movements. "I perform corporate credit research for basic industries such as metals, mining, chemicals, and forest products, following industry and company news and trends," Jason explains. Then he formulates an opinion and communicates purchase and sell recommendations to the portfolio managers.

One of the trends he watches is inflation, which affects the purchasing power of a given amount of money. When prices increase due to inflation, the value of a given amount of currency declines. Inflation therefore influences the interest rate a lender charges a borrower. "The interest rate charged is often fixed for a long period of time," says Jason. "Any unexpected change in inflation over that time period affects the purchasing power of those fixed future payments, so all interest rates include an inflation expectation. If inflation increases, the purchasing power of those fixed future payments decreases, and vice versa." This means that investors' inflation expectations influence the return they expect to receive when lending money. If they think inflation will rise, they will want a higher interest rate.

In addition, investors' interest rate expectations should be reflected in the length of time an investor is willing to lend funds. "If investors believe that interest rates will rise, they should choose a short-term investment, rather than tie up their money at the current lower interest rate," he says. "If investors believe interest rates will fall, they should choose a longer-term investment, locking in the current higher interest rate."

When economic activity slows and the financial climate is uncertain, as it was in 2008, investors seek lower-risk investment opportunities. "Lenders evaluate borrowers more closely," says Jason. "As a consumer currently seeking a loan for education expenses, a car, or a house, your perceived risk of default—not being able to repay the loan—is more important now than it was just a few years ago."

"As a consumer currently seeking a loan for education expenses, a car, or a house, your perceived risk of default—not being able to repay the loan—is more important now than it was just a few years ago."

Recall that an interest rate allows us to convert money at one point in time to another. But how do we determine that interest rate? In this chapter, we consider the factors that affect interest rates and discuss how to determine the appropriate discount rate for a set of cash flows. We begin by looking at the way interest is paid and interest rates are quoted, and we show how to calculate the effective interest paid in one year given different quoting conventions. We then consider some of the main determinants of interest rates—namely, inflation and economic growth. Because interest rates tend to change over time, investors will demand different interest rates for different investment horizons, based on their expectations and the risk involved in longer time horizons.

Interest Rate Quotes and Adjustments

If you spend some time looking through a newspaper, you will find literally dozens of interest rates discussed and advertised, from savings deposit rates to auto loan rates to interest rates being paid on the government's debt. Interest rates are clearly central to the functioning of any financial system. To understand interest rates, it's important to think of interest rates as a price—the price of using money. When you borrow money to buy a car, you are using the bank's money now to get the car and paying the money back over time. The interest rate on your loan is the price you pay to be able to convert your future loan payments into a car today. Similarly, when you deposit money into a savings account, you are letting the bank use your money until you withdraw it later. The interest the bank pays you on your deposit is the price it pays to have the use of your money (for things like making car loans).

Just like any other price, interest rates are set by market forces, in particular the supply of and demand for funds. When the supply (savings) is high and the demand (borrowing) is low, interest rates are low, other things being equal. Additionally, as we discuss later in the chapter, interest rates are also influenced by expected inflation and risk.

In order to be able to study and use interest rates, we have to understand how they are quoted. In practice, interest is paid, and interest rates are quoted, in different ways. For example, in mid-2006 ING Direct, an Internet bank, offered savings accounts with an interest rate of 5.25% paid at the end of one year, while New Century Bank offered an interest rate of 5.12%, but with the interest paid on a daily basis. Interest rates can also differ depending on the investment horizon. In January 2004, investors earned only about 1% on one-year risk-free investments, but could earn more than 5% on 15-year risk-free investments. Interest rates can also vary due to risk. For example, the U.S. government is able to borrow at a much lower interest rate than General Motors.

Because interest rates may be quoted for different time intervals, such as monthly, semiannual, or annual, it is often necessary to adjust the interest rate to a time period that matches that of our cash flows. We explore these mechanics of interest rates in this section.

The Effective Annual Rate

effective annual rate (EAR) or annual percentage yield (APY)
The total amount of interest that will be earned at the end of one year.

Interest rates are often reported as an **effective annual rate (EAR)** or **annual percentage yield (APY)**, which indicates the total amount of interest that will be earned at the end of one year.[1] With an EAR of 5%, a $100 investment grows to

$$\$100 \times (1 + r) = \$100 \times (1.05) = \$105$$

in one year. After two years it will grow to:

$$\$100 \times (1 + r)^2 = \$100 \times (1.05)^2 = \$110.25$$

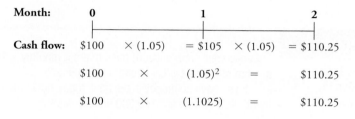

Adjusting the Discount Rate to Different Time Periods

The preceding example shows that earning an effective annual rate of 5% for two years is equivalent to earning 10.25% in total interest over the entire period:

$$\$100 \times (1.05)^2 = \$100 \times 1.1025 = \$110.25$$

In general, by raising the interest rate factor $(1 + r)$ to the appropriate power, we can compute an equivalent interest rate for a longer time period.

We can use the same method to find the equivalent interest rate for periods shorter than one year. In this case, we raise the interest rate factor $(1 + r)$ to the appropriate fractional power. For example, earning 5% interest in one year is equivalent to receiving

$$(1 + r)^{0.5} = (1.05)^{0.5} = \$1.0247$$

for each $1 invested every six months (0.5 years). That is, a 5% effective annual rate is equivalent to an interest rate of approximately 2.47% earned every six months. We can verify this result by computing the interest we would earn in one year by investing for two six-month periods at this rate:

$$(1 + r)^2 = (1.0247)^2 = \$1.05$$

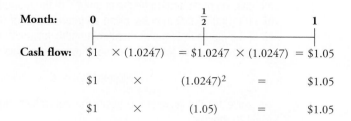

---

[1]The effective annual rate is also referred to as the *effective annual yield* (EAY).

In general, we can convert a discount rate of r for one period to an equivalent discount rate for n periods using the following formula:

$$\text{Equivalent } n\text{-period Discount Rate} = (1 + r)^n - 1 \qquad (1)$$

In this formula, n can be larger than 1 (to compute a rate over more than one period) or smaller than 1 (to compute a rate over a fraction of a period).

When computing present or future values, you should adjust the discount rate to match the time period of the cash flows.

This adjustment is necessary to apply the perpetuity or annuity formulas to non-annual cash flows, as in the following example.

EXAMPLE 1

Personal Finance
Valuing Monthly
Cash Flows

Problem

Suppose your bank account pays interest monthly with an effective annual rate of 6%. What amount of interest will you earn each month?

If you have no money in the bank today, how much will you need to save at the end of each month to accumulate $100,000 in 10 years?

Solution

▶ Plan

We can use Eq. (1) to convert the EAR to a monthly rate, answering the first part of the question. The second part of the question is a future value of an annuity question. It is asking how big a monthly annuity we would have to deposit in order to end up with $100,000 in 10 years. However, in order to do this problem, we need to write the timeline in terms of *monthly* periods because our cash flows (deposits) will be monthly:

Month:	0	1	2	⋯	120
Cash flow:		C	C		C

That is, we can view the savings plan as a monthly annuity with $10 \times 12 = 120$ monthly payments. We have the future value of the annuity ($100,000), the length of time (120 months), and we will have the monthly interest rate from the first part of the question. We can then use the future value of an annuity formula to solve for the monthly deposit.

▶ Execute

From Eq. (1), a 6% EAR is equivalent to earning $(1.06)^{1/12} - 1 = 0.4868\%$ per month. The exponent in this equation is 1/12 because the period is 1/12th of a year (a month).

To determine the amount to save each month to reach the goal of $100,000 in 120 months, we must determine the amount C of the monthly payment that will have a future value of $100,000 in 120 months, given an interest rate of 0.4868% per month. Now that we have all of the inputs in terms of months (monthly payment, monthly interest rate, and total number of months), we use the future value of annuity formula to solve this problem:

$$FV(\text{annuity}) = C \times \frac{1}{r}[(1 + r)^n - 1]$$

We solve for the payment C using the equivalent monthly interest rate $r = 0.4868\%$, and $n = 120$ months:

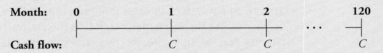

$$C = \frac{FV(\text{annuity})}{\frac{1}{r}[(1 + r)^n - 1]} = \frac{\$100,000}{\frac{1}{0.004868}[(1.004868)^{120} - 1]} = \$615.47 \text{ per month}$$

We can also compute this result using a financial calculator:

	N	I/Y	PV	PMT	FV
Given:	120	0.4868	0		100,000
Solve for:				−615.47	

Excel Formula: = PMT(RATE,NPER,PV,FV)=PMT(0.004868,120,0,100000)

▶ **Evaluate**

Thus, if we save $615.47 per month and we earn interest monthly at an effective annual rate of 6%, we will have $100,000 in 10 years. Notice that the timing in the annuity formula must be consistent for all of the inputs. In this case, we had a monthly deposit, so we needed to convert our interest rate to a monthly interest rate and then use total number of months (120) instead of years.

Annual Percentage Rates

annual percentage rate (APR) Indicates the amount of interest earned in one year without the effect of compounding.

simple interest Interest earned without the effect of compounding.

The most common way to quote interest rates is in terms of an **annual percentage rate (APR)**, which indicates the amount of **simple interest** earned in one year, that is, the amount of interest earned *without* the effect of compounding. Because it does not include the effect of compounding, the APR quote is typically less than the actual amount of interest that you will earn. To compute the actual amount that you will earn in one year, you must first convert the APR to an effective annual rate.

For example, suppose Granite Bank advertises savings accounts with an interest rate of "6% APR with monthly compounding." When it quotes a rate this way, Granite Bank really means that you will earn 6%/12 = 0.5% every month. That is, an APR with monthly compounding is actually a way of quoting a *monthly* interest rate, rather than an annual interest rate. In this case, the actual rate being quoted is 0.5% *per month,* and by convention, the bank states it as an APR by multiplying by 12 months. Because the interest compounds each month, you will actually have

$$\$1 \times (1.005)^{12} = \$1.061678$$

Common Mistake — Using the EAR in the Annuity Formula

At this point, many students make the mistake of trying to use the EAR in the annuity formula. The interest rate in the annuity formula must match the frequency of the cash flows. That's why in Example 1 we first converted the EAR into a monthly rate and then used the annuity formula to compute the monthly loan payments. The common mistake in this case would be to use the EAR in the annuity formula to obtain annual cash flows, and then divide those cash flows by 12 to obtain the monthly payments.

This process will produce the wrong answer. To see why, consider the timing of the first deposit in Example 1. With a monthly rate and monthly payments, the annuity formula assumes that the first payment will be made one month from now. It then assumes that you will be making 11 more monthly deposits before the end of the first year. Each of those deposits will start earning interest as soon you make it. In contrast, if you use an EAR and calculate an annual cash flow, the formula assumes that you will make your first deposit one *year* from now, so that you will forgo a whole year of interest before you start earning anything. Thus, you can see that the EAR approach misses the fact that you are making deposits earlier and more often than annually, so you are adding to your interest-earning principal more frequently than once per year.

at the end of one year, for an effective annual rate of 6.1678%. The 6.1678% that you earn on your deposit is higher than the quoted 6% APR due to compounding: In later months, you earn interest on the interest paid in earlier months. To summarize, an actual rate of 0.5% *per month* can be stated in either of the following ways:

- 6% APR, compounded monthly
- EAR of 6.1678%, which is the actual rate earned *per year*

It is important to remember that because the APR does not reflect the true amount you will earn over one year, *the APR itself cannot be used as a discount rate*. Instead, the APR is a way of quoting the actual interest earned each compounding period:

$$\text{Interest Rate per Compounding Period} = \frac{\text{APR}}{m} \tag{2}$$

(m = number of compounding periods per year)

Once we have computed the interest earned per compounding period from Eq. (2), we can compute the equivalent interest rate for any other time interval using Eq. (1). Thus, the effective annual rate corresponding to an APR is given by the following conversion formula:

Converting an APR to an EAR

$$1 + EAR = \left(1 + \frac{APR}{m}\right)^m \tag{3}$$

(m = number of compounding periods per year)

Table 1 shows the effective annual rates that correspond to an APR of 6% with different compounding intervals. The EAR increases with the frequency of compounding because of the ability to earn interest on interest sooner. Investments can compound even more frequently than daily. In principle, the compounding interval could be hourly or every second. As a practical matter, compounding more frequently than daily has a negligible impact on the effective annual rate and is rarely observed.

When working with APRs, we must first convert the APR to a discount rate per compounding interval using Eq. (2), or to an EAR using Eq. (3), before evaluating the present or future value of a set of cash flows.

TABLE 1
Effective Annual Rates for a 6% APR with Different Compounding Periods

Compounding Interval	Effective Annual Rate
Annual	$\left(1 + \frac{0.06}{1}\right)^1 - 1 = 6\%$
Semiannual	$\left(1 + \frac{0.06}{2}\right)^2 - 1 = 6.09\%$
Monthly	$\left(1 + \frac{0.06}{12}\right)^{12} - 1 = 6.1678\%$
Daily	$\left(1 + \frac{0.06}{365}\right)^{365} - 1 = 6.1831\%$

EXAMPLE 2

Converting the APR to a Discount Rate

Problem

Your firm is purchasing a new telephone system that will last for four years. You can purchase the system for an upfront cost of $150,000, or you can lease the system from the manufacturer for $4000 paid at the end of each month. The lease price is offered for a 48-month lease with no early termination—you cannot end the lease early. Your firm can borrow at an interest rate of 6% APR with monthly compounding. Should you purchase the system outright or pay $4000 per month?

Solution

▶ **Plan**

The cost of leasing the system is a 48-month annuity of $4000 per month:

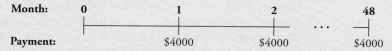

We can compute the present value of the lease cash flows using the annuity formula, but first we need to compute the discount rate that corresponds to a period length of one month. To do so, we convert the borrowing cost of 6% APR with monthly compounding to a monthly discount rate using Eq. (2). Once we have a monthly rate, we can use the present value of annuity formula to compute the present value of the monthly payments and compare it to the cost of buying the system.

▶ **Execute**

As Eq. (2) shows, the 6% APR with monthly compounding really means 6%/12 = 0.5% every month. The 12 comes from the fact that there are 12 monthly compounding periods per year. Now that we have the true rate corresponding to the stated APR, we can use that discount rate in the annuity formula to compute the present value of the monthly payments:

$$PV = 4000 \times \frac{1}{0.005}\left(1 - \frac{1}{1.005^{48}}\right) = \$170,321.27$$

Using a financial calculator or Excel:

	N	I/Y	PV	PMT	FV
Given:	48	0.5		−4000	0
Solve for:			170,321.27		

Excel Formula: =PV(RATE,NPER,PMT,FV)=PV(0.005,48,−4000,0)

▶ **Evaluate**

Thus, paying $4000 per month for 48 months is equivalent to paying a present value of $170,321.27 today. This cost is $170,321.27 − $150,000 = $20,321.27 higher than the cost of purchasing the system, so it is better to pay $150,000 for the system rather than lease it. One way to interpret this result is as follows: At a 6% APR with monthly compounding, by promising to repay $4000 per month your firm can borrow $170,321 today. With this loan it could purchase the phone system and have an additional $20,321 to use for other purposes.

Concept Check

1. What is the difference between an EAR and an APR quote?

2. Why can't the APR be used as a discount rate?

② Application: Discount Rates and Loans

Now that we have explained how to compute the discount rate from an interest rate quote, let's apply the concept to solve two common financial problems: calculating a loan payment and calculating the remaining balance on a loan.

amortizing loan A loan on which the borrower makes monthly payments that include interest on the loan plus some part of the loan balance.

Computing Loan Payments

Many loans, such as mortgages and car loans, have monthly payments and are quoted in terms of an APR with monthly compounding. These types of loans are **amortizing loans**, which means that each month you pay interest on the loan plus some part of the loan balance. Each monthly payment is the same, and the loan is fully repaid with the final payment. Typical terms for a new car loan might be "6.75% APR for 60 months." When the compounding interval for the APR is not stated explicitly, it is equal to the interval between the payments, or one month in this case. Thus, this quote means that the loan will be repaid with 60 equal monthly payments, computed using a 6.75% APR with monthly compounding. It sometimes helps to look at the loan from the bank's point of view: the bank will give you $30,000 in cash today to use to buy the car. In return, you will give the bank 60 equal payments each month for 60 months, starting one month from now. In order for the bank to be willing to accept this exchange, it must be true that the present value of what you will give the bank, discounted at the loan's interest rate, is equal to the amount of cash the bank is giving you now. Consider the timeline for a $30,000 car loan with these terms:

Month:	0	1	2		60
Cash flow:	$30,000	$-C$	$-C$	$\cdots$	$-C$

The payment, C, is set so that the present value of the cash flows, evaluated using the loan interest rate, equals the original principal amount of $30,000. In this case, the 6.75% APR with monthly compounding corresponds to a one-month discount rate of $6.75\%/12 = 0.5625\%$. It is important that the discount rate match the frequency of the cash flows—here we have a monthly discount rate and a monthly loan payment, so we can proceed. Because the loan payments are an annuity, we can use the following to find C:

$$C = \frac{P}{\frac{1}{r}\left(1 - \frac{1}{(1+r)^N}\right)} = \frac{30{,}000}{\frac{1}{0.005625}\left(1 - \frac{1}{(1+0.005625)^{60}}\right)} = \$590.50$$

Alternatively, we can solve for the payment C using a financial calculator or a spreadsheet:

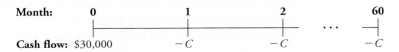

	N	I/Y	PV	PMT	FV
Given:	60	0.5625	30,000		0
Solve for:				−590.50	
Excel Formula: =PMT(RATE,NPER,PV,FV)=PMT(0.005625,60,30000,0)					

Your loan payment each month includes interest and repayment of part of the principal, reducing the amount you still owe. Because the loan balance (amount you still owe) is decreasing each month, the interest that accrues on that balance is decreasing. As a result, even though your payment stays the same over the entire 60-month life of the loan, the part of that payment needed to cover interest each month is constantly decreas-

FIGURE 1

Amortizing Loan

Panel (a) shows how the interest (red) and principal portions (turquoise) of the monthly payment on the $30,000 car loan change over the life of the loan. Panel (b) illustrates the effect on the outstanding balance (principal) of the loan. Note that as the balance decreases, the amount of the payment needed to cover interest on that balance decreases, allowing more of the payment to be used to reduce the principal.

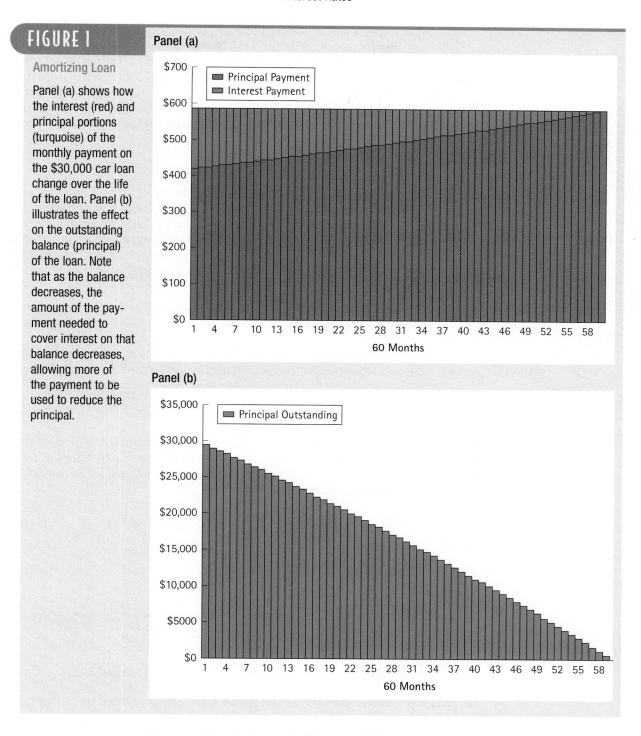

Panel (a)

Panel (b)

ing and the part left over to reduce the principal further is constantly increasing. We illustrate this effect in panel (a) of Figure 1, where we show the proportion of each monthly loan payment that covers interest (red) and the portion left over to reduce the principal (turquoise). As you can see, $168.75 of your first $590.50 payment is needed just to cover interest accrued over the first month ($30,000 × 0.005625 = $168.75). However, this amount steadily decreases so that by the end of the loan, nearly all of your payment is going toward principal.

Panel (b) of Figure 1 shows the effect of your payments on the loan balance. When you make your first payment of $590.50, $168.75 covers interest on the loan, leaving $421.75 to reduce the principal to $30,000 − $421.75 = $29,578.25. The next month, you owe interest only on the $29,578.25 loan balance, which is $166.38, leaving more of your $590.50 payment to reduce the principal further. This effect continues so that each month more of your payment is available to reduce the principal, causing the principal to decrease rapidly toward the end of the loan as you are taking bigger and bigger chunks out of the balance.

Computing the Outstanding Loan Balance

As Figure 1 shows, the outstanding balance on an amortizing loan is different each month. The amount you owe at any point in time can be calculated as the present value of your future obligations on the loan. So, the outstanding balance, also called the outstanding principal, is equal to the present value of the remaining future loan payments, again evaluated using the loan interest rate. We calculate the outstanding loan balance by determining the present value of the remaining loan payments using the loan rate as the discount rate.

EXAMPLE 3

Personal Finance
Computing the
Outstanding Loan
Balance

Problem
Let's say that you are now 3 years into your $30,000 car loan from the previous section and you decide to sell the car. When you sell the car, you will need to pay whatever the remaining balance is on your car loan. After 36 months of payments, how much do you still owe on your car loan?

Solution

▶ **Plan**
We have already determined that the monthly payments on the loan are $590.50. The remaining balance on the loan is the present value of the remaining 2 years, or 24 months, of payments. Thus, we can just use the annuity formula with the monthly rate of 0.5625%, a monthly payment of $590.50, and 24 months remaining.

▶ **Execute**

$$\text{Balance with 24 months remaining} = \$590.50 \times \frac{1}{0.005625}\left(1 - \frac{1}{1.005625^{24}}\right) = \$13{,}222.32$$

Thus, after 3 years, you owe $13,222.32 on the loan.
    Using a financial calculator or Excel:

	N	**I/Y**	**PV**	**PMT**	**FV**
Given:	24	0.5625		−590.50	0
Solve for:			**13,222.32**		
	Excel Formula: =PV(RATE,NPER,PMT,FV)=PV(0.005625,24,−590.50,0)				

You could also compute this as the FV of the original loan amount after deducting payments:

	N	**I/Y**	**PV**	**PMT**	**FV**
Given:	36	0.5625	30,000	−590.50	
Solve for:					**13,222.41**
	Excel Formula: =FV(RATE,NPER,PMT,PV)=FV(0.005625,36,−590.50,30000)				

The nine-cent difference is due to rounding on the payment amount.

> ▶ **Evaluate**
> At any point in time, including when you first take out the loan, you can calculate the balance of the loan as the present value of your remaining payments. Recall that when the bank gave you the $30,000 in the first place, it was willing to take 60 monthly payments of $590.50 in return only because the present value of those payments was equivalent to the cash it was giving you. Any time that you want to end the loan, the bank will charge you a lump sum equal to the present value of what it would receive if you continued making your payments as planned. As the second approach shows, the amount you owe can also be thought of as the future value of the original amount borrowed after deducting payments made along the way.

Concept Check

3. How is the principal repaid in an amortizing loan?

4. Why does the part of your loan payment covering interest change over time?

3 The Determinants of Interest Rates

Now that we understand how interest rates are quoted and used in loans, we turn to a broader question: How are interest rates determined? Fundamentally, interest rates are determined by market forces based on the relative supply and demand of funds. This supply and demand is in turn determined by the willingness of individuals, banks, and firms to borrow, save, and lend. Changes in interest rates affect consumer decisions, such as how much you can borrow for a car loan or mortgage. Because they change the present value of future cash flows, changes in interest rates also have a broad impact on capital budgeting decisions within the firm. In this section, we look at some of the factors that may influence interest rates, such as inflation, current economic activity, and expectations of future growth.

Inflation and Real Versus Nominal Rates

nominal interest rates
Interest rates quoted by banks and other financial institutions that indicate the rate at which money will grow if invested for a certain period of time.

Inflation measures how the purchasing power of a given amount of currency declines due to increasing prices. How many times have you heard the expression, "A dollar just doesn't buy what it used to"? We've all witnessed the steady upward climb of prices—for example, your morning coffee probably costs a little more today than it did five years ago. Inflation affects how we evaluate the interest rates being quoted by banks and other financial institutions. Those interest rates, and the ones we have used for discounting cash flows in this book, are **nominal interest rates**, which indicate the rate at which your money will grow if invested for a certain period. Of course, if prices in the economy are also increasing due to inflation, the nominal interest rate does not represent the true increase in purchasing power that will result from investing.

Grand Avenue by Steve Breen, October 20, 2003.

For example, let's say that a cup of coffee costs $1 this year. If you have $100, you could buy 100 coffees. Instead, if you put that $100 in a bank account earning 5.06% per year, you will have $105.06 at the end of the year. But how much better off will you really be? That depends on how much prices have increased over the same year. If inflation was 3% over the year, then that cup of coffee would cost 3% more, or $1.03 at the end of the year. Thus, you could take your $105.06 and buy $105.06/$1.03 = 102 coffees, so you're really only 2% better off.

real interest rate The rate of growth of purchasing power after adjusting for inflation.

That 2% is your **real interest rate**: the rate of growth of your purchasing power, after adjusting for inflation. Just as in the example, we can calculate the rate of growth of purchasing power as follows:

$$\text{Growth in Purchasing Power} = 1 + \text{real rate} = \frac{1 + \text{nominal rate}}{1 + \text{inflation rate}}$$

$$= \frac{\text{Growth of Money}}{\text{Growth of Prices}} \tag{4}$$

We can rearrange Eq. (4) to find the following formula for the real interest rate, together with a convenient approximation for the real interest rate when inflation rates are low:

The Real Interest Rate

$$\text{real rate} = \frac{\text{nominal rate} - \text{inflation rate}}{1 + \text{inflation rate}} \approx \text{nominal rate} - \text{inflation rate} \tag{5}$$

That is, the real interest rate is approximately equal to the nominal interest rate less the rate of inflation.[2]

EXAMPLE 4

Calculating the Real Interest Rate

Problem

In the year 2000, short-term U.S. government bond rates were about 5.8% and the rate of inflation was about 3.4%. In 2003, interest rates were about 1% and inflation was about 1.9%. What was the real interest rate in 2000 and 2003?

Solution

▶ **Plan**

The bond rates tell us the nominal rates. Given the nominal rates and inflation for each year, we can use Eq. (5) to calculate the real interest rate.

▶ **Execute**

Eq. (5) says:

$$\text{real rate} = \frac{\text{nominal rate} - \text{inflation rate}}{1 + \text{inflation rate}}$$

Thus, the real interest rate in 2000 was (5.8% − 3.4%)/(1.034) = 2.32% (which is approximately equal to the difference between the nominal rate and inflation: 5.8% − 3.4% = 2.4%). In 2003, the real interest rate was (1% − 1.9%)/(1.019) = −0.88%.

---

[2]The real interest rate should not be used as a discount rate for future cash flows. It can be used as a discount rate only if the cash flows are not the expected cash flows that will be paid, but are the equivalent cash flows before adjusting them for growth due to inflation (in that case, we say the cash flows are in real terms). This approach is error prone, however, so throughout this book we will always forecast cash flows including any growth due to inflation, and discount using nominal interest rates.

> **▶ Evaluate**
> Note that the real interest rate was negative in 2003, indicating that interest rates were insufficient to keep up with inflation. As a result, investors in U.S. government bonds were able to buy less at the end of the year than they could have purchased at the start of the year.

Figure 2 shows the history of nominal interest rates and inflation rates in the United States since 1955. Note that the nominal interest rate tends to move with inflation. Intuitively, individuals' willingness to save will depend on the growth in purchasing power they can expect (given by the real interest rate). Thus, when the inflation rate is high, a higher nominal interest rate is needed to induce individuals to save. This was evident in the late 1970s and early 1980s when inflation reached double-digits in the United States, and nominal rates increased in response.

Investment and Interest Rate Policy

Interest rates affect not only individuals' propensity to save, but also firms' incentive to raise capital and invest. Consider an opportunity that requires an upfront investment of $10 million and generates a cash flow of $3 million per year for four years. If the interest rate is 5%, this investment has an NPV of:

$$NPV = -10 + \frac{3}{1.05} + \frac{3}{1.05^2} + \frac{3}{1.05^3} + \frac{3}{1.05^4} = \$0.638 \text{ million}$$

If the interest rate is 9%, the NPV falls to

$$NPV = -10 + \frac{3}{1.09} + \frac{3}{1.09^2} + \frac{3}{1.09^3} + \frac{3}{1.09^4} = -\$0.281 \text{ million}$$

FIGURE 2

U.S. Interest Rates and Inflation Rates, 1955–2007

The graph shows U.S. nominal interest rates (in blue) and inflation rates (in red) from 1955–2007. Note that interest rates tend to be high when inflation is high. Interest rates are average three-month Treasury bill rates and inflation rates are based on annual increases in the U.S. Bureau of Labor Statistics' consumer price index.

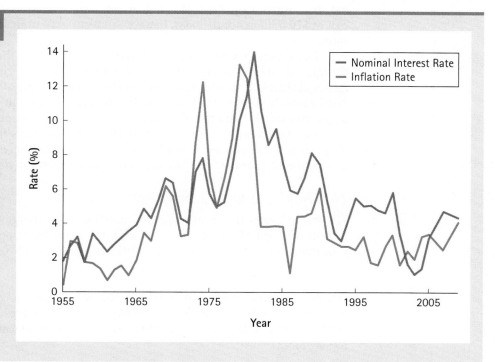

How Is Inflation Actually Calculated?

Inflation is calculated as the rate of change in the *Consumer Price Index* (CPI). The CPI measures what it costs each month to purchase a standard set of goods that the average consumer would buy. How controversial can price data be?

To gather the price information, data collectors visit stores and gather 80,000 retail price quotes and 5000 housing rent quotes. The data is sent daily to Washington, DC, where analysts at the Bureau of Labor Statistics seek to determine if part of a price change captures a change in quality or inflation. Because this adjustment can be subjective, herein lies the controversy in the CPI calculation. The *Wall Street Journal*, covering the controversy, reported the following examples:

▶ A 57-inch television in which the price dropped from $2238.99 to $1909.97. Going over the checklist, the data gatherer in the field discovered the old version had a built-in high-definition tuner. The new one did not. The analyst estimated that the tuner was valued at $513.69. This turned what appeared to be a 14.7% price decrease into a 10.7% increase.

▶ A 27-inch television where the price appeared to stay the same, but an analyst determined that the price had declined. The latest model had a flat screen, something that consumers value more than the curved screen in the old model. The newer TV also had a ten-watt stereo, compared with the weaker six-watt stereo in the older model.

Critics argue that this quality adjustment most often ends up making a price increase look smaller or even turning it into a decline. Thus, they conclude that the government underestimates the true rate of inflation. Supporters argue that these adjustments are necessary because paying more for a better product is not equivalent to paying more for the same product. This debate is important because many union contracts, for example, have wages linked to inflation, and investors need good inflation data to determine what interest rate to demand.

WSJ Source: Aeppel, T., New and Improved: An Inflation Debate Brews Over Intangibles at the Mall—Critics Say U.S. Plays Down CPI Through Adjustments For Quality, Not Just Price—Value of a TV's Flat Screen, 9 May 2005, A1

and the investment is no longer profitable. The reason, of course, is that we are discounting the positive cash flows at a higher rate, which reduces their present value. The cost of $10 million occurs today, however, so its present value is independent of the discount rate.

More generally, when the costs of an investment precede the benefits, an increase in the interest rate will decrease the investment's NPV. All else being equal, higher interest rates will therefore tend to shrink the set of positive-NPV investments available to firms. The Federal Reserve in the United States and central banks in other countries attempt to use this relationship between interest rates and investment incentives when trying to guide the economy. They will often lower interest rates in attempts to stimulate investment if the economy is slowing, and they will raise interest rates to reduce investment if the economy is "overheating" and inflation is on the rise.

The Yield Curve and Discount Rates

The interest rates that banks offer on investments or charge on loans depend on the horizon, or *term,* of the investment or loan. For example, suppose you are willing to put your money in a CD (certificate of deposit)[3] that matures in two years (meaning that you

---

[3]A certificate of deposit is a short- or medium-term debt instrument offered by banks. You deposit money in the bank for a stated period of time and normally receive a fixed rate of interest. The rate is higher than it would be on a savings account because you cannot withdraw your money early without paying a penalty.

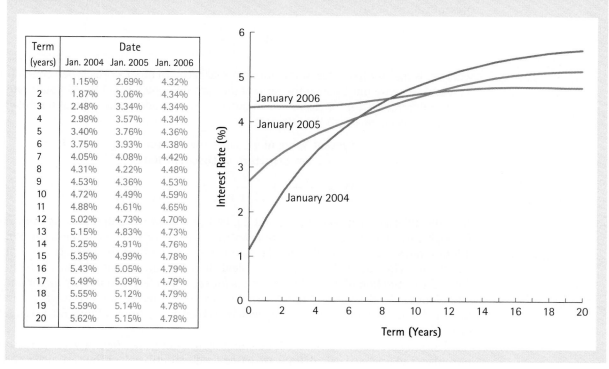

FIGURE 3

Term Structure of Risk-Free U.S. Interest Rates, January 2004, 2005, and 2006

The figure shows the interest rate available from investing in risk-free U.S. Treasury securities with different investment terms. In each case, the interest rates differ depending on the horizon. For example, in 2004, the interest rate on a 10-year loan (4.72%) was more than 4 times the rate on a 1-year loan (1.15%). (Data from U.S. Treasury securities.)

Term (years)	Date		
	Jan. 2004	Jan. 2005	Jan. 2006
1	1.15%	2.69%	4.32%
2	1.87%	3.06%	4.34%
3	2.48%	3.34%	4.34%
4	2.98%	3.57%	4.34%
5	3.40%	3.76%	4.36%
6	3.75%	3.93%	4.38%
7	4.05%	4.08%	4.42%
8	4.31%	4.22%	4.48%
9	4.53%	4.36%	4.53%
10	4.72%	4.49%	4.59%
11	4.88%	4.61%	4.65%
12	5.02%	4.73%	4.70%
13	5.15%	4.83%	4.73%
14	5.25%	4.91%	4.76%
15	5.35%	4.99%	4.78%
16	5.43%	5.05%	4.79%
17	5.49%	5.09%	4.79%
18	5.55%	5.12%	4.79%
19	5.59%	5.14%	4.78%
20	5.62%	5.15%	4.78%

term structure The relationship between the investment term and the interest rate.

yield curve A plot of bond yields as a function of the bonds' maturity date.

risk-free interest rate The interest rate at which money can be borrowed or lent without risk over a given period.

cannot get the money back before then without a penalty). The bank will offer you a higher rate of interest for this CD than if you put your money in a statement savings account, where you can withdraw your funds at any time. The relationship between the investment term and the interest rate is called the **term structure** of interest rates. We can plot this relationship on a graph called the **yield curve**. Figure 3 shows the term structure and corresponding yield curve of U.S. interest rates that were available to investors in January of 2004, 2005, and 2006. In each case, note that the interest rate depends on the horizon, and that the difference between short-term and long-term interest rates was especially pronounced in 2004. The rates plotted are interest rates for U.S. Treasury securities, which are considered to be free of any risk of default (the U.S. government will not default on its loans). Thus, each of these rates is a **risk-free interest rate**, which is the interest rate at which money can be borrowed or lent without risk over a given period.

We can use the term structure to compute the present and future values of a risk-free cash flow over different investment horizons. For example, $100 invested for one year at the one-year interest rate in January 2004 would grow to a future value of

$$\$100 \times 1.0115 = \$101.15$$

at the end of one year, and $100 invested for ten years at the ten-year interest rate in January 2004 would grow to[4]:

$$\$100 \times (1.0472)^{10} = \$158.60$$

We can apply the same logic when computing the present value of cash flows with different maturities. A risk-free cash flow received in two years should be discounted at the two-year interest rate, and a cash flow received in ten years should be discounted at the ten-year interest rate. In general, a risk-free cash flow of C_n received in n years has present value

$$PV = \frac{C_n}{(1 + r_n)^n} \qquad (6)$$

where r_n is the risk-free interest rate for an n-year term. In other words, when computing a present value we must match the term of the cash flow and term of the discount rate.

Combining Eq. (6) for cash flows in different years leads to the general formula for the present value of a cash flow stream:

**Present Value of a Cash Flow Stream Using
a Term Structure of Discount Rates**

$$PV = \frac{C_1}{1 + r_1} + \frac{C_2}{(1 + r_2)^2} + \cdots + \frac{C_N}{(1 + r_N)^N} \qquad (7)$$

Note the difference between Eq. (7) and Eq. (4.3). Here, we use a different discount rate for each cash flow, based on the rate from the yield curve with the same term. When interest rates are very similar across maturities, we say that the yield curve is flat, because it is close to a flat line. When the yield curve is relatively flat, as it was in January 2006, the distinction of using different rates for each cash flow is relatively minor and is often ignored by discounting using a single "average" interest rate r. But when short-term and long-term interest rates vary widely, as they did in January 2004, Eq. (7) should be used.

Warning: All of our shortcuts for computing present values (annuity and perpetuity formulas, and financial calculators) are based on discounting all of the cash flows *at the same rate*. They *cannot* be used in situations in which cash flows need to be discounted at different rates.

EXAMPLE 5

Using the Term
Structure to Compute
Present Values

Problem

Compute the present value of a risk-free 5-year annuity of $1000 per year, given the yield curve for January 2005 in Figure 3.

Solution

▶ **Plan**

The timeline of the cash flows of the annuity is:

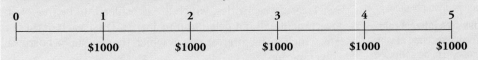

Footnote:

[4]We could also invest for ten years by investing at the one-year interest rate for ten years in a row. However, because we do not know what future interest rates will be, our ultimate payoff would not be risk free.

We can use the table next to the yield curve to identify the interest rate corresponding to each length of time: 1, 2, 3, 4, and 5 years. With the cash flows and those interest rates, we can compute the PV.

▶ **Execute**

From Figure 3, we see that the interest rates are: 2.69%, 3.06%, 3.34%, 3.57%, and 3.76%, for terms of 1, 2, 3, 4, and 5 years, respectively.

To compute the present value, we discount each cash flow by the corresponding interest rate:

$$PV = \frac{1000}{1.0269} + \frac{1000}{1.0306^2} + \frac{1000}{1.0334^3} + \frac{1000}{1.0357^4} + \frac{1000}{1.0376^5} = \$4522$$

▶ **Evaluate**

The yield curve tells us the market interest rate per year for each different maturity. In order to correctly calculate the PV of cash flows from five different maturities, we need to use the five different interest rates corresponding to those maturities. Note that we cannot use the annuity formula here because the discount rates differ for each cash flow.

Common Mistake — Using the Annuity Formula When Discount Rates Vary

When computing the present value of an annuity, a common mistake is to use the annuity formula with a single interest rate even though interest rates vary with the investment horizon. For example, we *cannot* compute the present value of the five-year annuity in Example 5 using the five-year interest rate from January 2005:

$$PV \neq \$1000 \times \frac{1}{0.0376}\left(1 - \frac{1}{1.0376^5}\right) = \$4482$$

If we want to find the single interest rate that we could use to value the annuity, we must first compute the present value of the annuity using Eq. (7) and then solve for its IRR. For the annuity in Example 5, we use a financial calculator or spreadsheet to find its IRR of 3.45%. The IRR of the annuity is always between the highest and lowest discount rates used to calculate its present value, as is the case in this example.

	N	I/Y	PV	PMT	FV
Given:	5		−4522	1000	0
Solve for:		3.45			
	Excel Formula: =RATE(NPER,PMT,PV,FV)=RATE(5,1000,−4522,0)				

The Yield Curve and the Economy

As Figure 4 illustrates, the yield curve changes over time. Sometimes, short-term rates are close to long-term rates, and at other times they may be very different. What accounts for the changing shape of the yield curve?

federal funds rate
The overnight loan rate charged by banks with excess reserves at a Federal Reserve bank (called federal funds) to banks that need additional funds to meet reserve requirements.

Interest Rate Determination. The Federal Reserve determines very short-term interest rates through its influence on the **federal funds rate**, which is the rate at which banks can borrow cash reserves on an overnight basis. All other interest rates on the yield curve are set in the market and are adjusted until the supply of lending matches the demand for borrowing at each loan term. As we shall see in a moment, expectations of future interest rate changes have a major effect on investors' willingness to lend or borrow for longer terms and, therefore, on the shape of the yield curve.

FIGURE 4

Yield Curve Shapes

The figure shows three different yield curve shapes. The blue line represents a "normal" yield curve. Most of the time the yield curve has this shape—moderately upward sloping. The red line depicts a steep yield curve—note the larger than normal difference between short-term rates (2%) and long-term rates (7%), making the yield curve look steeper than normal. This example of a steep yield curve is from October 1991. Finally, the green line depicts an inverted yield curve, so called because it slopes downward instead of upward. This happens when short-term rates are higher than long-term rates as they were in January 1981. We discuss why the shape of the yield curve changes over time in the rest of this section.

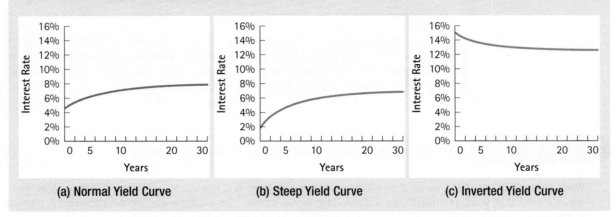

(a) Normal Yield Curve   (b) Steep Yield Curve   (c) Inverted Yield Curve

Suppose short-term interest rates are equal to long-term interest rates. If interest rates are expected to rise in the future, investors would not want to make long-term investments. Instead, they could do better by investing on a short-term basis and then reinvesting after interest rates rose. Thus, if interest rates are expected to rise, long-term interest rates will tend to be higher than short-term rates to attract investors.

Similarly, if interest rates are expected to fall in the future, then borrowers would not wish to borrow at long-term rates that are equal to short-term rates. They would do better by borrowing on a short-term basis, and then taking out a new loan after rates fall. So, if interest rates are expected to fall, long-term rates will tend to be lower than short-term rates to attract borrowers.

Yield Curve Shape.   These arguments indicate that the shape of the yield curve will be strongly influenced by interest rate expectations. A sharply increasing (*steep*) yield curve, with long-term rates much higher than short-term rates, generally indicates that interest rates are expected to rise in the future. A decreasing (*inverted*) yield curve, with long-term rates lower than short-term rates, generally signals an expected decline in future interest rates. Because interest rates tend to drop in response to a slowdown in the economy, an inverted yield curve is often interpreted as a negative forecast for economic growth. Indeed, as Figure 5 illustrates, each of the last six recessions in the United States was preceded by a period in which the yield curve was inverted (note the red shaded areas before the gray bars indicating a recession). Conversely, the yield curve tends to be steep (and therefore shaded blue) as the economy comes out of a recession and interest rates are expected to rise.

The normal shape of the yield curve is moderately upward sloping. This would be the case if investors almost always believed that interest rates were going to rise in the future. But that is unlikely, so there have to be other forces at work to cause long-term

162

FIGURE 5

Short-Term Versus Long-Term U.S. Interest Rates and Recessions

One-year and ten-year U.S. Treasury rates are plotted, with the spread between them shaded in green if the shape of the yield curve is increasing (the one-year rate is below the ten-year rate) and in red if the yield curve is inverted (the one-year rate exceeds the ten-year rate). Gray bars show the dates of U.S. recessions as determined by the National Bureau of Economic Research. Note that inverted yield curves tend to precede recessions as determined by the National Bureau of Economic Research. In recessions, interest rates tend to fall, with short-term rates dropping further. As a result, the yield curve tends to be steep coming out of a recession.

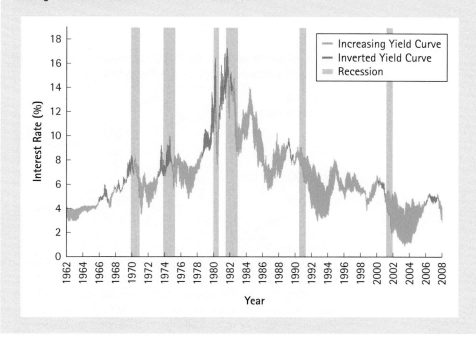

interest rates normally to be higher than short-term rates. The most commonly cited reason is that long-term loans are riskier than short-term loans. If you make a 30-year loan today and lock-in the interest rate, the present value of the payments you receive on the loan is very sensitive to even small changes in market interest rates. This sensitivity is due to the effect of compounding a change in interest rates over a 30-year period. To see this effect, consider the following example.

EXAMPLE 6

Long-term Versus Short-term Loans

Problem

You work for a bank that has just made two loans. In one, you loaned $909.09 today in return for $1000 in one year. In the other, you loaned $909.09 today in return for $15,863.08 in 30 years. The difference between the loan amount and repayment amount is based on an interest rate of 10% per year. Imagine that immediately after you make the loans, news about economic growth is announced that increases inflation expectations, so that the market interest rate for loans like these jumps to 11%. Loans make up a major part of a bank's assets, so you are naturally concerned about the value of these loans. What is the effect of the interest rate change on the value to the bank of the promised repayment of these loans?

Solution

▶ **Plan**

Each of these loans has only one repayment cash flow at the end of the loan. They differ only by the time to repayment:

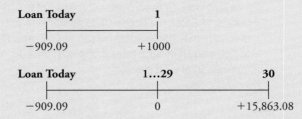

The effect on the value of the future repayment to the bank today is just the PV of the loan repayment, calculated at the new market interest rate.

▶ **Execute**

For the one-year loan:

$$PV = \frac{\$1,000}{(1.11)^1} = \$900.90$$

For the 30-year loan:

$$PV = \frac{\$15,863.08}{(1.11)^{30}} = \$692.94$$

▶ **Evaluate**

The value of the one-year loan decreased by $909.09 − $900.90 = $8.19, or 0.9%, but the value of the 30-year loan decreased by $909.09 − $692.94 = $216.15, or almost 24%! The small change in market interest rates, compounded over a longer period, resulted in a much larger change in the present value of the loan repayment. You can see why investors and banks view longer-term loans as being riskier than short-term loans.

In addition to specifying the discount rates for risk-free cash flows that occur at different horizons, it is also a potential leading indicator of future economic growth. Due to these qualities, the yield curve provides extremely important information for a business manager.

5. What is the difference between a nominal and real interest rate?

6. How are interest rates and the level of investment made by businesses related?

The Opportunity Cost of Capital

As we have seen in this chapter, the interest rates we observe in the market will vary based on quoting conventions, the term of the investment, and risk. In this chapter, we have developed the tools to account for these differences and gained some insights into how interest rates are determined. This knowledge will provide the foundation for our study of bonds in the next chapter.

The Valuation Principle tells us to use the "market interest rate" to compute present values and evaluate an investment opportunity. But with so many interest rates to choose from, the term "market interest rate" is inherently ambiguous. Therefore, going forward in the textbook, we will base the discount rate that we use to evaluate cash flows on the investor's **opportunity cost of capital** (or more simply, the **cost of capital**), which is *the best available expected return offered in the market on an investment of comparable risk and term to the cash flow being discounted.*

In order to understand the definition of opportunity cost of capital, it helps to think of yourself as a financial manager competing with financial managers at other firms to attract investors' funds (capital). In order to attract investors to invest in your firm or creditors to lend to your firm, you have to be able to offer them an expected return at least as good as what they could get elsewhere in the market for the same risk and length of investment. Now it is easier to see where the term (opportunity) cost of capital comes from—investors in your firm are giving up the opportunity to invest their funds elsewhere. This is an opportunity cost to them and to overcome it you must offer them a return equal to or better than their opportunity cost of capital. Even if you already have the funds internally in the firm to invest, the logic still applies. You could either return the funds to your shareholders to invest elsewhere, or reinvest them in a new project; however, you should only reinvest them if doing so provides a better return than the shareholders' other opportunities.

opportunity cost of capital or **cost of capital** The best available expected return offered in the market on an investment of comparable risk and term to the cash flow being discounted; the return the investor forgoes on an alternative investment of equivalent risk and term when the investor takes on a new investment.

Interest Rates, Discount Rates, and the Cost of Capital

By now, you may have noticed that we are using three terms to refer to rates of return. While many people use these three terms interchangeably, they are distinct. Throughout this book, we will use "interest rate" to mean a quoted rate in the market. A "discount rate" is the appropriate rate for discounting a given cash flow, *matched to the frequency of the cash flow.* Finally, we use "cost of capital" to indicate the rate of return on an investment of similar risk.

The opportunity cost of capital is the return the investor forgoes when the investor takes on a new investment. For a risk-free project, it will typically correspond to the interest rate on U.S. Treasury securities with a similar term. But the cost of capital is a much more general concept that can be applied to risky investments as well.

EXAMPLE 7

The Opportunity Cost of Capital

Problem

Suppose a friend offers to borrow $100 from you today and in return pay you $110 one year from today. Looking in the market for other options for investing the $100, you find your best alternative option that you view as equally risky as lending it to your friend. That option has an expected return of 8%. What should you do?

Solution

▶ **Plan**

Your decision depends on what the opportunity cost is of lending your money to your friend. If you lend her the $100, then you cannot invest it in the alternative with an 8% expected return. Thus, by making the loan, you are giving up the opportunity to invest for an 8% expected return. You can make your decision by using your 8% opportunity cost of capital to value the $110 in one year.

▶ **Execute**

The value of the $110 in one year is its present value, discounted at 8%:

$$PV = \frac{\$110}{(1.08)^1} = \$101.85$$

The $100 loan is worth $101.85 to you today, so you make the loan.

▶ **Evaluate**

The Valuation Principle tells us that we can determine the value of an investment by using market prices to value the benefits net of the costs. As this example shows, market prices determine what our best alternative opportunities are, so that we can decide whether an investment is worth the cost.

In this chapter, we have developed the fundamental tools a financial manager needs to value cash flows at different points in time. In this last section, we have reiterated the importance of using market information to determine the opportunity cost of capital, which is your discount rate in valuation calculations.

Concept Check

7. What is the opportunity cost of capital?

8. Can you ignore the cost of capital if you already have the funds inside the firm?

Here is what you should know after reading this chapter. MyFinanceLab will help you identify what you know, and where to go when you need to practice.

Key Points and Equations	Terms	Online Practice Opportunities
1 Interest Rate Quotes and Adjustments ▶ Just like any other price, interest rates are set by market forces, in particular the supply and demand of funds. ▶ The effective annual rate (EAR) indicates the actual amount of interest earned in one year. The EAR can be used as a discount rate for annual cash flows.	annual percentage rate (APR) effective annual rate (EAR) simple interest	MyFinanceLab Study Plan 5.1

▶ Given an EAR r, the equivalent discount rate for an n-year time interval, where n may be more than one year or less than or equal to one year (a fraction), is:

Equivalent n-period Discount Rate $=$
$$(1 + r)^n - 1 \qquad (1)$$

▶ An annual percentage rate (APR) is a common way of quoting interest rates. The actual interest rate per period is the APR/number of compounding periods per year. APRs cannot be used as discount rates.

▶ We need to know the compounding interval of an APR to determine the EAR:

$$1 + EAR = \left(1 + \frac{APR}{m}\right)^m \qquad (3)$$

$m =$ number of compounding periods per year

▶ For a given APR, the EAR increases with the compounding frequency.

2 Application: Discount Rates and Loans

▶ Loan rates are typically stated as APRs. The outstanding balance of a loan is equal to the present value of the loan cash flows, when evaluated using the actual interest rate per payment interval based on the loan rate.

▶ In each loan payment on an amortizing loan, you pay interest on the loan plus some part of the loan balance.

amortizing loans

MyFinanceLab
Study Plan 5.2

3 The Determinants of Interest Rates

▶ Quoted interest rates are nominal interest rates, which indicate the rate of growth of the money invested. The real interest rate indicates the rate of growth of one's purchasing power after adjusting for inflation.

▶ Given a nominal interest rate and an inflation rate, the real interest rate is:

$$\text{real rate} = \frac{\text{nominal rate} - \text{inflation rate}}{1 + \text{inflation rate}} \qquad (5)$$
$$\approx \text{real rate} - \text{inflation rate}$$

▶ Nominal interest rates tend to be high when inflation is high and low when inflation is low.

federal funds rate
nominal interest rates
real interest rate
risk-free interest rate
term structure
yield curve

MyFinanceLab
Study Plan 5.3
Interactive Yield
Curve

- Higher interest rates tend to reduce the NPV of typical investment projects. The U.S. Federal Reserve raises interest rates to moderate investment and combat inflation and lowers interest rates to stimulate investment and economic growth.
- Interest rates differ with the investment horizon according to the term structure of interest rates. The graph plotting interest rates as a function of the horizon is called the yield curve.
- Cash flows should be discounted using the discount rate that is appropriate for their horizon. Thus, the PV of a cash flow stream is:

$$PV = \frac{C_1}{1 + r_1} + \frac{C_2}{(1 + r_2)^2} + \cdots + \frac{C_N}{(1 + r_N)^N} \quad (7)$$

- Annuity and perpetuity formulas cannot be applied when discount rates vary with the horizon.
- The shape of the yield curve tends to vary with investors' expectations of future economic growth and interest rates. It tends to be inverted prior to recessions and to be steep coming out of a recession. Because investors view long-term loans as riskier, long-term rates are generally higher than short-term rates.

4 The Opportunity Cost of Capital

- An investor's opportunity cost of capital (or more simply, the cost of capital) is the best available expected return offered in the market on an investment of comparable risk and term to the cash flow being discounted.

(opportunity) cost of capital

MyFinanceLab
Study Plan 5.4

Review Questions

1. Explain how an interest rate is just a price.

2. Why is the EAR for 6% APR, with semi-annual compounding, higher than 6%?

3. Why is it so important to match the frequency of the interest rate to the frequency of the cash flows?

4. Why aren't the payments for a 15-year mortgage twice the payments for a 30-year mortgage at the same rate?

5. What mistake do you make when you discount real cash flows with nominal discount rates ?

6. How do changes in inflation expectations impact interest rates?

7. Can the nominal interest rate available to an investor be negative? (*Hint:* Consider the interest rate earned from saving cash "under the mattress.") Can the real interest rate be negative?

8. In the early 1980s, inflation was in the double-digits and the yield curve sloped sharply downward. What did the yield curve say about investors' expectations about future inflation rates?

9. What do we mean when we refer to the "opportunity cost" of capital?

Problems

All problems in this chapter are available in MyFinanceLab. An asterisk (*) indicates problems with a higher level of difficulty.

Interest Rate Quotes and Adjustments

1. Your bank is offering you an account that will pay 20% interest in total for a two-year deposit. Determine the equivalent discount rate for a period length of
   a. six months.
   b. one year.
   c. one month.

2. Which do you prefer: a bank account that pays 5% per year (EAR) for three years or
   a. an account that pays 2.5% every six months for three years?
   b. an account that pays 7.5% every 18 months for three years?
   c. an account that pays 0.5% per month for three years?

3. You have been offered a job with an unusual bonus structure. As long as you stay with the firm, you will get an extra $70,000 every seven years, starting seven years from now. What is the present value of this incentive if you plan to work for the company for a total of 42 years and the interest rate is 6% (EAR)?

4. You have found three investment choices for a one-year deposit: 10% APR compounded monthly, 10% APR compounded annually, and 9% APR compounded daily. Compute the EAR for each investment choice. (Assume that there are 365 days in the year.)

5. Your bank account pays interest with an EAR of 5%. What is the APR quote for this account based on semiannual compounding? What is the APR with monthly compounding?

6. Suppose the interest rate is 8% APR with monthly compounding. What is the present value of an annuity that pays $100 every six months for five years?

7. You have been accepted into college. The college guarantees that your tuition will not increase for the four years you attend college. The first $10,000 tuition payment is due in six months. After that, the same payment is due every six months until you have made a total of eight payments. The college offers a bank account that allows you to withdraw money every six months and has a fixed APR of 4% (semiannual) guaranteed to remain the same over the next four years. How much money must you deposit today if you intend to make no further deposits and would like to make all the tuition payments from this account, leaving the account empty when the last payment is made?

169

Application: Discount Rates and Loans

8. You make monthly payments on your car loan. It has a quoted APR of 5% (monthly compounding). What percentage of the outstanding principal do you pay in interest each month?

9. Suppose Capital One is advertising a 60-month, 5.99% APR motorcycle loan. If you need to borrow $8000 to purchase your dream Harley Davidson, what will your monthly payment be?

10. Suppose Oppenheimer Bank is offering a 30-year mortgage with an EAR of 6.80%. If you plan to borrow $150,000, what will your monthly payment be?

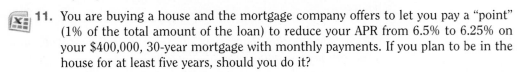

11. You are buying a house and the mortgage company offers to let you pay a "point" (1% of the total amount of the loan) to reduce your APR from 6.5% to 6.25% on your $400,000, 30-year mortgage with monthly payments. If you plan to be in the house for at least five years, should you do it?

12. You have decided to refinance your mortgage. You plan to borrow whatever is outstanding on your current mortgage. The current monthly payment is $2356 and you have made every payment on time. The original term of the mortgage was 30 years, and the mortgage is exactly four years and eight months old. You have just made your monthly payment. The mortgage interest rate is 6.375% (APR). How much do you owe on the mortgage today?

13. You have just sold your house for $1,000,000 in cash. Your mortgage was originally a 30-year mortgage with monthly payments and an initial balance of $800,000. The mortgage is currently exactly 18½ years old, and you have just made a payment. If the interest rate on the mortgage is 5.25% (APR), how much cash will you have from the sale once you pay off the mortgage?

14. You have just purchased a car and taken out a $50,000 loan. The loan has a five-year term with monthly payments and an APR of 6%.
    a. How much will you pay in interest, and how much will you pay in principal, during the first month, second month, and first year? (*Hint:* Compute the loan balance after one month, two months and one year.)
    b. How much will you pay in interest, and how much will you pay in principal, during the fourth year (i.e., between three and four years from now)?

*15. You have some extra cash this month and you are considering putting it toward your car loan. Your interest rate is 7%, your loan payments are $600 per month and you have 36 months left on your loan. If you pay an additional $1000 with your next regular $600 payment (due in one month), how much will it reduce the amount of time left to pay off your loan?

*16. You have an outstanding student loan with required payments of $500 per month for the next four years. The interest rate on the loan is 9% APR (monthly). You are considering making an extra payment of $100 today (i.e., you will pay an extra $100 that you are not required to pay). If you are required to continue to make payments of $500 per month until the loan is paid off, what is the amount of your final payment? What effective rate of return (expressed as an APR with monthly compounding) have you earned on the $100?

*17. Consider again the setting of Problem 16. Now that you realize your best investment is to prepay your student loan, you decide to prepay as much as you can each month. Looking at your budget, you can afford to pay an extra $250 per month in addition to your required monthly payments of $500, or $750 in total each month. How long will it take you to pay off the loan?

*18. If you decide to take the mortgage in Problem 10, Oppenheimer Bank will offer you the following deal: Instead of making the monthly payment you computed in that problem every month, you can make half the payment every two weeks (so that you will make $52/2 = 26$ payments per year). How long will it take to pay off the mortgage if the EAR remains the same at 6.80%.

*19. Your friend tells you he has a very simple trick for taking one-third off the time it takes to repay your mortgage: Use your Christmas bonus to make an extra payment on January 1 of each year (that is, pay your monthly payment due on that day twice). If you take out your mortgage on July 1, so your first monthly payment is due August 1, and you make an extra payment every January 1, how long will it take to pay off the mortgage? Assume that the mortgage has an original term of 30 years and an APR of 12%.

20. The mortgage on your house is five years old. It required monthly payments of $1402, had an original term of 30 years, and had an interest rate of 10% (APR). In the intervening five years, interest rates have fallen and so you have decided to refinance—that is, you will roll over the outstanding balance into a new mortgage. The new mortgage has a 30-year term, requires monthly payments, and has an interest rate of $6\frac{5}{8}$% (APR).
   a. What monthly repayments will be required with the new loan?
   b. If you still want to pay off the mortgage in 25 years, what monthly payment should you make after you refinance?
   c. Suppose you are willing to continue making monthly payments of $1402. How long will it take you to pay off the mortgage after refinancing?
   d. Suppose you are willing to continue making monthly payments of $1402, and want to pay off the mortgage in 25 years. How much additional cash can you borrow today as part of the refinancing?

21. You have credit card debt of $25,000 that has an APR (monthly compounding) of 15%. Each month you pay a minimum monthly payment only. You are required to pay only the outstanding interest. You have received an offer in the mail for an otherwise identical credit card with an APR of 12%. After considering all your alternatives, you decide to switch cards, roll over the outstanding balance on the old card into the new card, and borrow additional money as well. How much can you borrow today on the new card without changing the minimum monthly payment you will be required to pay?

22. Your firm has taken out a $500,000 loan with 9% APR (compounded monthly) for some commercial property. As is common in commercial real estate, the loan is a 5-year loan based on a 15-year amortization. This means that your loan payments will be calculated as if you will take 15 years to pay off the loan, but you actually must do so in 5 years. To do this, you will make 59 equal payments based on the 15-year amortization schedule and then make a final 60th payment to pay the remaining balance.
   a. What will your monthly payments be?
   b. What will your final payment be?

The Determinants of Interest Rates

23. In 1975, interest rates were 7.85% and the rate of inflation was 12.3% in the United States. What was the real interest rate in 1975? How would the purchasing power of your savings have changed over the year?

24. If the rate of inflation is 5%, what nominal interest rate is necessary for you to earn a 3% real interest rate on your investment?

25. Consider a project that requires an initial investment of $100,000 and will produce a single cash flow of $150,000 in five years.
   a. What is the NPV of this project if the five-year interest rate is 5% (EAR)?
   b. What is the NPV of this project if the five-year interest rate is 10% (EAR)?
   c. What is the highest five-year interest rate such that this project is still profitable?

 26. What is the shape of the yield curve given in the following term structure? What expectations are investors likely to have about future interest rates?

Term	1 year	2 years	3 years	5 years	7 years	10 years	20 years
Rate (EAR, %)	1.99	2.41	2.74	3.32	3.76	4.13	4.93

Chapter 6

Risk and Return

WHY THIS CHAPTER MATTERS TO YOU

In Your Professional Life

Accounting: You need to understand the relationship between risk and return because of the effect that riskier projects will have on the firm's annual net income and on your efforts to stabilize reported net income.

Information systems: You need to understand how to do scenario and correlation analyses to build decision packages that help management analyze the risk and return of various business opportunities.

Management: You need to understand the relationship between risk and return, and how to measure that relationship to evaluate data that come from finance personnel and translate those data into decisions that increase the value of the firm.

Marketing: You need to understand that although higher-risk projects may produce higher returns, they may not be the best choice for the firm if they produce an erratic earnings pattern and fail to optimize the value of the firm.

Operations: You need to understand why investments in plant, equipment, and systems need to be evaluated in light of their impact on the firm's risk and return, which together will affect the firm's value.

In Your Personal Life

The tradeoff between risk and return enters into numerous personal financial decisions. You will use risk and return concepts when you select savings vehicles, buy real estate, finance major purchases, purchase insurance, invest in securities, and implement retirement plans. Although risk and return are difficult to measure precisely, you can get a feel for them and make decisions based upon the tradeoffs between risk and return in light of your personal disposition toward risk.

LEARNING GOALS

LG 1 Understand the meaning and fundamentals of risk, return, and risk preferences.

LG 2 Describe procedures for assessing and measuring the risk of a single asset.

LG 3 Discuss risk measurement for a single asset using the standard deviation and coefficient of variation.

LG 4 Understand the risk and return characteristics of a portfolio in terms of correlation and diversification, and the impact of international assets on a portfolio.

LG 5 Review the two types of risk and the derivation and role of beta in measuring the relevant risk of both a security and a portfolio.

LG 6 Explain the capital asset pricing model (CAPM), its relationship to the security market line (SML).

From Chapter 5 of *Principles of Managerial Finance*, Brief 5th Edition. Lawrence J. Gitman. Copyright © 2009 by Pearson Prentice Hall. All rights reserved.

The concept that return should increase if risk increases is fundamental to modern management and finance. This relationship is regularly observed in the financial markets, and important clarification of it has led to Nobel prizes. In this chapter we discuss these two key factors in finance—risk and return—and introduce some quantitative tools and techniques used to measure risk and return for individual assets and for groups of assets.

1 | Risk and Return Fundamentals

To maximize share price, the financial manager must learn to assess two key determinants: risk and return. Each financial decision presents certain risk and return characteristics, and the unique combination of these characteristics has an impact on share price. Risk can be viewed as it is related either to a single asset or to a **portfolio**—a collection, or group, of assets. We will look at both, beginning with the risk of a single asset. First, though, it is important to introduce some fundamental ideas about risk, return, and risk preferences.

portfolio
A collection, or group, of assets.

Risk Defined

risk
The chance of financial loss or, more formally, the *variability of returns associated with a given asset.*

In the most basic sense, **risk** is the chance of financial loss. Assets having greater chances of loss are viewed as more risky than those with lesser chances of loss. More formally, the term *risk* is used interchangeably with *uncertainty* to refer to the *variability of returns associated with a given asset.* A $1,000 government bond that guarantees its holder $5 interest after 30 days has no risk, because there is no variability associated with the return. A $1,000 investment in a firm's common stock, which over the same 30 days may earn anywhere from $0 to $10, is very risky because of the high variability of its return. The more nearly certain the return from an asset, the less variability and therefore the less risk.

Some risks directly affect both financial managers and shareholders. Table 1 briefly describes the common sources of risk that affect both firms and their shareholders. As you can see, business risk and financial risk are more firm-specific and therefore are of greatest interest to financial managers. Interest rate, liquidity, and market risks are more shareholder-specific and therefore are of greatest interest to stockholders. Event, exchange rate, purchasing-power, and tax risk directly affect both firms and shareholders. The *Focus on Ethics* box addresses another risk that affects both firms and shareholders—moral risk. A number of these risks are discussed in more detail later in this text. Clearly, both financial managers and shareholders must assess these and other risks as they make investment decisions.

return
The total gain or loss experienced on an investment over a given period of time; calculated by dividing the asset's cash distributions during the period, plus change in value, by its beginning-of-period investment value.

Return Defined

Obviously, if we are going to assess risk on the basis of variability of return, we need to be certain we know what *return* is and how to measure it. The **return** is the total gain or loss experienced on an investment over a given period of time. It is commonly measured as cash distributions during the period plus the change in value, expressed as a percentage of the beginning-of-period investment value. The

TABLE 1	Popular Sources of Risk Affecting Financial Managers and Shareholders
Source of risk	Description
Firm-Specific Risks	
Business risk	The chance that the firm will be unable to cover its operating costs. Level is driven by the firm's revenue stability and the structure of its operating costs (fixed versus variable).
Financial risk	The chance that the firm will be unable to cover its financial obligations. Level is driven by the predictability of the firm's operating cash flows and its fixed-cost financial obligations.
Shareholder-Specific Risks	
Interest rate risk	The chance that changes in interest rates will adversely affect the value of an investment. Most investments lose value when the interest rate rises and increase in value when it falls.
Liquidity risk	The chance that an investment cannot be easily liquidated at a reasonable price. Liquidity is significantly affected by the size and depth of the market in which an investment is customarily traded.
Market risk	The chance that the value of an investment will decline because of market factors that are independent of the investment (such as economic, political, and social events). In general, the more a given investment's value responds to the market, the greater its risk; the less it responds, the smaller its risk.
Firm and Shareholder Risks	
Event risk	The chance that a totally unexpected event will have a significant effect on the value of the firm or a specific investment. These infrequent events, such as government-mandated withdrawal of a popular prescription drug, typically affect only a small group of firms or investments.
Exchange rate risk	The exposure of future expected cash flows to fluctuations in the currency exchange rate. The greater the chance of undesirable exchange rate fluctuations, the greater the risk of the cash flows and therefore the lower the value of the firm or investment.
Purchasing-power risk	The chance that changing price levels caused by inflation or deflation in the economy will adversely affect the firm's or investment's cash flows and value. Typically, firms or investments with cash flows that move with general price levels have a low purchasing-power risk, and those with cash flows that do not move with general price levels have a high purchasing-power risk.
Tax risk	The chance that unfavorable changes in tax laws will occur. Firms and investments with values that are sensitive to tax law changes are more risky.

expression for calculating the rate of return earned on any asset over period t, r_t, is commonly defined as

$$r_t = \frac{C_t + P_t - P_{t-1}}{P_{t-1}} \tag{1}$$

where

r_t = actual, expected, or required rate of return during period t

C_t = cash (flow) received from the asset investment in the time period $t-1$ to t

P_t = price (value) of asset at time t

P_{t-1} = price (value) of asset at time $t-1$

IN PRACTICE

Focus on Ethics   What about Moral Risk?

The poster boy for "moral risk," exemplifying the devastating effects of unethical behavior for a company's investors, has to be Nick Leeson. As a futures trader, Leeson violated his bank's investing rules while secretly placing huge bets on the direction of the Japanese stock market. When those bets proved wrong, the $1.24 billion losses resulted in the 1995 demise of the centuries-old Barings Bank. More than any other single episode in world financial history, Leeson's misdeeds proved the importance of character in the financial industry.

Problems with ethics can be found throughout the business world. In a survey conducted by *CFO* magazine, 41 percent of surveyed chief financial officers admitted ethical problems in their organizations, and 48 percent of surveyed employees admitted engaging in unethical practices such as cheating on expense accounts or forging signatures. In the 2004 survey, 47 percent of CFOs said that they felt pressure from CEOs to use aggressive accounting to "make the numbers work." One

of the main reasons cited for accounting fraud uncovered in recent years was the pressure to "hit the numbers" expected by some Wall Street security analysts. The good news was that the same survey found CFOs standing up to CEO pressure and improving ethical standards in their departments, thanks to the 2002 Sarbanes-Oxley Act.

What can be done to minimize moral risk? A first step is to build awareness through a code of ethics. Almost all *Fortune* 500 companies and about half of all companies have an ethics code that spells out general principles of right and wrong conduct. Because ethical codes are often faulted for being vague and abstract, companies such as **Texas Instruments** have written detailed standards of conduct. Organizations also reveal their ethical commitment in other ways. Some administer honesty tests prior to hiring new workers; others require ethics training of mid-level managers. Additional methods of strengthening corporate ethics include providing whistle-blower protection for employees with ethics-related

concerns, establishing an *ethics director,* and evaluating managers' ethics in performance reviews.

The trend may be toward higher ethical standards, according to a study conducted by five Baylor University professors. They surveyed 10,000 U.S. business professionals three times over a 20-year period, asking the respondents to judge acceptable responses to 16 common business situations with questionable ethical dimensions. The responses, compiled into a single "ethics index" for each survey year, show an upward trend, according to the study published in 2006. Debate continues, however, over whether there is a gap between attitudes and actual actions. People who otherwise might do the right thing can be pressured to do something wrong.

■ *Is "hitting the numbers" an appropriate goal, given the contrast of profit and shareholder wealth maximization? If not, why do executives emphasize it?*

The return, r_t, reflects the combined effect of cash flow, C_t, and changes in value, $P_t - P_{t-1}$, over period t.

Equation 1 is used to determine the rate of return over a time period as short as 1 day or as long as 10 years or more. However, in most cases, t is 1 year, and r therefore represents an annual rate of return.

Example

Robin's Gameroom, a high-traffic video arcade, wishes to determine the return on two of its video machines, Conqueror and Demolition. Conqueror was purchased 1 year ago for $20,000 and currently has a market value of $21,500. During the year, it generated $800 of after-tax cash receipts. Demolition was purchased

4 years ago; its value in the year just completed declined from $12,000 to $11,800. During the year, it generated $1,700 of after-tax cash receipts. Substituting into Equation 1, we can calculate the annual rate of return, r, for each video machine.

Conqueror (C):

$$r_C = \frac{\$800 + \$21,500 - \$20,000}{\$20,000} = \frac{\$2,300}{\$20,000} = \underline{11.5\%}$$

Demolition (D):

$$r_D = \frac{\$1,700 + \$11,800 - \$12,000}{\$12,000} = \frac{\$1,500}{\$12,000} = \underline{12.5\%}$$

Although the market value of Demolition declined during the year, its cash flow caused it to earn a higher rate of return than Conqueror earned during the same period. Clearly, the combined impact of cash flow and changes in value, as measured by the rate of return, is important.

Historical Returns

Investment returns vary both over time and between different types of investments. By averaging historical returns over a long period of time, it becomes possible to eliminate the impact of market and other types of risk. This enables the financial decision maker to focus on the differences in return that are attributable primarily to the types of investment. Table 2 shows the average annual rates of return for a number of popular security investments (and inflation) over the 81-year period January 1, 1926, through December 31, 2006. Each rate represents the average annual rate of return an investor would have realized had he or she purchased the investment on January 1, 1926, and sold it on December 31, 2006. You can see that significant differences exist between the average annual rates of return realized on the various types of stocks, bonds, and bills shown. Later in this chapter, we will see how these differences in return can be linked to differences in the risk of each of these investments.

TABLE 2	Historical Returns for Selected Security Investments (1926–2006)

Investment	Average annual return
Large-company stocks	12.3%
Small-company stocks	17.4
Long-term corporate bonds	6.2
Long-term government bonds	5.8
U.S. Treasury bills	3.8
Inflation	3.1%

Source: Stocks, Bonds, Bills, and Inflation, 2007 Yearbook (Chicago: Ibbotson Associates, Inc., 2007).

risk-averse
The attitude toward risk in which an increased return would be required for an increase in risk.

Hint Remember that most *shareholders* are risk-averse. Like risk-averse managers, for a given increase in risk, they require an increase in return on their investment in that firm.

Risk Aversion

Financial managers generally seek to avoid risk. Most managers are **risk-averse**; for a given increase in risk, they require an increase in return. This attitude is believed consistent with that of the owners for whom the firm is being managed. Managers generally tend to be conservative rather than aggressive when accepting risk for their firm. Accordingly, a *risk-averse financial manager requiring higher returns for greater risk is assumed throughout this text.*

REVIEW QUESTIONS

1   What is *risk* in the context of financial decision making?
2   Define *return,* and describe how to find the rate of return on an investment.
3   Describe the attitude toward return of a risk-averse financial manager.

---

    2 | # Risk of a Single Asset

The concept of risk can be developed by first considering a single asset held in isolation. We can look at expected-return behaviors to assess risk, and use statistics to measure it.

Risk Assessment

scenario analysis
An approach for assessing risk that uses several possible alternative outcomes (scenarios) to obtain a sense of the variability among returns.

range
A measure of an asset's risk, which is found by subtracting the return associated with the pessimistic (worst) outcome from the return associated with the optimistic (best) outcome.

Scenario analysis and probability distributions can be used to assess the general level of risk embodied in a given asset.

Scenario Analysis

Scenario analysis uses several possible alternative outcomes (scenarios) to obtain a sense of the variability among returns. One common method involves considering pessimistic (worst), most likely (expected), and optimistic (best) outcomes and the returns associated with them for a given asset. In this case, the asset's risk can be measured by the range of returns. The **range** is found by subtracting the return associated with the pessimistic outcome from the return associated with the optimistic outcome. The greater the range, the more variability, or risk, the asset is said to have.

Example

Norman Company, a custom golf equipment manufacturer, wants to choose the better of two investments, A and B. Each requires an initial outlay of $10,000, and each has a *most likely* annual rate of return of 15%. Management has estimated returns associated with each investment's *pessimistic* and *optimistic* outcomes. The three estimates for each asset, along with its range, are given in Table 3. Asset A appears to be less risky than asset B; its range of 4% (17% − 13%) is less than the range of 16% (23% − 7%) for asset B. The risk-averse decision maker would prefer asset A over asset B, because A offers the same most likely return as B (15%) with lower risk (smaller range).

TABLE 3	Assets A and B	
	Asset A	**Asset B**
Initial investment	$10,000	$10,000
Annual rate of return		
Pessimistic	13%	7%
Most likely	15%	15%
Optimistic	17%	23%
Range	4%	16%

Although the use of scenario analysis and the range is rather crude, it does give the decision maker a feel for the behavior of returns, which can be used to estimate the risk involved.

Probability Distributions

Probability distributions provide a more quantitative insight into an asset's risk. The **probability** of a given outcome is its *chance* of occurring. An outcome with an 80 percent probability of occurrence would be expected to occur 8 out of 10 times. An outcome with a probability of 100 percent is certain to occur. Outcomes with a probability of zero will never occur.

probability
The *chance* that a given outcome will occur.

Example

Norman Company's past estimates indicate that the probabilities of the pessimistic, most likely, and optimistic outcomes are 25%, 50%, and 25%, respectively. Note that the sum of these probabilities must equal 100%; that is, they must be based on all the alternatives considered.

probability distribution
A model that relates probabilities to the associated outcomes.

bar chart
The simplest type of probability distribution; shows only a limited number of outcomes and associated probabilities for a given event.

A **probability distribution** is a model that relates probabilities to the associated outcomes. The simplest type of probability distribution is the **bar chart**, which shows only a limited number of outcome–probability coordinates. The bar charts for Norman Company's assets A and B are shown in Figure 1. Although both assets have the same most likely return, the range of return is much greater, or more dispersed, for asset B than for asset A—16 percent versus 4 percent.

FIGURE 1	

Bar Charts
Bar charts for asset A's and asset B's returns

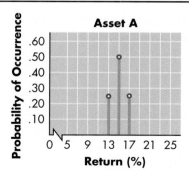
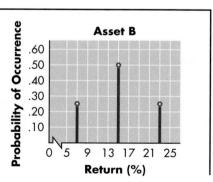

Continuous Probability Distributions
Continuous probability distributions for asset A's and asset B's returns

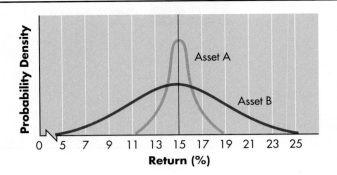

continuous probability distribution
A probability distribution showing all the possible outcomes and associated probabilities for a given event.

If we knew all the possible outcomes and associated probabilities, we could develop a **continuous probability distribution**. This type of distribution can be thought of as a bar chart for a very large number of outcomes. Figure 2 presents continuous probability distributions for assets A and B. Note that although assets A and B have the same most likely return (15 percent), the distribution of returns for asset B has much greater *dispersion* than the distribution for asset A. Clearly, asset B is more risky than asset A.

Risk Measurement

In addition to considering its *range,* the risk of an asset can be measured quantitatively by using statistics. Here we consider two statistics—the standard deviation and the coefficient of variation—that can be used to measure the variability of asset returns.

Standard Deviation

standard deviation (σ_r)
The most common statistical indicator of an asset's risk; it measures the dispersion around the *expected value.*

expected value
of a return ($\bar{r}$)
The most likely return on a given asset.

The most common statistical indicator of an asset's risk is the **standard deviation,** s_r, which measures the dispersion around the *expected value.* The **expected value of a return,** $\bar{r}$, is the most likely return on an asset. It is calculated as follows:[1]

$$\bar{r} = \sum_{j=1}^{n} r_j \times Pr_j \qquad (2)$$

where

r_j = return for the *j*th outcome

Pr_j = probability of occurrence of the *j*th outcome

n = number of outcomes considered

---

1. The formula for finding the expected value of return, $\bar{r}$, when all of the outcomes, r_j, are known *and* their related probabilities are assumed to be equal, is a simple arithmetic average:

$$\bar{r} = \frac{\sum_{j=1}^{n} r_j}{n} \qquad (2a)$$

where *n* is the number of observations. Equation 2 is emphasized in this chapter because returns and related probabilities are often available.

TABLE 4	Expected Values of Returns for Assets A and B		
Possible outcomes	Probability (1)	Returns (2)	Weighted value [(1) × (2)] (3)
Asset A			
Pessimistic	.25	13%	3.25%
Most likely	.50	15	7.50
Optimistic	.25	17	4.25
Total	1.00	Expected return	15.00%
Asset B			
Pessimistic	.25	7%	1.75%
Most likely	.50	15	7.50
Optimistic	.25	23	5.75
Total	1.00	Expected return	15.00%

Example

The expected values of returns for Norman Company's assets A and B are presented in Table 4. Column 1 gives the Pr_j's and column 2 gives the r_j's. In each case n equals 3. The expected value for each asset's return is 15%.

The expression for the *standard deviation of returns*, s_r, is[2]

$$\sigma_r = \sqrt{\sum_{j=1}^{n} (r_j - \bar{r})^2 \times Pr_j} \qquad (3)$$

In general, the higher the standard deviation, the greater the risk.

Example

Table 5 presents the standard deviations for Norman Company's assets A and B, based on the earlier data. The standard deviation for asset A is 1.41%, and the standard deviation for asset B is 5.66%. The higher risk of asset B is clearly reflected in its higher standard deviation.

Historical Returns and Risk   We can now use the standard deviation as a measure of risk to assess the historical (1926–2006) investment return data in Table 2. Table 6 repeats the historical returns in column 1 and shows the standard deviations associated with each of them in column 2. A close relationship

---

2. The formula that is commonly used to find the standard deviation of returns, s_r, in a situation in which *all* outcomes are known *and* their related probabilities are assumed equal, is

$$\sigma_r = \sqrt{\frac{\sum_{j=1}^{n} (r_j - \bar{r})^2}{n - 1}} \qquad (3a)$$

where n is the number of observations. Equation 3 is emphasized in this chapter because returns and related probabilities are often available.

TABLE 5	The Calculation of the Standard Deviation of the Returns for Assets A and B[a]

j	r_j	$\bar{r}$	$r_j - \bar{r}$	$(r_j - \bar{r})^2$	Pr_j	$(r_j - \bar{r})^2 \times Pr_j$
			Asset A			
1	13%	15%	−2%	4%	.25	1%
2	15	15	0	0	.50	0
3	17	15	2	4	.25	1

$$\sum_{j=1}^{3}(r_j - \bar{r})^2 \times Pr_j = 2\%$$

$$\sigma_{r_A} = \sqrt{\sum_{j=1}^{3}(r_j - \bar{r})^2 \times Pr_j} = \sqrt{2\%} = \underline{\underline{1.41\%}}$$

j	r_j	$\bar{r}$	$r_j - \bar{r}$	$(r_j - \bar{r})^2$	Pr_j	$(r_j - \bar{r})^2 \times Pr_j$
			Asset B			
1	7%	15%	−8%	64%	.25	16%
2	15	15	0	0	.50	0
3	23	15	8	64	.25	16

$$\sum_{j=1}^{3}(r_j - \bar{r})^2 \times Pr_j = 32\%$$

$$\sigma_{r_B} = \sqrt{\sum_{j=1}^{3}(r_j - \bar{r})^2 \times Pr_j} = \sqrt{32\%} = \underline{\underline{5.66\%}}$$

[a]Calculations in this table are made in percentage form rather than decimal form—e.g., 13% rather than 0.13. As a result, some of the intermediate computations may appear to be inconsistent with those that would result from using decimal form. Regardless, the resulting standard deviations are correct and identical to those that would result from using decimal rather than percentage form.

TABLE 6	Historical Returns, Standard Deviations, and Coefficients of Variation for Selected Security Investments (1926–2006)

Investment	Average annual return (1)	Standard deviation (2)	Coefficient of variation[a] (3)
Large-company stocks	12.3%	20.1%	1.63
Small-company stocks	17.4	32.7	1.88
Long-term corporate bonds	6.2	8.5	1.37
Long-term government bonds	5.8	9.2	1.59
U.S. Treasury bills	3.8	3.1	0.82
Inflation	3.1%	4.3%	1.39

[a]Calculated by dividing the standard deviation in column 2 by the average annual return in column 1.
Source: Stocks, Bonds, Bills, and Inflation, 2007 Yearbook (Chicago: Ibbotson Associates, Inc., 2007).

can be seen between the investment returns and the standard deviations: Investments with higher returns have higher standard deviations. Because higher standard deviations are associated with greater risk, the historical data confirm the existence of a positive relationship between risk and return. That relationship reflects *risk aversion* by market participants, who require higher returns as compensation for greater risk. The historical data in columns 1 and 2 of Table 6 clearly show that during the 1926–2006 period, investors were rewarded with higher returns on higher-risk investments.

Coefficient of Variation

coefficient of variation (CV)
A measure of relative dispersion that is useful in comparing the risks of assets with differing expected returns.

The **coefficient of variation**, *CV*, is a measure of relative dispersion that is useful in comparing the risks of assets with differing expected returns. Equation 4 gives the expression for the coefficient of variation:

$$CV = \frac{\sigma_r}{\bar{r}} \qquad (4)$$

The higher the coefficient of variation, the greater the risk and therefore the higher the expected return. This relationship can be seen by comparing the coefficients of variation in column 3 of Table 6, which shows historical 1926–2006 investment data, with the average annual returns in column 1. As with the standard deviations in column 2, higher returns are associated with higher coefficients of variation.

Example

When the standard deviations (from Table 5) and the expected returns (from Table 4) for assets A and B are substituted into Equation 4, the coefficients of variation for A and B are 0.094 (1.41% ÷ 15%) and 0.377 (5.66% ÷ 15%), respectively. Asset B has the higher coefficient of variation and is therefore more risky than asset A—which we already know from the standard deviation. (Because both assets have the same expected return, the coefficient of variation has not provided any new information.)

The real utility of the coefficient of variation comes in comparing the risks of assets that have *different* expected returns.

Example

A firm wants to select the less risky of two alternative assets—C and D. The expected return, standard deviation, and coefficient of variation for each of these assets' returns are

Statistics	Asset C	Asset D
(1) Expected return	12%	20%
(2) Standard deviation	9%[a]	10%
(3) Coefficient of variation [(2) ÷ (1)]	0.75	0.50[a]

[a]Preferred asset using the given risk measure.

Judging solely on the basis of their standard deviations, the firm would prefer asset C, which has a lower standard deviation than asset D (9% versus 10%). However, management would be making a serious error in choosing asset C over asset D, because the dispersion—the risk—of the asset, as reflected in the coefficient of variation, is lower for D (0.50) than for C (0.75). Clearly, using the coefficient of variation to compare asset risk is effective because it also considers the relative size, or expected return, of the assets.

Personal Finance Example   Marilyn Ansbro is reviewing stocks for inclusion in her investment portfolio. The stock she wishes to analyze is Danhaus Industries, Inc. (DII), a diversified manufacturer of pet products. One of her key concerns is risk; as a rule she will invest only in stocks with a coefficient of variation of returns below 0.75. She has gathered price and dividend data shown below for DII over the past 3 years, 2007–2009, and assumes that each year's return is equally probable.

| | Stock Price | | |
Year	Beginning	End	Dividend paid
2007	$35.00	$36.50	$3.50
2008	36.50	34.50	3.50
2009	34.50	35.00	4.00

Substituting the price and dividend data for each year into Equation 1, we get:

Year	Returns
2007	[$3.50 + ($36.50 − $35.00)]/$35.00 = $5.00 / $35.00 = 14.3%
2008	[$3.50 + ($34.50 − $36.50)]/$36.50 = $1.50 / $36.50 = 4.1%
2009	[$4.00 + ($35.00 − $34.50)]/$34.50 = $4.50 / $34.50 = 13.0%

Substituting into Equation 2a, given that the returns are equally probable, we get the average return, $\bar{r}_{2007-2009}$:

$$\bar{r}_{2007-2009} = (14.3\% + 4.1\% + 13.0\%)/3 = \mathbf{10.5\%}$$

Substituting the average return and annual returns into Equation 3a, we get the standard deviation, $\sigma_{r2007-2009}$:

$$\sigma_{r2007-2009} = \sqrt{[(14.3\% - 10.5\%)^2 + (4.1\% - 10.5\%)^2 + (13.0\% - 10.5\%)^2]/(3-1)}$$

$$= \sqrt{(14.44\% + 40.96\% + 6.25\%)/2} = \sqrt{30.825\%} = 5.6\%$$

Finally, substituting the standard deviation of returns and the average return into Equation 4, we get the coefficient of variation, CV:

$$CV = 5.6\%/10.5\% = \mathbf{0.53}$$

Because the coefficient of variation of returns on the DII stock over the 2007–2009 period of 0.53 is well below Marilyn's maximum coefficient of variation of 0.75, she concludes that the DII stock would be an acceptable investment.

REVIEW QUESTIONS

efficient portfolio
A portfolio that maximizes return for a given level of risk or minimizes risk for a given level of return.

correlation
A statistical measure of the relationship between any two series of numbers representing data of any kind.

4   Explain how the *range* is used in scenario analysis.
5   What does a plot of the *probability distribution* of outcomes show a decision maker about an asset's risk?
6   What relationship exists between the size of the *standard deviation* and the degree of asset risk?
7   When is the *coefficient of variation* preferred over the standard deviation for comparing asset risk?

3 | Risk of a Portfolio

In real-world situations, the risk of any single investment would not be viewed independently of other assets. (We did so for teaching purposes.) New investments must be considered in light of their impact on the risk and return of the *portfolio* of assets. The financial manager's goal is to create an **efficient portfolio,** one that maximizes return for a given level of risk or minimizes risk for a given level of return. First, we will look at the statistical concept of *correlation,* which underlies the process of diversification that is used to develop an efficient portfolio.

positively correlated
Describes two series that move in the same direction.

negatively correlated
Describes two series that move in opposite directions.

correlation coefficient
A measure of the degree of correlation between two series.

perfectly positively correlated
Describes two *positively correlated* series that have a *correlation coefficient* of +1.

perfectly negatively correlated
Describes two *negatively correlated* series that have a *correlation coefficient* of −1.

Correlation

Correlation is a statistical measure of the relationship between any two series of numbers. The numbers may represent data of any kind, from returns to test scores. If two series move in the same direction, they are **positively correlated.** If the series move in opposite directions, they are **negatively correlated.**

The degree of correlation is measured by the **correlation coefficient,** which ranges from +1 for **perfectly positively correlated** series to −1 for **perfectly negatively correlated** series. These two extremes are depicted for series M and N in Figure 3. The perfectly positively correlated series move exactly together; the perfectly negatively correlated series move in exactly opposite directions.

FIGURE 3	
Correlations The correlation between series M and series N	

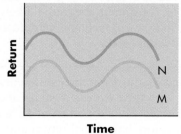

Perfectly Positively Correlated

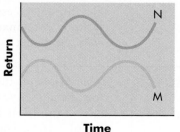

Perfectly Negatively Correlated

FIGURE 4

Diversification
Combining negatively
correlated assets to reduce,
or diversify, risk

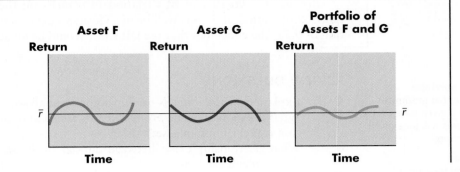

Diversification

The concept of correlation is essential to developing an efficient portfolio. To reduce overall risk, it is best to *diversify* by combining, or adding to the portfolio, assets that have a negative (or a low positive) correlation. Combining negatively correlated assets can reduce the overall variability of returns. Figure 4 shows that a portfolio containing the negatively correlated assets F and G, both of which have the same expected return, $\bar{r}$, also has that same return $\bar{r}$ but has less risk (variability) than either of the individual assets. Even if assets are not negatively correlated, the lower the positive correlation between them, the lower the resulting risk.

uncorrelated
Describes two series that lack
any interaction and therefore
have a *correlation coefficient*
close to zero.

Some assets are **uncorrelated**—that is, there is no interaction between their returns. Combining uncorrelated assets can reduce risk, not so effectively as combining negatively correlated assets, but more effectively than combining positively correlated assets. The *correlation coefficient for uncorrelated assets is close to zero* and acts as the midpoint between perfect positive and perfect negative correlation.

The creation of a portfolio that combines two assets with perfectly positively correlated returns results in overall portfolio risk that at minimum equals that of the least risky asset and at maximum equals that of the most risky asset. However, a portfolio combining two assets with less than perfectly positive correlation *can* reduce total risk to a level below that of either of the components, which in certain situations may be zero. For example, assume that you manufacture machine tools. The business is very *cyclical,* with high sales when the economy is expanding and low sales during a recession. If you acquired another machine-tool company, with sales positively correlated with those of your firm, the combined sales would still be cyclical and risk would remain the same. Alternatively, however, you could acquire a sewing machine manufacturer, whose sales are *countercyclical.* It typically has low sales during economic expansion and high sales during recession (when consumers are more likely to make their own clothes). Combination with the sewing machine manufacturer, which has negatively correlated sales, should reduce risk.

Example

Table 7 presents the forecasted returns from three different assets—X, Y, and Z— over the next 5 years, along with their expected values and standard deviations. Each of the assets has an expected value of return of 12% and a standard deviation of 3.16%. The assets therefore have equal return and equal risk. The return

| TABLE 7 | **Forecasted Returns, Expected Values, and Standard Deviations for Assets X, Y, and Z and Portfolios XY and XZ** |

	Assets			Portfolios	
Year	X	Y	Z	XY[a] (50% X + 50% Y)	XZ[b] (50% X + 50% Z)
2010	8%	16%	8%	12%	8%
2011	10	14	10	12	10
2012	12	12	12	12	12
2013	14	10	14	12	14
2014	16	8	16	12	16
Statistics:[c]					
Expected value	12%	12%	12%	12%	12%
Standard deviation[d]	3.16%	3.16%	3.16%	0%	3.16%

[a]Portfolio XY, which consists of 50% of asset X and 50% of asset Y, illustrates *perfect negative correlation* because these two return streams behave in completely opposite fashion over the 5-year period. Its return values are calculated as shown in the following table.

	Forecasted return			Expected portfolio
Year	Asset X (1)	Asset Y (2)	Portfolio return calculation[a] (3)	return, r_p (4)
2010	8%	16%	$(.50 \times 8\%) + (.50 \times 16\%) =$	12%
2011	10	14	$(.50 \times 10\%) + (.50 \times 14\%) =$	12
2012	12	12	$(.50 \times 12\%) + (.50 \times 12\%) =$	12
2013	14	10	$(.50 \times 14\%) + (.50 \times 10\%) =$	12
2014	16	8	$(.50 \times 16\%) + (.50 \times 8\%) =$	12

[b]Portfolio XZ, which consists of 50% of asset X and 50% of asset Z, illustrates *perfect positive correlation* because these two return streams behave identically over the 5-year period. Its return values are calculated using the same method demonstrated in note *a* above for portfolio XY.

[c]Because the probabilities associated with the returns are not given, the general equation, Equation 2a in footnote 1, is used to calculate expected values as demonstrated below for portfolio XY.

$$\bar{r}_{xy} = \frac{12\% + 12\% + 12\% + 12\% + 12\%}{5} = \frac{60\%}{5} = \underline{\underline{12\%}}$$

The same formula is applied to find the expected value of return for assets X, Y, and Z, and portfolio XZ.

[d]The portfolio standard deviations can be directly calculated from the standard deviations of the component assets with the following formula:

$$\sigma_{r_p} = \sqrt{w_1^2 \sigma_1^2 + w_2^2 \sigma_2^2 + 2w_1 w_2 c_{1,2} \sigma_1 \sigma_2}$$

where w_1 and w_2 are the proportions of component assets 1 and 2, σ_1 and σ_2 are the standard deviations of component assets 1 and 2, and $c_{1,2}$ is the correlation coefficient between the returns of component assets 1 and 2.

patterns of assets X and Y are perfectly negatively correlated. They move in exactly opposite directions over time. The returns of assets X and Z are perfectly positively correlated. They move in precisely the same direction. (*Note:* The returns for X and Z are identical.)[3]

Portfolio XY Portfolio XY (shown in Table 7) is created by combining equal portions of assets X and Y, the perfectly negatively correlated assets.[4] The risk in this portfolio, as reflected by its standard deviation, is reduced to 0%, whereas the expected return remains at 12%. Thus the combination results in the complete elimination of risk. Whenever assets are perfectly negatively correlated, an optimal combination (similar to the 50–50 mix in the case of assets X and Y) exists for which the resulting standard deviation will equal 0.

Portfolio XZ Portfolio XZ (shown in Table 7) is created by combining equal portions of assets X and Z, the perfectly positively correlated assets. The risk in this portfolio, as reflected by its standard deviation, is unaffected by this combination. Risk remains at 3.16%, and the expected return value remains at 12%. Because assets X and Z have the same standard deviation, the minimum and maximum standard deviations are the same (3.16%).

Correlation, Diversification, Risk, and Return

Hint Remember, low correlation between two series of numbers is less positive and more negative—indicating greater dissimilarity of behavior of the two series.

In general, the lower the correlation between asset returns, the greater the potential diversification of risk. (This should be clear from the behaviors illustrated in Table 7.) For each pair of assets, there is a combination that will result in the lowest risk (standard deviation) possible. The amount that risk can be reduced by this combination depends on the degree of correlation. Many potential combinations (assuming divisibility) could be made, but only one combination of the infinite number of possibilities will minimize risk.

Three possible correlations—perfect positive, uncorrelated, and perfect negative—illustrate the effect of correlation on the diversification of risk and return. Table 8 summarizes the impact of correlation on the range of return and risk for various two-asset portfolio combinations. The table shows that as we move from perfect positive correlation to uncorrelated assets to perfect negative correlation, the ability to reduce risk is improved. Note that in no case will a portfolio of assets be riskier than the riskiest asset included in the portfolio. Further discussion of these relationships can be found at the text's website.

International Diversification

The ultimate example of portfolio diversification involves including foreign assets in a portfolio. The inclusion of assets from countries with business cycles that are not highly correlated with the U.S. business cycle reduces the portfolio's responsiveness to market movements and to foreign currency fluctuations.

---

3. Identical return streams are used in this example to permit clear illustration of the concepts, but it is *not* necessary for return streams to be identical for them to be perfectly positively correlated. Any return streams that move (i.e., vary) exactly together—regardless of the relative magnitude of the returns—are perfectly positively correlated.

4. For illustrative purposes it has been assumed that each of the assets—X, Y, and Z—can be divided up and combined with other assets to create portfolios. This assumption is made only to permit clear illustration of the concepts. The assets are not actually divisible.

TABLE 8	Correlation, Return, and Risk for Various Two-Asset Portfolio Combinations	
Correlation coefficient	**Ranges of return**	**Ranges of risk**
+1 (perfect positive)	Between returns of two assets held in isolation	Between risk of two assets held in isolation
0 (uncorrelated)	Between returns of two assets held in isolation	Between risk of most risky asset and an amount less than risk of least risky asset but greater than 0
−1 (perfect negative)	Between returns of two assets held in isolation	Between risk of most risky asset and 0

Returns from International Diversification

Over long periods, returns from internationally diversified portfolios tend to be superior to those of purely domestic ones. This is particularly so if the U.S. economy is performing relatively poorly and the dollar is depreciating in value against most foreign currencies. At such times, the dollar returns to U.S. investors on a portfolio of foreign assets can be very attractive. However, over any single short or intermediate period, international diversification can yield subpar returns, particularly when the dollar is appreciating in value relative to other currencies. When the U.S. currency gains in value, the dollar value of a foreign-currency-denominated portfolio of assets declines. Even if this portfolio yields a satisfactory return in local currency, the return to U.S. investors will be reduced when translated into dollars. Subpar local currency portfolio returns, coupled with an appreciating dollar, can yield truly dismal dollar returns to U.S. investors.

Overall, though, the logic of international portfolio diversification assumes that these fluctuations in currency values and relative performance will average out over long periods. Compared to similar, purely domestic portfolios, an internationally diversified portfolio will tend to yield a comparable return at a lower level of risk.

Risks of International Diversification

political risk
Risk that arises from the possibility that a host government will take actions harmful to foreign investors or that political turmoil will endanger investments.

In addition to the risk induced by currency fluctuations, several other financial risks are unique to international investing. Most important is **political risk,** which arises from the possibility that a host government will take actions harmful to foreign investors or that political turmoil will endanger investments. Political risks are particularly acute in developing countries, where unstable or ideologically motivated governments may attempt to block return of profits by foreign investors or even seize (nationalize) their assets in the host country. For example, reflecting President Chavez's desire to broaden the country's socialist revolution, Venezuela issued a list of priority goods for import that excluded a large percentage of the necessary inputs to the automobile production process. As a result, Toyota halted auto production in Venezuela, and three other auto manufacturers temporarily closed or deeply cut their production there. Chavez also has forced most foreign energy firms to reduce their stakes and give up control of oil projects in Venezuela.

Even where governments do not impose exchange controls or seize assets, international investors may suffer if a shortage of hard currency prevents payment of dividends or interest to foreigners. When governments are forced to allocate scarce foreign exchange, they rarely give top priority to the interests of foreign investors. Instead, hard-currency reserves are typically used to pay for necessary imports such as food, medicine, and industrial materials and to pay interest on the government's debt. Because most of the debt of developing countries is held by banks rather than individuals, foreign investors are often badly harmed when a country experiences political or economic problems.

REVIEW QUESTIONS

8 Why must assets be evaluated in a portfolio context?

9 Why is the *correlation* between asset returns important? How does diversification allow risky assets to be combined so that the risk of the portfolio is less than the risk of the individual assets in it?

10 How does international diversification enhance risk reduction? When might international diversification result in subpar returns? What are *political risks,* and how do they affect international diversification?

4 | Risk and Return: The Capital Asset Pricing Model (CAPM)

capital asset pricing model (CAPM)
The basic theory that links risk and return for all assets.

The most important aspect of risk is the *overall risk* of the firm as viewed by investors in the marketplace. Overall risk significantly affects investment opportunities and—even more important—the owners' wealth. The basic theory that links risk and return for all assets is the **capital asset pricing model (CAPM).**[5] We will use CAPM to understand the basic risk–return tradeoffs involved in all types of financial decisions.

Types of Risk

To understand the basic types of risk, consider what happens to the risk of a portfolio consisting of a single security (asset), to which we add securities randomly selected from, say, the population of all actively traded securities. Using the standard deviation of return, s_{r_p}, to measure the total portfolio risk, Figure 5 depicts the behavior of the total portfolio risk (y axis) as more securities are added (x axis). With the addition of securities, the total portfolio risk declines, as a result of the effects of diversification, and tends to approach a lower limit. Research has shown that, on average, most of the risk-reduction benefits of diversification can be gained by forming portfolios containing 15 to 20 randomly selected securities.

5. The initial development of this theory is generally attributed to William F. Sharpe, "Capital Asset Prices: A Theory of Market Equilibrium Under Conditions of Risk," *Journal of Finance* 19 (September 1964), pp. 425–442, and John Lintner, "The Valuation of Risk Assets and the Selection of Risky Investments in Stock Portfolios and Capital Budgets," *Review of Economics and Statistics* 47 (February 1965), pp. 13–37. A number of authors subsequently advanced, refined, and tested this now widely accepted theory.

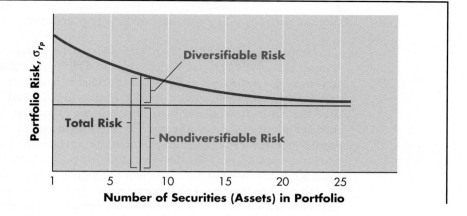

FIGURE 5

Risk Reduction
Portfolio risk and diversification

(Graph: vertical axis labeled "Portfolio Risk, σ_{r_p}"; horizontal axis labeled "Number of Securities (Assets) in Portfolio" with markings at 1, 5, 10, 15, 20, 25. Curve labeled "Diversifiable Risk", with "Total Risk" and "Nondiversifiable Risk" bracketed.)

The **total risk** of a security can be viewed as consisting of two parts:

$$\text{Total security risk} = \text{Nondiversifiable risk} + \text{Diversifiable risk} \tag{5}$$

Diversifiable risk (sometimes called *unsystematic risk*) represents the portion of an asset's risk that is associated with random causes that can be eliminated through diversification. It is attributable to firm-specific events, such as strikes, lawsuits, regulatory actions, and loss of a key account. **Nondiversifiable risk** (also called *systematic risk*) is attributable to market factors that affect all firms; it cannot be eliminated through diversification. (It is the shareholder-specific *market risk* described in Table 1.) Factors such as war, inflation, international incidents, and political events account for nondiversifiable risk.

Because any investor can create a portfolio of assets that will eliminate virtually all diversifiable risk, *the only relevant risk is nondiversifiable risk*. Any investor or firm therefore must be concerned solely with nondiversifiable risk. The measurement of nondiversifiable risk is thus of primary importance in selecting assets with the most desired risk–return characteristics.

The Model: CAPM

The capital asset pricing model (CAPM) links nondiversifiable risk and return for all assets. We will discuss the model in four sections. The first deals with the beta coefficient, which is a measure of nondiversifiable risk. The second section presents an equation of the model itself, and the third graphically describes the relationship between risk and return. The final section offers some comments on the CAPM.

Beta Coefficient

The **beta coefficient,** *b,* is a relative measure of nondiversifiable risk. It is an *index* of the degree of movement of an asset's return in response to a change in the *market return*. An asset's historical returns are used in finding the asset's beta coefficient. The **market return** is the return on the market portfolio of all traded securities. The *Standard & Poor's 500 Stock Composite Index* or some similar stock index is commonly used as the market return. Betas for actively traded stocks can be obtained from a variety of sources, but you should understand how they are derived and interpreted and how they are applied to portfolios.

Deriving Beta from Return Data   An asset's historical returns are used in finding the asset's beta coefficient. Figure 6 plots the relationship between the returns of two assets—R and S—and the market return. Note that the horizontal (*x*) axis measures the historical market returns and that the vertical (*y*) axis measures the individual asset's historical returns. The first step in deriving beta involves plotting the coordinates for the market return and asset returns from various points in time. Such annual "market return–asset return" coordinates are shown *for asset S only* for the years 2002 through 2009. For example, in 2009, asset S's return was 20 percent when the market return was 10 percent. By use of statistical techniques, the "characteristic line" that best explains the relationship between the asset return and the market return coordinates is fit to the data points. The slope of this line is *beta*. The beta for asset R is about .80 and that for asset S is about 1.30. Asset S's higher beta (steeper characteristic line slope) indicates that its return is more responsive to changing market returns. *Therefore asset S is more risky than asset R.*

Interpreting Betas   The beta coefficient for the market is considered to be equal to 1.0. All other betas are viewed in relation to this value. Asset betas may be positive or negative, but positive betas are the norm. The majority of beta coefficients fall between .5 and 2.0. The return of a stock that is half as responsive as the market ($b = .5$) is expected to change by .5 percent for each 1 percent

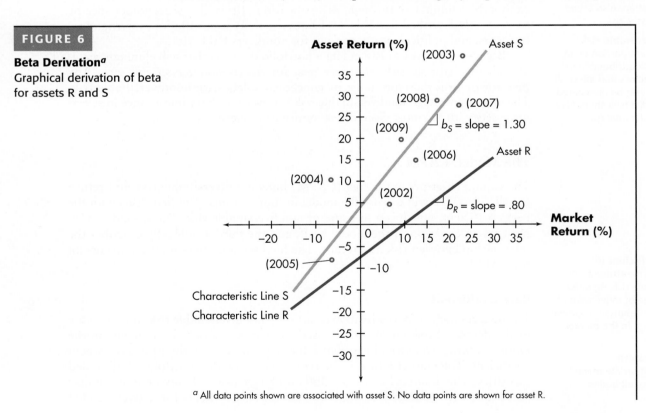

FIGURE 6

Beta Derivation*a*
Graphical derivation of beta
for assets R and S

a All data points shown are associated with asset S. No data points are shown for asset R.

TABLE 9	Selected Beta Coefficients and Their Interpretations	
Beta	Comment	Interpretation
2.0	Move in same direction as market	Twice as responsive as the market
1.0		Same response as the market
.5		Only half as responsive as the market
0		Unaffected by market movement
− .5	Move in opposite direction to market	Only half as responsive as the market
−1.0		Same response as the market
−2.0		Twice as responsive as the market

Hint Remember that published betas are calculated using historical data. When investors use beta for decision making, they should recognize that past performance relative to the market average may not accurately predict future performance.

change in the return of the market portfolio. A stock that is twice as responsive as the market ($b = 2.0$) is expected to experience a 2 percent change in its return for each 1 percent change in the return of the market portfolio. Table 9 provides various beta values and their interpretations. Beta coefficients for actively traded stocks can be obtained from published sources such as *Value Line Investment Survey,* via the Internet, or through brokerage firms. Betas for some selected stocks are given in Table 10.

Portfolio Betas The beta of a portfolio can be easily estimated by using the betas of the individual assets it includes. Letting w_j represent the proportion of the portfolio's total dollar value represented by asset j, and letting b_j equal the beta of asset j, we can use Equation 6 to find the portfolio beta, b_p:

$$b_p = (w_1 \times b_1) + (w_2 \times b_2) + \cdots + (w_n \times b_n) = \sum_{j=1}^{n} w_j \times b_j \qquad (6)$$

Of course, $\sum_{j=1}^{n} w_j = 1$, which means that 100 percent of the portfolio's assets must be included in this computation.

TABLE 10	Beta Coefficients for Selected Stocks (July 10, 2007)		
Stock	Beta	Stock	Beta
Amazon.com	1.20	JP Morgan Chase & Co.	1.40
Anheuser-Busch	.65	Merrill Lynch & Co.	1.35
DaimlerChrysler AG	1.30	Microsoft	.95
Disney	1.30	Nike, Inc.	.85
eBay	1.10	PepsiCo, Inc.	.75
ExxonMobil Corp.	.90	Qualcomm	1.00
Gap (The), Inc.	.95	Sempra Energy	1.05
General Electric	1.10	Wal-Mart Stores	.75
Intel	1.15	Xerox	1.40
Int'l Business Machines	1.05	Yahoo! Inc.	1.40

Source: Value Line Investment Survey (New York: Value Line Publishing, July 20, 2007).

Hint Mutual fund managers are key users of the portfolio beta and return concepts. They are continually evaluating what would happen to the fund's beta and return if the securities of a particular firm were added to or deleted from the fund's portfolio.

Portfolio betas are interpreted in the same way as the betas of individual assets. They indicate the degree of responsiveness of the *portfolio's* return to changes in the market return. For example, when the market return increases by 10 percent, a portfolio with a beta of .75 will experience a 7.5 percent increase in its return ($.75 \times 10\%$); a portfolio with a beta of 1.25 will experience a 12.5 percent increase in its return ($1.25 \times 10\%$). Clearly, a portfolio containing mostly low-beta assets will have a low beta, and one containing mostly high-beta assets will have a high beta.

Personal Finance Example   Mario Austino, an individual investor, wishes to assess the risk of two small portfolios he is considering—V and W. Both portfolios contain five assets, with the proportions and betas shown in Table 11. The betas for the two portfolios, b_v and b_w, can be calculated by substituting data from the table into Equation 7:

$$b_v = (.10 \times 1.65) + (.30 \times 1.00) + (.20 \times 1.30) + (.20 \times 1.10) + (.20 \times 1.25)$$
$$= .165 + .300 + .260 + .220 + .250 = 1.195 \approx \underline{\underline{1.20}}$$

$$b_w = (.10 \times .80) + (.10 \times 1.00) + (.20 \times .65) + (.10 \times .75) + (.50 \times 1.05)$$
$$= .080 + .100 + .130 + .075 + .525 = \underline{\underline{.91}}$$

Portfolio V's beta is about 1.20, and portfolio W's is .91. These values make sense, because portfolio V contains relatively high-beta assets, and portfolio W contains relatively low-beta assets. Mario's calculations show that portfolio V's returns are more responsive to changes in market returns and are therefore more risky than portfolio W's. He must now decide which, if either, portfolio he feels comfortable adding to his existing investments.

The Equation

Using the beta coefficient to measure nondiversifiable risk, the *capital asset pricing model (CAPM)* is given in Equation 7:

$$r_j = R_F + [b_j \times (r_m - R_F)] \tag{7}$$

TABLE 11	**Mario Austino's Portfolios V and W**			
	Portfolio V		Portfolio W	
Asset	Proportion	Beta	Proportion	Beta
1	.10	1.65	.10	.80
2	.30	1.00	.10	1.00
3	.20	1.30	.20	.65
4	.20	1.10	.10	.75
5	.20	1.25	.50	1.05
Totals	1.00		1.00	

where

r_j = required return on asset j

R_F = risk-free rate of return, commonly measured by the return
on a U.S. Treasury bill

b_j = beta coefficient or index of nondiversifiable risk for asset j

r_m = market return; return on the market portfolio of assets

risk-free rate of return, (R_F)
The required return on a *risk-free asset,* typically a 3-month U.S. Treasury bill.

U.S. Treasury bills (T-bills)
Short-term IOUs issued by the U.S. Treasury; considered the *risk-free asset.*

The CAPM can be divided into two parts: (1) the **risk-free rate of return, R_F,** which is the required return on a *risk-free asset,* typically a 3-month **U.S. Treasury bill (T-bill)**, a short-term IOU issued by the U.S. Treasury, and (2) the *risk premium.* These are, respectively, the two elements on either side of the plus sign in Equation 7. The $(r_m - R_F)$ portion of the risk premium is called the *market risk premium,* because it represents the premium the investor must receive for taking the average amount of risk associated with holding the market portfolio of assets.[6]

Historical Risk Premiums Using the historical return data for selected security investments for the 1926–2006 period shown in Table 2, we can calculate the risk premiums for each investment category. The calculation (consistent with Equation 7) involves merely subtracting the historical U.S. Treasury bill's average return from the historical average return for a given investment:

Investment	Risk premium[a]		
Large-company stocks	12.3%	− 3.8% =	8.5%
Small company stocks	17.4	− 3.8	= 13.6
Long-term corporate bonds	6.2	− 3.8	= 2.4
Long-term government bonds	5.8	− 3.8	= 2.0
U.S. Treasury bills	3.8	− 3.8	= 0.0

[a]Return values obtained from Table 2.

Reviewing the risk premiums calculated above, we can see that the risk premium is highest for small-company stocks, followed by large-company stocks, long-term corporate bonds, and long-term government bonds. This outcome makes sense intuitively because small-company stocks are riskier than large-company stocks, which are riskier than long-term corporate bonds (equity is riskier than debt investment). Long-term corporate bonds are riskier than long-term government bonds (because the government is less likely to renege on debt). And of course, U.S. Treasury bills, because of their lack of default risk and their very short maturity, are virtually risk-free, as indicated by their lack of any risk premium.

---

6. Although CAPM has been widely accepted, a broader theory, *arbitrage pricing theory (APT),* first described by Stephen A. Ross, "The Arbitrage Theory of Capital Asset Pricing," *Journal of Economic Theory* (December 1976), pp. 341–360, has received a great deal of attention in the financial literature. The theory suggests that the risk premium on securities may be better explained by a number of factors underlying and in place of the market return used in CAPM. The CAPM in effect can be viewed as being derived from APT. Although testing of APT confirms the importance of the market return, it has thus far failed to identify other risk factors clearly. As a result of this failure, as well as APT's lack of practical acceptance and usage, we concentrate our attention here on CAPM.

Example

Benjamin Corporation, a growing computer software developer, wishes to determine the required return on an asset Z, which has a beta of 1.5. The risk-free rate of return is 7%; the return on the market portfolio of assets is 11%. Substituting $b_Z = 1.5$, $R_F = 7\%$, and $r_m = 11\%$ into the capital asset pricing model given in Equation 7 yields a required return of

$$r_Z = 7\% + [1.5 \times (11\% - 7\%)] = 7\% + 6\% = \underline{\underline{13\%}}$$

The market risk premium of 4% ($11\% - 7\%$), when adjusted for the asset's index of risk (beta) of 1.5, results in a risk premium of 6% ($1.5 \times 4\%$). That risk premium, when added to the 7% risk-free rate, results in a 13% required return.

Other things being equal, *the higher the beta, the higher the required return, and the lower the beta, the lower the required return.*

The Graph: The Security Market Line (SML)

security market line (SML)
The depiction of the *capital asset pricing model* (*CAPM*) as a graph that reflects the required return in the marketplace for each level of nondiversifiable risk (beta).

When the capital asset pricing model (Equation 7) is depicted graphically, it is called the **security market line** (SML). The SML will, in fact, be a straight line. It reflects the required return in the marketplace for each level of nondiversifiable risk (beta). In the graph, risk as measured by beta, b, is plotted on the x axis, and required returns, r, are plotted on the y axis. The risk–return tradeoff is clearly represented by the SML.

Example

In the preceding example for Benjamin Corporation, the risk-free rate, R_F, was 7%, and the market return, r_m, was 11%. The SML can be plotted by using the two sets of coordinates for the betas associated with R_F and r_m, b_{R_F} and b_m (that is, $b_{R_F} = 0$,[7] $R_F = 7\%$; and $b_m = 1.0$, $r_m = 11\%$). Figure 7 presents the resulting security market line. As traditionally shown, the security market line in Figure 7 presents the required return associated with all positive betas. The market risk premium of 4% (r_m of 11% − R_F of 7%) has been highlighted. For a beta for asset Z, b_Z, of 1.5, its corresponding required return, r_Z, is 13%. Also shown in the figure is asset Z's risk premium of 6% (r_Z of 13% − R_F of 7%). It should be clear that for assets with betas greater than 1, the risk premium is greater than that for the market; for assets with betas less than 1, the risk premium is less than that for the market.

Some Comments on CAPM

The capital asset pricing model generally relies on historical data. The betas may or may not actually reflect the *future* variability of returns. Therefore, the required returns specified by the model can be viewed only as rough approximations. Users of betas commonly make subjective adjustments to the historically determined betas to reflect their expectations of the future.

The CAPM was developed to explain the behavior of security prices and provide a mechanism whereby investors could assess the impact of a proposed security investment on their portfolio's overall risk and return. It is based on an

---

7. Because R_F is the rate of return on a risk-free asset, the beta associated with the risk-free asset, b_{R_F}, would equal 0. The zero beta on the risk-free asset reflects not only its absence of risk but also that the asset's return is unaffected by movements in the market return.

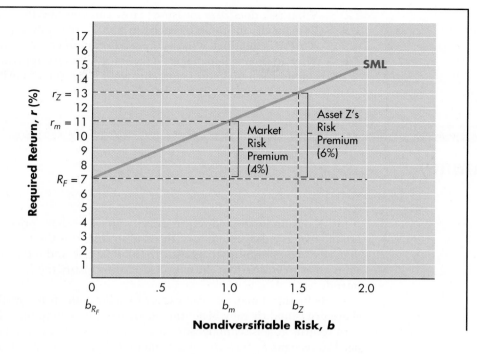

FIGURE 7

Security Market Line
Security market line (SML) with Benjamin Corporation's asset Z data shown

assumed **efficient market** with the following characteristics: many small investors, all having the same information and expectations with respect to securities; no restrictions on investment, no taxes, and no transaction costs; and rational investors, who view securities similarly and are risk-averse, preferring higher returns and lower risk.

Although the perfect world of the efficient market appears to be unrealistic, studies have provided support for the existence of the expectational relationship described by CAPM in active markets such as the New York Stock Exchange.[8] In the case of real corporate assets, such as plant and equipment, research thus far has failed to prove the general applicability of CAPM because of indivisibility, relatively large size, limited number of transactions, and absence of an efficient market for such assets.

Despite the limitations of CAPM, it provides a useful conceptual framework for evaluating and linking risk and return. An awareness of this tradeoff and an attempt to consider risk as well as return in financial decision making should help financial managers achieve their goals.

REVIEW QUESTIONS

11   How are total risk, nondiversifiable risk, and diversifiable risk related? Why is nondiversifiable risk the *only relevant risk*?

---

8. A study by Eugene F. Fama and Kenneth R. French, "The Cross-Section of Expected Stock Returns," *Journal of Finance* 47 (June 1992), pp. 427–465, raised serious questions about the validity of CAPM. The study failed to find a significant relationship between the *historical* betas and *historical* returns on over 2,000 stocks during 1963–1990. In other words, it found that the magnitude of a stock's *historical* beta had no relationship to the level of its *historical* return. Although Fama and French's study continues to receive attention, CAPM has not been abandoned because its rejection as a *historical* model fails to discredit its validity as an *expectational* model. Therefore, in spite of this challenge, CAPM continues to be viewed as a logical and useful framework—both conceptually and operationally—for linking *expected* nondiversifiable risk and return.

12   What risk does *beta* measure? How can you find the beta of a portfolio?
13   Explain the meaning of each variable in the *capital asset pricing model (CAPM)* equation. What is the *security market line (SML)?*
14   Why do financial managers have some difficulty applying CAPM in financial decision making? Generally, what benefit does CAPM provide them?

Summary

Focus on Value

A firm's risk and expected return directly affect its share price. Risk and return are the two key determinants of the firm's value. It is therefore the financial manager's responsibility to assess carefully the risk and return of all major decisions so as to ensure that the expected returns justify the level of risk being introduced.

The financial manager can expect to achieve **the firm's goal of increasing its share price** (and thereby benefiting its owners) by taking only those actions that earn returns at least commensurate with their risk. Clearly, financial managers need to recognize, measure, and evaluate risk–return tradeoffs to ensure that their decisions contribute to the creation of value for owners.

Review of Learning Goals

Key definitions and formulas for this chapter are summarized in Table 12.

LG 1 **Understand the meaning and fundamentals of risk, return, and risk preferences.** Risk is the chance of loss or, more formally, the variability of returns. A number of sources of firm-specific and shareholder-specific risks exist. Return is any cash distributions plus the change in value over a given period of time expressed as a percentage of the initial value. Investment returns vary both over time and between different types of investments. Most financial decision makers are risk-averse. They require higher expected returns in exchange for greater risk.

LG 2 **Describe procedures for assessing and measuring the risk of a single asset.** The risk of a single asset is measured in much the same way as the risk of a portfolio of assets. Scenario analysis and probability distributions can be used to assess risk. The range, the standard deviation, and the coefficient of variation can be used to measure risk quantitatively.

LG 3 **Discuss risk measurement for a single asset using the standard deviation and coefficient of variation.** In addition to the range, which is the optimistic (best) outcome minus the pessimistic (worst) outcome, the standard deviation and the coefficient of variation can be used to measure risk quantitatively. The standard deviation measures the dispersion around an asset's expected value, and the coefficient of variation uses the standard deviation to measure dispersion on a relative basis.

TABLE 12	Summary of Key Definitions and Formulas for Risk and Return

Definitions of variables

b_j = beta coefficient or index of nondiversifiable risk for asset j

b_p = portfolio beta

C_t = cash received from the asset investment in the time period $t-1$ to t

CV = coefficient of variation

$\bar{r}$ = expected value of a return

r_j = return for the jth outcome; return on asset j; required return on asset j

r_m = market return; the return on the market portfolio of assets

r_p = portfolio return

r_t = actual, expected, or required rate of return during period t

n = number of outcomes considered

P_t = price (value) of asset at time t

P_{t-1} = price (value) of asset at time $t-1$

Pr_j = probability of occurrence of the jth outcome

R_F = risk-free rate of return

σ_r = standard deviation of returns

w_j = proportion of total portfolio dollar value represented by asset j

Risk and return formulas

Rate of return during period t:

$$r_t = \frac{C_t + P_t - P_{t-1}}{P_{t-1}}$$ [Equation 1]

Expected value of a return:

For probabilistic data:

$$\bar{r} = \sum_{j=1}^{n} r_j \times Pr_j$$ [Equation 2]

General formula:

$$\bar{r} = \frac{\sum_{j=1}^{n} r_j}{n}$$ [Equation 2a]

Standard deviation of return:

For probabilistic data:

$$\sigma_r = \sqrt{\sum_{j=1}^{n} (r_j - \bar{r})^2 \times Pr_j}$$ [Equation 3]

General formula:

$$\sigma_r = \sqrt{\frac{\sum_{j=1}^{n} (r_j - \bar{r})^2}{n-1}}$$ [Equation 3a]

Coefficient of variation:

$$CV = \frac{\sigma_r}{\bar{r}}$$ [Equation 4]

Total security risk = Nondiversifiable risk + Diversifiable risk [Equation 5]

Portfolio beta:

$$b_p = \sum_{j=1}^{n} w_j \times b_j$$ [Equation 6]

Capital asset pricing model (CAPM):

$$r_j = R_F + [b_j \times (r_m - R_F)]$$ [Equation 7]

Understand the risk and return characteristics of a portfolio in terms of correlation and diversification, and the impact of international assets on a portfolio. The financial manager's goal is to create an efficient portfolio that maximizes return for a given level of risk. The risk of a portfolio of assets may be reduced by diversification—combining assets with low correlation to reduce the risk of the portfolio. Correlation, the statistical relationship between asset returns, affects diversification. The more negative (or less positive) the correlation, the greater the risk-reducing benefits.

International diversification can further reduce a portfolio's risk. Foreign assets have the risk of currency fluctuation and political risks.

Review the two types of risk and the derivation and role of beta in measuring the relevant risk of both a security and a portfolio. The total risk of a security consists of nondiversifiable and diversifiable risk. Diversifiable risk can be eliminated through diversification. Nondiversifiable risk is the only relevant risk. Nondiversifiable risk is measured by the beta coefficient, which is a relative measure of the relationship between an asset's return and the market return. Beta is derived by finding the slope of the "characteristic line" that best explains the historical relationship between the asset's return and the market return. The beta of a portfolio is a weighted average of the betas of the individual assets that it includes.

Explain the capital asset pricing model (CAPM) and its relationship to the security market line (SML). The capital asset pricing model (CAPM) uses beta to relate an asset's risk relative to the market to the asset's required return. The graphical depiction of CAPM is the security market line (SML). Although it has some shortcomings, CAPM provides a useful conceptual framework for evaluating and linking risk and return.

Self-Test Problems

ST5–1 **Portfolio analysis** You have been asked for your advice in selecting a portfolio of assets and have been given the following data:

	Expected return		
Year	Asset A	Asset B	Asset C
2010	12%	16%	12%
2011	14	14	14
2012	16	12	16

No probabilities have been supplied. You have been told that you can create two portfolios—one consisting of assets A and B and the other consisting of assets A and C—by investing equal proportions (50%) in each of the two component assets.
a. What is the expected return for each asset over the 3-year period?
b. What is the standard deviation for each asset's return?
c. What is the expected return for each of the two portfolios?

d. How would you characterize the correlations of returns of the two assets making up each of the two portfolios identified in part **c**?

e. What is the standard deviation for each portfolio?

f. Which portfolio do you recommend? Why?

 ST5–2 Beta and CAPM Currently under consideration is a project with a beta, *b*, of 1.50. At this time, the risk-free rate of return, R_F, is 7%, and the return on the market portfolio of assets, r_m, is 10%. The project is actually *expected* to earn an annual rate of return of 11%.

a. If the return on the market portfolio were to increase by 10%, what would you expect to happen to the project's *required return*? What if the market return were to decline by 10%?

b. Use the capital asset pricing model (CAPM) to find the *required return* on this investment.

c. On the basis of your calculation in part **b**, would you recommend this investment? Why or why not?

d. Assume that as a result of investors becoming less risk-averse, the market return drops by 1% to 9%. What impact would this change have on your responses in parts **b** and **c**?

Warm-Up Exercises   A blue box (■) indicates exercises available in 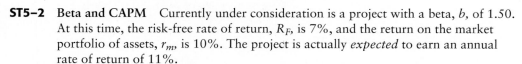.

 E5–1 An analyst predicted last year that the stock of Logistics, Inc., would offer a total return of at least 10% in the coming year. At the beginning of the year, the firm had a stock market value of $10 million. At the end of the year, it had a market value of $12 million even though it experienced a loss, or negative net income, of $2.5 million. Did the analyst's prediction prove correct? Explain using the values for total annual return.

E5–2 Four analysts cover the stock of Fluorine Chemical. One forecasts a 5% return for the coming year. A second expects the return to be negative 5%. A third predicts a 10% return. A fourth expects a 3% return in the coming year. You are relatively confident that the return will be positive but not large, so you arbitrarily assign probabilities of being correct of 35%, 5%, 20%, and 40%, respectively, to the analysts' forecasts. Given these probabilities, what is Fluorine Chemical's *expected return* for the coming year?

E5–3 The expected annual returns are 15% for investment 1 and 12% for investment 2. The standard deviation of the first investment's return is 10%; the second investment's return has a standard deviation of 5%. Which investment is less risky based solely on *standard deviation*? Which investment is less risky based on *coefficient of variation*? Which is a better measure given that the expected returns of the two investments are not the same?

E5–4 Your portfolio has three asset classes. U.S. government T-bills account for 45% of the portfolio, large-company stocks constitute another 40%, and small-company stocks make up the remaining 15%. If the expected returns are 3.8% for the T-bills, 12.3% for the large-company stocks, and 17.4% for the small-company stocks, what is the expected return of the portfolio?

E5–5 You wish to calculate the risk level of your portfolio based on its beta. The five stocks in the portfolio with their respective weights and betas are shown below. Calculate the beta of your portfolio.

Stock	Portfolio weight	Beta
Alpha	20%	1.15
Centauri	10	.85
Zen	15	1.6
Wren	20	1.35
Yukos	35	1.85

  E5–6 a. Calculate the required rate of return for an asset that has a beta of 1.8, given a risk-free rate of 5% and a market return of 10%.

b. If investors have become more risk-averse due to recent geopolitical events, and the market return rises to 13%, what is the required rate of return for the same asset?

c. Use your findings in part **a** to graph the initial *security market line (SML)*.

Problems

A blue box (■) indicates problems available in .

 P5–1 **Rate of return** Douglas Keel, a financial analyst for Orange Industries, wishes to estimate the rate of return for two similar-risk investments, X and Y. Douglas's research indicates that the immediate past returns will serve as reasonable estimates of future returns. A year earlier, investment X had a market value of $20,000; investment Y had a market value of $55,000. During the year, investment X generated cash flow of $1,500 and investment Y generated cash flow of $6,800. The current market values of investments X and Y are $21,000 and $55,000, respectively.

a. Calculate the expected rate of return on investments X and Y using the most recent year's data.

b. Assuming that the two investments are equally risky, which one should Douglas recommend? Why?

 P5–2 **Return calculations** For each of the investments shown in the following table, calculate the rate of return earned over the unspecified time period.

Investment	Cash flow during period	Beginning-of-period value	End-of-period value
A	− $ 100	$ 800	$ 1,100
B	15,000	120,000	118,000
C	7,000	45,000	48,000
D	80	600	500
E	1,500	12,500	12,400

P5–3 **Risk preferences** Sharon Smith, the financial manager for Barnett Corporation, wishes to evaluate three prospective investments: X, Y, and Z. Currently, the firm earns 12% on its investments, which have a risk index of 6%. The expected return and expected risk of the investments are shown below. If Sharon Smith is *risk-averse*, which investments would she select? Why?

Investment	Expected return	Expected risk index
X	14%	7%
Y	12	8
Z	10	9

P5–4 **Risk analysis** Solar Designs is considering an investment in an expanded product line. Two possible types of expansion are being considered. After investigating the possible outcomes, the company made the estimates shown in the following table:

	Expansion A	Expansion B
Initial investment	$12,000	$12,000
Annual rate of return		
Pessimistic	16%	10%
Most likely	20%	20%
Optimistic	24%	30%

a. Determine the *range* of the rates of return for each of the two projects.
b. Which project is less risky? Why?
c. If you were making the investment decision, which one would you choose? Why? What does this imply about your feelings toward risk?
d. Assume that expansion B's most likely outcome is 21% per year and that all other facts remain the same. Does this change your answer to part **c**? Why?

P5–5 **Risk and probability** Micro-Pub, Inc., is considering the purchase of one of two microfilm cameras, R and S. Both should provide benefits over a 10-year period, and each requires an initial investment of $4,000. Management has constructed the following table of estimates of rates of return and probabilities for pessimistic, most likely, and optimistic results.

	Camera R		Camera S	
	Amount	Probability	Amount	Probability
Initial investment	$4,000	1.00	$4,000	1.00
Annual rate of return				
Pessimistic	20%	.25	15%	.20
Most likely	25%	.50	25%	.55
Optimistic	30%	.25	35%	.25

a. Determine the *range* for the rate of return for each of the two cameras.
b. Determine the *expected value* of return for each camera.
c. Purchase of which camera is riskier? Why?

  P5–6 **Bar charts and risk** Swan's Sportswear is considering bringing out a line of designer jeans. Currently, it is negotiating with two different well-known designers. Because of the highly competitive nature of the industry, the two lines of jeans have been given code names. After market research, the firm has established the expectations shown in the following table about the annual rates of return:

		Annual rate of return	
Market acceptance	Probability	Line J	Line K
Very poor	.05	.0075	.010
Poor	.15	.0125	.025
Average	.60	.0850	.080
Good	.15	.1475	.135
Excellent	.05	.1625	.150

Use the table to:
a. Construct a bar chart for each line's annual rate of return.
b. Calculate the *expected value* of return for each line.
c. Evaluate the relative riskiness for each jean line's rate of return using the bar charts.

  P5–7 **Coefficient of variation** Metal Manufacturing has isolated four alternatives for meeting its need for increased production capacity. The following table summarizes data gathered relative to each of these alternatives.

Alternative	Expected return	Standard deviation of return
A	20%	7.0%
B	22	9.5
C	19	6.0
D	16	5.5

a. Calculate the *coefficient of variation* for each alternative.
b. If the firm wishes to minimize risk, which alternative do you recommend? Why?

PERSONAL FINANCE PROBLEM

  P5–8 **Rate of return, standard deviation, coefficient of variation** Mike is searching for a stock to include in his current stock portfolio. He is interested in Apple Inc.; he has been impressed with the company's computer products and believes Apple is an innovative market player. However, Mike realizes that any time you consider a so-called high-tech stock, risk is a major concern. The rule he follows is to include only securities with a coefficient of variation of returns below 0.90.

Mike has obtained the following price information for the period 2006 through 2009. Apple stock, being growth-oriented, did not pay any dividends during these 4 years.

	Stock price	
Year	Beginning	End
2006	$14.36	$21.55
2007	21.55	64.78
2008	64.78	72.38
2009	72.38	91.80

a. Calculate the *rate of return* for each year, 2006 through 2009, for Apple stock.
b. Assume that each year's return is equally probable and calculate the *average return* over this time period.
c. Calculate the *standard deviation* of returns over the past 4 years. (*Hint:* Treat this data as a sample.)
d. Based on **b** and **c** determine the *coefficient of variation* of returns for the security.
e. Given the calculation in **d** what should be Mike's decision regarding the inclusion of Apple stock in his portfolio?

  P5–9 **Assessing return and risk** Swift Manufacturing must choose between two asset purchases. The annual rate of return and the related probabilities given in the following table summarize the firm's analysis to this point.

Project 257		Project 432	
Rate of return	Probability	Rate of return	Probability
−10%	.01	10%	.05
10	.04	15	.10
20	.05	20	.10
30	.10	25	.15
40	.15	30	.20
45	.30	35	.15
50	.15	40	.10
60	.10	45	.10
70	.05	50	.05
80	.04		
100	.01		

a. For each project, compute:
   (1) The range of possible rates of return.
   (2) The expected value of return.
   (3) The standard deviation of the returns.
   (4) The coefficient of variation of the returns.
b. Construct a bar chart of each distribution of rates of return.
c. Which project would you consider less risky? Why?

P5–10 Integrative—Expected return, standard deviation, and coefficient of variation
Three assets—F, G, and H—are currently being considered by Perth Industries.
The probability distributions of expected returns for these assets are shown in the
following table.

	Asset F		Asset G		Asset H	
j	Pr_j	Return, r_j	Pr_j	Return, r_j	Pr_j	Return, r_j
1	.10	40%	.40	35%	.10	40%
2	.20	10	.30	10	.20	20
3	.40	0	.30	−20	.40	10
4	.20	− 5			.20	0
5	.10	−10			.10	−20

a. Calculate the expected value of return, $\bar{r}$, for each of the three assets.
   Which provides the largest expected return?
b. Calculate the standard deviation, s_r, for each of the three assets' returns.
   Which appears to have the greatest risk?
c. Calculate the coefficient of variation, CV, for each of the three assets' returns.
   Which appears to have the greatest *relative* risk?

PERSONAL FINANCE PROBLEM

P5–11 **Portfolio return and standard deviation** Jamie Wong is considering building
an investment portfolio containing two stocks, L and M. Stock L will represent 40%
of the dollar value of the portfolio, and stock M will account for the other 60%.
The expected returns over the next 6 years, 2010–2015, for each of these stocks
are shown in the following table:

	Expected return	
Year	Stock L	Stock M
2010	14%	20%
2011	14	18
2012	16	16
2013	17	14
2014	17	12
2015	19	10

a. Calculate the expected portfolio return, r_p, for *each* of the 6 years.
b. Calculate the expected value of portfolio returns, $\bar{r}_p$, over the 6-year period.
c. Calculate the standard deviation of expected portfolio returns, s_{r_p}, over the
   6-year period.
d. How would you characterize the correlation of returns of the two stocks L
   and M?
e. Discuss any benefits of diversification achieved by Jamie through creation of the
   portfolio.

P5–12 **Portfolio analysis** You have been given the expected return data shown in the first table on three assets—F, G, and H—over the period 2010–2013.

	Expected return		
Year	Asset F	Asset G	Asset H
2010	16%	17%	14%
2011	17	16	15
2012	18	15	16
2013	19	14	17

Using these assets, you have isolated the three investment alternatives shown in the following table:

Alternative	Investment
1	100% of asset F
2	50% of asset F and 50% of asset G
3	50% of asset F and 50% of asset H

a. Calculate the expected return over the 4-year period for each of the three alternatives.
b. Calculate the standard deviation of returns over the 4-year period for each of the three alternatives.
c. Use your findings in parts **a** and **b** to calculate the coefficient of variation for each of the three alternatives.
d. On the basis of your findings, which of the three investment alternatives do you recommend? Why?

P5–13 **Correlation, risk, and return** Matt Peters wishes to evaluate the risk and return behaviors associated with various combinations of assets V and W under three assumed degrees of correlation: perfect positive, uncorrelated, and perfect negative. The expected return and risk values calculated for each of the assets are shown in the following table.

Asset	Expected return, $\bar{r}$	Risk (standard deviation), σ_r
V	8%	5%
W	13	10

a. If the returns of assets V and W are *perfectly positively correlated* (correlation coefficient $= +1$), describe the *range* of (1) expected return and (2) risk associated with all possible portfolio combinations.
b. If the returns of assets V and W are *uncorrelated* (correlation coefficient $= 0$), describe the *approximate range* of (1) expected return and (2) risk associated with all possible portfolio combinations.

c. If the returns of assets V and W are *perfectly negatively correlated* (correlation coefficient = −1), describe the *range* of (1) expected return and (2) risk associated with all possible portfolio combinations.

PERSONAL FINANCE PROBLEM

P5–14 International investment returns   Joe Martinez, a U.S. citizen living in Brownsville, Texas, invested in the common stock of Telmex, a Mexican corporation. He purchased 1,000 shares at 20.50 pesos per share. Twelve months later, he sold them at 24.75 pesos per share. He received no dividends during that time.

  a. What was Joe's investment return (in percentage terms) for the year, on the basis of the peso value of the shares?
  b. The exchange rate for pesos was 9.21 pesos per US$1.00 at the time of the purchase. At the time of the sale, the exchange rate was 9.85 pesos per US$1.00. Translate the purchase and sale prices into US$.
  c. Calculate Joe's investment return on the basis of the US$ value of the shares.
  d. Explain why the two returns are different. Which one is more important to Joe? Why?

P5–15 Total, nondiversifiable, and diversifiable risk   David Talbot randomly selected securities from all those listed on the New York Stock Exchange for his portfolio. He began with a single security and added securities one by one until a total of 20 securities were held in the portfolio. After each security was added, David calculated the portfolio standard deviation, s_{r_p}. The calculated values are shown in the following table.

Number of securities	Portfolio risk, σ_{r_p}	Number of securities	Portfolio risk, σ_{r_p}
1	14.50%	11	7.00%
2	13.30	12	6.80
3	12.20	13	6.70
4	11.20	14	6.65
5	10.30	15	6.60
6	9.50	16	6.56
7	8.80	17	6.52
8	8.20	18	6.50
9	7.70	19	6.48
10	7.30	20	6.47

  a. On a set of "number of securities in portfolio (*x* axis)–portfolio risk (*y* axis)" axes, plot the portfolio risk data given in the preceding table.
  b. Divide the total portfolio risk in the graph into its *nondiversifiable* and *diversifiable* risk components and label each of these on the graph.
  c. Describe which of the two risk components is the *relevant risk*, and explain why it is relevant. How much of this risk exists in David Talbot's portfolio?

P5–16 Graphical derivation of beta   A firm wishes to estimate graphically the betas for two assets, A and B. It has gathered the return data shown in the following table for the market portfolio and for both assets over the last 10 years, 2000–2009.

Risk and Return

	Actual return		
Year	Market portfolio	Asset A	Asset B
2000	6%	11%	16%
2001	2	8	11
2002	−13	− 4	−10
2003	− 4	3	3
2004	− 8	0	− 3
2005	16	19	30
2006	10	14	22
2007	15	18	29
2008	8	12	19
2009	13	17	26

a. On a set of "market return (x axis)–asset return (y axis)" axes, use the data given to draw the characteristic line for asset A and for asset B.
b. Use the characteristic lines from part **a** to estimate the betas for assets A and B.
c. Use the betas found in part **b** to comment on the relative risks of assets A and B.

 P5–17 **Interpreting beta**   A firm wishes to assess the impact of changes in the market return on an asset that has a beta of 1.20.
  a. If the market return increased by 15%, what impact would this change be expected to have on the asset's return?
  b. If the market return decreased by 8%, what impact would this change be expected to have on the asset's return?
  c. If the market return did not change, what impact, if any, would be expected on the asset's return?
  d. Would this asset be considered more or less risky than the market? Explain.

 P5–18 **Betas**   Answer the questions below for assets A to D shown in the following table.

Asset	Beta
A	.50
B	1.60
C	− .20
D	.90

  a. What impact would a *10% increase* in the market return be expected to have on each asset's return?
  b. What impact would a *10% decrease* in the market return be expected to have on each asset's return?
  c. If you were certain that the market return would *increase* in the near future, which asset would you prefer? Why?
  d. If you were certain that the market return would *decrease* in the near future, which asset would you prefer? Why?

PERSONAL FINANCE PROBLEM

 P5–19 **Betas and risk rankings**   You are considering three stocks—A, B, and C—for possible inclusion in your investment portfolio. Stock A has a beta of .80, stock B has a beta of 1.40, and stock C has a beta of − .30.

a. Rank these stocks from the most risky to the least risky.

b. If the return on the market portfolio increased by 12%, what change would you expect in the return for each of the stocks?

c. If the return on the market portfolio decreased by 5%, what change would you expect in the return for each of the stocks?

d. If you felt that the stock market was getting ready to experience a significant decline, which stock would you probably add to your portfolio? Why?

e. If you anticipated a major stock market rally, which stock would you add to your portfolio? Why?

PERSONAL FINANCE PROBLEM

 P5–20 **Portfolio betas** Rose Berry is attempting to evaluate two possible portfolios, which consist of the same five assets held in different proportions. She is particularly interested in using beta to compare the risks of the portfolios, so she has gathered the data shown in the following table.

		Portfolio weights	
Asset	Asset beta	Portfolio A	Portfolio B
1	1.30	10%	30%
2	.70	30	10
3	1.25	10	20
4	1.10	10	20
5	.90	40	20
Totals		100%	100%

a. Calculate the betas for portfolios A and B.

b. Compare the risks of these portfolios to the market as well as to each other. Which portfolio is more risky?

 P5–21 **Capital asset pricing model (CAPM)** For each of the cases shown in the following table, use the capital asset pricing model to find the required return.

Case	Risk-free rate, R_F	Market return, r_m	Beta, b
A	5%	8%	1.30
B	8	13	.90
C	9	12	− .20
D	10	15	1.00
E	6	10	.60

PERSONAL FINANCE PROBLEM

 P5–22 **Beta coefficients and the capital asset pricing model** Katherine Wilson is wondering how much risk she must undertake to generate an acceptable return on her portfolio. The risk-free return currently is 5%. The return on the average stock (market return) is 16%. Use the CAPM to calculate the beta coefficient associated with each of the following portfolio returns.

a. 10%
b. 15%
c. 18%
d. 20%
e. Katherine is risk-averse. What is the highest return she can expect if she is unwilling to take more than an average risk?

P5–23 Manipulating CAPM Use the basic equation for the capital asset pricing model (CAPM) to work each of the following problems.
a. Find the *required return* for an asset with a beta of .90 when the risk-free rate and market return are 8% and 12%, respectively.
b. Find the *risk-free rate* for a firm with a required return of 15% and a beta of 1.25 when the market return is 14%.
c. Find the *market return* for an asset with a required return of 16% and a beta of 1.10 when the risk-free rate is 9%.
d. Find the *beta* for an asset with a required return of 15% when the risk-free rate and market return are 10% and 12.5%, respectively.

PERSONAL FINANCE PROBLEM

P5–24 Portfolio return and beta Jamie Peters invested $100,000 to set up the following portfolio one year ago:

Asset	Cost	Beta at purchase	Yearly income	Value today
A	$20,000	.80	$1,600	$20,000
B	35,000	.95	1,400	36,000
C	30,000	1.50	—	34,500
D	15,000	1.25	375	16,500

a. Calculate the portfolio beta on the basis of the original cost figures.
b. Calculate the percentage return of each asset in the portfolio for the year.
c. Calculate the percentage return of the portfolio on the basis of original cost, using income and gains during the year.
d. At the time Jamie made his investments, investors were estimating that the market return for the coming year would be 10%. The estimate of the risk-free rate of return averaged 4% for the coming year. Calculate an expected rate of return for each stock on the basis of its beta and the expectations of market and risk-free returns.
e. On the basis of the actual results, explain how each stock in the portfolio performed relative to those CAPM-generated expectations of performance. What factors could explain these differences?

P5–25 Security market line (SML) Assume that the risk-free rate, R_F, is currently 9% and that the market return, r_m, is currently 13%.
a. Draw the security market line (SML) on a set of "nondiversifiable risk (*x* axis)–required return (*y* axis)" axes.
b. Calculate and label the *market risk premium* on the axes in part **a**.
c. Given the previous data, calculate the required return on asset A having a beta of .80 and asset B having a beta of 1.30.

d. Draw in the betas and required returns from part **c** for assets A and B on the axes in part **a.** Label the *risk premium* associated with each of these assets, and discuss them.

P5–26 **Integrative—Risk, return, and CAPM** Wolff Enterprises must consider several investment projects, A through E, using the capital asset pricing model (CAPM) and its graphical representation, the security market line (SML). Relevant information is presented in the following table.

Item	Rate of return	Beta, *b*
Risk-free asset	9%	0
Market portfolio	14	1.00
Project A	—	1.50
Project B	—	.75
Project C	—	2.00
Project D	—	0
Project E	—	− .5

a. Calculate (1) the required rate of return and (2) the risk premium for each project, given its level of nondiversifiable risk.
b. Use your findings in part **a** to draw the security market line (required return relative to nondiversifiable risk).
c. Discuss the relative nondiversifiable risk of projects A through E.

P5–27 **ETHICS PROBLEM** Integrity, especially honesty, is trait number one for being hired as a CFO in corporate America today. How might you assess a job candidate's honesty if you were interviewing a potential CFO candidate?

Chapter Case

Analyzing Risk and Return on Chargers Products' Investments

Junior Sayou, a financial analyst for Chargers Products, a manufacturer of stadium benches, must evaluate the risk and return of two assets, X and Y. The firm is considering adding these assets to its diversified asset portfolio. To assess the return and risk of each asset, Junior gathered data on the annual cash flow and beginning- and end-of-year values of each asset over the immediately preceding 10 years, 2000–2009. These data are summarized in the following table. Junior's investigation suggests that both assets, on average, will tend to perform in the future just as they have during the past 10 years. He therefore believes that the expected annual return can be estimated by finding the average annual return for each asset over the past 10 years.

	Asset X			Asset Y		
		Value			Value	
Year	Cash flow	Beginning	Ending	Cash flow	Beginning	Ending
2000	$1,000	$20,000	$22,000	$1,500	$20,000	$20,000
2001	1,500	22,000	21,000	1,600	20,000	20,000
2002	1,400	21,000	24,000	1,700	20,000	21,000
2003	1,700	24,000	22,000	1,800	21,000	21,000
2004	1,900	22,000	23,000	1,900	21,000	22,000
2005	1,600	23,000	26,000	2,000	22,000	23,000
2006	1,700	26,000	25,000	2,100	23,000	23,000
2007	2,000	25,000	24,000	2,200	23,000	24,000
2008	2,100	24,000	27,000	2,300	24,000	25,000
2009	2,200	27,000	30,000	2,400	25,000	25,000

Return Data for Assets X and Y, 2000–2009

Junior believes that each asset's risk can be assessed in two ways: in isolation and as part of the firm's diversified portfolio of assets. The risk of the assets in isolation can be found by using the standard deviation and coefficient of variation of returns over the past 10 years. The capital asset pricing model (CAPM) can be used to assess the asset's risk as part of the firm's portfolio of assets. Applying some sophisticated quantitative techniques, Junior estimated betas for assets X and Y of 1.60 and 1.10, respectively. In addition, he found that the risk-free rate is currently 7% and that the market return is 10%.

To Do

a. Calculate the annual rate of return for each asset in *each* of the 10 preceding years, and use those values to find the average annual return for each asset over the 10-year period.

b. Use the returns calculated in part **a** to find (1) the standard deviation and (2) the coefficient of variation of the returns for each asset over the 10-year period 2000–2009.

c. Use your findings in parts **a** and **b** to evaluate and discuss the return and risk associated with each asset. Which asset appears to be preferable? Explain.

d. Use the CAPM to find the required return for each asset. Compare this value with the average annual returns calculated in part **a**.

e. Compare and contrast your findings in parts **c** and **d**. What recommendations would you give Junior with regard to investing in either of the two assets? Explain to Junior why he is better off using beta rather than the standard deviation and coefficient of variation to assess the risk of each asset.

f. Rework parts **d** and **e** under each of the following circumstances:
   (1) A rise of 1% in inflationary expectations causes the risk-free rate to rise to 8% and the market return to rise to 11%.
   (2) As a result of favorable political events, investors suddenly become less risk-averse, causing the market return to drop by 1%, to 9%.

Spreadsheet Exercise

Jane is considering investing in three different stocks or creating three distinct two-stock portfolios. Jane considers herself to be a rather conservative investor. She is able to obtain forecasted returns for the three securities for the years 2010 through 2016. The data are as follows:

Year	Stock A	Stock B	Stock C
2010	10%	10%	12%
2011	13	11	14
2012	15	8	10
2013	14	12	11
2014	16	10	9
2015	14	15	9
2016	12	15	10

In any of the possible two-stock portfolios, the weight of each stock in the portfolio will be 50%. The three possible portfolio combinations are AB, AC, and BC.

To Do

Create a spreadsheet similar to Tables 7 and 8 (which can be viewed at **www .prenhall.com/gitman** as Tables 5.7 and 5.8) to answer the following:

a. Calculate the expected return for each individual stock.
b. Calculate the standard deviation for each individual stock.
c. Calculate the expected returns for portfolio AB, AC, and BC.
d. Calculate the standard deviations for portfolios AB, AC, and BC.
e. Would you recommend that Jane invest in the single stock A or the portfolio consisting of stocks A and B? Explain your answer from a risk–return viewpoint.
f. Would you recommend that Jane invest in the single stock B or the portfolio consisting of stocks B and C? Explain your answer from a risk–return viewpoint.

Web Exercise

Go to the text's companion website at **www.prenhall.com/gitman** to find the Web Exercise for this chapter.

> Remember to check the text's website at **www.prenhall.com/gitman** to find additional resources, including Web Exercises and a Web Case.

Solutions to Self-Test Problems

ST5–1 **a.** Expected return, $\bar{r} = \dfrac{\Sigma \text{Returns}}{3}$ (*Equation 5.2a in footnote 9*)

$$\bar{r}_A = \frac{12\% + 14\% + 16\%}{3} = \frac{42\%}{3} = \underline{\underline{14\%}}$$

$$\bar{r}_B = \frac{16\% + 14\% + 12\%}{3} = \frac{42\%}{3} = \underline{\underline{14\%}}$$

$$\bar{r}_C = \frac{12\% + 14\% + 16\%}{3} = \frac{42\%}{3} = \underline{\underline{14\%}}$$

b. Standard deviation, $\sigma_r = \sqrt{\dfrac{\displaystyle\sum_{j=1}^{n}(r_i - \bar{r})^2}{n - 1}}$ (*Equation 5.3a in footnote 10*)

$$\sigma_{r_A} = \sqrt{\frac{(12\% - 14\%)^2 + (14\% - 14\%)^2 + (16\% - 14\%)^2}{3 - 1}}$$

$$= \sqrt{\frac{4\% + 0\% + 4\%}{2}} = \sqrt{\frac{8\%}{2}} = \underline{\underline{2\%}}$$

$$\sigma_{r_B} = \sqrt{\frac{(16\% - 14\%)^2 + (14\% - 14\%)^2 + (12\% - 14\%)^2}{3 - 1}}$$

$$= \sqrt{\frac{4\% + 0\% + 4\%}{2}} = \sqrt{\frac{8\%}{2}} = \underline{\underline{2\%}}$$

$$\sigma_{r_C} = \sqrt{\frac{(12\% - 14\%)^2 + (14\% - 14\%)^2 + (16\% - 14\%)^2}{3 - 1}}$$

$$= \sqrt{\frac{4\% + 0\% + 4\%}{2}} = \sqrt{\frac{8\%}{2}} = \underline{\underline{2\%}}$$

c.

	Annual expected returns	
Year	Portfolio AB	Portfolio AC
2010	$(0.50 \times 12\%) + (0.50 \times 16\%) = 14\%$	$(0.50 \times 12\%) + (0.50 \times 12\%) = 12\%$
2011	$(0.50 \times 14\%) + (0.50 \times 14\%) = 14\%$	$(0.50 \times 14\%) + (0.50 \times 14\%) = 14\%$
2012	$(0.50 \times 16\%) + (0.50 \times 12\%) = 14\%$	$(0.50 \times 16\%) + (0.50 \times 16\%) = 16\%$

Over the 3-year period:

$$\bar{r}_{AB} = \frac{14\% + 14\% + 14\%}{3} = \frac{42\%}{3} = \underline{\underline{14\%}}$$

$$\bar{r}_{AC} = \frac{12\% + 14\% + 16\%}{3} = \frac{42\%}{3} = \underline{\underline{14\%}}$$

d. AB is perfectly negatively correlated.

AC is perfectly positively correlated.

e. Standard deviation of the portfolios

$$\sigma_{r_{AB}} = \sqrt{\frac{(14\% - 14\%)^2 + (14\% - 14\%)^2 + (14\% - 14\%)^2}{3 - 1}}$$

$$= \sqrt{\frac{(0\% + 0\% + 0\%)}{2}} = \sqrt{\frac{0\%}{2}} = \underline{\underline{0\%}}$$

$$\sigma_{r_{AC}} = \sqrt{\frac{(12\% - 14\%)^2 + (14\% - 14\%)^2 + (16\% - 14\%)^2}{3 - 1}}$$

$$= \sqrt{\frac{4\% + 0\% + 4\%}{2}} = \sqrt{\frac{8\%}{2}} = \underline{\underline{2\%}}$$

f. Portfolio AB is preferred, because it provides the same return (14%) as AC but with less risk $[(\sigma_{r_{AB}} = 0\%) < (\sigma_{r_{AC}} = 2\%)]$.

ST5–2 a. When the market return increases by 10%, the project's required return would be expected to increase by 15% ($1.50 \times 10\%$). When the market return decreases by 10%, the project's required return would be expected to decrease by 15% [$1.50 \times (-10\%)$].

b. $r_j = R_F + [b_j \times (r_m - R_F)]$
   $= 7\% + [1.50 \times (10\% - 7\%)]$
   $= 7\% + 4.5\% = \underline{\underline{11.5\%}}$

c. No, the project should be rejected, because its *expected* return of 11% is less than the 11.5% return *required* from the project.

d. $r_j = 7\% + [1.50 \times (9\% - 7\%)]$
   $= 7\% + 3\% = \underline{\underline{10\%}}$

The project would now be acceptable, because its *expected* return of 11% is now in excess of the *required* return, which has declined to 10% as a result of investors in the marketplace becoming less risk-averse.

Answers to Selected End-of-Chapter Problems

5–1 a. X: 12.50%
        Y: 12.36%
5–2 A: 25%
5–4 a. A: 8%
        B: 20%
5–5 a. R: 10%
        S: 20%
     b. R: 25%
        S: 25.5%

5–8	**a.**	2008 return (hypothetical): 11.73%
5–9	**a.**	(4) Project 257 CV: .368
		Project 432 CV: .354
5–10	**a.**	F: 4%
	b.	F: 13.38%
	c.	F: 3.345
5–11	**b.**	Portfolio return: 15.5%
	c.	Standard deviation: 1.511%
5–14	**a.**	20.73%
	c.	12.89%
5–17	**a.**	18% increase
	b.	9.6% decrease
	c.	No change
5–21		A: 8.9%
		D: 15%
5–23	**b.**	10%

Chapter 7

Interest Rates and Bond Valuation

WHY THIS CHAPTER MATTERS TO YOU

In Your Professional Life

Accounting: You need to understand interest rates and the various types of bonds to be able to account properly for amortization of bond premiums and discounts and for bond purchases and retirements.

Information systems: You need to understand the data that you will need to track in bond amortization schedules and bond valuation.

Management: You need to understand the behavior of interest rates and how they will affect the types of funds the firm can raise and the timing and cost of bond issues and retirements.

Marketing: You need to understand how the interest rate level and the firm's ability to issue bonds may affect the availability of financing for marketing research projects and new-product development.

Operations: You need to understand how the interest rate level may affect the firm's ability to raise funds to maintain and grow the firm's production capacity.

In Your Personal Life

Interest rates have a direct impact on personal financial planning. Movements in interest rates occur frequently and affect the returns from and values of savings and investments. The rate of interest you are charged on credit cards and loans can have a profound effect on your personal finances. Understanding the basics of interest rates is important to your personal financial plans.

LEARNING GOALS

LG 1 Describe interest rate fundamentals, the term structure of interest rates, and risk premiums.

LG 2 Review the legal aspects of bond financing and bond cost.

LG 3 Discuss the general features, yields, prices, ratings, popular types, and international issues of corporate bonds.

LG 4 Understand the key inputs and basic model used in the valuation process.

LG 5 Apply the basic valuation model to bonds and describe the impact of required return and time to maturity on bond values.

LG 6 Explain yield to maturity (YTM), its calculation, and the procedure used to value bonds that pay interest semiannually.

From Chapter 6 of *Principles of Managerial Finance*, Brief 5th Edition. Lawrence J. Gitman. Copyright © 2009 by Pearson Prentice Hall. All rights reserved.

The interactions of suppliers and demanders of funds in the financial markets affect interest rates. The interest rates (returns) required by suppliers of funds also depend on the perceived risk of an asset. In this chapter, we apply the concepts of risk and return in a process called valuation. This chapter discusses interest rates, describes the key aspects of corporate bonds, and demonstrates the valuation process for the easiest financial asset to value, bonds.

1 | Interest Rates and Required Returns

Financial institutions and markets create the mechanism through which funds flow between savers (funds suppliers) and investors (funds demanders). The level of funds flow between suppliers and demanders can significantly affect economic growth. The interest rate level acts as a regulating device that controls the flow of funds between suppliers and demanders. The *Board of Governors of the Federal Reserve System* regularly assesses economic conditions and, when necessary, initiates actions to raise or lower interest rates to control inflation and economic growth. Generally, the lower the interest rate, the greater the funds flow and therefore the greater the economic growth; the higher the interest rate, the lower the funds flow and economic growth.

Interest Rate Fundamentals

The *interest rate* or *required return* represents the cost of money. It is the compensation that a demander of funds must pay a supplier. When funds are lent, the cost of borrowing the funds is the **interest rate**. When funds are obtained by selling an ownership interest—as in the sale of stock—the cost to the issuer (demander) is commonly called the **required return,** which reflects the funds supplier's level of expected return. In both cases the supplier is compensated for providing funds. Ignoring risk factors, the cost of funds results from the *real rate of interest* adjusted for inflationary expectations and **liquidity preferences**—general preferences of investors for shorter-term securities.

The Real Rate of Interest

Assume a *perfect world* in which there is no inflation and in which funds suppliers and demanders are indifferent to the term of loans or investments because they have no *liquidity preference* and all outcomes are certain.[1] At any given point in time in that perfect world, there would be one cost of money—the **real rate of interest.** The real rate of interest creates an equilibrium between the supply of savings and the demand for investment funds. It represents the most basic cost of money. The real rate of interest in the United States is assumed to be stable and

interest rate
The compensation paid by the borrower of funds to the lender; from the borrower's point of view, the cost of borrowing funds.

required return
The cost of funds obtained by selling an ownership interest; it reflects the funds supplier's level of expected return.

liquidity preferences
General preferences of investors for shorter-term securities.

real rate of interest
The rate that creates an equilibrium between the supply of savings and the demand for investment funds in a perfect world, without inflation, where funds suppliers and demanders are indifferent to the term of loans or investments because they have no *liquidity preference,* and where all outcomes are certain.

---

1. These assumptions are made to describe the most basic interest rate, the *real rate of interest*. Subsequent discussions relax these assumptions to develop the broader concept of the interest rate and required return.

FIGURE 1

Supply–Demand Relationship
Supply of savings and demand for investment funds

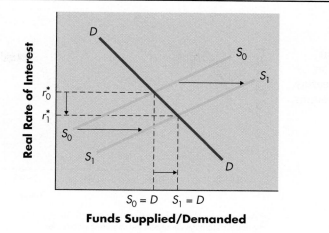

Funds Supplied/Demanded

equal to around 1 percent.[2] This supply–demand relationship is shown in Figure 1 by the supply function (labeled S_0) and the demand function (labeled D). An equilibrium between the supply of funds and the demand for funds ($S_0 = D$) occurs at a rate of interest r_0^*, the real rate of interest.

Clearly, the real rate of interest changes with changing economic conditions, tastes, and preferences. A trade surplus could result in an increased supply of funds, causing the supply function in Figure 1 to shift to, say, S_1. This could result in a lower real rate of interest, r_1^*, at equilibrium ($S_1 = D$). Likewise, a change in tax laws or other factors could affect the demand for funds, causing the real rate of interest to rise or fall to a new equilibrium level.

Inflation and the Cost of Money

Ignoring risk factors, the cost of funds—the interest rate or required return—is closely tied to inflationary expectations. This can be demonstrated by using the **risk-free rate of interest, R_F,** defined as the required return on the risk-free asset. The risk-free asset is typically considered to be a 3-month *U.S. Treasury bill (T-bill),* which is a short-term IOU issued regularly by the U.S. Treasury.

Figure 2 illustrates the annual movement of the rate of inflation and the risk-free rate of return during the period 1978–2007. During this period the two rates tended to move in a similar fashion. Between 1978 and the early 1980s, inflation and interest rates were quite high, peaking at over 13 percent in 1980–1981. Since 1981 these rates have declined to levels generally below those in 1978. Note that between 2002 and 2005 the annual rate of inflation actually exceeded the average 3-month Treasury bill rate. The data in Figure 2 clearly illustrate the significant impact of inflation on the actual rate of interest charged by the supplier of funds and paid by the demander for the risk-free asset.

risk-free rate of interest, R_F
The required return on a risk-free asset, typically a 3-month *U.S. Treasury bill (T-bill).*

---

2. Data in *Stocks, Bonds, Bills, and Inflation, 2007 Yearbook* (Chicago: Ibbotson Associates, Inc., 2007), show that over the period 1926–2006, U.S. Treasury bills provided an average annual real rate of return of about 0.70 percent. Because of certain major economic events that occurred during the 1926–2006 period, many economists believe that the real rate of interest during recent years has been about 1 percent.

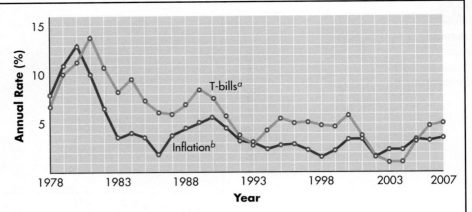

FIGURE 2

Impact of Inflation
Relationship between annual rate of inflation and 3-month U.S. Treasury bill average annual returns, 1978–2007

a Average annual rate of return on 3-month U.S. Treasury bills.
b Annual pecentage change in the consumer price index.

Sources: Data from selected *Federal Reserve Bulletins* and *U.S. Department of Labor Bureau of Labor Statistics.*

term structure of interest rates
The relationship between the interest rate or rate of return and the time to maturity.

yield to maturity
Compound annual rate of return earned on a debt security purchased on a given day and held to maturity.

yield curve
A graph of the relationship between the debt's remaining time to maturity (*x* axis) and its yield to maturity (*y* axis); it shows the yield to maturity for debts of equal quality and different maturities. Graphically depicts the *term structure of interest rates.*

inverted yield curve
A *downward-sloping* yield curve that indicates generally cheaper long-term borrowing costs than short-term borrowing costs.

normal yield curve
An *upward-sloping* yield curve that indicates generally cheaper short-term borrowing costs than long-term borrowing costs.

flat yield curve
A yield curve that reflects relatively similar borrowing costs for both short- and longer-term loans.

Term Structure of Interest Rates

For any class of similar-risk securities, the **term structure of interest rates** relates the interest rate or rate of return to the time to maturity. For convenience we will use Treasury securities as an example, but other classes could include securities that have similar overall quality or risk. The riskless nature of Treasury securities also provides a laboratory in which to develop the term structure.

Yield Curves

A debt security's **yield to maturity** (discussed later in this chapter) represents the compound annual rate of return earned on it assuming it is purchased on a given day and held to maturity. At any point in time, the relationship between the debt's remaining time to maturity and its yield to maturity is represented by the **yield curve.** The yield curve shows the yield to maturity for debts of equal quality and different maturities; it is a graphical depiction of the *term structure of interest rates.* Figure 3 shows three yield curves for all U.S. Treasury securities: one at May 22, 1981, a second at September 29, 1989, and a third at May 17, 2004. (Note that we purposefully kept the yield curve for 2004 because it better shows some key lessons than do more current yield curves, which are relatively flat.)

Observe that both the position and the shape of the yield curves change over time. The yield curve of May 22, 1981, indicates that short-term interest rates at that time were above longer-term rates. This curve is described as *downward-sloping,* reflecting long-term borrowing costs generally cheaper than short-term borrowing costs. Historically, the downward-sloping yield curve, which is often called an **inverted yield curve,** has been the exception. More frequently, yield curves similar to that of May 17, 2004, have existed. These *upward-sloping* or **normal yield curves** indicate that short-term borrowing costs are below long-term borrowing costs. Sometimes, a **flat yield curve,** similar to that of September 29, 1989, exists. It reflects relatively similar borrowing costs for both short- and longer-term loans. In mid-March 2007, the yield curve (not shown) was flat with yields over the 30 years ranging between 4.46 and 5.07 percent.

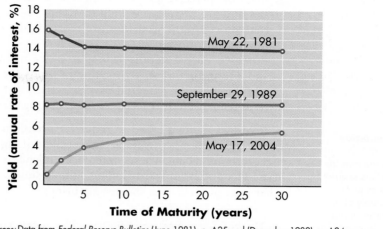

FIGURE 3

Treasury Yield Curves
Yield curves for U.S.
Treasury securities: May 22,
1981; September 29, 1989;
and May 17, 2004

Sources: Data from *Federal Reserve Bulletins* (June 1981), p. A25 and (December 1989), p. A24;
and U.S. Department of Treasury Office of Debt Management, www.ustreas.gov/
offices/domestic-finance/debt-management/interest-rate/yield.html

The shape of the yield curve may affect the firm's financing decisions. A financial manager who faces a downward-sloping yield curve is likely to rely more heavily on cheaper, long-term financing; when the yield curve is upward-sloping, the manager is more likely to use cheaper, short-term financing. Although a variety of other factors influence the choice of loan maturity, the shape of the yield curve provides useful insights into future interest rate expectations.

Theories of Term Structure

Three theories are frequently cited to explain the general shape of the yield curve: the expectations theory, the liquidity preference theory, and the market segmentation theory.

Expectations Theory   One theory of the term structure of interest rates, the **expectations theory,** suggests that the yield curve reflects investor expectations about future interest rates and inflation. Higher future rates of expected inflation will result in higher long-term interest rates; the opposite occurs with lower future rates. This widely accepted explanation of the term structure can be applied to the securities of any issuer.

Generally, under the expectations theory, an increasing inflation expectation results in an upward-sloping yield curve; a decreasing inflation expectation results in a downward-sloping yield curve; and a stable inflation expectation results in a flat yield curve. Although, as we'll see, other theories exist, the observed strong relationship between inflation and interest rates (see Figure 2) supports this widely accepted theory.

Liquidity Preference Theory   The tendency for yield curves to be upward-sloping can be further explained by the **liquidity preference theory.** This theory holds that for a given issuer, such as the U.S. Treasury, long-term rates tend to be higher than short-term rates. This belief is based on two behavioral facts:

expectations theory
The theory that the yield curve reflects investor expectations about future interest rates and inflation; an increasing inflation expectation results in an upward-sloping yield curve, and a decreasing inflation expectation results in a downward-sloping yield curve.

liquidity preference theory
Theory suggesting that for any given issuer, long-term interest rates tend to be higher than short-term rates because (1) lower liquidity and higher responsiveness to general interest rate movements of longer-term securities exists and (2) borrower willingness to pay a higher rate for long-term financing cause the yield curve to be upward-sloping.

227

1. Investors perceive less risk in short-term securities than in longer-term securities and are therefore willing to accept lower yields on them. The reason is that shorter-term securities are more liquid and less responsive to general interest rate movements.[3]
2. Borrowers are generally willing to pay a higher rate for long-term than for short-term financing. By locking in funds for a longer period of time, they can eliminate the potential adverse consequences of having to roll over short-term debt at unknown costs to obtain long-term financing.

Investors (lenders) tend to require a premium for tying up funds for longer periods, whereas borrowers are generally willing to pay a premium to obtain longer-term financing. These preferences of lenders and borrowers cause the yield curve to tend to be upward-sloping. Simply stated, longer maturities tend to have higher interest rates than shorter maturities.

market segmentation theory
Theory suggesting that the market for loans is segmented on the basis of maturity and that the supply of and demand for loans within each segment determine its prevailing interest rate; the slope of the yield curve is determined by the general relationship between the prevailing rates in each market segment.

Market Segmentation Theory The **market segmentation theory** suggests that the market for loans is segmented on the basis of maturity and that the supply of and demand for loans within each segment determine its prevailing interest rate. In other words, the equilibrium between suppliers and demanders of short-term funds, such as seasonal business loans, would determine prevailing short-term interest rates, and the equilibrium between suppliers and demanders of long-term funds, such as real estate loans, would determine prevailing long-term interest rates. The slope of the yield curve would be determined by the general relationship between the prevailing rates in each market segment. Simply stated, low rates in the short-term segment and high rates in the long-term segment cause the yield curve to be upward-sloping. The opposite occurs for high short-term rates and low long-term rates.

Hint An upward-sloping yield curve will result if the supply outstrips the demand for short-term loans, thereby resulting in relatively low short-term rates at a time when long-term rates are high because the demand for long-term loans is far above their supply.

All three theories of term structure have merit. From them we can conclude that at any time, the slope of the yield curve is affected by (1) inflationary expectations, (2) liquidity preferences, and (3) the comparative equilibrium of supply and demand in the short- and long-term market segments. Upward-sloping yield curves result from higher future inflation expectations, lender preferences for shorter-maturity loans, and greater supply of short-term loans than of long-term loans relative to demand. The opposite behaviors would result in a downward-sloping yield curve. At any time, the interaction of these three forces determines the prevailing slope of the yield curve.

risk premium
The amount by which the interest rate or required return on a security exceeds the risk-free rate of interest R_F; it varies with specific issuer and issue characteristics.

Risk Premiums: Issuer and Issue Characteristics

So far we have considered only risk-free U.S. Treasury securities. We now add the element of risk, in order to assess what effect it has on the cost of funds. The amount by which the interest rate or required return exceeds the risk-free rate of interest, R_F, is a security's **risk premium**. The risk premium varies with specific

---

3. Later in this chapter we demonstrate that debt instruments with longer maturities are more sensitive to changing market interest rates. For a given change in market rates, the price or value of longer-term debts will be more significantly changed (up or down) than the price or value of debts with shorter maturities.

TABLE 1	Debt-Specific Issuer- and Issue-Related Risk Premium Components
Component	**Description**
Default risk	The possibility that the issuer of debt will not pay the contractual interest or principal as scheduled. The greater the uncertainty as to the borrower's ability to meet these payments, the greater the risk premium. High bond ratings reflect low default risk, and low bond ratings reflect high default risk.
Maturity risk	The fact that the longer the maturity, the more the value of a security will change in response to a given change in interest rates. If interest rates on otherwise similar-risk securities suddenly rise as a result of a change in the money supply, the prices of long-term bonds will decline by more than the prices of short-term bonds, and vice versa.[a]
Contractual provision risk	Conditions that are often included in a debt agreement or a stock issue. Some of these reduce risk, whereas others may increase risk. For example, a provision allowing a bond issuer to retire its bonds prior to their maturity under favorable terms increases the bond's risk.

[a]A detailed discussion of the effects of interest rates on the price or value of bonds and other fixed-income securities is presented later in this chapter.

issuer and issue characteristics; it causes similar-maturity securities to have differing rates of interest.

The risk premium consists of a number of issuer- and issue-related components, including business risk, financial risk, interest rate risk, liquidity risk, and tax risk, and the purely debt-specific risks—default risk, maturity risk, and contractual provision risk, briefly defined in Table 1. In general, the highest risk premiums and therefore the highest returns result from securities issued by firms with a high risk of default and from long-term maturities that have unfavorable contractual provisions.

REVIEW QUESTIONS

1. What is the *real rate of interest?* Differentiate it from the *risk-free rate of interest* for a 3-month U.S. Treasury bill.

2. What is the *term structure of interest rates,* and how is it related to the *yield curve?*

3. For a given class of similar-risk securities, what does each of the following yield curves reflect about interest rates: (a) downward-sloping; (b) upward-sloping; and (c) flat? Which form has been historically dominant?

4. Briefly describe the following theories of the general shape of the yield curve: (a) expectations theory; (b) liquidity preference theory; and (c) market segmentation theory.

5. List and briefly describe the potential issuer- and issue-related risk components that are embodied in the risk premium. Which are the purely debt-specific risks?

2 | Corporate Bonds

corporate bond
A long-term debt instrument indicating that a corporation has borrowed a certain amount of money and promises to repay it in the future under clearly defined terms.

A **corporate bond** is a long-term debt instrument indicating that a corporation has borrowed a certain amount of money and promises to repay it in the future under clearly defined terms. Most bonds are issued with maturities of 10 to 30 years and with a par value, or face value, of $1,000. The **coupon interest rate** on a bond represents the percentage of the bond's par value that will be paid annually, typically in two equal semiannual payments, as interest. The bondholders, who are the lenders, are promised the semiannual interest payments and, at maturity, repayment of the principal amount.

coupon interest rate
The percentage of a bond's par value that will be paid annually, typically in two equal semiannual payments, as interest.

Legal Aspects of Corporate Bonds

Certain legal arrangements are required to protect purchasers of bonds. Bondholders are protected primarily through the indenture and the trustee.

Bond Indenture

bond indenture
A legal document that specifies both the rights of the bondholders and the duties of the issuing corporation.

A **bond indenture** is a legal document that specifies both the rights of the bondholders and the duties of the issuing corporation. Included in the indenture are descriptions of the amount and timing of all interest and principal payments, various standard and restrictive provisions, and, frequently, sinking-fund requirements and security interest provisions.

standard debt provisions
Provisions in a *bond indenture* specifying certain record-keeping and general business practices that the bond issuer must follow; normally, they do not place a burden on a financially sound business.

Standard Provisions The **standard debt provisions** in the bond indenture specify certain record-keeping and general business practices that the bond issuer must follow. Standard debt provisions do not normally place a burden on a financially sound business.

The borrower commonly must (1) *maintain satisfactory accounting records* in accordance with generally accepted accounting principles (GAAP); (2) periodically *supply audited financial statements*; (3) *pay taxes and other liabilities when due*; and (4) *maintain all facilities in good working order*.

restrictive covenants
Provisions in a *bond indenture* that place operating and financial constraints on the borrower.

Restrictive Provisions Bond indentures also normally include certain **restrictive covenants**, which place operating and financial constraints on the borrower. These provisions help protect the bondholder against increases in borrower risk. Without them, the borrower could increase the firm's risk but not have to pay increased interest to compensate for the increased risk.

The most common restrictive covenants do the following:

1. Require a *minimum level of liquidity*, to ensure against loan default.
2. *Prohibit the sale of accounts receivable* to generate cash. Selling receivables could cause a long-run cash shortage if proceeds were used to meet current obligations.
3. Impose *fixed-asset restrictions*. The borrower must maintain a specified level of fixed assets to guarantee its ability to repay the bonds.
4. *Constrain subsequent borrowing*. Additional long-term debt may be prohibited, or additional borrowing may be *subordinated* to the original loan. **Subordination** means that subsequent creditors agree to wait until all claims of the *senior debt* are satisfied.

subordination
In a bond indenture, the stipulation that subsequent creditors agree to wait until all claims of the *senior debt* are satisfied.

5. *Limit the firm's annual cash dividend payments* to a specified percentage or amount.

Other restrictive covenants are sometimes included in bond indentures.

The violation of any standard or restrictive provision by the borrower gives the bondholders the right to demand immediate repayment of the debt. Generally, bondholders evaluate any violation to determine whether it jeopardizes the loan. They may then decide to demand immediate repayment, continue the loan, or alter the terms of the bond indenture.

Sinking-Fund Requirements   Another common restrictive provision is a **sinking-fund requirement.** Its objective is to provide for the systematic retirement of bonds prior to their maturity. To carry out this requirement, the corporation makes semiannual or annual payments that are used to retire bonds by purchasing them in the marketplace.

Security Interest   The bond indenture identifies any collateral pledged against the bond and specifies how it is to be maintained. The protection of bond collateral is crucial to guarantee the safety of a bond issue.

sinking-fund requirement
A restrictive provision often included in a bond indenture, providing for the systematic retirement of bonds prior to their maturity.

Trustee

A **trustee** is a third party to a *bond indenture*. The trustee can be an individual, a corporation, or (most often) a commercial bank trust department. The trustee is paid to act as a "watchdog" on behalf of the bondholders and can take specified actions on behalf of the bondholders if the terms of the indenture are violated.

trustee
A paid individual, corporation, or commercial bank trust department that acts as the third party to a *bond indenture* and can take specified actions on behalf of the bondholders if the terms of the indenture are violated.

Cost of Bonds to the Issuer

The cost of bond financing is generally greater than the issuer would have to pay for short-term borrowing. The major factors that affect the cost, which is the rate of interest paid by the bond issuer, are the bond's maturity, the size of the offering, the issuer's risk, and the basic cost of money.

Impact of Bond Maturity

Generally, as we noted earlier, long-term debt pays higher interest rates than short-term debt. In a practical sense, the longer the maturity of a bond, the less accuracy there is in predicting future interest rates, and therefore the greater the bondholders' risk of giving up an opportunity to lend money at a higher rate. In addition, the longer the term, the greater the chance that the issuer might default.

Impact of Offering Size

The size of the bond offering also affects the interest cost of borrowing, but in an inverse manner: Bond flotation and administration costs per dollar borrowed are likely to decrease with increasing offering size. On the other hand, the risk to the bondholders may increase, because larger offerings result in greater risk of default.

Impact of Issuer's Risk

The greater the issuer's *default risk,* the higher the interest rate. Some of this risk can be reduced through inclusion of appropriate restrictive provisions in the bond indenture. Clearly, bondholders must be compensated with higher returns for taking greater risk. Frequently, bond buyers rely on bond ratings (discussed later) to determine the issuer's overall risk.

Impact of the Cost of Money

The cost of money in the capital market is the basis for determining a bond's coupon interest rate. Generally, the rate on U.S. Treasury securities of equal maturity is used as the lowest-risk cost of money. To that basic rate is added a *risk premium* (as described earlier in this chapter) that reflects the factors mentioned above (maturity, offering size, and issuer's risk).

General Features of a Bond Issue

Three features sometimes included in a corporate bond issue are a conversion feature, a call feature, and stock purchase warrants. These features provide the issuer or the purchaser with certain opportunities for replacing or retiring the bond or supplementing it with some type of equity issue.

conversion feature
A feature of *convertible bonds* that allows bondholders to change each bond into a stated number of shares of common stock.

Convertible bonds offer a **conversion feature** that allows bondholders to change each bond into a stated number of shares of common stock. Bondholders convert their bonds into stock only when the market price of the stock is such that conversion will provide a profit for the bondholder. Inclusion of the conversion feature by the issuer lowers the interest cost and provides for automatic conversion of the bonds to stock if future stock prices appreciate noticeably.

call feature
A feature included in nearly all corporate bond issues that gives the issuer the opportunity to repurchase bonds at a stated *call price* prior to maturity.

call price
The stated price at which a bond may be repurchased, by use of a *call feature,* prior to maturity.

call premium
The amount by which a bond's *call price* exceeds its par value.

The **call feature** is included in nearly all corporate bond issues. It gives the issuer the opportunity to repurchase bonds prior to maturity. The **call price** is the stated price at which bonds may be repurchased prior to maturity. Sometimes the call feature can be exercised only during a certain period. As a rule, the call price exceeds the par value of a bond by an amount equal to 1 year's interest. For example, a $1,000 bond with a 10 percent coupon interest rate would be callable for around $1,100 [$1,000 + (10% × $1,000)]. The amount by which the call price exceeds the bond's par value is commonly referred to as the **call premium.** This premium compensates bondholders for having the bond called away from them; to the issuer, it is the cost of calling the bonds.

The call feature enables an issuer to call an outstanding bond when interest rates fall and issue a new bond at a lower interest rate. When interest rates rise, the call privilege will not be exercised, except possibly to meet *sinking-fund requirements.* Of course, to sell a callable bond in the first place, the issuer must pay a higher interest rate than on noncallable bonds of equal risk, to compensate bondholders for the risk of having the bonds called away from them.

stock purchase warrants
Instruments that give their holders the right to purchase a certain number of shares of the issuer's common stock at a specified price over a certain period of time. Occasionally attached to bonds as "sweeteners."

Bonds occasionally have stock purchase warrants attached as "sweeteners" to make them more attractive to prospective buyers. **Stock purchase warrants** are instruments that give their holders the right to purchase a certain number of shares of the issuer's common stock at a specified price over a certain period of time. Their inclusion typically enables the issuer to pay a slightly lower coupon interest rate than would otherwise be required.

Bond Yields

The *yield*, or rate of return, on a bond is frequently used to assess a bond's performance over a given period of time, typically 1 year. Because there are a number of ways to measure a bond's yield, it is important to understand popular yield measures. The three most widely cited bond yields are (1) *current yield*, (2) *yield to maturity (YTM)*, and (3) *yield to call (YTC)*. Each of these yields provides a unique measure of the return on a bond.

The simplest yield measure is the **current yield**, the annual interest payment divided by the current price. For example, a $1,000 par value bond with an 8% coupon interest rate that currently sells for $970 would have a current yield of 8.25% [(0.08 × $1,000)/$970]. This measure indicates the cash return for the year from the bond. However, because current yield ignores any change in bond value, it does not measure the total return. As we'll see later in this chapter, both the yield to maturity and the yield to call measure the total return.

current yield
A measure of a bond's cash return for the year; calculated by dividing the bond's annual interest payment by its current price.

Bond Prices

Because most corporate bonds are purchased and held by institutional investors, such as banks, insurance companies, and mutual funds, rather than individual investors, bond trading and price data are not readily available to individuals. Table 2 includes some assumed current data on the bonds of five companies, noted A through E. Looking at the data for Company C's bond, which is highlighted in the table, we see that the bond has a coupon interest rate of 7.200% and a maturity date of January 15, 2014. These data identify a specific bond issued by Company C. (The company could have more than a single bond issue outstanding.) The price represents the final price at which the bond traded on the current day.

Although most corporate bonds are issued with a *par*, or *face*, *value* of $1,000, *all bonds are quoted as a percentage of par*. A $1,000-par-value bond quoted at 94.007 is priced at $940.07 (94.007% × $1,000). Corporate bonds are quoted in dollars and cents. Thus, Company C's price of 103.143 for the day was $1,031.43—that is, 103.143% × $1,000.

The final column of Table 2 represents the bond's *yield to maturity (YTM)*, which is the compound annual rate of return that would be earned on the bond if it were purchased on the given day and held to maturity. (YTM is discussed in detail later in this chapter.)

TABLE 2	Data on Selected Bonds			
Company	Coupon	Maturity	Price	Yield (YTM)
Company A	6.125%	Nov. 15, 2011	105.336	4.788%
Company B	6.000	Oct. 31, 2036	94.007	6.454
Company C	7.200	Jan. 15, 2014	103.143	6.606
Company D	5.150	Jan. 15, 2017	95.140	5.814
Company E	5.850	Jan. 14, 2012	100.876	5.631

Focus on Ethics — Can We Trust the Bond Raters?

Assessing default risk requires an evaluation of creditworthiness. Most investors have neither the time nor the expertise to do their own credit appraisals for potential bond investments, so they rely on credit-rating agencies for this service. But how reliable are their ratings?

"The dominant rating agencies failed millions of investors by neglecting to lower their ratings on Enron, WorldCom, and other companies heading for bankruptcy," said Alabama Senator Richard Shelby, past-chair of the Senate Banking Committee and sponsor of legislation to hold rating agencies more accountable. "The absence of timely downgrades in these cases was a product of an industry that was beset with conflicts of interest and a lack of competition. Ultimately, this compromised the integrity of the market and investors paid the price," he concluded.

On September 29, 2006, President Bush signed the *Credit Rating Agency Reform Act of 2006*, which abolished the SEC's authority to designate credit-rating agencies as "nationally recognized rating agencies (NRSROs)." Instead, a credit-rating company with 3 years of experience that meets certain standards would be allowed to register with the SEC as a "statistical ratings organization."

The new law is designed to curb alleged abusive practices cited by members of Congress and corporate trade groups, including the practice of sending a company unsolicited ratings with a bill; *notching*, which occurs when a firm lowers ratings on asset-backed securities unless the firm rates a substantial portion of the underlying assets; and tying ratings to the purchase of additional services.

"Importantly, the new law gives the SEC the tools necessary to hold recognized rating agencies accountable if they fail to produce credible and reliable ratings," declared Jim Kaitz, president of the Association for Financial Professionals (AFP), in a statement. AFP represents 15,000 members working in corporate treasury and financial management functions.

One credit-rating agency, S&P, voiced its objection to the original House bill, saying that ratings agencies are members of the financial press and that the proposed legislation represented an unconstitutional infringement of the company's free speech. Despite their objection, the legislation is now law.

Performing risk–return analysis in the bond markets depends on having accurate and timely information. The increased scrutiny from the SEC along with increased competition should add to the value of the ratings received by the investing public.

■ *What effect will the new legislation likely have on the market share of the largest rating agencies? How will the new legislation affect the process of finding ratings information for investors?*

Bond Ratings

Independent agencies such as Moody's and Standard & Poor's assess the riskiness of publicly traded bond issues. These agencies derive their ratings by using financial ratio and cash flow analyses to assess the likely payment of bond interest and principal. Table 3 summarizes these ratings. For discussion of ethical issues related to the bond-rating agencies, see the *Focus on Ethics* box above.

Normally an inverse relationship exists between the quality of a bond and the rate of return that it must provide bondholders: High-quality (high-rated) bonds provide lower returns than lower-quality (low-rated) bonds. This reflects the lender's risk–return tradeoff. When considering bond financing, the financial manager must be concerned with the expected ratings of the bond issue, because these ratings affect salability and cost.

Hint Note that Moody's has 9 major ratings; Standard & Poor's has 10.

TABLE 3	Moody's and Standard & Poor's Bond Ratings[a]			
Moody's	Interpretation	Standard & Poor's	Interpretation
Aaa	Prime quality	AAA	Bank investment quality
Aa	High grade	AA	
A	Upper medium grade	A	
Baa	Medium grade	BBB	
Ba	Lower medium grade	BB	Speculative
	or speculative	B	
B	Speculative		
Caa	From very speculative	CCC	
Ca	to near or in default	CC	
C	Lowest grade	C	Income bond
		D	In default

[a]Some ratings may be modified to show relative standing within a major rating category; for example, Moody's uses numerical modifiers (1, 2, 3), whereas Standard & Poor's uses plus (+) and minus (−) signs.
Sources: Moody's Investors Service, Inc. and Standard & Poor's Corporation.

Popular Types of Bonds

debentures
subordinated debentures
income bonds
mortgage bonds
collateral trust bonds
equipment trust certificates
See Table 4.

zero- (or low-) coupon
  bonds
junk bonds
floating-rate bonds
extendible notes
putable bonds
See Table 5.

Bonds can be classified in a variety of ways. Here we break them into traditional bonds (the basic types that have been around for years) and contemporary bonds (newer, more innovative types). The traditional types of bonds are summarized in terms of their key characteristics and priority of lender's claim in Table 4. Note that the first three types—**debentures, subordinated debentures,** and **income bonds**—are unsecured, whereas the last three—**mortgage bonds, collateral trust bonds,** and **equipment trust certificates**—are secured.

Table 5 describes the key characteristics of five contemporary types of bonds: **zero- (or low-) coupon bonds, junk bonds, floating-rate bonds, extendible notes,** and **putable bonds.** These bonds can be either unsecured or secured. Changing capital market conditions and investor preferences have spurred further innovations in bond financing in recent years and will probably continue to do so.

International Bond Issues

Eurobond
A bond issued by an international borrower and sold to investors in countries with currencies other than the currency in which the bond is denominated.

Companies and governments borrow internationally by issuing bonds in two principal financial markets: the Eurobond market and the foreign bond market. Both give borrowers the opportunity to obtain large amounts of long-term debt financing quickly, in the currency of their choice and with flexible repayment terms.

A **Eurobond** is issued by an international borrower and sold to investors in countries with currencies other than the currency in which the bond is denominated. An example is a dollar-denominated bond issued by a U.S. corporation

TABLE 4	Characteristics and Priority of Lender's Claim of Traditional Types of Bonds	
Bond type	Characteristics	Priority of lender's claim
Unsecured Bonds		
Debentures	Unsecured bonds that only creditworthy firms can issue. Convertible bonds are normally debentures.	Claims are the same as those of any general creditor. May have other unsecured bonds subordinated to them.
Subordinated debentures	Claims are not satisfied until those of the creditors holding certain (senior) debts have been fully satisfied.	Claim is that of a general creditor but not as good as a senior debt claim.
Income bonds	Payment of interest is required only when earnings are available. Commonly issued in reorganization of a failing firm.	Claim is that of a general creditor. Are not in default when interest payments are missed, because they are contingent only on earnings being available.
Secured Bonds		
Mortgage bonds	Secured by real estate or buildings.	Claim is on proceeds from sale of mortgaged assets; if not fully satisfied, the lender becomes a general creditor. The *first-mortgage* claim must be fully satisfied before distribution of proceeds to *second-mortgage* holders, and so on. A number of mortgages can be issued against the same collateral.
Collateral trust bonds	Secured by stock and (or) bonds that are owned by the issuer. Collateral value is generally 25% to 35% greater than bond value.	Claim is on proceeds from stock and (or) bond collateral; if not fully satisfied, the lender becomes a general creditor.
Equipment trust certificates	Used to finance "rolling stock"—airplanes, trucks, boats, railroad cars. A trustee buys the asset with funds raised through the sale of trust certificates and then leases it to the firm; after making the final scheduled lease payment, the firm receives title to the asset. A type of leasing.	Claim is on proceeds from the sale of the asset; if proceeds do not satisfy outstanding debt, trust certificate lenders become general creditors.

and sold to Belgian investors. From the founding of the Eurobond market in the 1960s until the mid-1980s, "blue chip" U.S. corporations were the largest single class of Eurobond issuers. Some of these companies were able to borrow in this market at interest rates below those the U.S. government paid on Treasury bonds. As the market matured, issuers became able to choose the currency in which they borrowed, and European and Japanese borrowers rose to prominence. In more recent years, the Eurobond market has become much more balanced in terms of the mix of borrowers, total issue volume, and currency of denomination.

foreign bond
A bond issued in a host country's financial market, in the host country's currency, by a foreign borrower.

In contrast, a **foreign bond** is issued in a host country's financial market, in the host country's currency, by a foreign borrower. A Swiss-franc–denominated bond issued in Switzerland by a U.S. company is an example of a foreign bond. The three largest foreign-bond markets are Japan, Switzerland, and the United States.

REVIEW QUESTIONS

6 What are typical maturities, denominations, and interest payments of a corporate bond? What mechanisms protect bondholders?

TABLE 5	Characteristics of Contemporary Types of Bonds
Bond type	**Characteristics**[a]
Zero- (or low-) coupon bonds	Issued with no (zero) or a very low coupon (stated interest) rate and sold at a large discount from par. A significant portion (or all) of the investor's return comes from gain in value (i.e., par value minus purchase price). Generally callable at par value. Because the issuer can annually deduct the current year's interest accrual without having to pay the interest until the bond matures (or is called), its cash flow each year is increased by the amount of the tax shield provided by the interest deduction.
Junk bonds	Debt rated Ba or lower by Moody's or BB or lower by Standard & Poor's. Commonly used by rapidly growing firms to obtain growth capital, most often as a way to finance mergers and takeovers. High-risk bonds with high yields—often yielding 2% to 3% more than the best-quality corporate debt.
Floating-rate bonds	Stated interest rate is adjusted periodically within stated limits in response to changes in specified money market or capital market rates. Popular when future inflation and interest rates are uncertain. Tend to sell at close to par because of the automatic adjustment to changing market conditions. Some issues provide for annual redemption at par at the option of the bondholder.
Extendible notes	Short maturities, typically 1 to 5 years, that can be renewed for a similar period at the option of holders. Similar to a floating-rate bond. An issue might be a series of 3-year renewable notes over a period of 15 years; every 3 years, the notes could be extended for another 3 years, at a new rate competitive with market interest rates at the time of renewal.
Putable bonds	Bonds that can be redeemed at par (typically, $1,000) at the option of their holder either at specific dates after the date of issue and every 1 to 5 years thereafter or when and if the firm takes specified actions, such as being acquired, acquiring another company, or issuing a large amount of additional debt. In return for its conferring the right to "put the bond" at specified times or when the firm takes certain actions, the bond's yield is lower than that of a nonputable bond.

[a]The claims of lenders (i.e., bondholders) against issuers of each of these types of bonds vary, depending on the bonds' other features. Each of these bonds can be unsecured or secured.

7. Differentiate between *standard debt provisions* and *restrictive covenants* included in a bond indenture. What are the consequences of violation of them by the bond issuer?

8. How is the cost of bond financing typically related to the cost of short-term borrowing? In addition to a bond's maturity, what other major factors affect its cost to the issuer?

9. What is a *conversion feature?* A *call feature? Stock purchase warrants?*

10. What is the *current yield* for a bond? How are bond prices quoted? How are bonds rated, and why?

11. Compare the basic characteristics of *Eurobonds* and *foreign bonds.*

3 | **Valuation Fundamentals**

valuation
The process that links risk and return to determine the worth of an asset.

Valuation is the process that links risk and return to determine the worth of an asset. It is a relatively simple process that can be applied to *expected* streams of benefits from bonds, stocks, income properties, oil wells, and so on. To determine an asset's worth at a given point in time, a financial manager uses the time-value-of-money techniques and the concepts of risk and return.

Key Inputs

There are three key inputs to the valuation process: (1) cash flows (returns), (2) timing, and (3) a measure of risk, which determines the required return. Each is described below.

Cash Flows (Returns)

The value of any asset depends on the cash flow(s) it is *expected* to provide over the ownership period. To have value, an asset does not have to provide an annual cash flow; it can provide an intermittent cash flow or even a single cash flow over the period.

Personal Finance Example   Celia Sargent wishes to estimate the value of three assets she is considering investing in: common stock in Michaels Enterprises, an interest in an oil well, and an original painting by a well-known artist. Her cash flow estimates for each are as follows:

> **Stock in Michaels Enterprises**   *Expect* to receive cash dividends of $300 per year indefinitely.
>
> **Oil well**   *Expect* to receive cash flow of $2,000 at the end of year 1, $4,000 at the end of year 2, and $10,000 at the end of year 4, when the well is to be sold.
>
> **Original painting**   *Expect* to be able to sell the painting in 5 years for $85,000.

With these cash flow estimates, Celia has taken the first step toward placing a value on each of the assets.

Timing

In addition to making cash flow estimates, we must know the timing of the cash flows.[4] For example, Celia expects the cash flows of $2,000, $4,000, and $10,000 for the oil well to occur at the ends of years 1, 2, and 4, respectively. The combination of the cash flow and its timing fully defines the return expected from the asset.

Risk and Required Return

Hint The required rate of return is the result of investors being risk-averse. For the risk-averse investor to purchase a given asset, the investor *must* *expect* at least enough return to compensate for the asset's perceived risk.

The level of risk associated with a given cash flow can significantly affect its value. In general, the greater the risk of (or the less certain) a cash flow, the lower its value. Greater risk can be incorporated into a valuation analysis by using a higher required return or discount rate. As in the previous chapter, the higher the risk, the greater the required return, and the lower the risk, the less the required return.

---

4. Although cash flows can occur at any time during a year, for computational convenience as well as custom, we will assume they occur at the *end of the year* unless otherwise noted.

Let's return to Celia Sargent's task of placing a value on the original painting and consider two scenarios.

Scenario 1—Certainty A major art gallery has contracted to buy the painting for $85,000 at the end of 5 years. Because this is considered a certain situation, Celia views this asset as "money in the bank." She thus would use the prevailing risk-free rate of 9% as the required return when calculating the value of the painting.

Scenario 2—High Risk The values of original paintings by this artist have fluctuated widely over the past 10 years. Although Celia expects to be able to sell the painting for $85,000, she realizes that its sale price in 5 years could range between $30,000 and $140,000. Because of the high uncertainty surrounding the painting's value, Celia believes that a 15% required return is appropriate.

These two estimates of the appropriate required return illustrate how this rate captures risk. The often subjective nature of such estimates is also clear.

Basic Valuation Model

Simply stated, the value of any asset is *the present value of all future cash flows it is expected to provide over the relevant time period*. The time period can be any length, even infinity. The value of an asset is therefore determined by discounting the expected cash flows back to their present value, using the required return commensurate with the asset's risk as the appropriate discount rate. Utilizing the present value techniques, we can express the value of any asset at time zero, V_0, as

$$V_0 = \frac{CF_1}{(1+r)^1} + \frac{CF_2}{(1+r)^2} + \cdots + \frac{CF_n}{(1+r)^n} \tag{1}$$

where

V_0 = value of the asset at time zero

CF_t = cash flow *expected* at the end of year t

r = appropriate required return (discount rate)

n = relevant time period

Using present value interest factor notation, $PVIF_{r,n}$, Equation 1 can be rewritten as

$$V_0 = [CF_1 \times (PVIF_{r,1})] + [CF_2 \times (PVIF_{r,2})] + \cdots + [CF_n \times (PVIF_{r,n})] \tag{2}$$

We can use Equation 2 to determine the value of any asset.

Celia Sargent used Equation 2 to calculate the value of each asset (using present value interest factors from Appendix: Financial Tables, Table A–2), as shown in Table 6. Michaels Enterprises stock has a value of $2,500, the oil well's

TABLE 6	Valuation of Assets by Celia Sargent			
Asset	Cash flow, CF		Appropriate required return	Valuation[a]
Michaels Enterprises stock[b]	$300/year indefinitely		12%	$V_0 = \$300 \times (PVIFA_{12\%,\infty})$ $= \$300 \times \dfrac{1}{0.12} = \underline{\underline{\$2,500}}$
Oil well[c]	Year (t)	CF_t	20%	$V_0 = [\$2,000 \times (PVIF_{20\%,1})]$
	1	$ 2,000		$\quad + [\$4,000 \times (PVIF_{20\%,2})] + [\$0 \times (PVIF_{20\%,3})]$
	2	4,000		$\quad + [\$10,000 \times (PVIF_{20\%,4})]$
	3	0		$= [\$2,000 \times (0.833)]$
	4	10,000		$\quad + [\$4,000 \times (0.694)] + [\$0 \times (0.579)]$
				$\quad + [\$10,000 \times (0.482)]$
				$= \$1,666 + \$2,776 + \$0 + \$4,820$
				$= \underline{\underline{\$9,262}}$
Original painting[d]	$85,000 at end of year 5		15%	$V_0 = \$85,000 \times (PVIF_{15\%,5})$ $= \$85,000 \times (0.497)$ $= \underline{\underline{\$42,245}}$

[a]Based on *PVIF* interest factors from Appendix: Financial Tables, Table A–2. If calculated using a calculator, the values of the oil well and original painting would have been $9,266.98 and $42,260.03, respectively.

[b]This is a perpetuity (infinite-lived annuity), and therefore the present value interest factor given in Equation $FV_n = PV \times \left(1 + \dfrac{i}{m}\right)^{m \times n}$ is applied.

[c]This is a mixed stream of cash flows and therefore requires a number of *PVIF*s, as noted.

[d]This is a single-amount cash flow and therefore requires a single *PVIF*.

value is $9,262, and the original painting has a value of $42,245. Note that regardless of the pattern of the expected cash flow from an asset, the basic valuation equation can be used to determine its value.

REVIEW QUESTIONS

12 Why is it important for financial managers to understand the valuation process?

13 What are the three key inputs to the valuation process?

14 Does the valuation process apply only to assets that provide an annual cash flow? Explain.

15 Define and specify the general equation for the value of any asset, V_0.

  4 | Bond Valuation

The basic valuation equation can be customized for use in valuing specific securities: bonds, common stock, and preferred stock. We describe bond valuation in this chapter.

Bond Fundamentals

As noted earlier in this chapter, *bonds* are long-term debt instruments used by business and government to raise large sums of money, typically from a diverse group of lenders. Most corporate bonds pay interest *semiannually* (every 6 months) at a stated *coupon interest rate,* have an initial *maturity* of 10 to 30 years, and have a *par value,* or *face value,* of $1,000 that must be repaid at maturity.

Example

Mills Company, a large defense contractor, on January 1, 2010, issued a 10% coupon interest rate, 10-year bond with a $1,000 par value that pays interest semiannually. Investors who buy this bond receive the contractual right to two cash flows: (1) $100 annual interest (10% coupon interest rate × $1,000 par value) distributed as $50 (1/2 × $100) at the end of each 6 months, and (2) the $1,000 par value at the end of the tenth year.

We will use data for Mills's bond issue to look at basic bond valuation.

Basic Bond Valuation

The value of a bond is the present value of the payments its issuer is contractually obligated to make, from the current time until it matures. The basic model for the value, B_0, of a bond is given by Equation 3:

$$B_0 = I \times \left[\sum_{t=1}^{n} \frac{1}{(1 + r_d)^t} \right] + M \times \left[\frac{1}{(1 + r_d)^n} \right] \qquad (3)$$

$$= I \times (PVIFA_{r_d,n}) + M \times (PVIF_{r_d,n}) \qquad (3a)$$

where

$B_0 =$ value of the bond at time zero
$I =$ *annual* interest paid in dollars[5]
$n =$ number of years to maturity
$M =$ par value in dollars
$r_d =$ required return on a bond

We can calculate bond value by using Equation 3a and a financial calculator or by using a spreadsheet or financial tables (Appendix: Financial Tables, Tables A–2 and A–4).

Personal Finance Example　Tim Sanchez wishes to determine the current value of the Mills Company bond. *Assuming that interest on the Mills Company bond issue is paid annually* and that the required return is equal to the bond's coupon interest rate, $I = 100, $r_d = 10\%$, $M = $1,000$, and $n = 10$ years.

The computations involved in finding the bond value are depicted graphically on the time line.

---

5. The payment of annual rather than semiannual bond interest is assumed throughout the following discussion. This assumption simplifies the calculations involved, while maintaining the conceptual accuracy of the valuation procedures presented.

Time line for bond valuation (Mills Company's 10% coupon interest rate, 10-year maturity, $1,000 par, January 1, 2010, issue paying annual interest; required return = 10%)

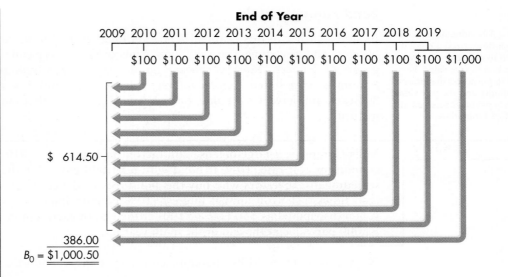

Calculator Use Using the Mills Company's inputs shown at the left, you should find the bond value to be exactly $1,000. Note that *the calculated bond value is equal to its par value; this will always be the case when the required return is equal to the coupon interest rate.*

Spreadsheet Use The value of the Mills Company bond also can be calculated as shown in the following Excel spreadsheet.

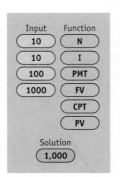

	A	B
1	BOND VALUE, ANNUAL INTEREST, REQUIRED RETURN = COUPON INTEREST RATE	
2	Annual interest payment	$100
3	Coupon interest rate	10%
4	Number of years to maturity	10
5	Par value	$1,000
6	Bond value	$1,000.00

Entry in Cell B6 is
(B2*(1-(1/(1+B3)^B4)))/B3 + (B6*(1/(1+B3)^B4))

The expression 1-(1/(1+B3)^B4))/B3 calculates the Present Value Interest Factor for an Annuity.
The expression 1/(1+B3)^B4 calculates the Present Value Interest Factor for a Single Amount.

Table Use Substituting the appropriate values into Equation 7a yields

$$B_0 = \$100 \times (PVIFA_{10\%,10yrs}) + \$1,000 \times (PVIF_{10\%,10yrs})$$
$$= \$100 \times (6.145) + \$1,000 \times (0.386)$$
$$= \$614.50 + \$386.00 = \underline{\$1,000.50}$$

The bond therefore has a value of approximately $1,000.[6]

---

6. Note that a slight rounding error ($0.50) results here from the use of the table factors, which are rounded to the nearest thousandth.

Bond Value Behavior

In practice, the value of a bond in the marketplace is rarely equal to its par value. In the bond data (see Table 2), it can be seen that the prices of bonds often differ from their par values of 100 (100 percent of par). Some bonds are valued below par (current price below 100), and others are valued above par (current price above 100). A variety of forces in the economy, as well as the passage of time, tend to affect value. Although these external forces are in no way controlled by bond issuers or investors, it is useful to understand the impact that required return and time to maturity have on bond value.

Required Returns and Bond Values

Whenever the required return on a bond differs from the bond's coupon interest rate, the bond's value will differ from its par value. The required return is likely to differ from the coupon interest rate because either (1) economic conditions have changed, causing a shift in the basic cost of long-term funds, or (2) the firm's risk has changed. Increases in the basic cost of long-term funds or in risk will raise the required return; decreases in the cost of funds or in risk will lower the required return.

discount
The amount by which a bond sells at a value that is less than its par value.

premium
The amount by which a bond sells at a value that is greater than its par value.

Regardless of the exact cause, what is important is the relationship between the required return and the coupon interest rate: When the required return is greater than the coupon interest rate, the bond value, B_0, will be less than its par value, M. In this case, the bond is said to sell at a **discount**, which will equal $M - B_0$. When the required return falls below the coupon interest rate, the bond value will be greater than par. In this situation, the bond is said to sell at a **premium**, which will equal $B_0 - M$.

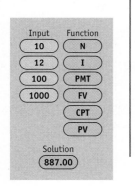

Example

The preceding example showed that when the required return equaled the coupon interest rate, the bond's value equaled its $1,000 par value. If for the same bond the required return were to rise to 12% or fall to 8%, its value in each case would be found as follows (using Equation 3a):

Calculator Use Using the inputs shown at the left and on the next page for the two different required returns, you will find the value of the bond to be below or above par. At a 12% required return, the bond would sell at a *discount* of $113.00 ($1,000 par value − $887.00 value). At the 8% required return, the bond would sell for a *premium* of about $134.00 ($1,134.00 value − $1,000 par value). The results of this and the following calculations for Mills Company's bond values are summarized in Table 7 and graphically depicted in Figure 4. The

TABLE 7	Bond Values for Various Required Returns (Mills Company's 10% Coupon Interest Rate, 10-Year Maturity, $1,000 Par, January 1, 2010, Issue Paying Annual Interest)		

Required return, r_d	Bond value, B_0	Status
12%	$ 887.00	Discount
10	1,000.00	Par value
8	1,134.20	Premium

FIGURE 4

Bond Values and Required Returns

Bond values and required returns (Mills Company's 10% coupon interest rate, 10-year maturity, $1,000 par, January 1, 2010, issue paying annual interest)

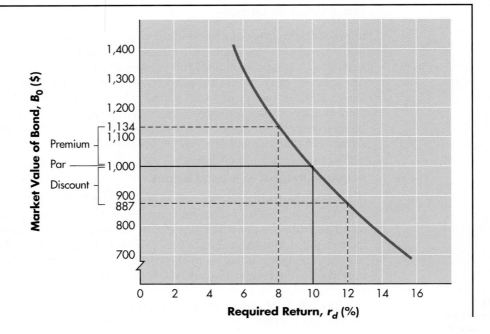

inverse relationship between bond value and required return is clearly shown in the figure.

Spreadsheet Use   The values for the Mills Company bond at required returns of 12% and 8% also can be calculated as shown in the following Excel spreadsheet. (See the text's website, **www.prenhall.com/gitman**, Chapter 6, for another spreadsheet model that computes the values of the Mills Company bond at a discount and a premium.)

	A	B	C
1	BOND VALUE, ANNUAL INTEREST, REQUIRED RETURN NOT EQUAL TO COUPON INTEREST RATE		
2	Annual interest payment	$100	$100
3	Coupon interest rate	10%	10%
4	Required return	12%	8%
5	Number of years to maturity	10	10
6	Par value	$1,000	$1,000
7	Bond value	$887.00	$1,134.20

Entry in Cell B7, a **bond discount**, is
(B2*(1-(1/(1+B4)^B5))/B4) + (B6*(1/(1+B4)^B5))
The expression 1-(1/(1+B4)^B5))/B4) calculates the Present Value Interest Factor for an Annuity.
The expression 1/(1+B4)^B5 calculates the Present Value Interest Factor for a Single Amount.

Entry in Cell C7, a **bond premium**, is
(C2*(1-(1/(1+C4)^C5))/C4) + (C6*(1/(1+C4)^C5))
The expression 1-(1/(1+C4)^C5))/C4) calculates the Present Value Interest Factor for an Annuity.
The expression 1/(1+C4)^C5 calculates the Present Value Interest Factor for a Single Amount.

Table Use

Required Return = 12%	Required Return = 8%
$B_0 = \$100 \times (PVIFA_{12\%,10yrs}) + \$1,000 \times (PVIF_{12\%,10yrs})$	$B_0 = \$100 \times (PVIFA_{8\%,10yrs}) + \$1,000 \times (PVIF_{8\%,10yrs})$
$= \$887.00$	$= \$1,134.00$

Time to Maturity and Bond Values

Whenever the required return is different from the coupon interest rate, the amount of time to maturity affects bond value. An additional factor is whether required returns are constant or change over the life of the bond.

Constant Required Returns   When the required return is different from the coupon interest rate and is assumed to be *constant until maturity,* the value of the bond will approach its par value as the passage of time moves the bond's value closer to maturity. (Of course, when the required return *equals* the coupon interest rate, the bond's value will remain at par until it matures.)

Example

interest rate risk
The chance that interest rates will change and thereby change the required return and bond value. Rising rates, which result in decreasing bond values, are of greatest concern.

Figure 5 depicts the behavior of the bond values calculated earlier and presented in Table 7 for Mills Company's 10% coupon interest rate bond paying annual interest and having 10 years to maturity. Each of the three required returns—12%, 10%, and 8%—is assumed to remain constant over the 10 years to the bond's maturity. The bond's value at both 12% and 8% approaches and ultimately equals the bond's $1,000 par value at its maturity, as the discount (at 12%) or premium (at 8%) declines with the passage of time.

Changing Required Returns   The chance that interest rates will change and thereby change the required return and bond value is called **interest rate risk.**

FIGURE 5

Time to Maturity and Bond Values
Relationship among time to maturity, required returns, and bond values (Mills Company's 10% coupon interest rate, 10-year maturity, $1,000 par, January 1, 2010, issue paying annual interest)

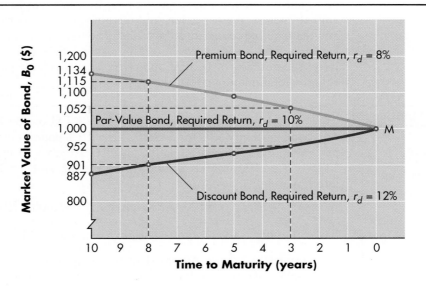

Bondholders are typically more concerned with rising interest rates because a rise in interest rates, and therefore in the required return, causes a decrease in bond value. The shorter the amount of time until a bond's maturity, the less responsive its market value to a given change in the required return. In other words, *short maturities have less interest rate risk than long maturities when all other features (coupon interest rate, par value, and interest payment frequency) are the same.* This is because of the mathematics of time value; the present values of short-term cash flows change far less than the present values of longer-term cash flows in response to a given change in the discount rate (required return).

Example	The effect of changing required returns on bonds with differing maturities can be illustrated by using Mills Company's bond and Figure 5. If the required return rises from 10% to 12% when the bond has 8 years to maturity (see the dashed line at 8 years), the bond's value decreases from $1,000 to $901—a 9.9% decrease. If the same change in required return had occurred with only 3 years to maturity (see the dashed line at 3 years), the bond's value would have dropped to just $952—only a 4.8% decrease. Similar types of responses can be seen for the change in bond value associated with decreases in required returns. The shorter the time to maturity, the less the impact on bond value caused by a given change in the required return.

Yield to Maturity (YTM)

yield to maturity (YTM)
The rate of return that investors earn if they buy a bond at a specific price and hold it until maturity. (Assumes that the issuer makes all scheduled interest and principal payments as promised.)

When investors evaluate bonds, they commonly consider **yield to maturity (YTM)**. This is the rate of return that investors earn if they buy the bond at a specific price and hold it until maturity. (The measure assumes, of course, that the issuer makes all scheduled interest and principal payments as promised.) The yield to maturity on a bond with a current price equal to its par value (that is, $B_0 = M$) will always equal the coupon interest rate. When the bond value differs from par, the yield to maturity will differ from the coupon interest rate.

Assuming that interest is paid annually, the yield to maturity on a bond can be found by solving Equation 3 for r_d. In other words, the current value, the annual interest, the par value, and the number of years to maturity are known, and the required return must be found. The required return is the bond's yield to maturity. The YTM can be found by using a financial calculator, by using an Excel spreadsheet, or by trial and error. The calculator provides accurate YTM values with minimum effort.

Personal Finance Example	Earl Washington wishes to find the YTM on the Mills Company bond. The bond currently sells for $1,080, has a 10% coupon interest rate and $1,000 par value, pays interest annually, and has 10 years to maturity. Because $B_0 = $1,080$, $I = 100 $(0.10 \times $1,000)$, $M = $1,000$, and $n = 10$ years, substituting into Equation 3a yields

$$\$1,080 = \$100 \times (PVIFA_{r_d,10\text{yrs}}) + \$1,000 \times (PVIF_{r_d,10\text{yrs}})$$

Earl's objective is to solve the equation for r_d, the YTM.

Calculator Use [*Note:* Most calculators require *either* the present value (B_0 in this case) or the future values (I and M in this case) to be input as negative num-

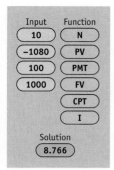

Input	Function
10	N
−1080	PV
100	PMT
1000	FV
	CPT
	I

Solution
8.766

bers to calculate yield to maturity. That approach is employed here.] Using the inputs shown at the left, you should find the YTM to be 8.766%.

Spreadsheet Use The yield to maturity of the 10% coupon rate Mills Company bond also can be calculated as shown in the following Excel spreadsheet.

	A	B
1	YIELD TO MATURITY, ANNUAL INTEREST	
2	Annual interest payment	$100
3	Coupon interest rate	10%
4	Number of years to maturity	10
5	Par value	$1,000
6	Current bond price	$1,080
7	Yield to maturity	8.77%
8	**Trial and error method:**	
9	Choose various required rates and place them in Cell A14	
10	The spreadsheet will recalculate each time. Continue the process	
11	until the value ofthe bond equals the currentprice of the bond	
12	(in this example, it is $1,080).	
13		
14	8.77%	
15	**Payments** **PVIFA** **PVIF**	**PV**
16	$ 100 6.4831	$ 648.31
17	1,000 0.4314	431.40
18	Bond Value	≈ $1,080.00

Trial and Error Because we know that a required return, r_d, of 10% (which equals the bond's 10% coupon interest rate) would result in a value of $1,000, the discount rate that would result in $1,080 must be less than 10%. (Remember that the lower the discount rate, the higher the present value, and the higher the discount rate, the lower the present value.) Trying 9%, we get

$$\$100 \times (PVIFA_{9\%,10yrs}) + \$1,000 \times (PVIF_{9\%,10yrs})$$
$$= \$100 \times (6.418) + \$1,000 \times (0.422)$$
$$= \$641.80 + \$422.00$$
$$= \$1,063.80$$

Because the 9% rate is not quite low enough to bring the value up to $1,080, we next try 8% and get

$$\$100 \times (PVIFA_{8\%,10yrs}) + \$1,000 \times (PVIF_{8\%,10yrs})$$
$$= \$100 \times (6.710) + \$1,000 \times (0.463)$$
$$= \$671.00 + \$463.00$$
$$= \$1,134.00$$

Because the value at the 8% rate is higher than $1,080 and the value at the 9% rate is lower than $1,080, the bond's yield to maturity must be between 8% and 9%. Because the $1,063.80 is closer to $1,080, the YTM to the nearest whole percent is 9%. (By using *interpolation*, we could eventually find the more precise YTM value to be 8.77%.)[7]

---

7. For information on how to interpolate to get a more precise answer, see the text's website at **www.prenhall.com/ gitman**.

Semiannual Interest and Bond Values

The procedure used to value bonds paying interest semiannually is similar to that for compounding interest more frequently than annually, except that here we need to find present value instead of future value. It involves

1. Converting annual interest, I, to semiannual interest by dividing I by 2.
2. Converting the number of years to maturity, n, to the number of 6-month periods to maturity by multiplying n by 2.
3. Converting the required stated (rather than effective) annual return for similar-risk bonds that also pay semiannual interest from an annual rate, r_d, to a semiannual rate by dividing r_d by 2.

Substituting these three changes into Equation 3 yields

$$B_0 = \frac{I}{2} \times \left[\sum_{t=1}^{2n} \frac{1}{\left(1 + \frac{r_d}{2}\right)^t} \right] + M \times \left[\frac{1}{\left(1 + \frac{r_d}{2}\right)^{2n}} \right] \quad \text{(4)}$$

$$= \frac{I}{2} \times (PVIFA_{r_d/2,2n}) + M \times (PVIF_{r_d/2,2n}) \quad \text{(4a)}$$

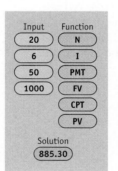

Input / Function

Input	Function
20	N
6	I
50	PMT
1000	FV
	CPT
	PV

Solution
885.30

Example

Assuming that the Mills Company bond pays interest semiannually and that the required stated annual return, r_d, is 12% for similar-risk bonds that also pay semiannual interest, substituting these values into Equation 4a yields

$$B_0 = \frac{\$100}{2} \times (PVIFA_{12\%/2,2 \times 10\text{yrs}}) + \$1,000 \times (PVIF_{12\%/2,2 \times 10\text{yrs}})$$

Calculator Use In using a calculator to find bond value when interest is paid semiannually, we must double the number of periods and divide both the required stated annual return and the annual interest by 2. For the Mills Company bond, we would use 20 periods (2×10 years), a required return of 6% ($12\% \div 2$), and an interest payment of $50 ($100 \div 2$). Using these inputs, you should find the bond value with semiannual interest to be $885.30, as shown at the left.

Spreadsheet Use The value of the Mills Company bond paying semiannual interest at a required return of 12% also can be calculated as shown in the following Excel spreadsheet.

	A	B
1	BOND VALUE, SEMIANNUAL INTEREST	
2	Annual interest payment	$100
3	Stated annual return	12%
4	Number of years to maturity	10
5	Par value	$1,000
6	Bond value	$885.30

Entry in Cell B6 is
(B2/2*(1-(1/(1+B3/2)^(2*B4)))/(B3/2) + (B5*(1/(1+B3/2)^(2*B4)))
The expression 1-(1/(1+B3/2)^(2*B4)))/(B3/2) calculates the Present Value Interest Factor for an Annuity (semiannual interest).
The expression 1/(1+B3/2)^(2*B4) calculates the Present Value Interest Factor for a Single Amount (semiannual interest).

Table Use

$$B_0 = \$50 \times (PVIFA_{6\%,20\text{periods}}) + \$1,000 \times (PVIF_{6\%,20\text{periods}})$$
$$= \$50 \times (11.470) + \$1,000 \times (0.312) = \underline{\underline{\$885.50}}$$

Note that this value is not as precise as that found using a financial calculator or spreadsheet.

Comparing this result with the $887.00 value found earlier for annual compounding (see Table 7), we can see that the bond's value is lower when semiannual interest is paid. *This will always occur when the bond sells at a discount.* For bonds selling at a premium, the opposite will occur: The value with semiannual interest will be greater than with annual interest.

REVIEW QUESTIONS

16 What basic procedure is used to value a bond that pays annual interest? Semiannual interest?

17 What relationship between the required return and the coupon interest rate will cause a bond to sell at a *discount?* At a *premium?* At its *par value?*

18 If the required return on a bond differs from its coupon interest rate, describe the behavior of the bond value over time as the bond moves toward maturity.

19 As a risk-averse investor, would you prefer bonds with short or long periods until maturity? Why?

20 What is a bond's *yield to maturity* (YTM)? Briefly describe the use of a financial calculator, the use of an Excel spreadsheet, and the trial-and-error approach for finding YTM.

Summary

Focus on Value

Interest rates and required returns embody the real cost of money, inflationary expectations, and issuer and issue risk. They reflect the level of return required by market participants as compensation for the risk perceived in a specific security or asset investment. Because these returns are affected by economic expectations, they vary as a function of time, typically rising for longer-term maturities. The yield curve reflects such market expectations at any point in time.

The value of an asset can be found by calculating the present value of its expected cash flows, using the required return as the discount rate. Bonds are the easiest financial assets to value; both the amounts and the timing of their cash flows are contractual and therefore known with certainty. The financial manager needs to understand how to apply valuation techniques to bonds, stocks, and tangible assets to make decisions that are consistent with the firm's **share price maximization goal.**

Review of Learning Goals

Key definitions and formulas for this chapter are summarized in Table 8.

LG 1 **Describe interest rate fundamentals, the term structure of interest rates, and risk premiums.** The flow of funds between savers and investors is regulated by the interest rate or required return. In a perfect, inflation-free, certain world there would be one cost of money—the real rate of interest.

For any class of similar-risk securities, the term structure of interest rates reflects the relationship between the interest rate or rate of return and the time to maturity. Yield curves can be downward-sloping (inverted), upward-sloping (normal), or flat. The expectations theory, liquidity preference theory, and market segmentation theory are cited to explain the shape of the yield curve. Risk premiums for non-Treasury debt issues result from business risk, financial risk, interest rate risk, liquidity risk, tax risk, default risk, maturity risk, and contractual provision risk.

LG 2 **Review the legal aspects of bond financing and bond cost.** Corporate bonds are long-term debt instruments indicating that a corporation has borrowed an amount that it promises to repay in the future under clearly defined terms. Most bonds are issued with maturities of 10 to 30 years and a par value of $1,000. The bond indenture, enforced by a trustee, states all conditions of the bond issue. It contains both standard debt provisions and restrictive covenants, which may include a sinking-fund requirement and/or a security interest. The cost of a bond to an issuer depends on its maturity, offering size, and issuer risk and on the basic cost of money.

LG 3 **Discuss the general features, yields, prices, ratings, popular types, and international issues of corporate bonds.** A bond issue may include a conversion feature, a call feature, or stock purchase warrants. The yield, or rate of return, on a bond can be measured by its current yield, yield to maturity (YTM), or yield to call (YTC). Bond prices are typically reported along with their coupon, maturity date, and yield to maturity (YTM). Bond ratings by independent agencies indicate the risk of a bond issue. Various types of traditional and contemporary bonds are available. Eurobonds and foreign bonds enable established creditworthy companies and governments to borrow large amounts internationally.

LG 4 **Understand the key inputs and basic model used in the valuation process.** Key inputs to the valuation process include cash flows (returns), timing, and risk and the required return. The value of any asset is equal to the present value of all future cash flows it is *expected* to provide over the relevant time period.

LG 5 **Apply the basic valuation model to bonds and describe the impact of required return and time to maturity on bond values.** The value of a bond is the present value of its interest payments plus the present value of its par

TABLE 8	Summary of Key Valuation Definitions and Formulas for Any Asset and for Bonds

Definitions of variables

B_0 = bond value

CF_t = cash flow *expected* at the end of year t

I = annual interest on a bond

r = appropriate required return (discount rate)

r_d = required return on a bond

M = par, or face, value of a bond

n = relevant time period, or number of years to maturity

V_0 = value of the asset at time zero

Valuation formulas

Value of any asset:

$$V_0 = \frac{CF_1}{(1+r)^1} + \frac{CF_2}{(1+r)^2} + \cdots + \frac{CF_n}{(1+r)^n}$$ [Equation 1]

$$= [CF_1 \times (PVIF_{r,1})] + [CF_2 \times (PVIF_{r,2})] + \cdots + [CF_n \times (PVIF_{r,n})]$$ [Equation 2]

Bond value:

$$B_0 = I \times \left[\sum_{t=1}^{n} \frac{1}{(1+r_d)^t}\right] + M \times \left[\frac{1}{(1+r_d)^n}\right]$$ [Equation 3]

$$= I \times (PVIFA_{r_d,n}) + M \times (PVIF_{r_d,n})$$ [Equation 3a]

value. The discount rate used to determine bond value is the required return, which may differ from the bond's coupon interest rate. A bond can sell at a discount, at par, or at a premium, depending on whether the required return is greater than, equal to, or less than its coupon interest rate. The amount of time to maturity affects bond values. The value of a bond will approach its par value as the bond moves closer to maturity. The chance that interest rates will change and thereby change the required return and bond value is called interest rate risk. The shorter the amount of time until a bond's maturity, the less responsive is its market value to a given change in the required return.

LG 6 **Explain yield to maturity (YTM), its calculation, and the procedure used to value bonds that pay interest semiannually.** Yield to maturity is the rate of return investors earn if they buy a bond at a specific price and hold it until maturity. YTM can be calculated by using a financial calculator, by using an Excel spreadsheet, or by trial and error. Bonds that pay interest semiannually are valued by using the same procedure used to value bonds paying annual interest, except that the interest payments are one-half of the annual interest payments, the number of periods is twice the number of years to maturity, and the required return is one-half of the stated annual required return on similar-risk bonds.

Self-Test Problems

  ST6–1 Bond valuation Lahey Industries has outstanding a $1,000 par-value bond with an 8% coupon interest rate. The bond has 12 years remaining to its maturity date.

  a. If interest is paid *annually*, find the value of the bond when the required return is (1) 7%, (2) 8%, and (3) 10%.

  b. Indicate for each case in part **a** whether the bond is selling at a discount, at a premium, or at its par value.

  c. Using the 10% required return, find the bond's value when interest is paid *semiannually*.

  ST6–2 Bond yields Elliot Enterprises' bonds currently sell for $1,150, have an 11% coupon interest rate and a $1,000 par value, pay interest *annually*, and have 18 years to maturity.

  a. Calculate the bonds' *current yield*.

  b. Calculate the bonds' *yield to maturity (YTM)*.

  c. Compare the YTM calculated in part **b** to the bonds' coupon interest rate and current yield (calculated in part **a**). Use a comparison of the bonds' current price and par value to explain these differences.

Warm-Up Exercises   A blue box (■) indicates exercises available in .

 E6–1 The yields for Treasuries with differing maturities on a recent day were as shown in the following table:

Maturity	Yield
3 months	1.41%
6 months	1.71
2 years	2.68
3 years	3.01
5 years	3.70
10 years	4.51
30 years	5.25

Use the information above to construct a *yield curve* for this date.

 E6–2 Recently, the annual inflation rate measured by the Consumer Price Index (CPI) was forecast to be 3.3%. How could a T-bill have had a negative real rate of return over the same period? How could it have had a zero real rate of return? What minimum rate of return must the T-bill have earned to meet your requirement of a 2% real rate of return?

E6–3 You have two assets and must calculate their values today based on their different payment streams and appropriate required returns. Asset 1 has a required return of 15% and will produce a stream of $500 at the end of each year indefinitely. Asset 2 has a required return of 10% and will produce an end-of-year cash flow of $1,200 in the first year, $1,500 in the second year, and $850 in its third and final year.

 E6–4 A bond with 5 years to maturity and a coupon rate of 6% has a par, or face, value of $20,000. Interest is paid annually. If you required a return of 8% on this bond, what is the value of this bond to you?

 E6–5 Assume a 5-year Treasury bond has a coupon rate of 4.5%.
a. Give examples of required rates of return that would make the bond sell at a discount, at a premium, and at par.
b. If this bond's par value is $10,000, calculate the differing values for this bond given the required rates you chose in part **a.**

Problems

A blue box (■) indicates problems available in ⟨myfinancelab⟩.

 P6–1 **Yield curve** A firm wishing to evaluate interest rate behavior has gathered yield data on five U.S. Treasury securities, each having a different maturity and all measured at the same point in time. The summarized data follow.

U.S. Treasury security	Time to maturity	Yield
A	1 year	12.6%
B	10 years	11.2
C	6 months	13.0
D	20 years	11.0
E	5 years	11.4

a. Draw the yield curve associated with these data.
b. Describe the resulting yield curve in part **a,** and explain the general expectations embodied in it.

 P6–2 **Term structure of interest rates** The following yield data for a number of highest-quality corporate bonds existed at each of the three points in time noted.

	Yield		
Time to maturity (years)	5 years ago	2 years ago	Today
1	9.1%	14.6%	9.3%
3	9.2	12.8	9.8
5	9.3	12.2	10.9
10	9.5	10.9	12.6
15	9.4	10.7	12.7
20	9.3	10.5	12.9
30	9.4	10.5	13.5

a. On the same set of axes, draw the yield curve at each of the three given times.
b. Label each curve in part **a** with its general shape (downward-sloping, upward-sloping, flat).
c. Describe the general inflationary and interest rate expectation existing at each of the three times.

P6–3 **Risk-free rate and risk premiums** The real rate of interest is currently 3%; the inflation expectation and risk premiums for a number of securities follow.

Security	Inflation expectation premium	Risk premium
A	6%	3%
B	9	2
C	8	2
D	5	4
E	11	1

a. Find the *risk-free rate of interest*, R_F, that is applicable to each security.
b. Although not noted, what factor must be the cause of the differing risk-free rates found in part **a**?

P6–4 **Risk premiums** Eleanor Burns is attempting to find the nominal rate of interest for each of two securities—A and B—issued by different firms at the same point in time. She has gathered the following data:

Characteristic	Security A	Security B
Time to maturity	3 years	15 years
Inflation expectation premium	9.0%	7.0%
Risk premium for:		
Liquidity risk	1.0%	1.0%
Default risk	1.0%	2.0%
Maturity risk	0.5%	1.5%
Other risk	0.5%	1.5%

a. If the real rate of interest is currently 2%, find the *risk-free rate of interest* applicable to each security.
b. Find the total risk premium attributable to each security's issuer and issue characteristics.

P6–5 **Bond interest payments before and after taxes** Charter Corp. has issued 2,500 debentures with a total principal value of $2,500,000. The bonds have a coupon interest rate of 7%.
a. What dollar amount of interest per bond can an investor expect to receive each year from Charter?
b. What is Charter's total interest expense per year associated with this bond issue?

c. Assuming that Charter is in a 35% corporate tax bracket, what is the company's net after-tax interest cost associated with this bond issue?

P6–6 **Bond prices and yields**   Assume that the Financial Management Corporation's $1,000-par-value bond had a 5.700% coupon, matured on May 15, 2017, had a current price quote of 97.708, and had a yield to maturity (YTM) of 6.034%. Given this information, answer the following questions.
a. What was the dollar price of the bond?
b. What is the bond's *current yield?*
c. Is the bond selling at par, at a discount, or at a premium? Why?
d. Compare the bond's current yield calculated in part **b** to its YTM and explain why they differ.

PERSONAL FINANCE PROBLEM

P6–7 **Valuation fundamentals**   Imagine that you are trying to evaluate the economics of purchasing an automobile. You expect the car to provide annual after-tax cash benefits of $1,200 at the end of each year, and assume that you can sell the car for after-tax proceeds of $5,000 at the end of the planned 5-year ownership period. All funds for purchasing the car will be drawn from your savings, which are currently earning 6% after taxes.
a. Identify the cash flows, their timing, and the required return applicable to valuing the car.
b. What is the maximum price you would be willing to pay to acquire the car? Explain.

P6–8 **Valuation of assets**   Using the information provided in the following table, find the value of each asset.

Asset	Cash flow End of year	Cash flow Amount	Appropriate required return
A	1	$ 5,000	18%
	2	5,000	
	3	5,000	
B	1 through ∞	$ 300	15%
C	1	$ 0	16%
	2	0	
	3	0	
	4	0	
	5	35,000	
D	1 through 5	$ 1,500	12%
	6	8,500	
E	1	$ 2,000	14%
	2	3,000	
	3	5,000	
	4	7,000	
	5	4,000	
	6	1,000	

PERSONAL FINANCE PROBLEM

P6–9 Asset valuation and risk   Laura Drake wishes to estimate the value of an asset expected to provide cash inflows of $3,000 per year at the end of years 1 through 4 and $15,000 at the end of year 5. Her research indicates that she must earn 10% on low-risk assets, 15% on average-risk assets, and 22% on high-risk assets.

a. Determine what is the most Laura should pay for the asset if it is classified as (1) low-risk, (2) average-risk, and (3) high-risk.

b. Suppose Laura is unable to assess the risk of the asset and wants to be certain she's making a good deal. On the basis of your findings in part **a**, what is the most she should pay? Why?

c. All else being the same, what effect does increasing risk have on the value of an asset? Explain in light of your findings in part **a**.

P6–10 Basic bond valuation   Complex Systems has an outstanding issue of $1,000-par-value bonds with a 12% coupon interest rate. The issue pays interest *annually* and has 16 years remaining to its maturity date.

a. If bonds of similar risk are currently earning a 10% rate of return, how much should the Complex Systems bond sell for today?

b. Describe the *two* possible reasons why the rate on similar-risk bonds is below the coupon interest rate on the Complex Systems bond.

c. If the required return were at 12% instead of 10%, what would the current value of Complex Systems' bond be? Contrast this finding with your findings in part **a** and discuss.

P6–11 Bond valuation—Annual interest   Calculate the value of each of the bonds shown in the following table, all of which pay interest *annually*.

Bond	Par value	Coupon interest rate	Years to maturity	Required return
A	$1,000	14%	20	12%
B	1,000	8	16	8
C	100	10	8	13
D	500	16	13	18
E	1,000	12	10	10

P6–12 Bond value and changing required returns   Midland Utilities has outstanding a bond issue that will mature to its $1,000 par value in 12 years. The bond has a coupon interest rate of 11% and pays interest *annually*.

a. Find the value of the bond if the required return is (1) 11%, (2) 15%, and (3) 8%.

b. Plot your findings in part **a** on a set of "required return (x axis)–market value of bond (y axis)" axes.

c. Use your findings in parts **a** and **b** to discuss the relationship between the coupon interest rate on a bond and the required return and the market value of the bond relative to its par value.

d. What *two* possible reasons could cause the required return to differ from the coupon interest rate?

P6-13 **Bond value and time—Constant required returns** Pecos Manufacturing has just issued a 15-year, 12% coupon interest rate, $1,000-par bond that pays interest *annually.* The required return is currently 14%, and the company is certain it will remain at 14% until the bond matures in 15 years.

a. Assuming that the required return does remain at 14% until maturity, find the value of the bond with (1) 15 years, (2) 12 years, (3) 9 years, (4) 6 years, (5) 3 years, and (6) 1 year to maturity.

b. Plot your findings on a set of "time to maturity (*x* axis)–market value of bond (*y* axis)" axes constructed similarly to Figure 5.

c. All else remaining the same, when the required return differs from the coupon interest rate and is assumed to be constant to maturity, what happens to the bond value as time moves toward maturity? Explain in light of the graph in part **b.**

PERSONAL FINANCE PROBLEM

P6-14 **Bond value and time—Changing required returns** Lynn Parsons is considering investing in either of two outstanding bonds. The bonds both have $1,000 par values and 11% coupon interest rates and pay *annual* interest. Bond A has exactly 5 years to maturity, and bond B has 15 years to maturity.

a. Calculate the value of bond A if the required return is (1) 8%, (2) 11%, and (3) 14%.

b. Calculate the value of bond B if the required return is (1) 8%, (2) 11%, and (3) 14%.

c. From your findings in parts **a** and **b,** complete the following table, and discuss the relationship between time to maturity and changing required returns.

Required return	Value of bond A	Value of bond B
8%	?	?
11	?	?
14	?	?

d. If Lynn wanted to minimize *interest rate risk,* which bond should she purchase? Why?

P6-15 **Yield to maturity** The relationship between a bond's yield to maturity and coupon interest rate can be used to predict its pricing level. For each of the bonds listed, state whether the price of the bond will be at a premium to par, at par, or at a discount to par.

Bond	Coupon interest rate	Yield to maturity	Price
A	6%	10%	_____
B	8	8	_____
C	9	7	_____
D	7	9	_____
E	12	10	_____

P6–16 **Yield to maturity** The Salem Company bond currently sells for $955, has a 12% coupon interest rate and a $1,000 par value, pays interest *annually,* and has 15 years to maturity.

a. Calculate the *yield to maturity (YTM)* on this bond.

b. Explain the relationship that exists between the coupon interest rate and yield to maturity and the par value and market value of a bond.

P6–17 **Yield to maturity** Each of the bonds shown in the following table pays interest *annually.*

Bond	Par value	Coupon interest rate	Years to maturity	Current value
A	$1,000	9%	8	$ 820
B	1,000	12	16	1,000
C	500	12	12	560
D	1,000	15	10	1,120
E	1,000	5	3	900

a. Calculate the *yield to maturity (YTM)* for each bond.

b. What relationship exists between the coupon interest rate and yield to maturity and the par value and market value of a bond? Explain.

P6–18 **Bond valuation—Semiannual interest** Find the value of a bond maturing in 6 years, with a $1,000 par value and a coupon interest rate of 10% (5% paid semiannually) if the required return on similar-risk bonds is 14% annual interest (7% paid semiannually).

P6–19 **Bond valuation—Semiannual interest** Calculate the value of each of the bonds shown in the following table, all of which pay interest *semiannually.*

Bond	Par value	Coupon interest rate	Years to maturity	Required stated annual return
A	$1,000	10%	12	8%
B	1,000	12	20	12
C	500	12	5	14
D	1,000	14	10	10
E	100	6	4	14

P6–20 **Bond valuation—Quarterly interest** Calculate the value of a $5,000-par-value bond paying quarterly interest at an annual coupon interest rate of 10% and having 10 years until maturity if the required return on similar-risk bonds is currently a 12% annual rate paid *quarterly.*

P6–21 **ETHICS PROBLEM** Bond rating agencies have invested significant sums of money in an effort to determine which quantitative and nonquantitative factors best predict bond defaults. Furthermore, some of the raters invest time and money to meet privately with corporate personnel to get nonpublic information that is used in assigning the issue's bond rating. In order to recoup those costs, some bond rating agencies have tied their ratings to the purchase of additional services. Do you believe that this is an acceptable practice? Defend your position.

Chapter Case

Evaluating Annie Hegg's Proposed Investment in Atilier Industries Bonds

Annie Hegg has been considering investing in the bonds of Atilier Industries. The bonds were issued 5 years ago at their $1,000 par value and have exactly 25 years remaining until they mature. They have an 8% coupon interest rate, are convertible into 50 shares of common stock, and can be called any time at $1,080. The bond is rated Aa by Moody's. Atilier Industries, a manufacturer of sporting goods, recently acquired a small athletic-wear company that was in financial distress. As a result of the acquisition, Moody's and other rating agencies are considering a rating change for Atilier bonds. Recent economic data suggest that expected inflation, currently at 5% annually, is likely to increase to a 6% annual rate.

Annie remains interested in the Atilier bond but is concerned about inflation, a potential rating change, and maturity risk. To get a feel for the potential impact of these factors on the bond value, she decided to apply the valuation techniques she learned in her finance course.

To Do

a. If the price of the common stock into which the bond is convertible rises to $30 per share after 5 years and the issuer calls the bonds at $1,080, should Annie let the bond be called away from her or should she convert it into common stock?

b. For each of the following required returns, calculate the bond's value, assuming annual interest. Indicate whether the bond will sell at a discount, at a premium, or at par value.
   (1) Required return is 6%.
   (2) Required return is 8%.
   (3) Required return is 10%.

c. Repeat the calculations in part b, assuming that interest is paid *semiannually* and that the semiannual required returns are one-half of those shown. Compare and discuss differences between the bond values for each required return calculated here and in part b under the annual versus semiannual payment assumptions.

d. If Annie strongly believes that expected inflation will rise by 1% during the next few months, what is the most she should pay for the bond, assuming annual interest?

e. If the Atilier bonds are downrated by Moody's from Aa to A, and if such a rating change will result in an increase in the required return from 8% to 8.75%, what impact will this have on the bond value, assuming annual interest?

f. If Annie buys the bond today at its $1,000 par value and holds it for exactly 3 years, at which time the required return is 7%, how much of a gain or loss will she experience in the value of the bond (ignoring interest already received and assuming annual interest)?

g. Rework part **f,** assuming that Annie holds the bond for 10 years and sells it when the required return is 7%. Compare your finding to that in part **f,** and comment on the bond's *maturity risk*.

h. Assume that Annie buys the bond at its current price of 98.380 and holds it until maturity. What will her *current yield* and *yield to maturity* (*YTM*) be, assuming annual interest?

i. After evaluating all of the issues raised above, what recommendation would you give Annie with regard to her proposed investment in the Atilier Industries bonds?

Spreadsheet Exercise

CSM Corporation has a bond issue outstanding at the end of 2009. The bond has 15 years remaining to maturity and carries a coupon interest rate of 6%. Interest on the bond is compounded on a semiannual basis. The par value of the CSM bond is $1,000 and it is currently selling for $874.42.

To Do

Create a spreadsheet similar to the spreadsheets for yield to maturity and semiannual interest that can be viewed at **www.prenhall.com/gitman**, to model the following:

a. Using the trial and error method, determine the *annual* required rate of return (r_d). Find one interest rate that results in a bond value greater than the current bond price, and then find another rate that results in a bond value lower than the current bond price.

b. What is the time to maturity (n)?

c. What is the semiannual coupon payment (pmt)?

d. What is the semiannual required rate of return ($r_d/2$)?

Web Exercise

Go to the text's companion website at **www.prenhall.com/gitman** to find the Web Exercise for this chapter.

> Remember to check the text's website at **www.prenhall.com/gitman** to find additional resources, including Web Exercises and a Web Case.

Solutions to Self-Test Problems

ST6–1 **a.** $B_0 = I \times (PVIFA_{r_d,n}) + M \times (PVIF_{r_d,n})$

$I = 0.08 \times \$1,000 = \$80$

$M = \$1,000$

$n = 12$ yrs

(1) $r_d = 7\%$

$B_0 = \$80 \times (PVIFA_{7\%,12\text{yrs}}) + \$1,000 \times (PVIF_{7\%,12\text{yrs}})$

$= (\$80 \times 7.943) + (\$1,000 \times 0.444)$

$= \$635.44 + \$444.00 = \underline{\$1,079.44}$

(Calculator solution = \$1,079.43)

(2) $r_d = 8\%$

$B_0 = \$80 \times (PVIFA_{8\%,12\text{yrs}}) + \$1,000 \times (PVIF_{8\%,12\text{yrs}})$

$= (\$80 \times 7.536) + (\$1,000 \times 0.397)$

$= \$602.88 + \$397.00 = \underline{\$999.88}$

(Calculator solution = \$1,000)

(3) $r_d = 10\%$

$B_0 = \$80 \times (PVIFA_{10\%,12\text{yrs}}) + \$1,000 \times (PVIF_{10\%,12\text{yrs}})$

$= (\$80 \times 6.814) + (\$1,000 \times 0.319)$

$= \$545.12 + \$319.00 = \underline{\$864.12}$

(Calculator solution = \$863.73)

b. (1) $r_d = 7\%$, $B_0 = \$1,079.44$; sells at a *premium*

(2) $r_d = 8\%$, $B_0 = \$999.88 < \$1,000.00$; sells at its *par value*

(3) $r_d = 10\%$, $B_0 = \$864.12$; sells at a *discount*

c. $B_0 = \dfrac{I}{2} \times (PVIFA_{r_d \div 2, 2n}) + M \times (PVIF_{r_d \div 2, 2n})$

$= \dfrac{\$80}{2} \times (PVIFA_{10\%/2, 2 \times 12\text{periods}}) + \$1,000 \times (PVIF_{10\%/2, 2 \times 12\text{periods}})$

$= \$40 \times (PVIFA_{5\%, 24\text{periods}}) + \$1,000 \times (PVIF_{5\%, 24\text{periods}})$

$= (\$40 \times 13.799) + (\$1,000 \times 0.310)$

$= \$551.96 + \$310.00 = \underline{\$861.96}$

(Calculator solution = \$862.01)

ST6–2 **a.** $B_0 = \$1,150$

$I = 0.11 \times \$1,000 = \$110$

$M = \$1,000$

$n = 18$ yrs

$$\text{Current yield} = \frac{\text{annual interest}}{\text{current price}}$$

$$= \frac{\$110}{\$1,150} = 9.57\%$$

b. $\$1,150 = \$110 \times (PVIFA_{r_d,18\text{yrs}}) + \$1,000 \times (PVIF_{r_d,18\text{yrs}})$

Because if $r_d = 11\%$, $B_0 = \$1,000 = M$, try $r_d = 10\%$.

$B_0 = \$110 \times (PVIFA_{10\%,18yrs}) + \$1,000 \times (PVIF_{10\%,18yrs})$

$\quad = (\$110 \times 8.201) + (\$1,000 \times 0.180)$

$\quad = \$902.11 + \$180.00 = \$1,082.11$

Because $\$1,082.11 < \$1,150$, try $r_d = 9\%$.

$B_0 = \$110 \times (PVIFA_{9\%,18yrs}) + \$1,000 \times (PVIF_{9\%,18yrs})$

$\quad = (\$110 \times 8.756) + (\$1,000 \times 0.212)$

$\quad = \$963.16 + \$212.00 = \$1,175.16$

Because the $1,175.16 value at 9% is higher than $1,150, and the $1,082.11 value at 10% rate is lower than $1,150, the bond's yield to maturity must
be between 9% and 10%. Because the $1,175.16 value is closer to $1,150, rounding to the nearest whole percent, the YTM is 9%. (By using interpolation, the more precise YTM value is 9.27%.)

(Calculator solution = 9.26%)

c. The calculated YTM of 9.26% is below both the bond's 11% coupon interest rate and its current yield of 9.57% calculated in part **a**, because the bond's market value of $1,150 is above its $1,000 par value. Whenever a bond's market value is above its par value (it sells at a *premium*), its YTM and current yield will be below its coupon interest rate; when a bond sells at *par*, the YTM and current yield will equal its coupon interest rate; and when the bond sells for less than par (at a *discount*), its YTM and current yield will be greater than its coupon interest rate.

Answers to Selected End-of-Chapter Problems

6–3 a. A: 9%
        B: 12%
6–5 b. $175,000
     c. $113,750
6–7 b. $8,789.40
6–8 C: $16,660.00
     D: $9,717.00
6–10 a. $1,156.88
6–14 a. (1) $1,120.23
          (2) $1,000.00
          (3) $896.63
6–17 a. A: approximate: 12.36%
             Calculator solution: 12.71%
          C: approximate: 10.38%
             Calculator solution: 10.22%
          E: approximate: 8.77%
             Calculator solution: 8.95%
6–19 A: $1,152.35
      C: $464.72
      E: $76.11

Chapter 8

Stock Valuation

WHY THIS CHAPTER MATTERS TO YOU

In Your Professional Life

Accounting: You need to understand the difference between debt and equity in terms of tax treatment; the ownership claims of capital providers, including venture capitalists and stockholders; and why book value per share is not a sophisticated basis for common stock valuation.

Information systems: You need to understand the procedures used to issue common stock; the information needed to value stock; and how proposed actions affect the share price.

Management: You need to understand the difference between debt and equity capital; the rights and claims of stockholders; the process of issuing common stock; and the stock valuation models used to value the firm's common stock.

Marketing: You need to understand that the firm's ideas for products and services will greatly affect its ability to raise capital and that a perceived increase in risk from new projects may negatively affect the firm's stock value.

Operations: You need to understand that the amount of capital the firm has to invest in plant assets and inventory will depend on the evaluations of venture capitalists and would-be investors; the better the prospects look for growth, the more money the firm will have for operations.

In Your Personal Life

At some point, you are likely to hold stocks as an asset in your retirement program. You may want to estimate a stock's value. If the stock is selling below its estimated value, you may buy the stock; if its market price is above its value, you may sell it. Some individuals rely on financial advisors to make such buy or sell recommendations. Regardless of how you approach investment decisions, it will be helpful for you to understand how stocks are valued.

LEARNING GOALS

LG 1 Differentiate between debt and equity capital.

LG 2 Discuss the rights, characteristics, and features of both common and preferred stock.

LG 3 Describe the process of issuing common stock, including venture capital, going public, and the investment banker, and interpreting stock quotations.

LG 4 Understand the concept of market efficiency and basic common stock valuation using zero-growth and constant-growth models.

LG 5 Discuss the free cash flow valuation model and the book value, liquidation value, and price/earnings (P/E) multiple approaches.

LG 6 Explain the relationships among financial decisions, return, risk, and the firm's value.

From Chapter 7 of *Principles of Managerial Finance*, Brief 5th Edition. Lawrence J. Gitman. Copyright © 2009 by Pearson Prentice Hall. All rights reserved.

Owning corporate stock is a popular investment activity. Each weekday, the news media report on the movements of stock prices in the financial markets. The price of each share of a firm's common stock is driven by the cash flows (dividends) owners expect to receive from owning the stock and the perceived riskiness of those forecasted cash flows. This chapter describes the key aspects of corporate stock and continues our discussion of the valuation process—this time, of the valuation of stock.

1 | Differences between Debt and Equity Capital

capital
The long-term funds of a firm; all items on the right-hand side of the firm's balance sheet, *excluding current liabilities.*

debt capital
All long-term borrowing incurred by a firm, including bonds.

equity capital
The long-term funds provided by the firm's owners, the stockholders.

The term **capital** denotes the long-term funds of a firm. All items on the right-hand side of the firm's balance sheet, *excluding current liabilities,* are sources of capital. **Debt capital** includes all long-term borrowing incurred by a firm, including bonds. **Equity capital** consists of long-term funds provided by the firm's owners, the stockholders. A firm can obtain equity capital either *internally,* by retaining earnings rather than paying them out as dividends to its stockholders, or *externally,* by selling common or preferred stock. The key differences between debt and equity capital are summarized in Table 1 and discussed below.

Voice in Management

Unlike creditors (lenders), holders of equity capital (common and preferred stockholders) are owners of the firm. Holders of common stock have voting rights that permit them to select the firm's directors and to vote on special issues. In contrast, debtholders and preferred stockholders may receive voting privileges only when the firm has violated its stated contractual obligations to them.

Claims on Income and Assets

Holders of equity have claims on both income and assets that are secondary to the claims of creditors. Their *claims on income* cannot be paid until the claims of all creditors (including both interest and scheduled principal payments) have been satisfied. After satisfying these claims, the firm's board of directors decides whether to distribute dividends to the owners.

The equity holders' *claims on assets* also are secondary to the claims of creditors. If the firm fails, its assets are sold, and the proceeds are distributed in this order: employees and customers, the government, creditors, and (finally) equity holders. Because equity holders are the last to receive any distribution of assets, they expect greater returns from dividends and/or increases in stock price.

The costs of equity financing are generally higher than debt costs. One reason is that the suppliers of equity capital take more risks because of their subordinate claims on income and assets. Despite being more costly, equity capital is necessary for a firm to grow. All corporations must initially be financed with some common stock equity.

TABLE 1	Key Differences between Debt and Equity Capital	
	Type of capital	
Characteristic	Debt	Equity
Voice in management[a]	No	Yes
Claims on income and assets	Senior to equity	Subordinate to debt
Maturity	Stated	None
Tax treatment	Interest deduction	No deduction

[a]In the event that the issuer violates its stated contractual obligations to them, debtholders and preferred stockholders *may* receive a voice in management; otherwise, only common stockholders have voting rights.

Maturity

Unlike debt, equity capital is a *permanent form* of financing for the firm. It does not "mature" so repayment is not required. Because equity is liquidated only during bankruptcy proceedings, stockholders must recognize that although a ready market may exist for their shares, the price that can be realized may fluctuate. This fluctuation of the market price of equity makes the overall returns to a firm's stockholders even more risky.

Tax Treatment

Interest payments to debtholders are treated as tax-deductible expenses by the issuing firm, whereas dividend payments to a firm's common and preferred stockholders are not tax-deductible. The tax deductibility of interest lowers the corporation's cost of debt financing, further causing it to be lower than the cost of equity financing.

REVIEW QUESTION

1   What are the key differences between *debt capital* and *equity capital*?

2 | # Common and Preferred Stock

A firm can obtain equity capital by selling either common or preferred stock. All corporations initially issue common stock to raise equity capital. Some of these firms later issue either additional common stock or preferred stock to raise more equity capital. Although both common and preferred stock are forms of equity capital, preferred stock has some similarities to debt capital that significantly differentiate it from common stock. Here we first consider the features of both common and preferred stock and then describe the process of issuing common stock, including the use of venture capital.

Common Stock

The true owners of business firms are the common stockholders. Common stockholders are sometimes referred to as *residual owners* because they receive what is left—the residual—after all other claims on the firm's income and assets have been satisfied. They are assured of only one thing: that they cannot lose any more than they have invested in the firm. As a result of this generally uncertain position, common stockholders expect to be compensated with adequate dividends and, ultimately, capital gains.

Ownership

privately owned (stock)
All common stock of a firm owned by a single individual.

closely owned (stock)
All common stock of a firm owned by a small group of investors (such as a family).

publicly owned (stock)
Common stock of a firm owned by a broad group of unrelated individual or institutional investors.

The common stock of a firm can be **privately owned** by a single individual, **closely owned** by a small group of investors (such as a family), or **publicly owned** by a broad group of unrelated individual or institutional investors. Typically, small corporations are privately or closely owned; if their shares are traded, this trading occurs infrequently and in small amounts. Large corporations, which are emphasized in the following discussions, are publicly owned, and their shares are generally actively traded in broker or dealer markets.

Par Value

par value (stock)
A relatively useless value for a stock established for legal purposes in the firm's corporate charter.

Unlike bonds, which always have a par value, common stock may be sold with or without a par value. The **par value** of a common stock is a relatively useless value established for legal purposes in the firm's corporate charter. It is generally quite low, about $1.

Firms often issue stock with no par value, in which case they may assign the stock a value or record it on the books at the price at which it is sold. A low par value may be advantageous in states where certain corporate taxes are based on the par value of stock; if a stock has no par value, the tax may be based on an arbitrarily determined per-share figure.

Preemptive Rights

preemptive right
Allows common stockholders to maintain their *proportionate* ownership in the corporation when new shares are issued.

dilution of ownership
Occurs when a new stock issue results in each present shareholder having a claim on a *smaller* part of the firm's earnings than previously.

rights
Financial instruments that allow stockholders to purchase additional shares at a price below the market price, in direct proportion to their number of owned shares.

The **preemptive right** allows common stockholders to maintain their *proportionate* ownership in the corporation when new shares are issued. It allows existing shareholders to maintain voting control and protects them against the dilution of their ownership. **Dilution of ownership** usually results in the dilution of earnings, because each present shareholder has a claim on a *smaller* part of the firm's earnings than previously.

In a *rights offering,* the firm grants **rights** to its shareholders. These financial instruments allow stockholders to purchase additional shares at a price below the market price, in direct proportion to their number of owned shares. Rights are used primarily by smaller corporations whose shares are either *closely owned* or *publicly owned* and not actively traded. In these situations, rights are an important financing tool without which shareholders would run the risk of losing their proportionate control of the corporation. From the firm's viewpoint, the use of rights offerings to raise new equity capital may be less costly and may generate more interest than a public offering of stock.

Example

Dominic Company, a regional advertising firm, currently has 100,000 shares of common stock outstanding and is contemplating a rights offering of an additional 10,000 shares. Each existing shareholder will receive one right per share, and each right will entitle the shareholder to purchase one-tenth of a share of new common stock (10,000 ÷ 100,000), so 10 rights will be required to purchase one share of the stock. The holder of 1,000 shares (1 percent) of the outstanding common stock will receive 1,000 rights, each permitting the purchase of one-tenth of a share of new common stock, for a total of 100 new shares. If the shareholder exercises the rights, he or she will end up with a total of 1,100 shares of common stock, or 1 percent of the total number of shares then outstanding (110,000). Thus, the shareholder maintains the same proportion of ownership he or she had prior to the rights offering.

Authorized, Outstanding, and Issued Shares

authorized shares
The number of shares of common stock that a firm's corporate charter allows it to issue.

A firm's corporate charter indicates how many **authorized shares** it can issue. The firm cannot sell more shares than the charter authorizes without obtaining approval through a shareholder vote. To avoid later having to amend the charter, firms generally attempt to authorize more shares than they initially plan to issue.

outstanding shares
The number of shares of common stock held by the public.

Authorized shares become **outstanding shares** when they are held by the public. If the *firm* repurchases any of its outstanding shares, these shares are recorded as **treasury stock** and are no longer considered to be outstanding shares. **Issued shares** are the shares of common stock that have been put into circulation; they represent the sum of *outstanding shares* and *treasury stock*.

treasury stock
The number of shares of outstanding stock that have been repurchased by the firm.

issued shares
The number of shares of common stock that have been put into circulation; the sum of *outstanding shares* and *treasury stock*.

Example

Golden Enterprises, a producer of medical pumps, has the following stockholders' equity account on December 31:

Stockholders' Equity

Common stock—$0.80 par value:	
Authorized 35,000,000 shares; issued 15,000,000 shares	$ 12,000,000
Paid-in capital in excess of par	63,000,000
Retained earnings	31,000,000
	$106,000,000
Less: Cost of treasury stock (1,000,000 shares)	4,000,000
Total stockholders' equity	$102,000,000

How many shares of additional common stock can Golden sell without gaining approval from its shareholders? The firm has 35 million authorized shares, 15 million issued shares, and 1 million shares of treasury stock. Thus 14 million shares are outstanding (15 million issued shares − 1 million shares of treasury stock), and Golden can issue 21 million additional shares (35 million authorized shares − 14 million outstanding shares) without seeking shareholder approval. This total includes the treasury shares currently held, which the firm can reissue to the public without obtaining shareholder approval.

Voting Rights

Generally, each share of common stock entitles its holder to one vote in the election of directors and on special issues. Votes are generally assignable and may be cast at the annual stockholders' meeting.

In recent years, many firms have issued two or more classes of common stock; they differ mainly in having unequal voting rights. A firm can use different classes of stock as a defense against a *hostile takeover* in which an outside group, without management support, tries to gain voting control of the firm by buying its shares in the marketplace. **Supervoting shares** of stock give each owner multiple votes. Supervoting shares allow "insiders" to maintain control against an outside group whose shares have only one vote each. At other times, a class of **nonvoting common stock** is issued when the firm wishes to raise capital through the sale of common stock but does not want to give up its voting control.

When different classes of common stock are issued on the basis of unequal voting rights, class A common is typically—but not universally—designated as nonvoting, and class B common has voting rights. Generally, higher classes of shares (class A, for example) are given preference in the distribution of earnings (dividends) and assets; lower-class shares, in exchange, receive voting rights. Treasury stock, which is held within the corporation, generally *does not* have voting rights, *does not* earn dividends, and *does not* have a claim on assets in liquidation.

Because most small stockholders do not attend the annual meeting to vote, they may sign a **proxy statement** transferring their votes to another party. The solicitation of proxies from shareholders is closely controlled by the Securities and Exchange Commission to ensure that proxies are not being solicited on the basis of false or misleading information. Existing management generally receives the stockholders' proxies, because it is able to solicit them at company expense.

Occasionally, when the firm is widely owned, outsiders may wage a **proxy battle** to unseat the existing management and gain control. To win a corporate election, votes from a majority of the shares voted are required. However, the odds of a nonmanagement group winning a proxy battle are generally slim.

supervoting shares
Stock that carries with it multiple votes per share rather than the single vote per share typically given on regular shares of common stock.

nonvoting common stock
Common stock that carries no voting rights; issued when the firm wishes to raise capital through the sale of common stock but does not want to give up its voting control.

proxy statement
A statement transferring the votes of a stockholder to another party.

proxy battle
The attempt by a non-management group to gain control of the management of a firm by soliciting a sufficient number of proxy votes.

Dividends

The payment of dividends to the firm's shareholders is at the discretion of the corporation's board of directors. Most corporations pay dividends quarterly. Dividends may be paid in cash, stock, or merchandise. Cash dividends are the most common, merchandise dividends the least.

Common stockholders are not promised a dividend, but they come to expect certain payments on the basis of the historical dividend pattern of the firm. Before dividends are paid to common stockholders, the claims of the government, all creditors, and preferred stockholders must be satisfied. Since passage of the *Jobs and Growth Tax Relief Reconciliation Act of 2003*, many firms now pay larger dividends to shareholders, who are subject to a maximum tax rate of 15 percent on dividends rather than the maximum tax rate of 39 percent in effect prior to passage of the act.

International Stock Issues

Although the international market for common stock is not as large as the international market for bonds, cross-border issuance and trading of common stock have increased dramatically in the past 30 years.

Some corporations *issue stock in foreign markets*. For example, the stock of General Electric trades in Frankfurt, London, Paris, and Tokyo; the stocks of Time Warner and Microsoft trade in Frankfurt and London; and the stock of McDonalds trades in Frankfurt, London, and Paris. The Frankfurt, London, and Tokyo markets are the most popular. Issuing stock internationally broadens the ownership base and helps a company to integrate itself into the local business scene. A listing on a foreign stock exchange both increases local business press coverage and serves as effective corporate advertising. Having locally traded stock can also facilitate corporate acquisitions, because shares can be used as an acceptable method of payment.

Foreign corporations have also discovered the benefits of trading their stock in the United States. The disclosure and reporting requirements mandated by the U.S. Securities and Exchange Commission have historically discouraged all but the largest foreign firms from directly listing their shares on the New York Stock Exchange or the American Stock Exchange. For example, in 1993, Daimler-Benz (now DaimlerChrysler) became the first large German company to be listed on the NYSE.

As an alternative, most foreign companies choose to tap the U.S. market through **American depositary receipts (ADRs)**. These are dollar-denominated receipts for the stocks of foreign companies that are held in the vaults of banks in the companies' home countries. They serve as backing for **American depositary shares (ADSs)**, which are securities that permit U.S. investors to hold shares of non-U.S. companies and trade them in U.S. markets. Because ADSs are issued, in dollars, to U.S. investors, they are subject to U.S. securities laws. At the same time, they give investors the opportunity to diversify their portfolios internationally.

Preferred Stock

Preferred stock gives its holders certain privileges that make them senior to common stockholders. Preferred stockholders are promised a fixed periodic dividend, which is stated either as a percentage or as a dollar amount. How the dividend is specified depends on whether the preferred stock has a *par value*. **Par-value preferred stock** has a stated face value, and its annual dividend is specified as a percentage of this value. **No-par preferred stock** has no stated face value, but its annual dividend is stated in dollars. Preferred stock is most often issued by public utilities, by acquiring firms in merger transactions, and by firms that are experiencing losses and need additional financing.

Basic Rights of Preferred Stockholders

The basic rights of preferred stockholders are somewhat more favorable than the rights of common stockholders. Preferred stock is often considered *quasi-debt* because, much like interest on debt, it specifies a fixed periodic payment (dividend). Of course, as ownership, preferred stock is unlike debt in that it has no maturity date. Because they have a fixed claim on the firm's income that takes precedence over the claim of common stockholders, preferred stockholders are exposed to less risk. They are consequently *not normally given a voting right*.

Preferred stockholders have *preference over common stockholders in the distribution of earnings*. If the stated preferred stock dividend is "passed" (not paid)

American depositary receipts (ADRs)
Dollar-denominated receipts for the stocks of foreign companies that are held in the vaults of banks in the companies' home countries.

American depositary shares (ADSs)
Securities, backed by *American depositary receipts (ADRs)*, that permit U.S. investors to hold shares of non-U.S. companies and trade them in U.S. markets.

par-value preferred stock
Preferred stock with a stated face value that is used with the specified dividend percentage to determine the annual dollar dividend.

no-par preferred stock
Preferred stock with no stated face value but with a stated annual dollar dividend.

by the board of directors, the payment of dividends to common stockholders is prohibited. It is this preference in dividend distribution that makes common stockholders the true risk takers.

Preferred stockholders are also usually given *preference over common stockholders in the liquidation of assets* in a legally bankrupt firm, although they must "stand in line" behind creditors. The amount of the claim of preferred stockholders in liquidation is normally equal to the par or stated value of the preferred stock.

Features of Preferred Stock

A preferred stock issue generally includes a number of features, which, along with the stock's par value, the amount of dividend payments, the dividend payment dates, and any restrictive covenants, are specified in an agreement similar to a *bond indenture.*

Restrictive Covenants   The restrictive covenants in a preferred stock issue focus on ensuring the firm's continued existence and regular payment of the dividend. These covenants include provisions about passing dividends, the sale of senior securities, mergers, sales of assets, minimum liquidity requirements, and repurchases of common stock. The violation of preferred stock covenants usually permits preferred stockholders either to obtain representation on the firm's board of directors or to force the retirement of their stock at or above its par or stated value.

cumulative (preferred stock)
Preferred stock for which all passed (unpaid) dividends in arrears, along with the current dividend, must be paid before dividends can be paid to common stockholders.

noncumulative (preferred stock)
Preferred stock for which passed (unpaid) dividends do not accumulate.

Cumulation   Most preferred stock is **cumulative** with respect to any dividends passed. That is, all dividends in arrears, along with the current dividend, must be paid before dividends can be paid to common stockholders. If preferred stock is **noncumulative,** passed (unpaid) dividends do not accumulate. In this case, only the current dividend must be paid before dividends can be paid to common stockholders. Because the common stockholders can receive dividends only after the dividend claims of preferred stockholders have been satisfied, it is in the firm's best interest to pay preferred dividends when they are due.[1]

Example

Utley Corporation, a manufacturer of specialty automobiles, currently has outstanding an issue of $6 preferred stock on which quarterly dividends of $1.50 are to be paid. Because of a cash shortage, the last two quarterly dividends were passed. The directors of the company have been receiving a large number of complaints from common stockholders, who have, of course, not received any dividends in the past two quarters either. If the preferred stock is *cumulative*, the company will have to pay its preferred stockholders $4.50 per share ($3.00 of dividends in arrears plus the current $1.50 dividend) prior to paying dividends to its common stockholders. If the preferred stock is *noncumulative*, the firm must pay only the current $1.50 dividend to its preferred stockholders prior to paying dividends to its common stockholders.

Other Features   Preferred stock is generally *callable*—the issuer can retire outstanding stock within a certain period of time at a specified price. The call

---

1. Most preferred stock is cumulative, because it is difficult to sell noncumulative stock. Common stockholders obviously prefer issuance of noncumulative preferred stock, because it does not place them in quite so risky a position. But it is often in the best interest of the firm to sell cumulative preferred stock because of its lower cost.

option generally cannot be exercised until after a specified date. The call price is normally set above the initial issuance price, but it may decrease as time passes. Making preferred stock callable provides the issuer with a way to bring the fixed-payment commitment of the preferred issue to an end if conditions in the financial markets make it desirable to do so.

conversion feature (preferred stock)
A feature of *convertible preferred stock* that allows holders to change each share into a stated number of shares of common stock.

Preferred stock quite often contains a **conversion feature** that allows *holders of convertible preferred stock* to change each share into a stated number of shares of common stock. Sometimes the number of shares of common stock that the preferred stock can be exchanged for changes according to a prespecified formula.

Issuing Common Stock

Because of the high risk associated with a business startup, a firm's initial financing typically comes from its founders in the form of a common stock investment. Until the founders have made an equity investment, it is highly unlikely that others will contribute either equity or debt capital. Early-stage investors in the firm's equity, as well as lenders who provide debt capital, want to be assured that they are taking no more risk than the founding owner(s). In addition, they want confirmation that the founders are confident enough in their vision for the firm that they are willing to risk their own money.

The initial nonfounder financing for business startups with attractive growth prospects comes from private equity investors. Then, as the firm establishes the viability of its product or service offering and begins to generate revenues, cash flow, and profits, it will often "go public" by issuing shares of common stock to a much broader group of investors.

Before we consider the initial *public* sales of equity, let's review some of the key aspects of early-stage equity financing in firms that have attractive growth prospects.

Venture Capital

venture capital
Privately raised external equity capital used to fund early-stage firms with attractive growth prospects.

venture capitalists (VCs)
Providers of venture capital; typically, formal businesses that maintain strong oversight over the firms they invest in and that have clearly defined exit strategies.

angel capitalists (angels)
Wealthy individual investors who do not operate as a business but invest in promising early-stage companies in exchange for a portion of the firm's equity.

The initial external equity financing privately raised by firms, typically early-stage firms with attractive growth prospects, is called **venture capital**. Those who provide venture capital are known as **venture capitalists (VCs)**. They typically are formal business entities that maintain strong oversight over the firms they invest in and that have clearly defined exit strategies. Less visible early-stage investors called **angel capitalists** (or **angels**) tend to be investors who do not actually operate as a business; they are often wealthy individual investors who are willing to invest in promising early-stage companies in exchange for a portion of the firm's equity. Although angels play a major role in early-stage equity financing, we will focus on VCs because of their more formal structure and greater public visibility.

Organization and Investment Stages Institutional venture capital investors tend to be organized in one of four basic ways, as described in Table 2. The *VC limited partnership* is by far the dominant structure. These funds have as their sole objective to earn high returns, rather than to obtain access to the companies in order to sell or buy other products or services.

VCs can invest in early-stage companies, later-stage companies, or buyouts and acquisitions. Generally, about 40 to 50 percent of VC investments are devoted to early-stage companies (for startup funding and expansion) and a similar percentage to later-stage companies (for marketing, production expansion, and

TABLE 2	Organization of Institutional Venture Capital Investors
Organization	**Description**
Small business investment companies (SBICs)	Corporations chartered by the federal government that can borrow at attractive rates from the U.S. Treasury and use the funds to make venture capital investments in private companies.
Financial VC funds	Subsidiaries of financial institutions, particularly banks, set up to help young firms grow and, it is hoped, become major customers of the institution.
Corporate VC funds	Firms, sometimes subsidiaries, established by nonfinancial firms, typically to gain access to new technologies that the corporation can access to further its own growth.
VC limited partnerships	Limited partnerships organized by professional VC firms, which serve as the general partner and organize, invest, and manage the partnership using the limited partners' funds; the professional VCs ultimately liquidate the partnership and distribute the proceeds to all partners.

preparation for public offering); the remaining 5 to 10 percent are devoted to the buyout or acquisition of other companies. Generally, VCs look for compound annual rates of return ranging from 20 to 50 percent or more, depending on both the development stage and the attributes of each company. Earlier-stage investments tend to demand higher returns than later-stage investments because of the higher risk associated with the earlier stages of a firm's growth.

Deal Structure and Pricing Regardless of the development stage, venture capital investments are made under a legal contract that clearly allocates responsibilities and ownership interests between existing owners (founders) and the VC fund or limited partnership. The terms of the agreement will depend on numerous factors related to the founders; the business structure, stage of development, and outlook; and other market and timing issues. The specific financial terms will, of course, depend on the value of the enterprise, the amount of funding, and the perceived risk. To control the VC's risk, various covenants are included in the agreement, and the actual funding may be pegged to the achievement of *measurable milestones*. The VC will negotiate numerous other provisions into the contract, both to ensure the firm's success and to control its risk exposure. The contract will have an explicit exit strategy for the VC that may be tied both to measurable milestones and to time.

The amount of equity to which the VC is entitled will, of course, depend on the value of the firm, the terms of the contract, the exit terms, and the minimum compound annual rate of return required by the VC on its investment. Although each VC investment is unique and no standard contract exists, the transaction will be structured to provide the VC with a high rate of return that is consistent with the typically high risk of such transactions. The exit strategy of most VC investments is to take the firm public through an initial public offering.

Going Public

When a firm wishes to sell its stock in the primary market, it has three alternatives. It can make (1) a *public offering*, in which it offers its shares for sale to the general public; (2) a *rights offering,* in which new shares are sold to existing stockholders; or (3) a *private placement,* in which the firm sells new securities directly to an investor or group of investors. Here we focus on public offerings, particularly the **initial public offering (IPO)**, which is the first public sale of a firm's stock. IPOs are typically made by small, rapidly growing companies that either require additional capital to continue expanding or have met a milestone for going public that was established in a contract signed earlier in order to obtain VC funding.

initial public offering (IPO)
The first public sale of a firm's stock.

To go public, the firm must first obtain the approval of its current shareholders, the investors who own its privately issued stock. Next, the company's auditors and lawyers must certify that all documents for the company are legitimate. The company then finds an investment bank willing to *underwrite* the offering. This underwriter is responsible for promoting the stock and facilitating the sale of the company's IPO shares. The underwriter often brings in other investment banking firms as participants. We'll discuss the role of the investment banker in more detail in the next section.

The company files a registration statement with the SEC. One portion of the registration statement is called the **prospectus.** It describes the key aspects of the issue, the issuer, and its management and financial position. During the waiting period between the statement's filing and its approval, prospective investors can receive a preliminary prospectus. This preliminary version is called a **red herring,** because a notice printed in red on the front cover indicates the tentative nature of the offer. The cover of the preliminary prospectus describing the 2007 stock issue of Metro PCS Communications, Inc., is shown in Figure 1. Note the red herring printed vertically on its left edge.

prospectus
A portion of a security registration statement that describes the key aspects of the issue, the issuer, and its management and financial position.

red herring
A preliminary prospectus made available to prospective investors during the waiting period between the registration statement's filing with the SEC and its approval.

After the SEC approves the registration statement, the investment community can begin analyzing the company's prospects. However, from the time it files until at least one month after the IPO is complete, the company must observe a *quiet period,* during which there are restrictions on what company officials may say about the company. The purpose of the quiet period is to make sure that all potential investors have access to the same information about the company—the information presented in the preliminary prospectus—and not to any unpublished data that might give them an unfair advantage.

The investment bankers and company executives promote the company's stock offering through a *road show,* a series of presentations to potential investors around the country and sometimes overseas. In addition to providing investors with information about the new issue, road show sessions help the investment bankers gauge the demand for the offering and set an expected pricing range. After the underwriter sets terms and prices the issue, the SEC must approve the offering.

The Investment Banker's Role

investment banker
Financial intermediary that specializes in selling new security issues and advising firms with regard to major financial transactions.

underwriting
The role of the *investment banker* in bearing the risk of reselling, at a profit, the securities purchased from an issuing corporation at an agreed-on price.

Most public offerings are made with the assistance of an **investment banker.** The investment banker is a financial intermediary (such as Morgan Stanley or Goldman, Sachs) that specializes in selling new security issues and advising firms with regard to major financial transactions. The main activity of the investment banker is **underwriting.** This process involves purchasing the security issue from the issuing corporation at an agreed-on price and bearing the risk of reselling it to the public at a profit. The investment banker also provides the issuer with advice about pricing and other important aspects of the issue.

FIGURE 1

Cover of a Preliminary Prospectus for a Stock Issue

Some of the key factors related to the 2007 common stock issue by Metro PCS Communications, Inc., are summarized on the cover of the prospectus. The type printed vertically on the left edge is normally red, which explains its name "red herring." (*Source:* Metro PCS Communications, Inc., April 3, 2007, p. 1.)

SUBJECT TO COMPLETION, DATED APRIL 3, 2007

PROSPECTUS

50,000,000 Shares

MetroPCS Communications, Inc.

Common Stock

This is our initial public offering. We are offering 37,500,000 shares of our common stock and the selling stockholders identified in this prospectus are offering an additional 12,500,000 shares of our common stock. We will not receive any proceeds from the sale of our common stock by the selling stockholders. We currently expect the initial public offering price for our stock will be between $19.00 and $21.00 per share.

Unless otherwise indicated, all share numbers and per share prices in this prospectus give effect to a 3 for 1 stock split effected by means of a stock dividend of two shares of common stock for each share of common stock issued and outstanding at the close of business on March 14, 2007.

Prior to this offering, there has been no public market for our common stock. We have applied to list our common stock on the New York Stock Exchange under the symbol "PCS".

Investing in our common stock involves risks. See "Risk Factors" beginning on page 12.

	Per Share	Total
Public offering price..	$	$
Underwriting discounts...	$	$
Proceeds, before expenses, to us	$	$
Proceeds to the selling stockholders	$	$

Neither the Securities and Exchange Commission nor any state securities commission has approved or disapproved of these securities or passed upon the adequacy or accuracy of this prospectus. Any representation to the contrary is a criminal offense.

The underwriters expect to deliver the shares against payment in New York, New York on or about   , 2007.

The underwriters have a 30-day option to purchase up to 7,500,000 additional shares of common stock from the selling stockholders to cover over-allotments, if any. We will not receive any proceeds from the exercise of the over-allotment option.

Bear, Stearns & Co. Inc.
    Banc of America Securities LLC
        Merrill Lynch & Co.
            Morgan Stanley

UBS Investment Bank
    Thomas Weisel Partners LLC
        Wachovia Securities
            Raymond James

The date of this prospectus is   , 2007.

underwriting syndicate
A group of other bankers formed by an investment banker to share the financial risk associated with *underwriting* new securities.

selling group
A large number of brokerage firms that join the originating investment banker(s); each accepts responsibility for selling a certain portion of a new security issue on a commission basis.

In the case of very large security issues, the investment banker brings in other bankers as partners to form an **underwriting syndicate.** The syndicate shares the financial risk associated with buying the entire issue from the issuer and reselling the new securities to the public. The originating investment banker and the syndicate members put together a **selling group,** normally made up of themselves and a large number of brokerage firms. Each member of the selling group accepts the responsibility for selling a certain portion of the issue and is paid a commission on the securities it sells. The selling process for a large security issue is depicted in Figure 2.

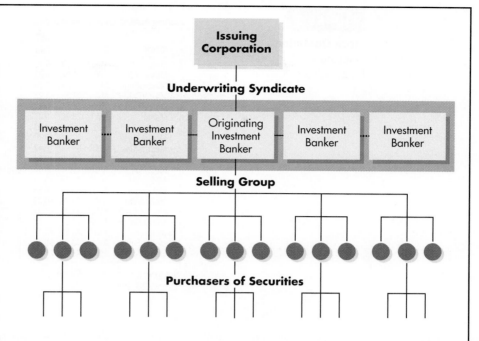

FIGURE 2

The Selling Process for a Large Security Issue
The investment banker hired by the issuing corporation may form an underwriting syndicate. The underwriting syndicate buys the entire security issue from the issuing corporation at an agreed-on price. The underwriters then have the opportunity (and bear the risk) of reselling the issue to the public at a profit. Both the originating investment banker and the other syndicate members put together a selling group to sell the issue on a commission basis to investors.

Compensation for underwriting and selling services typically comes in the form of a discount on the sale price of the securities. For example, an investment banker may pay the issuing firm $24 per share for stock that will be sold for $26 per share. The investment banker may then sell the shares to members of the selling group for $25.25 per share. In this case, the original investment banker earns $1.25 per share ($25.25 sale price − $24 purchase price). The members of the selling group earn 75 cents for each share they sell ($26 sale price − $25.25 purchase price). Although some primary security offerings are directly placed by the issuer, the majority of new issues are sold through public offering via the mechanism just described.

Interpreting Stock Quotations

The financial manager needs to stay abreast of the market values of the firm's outstanding stock, whether it is traded domestically or in international markets. Similarly, existing and prospective stockholders need to monitor the prices of the securities they own because these prices represent the current value of their investments. Price *quotations,* which include current price data along with statistics on recent price behavior, are readily available for actively traded stocks. The most up-to-date "quotes" can be obtained electronically, via a personal computer. Price information is available from stockbrokers and is widely published in news media. Popular sources of daily security price quotations include financial newspapers, such as the *Wall Street Journal* and *Investor's Business Daily,* and the business sections of daily general newspapers.

Figure 3 includes an excerpt from the NYSE quotations, reported in the *Wall Street Journal* on March 28, 2007, for transactions through the close of trading

FIGURE 3

Stock Quotations
Selected stock quotations for March 27, 2007

STOCK	SYM	CLOSE	NET CHG
Masco	MAS	27.80	-0.15
Masisa ADS	MYS	11.24	-0.03
MasseyEngy	MEE	24.20	-0.64
MasterCard	MA	107.25	-1.23
MatsuElec	MC	20.74	-0.22
Mattel	MAT	28.26	-0.47
McAfee	MFE	29.82	-0.07
↑ McClatchy A	MNI	37.61	-0.37
McCrmkCo	MKC	38.68	-0.43
McDermInt	MDR	49.82	-0.64
McDonalds	MCD	45.04	-0.08
McGrawH	MHP	63.33	-0.26
McKesson	MCK	58.50	0.58
MeadWVaco	MWV	30.66	-0.03
Mechel OAO	MTL	31.75	-0.31
MedcoHlthSol	MHS	71.80	-0.57
♣ Medtronic	MDT	48.68	-1.15
MellonFnl	MEL	43.11	-0.47
MensWearhs	MW	48.26	-0.05

← McDonald's

Source: Wall Street Journal, March 28, 2007, p. C13.

Hint Preferred stock quotations typically are not listed in the financial press, but can be obtained online or through a stockbroker.

on Tuesday, March 27, 2007. We'll look at the quotation for the common stock of McDonald's, highlighted in the figure. The quotations show that stock prices are quoted in dollars and cents. Listed to the right of the company's name is its *stock symbol;* McDonald's goes by "MCD." The next column, labeled "CLOSE," contains the closing (last) price at which the stock sold on the given day. The value for McDonald's was \$45.04. The final column, "NET CHG," indicates the change in the closing price from that on the prior trading day. McDonald's closed down \$0.08 from March 26, 2007, which means the closing price on that day was \$45.12.

Similar quotations systems are used for stocks that trade in other markets such as the Nasdaq market. Also note that when a stock issue is not traded on a given day, it generally is not quoted in the financial and business press.

REVIEW QUESTIONS

2 What risks do common stockholders take that other suppliers of long-term capital do not?

3 How does a *rights offering* protect a firm's stockholders against the *dilution of ownership?*

4 Explain the relationships among authorized shares, outstanding shares, treasury stock, and issued shares.

5 What are the advantages to both U.S.-based and foreign corporations of issuing stock outside their home markets? What are *American depositary receipts (ADRs)*? What are *American depositary shares (ADSs)*?

6 What claims do preferred stockholders have with respect to distribution of earnings (dividends) and assets?

7 Explain the *cumulative feature* of preferred stock. What is the purpose of a *call feature* in a preferred stock issue?

8   What is the difference between a *venture capitalist* (*VC*) and an *angel capitalist* (*angel*)?

9   Into what bodies are institutional VCs most commonly organized? How are their deals structured and priced?

10 What general procedures must a private firm follow to go public via an *initial public offering* (*IPO*)?

11 What role does an *investment banker* play in a public offering? Explain the sequence of events in the issuing of stock.

12 What are the key sources of *stock quotations*? Describe the items of information included in a published stock quotation.

---

3 | Common Stock Valuation

Common stockholders expect to be rewarded through periodic cash dividends and an increasing—or at least nondeclining—share value. Like current owners, prospective owners and security analysts frequently estimate the firm's value. Investors purchase the stock when they believe that it is *undervalued*—when its true value is greater than its market price. They sell the stock when they feel that it is *overvalued*—when its market price is greater than its true value.

In this section, we will describe specific stock valuation techniques. First, though, we will look at the concept of an efficient market, which questions whether the prices of actively traded stocks can differ from their true values.

Market Efficiency

Economically rational buyers and sellers use their assessment of an asset's risk and return to determine its value. To a buyer, the asset's value represents the maximum price that he or she would pay to acquire it; a seller views the asset's value as a minimum sale price. In competitive markets with many active participants, such as the New York Stock Exchange, the interactions of many buyers and sellers result in an equilibrium price—the *market value*—for each security. This price reflects the collective actions that buyers and sellers take on the basis of all available information. Buyers and sellers are assumed to digest new information immediately as it becomes available and, through their purchase and sale activities, to create a new market equilibrium price quickly. This general concept is known as *market efficiency*.

efficient-market hypothesis (EMH) Theory describing the behavior of an assumed "perfect" market in which (1) securities are typically in equilibrium, (2) security prices fully reflect all public information available and react swiftly to new information, and, (3) because stocks are fully and fairly priced, investors need not waste time looking for mispriced securities.

The Efficient-Market Hypothesis

Active broker and dealer markets, such as the New York Stock Exchange and the Nasdaq market, are *efficient*—they are made up of many rational investors who react quickly and objectively to new information. The **efficient-market hypothesis (EMH)**, which is the basic theory describing the behavior of such a "perfect" market, specifically states that

1. Securities are typically in equilibrium, which means that they are fairly priced and that their expected returns equal their required returns.

2. At any point in time, security prices fully reflect all public information available about the firm and its securities,[2] and these prices react swiftly to new information.

3. Because stocks are fully and fairly priced, investors need not waste their time trying to find mispriced (undervalued or overvalued) securities.

Not all market participants are believers in the efficient-market hypothesis. Some feel that it is worthwhile to search for undervalued or overvalued securities and to trade them to profit from market inefficiencies. Others argue that it is mere luck that would allow market participants to anticipate new information correctly and as a result earn *excess returns*—that is, actual returns greater than required returns. They believe it is unlikely that market participants can *over the long run* earn excess returns. Contrary to this belief, some well-known investors such as Warren Buffett and Peter Lynch *have* over the long run consistently earned excess returns on their portfolios. It is unclear whether their success is the result of their superior ability to anticipate new information or of some form of market inefficiency.

The Behavioral Finance Challenge

Although considerable evidence supports the concept of market efficiency, a growing body of academic evidence has begun to cast doubt on the validity of this notion. The research documents various *anomalies*—deviations from accepted beliefs—in stock returns. A number of academics and practitioners have also recognized that emotions and other subjective factors play a role in investment decisions.

behavioral finance
A growing body of research that focuses on investor behavior and its impact on investment decisions and stock prices. Advocates are commonly referred to as "behaviorists."

This focus on investor behavior has resulted in a significant body of research, collectively referred to as **behavioral finance**. Advocates of behavioral finance are commonly referred to as "behaviorists." Daniel Kahneman was awarded the 2002 Nobel Prize in economics for his work in behavioral finance, specifically for integrating insights from psychology and economics. Ongoing research into the psychological factors that can affect investor behavior and the resulting effects on stock prices will likely result in growing acceptance of behavioral finance. For further discussion of some of the findings of behavioral finance, see the text's website.

Throughout this text we ignore both disbelievers and behaviorists and continue to assume market efficiency. This means that *the terms "expected return" and "required return" are used interchangeably,* because they should be equal in an efficient market. This also means that stock prices accurately reflect true value based on risk and return. In other words, we will operate under the assumption that a stock's market price at any point in time is the best estimate of its value. We're now ready to look closely at the mechanics of common stock valuation.

---

2. Those market participants who have nonpublic—*inside*—information may have an unfair advantage that enables them to earn an excess return. Since the mid-1980s disclosure of the insider-trading activities of a number of well-known financiers and investors, major national attention has been focused on the "problem" of insider trading and its resolution. Clearly, those who trade securities on the basis of inside information have an unfair and illegal advantage. Empirical research has confirmed that those with inside information do indeed have an opportunity to earn an excess return. Here we ignore this possibility, given its illegality and the fact that enhanced surveillance and enforcement by the securities industry and the government have in recent years (it appears) significantly reduced insider trading. We, in effect, assume that all relevant information is public and that therefore the market is efficient.

Basic Common Stock Valuation Equation

Like the value of a bond, *the value of a share of common stock is equal to the present value of all future cash flows (dividends) that it is expected to provide over an infinite time horizon.* Although a stockholder can earn capital gains by selling stock at a price above that originally paid, what is really sold is the right to all future dividends. What about stocks that are not expected to pay dividends in the foreseeable future? Such stocks have a value attributable to a distant dividend expected to result from sale of the company or liquidation of its assets. Therefore, *from a valuation viewpoint, only dividends are relevant.*

The basic valuation model can be specified for common stock, as given in Equation 1:

$$P_0 = \frac{D_1}{(1 + r_s)^1} + \frac{D_2}{(1 + r_s)^2} + \cdots + \frac{D_\infty}{(1 + r_s)^\infty} \tag{1}$$

where

P_0 = value of common stock

D_t = per-share dividend *expected* at the end of year t

r_s = required return on common stock

The equation can be simplified somewhat by redefining each year's dividend, D_t, in terms of anticipated growth. We will consider two models here: zero-growth and constant-growth. A third model—variable-growth—is defined below and discussed more fully at the text's website.

Zero-Growth Model

The simplest approach to dividend valuation, the **zero-growth model,** assumes a constant, nongrowing dividend stream. In terms of the notation already introduced,

$$D_1 = D_2 = \cdots = D_\infty$$

When we let D_1 represent the amount of the annual dividend, Equation 1 under zero growth reduces to

$$P_0 = D_1 \times \sum_{t=1}^{\infty} \frac{1}{(1 + r_s)^t} = D_1 \times (PVIFA_{r_s, \infty}) = D_1 \times \frac{1}{r_s} = \frac{D_1}{r_s} \tag{2}$$

The equation shows that with zero growth, the value of a share of stock would equal the present value of a perpetuity of D_1 dollars discounted at a rate r_s. (Equation for present value interest factor for a perpetuity discounted at the rate i is: $PVIFA_{i, \infty} = \frac{1}{i}$)

zero-growth model
An approach to dividend valuation that assumes a constant, nongrowing dividend stream.

Personal Finance Example Chuck Swimmer estimates that the dividend of Denham Company, an established textile producer, is expected to remain constant at $3 per share indefinitely. If his required return on its stock is 15%, the stock's value is $20 ($3 ÷ 0.15) per share.

Preferred Stock Valuation Because preferred stock typically provides its holders with a fixed annual dividend over its assumed infinite life, *Equation 2 can be used to find the value of preferred stock*. The value of preferred stock can be estimated by substituting the stated dividend on the preferred stock for D_1 and the required return for r_s in Equation 2. For example, a preferred stock paying a $5 stated annual dividend and having a required return of 13 percent would have a value of $38.46 ($5 ÷ 0.13) per share.

Constant-Growth Model

constant-growth model
A widely cited dividend valuation approach that assumes that dividends will grow at a constant rate, but a rate that is less than the required return.

The most widely cited dividend valuation approach, the **constant-growth model,** assumes that dividends will grow at a constant rate, but a rate that is less than the required return. (The assumption that the constant rate of growth, *g*, is less than the required return, r_s, is a necessary mathematical condition for deriving this model.) By letting D_0 represent the most recent dividend, we can rewrite Equation 1 as follows:

$$P_0 = \frac{D_0 \times (1 + g)^1}{(1 + r_s)^1} + \frac{D_0 \times (1 + g)^2}{(1 + r_s)^2} + \cdots + \frac{D_0 \times (1 + g)^\infty}{(1 + r_s)^\infty} \tag{3}$$

If we simplify Equation 3, it can be rewritten as[3]

Gordon model
A common name for the *constant-growth model* that is widely cited in dividend valuation.

$$P_0 = \frac{D_1}{r_s - g} \tag{4}$$

The constant-growth model in Equation 4 is commonly called the **Gordon model.** An example will show how it works.

Example

Lamar Company, a small cosmetics company, from 2004 through 2009 paid the following per-share dividends:

Year	Dividend per share
2009	$1.40
2008	1.29
2007	1.20
2006	1.12
2005	1.05
2004	1.00

---

3. For the interested reader, the calculations necessary to derive Equation 4 from Equation 3 follow. The first step is to multiply each side of Equation 3 by $(1 + r_s)/(1 + g)$ and subtract Equation 3 from the resulting expression. This yields

$$\frac{P_0 \times (1 + r_s)}{1 + g} - P_0 = D_0 - \frac{D_0 \times (1 + g)^\infty}{(1 + r_s)^\infty} \tag{1}$$

Because r_s is assumed to be greater than *g*, the second term on the right side of Equation 1 should be zero. Thus

$$P_0 \times \left(\frac{1 + r_s}{1 + g} - 1\right) = D_0 \tag{2}$$

Equation 2 is simplified as follows:

$$P_0 \times \left[\frac{(1 + r_s) - (1 + g)}{1 + g}\right] = D_0 \tag{3}$$

$$P_0 \times (r_s - g) = D_0 \times (1 + g) \tag{4}$$

$$P_0 = \frac{D_1}{r_s - g} \tag{5}$$

Equation 5 equals Equation 4.

We assume that the historical compound annual growth rate of dividends is an accurate estimate of the future constant annual rate of dividend growth, g. Using a financial calculator, a spreadsheet, or Appendix: Financial Tables, Table A–2, we find that the historical compound annual growth rate of Lamar Company dividends equals 7%.[4] The company estimates that its dividend in 2010, D_1, will equal $1.50. The required return, r_s, is assumed to be 15%. By substituting these values into Equation 5, we find the value of the stock to be

$$P_0 = \frac{\$1.50}{0.15 - 0.07} = \frac{\$1.50}{0.08} = \underline{\underline{\$18.75}} \text{ per share}$$

Assuming that the values of D_1, r_s, and g are accurately estimated, Lamar Company's stock value is $18.75 per share.

Variable-Growth Model

variable-growth model
A dividend valuation approach that allows for a change in the dividend growth rate.

The zero- and constant-growth common stock models do not allow for any shift in expected growth rates. Because future growth rates might shift up or down because of changing expectations, it is useful to consider a **variable-growth model** that allows for a change in the dividend growth rate. For an explanation of how to use the variable-growth model to determine the value of a share of stock, see the text's website.

Free Cash Flow Valuation Model

free cash flow valuation model
A model that determines the value of an entire company as the present value of its expected *free cash flows* discounted at the firm's *weighted average cost of capital,* which is its expected average future cost of funds over the long run.

As an alternative to the dividend valuation models presented above, a firm's value can be estimated by using its projected *free cash flows* (FCFs). This approach is appealing when one is valuing firms that have no dividend history or are startups or when one is valuing an operating unit or division of a larger public company. Although dividend valuation models are widely used and accepted, in these situations it is preferable to use a more general free cash flow valuation model.

The **free cash flow valuation model** is based on the same basic premise as dividend valuation models: The value of a share of common stock is the present value of all future cash flows it is expected to provide over an infinite time horizon. However, in the free cash flow valuation model, instead of valuing the firm's expected dividends, we value the firm's expected *free cash flows,* defined as free cash flow equals operating cash flow minus net fixed asset investment minus net current asset investment. They represent the amount of cash flow available to

4. The technique involves solving the following equation for g:

$$D_{2009} = D_{2004} \times (1 + g)^5$$

$$\frac{D_{2004}}{D_{2009}} = \frac{1}{(1 + g)^5} = PVIF_{g,5}$$

To do so, we can use a financial calculator, a spreadsheet, or financial tables.

A financial calculator can be used. (*Note:* Most calculators require *either* the PV or FV value to be input as a negative number to calculate an unknown interest or growth rate. That approach is used here.) Using the inputs shown at the left, you should find the growth rate to be 6.96%, which we round to 7%.

An electronic spreadsheet could also be used to make this computation. Given space considerations, we have forgone that computational aid here.

We could also use a financial table. Two basic steps can be followed using the present value table. First, dividing the earliest dividend ($D_{2004} = \$1.00$) by the most recent dividend ($D_{2009} = \$1.40$) yields a factor for the present value of one dollar, *PVIF*, of 0.714 ($1.00 ÷ $1.40). Although six dividends are shown, *they reflect only 5 years of growth.* (The number of years of growth can also be found by subtracting the earliest year from the most recent year—that is, $2009 - 2004 = 5$ *years of growth.*) By looking across the Appendix: Financial Tables, Table A–2 at the *PVIF* for 5 years, we find that the factor closest to 0.714 occurs at 7% (0.713). Therefore, the growth rate of the dividends, rounded to the nearest whole percent, is 7%.

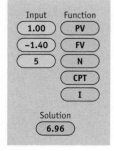

Input	Function
1.00	PV
-1.40	FV
5	N
	CPT
	I

Solution
6.96

investors—the providers of debt (creditors) and equity (owners)—after all other obligations have been met.

The free cash flow valuation model estimates the value of the entire company by finding the present value of its expected free cash flows discounted at its *weighted average cost of capital,* which is its expected average future cost of funds over the long run, as specified in Equation 5.

$$V_C = \frac{FCF_1}{(1 + r_a)^1} + \frac{FCF_2}{(1 + r_a)^2} + \cdots + \frac{FCF_\infty}{(1 + r_a)^\infty} \tag{5}$$

where

V_C = value of the entire company

FCF_t = free cash flow *expected* at the end of year t

r_a = the firm's weighted average cost of capital

Note the similarity between Equations 5 and 1, the general stock valuation equation.

Because the value of the entire company, V_C, is the market value of the entire enterprise (that is, of all assets), to find common stock value, V_S, we must subtract the market value of all of the firm's debt, V_D, and the market value of preferred stock, V_P, from V_C.

$$V_S = V_C - V_D - V_P \tag{6}$$

Because it is difficult to forecast a firm's free cash flow, specific annual cash flows are typically forecast for only about 5 years, beyond which a constant growth rate is assumed. Here we assume that the first 5 years of free cash flows are explicitly forecast and that a constant rate of free cash flow growth occurs beyond the end of year 5 to infinity. This model is methodologically similar to the variable-growth model presented earlier. Its application is best demonstrated with an example.

Example

Dewhurst, Inc., wishes to determine the value of its stock by using the free cash flow valuation model. To apply the model, the firm's CFO developed the data given in Table 3. Application of the model can be performed in four steps.

Step 1 Calculate the present value of the free cash flow occurring from the end of 2015 to infinity, measured at the beginning of 2015 (that is, at the end of 2014). Because a constant rate of growth in FCF is forecast beyond 2014, we can use the constant-growth dividend valuation model (Equation 4) to calculate the value of the free cash flows from the end of 2015 to infinity.

$$\text{Value of } FCF_{2015\to\infty} = \frac{FCF_{2015}}{r_a - g_{FCF}}$$

$$= \frac{\$600,000 \times (1 + 0.03)}{0.09 - 0.03}$$

$$= \frac{\$618,000}{0.06} = \underline{\$10,300,000}$$

Note that to calculate the FCF in 2015, we had to increase the 2014 FCF value of $600,000 by the 3% FCF growth rate, g_{FCF}.

TABLE 3	Dewhurst, Inc.'s Data for the Free Cash Flow Valuation Model	

	Free cash flow	
Year (t)	$(FCF_t)^a$	Other data
2010	$400,000	Growth rate of FCF, beyond 2014 to infinity, $g_{FCF} = 3\%$
2011	450,000	Weighted average cost of capital, $r_a = 9\%$
2012	520,000	Market value of all debt, $V_D = \$3,100,000$
2013	560,000	Market value of preferred stock, $V_P = \$800,000$
2014	600,000	Number of shares of common stock outstanding = 300,000

^{a}Developed using Equations 4 and 5 (Chapter: Cash Flow and Financial Planning).

Step 2   Add the present value of the FCF from 2015 to infinity, which is measured at the end of 2014, to the 2014 FCF value to get the total FCF in 2014.

Total $FCF_{2014} = \$600,000 + \$10,300,000 = \$10,900,000$

Step 3   Find the sum of the present values of the FCFs for 2010 through 2014 to determine the value of the entire company, V_C. This calculation is shown in Table 4, using present value interest factors, PVIFs, from Appendix: Financial Tables, Table A–2.

Step 4   Calculate the value of the common stock using Equation 6. Substituting into Equation 6 the value of the entire company, V_C, calculated in Step 3, and the market values of debt, V_D, and preferred stock, V_P, given in Table 3, yields the value of the common stock, V_S:

$V_S = \$8,628,620 - \$3,100,000 - \$800,000 = \underline{\$4,728,620}$

The value of Dewhurst's common stock is therefore estimated to be $4,728,620. By dividing this total by the 300,000 shares of common stock that the firm has outstanding, we get a common stock value of *$15.76 per share* ($4,728,620 ÷ 300,000).

TABLE 4	Calculation of the Value of the Entire Company for Dewhurst, Inc.		

Year (t)	FCF_t (1)	$PVIF_{9\%,t}$ (2)	Present value of FCF_t [(1) × (2)] (3)
2010	$ 400,000	0.917	$ 366,800
2011	450,000	0.842	378,900
2012	520,000	0.772	401,440
2013	560,000	0.708	396,480
2014	10,900,000^a	0.650	7,085,000
		Value of entire company, $V_C =$	$\underline{\$8,628,620}$

^{a}This amount is the sum of the FCF_{2014} of $600,000 from Table 3 and the $10,300,000 value of the $FCF_{2015\ \infty}$ calculated in Step 1.

It should now be clear that the free cash flow valuation model is consistent with the dividend valuation models presented earlier. The appeal of this approach is its focus on the free cash flow estimates rather than on forecast dividends, which are far more difficult to estimate, given that they are paid at the discretion of the firm's board. The more general nature of the free cash flow model is responsible for its growing popularity, particularly with CFOs and other financial managers.

Other Approaches to Common Stock Valuation

Many other approaches to common stock valuation exist. The more popular approaches include book value, liquidation value, and some type of price/earnings multiple.

book value per share
The amount per share of common stock that would be received if all of the firm's assets were *sold for their exact book (accounting) value* and the proceeds remaining after paying all liabilities (including preferred stock) were divided among the common stockholders.

Book Value

Book value per share is simply the amount per share of common stock that would be received if all of the firm's assets were *sold for their exact book (accounting) value* and the proceeds remaining after paying all liabilities (including preferred stock) were divided among the common stockholders. This method lacks sophistication and can be criticized on the basis of its reliance on historical balance sheet data. It ignores the firm's expected earnings potential and generally lacks any true relationship to the firm's value in the marketplace. Let us look at an example.

Example

At year-end 2009, Lamar Company's balance sheet shows total assets of $6 million, total liabilities (including preferred stock) of $4.5 million, and 100,000 shares of common stock outstanding. Its book value per share therefore would be

$$\frac{\$6,000,000 - \$4,500,000}{100,000 \text{ shares}} = \underline{\underline{\$15}} \text{ per share}$$

Because this value assumes that assets could be sold for their book value, it may not represent the minimum price at which shares are valued in the marketplace. As a matter of fact, although most stocks sell above book value, it is not unusual to find stocks selling below book value when investors believe either that assets are overvalued or that the firm's liabilities are understated.

---

liquidation value per share
The *actual amount* per share of common stock that would be received if all of the firm's assets were *sold for their market value,* liabilities (including preferred stock) were paid, and any remaining money were divided among the common stockholders.

Liquidation Value

Liquidation value per share is the *actual amount* per share of common stock that would be received if all of the firm's assets were *sold for their market value,* liabilities (including preferred stock) were paid, and any remaining money were divided among the common stockholders.[5] This measure is more realistic than book value—because it is based on the current market value of the firm's assets—but it still fails to consider the earning power of those assets. An example will illustrate.

---

5. In the event of liquidation, creditors' claims must be satisfied first, then those of the preferred stockholders. Anything left goes to common stockholders.

Example

Lamar Company found upon investigation that it could obtain only $5.25 million if it sold its assets today. The firm's liquidation value per share therefore would be

$$\frac{\$5,250,000 - \$4,500,000}{100,000 \text{ shares}} = \underline{\underline{\$7.50}} \text{ per share}$$

Ignoring liquidation expenses, this amount would be the firm's minimum value.

Price/Earnings (P/E) Multiples

The *price/earnings (P/E) ratio* reflects the amount investors are willing to pay for each dollar of earnings. The average P/E ratio in a particular industry can be used as the guide to a firm's value—if it is assumed that investors value the earnings of that firm in the same way they do the "average" firm in the industry. The **price/earnings multiple approach** is a popular technique used to estimate the firm's share value; it is calculated by multiplying the firm's expected earnings per share (EPS) by the average price/earnings (P/E) ratio for the industry. The average P/E ratio for the industry can be obtained from a source such as *Standard & Poor's Industrial Ratios*.

price/earnings multiple approach
A popular technique used to estimate the firm's share value; calculated by multiplying the firm's expected earnings per share (EPS) by the average price/earnings (P/E) ratio for the industry.

The P/E ratio valuation technique is a simple method of determining a stock's value and can be quickly calculated after firms make earnings announcements, which accounts for its popularity. Naturally, this has increased the demand for more frequent announcements or "guidance" regarding future earnings. Some firms feel that pre-earnings guidance creates additional costs and can lead to ethical issues, as discussed in the *Focus on Ethics* box.

The use of P/E multiples is especially helpful in valuing firms that are not publicly traded, whereas market price quotations can be used to value publicly traded firms. In any case, the price/earnings multiple approach is considered superior to the use of book or liquidation values because it considers *expected* earnings. An example will demonstrate the use of price/earnings multiples.

Personal Finance Example Ann Perrier plans to use the price/earnings multiple approach to estimate the value of Lamar Company's stock, which she currently holds in her retirement account. She estimates that Lamar Company will earn $2.60 per share next year (2010). This expectation is based on an analysis of the firm's historical earnings trend and of expected economic and industry conditions. She finds the price/earnings (P/E) ratio for firms in the same industry to average 7. Multiplying Lamar's expected earnings per share (EPS) of $2.60 by this ratio gives her a value for the firm's shares of $18.20, assuming that investors will continue to value the average firm at 7 times its earnings.

So how much is Lamar Company's stock really worth? That's a trick question, because there's no one right answer. It is important to recognize that the answer depends on the assumptions made and the techniques used. Professional securities analysts typically use a variety of models and techniques to value stocks. For example, an analyst might use the constant-growth model, liquidation value, and a price/earnings (P/E) multiple to estimate the worth of a given stock. If the analyst feels comfortable with his or her estimates, the stock would be valued at no more than the largest estimate. Of course, should the firm's estimated liquidation value

Focus on Ethics

Psst—Have You Heard Any Good Quarterly Earnings Forecasts Lately?

Corporate managers have long complained about the pressure to focus on the short term, and now business groups are coming to their defense. "The focus on the short term is a huge problem," says William Donaldson, former chairman of the Securities and Exchange Commission. "With all of the attention paid to quarterly performance, managers are taking their eyes off long-term strategic goals."

Donaldson, the U.S. Chamber of Commerce, and others believe that the best way to focus companies toward long-term goals is to do away with the practice of giving quarterly earnings guidance. In March 2007 the CFA Centre for Financial Market Integrity and the Business Roundtable Institute for Corporate Ethics proposed a template for quarterly earnings reports that would, in their view, obviate the need for earnings guidance.

Meanwhile, many companies are hesitant to give up issuing quarterly guidance. The practice of issuing earnings forecasts began in the early 1980s, a few years after the SEC's decision to allow companies to include forward-looking projections, provided they were accompanied by appropriate cautionary language. The result was what former SEC chairman Arthur Levitt once called a "game of winks and nods." Companies used earnings guidance to lower analysts' estimates; when the actual numbers came in higher, their stock prices jumped. The practice reached a fever pitch during the late 1990s when companies that missed the consensus earnings estimate, even by just a penny, saw their stock prices tumble.

One of the first companies to stop issuing earnings guidance was **Gillette,** in 2001. Others that abandoned quarterly guidance were **Coca-Cola, Intel,** and **McDonald's.** It became a trend. By 2005, just 61 percent of companies were offering quarterly projections to the public; according to the National Investor Relations Institute, the number declined to 52 percent in 2006.

Not everyone agrees with eliminating quarterly guidance. A survey conducted by New York University's Stern School of Business finance professor Baruch Lev, along with University of Florida professors Joel Houston and Jennifer Tucker, showed that companies that ended quarterly guidance reaped almost no benefit from doing so. Their study found no evidence that guidance-stoppers increased capital investments or research and development. So when should companies give up earnings guidance? According to Lev, they should do so only when they are not very good at predicting their earnings. "If you are not better than others at forecasting, then don't bother," he says.

■ *What are some of the real costs a company must face in preparing quarterly earnings guidance?*

Hint From an investor's perspective, the stock in this situation would be an attractive investment only if it could be purchased at a price below its liquidation value—which in an efficient market could never occur.

per share exceed its "going concern" value per share, estimated by using one of the valuation models (zero-, constant-, or variable-growth or free cash flow) or the P/E multiple approach, the firm would be viewed as being "worth more dead than alive." In such an event, the firm would lack sufficient earning power to justify its existence and should probably be liquidated.

REVIEW QUESTIONS

13 What does the *efficient-market hypothesis (EMH)* say about (a) securities prices, (b) their reaction to new information, and (c) investor opportunities to profit? What is the *behavioral finance* challenge to this hypothesis?

14 Describe, compare, and contrast the following common stock dividend valuation models: (a) zero-growth and (b) constant-growth.

15   Describe the *free cash flow valuation model* and explain how it differs from the dividend valuation models. What is the appeal of this model?

16   Explain each of the three other approaches to common stock valuation: (a) book value, (b) liquidation value, and (c) price/earnings (P/E) multiples. Which of these is considered the best?

4 | # Decision Making and Common Stock Value

Valuation equations measure the stock value at a point in time based on expected return and risk. Any decisions of the financial manager that affect these variables can cause the value of the firm to change. Figure 4 depicts the relationship among financial decisions, return, risk, and stock value.

Changes in Expected Return

Assuming that economic conditions remain stable, any management action that would cause current and prospective stockholders to raise their dividend expectations should increase the firm's value. In Equation 4, we can see that P_0 will increase for any increase in D_1 or g. Any action of the financial manager that will increase the level of expected returns without changing risk (the required return) should be undertaken, because it will positively affect owners' wealth.

Example

Using the constant-growth model in an earlier example, we found Lamar Company to have a share value of $18.75. On the following day, the firm announced a major technological breakthrough that would revolutionize its industry. Current and prospective stockholders would not be expected to adjust their required return of 15%, but they would expect that future dividends will increase. Specifically, they expect that although the dividend next year, D_1, will remain at $1.50, the expected rate of growth thereafter will increase from 7% to 9%. If we substitute $D_1 = \$1.50$, $r_s = 0.15$, and $g = 0.09$ into Equation 4, the resulting share value is $25 [\$1.50 \div (0.15 - 0.09)]$. The increased value therefore resulted from the higher expected future dividends reflected in the increase in the growth rate.

FIGURE 4

Decision Making and Stock Value
Financial decisions, return, risk, and stock value

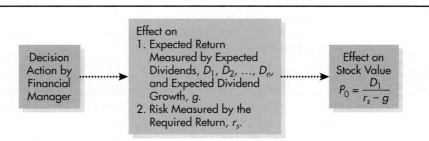

Changes in Risk

Although r_s is defined as the required return, it is directly related to the nondiversifiable risk, which can be measured by beta. The *capital asset pricing model (CAPM)* is stated here as Equation 7:

$$r_s = R_F + [b \times (r_m - R_F)] \tag{7}$$

With the risk-free rate, R_F, and the market return, r_m, held constant, the required return, r_s, depends directly on beta. Any action taken by the financial manager that increases risk (beta) will also increase the required return. In Equation 4, we can see that with everything else constant, an increase in the required return, r_s, will reduce share value, P_0. Likewise, a decrease in the required return will increase share value. Thus any action of the financial manager that increases risk contributes to a reduction in value, and any action that decreases risk contributes to an increase in value.

Example

Assume that Lamar Company's 15% required return resulted from a risk-free rate of 9%, a market return of 13%, and a beta of 1.50. Substituting into the capital asset pricing model, Equation 7, we get a required return, r_s, of 15%:

$$r_s = 9\% + [1.50 \times (13\% - 9\%)] = \underline{\underline{15\%}}$$

With this return, the firm's share value was calculated in an earlier example to be $18.75.

Now imagine that the financial manager makes a decision that, without changing expected dividends, causes the firm's beta to increase to 1.75. Assuming that R_F and r_m remain at 9% and 13%, respectively, the required return will increase to 16% (9% + [1.75 × (13% − 9%)]) to compensate stockholders for the increased risk. Substituting $D_1 = \$1.50$, $r_s = 0.16$, and $g = 0.07$ into the valuation equation, Equation 4, results in a share value of $16.67 [$1.50 ÷ (0.16 − 0.07)]. As expected, raising the required return, without any corresponding increase in expected return, causes the firm's stock value to decline. Clearly, the financial manager's action was not in the owners' best interest.

Combined Effect

A financial decision rarely affects return and risk independently; most decisions affect both factors. In terms of the measures presented, with an increase in risk (b), one would expect an increase in return (D_1 or g, or both), assuming that R_F and r_m remain unchanged. The net effect on value depends on the size of the changes in these variables.

Example

If we assume that the two changes illustrated for Lamar Company in the preceding examples occur simultaneously, key variable values would be $D_1 = \$1.50$, $r_s = 0.16$, and $g = 0.09$. Substituting into the valuation model, we obtain a share price of $21.43 [$1.50 ÷ (0.16 − 0.09)]. The net result of the decision, which increased return (g, from 7% to 9%) as well as risk (b, from 1.50 to 1.75 and therefore r_s from 15% to 16%), is positive: The share price increased from $18.75 to $21.43. The decision appears to be in the best interest of the firm's owners, because it increases their wealth.

REVIEW QUESTIONS

17 Explain the linkages among financial decisions, return, risk, and stock value.

18 Assuming that all other variables remain unchanged, what impact would *each* of the following have on stock price? (a) The firm's beta increases. (b) The firm's required return decreases. (c) The dividend expected next year decreases. (d) The rate of growth in dividends is expected to increase.

Summary

Focus on Value

The price of each share of a firm's common stock is the value of each ownership interest. Although common stockholders typically have voting rights, which indirectly give them a say in management, their only significant right is their claim on the residual cash flows of the firm. This claim is subordinate to those of vendors, employees, customers, lenders, the government (for taxes), and preferred stockholders. The value of the common stockholders' claim is embodied in the cash flows they are entitled to receive from now to infinity. The present value of those expected cash flows is the firm's share value.

To determine this present value, forecast cash flows are discounted at a rate that reflects their risk. Riskier cash flows are discounted at higher rates, resulting in lower present values than less risky expected cash flows, which are discounted at lower rates. The value of the firm's common stock is therefore driven by its expected cash flows (returns) and risk (certainty of the expected cash flows).

In pursuing the firm's goal of **maximizing the stock price,** the financial manager must carefully consider the balance of return and risk associated with each proposal and must undertake only those actions that create value for owners. By focusing on value creation and by managing and monitoring the firm's cash flows and risk, the financial manager should be able to achieve the firm's goal of share price maximization.

Review of Learning Goals

Key definitions and formulas for this chapter are summarized in Table 5.

LG 1 **Differentiate between debt and equity capital.** Holders of equity capital (common and preferred stock) are owners of the firm. Typically, only common stockholders have a voice in management. Equity holders' claims on income and assets are secondary to creditors' claims, there is no maturity date, and dividends paid to stockholders are not tax-deductible.

TABLE 5	Summary of Key Valuation Definitions and Formulas for Common Stock

Definitions of variables

D_t = per-share dividend *expected* at the end of year t

FCF_t = free cash flow *expected* at the end of year t

g = constant rate of growth in dividends

g_1 = initial dividend growth rate (in variable-growth model)

g_2 = subsequent dividend growth rate (in variable-growth model)

r_a = weighted average cost of capital

r_s = required return on common stock

N = last year of initial growth period (in variable-growth model)

P_0 = value of common stock

V_C = value of the entire company

V_D = market value of all the firm's debt

V_P = market value of preferred stock

V_S = value of common stock

Valuation formulas

Basic stock value:

$$P_0 = \frac{D_1}{(1 + r_s)^1} + \frac{D_2}{(1 + r_s)^2} + \cdots + \frac{D_\infty}{(1 + r_s)^\infty} \qquad \text{[Equation 1]}$$

Common stock value:

  Zero-growth:

$$P_0 = \frac{D_1}{r_s} \text{ (also used to value preferred stock)} \qquad \text{[Equation 2]}$$

  Constant-growth:

$$P_0 = \frac{D_1}{r_s - g} \qquad \text{[Equation 4]}$$

  Variable-growth: *See the book's website.*

  FCF value of entire company:

$$V_C = \frac{FCF_1}{(1 + r_a)^1} + \frac{FCF_2}{(1 + r_a)^2} + \cdots + \frac{FCF_\infty}{(1 + r_a)^\infty} \qquad \text{[Equation 5]}$$

  FCF common stock value:

$$V_S = V_C - V_D - V_P \qquad \text{[Equation 6]}$$

LG 2 **Discuss the rights, characteristics, and features of both common and preferred stock.** The common stock of a firm can be privately owned, closely owned, or publicly owned. It can be sold with or without a par value. Preemptive rights allow common stockholders to avoid dilution of ownership when new shares are issued. Not all shares authorized in the corporate charter are outstanding. If a firm has treasury stock, it will have issued more shares than are outstanding. Some firms have two or more classes of common stock that differ mainly in having unequal voting rights. Proxies transfer voting rights from one party to another. The decision to pay dividends to common stockholders is made by the firm's board of directors. Firms can issue stock in foreign markets. The stock of many foreign corporations is traded in U.S. markets in the form of American depositary shares (ADSs), which are backed by American depositary receipts (ADRs).

Preferred stockholders have preference over common stockholders with respect to the distribution of earnings and assets. They do not normally have voting privileges. Preferred stock issues may have certain restrictive covenants, cumulative dividends, a call feature, and a conversion feature.

LG 3 **Describe the process of issuing common stock, including venture capital, going public, and the investment banker, and interpreting stock quotations.** The initial nonfounder financing for business startups with attractive growth prospects typically comes from private equity investors. These investors can be either angel capitalists or venture capitalists (VCs). VCs usually invest in both early-stage and later-stage companies that they hope to take public so as to cash out their investments.

The first public issue of a firm's stock is called an initial public offering (IPO). The company selects an investment banker to advise it and to sell the securities. The lead investment banker may form a selling syndicate with other investment bankers. The IPO process includes getting SEC approval, promoting the offering to investors, and pricing the issue.

Stock quotations provide information on the closing (last) price at which the stock sold on the given day and the net price change from the prior trading day.

LG 4 **Understand the concept of market efficiency and basic common stock valuation using zero-growth and constant-growth models.** Market efficiency assumes that the quick reactions of rational investors to new information cause the market value of common stock to adjust quickly. The efficient-market hypothesis (EMH) suggests that securities are fairly priced, that they reflect fully all publicly available information, and that investors should therefore not waste time trying to find and capitalize on mispriced securities. Behavioral finance advocates challenge this hypothesis by arguing that emotion and other factors play a role in investment decisions.

The value of a share of common stock is the present value of all future dividends it is expected to provide over an infinite time horizon. Two dividend growth models—zero-growth and constant-growth—can be considered in common stock valuation. The most widely cited model is the constant-growth model. (A third model, the variable-growth model, allows for a change in the dividend growth rate.)

LG 5 Discuss the free cash flow valuation model and the book value, liquidation value, and price/earnings (P/E) multiple approaches. The free cash flow valuation model values firms that have no dividend history, startups, or an operating unit or division of a larger public company. The model finds the value of the entire company by discounting the firm's expected free cash flow at its weighted average cost of capital. The common stock value is found by subtracting the market values of the firm's debt and preferred stock from the value of the entire company.

Book value per share is the amount per share of common stock that would be received if all of the firm's assets were *sold for their exact book (accounting) value* and the proceeds remaining after paying all liabilities (including preferred stock) were divided among the common stockholders. Liquidation value per share is the *actual amount* per share of common stock that would be received if all of the firm's assets were *sold for their market value,* liabilities (including preferred stock) were paid, and the remaining money were divided among the common stockholders. The price/earnings (P/E) multiple approach estimates stock value by multiplying the firm's expected earnings per share (EPS) by the average price/earnings (P/E) ratio for the industry.

LG 6 Explain the relationships among financial decisions, return, risk, and the firm's value. In a stable economy, any action of the financial manager that increases the level of expected return without changing risk should increase share value; any action that reduces the level of expected return without changing risk should reduce share value. Similarly, any action that increases risk (required return) will reduce share value; any action that reduces risk will increase share value. An assessment of the combined effect of return and risk on stock value must be part of the financial decision-making process.

Self-Test Problems

ST7–1 **Common stock valuation**   Perry Motors' common stock currently pays an annual dividend of $1.80 per share. The required return on the common stock is 12%. Estimate the value of the common stock under each of the following assumptions about the dividend.
a. Dividends are expected to grow at an annual rate of 0% to infinity.
b. Dividends are expected to grow at a constant annual rate of 5% to infinity.

ST7–2 **Free cash flow valuation**   Erwin Footwear wishes to assess the value of its Active Shoe Division. This division has debt with a market value of $12,500,000 and no preferred stock. Its weighted average cost of capital is 10%. The Active Shoe Division's estimated free cash flow each year from 2010 through 2013 is given in the following table. Beyond 2013 to infinity, the firm expects its free cash flow to grow at 4% annually.

Year (t)	Free cash flow (FCF_t)
2010	$ 800,000
2011	1,200,000
2012	1,400,000
2013	1,500,000

a. Use the *free cash flow valuation model* to estimate the value of Erwin's entire Active Shoe Division.

b. Use your finding in part **a** along with the data provided above to find this division's common stock value.

c. If the Active Shoe Division as a public company will have 500,000 shares outstanding, use your finding in part **b** to calculate its value per share.

Warm-Up Exercises

A blue box (■) indicates exercises available in .

LG 1

E7–1 A balance sheet balances assets with their sources of debt and equity financing. If a corporation has assets equal to $5.2 million and a debt ratio of 75.0%, how much debt does the corporation have on its books?

LG 2

E7–2 Angina, Inc., has 5 million shares outstanding. The firm is considering issuing an additional 1 million shares. After selling these shares at their $20 per share offering price and netting 95% of the sale proceeds, the firm is obligated by an earlier agreement to sell an additional 250,000 shares at 90% of the offering price. In total, how much cash will the firm net from these stock sales?

LG 2

E7–3 Figurate Industries has 750,000 shares of cumulative preferred stock outstanding. It has passed the last three quarterly dividends of $2.50 per share and now (at the end of the current quarter) wishes to distribute a total of $12 million to its shareholders. If Figurate has 3 million shares of common stock outstanding, how large a per-share common stock dividend will it be able to pay?

LG 3

E7–4 Today the common stock of Gresham Technology closed at $24.60 per share, down $0.35 from yesterday. If the company has 4.6 million shares outstanding and annual earnings of $11.2 million, what is its P/E ratio today? What was its P/E ratio yesterday?

LG 4

E7–5 Stacker Weight Loss currently pays an annual year-end dividend of $1.20 per share. It plans to increase this dividend by 5% next year and maintain it at the new level for the foreseeable future. If the required return on this firm's stock is 8%, what is the value of Stacker's stock?

LG 6

E7–6 Brash Corporation initiated a new corporate strategy that fixes its annual dividend at $2.25 per share forever. Currently the risk-free rate is 4.5%, and Brash has a beta of 1.8. If the market return is 10.5%, what is the value of Brash's stock?

Problems

A blue box (■) indicates problems available in .

P7–1 **Authorized and available shares** Aspin Corporation's charter authorizes issuance of 2,000,000 shares of common stock. Currently, 1,400,000 shares are outstanding and 100,000 shares are being held as treasury stock. The firm wishes to raise $48,000,000 for a plant expansion. Discussions with its investment bankers indicate that the sale of new common stock will net the firm $60 per share.

    a. What is the maximum number of new shares of common stock that the firm can sell without receiving further authorization from shareholders?

    b. Judging on the basis of the data given and your finding in part **a**, will the firm be able to raise the needed funds without receiving further authorization?

    c. What must the firm do to obtain authorization to issue more than the number of shares found in part **a**?

P7–2 **Preferred dividends** Slater Lamp Manufacturing has an outstanding issue of preferred stock with an $80 par value and an 11% annual dividend.

    a. What is the annual dollar dividend? If it is paid quarterly, how much will be paid each quarter?

    b. If the preferred stock is *noncumulative* and the board of directors has passed the preferred dividend for the last 3 quarters, how much must be paid to preferred stockholders in the current quarter before dividends are paid to common stockholders?

    c. If the preferred stock is *cumulative* and the board of directors has passed the preferred dividend for the last 3 quarters, how much must be paid to preferred stockholders in the current quarter before dividends are paid to common stockholders?

P7–3 **Preferred dividends** In each case in the following table, how many dollars of preferred dividends per share must be paid to preferred stockholders in the current period before common stock dividends are paid?

Case	Type	Par value	Dividend per share per period	Periods of dividends passed
A	Cumulative	$ 80	$ 5	2
B	Noncumulative	110	8%	3
C	Noncumulative	100	$11	1
D	Cumulative	60	8.5%	4
E	Cumulative	90	9%	0

P7–4 **Convertible preferred stock** Valerian Corp. convertible preferred stock has a fixed conversion ratio of 5 common shares per 1 share of preferred stock. The preferred stock pays a dividend of $10.00 per share per year. The common stock currently sells for $20.00 per share and pays a dividend of $1.00 per share per year.

    a. Judging on the basis of the conversion ratio and the price of the common shares, what is the current conversion value of each preferred share?

b. If the preferred shares are selling at $96.00 each, should an investor convert the preferred shares to common shares?

c. What factors might cause an investor not to convert from preferred to common stock?

PERSONAL FINANCE PROBLEM

P7–5 Stock quotation   Assume that the following quote for the Advanced Business Machines stock (traded on the NYSE) was found in the Thursday, December 14, issue of the *Wall Street Journal.*

AdvBusMach   ABM   81.75   1.63

Given this information, answer the following questions:

a. On what day did the trading activity occur?

b. At what price did the stock sell at the end of the day on Wednesday, December 13?

c. What is the last price at which the stock traded on the day quoted?

d. How much, if any, of a change in stock price took place between the day quoted and the day before? At what price did the stock close on the day before?

P7–6 Common stock valuation—Zero growth   Scotto Manufacturing is a mature firm in the machine tool component industry. The firm's most recent common stock dividend was $2.40 per share. Because of its maturity as well as its stable sales and earnings, the firm's management feels that dividends will remain at the current level for the foreseeable future.

a. If the required return is 12%, what will be the value of Scotto's common stock?

b. If the firm's risk as perceived by market participants suddenly increases, causing the required return to rise to 20%, what will be the common stock value?

c. Judging on the basis of your findings in parts **a** and **b,** what impact does risk have on value? Explain.

PERSONAL FINANCE PROBLEM

P7–7 Common stock value—Zero growth   Kelsey Drums, Inc., is a well-established supplier of fine percussion instruments to orchestras all over the United States. The company's class A common stock has paid a dividend of $5.00 per share per year for the last 15 years. Management expects to continue to pay at that amount for the foreseeable future. Sally Talbot purchased 100 shares of Kelsey class A common 10 years ago at a time when the required rate of return for the stock was 16%. She wants to sell her shares today. The current required rate of return for the stock is 12%. How much capital gain or loss will Sally have on her shares?

P7–8 Preferred stock valuation   Jones Design wishes to estimate the value of its outstanding preferred stock. The preferred issue has an $80 par value and pays an annual dividend of $6.40 per share. Similar-risk preferred stocks are currently earning a 9.3% annual rate of return.

a. What is the market value of the outstanding preferred stock?

b. If an investor purchases the preferred stock at the value calculated in part **a,** how much does she gain or lose per share if she sells the stock when the required return on similar-risk preferreds has risen to 10.5%? Explain.

P7–9 **Common stock value—Constant growth** Use the constant-growth model (Gordon model) to find the value of each firm shown in the following table.

Firm	Dividend expected next year	Dividend growth rate	Required return
A	$1.20	8%	13%
B	4.00	5	15
C	0.65	10	14
D	6.00	8	9
E	2.25	8	20

P7–10 **Common stock value—Constant growth** McCracken Roofing, Inc., common stock paid a dividend of $1.20 per share last year. The company expects earnings and dividends to grow at a rate of 5% per year for the foreseeable future.
a. What required rate of return for this stock would result in a price per share of $28?
b. If McCracken expects both earnings and dividends to grow at an annual rate of 10%, what required rate of return would result in a price per share of $28?

PERSONAL FINANCE PROBLEM

P7–11 **Common stock value—Constant growth** Elk County Telephone has paid the dividends shown in the following table over the past 6 years.

Year	Dividend per share
2009	$2.87
2008	2.76
2007	2.60
2006	2.46
2005	2.37
2004	2.25

The firm's dividend per share next year is expected to be $3.02.
a. If you can earn 13% on similar-risk investments, what is the most you would be willing to pay per share?
b. If you can earn only 10% on similar-risk investments, what is the most you would be willing to pay per share?
c. Compare and contrast your findings in parts **a** and **b**, and discuss the impact of changing risk on share value.

PERSONAL FINANCE PROBLEM

P7–12 **Common stock value—Both growth models** You are evaluating the potential purchase of a small business currently generating $42,500 of after-tax cash flow $(D_0 = \$42,500)$. On the basis of a review of similar-risk investment opportunities, you must earn an 18% rate of return on the proposed purchase. Because you are relatively uncertain about future cash flows, you decide to estimate the firm's value using two possible assumptions about the growth rate of cash flows.
a. What is the firm's value if cash flows are expected to grow at an annual rate of 0% from now to infinity?

b. What is the firm's value if cash flows are expected to grow at a constant annual rate of 7% from now to infinity?

 P7–13 **Free cash flow valuation** Nabor Industries is considering going public but is unsure of a fair offering price for the company. Before hiring an investment banker to assist in making the public offering, managers at Nabor have decided to make their own estimate of the firm's common stock value. The firm's CFO has gathered data for performing the valuation using the free cash flow valuation model.

The firm's weighted average cost of capital is 11%, and it has $1,500,000 of debt at market value and $400,000 of preferred stock at its assumed market value. The estimated free cash flows over the next 5 years, 2010 through 2014, are given below. Beyond 2014 to infinity, the firm expects its free cash flow to grow by 3% annually.

Year (t)	Free cash flow (FCF_t)
2010	$200,000
2011	250,000
2012	310,000
2013	350,000
2014	390,000

a. Estimate the value of Nabor Industries' entire company by using the *free cash flow valuation model.*
b. Use your finding in part **a,** along with the data provided above, to find Nabor Industries' common stock value.
c. If the firm plans to issue 200,000 shares of common sock, what is its estimated value per share?

PERSONAL FINANCE PROBLEM

 P7–14 **Using the free cash flow valuation model to price an IPO** Assume that you have an opportunity to buy the stock of CoolTech, Inc., an IPO being offered for $12.50 per share. Although you are very much interested in owning the company, you are concerned about whether it is fairly priced. To determine the value of the shares, you have decided to apply the free cash flow valuation model to the firm's financial data that you've developed from a variety of data sources. The key values you have compiled are summarized in the following table.

Year (t)	Free cash flow FCF_t	Other data
2010	$ 700,000	Growth rate of FCF, beyond 2013 to infinity = 2%
2011	800,000	Weighted average cost of capital = 8%
2012	950,000	Market value of all debt = $2,700,000
2013	1,100,000	Market value of preferred stock = $1,000,000
		Number of shares of common stock outstanding = 1,100,000

a. Use the *free cash flow valuation model* to estimate CoolTech's common stock value per share.

b. Judging on the basis of your finding in part **a** and the stock's offering price, should you buy the stock?

c. Upon further analysis, you find that the growth rate in FCF beyond 2013 will be 3% rather than 2%. What effect would this finding have on your responses in parts **a** and **b**?

 P7–15 **Book and liquidation value** The balance sheet for Gallinas Industries is as follows.

Gallinas Industries Balance Sheet December 31			
Assets		**Liabilities and Stockholders' Equity**	
Cash	$ 40,000	Accounts payable	$100,000
Marketable securities	60,000	Notes payable	30,000
Accounts receivable	120,000	Accrued wages	30,000
Inventories	160,000	Total current liabilities	$160,000
Total current assets	$380,000	Long-term debt	$180,000
Land and buildings (net)	$150,000	Preferred stock	$ 80,000
Machinery and equipment	250,000	Common stock (10,000 shares)	260,000
Total fixed assets (net)	$400,000	Retained earnings	100,000
Total assets	$780,000	Total liabilities and stockholders' equity	$780,000

Additional information with respect to the firm is available:

(1) Preferred stock can be liquidated at book value.

(2) Accounts receivable and inventories can be liquidated at 90% of book value.

(3) The firm has 10,000 shares of common stock outstanding.

(4) All interest and dividends are currently paid up.

(5) Land and buildings can be liquidated at 130% of book value.

(6) Machinery and equipment can be liquidated at 70% of book value.

(7) Cash and marketable securities can be liquidated at book value.

Given this information, answer the following:

a. What is Gallinas Industries' *book value per share*?

b. What is its *liquidation value per share*?

c. Compare, contrast, and discuss the values found in parts **a** and **b**.

 P7–16 **Valuation with price/earnings multiples** For each of the firms shown in the following table, use the data given to estimate its common stock value employing price/earnings (P/E) multiples.

Firm	Expected EPS	Price/earnings multiple
A	$3.00	6.2
B	4.50	10.0
C	1.80	12.6
D	2.40	8.9
E	5.10	15.0

P7–17 **Management action and stock value** REH Corporation's most recent dividend was $3 per share, its expected annual rate of dividend growth is 5%, and the required return is now 15%. A variety of proposals are being considered by management to redirect the firm's activities. Determine the impact on share price for each of the following proposed actions, and indicate the best alternative.

a. Do nothing, which will leave the key financial variables unchanged.

b. Invest in a new machine that will increase the dividend growth rate to 6% and lower the required return to 14%.

c. Eliminate an unprofitable product line, which will increase the dividend growth rate to 7% and raise the required return to 17%.

d. Merge with another firm, which will reduce the growth rate to 4% and raise the required return to 16%.

e. Acquire a subsidiary operation from another manufacturer. The acquisition should increase the dividend growth rate to 8% and increase the required return to 17%.

  P7–18 **Integrative—Valuation and CAPM formulas** Given the following information for the stock of Foster Company, calculate its beta.

Current price per share of common	$50.00
Expected dividend per share next year	$ 3.00
Constant annual dividend growth rate	9%
Risk-free rate of return	7%
Return on market portfolio	10%

  P7–19 **Integrative—Risk and valuation** Giant Enterprises has a beta of 1.20, the risk-free rate of return is currently 10%, and the market return is 14%. The company, which plans to pay a dividend of $2.60 per share in the coming year, anticipates that its future dividends will increase at an annual rate consistent with that experienced over the 2003–2009 period, when the following dividends were paid:

Year	Dividend per share
2009	$2.45
2008	2.28
2007	2.10
2006	1.95
2005	1.82
2004	1.80
2003	1.73

a. Use the capital asset pricing model (CAPM) to determine the required return on Giant's stock.

b. Using the constant-growth model and your finding in part **a**, estimate the value of Giant's stock.

c. Explain what effect, if any, a decrease in beta would have on the value of Giant's stock.

  P7–20 **Integrative—Valuation and CAPM** Hamlin Steel Company wishes to determine the value of Craft Foundry, a firm that it is considering acquiring for cash. Hamlin wishes to use the capital asset pricing model (CAPM) to determine the applicable discount rate to use as an input to the constant-growth valuation model. Craft's stock is not publicly traded. After studying the betas of firms similar to Craft that are publicly traded, Hamlin believes that an appropriate beta for Craft's stock would be 1.25. The risk-free rate is currently 9%, and the market return is 13%. Craft's dividend per share for each of the past 6 years is shown in the following table.

Year	Dividend per share
2009	$3.44
2008	3.28
2007	3.15
2006	2.90
2005	2.75
2004	2.45

a. Given that Craft is expected to pay a dividend of $3.68 next year, determine the maximum cash price that Hamlin should pay for each share of Craft.
b. Discuss the use of the CAPM for estimating the value of common stock, and describe the effect on the resulting value of Craft of:
   (1) A decrease in its dividend growth rate of 2% from that exhibited over the 2004–2009 period.
   (2) A decrease in its beta to 1.

P7–21 **ETHICS PROBLEM**   Melissa is trying to value Generic Utility, Inc.'s stock, which is clearly not growing at all. Generic declared and paid a $5 dividend last year. The required rate of return for utility stocks is 11%, but Melissa is unsure about the financial reporting integrity of Generic's finance team. She decides to add an extra 1% "credibility" risk premium to the required return as part of her valuation analysis.
a. What is the value of Generic's stock, assuming that the financials are trustworthy?
b. What is the value of Generic's stock, assuming that Melissa includes the extra 1% "credibility" risk premium?
c. What is the difference between the values found in parts **a** and **b**, and how might one interpret that difference?

Chapter Case

Assessing the Impact of Suarez Manufacturing's Proposed Risky Investment on Its Stock Value

Early in 2010, Inez Marcus, the chief financial officer for Suarez Manufacturing, was given the task of assessing the impact of a proposed risky investment on the firm's stock value. To perform the necessary analysis, Inez gathered the following information on the firm's stock.

During the immediate past 5 years (2005–2009), the annual dividends paid on the firm's common stock were as follows:

Year	Dividend per share
2009	$1.90
2008	1.70
2007	1.55
2006	1.40
2005	1.30

The firm expects that without the proposed investment, the dividend in 2010 will be $2.09 per share and the historical annual rate of growth (rounded to the nearest whole percent) will continue in the future. Currently, the required return on the common stock is 14%. Inez's research indicates that if the proposed investment is undertaken, the 2010 dividend will rise to $2.15 per share and the annual rate of dividend growth will increase to 13%. She feels that in the *best case*, the dividend would continue to grow at this rate each year into the future and that in the *worst case*, the 13% annual rate of growth in dividends would continue only through 2012, and then, at the beginning of 2013, would return to the rate that was experienced between 2005 and 2009. As a result of the increased risk associated with the proposed risky investment, the required return on the common stock is expected to increase by 2% to an annual rate of 16%, regardless of which dividend growth outcome occurs.

Armed with the preceding information, Inez must now assess the impact of the proposed risky investment on the market value of Suarez's stock. To simplify her calculations, she plans to round the historical growth rate in common stock dividends to the nearest whole percent.

To Do

a. Find the *current* value per share of Suarez Manufacturing's common stock.

b. Find the value of Suarez's common stock in the event that it *undertakes the proposed risky investment* and assuming that the dividend growth rate stays at 13% forever. Compare this value to that found in part a. What effect would the proposed investment have on the firm's stockholders? Explain.

c. On the basis of your findings in part b, do the stockholders win or lose as a result of undertaking the proposed risky investment? Should the firm do it? Why?

d. Rework parts b and c assuming that at the beginning of 2013 the annual dividend growth rate returns to the rate experienced between 2005 and 2009.

Spreadsheet Exercise

You are interested in purchasing the common stock of Azure Corporation. The firm recently paid a dividend of $3 per share. It expects its earnings—and hence its dividends—to grow at a rate of 7% for the foreseeable future. Currently, similar-risk stocks have required returns of 10%.

To Do

a. Given the data above, calculate the present value of this security. Use the constant-growth model (Equation 5) to find the stock value.

b. One year later, your broker offers to sell you additional shares of Azure at $73. The most recent dividend paid was $3.21, and the expected growth rate for earnings remains at 7%. To determine the required rate of return, you decide to use the capital asset pricing model (CAPM). The risk-free rate, R_F, is currently 5.25%; the market return, r_m, is 11.55%; and the stock's beta, b_{Azure}, is 1.07. Substitute the appropriate values into the CAPM (Equation 7) to determine the firm's current required return, r_{Azure}.

c. Applying Equation 5, determine the value of the stock using the new dividend and required return from part **b**.

d. Given your calculation in part **c**, would you buy the additional shares from your broker at $73 per share? Explain.

e. Given your calculation in part **c**, would you sell your old shares for $73? Explain.

Web Exercise

Go to the text's companion website at **www.prenhall.com/gitman** to find the Web Exercise for this chapter.

> Remember to check the text's website at **www.prenhall.com/gitman** to find additional resources, including Web Exercises and a Web Case.

Solutions to Self-Test Problems

ST7–1 $D_0 = \$1.80$/share

$r_s = 12\%$

a. *Zero growth:*

$$P_0 = \frac{D_1}{r_s} = \frac{D_1 = D_0 = \$1.80}{0.12} = \underline{\underline{\$15}}\text{/share}$$

b. *Constant growth, g = 5%:*

$$D_1 = D_0 \times (1 + g) = \$1.80 = (1 + 0.05) = \$1.89\text{/share}$$

$$P_0 = \frac{D_1}{r_s - g} = \frac{\$1.89}{0.12 - 0.05} = \frac{\$1.89}{0.07} = \underline{\underline{\$27}}\text{/share}$$

ST7–2 **a. Step 1:** Present value of free cash flow from end of 2011 to infinity measured at the end of 2010.

$$FCF_{2014} = \$1,500,000 \times (1 + 0.04) = \$1,560,000$$

$$\text{Value of } FCF_{2014 \to \infty} = \frac{\$1,560,000}{0.10 - 0.04} = \frac{\$1,560,000}{0.06} = \underline{\underline{\$26,000,000}}$$

Step 2: Add the value found in Step 1 to the 2013 FCF.

Total $FCF_{2013} = \$1,500,000 + \$26,000,000 = \underline{\underline{\$27,500,000}}$

Step 3: Find the sum of the present values of the FCFs for 2010 through 2013 to determine company value, V_C.

Year (t)	FCF_t (1)	$PVIF_{10\%,t}$ (2)	Present value of FCF_t [(1) × (2)] (3)
2010	$ 800,000	0.909	$ 727,200
2011	1,200,000	0.826	991,200
2012	1,400,000	0.751	1,051,400
2013	27,500,000	0.683	18,782,500
		Value of entire company, $V_C =$	$\underline{\underline{\$21,552,300}}$

(Calculator solution = $21,553,719)

b. Common Stock value, $V_S = V_C - V_D - V_P$

$V_C = \$21,552,300$ (calculated in part **a**)

$V_D = \$12,500,000$ (given)

$V_P = \$0$ (given)

$V_S = \$21,552,300 - \$12,500,000 - \$0 = \underline{\underline{\$9,052,300}}$

(Calculator solution = $9,053,719)

c. Price per share $= \dfrac{\$9,052,300}{500,000} = \underline{\underline{\$18.10}}\text{/share}$

(Calculator solution = $18.11/share)

Answers to Selected End-of-Chapter Problems

7–1	**b.**	800,000 shares
7–3	A:	$15.00
	C:	$11.00
	D:	$25.50
7–6	**a.**	$20
	b.	$12
7–8	**a.**	$68.82
	b.	$60.95
7–9	A:	$24.00
	B:	$40.00
	E:	$18.75
7–10	**a.**	$37.75
	b.	$60.40
7–13	**a.**	(1) $5,021,250
		(2) $5,411,250
		(3) $4,049,331
	b.	$2,191,331
	c.	$10.96
7–15	**a.**	Book value: $36.00
	b.	Liquidation value: $30.20

Chapter 9

Financial Statements and Analysis

Financial Statements and Analysis

WHY THIS CHAPTER MATTERS TO YOU

In Your Professional Life

Accounting: You need to understand the stockholders' report and preparation of the four key financial statements; how firms consolidate international financial statements; and how to calculate and interpret financial ratios for decision making.

Information systems: You need to understand what data are included in the firm's financial statements to design systems that will supply such data to those who prepare the statements and to those in the firm who use the data for ratio calculations.

Management: You need to understand what parties are interested in the stockholders' report and why; how the financial statements will be analyzed by those both inside and outside the firm to assess various aspects of performance; the caution that should be exercised in using financial ratio analysis; and how the financial statements affect the value of the firm.

Marketing: You need to understand the effects your decisions will have on the financial statements, particularly the income statement and the statement of cash flows, and how analysis of ratios, especially those involving sales figures, will affect the firm's decisions about levels of inventory, credit policies, and pricing decisions.

Operations: You need to understand how the costs of operations are reflected in the firm's financial statements and how analysis of ratios, particularly those involving assets, cost of goods sold, or inventory, may affect requests for new equipment or facilities.

In Your Personal Life

A routine step in personal financial planning is to prepare and analyze personal financial statements, so that you can monitor progress toward your financial goals. Also, you need to understand and analyze corporate financial statements to build and monitor your investment portfolio.

LEARNING GOALS

LG 1 Review the contents of the stockholders' report and the procedures for consolidating international financial statements.

LG 2 Understand who uses financial ratios, and how.

LG 3 Use ratios to analyze a firm's liquidity and activity.

LG 4 Discuss the relationship between debt and financial leverage and the ratios used to analyze a firm's debt.

LG 5 Use ratios to analyze a firm's profitability and its market value.

LG 6 Use a summary of financial ratios and the DuPont system of analysis to perform a complete ratio analysis.

All companies gather financial data about their operations and report this information in financial statements for interested parties. These statements are widely standardized, and so we can use the data in them to make comparisons between firms and over time. Analysis of certain items of financial data can identify areas where the firm excels and, also, areas of opportunity for improvement. This chapter reviews the content of financial statements and explains categories of financial ratios and their use.

LG 1 | 1 | The Stockholders' Report

generally accepted accounting principles (GAAP)
The practice and procedure guidelines used to prepare and maintain financial records and reports; authorized by the *Financial Accounting Standards Board (FASB)*.

Financial Accounting Standards Board (FASB)
The accounting profession's rule-setting body, which authorizes *generally accepted accounting principles (GAAP)*.

Public Company Accounting Oversight Board (PCAOB)
A not-for-profit corporation established by the *Sarbanes-Oxley Act of 2002* to protect the interests of investors and further the public interest in the preparation of informative, fair, and independent audit reports.

Securities and Exchange Commission (SEC)
The federal regulatory body that governs the sale and listing of securities.

stockholders' report
Annual report that publicly owned corporations must provide to stockholders; it summarizes and documents the firm's financial activities during the past year.

letter to stockholders
Typically, the first element of the annual stockholders' report and the primary communication from management.

Every corporation has many and varied uses for the standardized records and reports of its financial activities. Periodically, reports must be prepared for regulators, creditors (lenders), owners, and management. The guidelines used to prepare and maintain financial records and reports are known as **generally accepted accounting principles (GAAP)**. These accounting practices and procedures are authorized by the accounting profession's rule-setting body, the **Financial Accounting Standards Board (FASB)**.

In addition, the *Sarbanes-Oxley Act of 2002*, enacted in an effort to eliminate the many disclosure and conflict of interest problems of corporations, established the **Public Company Accounting Oversight Board (PCAOB)**, a not-for-profit corporation that oversees auditors of public corporations. The PCAOB is charged with protecting the interes ts of investors and furthering the public interest in the preparation of informative, fair, and independent audit reports. The expectation is that it will instill confidence in investors with regard to the accuracy of the audited financial statements of public companies.

Publicly owned corporations with more than $5 million in assets and 500 or more stockholders[1] are required by the **Securities and Exchange Commission (SEC)**—the federal regulatory body that governs the sale and listing of securities—to provide their stockholders with an annual **stockholders' report.** The stockholders' report summarizes and documents the firm's financial activities during the past year. It begins with a letter to the stockholders from the firm's president and/or chairman of the board.

The Letter to Stockholders

The **letter to stockholders** is the primary communication from management. It describes the events that are considered to have had the greatest effect on the firm during the year. It also generally discusses management philosophy, corporate governance issues, strategies, and actions, as well as plans for the coming year. Links at this book's website (**www.prenhall.com/gitman**) will take you to some representative letters to stockholders.

---

1. Although the Securities and Exchange Commission (SEC) does not have an official definition of *publicly owned*, these financial measures mark the cutoff point it uses to require informational reporting, regardless of whether the firm publicly sells its securities. Firms that do not meet these requirements are commonly called "closely owned" firms.

The Four Key Financial Statements

The four key financial statements required by the SEC for reporting to shareholders are (1) the income statement, (2) the balance sheet, (3) the statement of stockholders' equity, and (4) the statement of cash flows.[2] The financial statements from the 2009 stockholders' report of Bartlett Company, a manufacturer of metal fasteners, are presented and briefly discussed. Most likely, you have studied these four financial statements in an accounting course, so the purpose of looking at them here is to refresh your memory of the basics, rather than provide an exhaustive review.

Income Statement

income statement
Provides a financial summary of the firm's operating results during a specified period.

The **income statement** provides a financial summary of the firm's operating results during a specified period. Most common are income statements covering a 1-year period ending at a specified date, ordinarily December 31 of the calendar year. Many large firms, however, operate on a 12-month financial cycle, or *fiscal year,* that ends at a time other than December 31. In addition, monthly income statements are typically prepared for use by management, and quarterly statements must be made available to the stockholders of publicly owned corporations.

Hint Some firms, such as retailers and agricultural firms, end their fiscal year at the end of their operating cycle rather than at the end of the calendar year—for example, retailers at the end of January and agricultural firms at the end of September.

Table 1 presents Bartlett Company's income statements for the years ended December 31, 2009 and 2008. The 2009 statement begins with *sales revenue*—the total dollar amount of sales during the period—from which the *cost of goods sold* is deducted. The resulting *gross profits* of $986,000 represent the amount remaining to satisfy operating, financial, and tax costs. Next, *operating expenses,* which include selling expense, general and administrative expense, lease expense, and depreciation expense, are deducted from gross profits.[3] The resulting *operating profits* of $418,000 represent the profits earned from producing and selling products; this amount does not consider financial and tax costs. (Operating profit is often called *earnings before interest and taxes,* or *EBIT.*) Next, the financial cost—*interest expense*—is subtracted from operating profits to find *net profits* (or *earnings*) *before taxes.* After subtracting $93,000 in 2009 interest, Bartlett Company had $325,000 of net profits before taxes.

Next, taxes are calculated at the appropriate tax rates and deducted to determine *net profits* (or *earnings*) *after taxes.* Bartlett Company's net profits after taxes for 2009 were $231,000. Any preferred stock dividends must be subtracted from net profits after taxes to arrive at *earnings available for common stockholders.* This is the amount earned by the firm on behalf of the common stockholders during the period.

Dividing earnings available for common stockholders by the number of shares of common stock outstanding results in *earnings per share (EPS).* EPS represent the number of dollars earned during the period on behalf of each outstanding

2. Whereas these statement titles are consistently used throughout this text, it is important to recognize that in practice, companies frequently use different titles. For example, General Electric uses "Statement of Earnings" rather than "Income Statement" and "Statement of Financial Position" rather than "Balance Sheet." Both Sprint Nextel and Qualcomm use "Statement of Operations" rather than "Income Statement."

3. Depreciation expense can be, and frequently is, included in manufacturing costs—cost of goods sold—to calculate gross profits. Depreciation is shown as an expense in this text to isolate its effect on cash flows.

TABLE 1	Bartlett Company Income Statements ($000)		
		For the years ended December 31	
		2009	2008
Sales revenue		$3,074	$2,567
Less: Cost of goods sold		2,088	1,711
Gross profits		$ 986	$ 856
Less: Operating expenses			
Selling expense		$ 100	$ 108
General and administrative expenses		194	187
Lease expense[a]		35	35
Depreciation expense		239	223
Total operating expense		$ 568	$ 553
Operating profits		$ 418	$ 303
Less: Interest expense		93	91
Net profits before taxes		$ 325	$ 212
Less: Taxes (rate = 29%)[b]		94	64
Net profits after taxes		$ 231	$ 148
Less: Preferred stock dividends		10	10
Earnings available for common stockholders		$ 221	$ 138
Earnings per share (EPS)[c]		$2.90	$1.81
Dividend per share (DPS)[d]		$1.29	$0.75

[a]Lease expense is shown here as a separate item rather than being included as part of interest expense, as specified by the FASB for financial reporting purposes. The approach used here is consistent with tax reporting rather than financial reporting procedures.

[b]The 29% tax rate for 2009 results because the firm has certain special tax write-offs that do not show up directly on its income statement.

[c]Calculated by dividing the earnings available for common stockholders by the number of shares of common stock outstanding—76,262 in 2009 and 76,244 in 2008. Earnings per share in 2009: $221,000 ÷ 76,262 = $2.90; in 2008: $138,000 ÷ 76,244 = $1.81.

[d]Calculated by dividing the dollar amount of dividends paid to common stockholders by the number of shares of common stock outstanding. Dividends per share in 2009: $98,000 ÷ 76,262 = $1.29; in 2008: $57,183 ÷ 76,244 = $0.75.

dividend per share (DPS)
The dollar amount of cash distributed during the period on behalf of each outstanding share of common stock.

share of common stock. In 2009, Bartlett Company earned $221,000 for its common stockholders, which represents $2.90 for each outstanding share. The actual cash **dividend per share (DPS)**, which is the dollar amount of cash distributed during the period on behalf of each outstanding share of common stock, paid in 2009 was $1.29.

Personal Finance Example   Jan and Jon Smith, a mid-30s married couple with no children, prepared a personal income and expense statement, which is similar to a corporate income statement. A condensed version of their income and expense statement appears on the next page. A more detailed version appears at the text's website.

Jan and Jon Smith
Income and Expense Statement
for the year ended December 31, 2009

Income

Salaries (incl. sales commissions)	$72,725
Interest received	195
Dividends received	120
(1) Total income	$73,040

Expenses

Mortgage payments	$16,864
Auto loan payments	2,520
Utilities (incl. cable)	2,470
Home repairs & maintenance	1,050
Food (incl. dining out)	5,825
Car expense	2,265
Health care and insurance	1,505
Clothes, shoes, accessories	1,700
Insurance (homeowners, auto, & life)	1,380
Taxes (income, Soc. Security, prop.)	16,430
Appliance and furniture payments	1,250
Recreation and entertainment	4,630
Tuition and books for Jan	1,400
Personal care & other items	2,415
(2) Total expenses	$61,704
(3) Cash surplus (or deficit) [(1) − (2)]	$11,336

During the year, the Smiths had total income of $73,040 and total expenses of $61,704, which left them with a cash surplus of $11,336. They can use the surplus to increase their savings and investments.

Balance Sheet

balance sheet
Summary statement of the firm's financial position at a given point in time.

The **balance sheet** presents a summary statement of the firm's financial position at a given point in time. The statement balances the firm's *assets* (what it owns) against its financing, which can be either *debt* (what it owes) or *equity* (what was provided by owners). Bartlett Company's balance sheets as of December 31 of 2009 and 2008 are presented in Table 2. They show a variety of asset, liability (debt), and equity accounts.

An important distinction is made between short-term and long-term assets and liabilities. The **current assets** and **current liabilities** are *short-term* assets and liabilities. This means that they are expected to be converted into cash (current assets) or paid (current liabilities) within 1 year or less. All other assets and liabilities, along with stockholders' equity, which is assumed to have an infinite life, are considered *long-term,* or *fixed,* because they are expected to remain on the firm's books for more than 1 year.

current assets
Short-term assets, expected to be converted into cash within 1 year or less.

current liabilities
Short-term liabilities, expected to be paid within 1 year or less.

As is customary, the assets are listed from the most liquid—*cash*—down to the least liquid. *Marketable securities* are very liquid short-term investments, such

TABLE 2   Bartlett Company Balance Sheets ($000)

Assets	December 31 2009	December 31 2008
Current assets		
Cash	$ 363	$ 288
Marketable securities	68	51
Accounts receivable	503	365
Inventories	289	300
Total current assets	$1,223	$1,004
Gross fixed assets (at cost)[a]		
Land and buildings	$2,072	$1,903
Machinery and equipment	1,866	1,693
Furniture and fixtures	358	316
Vehicles	275	314
Other (includes financial leases)	98	96
Total gross fixed assets (at cost)	$4,669	$4,322
Less: Accumulated depreciation	2,295	2,056
Net fixed assets	$2,374	$2,266
Total assets	$3,597	$3,270

Liabilities and Stockholders' Equity		
Current liabilities		
Accounts payable	$ 382	$ 270
Notes payable	79	99
Accruals	159	114
Total current liabilities	$ 620	$ 483
Long-term debt (includes financial leases)[b]	$1,023	$ 967
Total liabilities	$1,643	$1,450
Stockholders' equity		
Preferred stock—cumulative 5%, $100 par, 2,000 shares authorized and issued[c]	$ 200	$ 200
Common stock—$2.50 par, 100,000 shares authorized, shares issued and outstanding in 2009: 76,262; in 2008: 76,244	191	190
Paid-in capital in excess of par on common stock	428	418
Retained earnings	1,135	1,012
Total stockholders' equity	$1,954	$1,820
Total liabilities and stockholders' equity	$3,597	$3,270

[a]In 2009, the firm has a 6-year financial lease requiring annual beginning-of-year payments of $35,000. Four years of the lease have yet to run.

[b]Annual principal repayments on a portion of the firm's total outstanding debt amount to $71,000.

[c]The annual preferred stock dividend would be $5 per share (5% × $100 par), or a total of $10,000 annually ($5 per share × 2,000 shares).

Hint Another interpretation of the balance sheet is that on one side are the assets that have been purchased to be used to increase the profit of the firm. The other side indicates how these assets were acquired, either by borrowing or by investing the owners' money.

long-term debt
Debts for which payment is not due in the current year.

paid-in capital in excess of par
The amount of proceeds in excess of the par value received from the original sale of common stock.

retained earnings
The cumulative total of all earnings, net of dividends, that have been retained and reinvested in the firm since its inception.

as U.S. Treasury bills or certificates of deposit, held by the firm. Because they are highly liquid, marketable securities are viewed as a form of cash ("near cash"). *Accounts receivable* represent the total monies owed the firm by its customers on credit sales made to them. *Inventories* include raw materials, work in process (partially finished goods), and finished goods held by the firm. The entry for *gross fixed assets* is the original cost of all fixed (long-term) assets owned by the firm.[4] *Net fixed assets* represent the difference between gross fixed assets and *accumulated depreciation*—the total expense recorded for the depreciation of fixed assets. (The net value of fixed assets is called their *book value*.)

Like assets, the liabilities and equity accounts are listed from short-term to long-term. Current liabilities include *accounts payable,* amounts owed for credit purchases by the firm; *notes payable,* outstanding short-term loans, typically from commercial banks; and *accruals,* amounts owed for services for which a bill may not or will not be received. (Examples of accruals include taxes due the government and wages due employees.) **Long-term debt** represents debt for which payment is not due in the current year. *Stockholders' equity* represents the owners' claims on the firm. The *preferred stock* entry shows the historical proceeds from the sale of preferred stock ($200,000 for Bartlett Company).

Next, the amount paid by the original purchasers of common stock is shown by two entries: common stock and paid-in capital in excess of par on common stock. The *common stock* entry is the *par value* of common stock. **Paid-in capital in excess of par** represents the amount of proceeds in excess of the par value received from the original sale of common stock. The sum of the common stock and paid-in capital accounts divided by the number of shares outstanding represents the original price per share received by the firm on a single issue of common stock. Bartlett Company therefore received about $8.12 per share [($191,000 par + $428,000 paid-in capital in excess of par) ÷ 76,262 shares] from the sale of its common stock.

Finally, **retained earnings** represent the cumulative total of all earnings, net of dividends, that have been retained and reinvested in the firm since its inception. It is important to recognize that retained earnings *are not cash* but rather have been utilized to finance the firm's assets.

Bartlett Company's balance sheets in Table 2 show that the firm's total assets increased from $3,270,000 in 2008 to $3,597,000 in 2009. The $327,000 increase was due primarily to the $219,000 increase in current assets. The asset increase, in turn, appears to have been financed primarily by an increase of $193,000 in total liabilities. Better insight into these changes can be derived from the statement of cash flows, which we will discuss shortly.

Personal Finance Example

The following personal balance sheet for Jan and Jon Smith—the couple introduced earlier, who are married, in their mid-30s, and have no children—is similar to a corporate balance sheet. Again, a more detailed version appears at the text's website.

---

4. For convenience the term *fixed assets* is used throughout this text to refer to what, in a strict accounting sense, is captioned "property, plant, and equipment." This simplification of terminology permits certain financial concepts to be more easily developed.

Jan and Jon Smith
Balance Sheet
December 31, 2009

Assets			Liabilities and Net Worth		
Cash on hand	$	90	Credit card balances	$	665
Checking accounts		575	Utility bills		120
Savings accounts		760	Medical bills		75
Money market funds		800	Other current liab.		45
Total liquid assets	$	2,225	Total cur. liab.	$	905
Stocks & bonds	$	2,250	Real estate mortg.		$ 92,000
Mutual funds		1,500	Auto loans		4,250
Retirement funds, IRA		2,000	Education loan		3,800
Total investments	$	5,750	Personal loan		4,000
Real estate		$120,000	Furniture loan		800
Cars		14,000	Tot. L-T liab.		$104,850
Household furnishings		3,700	Tot. liab.		$105,755
Jewelry & artwork		1,500	Net worth (N/W)		$ 41,420
Total personal prop.		$139,200	Tot. liab.		
Total assets		$147,175	& N/W		$147,175

statement of stockholders' equity
Shows all equity account transactions that occurred during a given year.

statement of retained earnings
Reconciles the net income earned during a given year, and any cash dividends paid, with the change in retained earnings between the start and the end of that year. An abbreviated form of the *statement of stockholders' equity.*

The Smiths have total assets of $147,175 and total liabilities of $105,755. Personal net worth (N/W) is a "plug figure"—the difference between total assets and total liabilities—which in the case of Jan and Jon Smith is $41,420.

Statement of Retained Earnings

The *statement of retained earnings* is an abbreviated form of the statement of stockholders' equity. Unlike the **statement of stockholders' equity,** which shows all equity account transactions that occurred during a given year, the **statement of retained earnings** reconciles the net income earned during a given year, and any cash dividends paid, with the change in retained earnings between the start and the end of that year. Table 3 presents this statement for Bartlett Company for the year ended December 31, 2009. The statement shows that the company began the year with $1,012,000 in retained earnings and had net profits after taxes of $231,000,

TABLE 3	Bartlett Company Statement of Retained Earnings ($000) for the Year Ended December 31, 2009		
Retained earnings balance (January 1, 2009)			$1,012
Plus: Net profits after taxes (for 2009)			231
Less: Cash dividends (paid during 2009)			
Preferred stock		$10	
Common stock		98	
Total dividends paid			108
Retained earnings balance (December 31, 2009)			$1,135

from which it paid a total of $108,000 in dividends, resulting in year-end retained earnings of $1,135,000. Thus the net increase for Bartlett Company was $123,000 ($231,000 net profits after taxes minus $108,000 in dividends) during 2009.

Statement of Cash Flows

statement of cash flows
Provides a summary of the firm's operating, investment, and financing cash flows and reconciles them with changes in its cash and marketable securities during the period.

notes to the financial statements
Explanatory notes keyed to relevant accounts in the statements; they provide detailed information on the accounting policies, procedures, calculations, and transactions underlying entries in the financial statements.

The **statement of cash flows** is a summary of the cash flows over the period of concern. The statement provides insight into the firm's operating, investment, and financing cash flows and reconciles them with changes in its cash and marketable securities during the period. Bartlett Company's statement of cash flows for the year ended December 31, 2009, is presented in Table 4.

Notes to the Financial Statements

Included with published financial statements are explanatory notes keyed to the relevant accounts in the statements. These **notes to the financial statements** provide detailed information on the accounting policies, procedures, calculations, and transactions underlying entries in the financial statements. Common issues

TABLE 4	Bartlett Company Statement of Cash Flows ($000) for the Year Ended December 31, 2009		
Cash Flow from Operating Activities			
Net profits after taxes	$231		
Depreciation	239		
Increase in accounts receivable	(138)*a*		
Decrease in inventories	11		
Increase in accounts payable	112		
Increase in accruals	45		
Cash provided by operating activities			$500
Cash Flow from Investment Activities			
Increase in gross fixed assets	($347)		
Change in equity investments in other firms	0		
Cash provided by investment activities			(347)
Cash Flow from Financing Activities			
Decrease in notes payable	($ 20)		
Increase in long-term debts	56		
Changes in stockholders' equity*b*	11		
Dividends paid	(108)		
Cash provided by financing activities			(61)
Net increase in cash and marketable securities			$ 92

*a*As is customary, parentheses are used to denote a negative number, which in this case is a cash outflow.

*b*Retained earnings are excluded here, because their change is actually reflected in the combination of the "net profits after taxes" and "dividends paid" entries.

IN PRACTICE

Focus on Practice — Is It Time to Change SOX?

In 2000 and 2001, accounting irregularities at a number of large corporations forced Congress to take action, passing the Sarbanes-Oxley Act of 2002 (SOX). However, not everyone is pleased with the law. Many companies complain that compliance with the Sarbanes-Oxley corporate reporting regulations require them to spend much time and money. Large corporations, for example, spent an average of $3.8 million in 2005 to comply with the law. The most onerous aspect of SOX appears to be Section 404, which requires companies to first review their own systems for ensuring accurate financial reports and then have them tested by outside auditors.

Several high-ranking government officials have weighed in on the debate. In a speech to the Economic Club in November 2006, U.S. Treasury Secretary Henry Paulson acknowledged the impact of the accounting provi-sions, especially on small businesses. Rather than passing a new law to amend the act, he said, Section 404 should be implemented in a more efficient and cost-effective manner. Also, Securities and Exchange Commission (SEC) Chairman Christopher Cox wrote a letter to the Public Company Accounting Oversight Board (the auditing industry's overseer) urging that the rule be adapted to companies based on company size.

Supporters of SOX claim that the law and related reforms have produced more reliable corporate financial statements, which investors rely on when deciding whether to buy or sell shares. According to Duncan W. Richardson, chief equity investment officer at Eaton Vance Management and overseer of $80 billion in stock holdings, even the act's much-disparaged requirements for testing internal financial controls could drive gains in corporate productivity and profits. Thompson Financial's Earnings Purity Index, which tracks earnings adjusted for unusual charges and write-offs—techniques used to make earnings look better—reports that improvements have been shown in each of the past 4 years.

The jury is still out on whether Sarbanes-Oxley will be changed to alleviate the burden on U.S. corporations. However, consider this: On the day SOX was signed into law, the market value of the Wilshire 5000, a proxy for all public companies in the United States, stood at $10.5 trillion. By April 2007, the value of the Wilshire 5000 was $14.5 trillion. While the markets factor in many events, the passage of SOX has not had a significantly negative impact, as some might argue.

■ *In addition to investors, who else might be benefiting directly from the implementation of the Sarbanes-Oxley Act?*

---

addressed by these notes include revenue recognition, income taxes, breakdowns of fixed asset accounts, debt and lease terms, and contingencies. Since passage of Sarbanes-Oxley, notes to the financial statements have also included some details about compliance with that law. The *Focus on Practice* box above discusses issues relating to SOX compliance. Professional securities analysts use the data in the statements and notes to develop estimates of the value of securities that the firm issues, and these estimates influence the actions of investors and therefore the firm's share value.

Consolidating International Financial Statements

Financial Accounting Standards Board (FASB) Standard No. 52
Mandates that U.S.-based companies translate their foreign-currency-denominated assets and liabilities into dollars, for consolidation with the parent company's financial statements. This is done by using the *current rate (translation) method.*

So far, we've discussed financial statements involving only one currency, the U.S. dollar. The issue of how to consolidate a company's foreign and domestic financial statements has bedeviled the accounting profession for many years. The current policy is described in **Financial Accounting Standards Board (FASB) Standard No. 52,** which mandates that U.S.-based companies translate their

current rate (translation) method
Technique used by U.S.-based companies to translate their foreign-currency-denominated assets and liabilities into dollars, for consolidation with the parent company's financial statements, using the year-end (current) exchange rate.

foreign-currency-denominated assets and liabilities into dollars, for consolidation with the parent company's financial statements. This is done by using a technique called the **current rate (translation) method**, under which all of a U.S. parent company's foreign-currency-denominated assets and liabilities are converted into dollar values using the exchange rate prevailing at the fiscal year ending date (the current rate). Income statement items are treated similarly. Equity accounts, on the other hand, are translated into dollars by using the exchange rate that prevailed when the parent's equity investment was made (the historical rate). Retained earnings are adjusted to reflect each year's operating profits or losses. For an example that demonstrates consolidation of international financial statements, go to the text's website.

REVIEW QUESTIONS

1   What roles do GAAP, the FASB, and the PCAOB play in the financial reporting activities of public companies?
2   Describe the purpose of each of the four major financial statements.
3   Why are the notes to the financial statements important to professional securities analysts?
4   How is the *current rate (translation) method* used to consolidate a firm's foreign and domestic financial statements?

LG 2   2 | Using Financial Ratios

The information contained in the four basic financial statements is of major significance to a variety of interested parties who regularly need to have relative measures of the company's performance. *Relative* is the key word here, because the analysis of financial statements is based on the use of *ratios* or *relative values*. **Ratio analysis** involves methods of calculating and interpreting financial ratios to analyze and monitor the firm's performance. The basic inputs to ratio analysis are the firm's income statement and balance sheet.

ratio analysis
Involves methods of calculating and interpreting financial ratios to analyze and monitor the firm's performance.

Interested Parties

Hint Management should be the most interested party of this group. Managers not only have to worry about the financial situation of the firm, but they are also critically interested in what the other parties think about the firm.

Ratio analysis of a firm's financial statements is of interest to shareholders, creditors, and the firm's own management. Both current and prospective shareholders are interested in the firm's current and future level of risk and return, which directly affect share price. The firm's creditors are interested primarily in the short-term liquidity of the company and its ability to make interest and principal payments. A secondary concern of creditors is the firm's profitability; they want assurance that the business is healthy. Management, like stockholders, is concerned with all aspects of the firm's financial situation, and it attempts to produce financial ratios that will be considered favorable by both owners and creditors. In addition, management uses ratios to monitor the firm's performance from period to period.

Types of Ratio Comparisons

Ratio analysis is not merely the calculation of a given ratio. More important is the *interpretation* of the ratio value. A meaningful basis for comparison is needed to answer such questions as "Is it too high or too low?" and "Is it good or bad?" Two types of ratio comparisons can be made: cross-sectional and time-series.

Cross-Sectional Analysis

cross-sectional analysis
Comparison of different firms' financial ratios at the same point in time; involves comparing the firm's ratios to those of other firms in its industry or to industry averages.

benchmarking
A type of *cross-sectional analysis* in which the firm's ratio values are compared to those of a key competitor or group of competitors that it wishes to emulate.

Cross-sectional analysis involves the comparison of different firms' financial ratios at the same point in time. Analysts are often interested in how well a firm has performed in relation to other firms in its industry. Frequently, a firm will compare its ratio values to those of a key competitor or group of competitors that it wishes to emulate. This type of cross-sectional analysis, called **benchmarking**, has become very popular.

Comparison to industry averages is also popular. These figures can be found in the *Almanac of Business and Industrial Financial Ratios, Dun & Bradstreet's Industry Norms and Key Business Ratios, RMA Annual Statement Studies, Value Line,* and industry sources.[5] A sample from one available source of industry averages is given in Table 5.

TABLE 5	Industry Average Ratios for Selected Lines of Business[a]								
Line of business (number of concerns reporting)[b]	Current ratio (X)	Quick ratio (X)	Sales to inventory (X)	Collection period (days)	Total assets to sales (%)	Total liabilities to net worth (%)	Return on sales (%)	Return on total assets (%)	Return on net worth (%)
Department	4.9	1.4	6.6	1.8	32.0	25.1	2.8	6.8	16.2
stores	2.6	0.6	4.6	6.1	43.8	76.6	1.0	2.3	4.5
(143)	1.6	0.2	3.5	21.2	64.9	176.9	0.1	0.1	0.2
Electronic	2.3	1.5	31.6	27.4	24.6	54.3	3.4	7.3	20.6
computers	1.6	0.9	11.3	40.9	58.9	114.3	0.5	1.3	4.6
(76)	1.2	0.7	6.8	68.5	104.1	238.3	(9.7)	(10.4)	(20.6)
Grocery	2.6	1.0	29.6	1.1	15.3	48.5	2.2	9.4	24.8
stores	1.6	0.5	19.6	2.9	21.3	105.2	1.0	4.4	10.0
(455)	1.1	0.2	13.9	6.9	31.2	277.3	0.3	1.4	3.5
Motor	2.9	1.1	11.4	16.1	27.8	56.4	4.2	10.3	26.9
vehicles	1.7	0.7	8.3	24.1	37.4	150.8	1.5	4.1	9.6
(42)	1.2	0.5	5.5	40.5	47.3	357.2	0.2	0.8	1.2

[a]These values are given for each ratio for each line of business. The center value is the median, and the values immediately above and below it are the upper and lower quartiles, respectively.

[b]Standard Industrial Classification (SIC) codes for the lines of business shown are, respectively: SIC #5311, SIC #3571, SIC #5411, SIC #3711.

Source: "Industry Norms and Key Business Ratios," Dun & Bradstreet, Inc. Reprinted with permission.

---

5. Cross-sectional comparisons of firms operating in several lines of business are difficult to perform. Weighted-average industry average ratios based on the firm's product-line mix can be used or, if data are available, analysis of the firm on a product-line basis can be performed to evaluate a multiproduct firm.

Many people mistakenly believe that as long as the firm being analyzed has a value "better than" the industry average, it can be viewed favorably. However, this "better than average" viewpoint can be misleading. Quite often a ratio value that is far better than the norm can indicate problems that, on more careful analysis, may be more severe than had the ratio been worse than the industry average. It is therefore important to investigate significant deviations *to either side* of the industry standard.

Example

In early 2010, Mary Boyle, the chief financial analyst at Caldwell Manufacturing, a producer of heat exchangers, gathered data on the firm's financial performance during 2009, the year just ended. She calculated a variety of ratios and obtained industry averages. She was especially interested in inventory turnover, which reflects the speed with which the firm moves its inventory from raw materials through production into finished goods and to the customer as a completed sale. Generally, higher values of this ratio are preferred, because they indicate a quicker turnover of inventory. Caldwell Manufacturing's calculated inventory turnover for 2009 and the industry average inventory turnover were as follows:

	Inventory turnover, 2009
Caldwell Manufacturing	14.8
Industry average	9.7

Mary's initial reaction to these data was that the firm had managed its inventory significantly *better than* the average firm in the industry. The turnover was nearly 53% faster than the industry average. Upon reflection, however, she realized that a very high inventory turnover could also mean very low levels of inventory. The consequence of low inventory could be excessive stockouts (insufficient inventory). Discussions with people in the manufacturing and marketing departments did, in fact, uncover such a problem: Inventories during the year were extremely low, the result of numerous production delays that hindered the firm's ability to meet demand and resulted in lost sales. A ratio that initially appeared to reflect extremely efficient inventory management was actually the symptom of a major problem.

Time-Series Analysis

Time-series analysis evaluates performance over time. Comparison of current to past performance, using ratios, enables analysts to assess the firm's progress. Developing trends can be seen by using multiyear comparisons. Any significant year-to-year changes may be symptomatic of a major problem.

Combined Analysis

The most informative approach to ratio analysis combines cross-sectional and time-series analyses. A combined view makes it possible to assess the trend in the behavior of the ratio in relation to the trend for the industry. Figure 1 depicts this type of approach using the average collection period ratio of Bartlett Company, over the years 2006–2009. This ratio reflects the average amount of time (in days) it takes the firm to collect bills, and lower values of this ratio generally are preferred. The figure quickly discloses that (1) Bartlett's effectiveness in collecting

FIGURE 1

Combined Analysis
Combined cross-sectional and time-series view of Bartlett Company's average collection period, 2006–2009

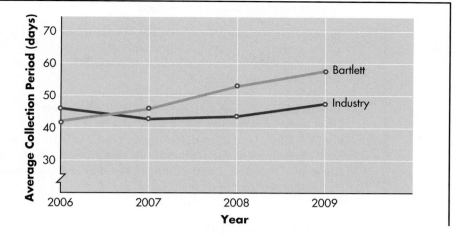

its receivables is poor in comparison to the industry, and (2) Bartlett's trend is toward longer collection periods. Clearly, Bartlett needs to shorten its collection period.

Cautions about Using Ratio Analysis

Before discussing specific ratios, we should consider the following cautions about their use:

1. Ratios that reveal large deviations from the norm merely indicate *symptoms* of a problem. Additional analysis is typically needed to isolate the *causes* of the problem.
2. A single ratio does not generally provide sufficient information from which to judge the *overall* performance of the firm. However, if an analysis is concerned only with certain *specific* aspects of a firm's financial position, one or two ratios may suffice.
3. The ratios being compared should be calculated using financial statements dated at the same point in time during the year. If they are not, the effects of *seasonality* may produce erroneous conclusions and decisions.
4. It is preferable to use *audited financial statements* for ratio analysis. If they have not been audited, the data in them may not reflect the firm's true financial condition.
5. The financial data being compared should have been developed in the same way. The use of differing accounting treatments—especially relative to inventory and depreciation—can distort the results of ratio comparisons, regardless of whether cross-sectional or time-series analysis is used.
6. Results can be distorted by *inflation*, which can cause the book values of inventory and depreciable assets to differ greatly from their replacement values. Additionally, inventory costs and depreciation write-offs can differ from their true values, thereby distorting profits. Without adjustment, inflation tends to cause older firms (older assets) to appear more efficient and profitable than newer firms (newer assets). Clearly, in using ratios, you must be careful when comparing older to newer firms or a firm to itself over a long period of time.

323

Categories of Financial Ratios

Financial ratios can be divided for convenience into five basic categories: liquidity, activity, debt, profitability, and market ratios. Liquidity, activity, and debt ratios primarily measure risk. Profitability ratios measure return. Market ratios capture both risk and return.

As a rule, the inputs necessary for an effective financial analysis include, at a minimum, the income statement and the balance sheet. We will use the 2009 and 2008 income statements and balance sheets for Bartlett Company, presented earlier in Tables 1 and 2, to demonstrate ratio calculations. Note, however, that the ratios presented in the remainder of this chapter can be applied to almost any company. Of course, many companies in different industries use ratios that focus on aspects peculiar to their industry.

REVIEW QUESTIONS

5   With regard to financial ratio analysis, how do the viewpoints held by the firm's present and prospective shareholders, creditors, and management differ?

6   What is the difference between *cross-sectional* and *time-series* ratio analysis? What is *benchmarking?*

7   What types of deviations from the norm should the analyst pay primary attention to when performing cross-sectional ratio analysis? Why?

8   Why is it preferable to compare ratios calculated using financial statements that are dated at the same point in time during the year?

3 | Liquidity Ratios

liquidity
A firm's ability to satisfy its short-term obligations *as they come due.*

The **liquidity** of a firm is measured by its ability to satisfy its short-term obligations *as they come due.* Liquidity refers to the solvency of the firm's *overall* financial position—the ease with which it can pay its bills. Because a common precursor to financial distress and bankruptcy is low or declining liquidity, these ratios can provide early signs of cash flow problems and impending business failure. The two basic measures of liquidity are the current ratio and the quick (acid-test) ratio.

Current Ratio

current ratio
A measure of liquidity calculated by dividing the firm's current assets by its current liabilities.

The **current ratio,** one of the most commonly cited financial ratios, measures the firm's ability to meet its short-term obligations. It is expressed as follows:

$$\text{Current ratio} = \frac{\text{Current assets}}{\text{Current liabilities}}$$

The current ratio for Bartlett Company in 2009 is

$$\frac{\$1,223,000}{\$620,000} = 1.97$$

Generally, the higher the current ratio, the more liquid the firm is considered to be. A current ratio of 2.0 is occasionally cited as acceptable, but a value's acceptability depends on the industry in which the firm operates. For example, a current ratio of 1.0 would be considered acceptable for a public utility but might be unacceptable for a manufacturing firm. The more predictable a firm's cash flows, the lower the acceptable current ratio. Because Bartlett Company is in a business with a relatively predictable annual cash flow, its current ratio of 1.97 should be quite acceptable.

Personal Finance Example   Individuals, like corporations, can use financial ratios to analyze and monitor their performance. Typically personal finance ratios are calculated using the personal income and expense statement and personal balance sheet for the period of concern. Here we use these statements, presented in the preceding personal finance examples, to demonstrate calculation of Jan and Jon Smith's liquidity ratio for calendar year 2009.

The personal *liquidity ratio* is calculated by dividing total liquid assets by total current debt. It indicates the percent of annual debt obligations that an individual can meet using current liquid assets. The Smiths' total liquid assets were $2,225. Their total current debts are $21,539 (total current liabilities of $905 + mortgage payments of $16,864 + auto loan payments of $2,520 + appliance and furniture payments of $1,250). Substituting these values into the ratio formula, we get:

$$\text{Liquidity ratio} = \frac{\text{Total liquid assets}}{\text{Total current debts}} = \frac{\$2,225}{\$21,539} = 0.1033, \text{ or } 10.3\%$$

That ratio indicates that the Smiths can cover only about 10 percent of their existing 1-year debt obligations with their current liquid assets. Clearly, the Smiths plan to meet these debt obligations from their income, but this ratio suggests that their liquid funds do not provide a large cushion. One of their goals should probably be to build up a larger fund of liquid assets to meet unexpected expenses.

Quick (Acid-Test) Ratio

quick (acid-test) ratio
A measure of liquidity calculated by dividing the firm's current assets minus inventory by its current liabilities.

The **quick (acid-test) ratio** is similar to the current ratio except that it excludes inventory, which is generally the least liquid current asset. The generally low liquidity of inventory results from two primary factors: (1) many types of inventory cannot be easily sold because they are partially completed items, special-purpose items, and the like; and (2) inventory is typically sold on credit, which means that it becomes an account receivable before being converted into cash. The quick ratio is calculated as follows:[6]

$$\text{Quick ratio} = \frac{\text{Current assets} - \text{Inventory}}{\text{Current liabilities}}$$

---

6. Sometimes the quick ratio is defined as (cash + marketable securities + accounts receivable) ÷ current liabilities. If a firm were to show as current assets items other than cash, marketable securities, accounts receivable, and inventories, its quick ratio might vary, depending on the method of calculation.

The quick ratio for Bartlett Company in 2009 is

$$\frac{\$1,223,000 - \$289,000}{\$620,000} = \frac{\$934,000}{\$620,000} = 1.51$$

A quick ratio of 1.0 or greater is occasionally recommended, but as with the current ratio, what value is acceptable depends largely on the industry. The quick ratio provides a better measure of overall liquidity only when a firm's inventory cannot be easily converted into cash. If inventory is liquid, the current ratio is a preferred measure of overall liquidity.

REVIEW QUESTION

9   Under what circumstances would the current ratio be the preferred measure of overall firm liquidity? Under what circumstances would the quick ratio be preferred?

4 | Activity Ratios

activity ratios
Measure the speed with which various accounts are converted into sales or cash—inflows or outflows.

Activity ratios measure the speed with which various accounts are converted into sales or cash—inflows or outflows. With regard to current accounts, measures of liquidity are generally inadequate because differences in the *composition* of a firm's current assets and current liabilities can significantly affect its "true" liquidity. It is therefore important to look beyond measures of overall liquidity and to assess the activity (liquidity) of specific current accounts. A number of ratios are available for measuring the activity of the most important current accounts, which include inventory, accounts receivable, and accounts payable.[7] The efficiency with which total assets are used can also be assessed.

Inventory Turnover

inventory turnover
Measures the activity, or liquidity, of a firm's inventory.

Inventory turnover commonly measures the activity, or liquidity, of a firm's inventory. It is calculated as follows:

$$\text{Inventory turnover} = \frac{\text{Cost of goods sold}}{\text{Inventory}}$$

---

7. For convenience, the activity ratios involving these current accounts assume that their end-of-period values are good approximations of the average account balance during the period—typically 1 year. Technically, when the month-end balances of inventory, accounts receivable, or accounts payable vary during the year, the average balance, calculated by summing the 12 month-end account balances and dividing the total by 12, should be used instead of the year-end value. If month-end balances are unavailable, the average can be approximated by dividing the sum of the beginning-of-year and end-of-year balances by 2. These approaches ensure a ratio that on the average better reflects the firm's circumstances. Because the data needed to find averages are generally unavailable to the external analyst, year-end values are frequently used to calculate activity ratios for current accounts.

Applying this relationship to Bartlett Company in 2009 yields

$$\text{Inventory turnover} = \frac{\$2,088,000}{\$289,000} = 7.2$$

The resulting turnover is meaningful only when it is compared with that of other firms in the same industry or to the firm's past inventory turnover. An inventory turnover of 20.0 would not be unusual for a grocery store, whereas a common inventory turnover for an aircraft manufacturer is 4.0.

average age of inventory
Average number of days' sales in inventory.

Inventory turnover can be easily converted into an **average age of inventory** by dividing it into 365—the assumed number of days in a year.[8] For Bartlett Company, the average age of inventory in 2009 is 50.7 days (365 ÷ 7.2). This value can also be viewed as the average number of days' sales in inventory.

Average Collection Period

average collection period
The average amount of time needed to collect accounts receivable.

The **average collection period,** or average age of accounts receivable, is useful in evaluating credit and collection policies.[9] It is arrived at by dividing the average daily sales[10] into the accounts receivable balance:

$$\text{Average collection period} = \frac{\text{Accounts receivable}}{\text{Average sales per day}}$$

$$= \frac{\text{Accounts receivable}}{\dfrac{\text{Annual sales}}{365}}$$

The average collection period for Bartlett Company in 2009 is

$$\frac{\$503,000}{\dfrac{\$3,074,000}{365}} = \frac{\$503,000}{\$8,422} = 59.7 \text{ days}$$

On the average, it takes the firm 59.7 days to collect an account receivable.

The average collection period is meaningful only in relation to the firm's credit terms. If Bartlett Company extends 30-day credit terms to customers, an average collection period of 59.7 days may indicate a poorly managed credit or collection department, or both. It is also possible that the lengthened collection period resulted from an intentional relaxation of credit-term enforcement in response to competitive pressures. If the firm had extended 60-day credit terms, the 59.7-day average collection period would be quite acceptable. Clearly, additional information is needed to evaluate the effectiveness of the firm's credit and collection policies.

---

8. Unless otherwise specified, a 365-day year is used throughout this textbook. This assumption makes the calculations more realistic than would use of a 360-day year consisting of twelve 30-day months.

9. The average collection period is sometimes called the *days' sales outstanding (DSO)*.

10. The formula as presented assumes, for simplicity, that all sales are made on a credit basis. If this is not the case, *average credit sales per day* should be substituted for average sales per day.

Average Payment Period

average payment period
The average amount of time needed to pay accounts payable.

The **average payment period,** or average age of accounts payable, is calculated in the same manner as the average collection period:

$$\text{Average payment period} = \frac{\text{Accounts payable}}{\text{Average purchases per day}}$$

$$= \frac{\text{Accounts payable}}{\dfrac{\text{Annual purchases}}{365}}$$

The difficulty in calculating this ratio stems from the need to find annual purchases,[11] a value not available in published financial statements. Ordinarily, purchases are estimated as a given percentage of cost of goods sold. If we assume that Bartlett Company's purchases equaled 70 percent of its cost of goods sold in 2009, its average payment period is

$$\frac{\$382,000}{\dfrac{0.70 \times \$2,088,000}{365}} = \frac{\$382,000}{\$4,004} = 95.4 \text{ days}$$

This figure is meaningful only in relation to the average credit terms extended to the firm. If Bartlett Company's suppliers have extended, on average, 30-day credit terms, an analyst would give Bartlett a low credit rating. Prospective lenders and suppliers of trade credit are most interested in the average payment period because it provides insight into the firm's bill-paying patterns.

Total Asset Turnover

total asset turnover
Indicates the efficiency with which the firm uses its assets to generate sales.

The **total asset turnover** indicates the efficiency with which the firm uses its assets to generate sales. Total asset turnover is calculated as follows:

$$\text{Total asset turnover} = \frac{\text{Sales}}{\text{Total assets}}$$

The value of Bartlett Company's total asset turnover in 2009 is

$$\frac{\$3,074,000}{\$3,597,000} = 0.85$$

Hint The higher the cost of the new assets, the larger the denominator and thus the smaller the ratio. Therefore, because of inflation and the use of historical costs, firms with newer assets will tend to have lower turnovers than those with older assets.

This means the company turns over its assets 0.85 times per year.

Generally, the higher a firm's total asset turnover, the more efficiently its assets have been used. This measure is probably of greatest interest to management, because it indicates whether the firm's operations have been financially efficient.

---

11. Technically, annual *credit* purchases—rather than annual purchases—should be used in calculating this ratio. For simplicity, this refinement is ignored here.

REVIEW QUESTION

10   To assess the firm's average collection period and average payment period ratios, what additional information is needed, and why?

---

5 | Debt Ratios

The *debt position* of a firm indicates the amount of other people's money being used to generate profits. In general, the financial analyst is most concerned with long-term debts, because these commit the firm to a stream of contractual payments over the long run. The more debt a firm has, the greater its risk of being unable to meet its contractual debt payments. Because creditors' claims must be satisfied before the earnings can be distributed to shareholders, current and prospective shareholders pay close attention to the firm's ability to repay debts. Lenders are also concerned about the firm's indebtedness.

financial leverage
The magnification of risk and return through the use of fixed-cost financing, such as debt and preferred stock.

In general, the more debt a firm uses in relation to its total assets, the greater its *financial leverage*. **Financial leverage** is the magnification of risk and return through the use of fixed-cost financing, such as debt and preferred stock. The more fixed-cost debt a firm uses, the greater will be its expected risk and return.

Example

Patty Akers is in the process of incorporating her new business. After much analysis she determined that an initial investment of $50,000—$20,000 in current assets and $30,000 in fixed assets—is necessary. These funds can be obtained in either of two ways. The first is the *no-debt plan*, under which she would invest the full $50,000 without borrowing. The other alternative, the *debt plan*, involves investing $25,000 and borrowing the balance of $25,000 at 12% annual interest.

Regardless of which alternative she chooses, Patty expects sales to average $30,000, costs and operating expenses to average $18,000, and earnings to be taxed at a 40% rate. Projected balance sheets and income statements associated with the two plans are summarized in Table 6. The no-debt plan results in after-tax profits of $7,200, which represent a 14.4% rate of return on Patty's $50,000 investment. The debt plan results in $5,400 of after-tax profits, which represent a 21.6% rate of return on Patty's investment of $25,000. The debt plan provides Patty with a higher rate of return, but the risk of this plan is also greater, because the annual $3,000 of interest must be paid before receipt of earnings.

The example demonstrates that *with increased debt comes greater risk as well as higher potential return.* Therefore, the greater the financial leverage, the greater the potential risk and return. Here, we emphasize the use of financial debt ratios to assess externally a firm's debt position.

degree of indebtedness
Measures the amount of debt relative to other significant balance sheet amounts.

There are two general types of debt measures: measures of the degree of indebtedness and measures of the ability to service debts. The **degree of indebtedness** measures the amount of debt relative to other significant balance sheet amounts. A popular measure of the degree of indebtedness is the debt ratio.

TABLE 6	Financial Statements Associated with Patty's Alternatives	
	No-debt plan	Debt plan
Balance Sheets		
Current assets	$20,000	$20,000
Fixed assets	30,000	30,000
Total assets	$50,000	$50,000
Debt (12% interest)	$ 0	$25,000
(1) Equity	50,000	25,000
Total liabilities and equity	$50,000	$50,000
Income Statements		
Sales	$30,000	$30,000
Less: Costs and operating expenses	18,000	18,000
Operating profits	$12,000	$12,000
Less: Interest expense	0 $0.12 \times \$25,000 =$	3,000
Net profits before taxes	$12,000	$ 9,000
Less: Taxes (rate = 40%)	4,800	3,600
(2) Net profits after taxes	$ 7,200	$ 5,400
Return on equity [(2) ÷ (1)]	$\dfrac{\$7,200}{\$50,000} = 14.4\%$	$\dfrac{\$5,400}{\$25,000} = 21.6\%$

ability to service debts
The ability of a firm to make the payments required on a scheduled basis over the life of a debt.

coverage ratios
Ratios that measure the firm's ability to pay certain fixed charges.

The second type of debt measure, the **ability to service debts**, reflects a firm's ability to make the payments required on a scheduled basis over the life of a debt.[12] The firm's ability to pay certain fixed charges is measured using **coverage ratios.** Typically, higher coverage ratios are preferred, but too high a ratio (above industry norms) may result in unnecessarily low risk and return. In general, the lower the firm's coverage ratios, the less certain it is to be able to pay fixed obligations. If a firm is unable to pay these obligations, its creditors may seek immediate repayment, which in most instances would force a firm into bankruptcy. Two popular coverage ratios are the times interest earned ratio and the fixed-payment coverage ratio.

Debt Ratio

debt ratio
Measures the proportion of total assets financed by the firm's creditors.

The **debt ratio** measures the proportion of total assets financed by the firm's creditors. The higher this ratio, the greater the amount of other people's money being used to generate profits. The ratio is calculated as follows:

$$\text{Debt ratio} = \frac{\text{Total liabilities}}{\text{Total assets}}$$

---

12. The term *service* refers to the payment of interest and repayment of principal associated with a firm's debt obligations. When a firm services its debts, it pays—or fulfills—these obligations.

The debt ratio for Bartlett Company in 2009 is

$$\frac{\$1,643,000}{\$3,597,000} = 0.457 = 45.7\%$$

This value indicates that the company has financed close to half of its assets with debt. The higher this ratio, the greater the firm's degree of indebtedness and the more financial leverage it has.

Times Interest Earned Ratio

times interest earned ratio
Measures the firm's ability to make contractual interest payments; sometimes called the *interest coverage ratio*.

The **times interest earned ratio,** sometimes called the *interest coverage ratio,* measures the firm's ability to make contractual interest payments. The higher its value, the better able the firm is to fulfill its interest obligations. The times interest earned ratio is calculated as follows:

$$\text{Times interest earned ratio} = \frac{\text{Earnings before interest and taxes}}{\text{Interest}}$$

The figure for *earnings before interest and taxes* is the same as that for *operating profits* shown in the income statement. Applying this ratio to Bartlett Company yields the following 2009 value:

$$\text{Times interest earned ratio} = \frac{\$418,000}{\$93,000} = 4.5$$

The times interest earned ratio for Bartlett Company seems acceptable. A value of at least 3.0—and preferably closer to 5.0—is often suggested. The firm's earnings before interest and taxes could shrink by as much as 78 percent [$(4.5 - 1.0) \div 4.5$], and the firm would still be able to pay the $93,000 in interest it owes. Thus it has a good margin of safety.

Fixed-Payment Coverage Ratio

fixed-payment coverage ratio
Measures the firm's ability to meet all fixed-payment obligations.

The **fixed-payment coverage ratio** measures the firm's ability to meet all fixed-payment obligations, such as loan interest and principal, lease payments, and preferred stock dividends.[13] As is true of the times interest earned ratio, the higher this value, the better. The formula for the fixed-payment coverage ratio is

$$\frac{\text{Fixed-payment coverage ratio}}{} = \frac{\text{Earnings before interest and taxes} + \text{Lease payments}}{\text{Interest} + \text{Lease payments} + \{(\text{Principal payments} + \text{Preferred stock dividends}) \times [1/(1 - T)]\}}$$

where T is the corporate tax rate applicable to the firm's income. The term $1/(1 - T)$ is included to adjust the after-tax principal and preferred stock dividend payments

13. Although preferred stock dividends, which are stated at the time of issue, can be "passed" (not paid) at the option of the firm's directors, it is generally believed that the payment of such dividends is necessary. *This text therefore treats the preferred stock dividend as a contractual obligation, to be paid as a fixed amount, as scheduled.*

back to a before-tax equivalent that is consistent with the before-tax values of all other terms. Applying the formula to Bartlett Company's 2009 data yields

$$\frac{\text{Fixed-payment}}{\text{coverage ratio}} = \frac{\$418,000 + \$35,000}{\$93,000 + \$35,000 + \{(\$71,000 + \$10,000) \times [1/(1 - 0.29)]\}}$$

$$= \frac{\$453,000}{\$242,000} = 1.9$$

Because the earnings available are nearly twice as large as its fixed-payment obligations, the firm appears safely able to meet the latter.

Like the times interest earned ratio, the fixed-payment coverage ratio measures risk. The lower the ratio, the greater the risk to both lenders and owners; the greater the ratio, the lower the risk. This ratio allows interested parties to assess the firm's ability to meet additional fixed-payment obligations without being driven into bankruptcy.

REVIEW QUESTIONS

11 What is *financial leverage?*

12 What ratio measures the firm's *degree of indebtedness?* What ratios assess the firm's *ability to service debts?*

---

6 | Profitability Ratios

There are many measures of profitability. As a group, these measures enable analysts to evaluate the firm's profits with respect to a given level of sales, a certain level of assets, or the owners' investment. Without profits, a firm could not attract outside capital. Owners, creditors, and management pay close attention to boosting profits because of the great importance the market places on earnings.

Common-Size Income Statements

common-size income statement
An income statement in which each item is expressed as a percentage of sales.

A popular tool for evaluating profitability in relation to sales is the **common-size income statement.** Each item on this statement is expressed as a percentage of sales. Common-size income statements are especially useful in comparing performance across years. Three frequently cited ratios of profitability that can be read directly from the common-size income statement are (1) the gross profit margin, (2) the operating profit margin, and (3) the net profit margin.

Common-size income statements for 2009 and 2008 for Bartlett Company are presented and evaluated in Table 7. These statements reveal that the firm's cost of goods sold increased from 66.7 percent of sales in 2008 to 67.9 percent in 2009, resulting in a worsening gross profit margin. However, thanks to a decrease in total operating expenses, the firm's net profit margin rose from 5.4 percent of sales in 2008 to 7.2 percent in 2009. The decrease in expenses more than compensated for the increase in the cost of goods sold. A decrease in the firm's 2009 interest expense (3.0 percent of sales versus 3.5 percent in 2008) added to the increase in 2009 profits.

TABLE 7	Bartlett Company Common-Size Income Statements		
		For the years ended December 31		Evaluation[a]
	2009	2008	2008–2009
Sales revenue	100.0%	100.0%	same
Less: Cost of goods sold	67.9	66.7	worse
(1) Gross profit margin	32.1%	33.3%	worse
Less: Operating expenses			
Selling expense	3.3%	4.2%	better
General and administrative expenses	6.8	6.7	better
Lease expense	1.1	1.3	better
Depreciation expense	7.3	9.3	better
Total operating expense	18.5%	21.5%	better
(2) Operating profit margin	13.6%	11.8%	better
Less: Interest expense	3.0	3.5	better
Net profits before taxes	10.6%	8.3%	better
Less: Taxes	3.1	2.5	worse[b]
Net profits after taxes	7.5%	5.8%	better
Less: Preferred stock dividends	0.3	0.4	better
(3) Net profit margin	7.2%	5.4%	better

[a]Subjective assessments based on data provided.

[b]Taxes as a percentage of sales increased noticeably between 2008 and 2009 because of differing costs and expenses, whereas the average tax rates (taxes ÷ net profits before taxes) for 2008 and 2009 remained about the same—30% and 29%, respectively.

Gross Profit Margin

gross profit margin
Measures the percentage of each sales dollar remaining after the firm has paid for its goods.

The **gross profit margin** measures the percentage of each sales dollar remaining after the firm has paid for its goods. The higher the gross profit margin, the better (that is, the lower the relative cost of merchandise sold). The gross profit margin is calculated as follows:

$$\text{Gross profit margin} = \frac{\text{Sales} - \text{Cost of goods sold}}{\text{Sales}} = \frac{\text{Gross profits}}{\text{Sales}}$$

Hint This is a very significant ratio for small retailers, especially during times of inflationary prices. If the owner of the firm does not raise prices when the cost of sales is rising, the gross profit margin will erode.

Bartlett Company's gross profit margin for 2009 is

$$\frac{\$3,074,000 - \$2,088,000}{\$3,074,000} = \frac{\$986,000}{\$3,074,000} = 32.1\%$$

This value is labeled (1) on the common-size income statement in Table 7.

Operating Profit Margin

operating profit margin
Measures the percentage of each sales dollar remaining after all costs and expenses *other than* interest, taxes, and preferred stock dividends are deducted; the "pure profits" earned on each sales dollar.

The **operating profit margin** measures the percentage of each sales dollar remaining after all costs and expenses *other than* interest, taxes, and preferred stock dividends are deducted. It represents the "pure profits" earned on each sales dollar.

Operating profits are "pure" because they measure only the profits earned on operations and ignore interest, taxes, and preferred stock dividends. A high operating profit margin is preferred. The operating profit margin is calculated as follows:

$$\text{Operating profit margin} = \frac{\text{Operating profits}}{\text{Sales}}$$

Bartlett Company's operating profit margin for 2009 is

$$\frac{\$418,000}{\$3,074,000} = 13.6\%$$

This value is labeled (2) on the common-size income statement in Table 7.

Net Profit Margin

net profit margin
Measures the percentage of each sales dollar remaining after all costs and expenses, *including* interest, taxes, and preferred stock dividends, have been deducted.

The **net profit margin** measures the percentage of each sales dollar remaining after all costs and expenses, *including* interest, taxes, and preferred stock dividends, have been deducted. The higher the firm's net profit margin, the better. The net profit margin is calculated as follows:

$$\text{Net profit margin} = \frac{\text{Earnings available for common stockholders}}{\text{Sales}}$$

Bartlett Company's net profit margin for 2009 is

$$\frac{\$221,000}{\$3,074,000} = 7.2\%$$

Hint The net profit margin is sometimes defined as net profits after taxes divided by sales. The formula used here places greater emphasis on the common stockholders.

This value is labeled (3) on the common-size income statement in Table 7.

The net profit margin is a commonly cited measure of the firm's success with respect to earnings on sales. "Good" net profit margins differ considerably across industries. A net profit margin of 1 percent or less would not be unusual for a grocery store, whereas a net profit margin of 10 percent would be low for a retail jewelry store.

Earnings per Share (EPS)

Hint EPS represents the dollar amount earned *on behalf of* each outstanding share of common stock—not the amount of earnings *actually distributed* to shareholders.

The firm's *earnings per share (EPS)* is generally of interest to present or prospective stockholders and management. As we noted earlier, EPS represents the number of dollars earned during the period on behalf of each outstanding share of common stock. Earnings per share is calculated as follows:

$$\text{Earnings per share} = \frac{\text{Earnings available for common stockholders}}{\text{Number of shares of common stock outstanding}}$$

Bartlett Company's earnings per share in 2009 is

$$\text{Earnings per share} = \frac{\text{Earnings available for common stockholders}}{\text{Number of shares of common stock outstanding}}$$

This figure represents the dollar amount earned *on behalf of* each outstanding share of common stock. The dollar amount of cash *actually distributed* to each shareholder is the *dividend per share (DPS)*, which, as noted in Bartlett Company's income statement (Table 1), rose to $1.29 in 2009 from $0.75 in 2008. EPS is closely watched by the investing public and is considered an important indicator of corporate success.

Return on Total Assets (ROA)

return on total assets (ROA)
Measures the overall effectiveness of management in generating profits with its available assets; also called the *return on investment (ROI)*.

The **return on total assets (ROA)**, often called the *return on investment (ROI)*, measures the overall effectiveness of management in generating profits with its available assets. The higher the firm's return on total assets, the better. The return on total assets is calculated as follows:

$$\text{Return on total assets} = \frac{\text{Earnings available for common stockholders}}{\text{Total assets}}$$

Hint Some firms use this measure as a simple decision technique for evaluating proposed fixed-asset investments.

Bartlett Company's return on total assets in 2009 is

$$\frac{\$221,000}{\$3,597,000} = 6.1\%$$

This value indicates that the company earned 6.1 cents on each dollar of asset investment.

Return on Common Equity (ROE)

return on common equity (ROE)
Measures the return earned on the common stockholders' investment in the firm.

The **return on common equity (ROE)** measures the return earned on the common stockholders' investment in the firm. Generally, the higher this return, the better off are the owners. Return on common equity is calculated as follows:

$$\text{Return on common equity} = \frac{\text{Earnings available for common stockholders}}{\text{Common stock equity}}$$

This ratio for Bartlett Company in 2009 is

$$\frac{\$221,000}{\$1,754,000} = 12.6\%$$

Note that the value for common stock equity ($1,754,000) was found by subtracting the $200,000 of preferred stock equity from the total stockholders' equity of $1,954,000 (see Bartlett Company's 2009 balance sheet in Table 2). The calculated ROE of 12.6 percent indicates that during 2009 Bartlett earned 12.6 cents on each dollar of common stock equity.

REVIEW QUESTIONS

13 What three ratios of profitability are found on a *common-size income statement?*

14 What would explain a firm's having a high gross profit margin and a low net profit margin?

15 Which measure of profitability is probably of greatest interest to the investing public? Why?

7 | Market Ratios

market ratios
Relate a firm's market value, as measured by its current share price, to certain accounting values.

Market ratios relate the firm's market value, as measured by its current share price, to certain accounting values. These ratios give insight into how well investors in the marketplace feel the firm is doing in terms of risk and return. They tend to reflect, on a relative basis, the common stockholders' assessment of all aspects of the firm's past and expected future performance. Here we consider two popular market ratios, one that focuses on earnings and another that considers book value.

Price/Earnings (P/E) Ratio

price/earnings (P/E) ratio
Measures the amount that investors are willing to pay for each dollar of a firm's earnings; the higher the P/E ratio, the greater the investor confidence.

The **price/earnings (P/E) ratio** is commonly used to assess the owners' appraisal of share value. The P/E ratio measures the amount that investors are willing to pay for each dollar of a firm's earnings. The level of this ratio indicates the degree of confidence that investors have in the firm's future performance. The higher the P/E ratio, the greater the investor confidence. The P/E ratio is calculated as follows:

$$\text{Price/earnings (P/E) ratio} = \frac{\text{Market price per share of common stock}}{\text{Earnings per share}}$$

If Bartlett Company's common stock at the end of 2009 was selling at $32.25, using the EPS of $2.90, the P/E ratio at year-end 2009 is

$$\frac{\$32.25}{\$2.90} = 11.1$$

This figure indicates that investors were paying $11.10 for each $1.00 of earnings. The P/E ratio is most informative when applied in cross-sectional analysis using an industry average P/E ratio or the P/E ratio of a benchmark firm.

Market/Book (M/B) Ratio

market/book (M/B) ratio
Provides an assessment of how investors view the firm's performance. Firms expected to earn high returns relative to their risk typically sell at higher M/B multiples.

The **market/book (M/B) ratio** provides an assessment of how investors view the firm's performance. It relates the market value of the firm's shares to their book—strict accounting—value. To calculate the firm's M/B ratio, we first need to find the *book value per share of common stock:*

$$\frac{\text{Book value per share}}{\text{of common stock}} = \frac{\text{Common stock equity}}{\text{Number of shares of common stock outstanding}}$$

Substituting the appropriate values for Bartlett Company from its 2009 balance sheet, we get

$$\frac{\text{Book value per share}}{\text{of common stock}} = \frac{\$1,754,000}{76,262} = \$23.00$$

The formula for the market/book ratio is

$$\frac{\$221,000}{76,262} = \$2.90$$

Substituting Bartlett Company's end of 2009 common stock price of $32.25 and its $23.00 book value per share of common stock (calculated above) into the M/B ratio formula, we get

$$\text{Market/book (M/B) ratio} = \frac{\$32.25}{\$23.00} = 1.40$$

This M/B ratio means that investors are currently paying $1.40 for each $1.00 of book value of Bartlett Company's stock.

The stocks of firms that are expected to perform well—improve profits, increase their market share, or launch successful products—typically sell at higher M/B ratios than the stocks of firms with less attractive outlooks. Simply stated, firms expected to earn high returns relative to their risk typically sell at higher M/B multiples. Clearly, Bartlett's future prospects are being viewed favorably by investors, who are willing to pay more than its book value for the firm's shares. Like P/E ratios, M/B ratios are typically assessed cross-sectionally, to get a feel for the firm's return and risk compared to peer firms.

REVIEW QUESTION

16 How do the *price/earnings (P/E) ratio* and the *market/book (M/B) ratio* provide a feel for the firm's return and risk?

8 | A Complete Ratio Analysis

Analysts frequently wish to take an overall look at the firm's financial performance and status. Here we consider two popular approaches to a complete ratio analysis: (1) summarizing all ratios and (2) the DuPont system of analysis. The summary analysis approach tends to view *all aspects* of the firm's financial activities to isolate key areas of responsibility. The DuPont system acts as a search technique aimed at finding the *key areas* responsible for the firm's financial condition.

Summarizing All Ratios

We can use Bartlett Company's ratios to perform a complete ratio analysis using both cross-sectional and time-series analysis approaches. The 2009 ratio values calculated earlier and the ratio values calculated for 2007 and 2008 for Bartlett Company, along with the industry average ratios for 2009, are summarized in Table 8, which also shows the formula used to calculate each ratio. Using these data, we can discuss the five key aspects of Bartlett's performance—liquidity, activity, debt, profitability, and market.

Liquidity

The overall liquidity of the firm seems to exhibit a reasonably stable trend, having been maintained at a level that is relatively consistent with the industry average in 2009. The firm's liquidity seems to be good.

TABLE 8   Summary of Bartlett Company Ratios (2007–2009, Including 2009 Industry Averages)

Ratio	Formula	Year			Industry average 2009[c]	Evaluation[d]		
		2007[a]	2008[b]	2009[b]		Cross-sectional 2009	Time-series 2007–2009	Overall
Liquidity								
Current ratio	$\dfrac{\text{Current assets}}{\text{Current liabilities}}$	2.04	2.08	1.97	2.05	OK	OK	OK
Quick (acid-test) ratio	$\dfrac{\text{Current assets} - \text{Inventory}}{\text{Current liabilities}}$	1.32	1.46	1.51	1.43	OK	good	good
Activity								
Inventory turnover	$\dfrac{\text{Cost of goods sold}}{\text{Inventory}}$	5.1	5.7	7.2	6.6	good	good	good
Average collection period	$\dfrac{\text{Accounts receivable}}{\text{Average sales per day}}$	43.9 days	51.2 days	59.7 days	44.3 days	poor	poor	poor
Average payment period	$\dfrac{\text{Accounts payable}}{\text{Average purchases per day}}$	75.8 days	81.2 days	95.4 days	66.5 days	poor	poor	poor
Total asset turnover	$\dfrac{\text{Sales}}{\text{Total assets}}$	0.94	0.79	0.85	0.75	OK	OK	OK
Debt								
Debt ratio	$\dfrac{\text{Total liabilities}}{\text{Total assets}}$	36.8%	44.3%	45.7%	40.0%	OK	OK	OK
Times interest earned ratio	$\dfrac{\text{Earnings before interest and taxes}}{\text{Interest}}$	5.6	3.3	4.5	4.3	good	OK	OK
Fixed-payment coverage ratio	$\dfrac{\text{Earnings before interest and taxes} + \text{Lease payments}}{\text{Int.} + \text{Lease pay.} + \{(\text{Prin.} + \text{Pref. div.}) \times [1/(1 - T)]\}}$	2.4	1.4	1.9	1.5	good	OK	good

| Ratio | Formula | Year | | | Industry average 2009[c] | Evaluation[d] | | |
		2007[a]	2008[b]	2009[b]		Cross-sectional 2009	Time-series 2007–2009	Overall
Profitability								
Gross profit margin	$\dfrac{\text{Gross profits}}{\text{Sales}}$	31.4%	33.3%	32.1%	30.0%	OK	OK	OK
Operating profit margin	$\dfrac{\text{Operating profits}}{\text{Sales}}$	14.6%	11.8%	13.6%	11.0%	good	OK	good
Net profit margin	$\dfrac{\text{Earnings available for common stockholders}}{\text{Sales}}$	8.2%	5.4%	7.2%	6.2%	good	OK	good
Earnings per share (EPS)	$\dfrac{\text{Earnings available for common stockholders}}{\text{Number of shares of common stock outstanding}}$	$3.26	$1.81	$2.90	$2.26	good	OK	good
Return on total assets (ROA)	$\dfrac{\text{Earnings available for common stockholders}}{\text{Total assets}}$	7.8%	4.2%	6.1%	4.6%	good	OK	good
Return on common equity (ROE)	$\dfrac{\text{Earnings available for common stockholders}}{\text{Common stock equity}}$	13.7%	8.5%	12.6%	8.5%	good	OK	good
Market								
Price/earnings (P/E) ratio	$\dfrac{\text{Market price per share of common stock}}{\text{Earnings per share}}$	10.5	10.0[e]	11.1	12.5	OK	OK	OK
Market/book (M/B) ratio	$\dfrac{\text{Market price per share of common stock}}{\text{Book value per share of common stock}}$	1.25	0.85[e]	1.40	1.30	OK	OK	OK

[a] Calculated from data not included in the chapter.
[b] Calculated by using the financial statements presented in Tables 1 and 2.
[c] Obtained from sources not included in this chapter.
[d] Subjective assessments based on data provided.
[e] The market price per share at the end of 2008 was $18.06.

Activity

Bartlett Company's inventory appears to be in good shape. Its inventory management seems to have improved, and in 2009 it performed at a level above that of the industry. The firm may be experiencing some problems with accounts receivable. The average collection period seems to have crept up above that of the industry. Bartlett also appears to be slow in paying its bills; it pays nearly 30 days slower than the industry average. This could adversely affect the firm's credit standing. Although overall liquidity appears to be good, the management of receivables and payables should be examined. Bartlett's total asset turnover reflects a decline in the efficiency of total asset utilization between 2007 and 2008. Although in 2009 it rose to a level considerably above the industry average, it appears that the pre-2008 level of efficiency has not yet been achieved.

Debt

Bartlett Company's indebtedness increased over the 2007–2009 period and is currently above the industry average. Although this increase in the debt ratio could be cause for alarm, the firm's ability to meet interest and fixed-payment obligations improved, from 2008 to 2009, to a level that outperforms the industry. The firm's increased indebtedness in 2008 apparently caused a deterioration in its ability to pay debt adequately. However, Bartlett has evidently improved its income in 2009 so that it is able to meet its interest and fixed-payment obligations at a level consistent with the average in the industry. In summary, it appears that although 2008 was an off year, the company's improved ability to pay debts in 2009 compensates for its increased degree of indebtedness.

Profitability

Bartlett's profitability relative to sales in 2009 was better than the average company in the industry, although it did not match the firm's 2007 performance. Although the *gross* profit margin was better in 2008 and 2009 than in 2007, higher levels of operating and interest expenses in 2008 and 2009 appear to have caused the 2009 *net* profit margin to fall below that of 2007. However, Bartlett Company's 2009 net profit margin is quite favorable when compared to the industry average.

The firm's earnings per share, return on total assets, and return on common equity behaved much as its net profit margin did over the 2007–2009 period. Bartlett appears to have experienced either a sizable drop in sales between 2007 and 2008 or a rapid expansion in assets during that period. The exceptionally high 2009 level of return on common equity suggests that the firm is performing quite well. The firm's above-average returns—net profit margin, EPS, ROA, and ROE—may be attributable to the fact that it is more risky than average. A look at market ratios is helpful in assessing risk.

Market

Investors have greater confidence in the firm in 2009 than in the prior two years, as reflected in the price/earnings (P/E) ratio of 11.1. However, this ratio is below the industry average. The P/E ratio suggests that the firm's risk has declined but remains above that of the average firm in its industry. The firm's market/book

(M/B) ratio has increased over the 2007–2009 period, and in 2009 it exceeds the industry average. This implies that investors are optimistic about the firm's future performance. The P/E and M/B ratios reflect the firm's increased profitability over the 2007–2009 period: Investors expect to earn high future returns as compensation for the firm's above-average risk.

In summary, the firm appears to be growing and has recently undergone an expansion in assets, financed primarily through the use of debt. The 2008–2009 period seems to reflect a phase of adjustment and recovery from the rapid growth in assets. Bartlett's sales, profits, and other performance factors seem to be growing with the increase in the size of the operation. In addition, the market response to these accomplishments appears to have been positive. In short, the firm seems to have done well in 2009.

DuPont System of Analysis

DuPont system of analysis
System used to dissect the firm's financial statements and to assess its financial condition.

The **DuPont system of analysis** is used to dissect the firm's financial statements and to assess its financial condition. It merges the income statement and balance sheet into two summary measures of profitability: return on total assets (ROA) and return on common equity (ROE). Figure 2 depicts the basic DuPont system with Bartlett Company's 2009 monetary and ratio values. The upper portion of the chart summarizes the income statement activities; the lower portion summarizes the balance sheet activities.

DuPont Formula

DuPont formula
Multiplies the firm's *net profit margin* by its *total asset turnover* to calculate the firm's *return on total assets (ROA).*

The DuPont system first brings together the *net profit margin,* which measures the firm's profitability on sales, with its *total asset turnover,* which indicates how efficiently the firm has used its assets to generate sales. In the **DuPont formula,** the product of these two ratios results in the *return on total assets (ROA):*

$$\text{ROA} = \text{Net profit margin} \times \text{Total asset turnover}$$

Substituting the appropriate formulas into the equation and simplifying results in the formula given earlier,

$$\text{ROA} = \frac{\text{Earnings available for common stockholders}}{\text{Sales}} \times \frac{\text{Sales}}{\text{Total assets}} = \frac{\text{Earnings available for common stockholders}}{\text{Total assets}}$$

When the 2009 values of the net profit margin and total asset turnover for Bartlett Company, calculated earlier, are substituted into the DuPont formula, the result is

$$\text{ROA} = 7.2\% \times 0.85 = 6.1\%$$

This value is the same as that calculated directly in an earlier section. The DuPont formula enables the firm to break down its return into profit-on-sales and efficiency-of-asset-use components. Typically, a firm with a low net profit margin has a high total asset turnover, which results in a reasonably good return on total assets. Often, the opposite situation exists.

FIGURE 2   DuPont System of Analysis

The DuPont system of analysis with application to Bartlett Company (2009)

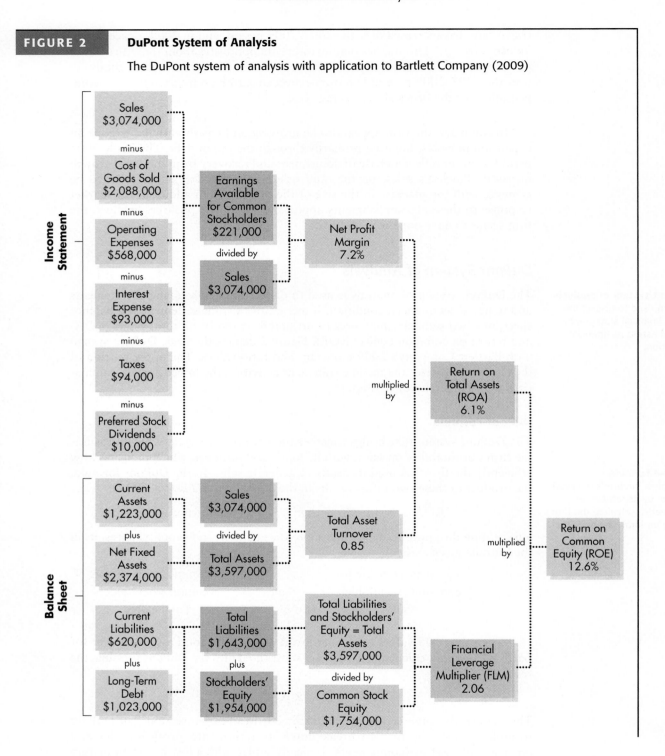

Modified DuPont Formula

The second step in the DuPont system employs the **modified DuPont formula.** This formula relates the firm's *return on total assets (ROA)* to its *return on common equity (ROE)*. The latter is calculated by multiplying the return on total assets (ROA) by the **financial leverage multiplier (FLM)**, which is the ratio of total assets to common stock equity:

$$\text{ROE} = \text{ROA} \times \text{FLM}$$

Substituting the appropriate formulas into the equation and simplifying results in the formula given earlier,

$$\text{ROE} = \frac{\text{Earnings available for common stockholders}}{\text{Total assets}} \times \frac{\text{Total assets}}{\text{Common stock equity}} = \frac{\text{Earnings available for common stockholders}}{\text{Common stock equity}}$$

Use of the financial leverage multiplier (FLM) to convert the ROA into the ROE reflects the impact of financial leverage on owners' return. Substituting the values for Bartlett Company's ROA of 6.1 percent, calculated earlier, and Bartlett's FLM of 2.06 ($3,597,000 total assets ÷ $1,754,000 common stock equity) into the modified DuPont formula yields

$$\text{ROE} = 6.1\% \times 2.06 = 12.6\%$$

The 12.6 percent ROE calculated by using the modified DuPont formula is the same as that calculated directly.

Applying the DuPont System

The advantage of the DuPont system is that it allows the firm to break its return on equity into a profit-on-sales component (net profit margin), an efficiency-of-asset-use component (total asset turnover), and a use-of-financial-leverage component (financial leverage multiplier). The total return to owners therefore can be analyzed in these important dimensions.

The use of the DuPont system of analysis as a diagnostic tool is best explained using Figure 2. Beginning with the rightmost value—the ROE—the financial analyst moves to the left, dissecting and analyzing the inputs to the formula to isolate the probable cause of the resulting above-average (or below-average) value.

Example

For the sake of demonstration, let's ignore all industry average data in Table 8 and assume that Bartlett's ROE of 12.6 % is actually below the industry average. Moving to the left in Figure 2, we would examine the inputs to the ROE—the ROA and the FLM—relative to the industry averages. Let's assume that the FLM is in line with the industry average, but the ROA is below the industry average. Moving farther to the left, we examine the two inputs to the ROA—the net profit margin and total asset turnover. Assume that the net profit margin is in line with the industry average, but the total asset turnover is below the industry average. Moving still farther to the left, we find that whereas the firm's sales are consistent with the industry value, Bartlett's total assets have grown significantly during the past year. Looking farther to the left, we would review the firm's activity ratios for current assets. Let's say that whereas the firm's inventory turnover is in line with the industry average, its average collection period is well above the industry average.

We can readily trace the possible problem back to its cause: Bartlett's low ROE is primarily the consequence of slow collections of accounts receivable, which resulted in high levels of receivables and therefore high levels of total assets. The high total assets slowed Bartlett's total asset turnover, driving down its ROA, which then drove down its ROE. By using the DuPont system of analysis to dissect Bartlett's overall returns as measured by its ROE, we found that slow collections of receivables caused the below-industry-average ROE. Clearly, the firm needs to better manage its credit operations.

REVIEW QUESTIONS

17 Financial ratio analysis is often divided into five areas: *liquidity, activity, debt, profitability,* and *market* ratios. Differentiate each of these areas of analysis from the others. Which is of the greatest concern to creditors?

18 Describe how you would use a large number of ratios to perform a complete ratio analysis of the firm.

19 What three areas of analysis are combined in the *modified DuPont formula?* Explain how the *DuPont system of analysis* is used to dissect the firm's results and isolate their causes.

Summary

Focus on Value

Financial managers review and analyze the firm's financial statements periodically, both to uncover developing problems and to assess the firm's progress toward achieving its goals. These actions are aimed at **preserving and creating value for the firm's owners.** Financial ratios enable financial managers to monitor the pulse of the firm and its progress toward its strategic goals. Although financial statements and financial ratios rely on accrual concepts, they can provide useful insights into important aspects of risk and return (cash flow) that affect share price.

Review of Learning Goals

LG 1 **Review the contents of the stockholders' report and the procedures for consolidating international financial statements.** The annual stockholders' report, which publicly owned corporations must provide to stockholders, documents the firm's financial activities of the past year. It includes the letter to stockholders and various subjective and factual information. It also contains four key financial statements: the income statement, the balance sheet, the statement of stockholders' equity (or its abbreviated form, the statement of retained earnings), and the statement of cash flows. Notes describing the technical aspects of the financial statements follow. Financial statements of companies that have operations whose cash flows are denominated in one or more foreign currencies must be translated into dollars in accordance with *FASB Standard No. 52.*

LG 2 Understand who uses financial ratios, and how. Ratio analysis enables stockholders, lenders, and the firm's managers to evaluate the firm's financial performance. It can be performed on a cross-sectional or a time-series basis. Benchmarking is a popular type of cross-sectional analysis. Users of ratios should understand the cautions that apply to their use.

LG 3 Use ratios to analyze a firm's liquidity and activity. Liquidity, or the ability of the firm to pay its bills as they come due, can be measured by the current ratio and the quick (acid-test) ratio. Activity ratios measure the speed with which accounts are converted into sales or cash—inflows or outflows. The activity of inventory can be measured by its turnover; that of accounts receivable by the average collection period; and that of accounts payable by the average payment period. Total asset turnover measures the efficiency with which the firm uses its assets to generate sales.

LG 4 Discuss the relationship between debt and financial leverage and the ratios used to analyze a firm's debt. The more debt a firm uses, the greater its financial leverage, which magnifies both risk and return. Financial debt ratios measure both the degree of indebtedness and the ability to service debts. A common measure of indebtedness is the debt ratio. The ability to pay fixed charges can be measured by times interest earned and fixed-payment coverage ratios.

LG 5 Use ratios to analyze a firm's profitability and its market value. The common-size income statement, which shows all items as a percentage of sales, can be used to determine gross profit margin, operating profit margin, and net profit margin. Other measures of profitability include earnings per share, return on total assets, and return on common equity. Market ratios include the price/earnings ratio and the market/book ratio.

LG 6 Use a summary of financial ratios and the DuPont system of analysis to perform a complete ratio analysis. A summary of all ratios can be used to perform a complete ratio analysis using cross-sectional and time-series analysis. The DuPont system of analysis is a diagnostic tool used to find the key areas responsible for the firm's financial performance. It enables the firm to break the return on common equity into three components: profit on sales, efficiency of asset use, and use of financial leverage.

Self-Test Problems

ST2–1 Ratio formulas and interpretations Without referring to the text, indicate for each of the following ratios the formula for calculating it and the kinds of problems, if any, the firm is likely to have if that ratio is too high relative to the industry average. What if the ratio is too low relative to the industry average? Create a table similar to the one on the next page and fill in the empty blocks.

Ratio	Too high	Too low
Current ratio =		
Inventory turnover =		
Times interest earned =	$\times$	
Gross profit margin =		
Return on total assets =	$\times$	
Price/earnings (P/E) ratio =		

   ST2–2 Balance sheet completion using ratios Complete the 2009 balance sheet for O'Keefe Industries using the information that follows it.

O'Keefe Industries
Balance Sheet
December 31, 2009

Assets		Liabilities and Stockholders' Equity	
Cash	$32,720	Accounts payable	$120,000
Marketable securities	25,000	Notes payable	_____
Accounts receivable	_____	Accruals	20,000
Inventories	_____	Total current liabilities	_____
Total current assets	_____	Long-term debt	_____
Net fixed assets	_____	Stockholders' equity	$600,000
Total assets	$ _____	Total liabilities and stockholders' equity	$ _____

The following financial data for 2009 are also available:
(1) Sales totaled $1,800,000.
(2) The gross profit margin was 25%.
(3) Inventory turnover was 6.0.
(4) There are 365 days in the year.
(5) The average collection period was 40 days.
(6) The current ratio was 1.60.
(7) The total asset turnover ratio was 1.20.
(8) The debt ratio was 60%.

Warm-Up Exercises
A blue box (■) indicates exercises available in .

 E2–1 You are a summer intern at the office of a local tax-preparer. To test your basic knowledge of financial statements, your manager, who graduated from your alma mater 2 years ago, gives you the following list of accounts and asks you to prepare a simple income statement using those accounts.

Accounts	($000,000)
Depreciation	25
General and administrative expenses	22
Sales	345
Sales expenses	18
Cost of goods sold	255
Lease expense	4
Interest expense	3

a. Arrange the accounts into a well-labeled income statement. Make sure you label and solve for gross profit, operating profit, and net profit before taxes.

b. Using a 35% tax rate, calculate taxes paid and net profit after taxes.

c. Assuming a dividend of $1.10 per share with 4.25 million shares outstanding, calculate EPS and additions to retained earnings.

E2–2 Explain why the income statement can also be called a "profit and loss statement." What exactly does the word "balance" mean in the title of the balance sheet? Why do we balance the two halves?

E2–3 Cooper Industries, Inc., began 2009 with retained earnings of $25.32 million. During the year it paid four quarterly dividends of $0.35 per share to 2.75 million common stockholders. Preferred stockholders, holding 500,000 shares, were paid two semiannual dividends of $0.75 per share. The firm had a net profit after taxes of $5.15 million. Prepare the statement of retained earnings for the year ended December 31, 2009.

E2–4 Bluestone Metals, Inc., is a metal fabrication firm which manufactures prefabricated metal parts for customers in a variety of industries. The firm's motto is "If you need it, we can make it." The CEO of Bluestone recently held a board meeting during which he extolled the virtues of the corporation. The company, he stated confidently, had the capability to build any product and could do so using a lean manufacturing model. The firm would soon be profitable, claimed the CEO, because the company used state-of-the-art technology to build a variety of products while keeping inventory levels low. As a business press reporter, you have calculated some ratios to analyze the financial health of the firm. Bluestone's current ratios and quick ratios for the past 6 years are shown in the table below:

	2004	2005	2006	2007	2008	2009
Current ratio	1.2	1.4	1.3	1.6	1.8	2.2
Quick ratio	1.1	1.3	1.2	0.8	0.6	0.4

What do you think of the CEO's claim that the firm is lean and soon to be profitable? (*Hint:* Is there a possible warning sign in the relationship between the two ratios?)

E2–5 If we know that a firm has a net profit margin of 4.5%, total asset turnover of 0.72, and a financial leverage multiplier of 1.43, what is its ROE? What is the advantage to using the DuPont system to calculate ROE over the direct calculation of earnings available for common stockholders divided by common stock equity?

Problems

A blue box (■) indicates problems available in .

P2–1 **Reviewing basic financial statements** The income statement for the year ended December 31, 2009, the balance sheets for December 31, 2009 and 2008, and the statement of retained earnings for the year ended December 31, 2009, for Technica, Inc., are given below and on the next page. Briefly discuss the form and informational content of each of these statements.

Technica, Inc. Income Statement for the Year Ended December 31, 2009		
Sales revenue		$600,000
Less: Cost of goods sold		460,000
Gross profits		$140,000
Less: Operating expenses		
General and administrative expenses	$30,000	
Depreciation expense	30,000	
Total operating expense		60,000
Operating profits		$ 80,000
Less: Interest expense		10,000
Net profits before taxes		$ 70,000
Less: Taxes		27,100
Earnings available for common stockholders		$ 42,900
Earnings per share (EPS)		$2.15

Technica, Inc. Balance Sheets					
	December 31			**December 31**	
Assets	**2009**	**2008**	**Liabilities and Stockholders' Equity**	**2009**	**2008**
Cash	$ 15,000	$ 16,000	Accounts payable	$ 57,000	$ 49,000
Marketable securities	7,200	8,000	Notes payable	13,000	16,000
Accounts receivable	34,100	42,200	Accruals	5,000	6,000
Inventories	82,000	50,000	Total current liabilities	$ 75,000	$ 71,000
Total current assets	$138,300	$116,200	Long-term debt	$150,000	$160,000
Land and buildings	$150,000	$150,000	Stockholders' equity		
Machinery and equipment	200,000	190,000	Common stock equity (shares		
Furniture and fixtures	54,000	50,000	outstanding: 19,500 in 2009		
Other	11,000	10,000	and 20,000 in 2008)	$110,200	$120,000
Total gross fixed assets	$415,000	$400,000	Retained earnings	73,100	50,200
Less: Accumulated depreciation	145,000	115,000	Total stockholders' equity	$183,300	$170,200
Net fixed assets	$270,000	$285,000	Total liabilities and		
Total assets	$408,300	$401,200	stockholders' equity	$408,300	$401,200

Technica, Inc.	
Statement of Retained Earnings	
for the Year Ended December 31, 2009	
Retained earnings balance (January 1, 2009)	$50,200
Plus: Net profits after taxes (for 2009)	42,900
Less: Cash dividends (paid during 2009)	20,000
Retained earnings balance (December 31, 2009)	$73,100

P2–2 **Financial statement account identification**   Mark each of the accounts listed in the following table as follows:
  a. In column (1), indicate in which statement—income statement (IS) or balance sheet (BS)—the account belongs.
  b. In column (2), indicate whether the account is a current asset (CA), current liability (CL), expense (E), fixed asset (FA), long-term debt (LTD), revenue (R), or stockholders' equity (SE).

Account name	(1) Statement	(2) Type of account
Accounts payable	_____	_____
Accounts receivable	_____	_____
Accruals	_____	_____
Accumulated depreciation	_____	_____
Administrative expense	_____	_____
Buildings	_____	_____
Cash	_____	_____
Common stock (at par)	_____	_____
Cost of goods sold	_____	_____
Depreciation	_____	_____
Equipment	_____	_____
General expense	_____	_____
Interest expense	_____	_____
Inventories	_____	_____
Land	_____	_____
Long-term debts	_____	_____
Machinery	_____	_____
Marketable securities	_____	_____
Notes payable	_____	_____
Operating expense	_____	_____
Paid-in capital in excess of par	_____	_____
Preferred stock	_____	_____
Preferred stock dividends	_____	_____
Retained earnings	_____	_____
Sales revenue	_____	_____
Selling expense	_____	_____
Taxes	_____	_____
Vehicles	_____	_____

P2-3 **Income statement preparation** On December 31, 2009, Cathy Chen, a self-employed certified public accountant (CPA), completed her first full year in business. During the year, she billed $360,000 for her accounting services. She had two employees: a bookkeeper and a clerical assistant. In addition to her *monthly* salary of $8,000, Ms. Chen paid *annual* salaries of $48,000 and $36,000 to the bookkeeper and the clerical assistant, respectively. Employment taxes and benefit costs for Ms. Chen and her employees totaled $34,600 for the year. Expenses for office supplies, including postage, totaled $10,400 for the year. In addition, Ms. Chen spent $17,000 during the year on tax-deductible travel and entertainment associated with client visits and new business development. Lease payments for the office space rented (a tax-deductible expense) were $2,700 *per month*. Depreciation expense on the office furniture and fixtures was $15,600 for the year. During the year, Ms. Chen paid interest of $15,000 on the $120,000 borrowed to start the business. She paid an average tax rate of 30% during 2009.

a. Prepare an income statement for Cathy Chen, CPA, for the year ended December 31, 2009.

b. Evaluate her 2009 financial performance.

PERSONAL FINANCE PROBLEM

P2-4 **Income statement preparation** Adam and Arin Adams have collected their personal income and expense information and have asked you to put together an income and expense statement for the year ended December 31, 2009. The following information is received from the Adams family.

Adam's salary	$45,000	Utilities	$ 3,200
Arin's salary	30,000	Groceries	2,200
Interest received	500	Medical	1,500
Dividends received	150	Property taxes	1,659
Auto insurance	600	Income tax, soc. security	13,000
Home insurance	750	Clothes & accessories	2,000
Auto loan payment	3,300	Gas and auto repair	2,100
Mortgage payment	14,000	Entertainment	2,000

a. Create a personal *income and expense statement* for the period ended December 31, 2009. It should be similar to a corporate income statement.

b. Did the Adams family have a cash surplus or cash deficit?

c. If the result is a surplus, how can the Adams family use that surplus?

P2-5 **Calculation of EPS and retained earnings** Philagem, Inc., ended 2009 with a net profit *before* taxes of $218,000. The company is subject to a 40% tax rate and must pay $32,000 in preferred stock dividends before distributing any earnings on the 85,000 shares of common stock currently outstanding.

a. Calculate Philagem's 2009 earnings per share (EPS).

b. If the firm paid common stock dividends of $0.80 per share, how many dollars would go to retained earnings?

Financial Statements and Analysis

P2–6 **Balance sheet preparation** Use the *appropriate items* from the following list to pre-pare in good form Owen Davis Company's balance sheet at December 31, 2009.

Item	Value ($000) at December 31, 2009	Item	Value ($000) at December 31, 2009
Accounts payable	$ 220	Inventories	$ 375
Accounts receivable	450	Land	100
Accruals	55	Long-term debts	420
Accumulated depreciation	265	Machinery	420
Buildings	225	Marketable securities	75
Cash	215	Notes payable	475
Common stock (at par)	90	Paid-in capital in excess	
Cost of goods sold	2,500	of par	360
Depreciation expense	45	Preferred stock	100
Equipment	140	Retained earnings	210
Furniture and fixtures	170	Sales revenue	3,600
General expense	320	Vehicles	25

PERSONAL FINANCE PROBLEM

P2–7 **Balance sheet preparation** Adam and Arin Adams have collected their personal asset and liability information and have asked you to put together a balance sheet as of December 31, 2009. The following information is received from the Adams family.

Cash	$ 300	Retirement funds, IRA	$ 2,000
Checking	3,000	2008 Sebring	15,000
Savings	1,200	2007 Jeep	8,000
IBM stock	2,000	Money market funds	1,200
Auto loan	8,000	Jewelry & artwork	3,000
Mortgage	100,000	Net worth	76,500
Medical bills payable	250	Household furnishings	4,200
Utility bills payable	150	Credit card balance	2,000
Real estate	150,000	Personal loan	3,000

a. Create a personal balance sheet as of December 31, 2009. It should be similar to a corporate balance sheet.
b. What must the total assets of the Adams family be equal to by December 31, 2009?
c. What was their *net working capital (NWC)* for the year? (*Hint:* NWC is the difference between total liquid assets and total current liabilities.)

P2–8 **Impact of net income on a firm's balance sheet** Conrad Air, Inc., reported net income of $1,365,000 for the year ended December 31, 2009. Show the effect of these funds on the firm's balance sheet for the previous year in each of the scenarios following the balance sheet.

351

Conrad Air, Inc. Balance Sheet as of December 31, 2009			
Assets		**Liabilities and Stockholders' Equity**	
Cash	$ 120,000	Accounts payable	$ 70,000
Marketable securities	35,000	Short-term notes	55,000
Accounts receivable	45,000	Current liabilities	$ 125,000
Inventories	130,000	Long-term debt	$2,700,000
Current assets	$ 330,000	Total liabilities	$2,825,000
Equipment	$2,970,000	Common stock	$ 500,000
Buildings	1,600,000	Retained earnings	1,575,000
Fixed assets	$4,570,000	Stockholders' equity	$2,075,000
Total assets	$4,900,000	Total liabilities and equity	$4,900,000

a. Conrad paid no dividends during the year and invested the funds in marketable securities.

b. Conrad paid dividends totaling $500,000 and used the balance of the net income to retire (pay off) long-term debt.

c. Conrad paid dividends totaling $500,000 and invested the balance of the net income in building a new hangar.

d. Conrad paid out all $1,365,000 as dividends to its stockholders.

 P2-9 **Initial sale price of common stock** Beck Corporation has one issue of preferred stock and one issue of common stock outstanding. Given Beck's stockholders' equity account that follows, determine the original price per share at which the firm sold its single issue of common stock.

Stockholders' equity ($000)	
Preferred stock	$ 125
Common stock ($0.75 par, 300,000 shares outstanding)	225
Paid-in capital in excess of par on common stock	2,625
Retained earnings	900
Total stockholders' equity	$3,875

 P2-10 **Statement of retained earnings** Hayes Enterprises began 2009 with a retained earnings balance of $928,000. During 2009, the firm earned $377,000 after taxes. From this amount, preferred stockholders were paid $47,000 in dividends. At year-end 2009, the firm's retained earnings totaled $1,048,000. The firm had 140,000 shares of common stock outstanding during 2009.

a. Prepare a statement of retained earnings for the year ended December 31, 2009, for Hayes Enterprises. (*Note:* Be sure to calculate and include the amount of cash dividends paid in 2009.)

b. Calculate the firm's 2009 earnings per share (EPS).

c. How large a per-share cash dividend did the firm pay on common stock during 2009?

P2–11 **Ratio comparisons** Robert Arias recently inherited a stock portfolio from his uncle. Wishing to learn more about the companies in which he is now invested, Robert performs a ratio analysis on each one and decides to compare them to each other. Some of his ratios are listed below.

Ratio	Island Electric Utility	Burger Heaven	Fink Software	Roland Motors
Current ratio	1.10	1.3	6.8	4.5
Quick ratio	0.90	0.82	5.2	3.7
Debt ratio	0.68	0.46	0	0.35
Net profit margin	6.2%	14.3%	28.5%	8.4%

Assuming that his uncle was a wise investor who assembled the portfolio with care, Robert finds the wide differences in these ratios confusing. Help him out.

a. What problems might Robert encounter in comparing these companies to one another on the basis of their ratios?

b. Why might the current and quick ratios for the electric utility and the fast-food stock be so much lower than the same ratios for the other companies?

c. Why might it be all right for the electric utility to carry a large amount of debt, but not the software company?

d. Why wouldn't investors invest all of their money in software companies instead of in less profitable companies? (Focus on risk and return.)

 P2–12 **Liquidity management** Bauman Company's total current assets, total current liabilities, and inventory for each of the past 4 years follow:

Item	2006	2007	2008	2009
Total current assets	$16,950	$21,900	$22,500	$27,000
Total current liabilities	9,000	12,600	12,600	17,400
Inventory	6,000	6,900	6,900	7,200

a. Calculate the firm's current and quick ratios for each year. Compare the resulting time series for these measures of liquidity.

b. Comment on the firm's liquidity over the 2006–2009 period.

c. If you were told that Bauman Company's inventory turnover for each year in the 2006–2009 period and the industry averages were as follows, would this information support or conflict with your evaluation in part **b**? Why?

Inventory turnover	2006	2007	2008	2009
Bauman Company	6.3	6.8	7.0	6.4
Industry average	10.6	11.2	10.8	11.0

353

PERSONAL FINANCE PROBLEM

P2–13 **Liquidity ratio**   Josh Smith has compiled some of his personal financial data in order to determine his liquidity position. The data are as follows.

Account	Amount
Cash	$3,200
Marketable securities	1,000
Checking account	800
Credit card payables	1,200
Short-term notes payable	900

    a. Calculate Josh's *liquidity ratio.*
    b. Several of Josh's friends have told him that they have liquidity ratios of about 1.8. How would you analyze Josh's liquidity relative to his friends?

P2–14 **Inventory management**   Wilkins Manufacturing has annual sales of $4 million and a gross profit margin of 40%. Its *end-of-quarter inventories* are

Quarter	Inventory
1	$ 400,000
2	800,000
3	1,200,000
4	200,000

    a. Find the average quarterly inventory and use it to calculate the firm's inventory turnover and the average age of inventory.
    b. Assuming that the company is in an industry with an average inventory turnover of 2.0, how would you evaluate the activity of Wilkins' inventory?

P2–15 **Accounts receivable management**   An evaluation of the books of Blair Supply, which follows, gives the end-of-year accounts receivable balance, which is believed to consist of amounts originating in the months indicated. The company had annual sales of $2.4 million. The firm extends 30-day credit terms.

Month of origin	Amounts receivable
July	$ 3,875
August	2,000
September	34,025
October	15,100
November	52,000
December	193,000
Year-end accounts receivable	$300,000

    a. Use the year-end total to evaluate the firm's collection system.
    b. If 70% of the firm's sales occur between July and December, would this affect the validity of your conclusion in part **a?** Explain.

P2–16 **Debt analysis** Springfield Bank is evaluating Creek Enterprises, which has requested a $4,000,000 loan, to assess the firm's financial leverage and financial risk. On the basis of the debt ratios for Creek, along with the industry averages and Creek's recent financial statements (below), evaluate and recommend appropriate action on the loan request.

Creek Enterprises Income Statement for the Year Ended December 31, 2009		
Sales revenue		$30,000,000
Less: Cost of goods sold		21,000,000
Gross profits		$ 9,000,000
Less: Operating expenses		
Selling expense	$3,000,000	
General and administrative expenses	1,800,000	
Lease expense	200,000	
Depreciation expense	1,000,000	
Total operating expense		6,000,000
Operating profits		$ 3,000,000
Less: Interest expense		1,000,000
Net profits before taxes		$ 2,000,000
Less: Taxes (rate = 40%)		800,000
Net profits after taxes		$ 1,200,000
Less: Preferred stock dividends		100,000
Earnings available for common stockholders		$ 1,100,000

Creek Enterprises Balance Sheet December 31, 2009			
Assets		**Liabilities and Stockholders' Equity**	
Current assets		Current liabilities	
Cash	$ 1,000,000	Accounts payable	$ 8,000,000
Marketable securities	3,000,000	Notes payable	8,000,000
Accounts receivable	12,000,000	Accruals	500,000
Inventories	7,500,000	Total current liabilities	$16,500,000
Total current assets	$23,500,000	Long-term debt (includes financial leases)[b]	$20,000,000
Gross fixed assets (at cost)[a]		Stockholders' equity	
Land and buildings	$11,000,000	Preferred stock (25,000 shares,	
Machinery and equipment	20,500,000	$4 dividend)	$ 2,500,000
Furniture and fixtures	8,000,000	Common stock (1 million shares at $5 par)	5,000,000
Gross fixed assets	$39,500,000	Paid-in capital in excess of par value	4,000,000
Less: Accumulated depreciation	13,000,000	Retained earnings	2,000,000
Net fixed assets	$26,500,000	Total stockholders' equity	$13,500,000
Total assets	$50,000,000	Total liabilities and stockholders' equity	$50,000,000

[a]The firm has a 4-year financial lease requiring annual beginning-of-year payments of $200,000. Three years of the lease have yet to run.
[b]Required annual principal payments are $800,000.

Industry averages	
Debt ratio	0.51
Times interest earned ratio	7.30
Fixed-payment coverage ratio	1.85

P2–17 **Common-size statement analysis** A common-size income statement for Creek Enterprises' 2008 operations follows. Using the firm's 2009 income statement presented in Problem 2–16, develop the 2009 common-size income statement and compare it to the 2008 statement. Which areas require further analysis and investigation?

Creek Enterprises Common-Size Income Statement for the Year Ended December 31, 2008		
Sales revenue ($35,000,000)		100.0%
Less: Cost of goods sold		65.9
Gross profits		34.1%
Less: Operating expenses		
Selling expense	12.7%	
General and administrative expenses	6.3	
Lease expense	0.6	
Depreciation expense	3.6	
Total operating expense		23.2
Operating profits		10.9%
Less: Interest expense		1.5
Net profits before taxes		9.4%
Less: Taxes (rate = 40%)		3.8
Net profits after taxes		5.6%
Less: Preferred stock dividends		0.1
Earnings available for common stockholders		5.5%

P2–18 **Ratio proficiency** McDougal Printing, Inc., had sales totaling $40,000,000 in fiscal year 2009. Some ratios for the company are listed below. Use this information to determine the dollar values of various income statement and balance sheet accounts as requested.

McDougal Printing, Inc. Year Ended December 31, 2009	
Sales	$40,000,000
Gross profit margin	80%
Operating profit margin	35%
Net profit margin	8%
Return on total assets	16%
Return on common equity	20%
Total asset turnover	2
Average collection period	62.2 days

Calculate values for the following:
- **a.** Gross profits
- **b.** Cost of goods sold
- **c.** Operating profits
- **d.** Operating expenses
- **e.** Earnings available for common stockholders
- **f.** Total assets
- **g.** Total common stock equity
- **h.** Accounts receivable

P2–19 **Cross-sectional ratio analysis**   Use the financial statements below for Fox Manufacturing Company for the year ended December 31, 2009, along with the industry average ratios at the top of the next page, to:
- **a.** Prepare and interpret a complete ratio analysis of the firm's 2009 operations.
- **b.** Summarize your findings and make recommendations.

Fox Manufacturing Company Income Statement for the Year Ended December 31, 2009		
Sales revenue		$600,000
Less: Cost of goods sold		460,000
Gross profits		$140,000
Less: Operating expenses		
General and administrative expenses	$30,000	
Depreciation expense	30,000	
Total operating expense		60,000
Operating profits		$ 80,000
Less: Interest expense		10,000
Net profits before taxes		$ 70,000
Less: Taxes		27,100
Net profits after taxes (earnings available for common stockholders)		$ 42,900
Earnings per share (EPS)		$2.15

Fox Manufacturing Company
Balance Sheet
December 31, 2009

Assets		Liabilities and Stockholders' Equity	
Cash	$ 15,000	Accounts payable	$ 57,000
Marketable securities	7,200	Notes payable	13,000
Accounts receivable	34,100	Accruals	5,000
Inventories	82,000	Total current liabilities	$ 75,000
Total current assets	$138,300	Long-term debt	$150,000
Net fixed assets	$270,000	Stockholders' equity	
Total assets	$408,300	Common stock equity (20,000 shares outstanding)	$110,200
		Retained earnings	73,100
		Total stockholders' equity	$183,300
		Total liabilities and stockholders' equity	$408,300

Ratio	Industry average, 2009
Current ratio	2.35
Quick ratio	0.87
Inventory turnover[a]	4.55
Average collection period[a]	35.8 days
Total asset turnover	1.09
Debt ratio	0.300
Times interest earned ratio	12.3
Gross profit margin	0.202
Operating profit margin	0.135
Net profit margin	0.091
Return on total assets (ROA)	0.099
Return on common equity (ROE)	0.167
Earnings per share (EPS)	$3.10

[a]Based on a 365-day year and on end-of-year figures.

P2–20 **Financial statement analysis** The financial statements of Zach Industries for the year ended December 31, 2009, follow.

Zach Industries Income Statement for the Year Ended December 31, 2009	
Sales revenue	$160,000
Less: Cost of goods sold	106,000
Gross profits	$ 54,000
Less: Operating expenses	
Selling expense	$ 16,000
General and administrative expenses	10,000
Lease expense	1,000
Depreciation expense	10,000
Total operating expense	$ 37,000
Operating profits	$ 17,000
Less: Interest expense	6,100
Net profits before taxes	$ 10,900
Less: Taxes	4,360
Net profits after taxes	$ 6,540

Zach Industries Balance Sheet December 31, 2009	
Assets	
Cash	$ 500
Marketable securities	1,000
Accounts receivable	25,000
Inventories	45,500
Total current assets	$ 72,000
Land	$ 26,000
Buildings and equipment	90,000
Less: Accumulated depreciation	38,000
Net fixed assets	$ 78,000
Total assets	$150,000
Liabilities and Stockholders' Equity	
Accounts payable	$ 22,000
Notes payable	47,000
Total current liabilities	$ 69,000
Long-term debt	$ 22,950
Common stock[a]	$ 31,500
Retained earnings	$ 26,550
Total liabilities and stockholders' equity	$150,000

[a]The firm's 3,000 outstanding shares of common stock closed 2009 at a price of $25 per share.

a. Use the preceding financial statements to complete the following table. Assume the industry averages given in the table are applicable for both 2008 and 2009.

Ratio	Industry average	Actual 2008	Actual 2009
Current ratio	1.80	1.84	_____
Quick ratio	0.70	0.78	_____
Inventory turnover[a]	2.50	2.59	_____
Average collection period[a]	37.5 days	36.5 days	_____
Debt ratio	65%	67%	_____
Times interest earned ratio	3.8	4.0	_____
Gross profit margin	38%	40%	_____
Net profit margin	3.5%	3.6%	_____
Return on total assets	4.0%	4.0%	_____
Return on common equity	9.5%	8.0%	_____
Market/book ratio	1.1	1.2	_____

[a]Based on a 365-day year and on end-of-year figures.

b. Analyze Zach Industries' financial condition as it is related to (1) liquidity, (2) activity, (3) debt, (4) profitability, and (5) market. Summarize the company's overall financial condition.

 P2–21 **DuPont system of analysis** Use the following ratio information for Johnson International and the industry averages for Johnson's line of business to:

a. Construct the DuPont system of analysis for both Johnson and the industry.
b. Evaluate Johnson (and the industry) over the 3-year period.
c. Indicate in which areas Johnson requires further analysis. Why?

Johnson	2007	2008	2009
Financial leverage multiplier	1.75	1.75	1.85
Net profit margin	0.059	0.058	0.049
Total asset turnover	2.11	2.18	2.34

Industry Averages			
Financial leverage multiplier	1.67	1.69	1.64
Net profit margin	0.054	0.047	0.041
Total asset turnover	2.05	2.13	2.15

 P2–22 **ETHICS PROBLEM** Do some reading in periodicals and/or on the Internet to find out more about the Sarbanes-Oxley Act's provisions for companies. Select one of those provisions, and indicate why you think financial statements will be more trustworthy if company financial executives implement this provision of SOX.

Chapter Case

Assessing Martin Manufacturing's Current Financial Position

Terri Spiro, an experienced budget analyst at Martin Manufacturing Company, has been charged with assessing the firm's financial performance during 2009 and its financial position at year-end 2009. To complete this assignment, she gathered the firm's 2009 financial statements (below and on the following page). In addition, Terri obtained the firm's ratio values for 2007 and 2008, along with the 2009 industry average ratios (also applicable to 2007 and 2008).

Martin Manufacturing Company Income Statement for the Year Ended December 31, 2009		
Sales revenue		$5,075,000
Less: Cost of goods sold		3,704,000
Gross profits		$1,371,000
Less: Operating expenses		
Selling expense	$650,000	
General and administrative expenses	416,000	
Depreciation expense	152,000	
Total operating expense		1,218,000
Operating profits		$ 153,000
Less: Interest expense		93,000
Net profits before taxes		$ 60,000
Less: Taxes (rate = 40%)		24,000
Net profits after taxes		$ 36,000
Less: Preferred stock dividends		3,000
Earnings available for common stockholders		$ 33,000
Earnings per share (EPS)		$0.33

Martin Manufacturing Company Balance Sheets		
	December 31	
Assets	2009	2008
Current assets		
Cash	$ 25,000	$ 24,100
Accounts receivable	805,556	763,900
Inventories	700,625	763,445
Total current assets	$1,531,181	$1,551,445
Gross fixed assets (at cost)	$2,093,819	$1,691,707
Less: Accumulated depreciation	500,000	348,000
Net fixed assets	$1,593,819	$1,343,707
Total assets	$3,125,000	$2,895,152
Liabilities and Stockholders' Equity		
Current liabilities		
Accounts payable	$ 230,000	$ 400,500
Notes payable	311,000	370,000
Accruals	75,000	100,902
Total current liabilities	$ 616,000	$ 871,402
Long-term debt	$1,165,250	$ 700,000
Total liabilities	$1,781,250	$1,571,402
Stockholders' equity		
Preferred stock (2,500 shares, $1.20 dividend)	$ 50,000	$ 50,000
Common stock (100,000 shares at $4 par)[a]	400,000	400,000
Paid-in capital in excess of par value	593,750	593,750
Retained earnings	300,000	280,000
Total stockholders' equity	$1,343,750	$1,323,750
Total liabilities and stockholders' equity	$3,125,000	$2,895,152

[a]The firm's 100,000 outstanding shares of common stock closed 2009 at a price of $11.38 per share.

	Martin Manufacturing Company Historical and Industry Average Ratios			
Ratio	Actual 2007	Actual 2008	Actual 2009	Industry average 2009
Current ratio	1.7	1.8	_____	1.5
Quick ratio	1.0	0.9	_____	1.2
Inventory turnover (times)	5.2	5.0	_____	10.2
Average collection period	50.7 days	55.8 days	_____	46 days
Total asset turnover (times)	1.5	1.5	_____	2.0
Debt ratio	45.8%	54.3%	_____	24.5%
Times interest earned ratio	2.2	1.9	_____	2.5
Gross profit margin	27.5%	28.0%	_____	26.0%
Net profit margin	1.1%	1.0%	_____	1.2%
Return on total assets (ROA)	1.7%	1.5%	_____	2.4%
Return on common equity (ROE)	3.1%	3.3%	_____	3.2%
Price/earnings (P/E) ratio	33.5	38.7	_____	43.4
Market/book (M/B) ratio	1.0	1.1	_____	1.2

To Do

a. Calculate the firm's 2009 financial ratios, and then fill in the preceding table. (Assume a 365-day year.)
b. Analyze the firm's current financial position from both a cross-sectional and a time-series viewpoint. Break your analysis into evaluations of the firm's liquidity, activity, debt, profitability, and market.
c. Summarize the firm's overall financial position on the basis of your findings in part b.

Spreadsheet Exercise

The income statement and balance sheet are the basic reports that a firm constructs for use by management and for distribution to stockholders, regulatory bodies, and the general public. They are the primary sources of historical financial information about the firm. Dayton Products, Inc., is a moderate-sized manufacturer. The company's management has asked you to perform a detailed financial statement analysis of the firm.

The income statement data for the years ending December 31, 2009 and 2008, respectively, is presented in the table at the top of next page. (*Note:* Purchases of inventory during 2009 amounted to $109,865.)

Annual Income Statement (Values in millions)		
	For the year ended	
	December 31, 2009	December 31, 2008
Sales	$178,909.00	$187,510.00
Cost of goods sold	?	111,631.00
Selling, general, and administrative expenses	12,356.00	12,900.00
Other tax expense	33,572.00	33,377.00
Depreciation and amortization	12,103.00	7,944.00
Other income (add to EBIT to arrive at EBT)	3,147.00	3,323.00
Interest expense	398	293
Income tax rate (average)	35.324%	37.945%
Dividends paid per share	$1.47	$0.91
Basic EPS from total operations	$1.71	$2.25

You also have the following balance sheet information as of December 31, 2009 and 2008, respectively.

Annual Balance Sheet (Values in millions)		
	December 31, 2009	December, 31, 2008
Cash and equivalents	$ 7,229.00	$ 6,547.00
Receivables	21,163.00	19,549.00
Inventories	8,068.00	7,904.00
Other current assets	1,831.00	1,681.00
Property, plant, and equipment, gross	204,960.00	187,519.00
Accumulated depreciation and depletion	110,020.00	97,917.00
Other noncurrent assets	19,413.00	17,891.00
Accounts payable	$ 13,792.00	$ 22,862.00
Short-term debt payable	4,093.00	3,703.00
Other current liabilities	15,290.00	3,549.00
Long-term debt payable	6,655.00	7,099.00
Deferred income taxes	16,484.00	16,359.00
Other noncurrent liabilities	21,733.00	16,441.00
Retained earnings	$ 74,597.00	$ 73,161.00
Total common shares outstanding	6.7 billion	6.8 billion

To Do

a. Create a spreadsheet similar to the spreadsheet in Table 1 (which can be viewed at **www.prenhall.com/gitman**, Table 2.1) to model the following:
   (1) A multiple-step comparative income statement for Dayton, Inc., for the periods ending December 31, 2009 and 2008. You must calculate the cost of goods sold for the year 2009.
   (2) A common-size income statement for Dayton, Inc., covering the years 2009 and 2008.

b. Create a spreadsheet similar to the spreadsheet in Table 2 (which can be viewed at **www.prenhall.com/gitman**, Table 2.1) to model the following:
   (1) A detailed, comparative balance sheet for Dayton, Inc., for the years ended December 31, 2009 and 2008.
   (2) A common-size balance sheet for Dayton, Inc., covering the years 2009 and 2008.

c. Create a spreadsheet similar to the spreadsheet in Table 8 (which can be viewed at **www.prenhall.com/gitman**, Table 2.1) to perform the following analysis:
   (1) Create a table that reflects both 2009 and 2008 operating ratios for Dayton, Inc., segmented into (a) liquidity, (b) activity, (c) debt, (d) profitability, and (e) market. Assume that the current market price for the stock is $90.
   (2) Compare the 2009 ratios to the 2008 ratios. Indicate whether the results "outperformed the prior year" or "underperformed relative to the prior year."

Web Exercise

Go to the text's companion website at **www.prenhall.com/gitman** to find the Web Exercise for this chapter.

> Remember to check the text's website at **www.prenhall.com/gitman** to find additional resources, including Web Exercises and a Web Case.

Solutions to Self-Test Problems

ST2–1

Ratio	Too high	Too low
Current ratio = current assets/ current liabilities	May indicate that the firm is holding excessive cash, accounts receivable, or inventory.	May indicate poor ability to satisfy short-term obligations.
Inventory turnover = CGS/inventory	May indicate lower level of inventory, which may cause stockouts and lost sales.	May indicate poor inventory management, excessive inventory, or obsolete inventory.
Times interest earned = earnings before interest and taxes/interest		May indicate poor ability to pay contractual interest payments.
Gross profit margin = gross profits/sales	Indicates the low cost of merchandise sold relative to the sales price; may indicate noncompetitive pricing and potential lost sales.	Indicates the high cost of the merchandise sold relative to the sales price; may indicate either a low sales price or a high cost of goods sold.
Return on total assets = net profits after taxes/total assets		Indicates ineffective management in generating profits with the available assets.
Price/earnings (P/E) ratio = market price per share of common stock/earnings per share	Investors may have an excessive degree of confidence in the firm's future and underestimate its risk.	Investors lack confidence in the firm's future outcomes and feel that the firm has an excessive level of risk.

ST2–2

O'Keefe Industries
Balance Sheet
December 31, 2009

Assets		Liabilities and Stockholders' Equity	
Cash	$ 32,720	Accounts payable	$ 120,000
Marketable securities	25,000	Notes payable	160,000[e]
Accounts receivable	197,280[a]	Accruals	20,000
Inventories	225,000[b]	Total current liabilities	$ 300,000[d]
Total current assets	$ 480,000	Long-term debt	$ 600,000[f]
Net fixed assets	$1,020,000[c]	Stockholders' equity	$ 600,000
Total assets	$1,500,000	Total liabilities and stockholders' equity	$1,500,000

[a]Average collection period (ACP) = 40 days
ACP = Accounts receivable/Average sales per day
$40 = \text{Accounts receivable}/(\$1,800,000/365)$
$40 = \text{Accounts receivable}/\$4,932$
$\$197,280 = \text{Accounts receivable}$

[b]Inventory turnover = 6.0
Inventory turnover = Cost of goods sold/Inventory
$6.0 = [\text{Sales} \times (1 = \text{Gross profit margin})]/\text{Inventory}$
$6.0 = [\$1,800,000 \times (1 = 0.25)]/\text{Inventory}$
$\$225,000 = \text{Inventory}$

[c]Total asset turnover = 1.20
Total asset turnover = Sales/Total assets
$1.20 = \$1,800,000/\text{Total assets}$
$\$1,500,000 = \text{Total assets}$
Total assets = Current assets + Net fixed assets
$\$1,500,000 = \$480,000 + \text{Net fixed assets}$
$\$1,020,000 = \text{Net fixed assets}$

[d]Current ratio = 1.60
Current ratio = Current assets/Current liabilities
$1.60 = \$480,000/\text{Current liabilities}$
$\$300,000 = \text{Current liabilities}$

[e]Notes = Total current − Accounts − Accruals
payable   liabilities   payable
$= \$300,000 - \$120,000 - \$20,000$
$= \$160,000$

[f]Debt ratio = 0.60
Debt ratio = Total liabilities/Total assets
$0.60 = \text{Total liabilities}/\$1,500,000$
$\$900,000 = \text{Total liabilities}$

Total   Current
liabilities = liabilities + Long-term debt
$\$900,000 = \$300,000 + \text{Long-term debt}$
$\$600,000 = \text{Long-term debt}$

Answers to Selected End-of-Chapter Problems

2–3	a.	Net profit after tax: $38,500	
2–5	a.	Earnings per share: $1.162	
2–7	a.	Total liquid assets: $5,700	
		Total current liabilities: $2,400	
2–9		Initial sales price: $9.50	
2–10	b.	Earnings per share: $2.36	
	c.	Cash dividend per share: $1.50	
2–12	a.		

Current ratio	2006: 1.88	2008: 1.79
Quick ratio	2006: 1.22	2008: 1.24

2–15 a. 45.62 days

2–16	*Creek*	*Industry*
Debt ratio	0.73	0.51
Times interest earned	3.00	7.30

2–20 a.

	Actual 2009
Current ratio:	1.04
Average collection period:	57 days
Debt ratio:	61.3%
Net profit margin:	4.1%
Return on equity:	11.3%

2–21 a. 2006 Johnson ROE = 21.21%
                Industry ROE = 14.46%

Chapter 10

Cash Flow and
Financial Planning

From Chapter 3 of *Principles of Managerial Finance*, Brief 5th Edition. Lawrence J. Gitman. Copyright © 2009 by Pearson Prentice Hall. All rights reserved.

WHY THIS CHAPTER MATTERS TO YOU

In Your Professional Life

Accounting: You need to understand how depreciation is used for both tax and financial reporting purposes; how to develop the statement of cash flows; the primary focus on cash flows, rather than accruals, in financial decision making; and how pro forma financial statements are used within the firm.

Information systems: You need to understand the data that must be kept to record depreciation for tax and financial reporting; the information needs for strategic and operating plans; and what data are needed as inputs for preparing cash plans and profit plans.

Management: You need to understand the difference between strategic and operating plans, and the role of each; the importance of focusing on the firm's cash flows; and how use of pro forma statements can head off trouble for the firm.

Marketing: You need to understand the central role that marketing plays in formulating the firm's long-term, strategic plans, and the importance of the sales forecast as the key input for both cash planning and profit planning.

Operations: You need to understand how depreciation affects the value of the firm's plant assets; how the results of operations are captured in the statement of cash flows; that operations provide key inputs into the firm's short-term financial plans; and the distinction between fixed and variable operating costs.

In Your Personal Life

Individuals, like corporations, should focus on cash flow when planning and monitoring finances. You should establish short- and long-term financial goals (destinations) and develop personal financial plans (road maps) that will guide their achievement. Cash flows and financial plans are as important for individuals as for corporations.

LEARNING GOALS

LG 1 Understand tax depreciation procedures and the effect of depreciation on the firm's cash flows.

LG 2 Discuss the firm's statement of cash flows, operating cash flow, and free cash flow.

LG 3 Understand the financial planning process, including long-term (strategic) financial plans and short-term (operating) financial plans.

LG 4 Discuss the cash-planning process and the preparation, evaluation, and use of the cash budget.

LG 5 Explain the simplified procedures used to prepare and evaluate the pro forma income statement and the pro forma balance sheet.

LG 6 Evaluate the simplified approaches to pro forma financial statement preparation and the common uses of pro forma statements.

Cash flow is the primary focus of financial management. The goal is twofold: to meet the firm's financial obligations and to generate positive cash flow for its owners. Financial planning focuses on the firm's cash and profits—both of which are key elements of continued financial success, and even survival. This chapter outlines how the firm analyzes its cash flows, including the effects of depreciation and the roles of operating and free cash flows, and how it uses cash budgets and pro forma statements in the financial planning process.

1 | Analyzing the Firm's Cash Flow

Cash flow, the lifeblood of the firm, is the primary focus of the financial manager both in managing day-to-day finances and in planning and making strategic decisions focused on creating shareholder value. We therefore place major emphasis on estimating and analyzing the cash flows associated with the major financial decisions discussed and demonstrated throughout this text.

An important factor affecting a firm's cash flow is depreciation (and any other noncash charges). From an accounting perspective, a firm's cash flows can be summarized in the statement of cash flows. From a strict financial perspective, firms often focus on both *operating cash flow*, which is used in managerial decision making, and *free cash flow*, which is closely watched by participants in the capital market. We begin our analysis of cash flow by considering the key aspects of depreciation, which is closely related to the firm's cash flow.

Depreciation

depreciation
The systematic charging of a portion of the costs of fixed assets against annual revenues over time.

Business firms are permitted for tax and financial reporting purposes to charge a portion of the costs of fixed assets systematically against annual revenues. This allocation of historical cost over time is called **depreciation.** For tax purposes, the depreciation of business assets is regulated by the Internal Revenue Code. Because the objectives of financial reporting sometimes differ from those of tax legislation, firms often use different depreciation methods for financial reporting than those required for tax purposes. Keeping two different sets of records for these two different purposes is legal.

modified accelerated cost recovery system (MACRS)
System used to determine the depreciation of assets for tax purposes.

Depreciation for tax purposes is determined by using the **modified accelerated cost recovery system (MACRS);** a variety of depreciation methods are available for financial reporting purposes. Before we discuss the methods of depreciating an asset, you must understand the depreciable value of an asset and the depreciable life of an asset.

Depreciable Value of an Asset

Under the basic MACRS procedures, the depreciable value of an asset (the amount to be depreciated) is its *full* cost, including outlays for installation.[1] No adjustment is required for expected salvage value.

---

1. Land values are *not* depreciable. Therefore, to determine the depreciable value of real estate, the value of the land is subtracted from the cost of real estate. In other words, only buildings and other improvements are depreciable.

TABLE 1	First Four Property Classes under MACRS
Property class (recovery period)	**Definition**
3 years	Research equipment and certain special tools
5 years	Computers, typewriters, copiers, duplicating equipment, cars, light-duty trucks, qualified technological equipment, and similar assets
7 years	Office furniture, fixtures, most manufacturing equipment, railroad track, and single-purpose agricultural and horticultural structures
10 years	Equipment used in petroleum refining or in the manufacture of tobacco products and certain food products

Example

Baker Corporation acquired a new machine at a cost of $38,000, with installation costs of $2,000. Regardless of its expected salvage value, the depreciable value of the machine is $40,000: $38,000 cost + $2,000 installation cost.

Depreciable Life of an Asset

depreciable life
Time period over which an asset is depreciated.

The time period over which an asset is depreciated—its **depreciable life**—can significantly affect the pattern of cash flows. The shorter the depreciable life, the more quickly the cash flow created by the depreciation write-off will be received. Given the financial manager's preference for faster receipt of cash flows, a shorter depreciable life is preferred to a longer one. However, the firm must abide by certain Internal Revenue Service (IRS) requirements for determining depreciable life. These MACRS standards, which apply to both new and used assets, require the taxpayer to use as an asset's depreciable life the appropriate MACRS **recovery period**.[2] There are six MACRS recovery periods—3, 5, 7, 10, 15, and 20 years—excluding real estate. It is customary to refer to the property classes as 3-, 5-, 7-, 10-, 15-, and 20-year property. The first four property classes—those routinely used by business—are defined in Table 1.

recovery period
The appropriate depreciable life of a particular asset as determined by MACRS.

Depreciation Methods

For *financial reporting purposes,* companies can use a variety of depreciation methods (straight-line, double-declining balance, and sum-of-the-years'-digits[3]). For *tax purposes,* assets in the first four MACRS property classes are depreciated by the double-declining balance (200%) method, using the half-year convention and switching to straight-line when advantageous. The *approximate percentages* (rounded to the nearest whole percent) written off each year for the first four property classes are shown in Table 2. Rather than using the percentages in the table, the firm can either use straight-line depreciation over the asset's recovery period with the half-year convention or use the alternative depreciation system. For purposes of this text, we will use the MACRS depreciation percentages, because they generally provide for the fastest write-off and therefore the best cash flow effects for the profitable firm.

---

2. An exception occurs in the case of assets depreciated under the *alternative depreciation system.* For convenience, in this text we ignore the depreciation of assets under this system.

3. For a review of these depreciation methods as well as other aspects of financial reporting, see any recently published financial accounting text.

TABLE 2	Rounded Depreciation Percentages by Recovery Year Using MACRS for First Four Property Classes

	Percentage by recovery year[a]			
Recovery year	3 years	5 years	7 years	10 years
1	33%	20%	14%	10%
2	45	32	25	18
3	15	19	18	14
4	7	12	12	12
5		12	9	9
6		5	9	8
7			9	7
8			4	6
9				6
10				6
11				4
Totals	100%	100%	100%	100%

[a]These percentages have been rounded to the nearest whole percent to simplify calculations while retaining realism. To calculate the *actual* depreciation for tax purposes, be sure to apply the actual unrounded percentages or directly apply double-declining balance (200%) depreciation using the half-year convention.

Because MACRS requires use of the half-year convention, assets are assumed to be acquired in the middle of the year; therefore only one-half of the first year's depreciation is recovered in the first year. As a result, the final half-year of depreciation is recovered in the year immediately following the asset's stated recovery period. In Table 2, the depreciation percentages for an n-year class asset are given for $n + 1$ years. For example, a 5-year asset is depreciated over 6 recovery years. The application of the tax depreciation percentages given in Table 2 can be demonstrated by a simple example.

Example

Baker Corporation acquired, for an installed cost of $40,000, a machine having a recovery period of 5 years. Using the applicable percentages from Table 2, Baker calculates the depreciation in each year as follows:

Year	Cost (1)	Percentages (from Table 2) (2)	Depreciation [(1) × (2)] (3)
1	$40,000	20%	$ 8,000
2	40,000	32	12,800
3	40,000	19	7,600
4	40,000	12	4,800
5	40,000	12	4,800
6	40,000	5	2,000
Totals		100%	$40,000

> Column 3 shows that the full cost of the asset is written off over 6 recovery years.

Because financial managers focus primarily on cash flows, *only tax depreciation methods will be utilized throughout this text.*

Developing the Statement of Cash Flows

The *statement of cash flows* summarizes the firm's cash flow over a given period of time. Before discussing the statement and its interpretation, we will review the cash flow through the firm and the classification of inflows and outflows of cash.

The Firm's Cash Flows

Hint In finance, cash is king. Income statement profits are good, but they don't pay the bills, nor do asset owners accept them in place of cash.

operating flows
Cash flows directly related to sale and production of the firm's products and services.

investment flows
Cash flows associated with purchase and sale of both fixed assets and equity investments in other firms.

financing flows
Cash flows that result from debt and equity financing transactions; include incurrence and repayment of debt, cash inflow from the sale of stock, and cash outflows to repurchase stock or pay cash dividends.

Figure 1 illustrates the firm's cash flows. Note that marketable securities are considered the same as cash because of their highly liquid nature. Both cash and marketable securities represent a reservoir of liquidity that is *increased by cash inflows* and *decreased by cash outflows.*

Also note that the firm's cash flows can be divided into (1) operating flows, (2) investment flows, and (3) financing flows. The **operating flows** are cash inflows and outflows directly related to the sale and production of the firm's products and services. **Investment flows** are cash flows associated with the purchase and sale of both fixed assets and equity investments in other firms. Clearly, purchase transactions would result in cash outflows, whereas sales transactions would generate cash inflows. The **financing flows** result from debt and equity financing transactions. Incurring either short-term or long-term debt would result in a corresponding cash inflow; repaying debt would result in an outflow. Similarly, the sale of the company's stock would result in a cash inflow; the repurchase of stock or payment of cash dividends would result in an outflow.

Classifying Inflows and Outflows of Cash

The statement of cash flows, in effect, summarizes the inflows and outflows of cash during a given period. Table 3 classifies the basic inflows (sources) and outflows (uses) of cash. For example, if a firm's accounts payable balance increased by $1,000 during the year, the change would be an *inflow of cash.* If the firm's inventory increased by $2,500, the change would be an *outflow of cash.*

A few additional points can be made with respect to the classification scheme in Table 3:

noncash charge
An expense that is deducted on the income statement but does not involve the actual outlay of cash during the period; includes depreciation, amortization, and depletion.

1. A *decrease* in an asset, such as the firm's cash balance, is an *inflow of cash.* Why? Because cash that has been tied up in the asset is released and can be used for some other purpose, such as repaying a loan. On the other hand, an *increase* in the firm's cash balance is an *outflow of cash,* because additional cash is being tied up in the firm's cash balance.
2. Depreciation (like amortization and depletion) is a **noncash charge**—an expense that is deducted on the income statement but does not involve the

373

FIGURE 1 Cash Flows

The firm's cash flows

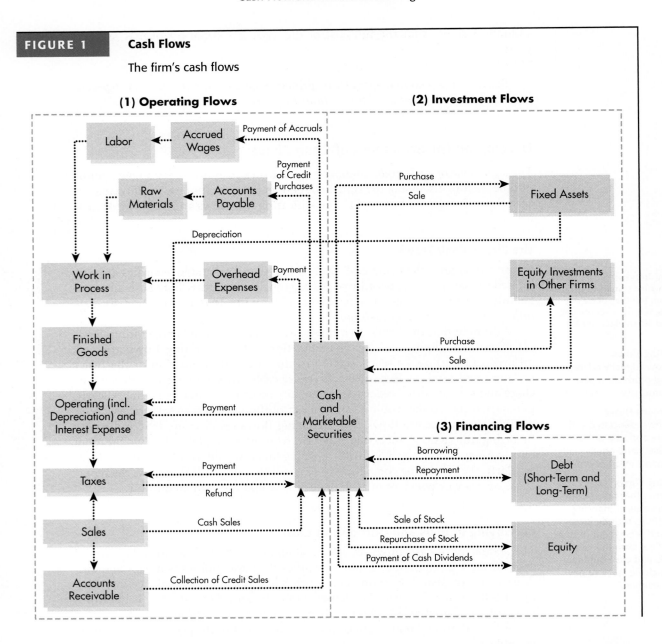

TABLE 3 Inflows and Outflows of Cash

Inflows (sources)	Outflows (uses)
Decrease in any asset	Increase in any asset
Increase in any liability	Decrease in any liability
Net profits after taxes	Net loss
Depreciation and other noncash charges	Dividends paid
Sale of stock	Repurchase or retirement of stock

actual outlay of cash during the period. Because it shields the firm from taxes by lowering taxable income, the noncash charge is considered a cash inflow. From a strict accounting perspective, adding depreciation back to the firm's net profits after taxes provides an estimate of cash flow from operations:[4]

Cash flow from operations =
   Net profits after taxes + Depreciation and other noncash charges   (1)

Note that a firm can have a *net loss* (negative net profits after taxes) and still have positive cash flow from operations when depreciation (and other noncash charges) during the period is greater than the net loss. In the statement of cash flows, net profits after taxes (or net losses) and depreciation (and other noncash charges) are therefore treated as separate entries.

3. We will refine Equation 1 in the next section (Equation 4).
4. Because depreciation is treated as a separate cash inflow, only *gross* rather than *net* changes in fixed assets appear on the statement of cash flows. This treatment avoids the potential double counting of depreciation.
5. Direct entries of changes in retained earnings are not included on the statement of cash flows. Instead, entries for items that affect retained earnings appear as net profits or losses after taxes and dividends paid.

Preparing the Statement of Cash Flows

The statement of cash flows for a given period is developed using the income statement for the period, along with the beginning- and end-of-period balance sheets. The income statement for the year ended December 31, 2009, and the December 31 balance sheets for 2008 and 2009 for Baker Corporation are given in Tables 4 and 5, respectively. The statement of cash flows for the year ended December 31, 2009, for Baker Corporation is presented in Table 6. Note that all cash inflows as well as net profits after taxes and depreciation are treated as positive values. All cash outflows, any losses, and dividends paid are treated as negative values. The items in each category—operating, investment, and financing—are totaled, and the three totals are added to get the "Net increase (decrease) in cash and marketable securities" for the period. As a check, this value should reconcile with the actual change in cash and marketable securities for the year, which is obtained from the beginning- and end-of-period balance sheets. A detailed description of the procedures used to prepare Baker Corporation's statement of cash flows is posted on this text's website.

Interpreting the Statement

The statement of cash flows allows the financial manager and other interested parties to analyze the firm's cash flow. The manager should pay special attention both to the major categories of cash flow and to the individual items of cash

---

4. This equation is merely an estimate because it is based on the assumption that the firm's accounts receivable, inventory, accounts payable, and accruals remain unchanged during the period. Generally, these account balances will change over the period.

TABLE 4	Baker Corporation Income Statement ($000) for the Year Ended December 31, 2009	
Sales revenue		$1,700
Less: Cost of goods sold		1,000
Gross profits		$ 700
Less: Operating expenses		
Selling expense	$ 70	
General and administrative expenses	120	
Lease expense[a]	40	
Depreciation expense	100	
Total operating expense		$ 330
Earnings before interest and taxes (EBIT)		$ 370
Less: Interest expense		70
Net profits before taxes		$ 300
Less: Taxes (rate = 40%)		120
Net profits after taxes		$ 180
Less: Preferred stock dividends		10
Earnings available for common stockholders		$ 170
Earnings per share (EPS)[b]		$1.70

[a]Lease expense is shown here as a separate item rather than included as interest expense as specified by the FASB for financial reporting purposes. The approach used here is consistent with tax reporting rather than financial reporting procedures.

[b]Calculated by dividing the earnings available for common stockholders by the number of shares of common stock outstanding ($170,000 ÷ 100,000 shares = $1.70 per share).

inflow and outflow, to assess whether any developments have occurred that are contrary to the company's financial policies. In addition, the statement can be used to evaluate progress toward projected goals or to isolate inefficiencies. The financial manager also can prepare a statement of cash flows developed from projected financial statements to determine whether planned actions are desirable in view of the resulting cash flows.

Operating Cash Flow

operating cash flow (OCF)
The cash flow a firm generates from its normal operations; calculated as *net operating profits after taxes (NOPAT)* plus depreciation.

A firm's **operating cash flow (OCF)** is the cash flow it generates from its normal operations—producing and selling its output of goods or services. A variety of definitions of OCF can be found in the financial literature. Equation 1 introduced the simple accounting definition of cash flow from operations. Here we refine this definition to estimate cash flows more accurately. Unlike the earlier definition, this one excludes interest and taxes to enable us to focus on the true cash flow resulting from operations without regard to interest expense and taxes. The

TABLE 5	Baker Corporation Balance Sheets ($000)		
		December 31	
Assets		2009	2008
Current assets			
Cash		$ 400	$ 300
Marketable securities		600	200
Accounts receivable		400	500
Inventories		600	900
Total current assets		$2,000	$1,900
Gross fixed assets (at cost)			
Land and buildings		$1,200	$1,050
Machinery and equipment		850	800
Furniture and fixtures		300	220
Vehicles		100	80
Other (includes certain leases)		50	50
Total gross fixed assets (at cost)		$2,500	$2,200
Less: Accumulated depreciation		1,300	1,200
Net fixed assets		$1,200	$1,000
Total assets		$3,200	$2,900
Liabilities and Stockholders' Equity			
Current liabilities			
Accounts payable		$ 700	$ 500
Notes payable		600	700
Accruals		100	200
Total current liabilities		$1,400	$1,400
Long-term debt		$ 600	$ 400
Total liabilities		$2,000	$1,800
Stockholders' equity			
Preferred stock		$ 100	$ 100
Common stock—$1.20 par, 100,000 shares outstanding in 2009 and 2008		120	120
Paid-in capital in excess of par on common stock		380	380
Retained earnings		600	500
Total stockholders' equity		$1,200	$1,100
Total liabilities and stockholders' equity		$3,200	$2,900

net operating profits after taxes (NOPAT) A firm's earnings before interest and after taxes, $EBIT \times (1 - T)$.

first step is to calculate **net operating profits after taxes (NOPAT),** which represent the firm's earnings before interest and after taxes. Letting T equal the applicable corporate tax rate, NOPAT is calculated as follows:

$$NOPAT = EBIT \times (1 - T) \tag{2}$$

To convert NOPAT to operating cash flow (OCF), we merely add back depreciation:

$$OCF = NOPAT + Depreciation \tag{3}$$

TABLE 6	Baker Corporation Statement of Cash Flows ($000) for the Year Ended December 31, 2009		
Cash Flow from Operating Activities			
Net profits after taxes		$180	
Depreciation		100	
Decrease in accounts receivable		100	
Decrease in inventories		300	
Increase in accounts payable		200	
Decrease in accruals		(100)[a]	
Cash provided by operating activities			$780
Cash Flow from Investment Activities			
Increase in gross fixed assets		($300)	
Changes in equity investments in other firms		0	
Cash provided by investment activities			(300)
Cash Flow from Financing Activities			
Decrease in notes payable		($100)	
Increase in long-term debts		200	
Changes in stockholders' equity[b]		0	
Dividends paid		(80)	
Cash provided by financing activities			20
Net increase in cash and marketable securities			$500

[a]As is customary, parentheses are used to denote a negative number, which in this case is a cash outflow.

[b]Retained earnings are excluded here, because their change is actually reflected in the combination of the "Net profits after taxes" and "Dividends paid" entries.

We can substitute the expression for NOPAT from Equation 2 into Equation 3 to get a single equation for OCF:

$$\text{OCF} = [\text{EBIT} \times (1 - T)] + \text{Depreciation} \qquad (4)$$

Example

Substituting the values for Baker Corporation from its income statement (Table 4) into Equation 4, we get

$$\text{OCF} = [\$370 \times (1.00 - 0.40)] + \$100 = \$222 + \$100 = \$322$$

During 2009, Baker Corporation generated $322,000 of cash flow from producing and selling its output. Therefore, we can conclude that Baker's operations are generating positive cash flows.

Comparing Equations 1 and 4 reveals the key difference between the accounting and finance definitions of operating cash flow: The finance definition excludes interest—a financing cost—as an operating cash flow, whereas the accounting definition includes it as an operating flow. In the unlikely case that a firm has no interest expense, the accounting definition (Equation 1) and the finance definition (Equation 4) of operating cash flow would be the same.

Free Cash Flow

The firm's **free cash flow (FCF)** represents the amount of cash flow available to investors—the providers of debt (creditors) and equity (owners)—after the firm has met all operating needs and paid for investments in net fixed assets and net current assets. It represents the summation of the net amount of cash flow available to creditors and owners during the period. Free cash flow can be defined as follows:

$$\text{FCF} = \text{OCF} - \text{Net fixed asset investment (NFAI)}$$
$$- \text{Net current asset investment (NCAI)} \tag{5}$$

The *net fixed asset investment (NFAI)* can be calculated as shown here:

$$\text{NFAI} = \text{Change in net fixed assets} + \text{Depreciation} \tag{6}$$

Example

Using the Baker Corporation's balance sheets in Table 5, we see that its change in net fixed assets between 2008 and 2009 was +$200 ($1,200 in 2009 − $1,000 in 2008). Substituting this value and the $100 of depreciation for 2009 into Equation 6, we get Baker's net fixed asset investment (NFAI) for 2009:

$$\text{NFAI} = \$200 + \$100 = \$300$$

Baker Corporation therefore invested a net $300,000 in fixed assets during 2009. This amount would, of course, represent a net cash outflow to acquire fixed assets during 2009.

Looking at Equation 6, we can see that if the depreciation during a year is less than the *decrease* during that year in net fixed assets, the NFAI would be negative. A negative NFAI represents a net cash *inflow* attributable to the fact that the firm sold more assets than it acquired during the year.

The *net current asset investment (NCAI)* represents the net investment made by the firm in its current (operating) assets. "Net" refers to the difference between current assets and the sum of accounts payable and accruals. Notes payable are not included in the NCAI calculation because they represent a negotiated creditor claim on the firm's free cash flow. Equation 7 shows the NCAI calculation.

$$\text{NCAI} = \text{Change in current assets} -$$
$$\text{Change in (accounts payable} + \text{accruals)} \tag{7}$$

Example

Looking at the Baker Corporation's balance sheets for 2008 and 2009 in Table 5, we see that the change in current assets between 2008 and 2009 is +$100 ($2,000 in 2009 − $1,900 in 2008). The difference between Baker's accounts payable plus accruals of $800 in 2009 ($700 in accounts payable + $100 in accruals) and of $700 in 2008 ($500 in accounts payable + $200 in accruals) is +$100 ($800 in 2009 − $700 in 2008). Substituting into Equation 7 the change in current assets and the change in the sum of accounts payable plus accruals for Baker Corporation, we get its 2009 NCAI:

$$\text{NCAI} = \$100 - \$100 = \$0$$

Focus on Practice — Free Cash Flow at eBay

Free cash flow is the lifeblood of any company and is the only true way to measure how much cash a company is generating. Free cash flow is, broadly, operating cash flow minus investments in net fixed assets and net current assets. It represents the net amount of cash flow available to creditors and owners. Free cash flow is an ideal way to measure a company's health and cash-generating growth.

Take **eBay,** for example. The company which brings together millions of people every day in its online marketplace produced $1.73 billion in free cash flow for the year ending December 31, 2006. Net cash provided by operating activities was $2.24 billion, and the company invested $0.51 billion in property, equipment, and net current assets during 2006, leaving $1.73 billion in free cash flow, a 10.09 percent increase over the previous year.

However, despite the increase in free cash flow, eBay faces some challenges. Users

of eBay generated a total of 610 million listings in the fourth quarter of 2006, a 12 percent increase over the fourth quarter of 2005. But the company is spending more and more, mostly paying Google, a chief competitor, to draw traffic to the site. When expenses start to increase more than free cash flow, it suggests that a company's competitive edge is under attack.

Having free cash flows is one thing; what a company does with it is quite another. According to the Motley Fool (www.fool.com), as an investor you are much better served by companies that use free cash flow to buy back their stock (if the stock is undervalued) or, better yet, use it toward a regular cash dividend. The investor then has the option to reinvest the dividend back into the company or use the dividend to pursue a different opportunity.

In 2006, eBay chose to use its excess cash to buy back stock. Since announcing a share buyback program in July 2006, the

company repurchased approximately 50 million shares of its common stock at a total cost of nearly $1.7 billion. In addition, the company has the capacity to buy back an additional $300 million of stock under the initial plan, and the company's board of directors has authorized an expansion of the stock repurchase program to provide for the repurchase of up to an additional $2 billion of the company's common stock within the next 2 years. For the time being, stockholders expecting the start of a dividend stream can put those expectations on hold. The company's intentions are clearly not to begin paying dividends for the foreseeable future.

■ *Free cash flow is often considered a more reliable measure of a company's income than reported earnings. What are some possible ways that corporate accountants might be able to change their earnings to portray a more favorable earnings statement?*

This means that during 2009 Baker Corporation made no investment ($0) in its current assets net of accounts payable and accruals.

Now we can substitute Baker Corporation's 2009 operating cash flow (OCF) of $322, its net fixed asset investment (NFAI) of $300, and its net current asset investment (NCAI) of $0 into Equation 5 to find its free cash flow (FCF):

$$FCF = \$322 - \$300 - \$0 = \$22$$

We can see that during 2009 Baker generated $22,000 of free cash flow, which it can use to pay its investors—creditors (payment of interest) and owners (payment of dividends). Thus, the firm generated adequate cash flow to cover all of its operating costs and investments and had free cash flow available to pay investors.

Clearly, cash flow is the lifeblood of the firm. The *Focus on Practice* box at the top of this page discusses eBay's free cash flow.

In the next section, we consider various aspects of financial planning for cash flow and profit.

REVIEW QUESTIONS

1   Briefly describe the first four *modified accelerated cost recovery system (MACRS)* property classes and recovery periods. Explain how the depreciation percentages are determined by using the MACRS recovery periods.

2   Describe the overall cash flow through the firm in terms of operating flows, investments flows, and financing flows.

3   Explain why a decrease in cash is classified as a *cash inflow (source)* and why an increase in cash is classified as a *cash outflow (use)* in preparing the statement of cash flows.

4   Why is depreciation (as well as amortization and depletion) considered a *noncash charge*? How do accountants estimate *cash flow from operations*?

5   Describe the general format of the statement of cash flows. How are cash inflows differentiated from cash outflows on this statement?

6   What is the difference between the accounting and finance definitions of *operating cash flow*? Under what circumstances are they the same?

7   From a strict financial perspective, define and differentiate between a firm's *operating cash flow (OCF)* and its *free cash flow (FCF)*.

---

 2 | # The Financial Planning Process

Financial planning is an important aspect of the firm's operations because it provides road maps for guiding, coordinating, and controlling the firm's actions to achieve its objectives. Two key aspects of the financial planning process are *cash planning* and *profit planning*. Cash planning involves preparation of the firm's cash budget. Profit planning involves preparation of pro forma statements. Both the cash budget and the pro forma statements are useful for internal financial planning; they also are routinely required by existing and prospective lenders.

financial planning process
Planning that begins with long-term, or *strategic*, financial plans that in turn guide the formulation of short-term, or *operating*, plans and budgets.

The **financial planning process** begins with long-term, or *strategic*, financial plans. These, in turn, guide the formulation of short-term, or *operating*, plans and budgets. Generally, the short-term plans and budgets implement the firm's long-term strategic objectives. Although the remainder of this chapter places primary emphasis on short-term financial plans and budgets, a few preliminary comments on long-term financial plans are in order.

Long-Term (Strategic) Financial Plans

long-term (strategic) financial plans
Lay out a company's planned financial actions and the anticipated impact of those actions over periods ranging from 2 to 10 years.

Long-term (strategic) financial plans lay out a company's planned financial actions and the anticipated impact of those actions over periods ranging from 2 to 10 years. Five-year strategic plans, which are revised as significant new information becomes available, are common. Generally, firms that are subject to high degrees of operating uncertainty, relatively short production cycles, or both, tend to use shorter planning horizons.

Long-term financial plans are part of an integrated strategy that, along with production and marketing plans, guides the firm toward strategic goals. Those long-term plans consider proposed outlays for fixed assets, research and development activities, marketing and product development actions, capital structure, and major sources of financing. Also included would be termination of existing projects, product lines, or lines of business; repayment or retirement of outstanding debts; and any planned acquisitions. Such plans tend to be supported by a series of annual budgets.

Hint Preparation of the annual budget is an important part of the firm's planning process that involves all managers. It represents a tedious but important management activity.

Short-Term (Operating) Financial Plans

Short-term (operating) financial plans specify short-term financial actions and the anticipated impact of those actions. These plans most often cover a 1- to 2-year period. Key inputs include the sales forecast and various forms of operating and financial data. Key outputs include a number of operating budgets, the cash budget, and pro forma financial statements. The entire short-term financial planning process is outlined in Figure 2. Here we focus solely on cash and profit planning from the financial manager's perspective.

short-term (operating) financial plans
Specify short-term financial actions and the anticipated impact of those actions.

Short-term financial planning begins with the sales forecast. From it, companies develop production plans that take into account lead (preparation) times and include estimates of the required raw materials. Using the production plans, the firm can estimate direct labor requirements, factory overhead outlays, and operating expenses. Once these estimates have been made, the firm can prepare a pro forma income statement and cash budget. With these basic inputs, the firm can finally develop a pro forma balance sheet.

Hint Excel spreadsheets are widely used to streamline the process of preparing and evaluating these short-term financial planning statements.

Personal Finance Example The first step in personal financial planning requires you to define your goals. Whereas in a corporation, the goal is to maximize owner wealth (i.e., share price), individuals typically have a number of major goals.

Generally personal goals can be short-term (1 year), intermediate-term (2–5 years), or long-term (6+ years). The short- and intermediate-term goals support the long-term goals. Clearly, types of long-term personal goals depend on the individual's or family's age, and goals will continue to change with one's life situation.

You should set your personal financial goals carefully and realistically. Each goal should be clearly defined and have a priority, time frame, and cost estimate. For example, a college senior's intermediate-term goal in 2009 might include earning a master's degree at a cost of $40,000 by 2012, and his or her long-term goal might be to buy a condominium at a cost of $125,000 by 2016.

Throughout the remainder of this chapter, we will concentrate on the key outputs of the short-term financial planning process: the cash budget, the pro forma income statement, and the pro forma balance sheet.

REVIEW QUESTIONS

8   What is the *financial planning process?* Contrast *long-term (strategic) financial plans* and *short-term (operating) financial plans.*

9   Which three statements result as part of the short-term (operating) financial planning process?

FIGURE 2

Short-Term Financial Planning
The short-term (operating) financial planning process

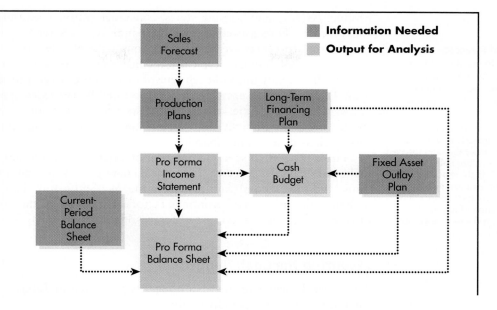

3 | Cash Planning: Cash Budgets

cash budget (cash forecast)
A statement of the firm's planned inflows and outflows of cash that is used to estimate its short-term cash requirements.

The **cash budget,** or **cash forecast,** is a statement of the firm's planned inflows and outflows of cash. It is used by the firm to estimate its short-term cash requirements, with particular attention being paid to planning for surplus cash and for cash shortages.

Typically, the cash budget is designed to cover a 1-year period, divided into smaller time intervals. The number and type of intervals depend on the nature of the business. The more seasonal and uncertain a firm's cash flows, the greater the number of intervals. Because many firms are confronted with a seasonal cash flow pattern, the cash budget is quite often presented on a *monthly basis*. Firms with stable patterns of cash flow may use quarterly or annual time intervals.

The Sales Forecast

sales forecast
The prediction of the firm's sales over a given period, based on external and/or internal data; used as the key input to the short-term financial planning process.

The key input to the short-term financial planning process is the firm's **sales forecast.** This prediction of the firm's sales over a given period is ordinarily prepared by the marketing department. On the basis of the sales forecast, the financial manager estimates the monthly cash flows that will result from projected sales and from outlays related to production, inventory, and sales. The manager also determines the level of fixed assets required and the amount of financing, if any, needed to support the forecast level of sales and production. In practice, obtaining good data is the most difficult aspect of forecasting. The sales forecast may be based on an analysis of external data, internal data, or a combination of the two.

external forecast
A sales forecast based on the relationships observed between the firm's sales and certain key external economic indicators.

An **external forecast** is based on the relationships observed between the firm's sales and certain key external economic indicators such as the gross domestic product (GDP), new housing starts, consumer confidence, and disposable personal income. Forecasts containing these indicators are readily available.

internal forecast
A sales forecast based on a buildup, or consensus, of sales forecasts through the firm's own sales channels.

Internal forecasts are based on a consensus of sales forecasts through the firm's own sales channels. Typically, the firm's salespeople in the field are asked to estimate how many units of each type of product they expect to sell in the coming year. These forecasts are collected and totaled by the sales manager, who may adjust the figures using knowledge of specific markets or of the salesperson's forecasting ability. Finally, adjustments may be made for additional internal factors, such as production capabilities.

Hint The firm needs to spend a great deal of time and effort to make the sales forecast as precise as possible. An "after-the-fact" analysis of the prior year's forecast can help the firm determine which approach or combination of approaches will give it the most accurate forecasts.

Firms generally use a combination of external and internal forecast data to make the final sales forecast. The internal data provide insight into sales expectations, and the external data provide a means of adjusting these expectations to take into account general economic factors. The nature of the firm's product also often affects the mix and types of forecasting methods used.

Preparing the Cash Budget

The general format of the cash budget is presented in Table 7. We will discuss each of its components individually.

Cash Receipts

cash receipts
All of a firm's inflows of cash during a given financial period.

Cash receipts include all of a firm's inflows of cash during a given financial period. The most common components of cash receipts are cash sales, collections of accounts receivable, and other cash receipts.

Example

Coulson Industries, a defense contractor, is developing a cash budget for October, November, and December. Coulson's sales in August and September were $100,000 and $200,000, respectively. Sales of $400,000, $300,000, and $200,000 have been forecast for October, November, and December, respectively. Historically, 20% of the firm's sales have been for cash, 50% have generated accounts receivable collected after 1 month, and the remaining 30% have generated accounts receivable collected after 2 months. Bad-debt expenses (uncol-

TABLE 7	The General Format of the Cash Budget					
	Jan.	Feb.	. . .	Nov.	Dec.
Cash receipts	$XXX	$XXG		$XXM	$XXT
Less: Cash disbursements	XXA	XXH	. . .	XXN	XXU
Net cash flow	$XXB	$XXI		$XXO	$XXV
Add: Beginning cash	XXC	XXD	XXJ	XXP	XXQ
Ending cash	$XXD	$XXJ		$XXQ	$XXW
Less: Minimum cash balance	XXE	XXK	. . .	XXR	XXY
Required total financing		$XXL		$XXS	
Excess cash balance	$XXF				$XXZ

TABLE 8	A Schedule of Projected Cash Receipts for Coulson Industries ($000)				
	Aug.	**Sept.**	**Oct.**	**Nov.**	**Dec.**
Forecast sales	$100	$200	$400	$300	$200
Cash sales (0.20)	$20	$40	$ 80	$ 60	$ 40
Collections of A/R:					
Lagged 1 month (0.50)		50	100	200	150
Lagged 2 months (0.30)			30	60	120
Other cash receipts					30
Total cash receipts			$210	$320	$340

lectible accounts) have been negligible.[5] In December, the firm will receive a $30,000 dividend from stock in a subsidiary. The schedule of expected cash receipts for the company is presented in Table 8. It contains the following items:

Forecast sales This initial entry is *merely informational.* It is provided as an aid in calculating other sales-related items.

Cash sales The cash sales shown for each month represent 20% of the total sales forecast for that month.

Collections of A/R These entries represent the collection of accounts receivable (A/R) resulting from sales in earlier months.

Lagged 1 month These figures represent sales made in the preceding month that generated accounts receivable collected in the current month. Because 50% of the current month's sales are collected 1 month later, the collections of A/R with a 1-month lag shown for September represent 50% of the sales in August, collections for October represent 50% of September sales, and so on.

Lagged 2 months These figures represent sales made 2 months earlier that generated accounts receivable collected in the current month. Because 30% of sales are collected 2 months later, the collections with a 2-month lag shown for October represent 30% of the sales in August, and so on.

Other cash receipts These are cash receipts expected from sources other than sales. Interest received, dividends received, proceeds from the sale of equipment, stock and bond sale proceeds, and lease receipts may show up here. For Coulson Industries, the only other cash receipt is the $30,000 dividend due in December.

Total cash receipts This figure represents the total of all the cash receipts listed for each month. For Coulson Industries, we are concerned only with October, November, and December, as shown in Table 8.

---

5. Normally, it would be expected that the collection percentages would total slightly less than 100%, because some of the accounts receivable would be uncollectible. In this example, the sum of the collection percentages is 100% (20% + 50% + 30%), which reflects the fact that all sales are assumed to be collected.

Cash Disbursements

cash disbursements
All outlays of cash by the firm during a given financial period.

Cash disbursements include all outlays of cash by the firm during a given financial period. The most common cash disbursements are

Cash purchases	Fixed-asset outlays
Payments of accounts payable	Interest payments
Rent (and lease) payments	Cash dividend payments
Wages and salaries	Principal payments (loans)
Tax payments	Repurchases or retirements of stock

It is important to recognize that *depreciation and other noncash charges are NOT included in the cash budget,* because they merely represent a scheduled write-off of an earlier cash outflow. The impact of depreciation, as we noted earlier, is reflected in the reduced cash outflow for tax payments.

Example

Coulson Industries has gathered the following data needed for the preparation of a cash disbursements schedule for October, November, and December.

Purchases The firm's purchases represent 70% of sales. Of this amount, 10% is paid in cash, 70% is paid in the month immediately following the month of purchase, and the remaining 20% is paid 2 months following the month of purchase.[6]

Rent payments Rent of $5,000 will be paid each month.

Wages and salaries Fixed salary cost for the year is $96,000, or $8,000 per month. In addition, wages are estimated as 10% of monthly sales.

Tax payments Taxes of $25,000 must be paid in December.

Fixed-asset outlays New machinery costing $130,000 will be purchased and paid for in November.

Interest payments An interest payment of $10,000 is due in December.

Cash dividend payments Cash dividends of $20,000 will be paid in October.

Principal payments (loans) A $20,000 principal payment is due in December.

Repurchases or retirements of stock No repurchase or retirement of stock is expected between October and December.

The firm's cash disbursements schedule, using the preceding data, is shown in Table 9. Some items in the table are explained in greater detail below.

Purchases This entry is *merely informational.* The figures represent 70% of the forecast sales for each month. They have been included to facilitate calculation of the cash purchases and related payments.

Cash purchases The cash purchases for each month represent 10% of the month's purchases.

Payments of A/P These entries represent the payment of accounts payable (A/P) resulting from purchases in earlier months.

---

6. Unlike the collection percentages for sales, the total of the payment percentages should equal 100%, because it is expected that the firm will pay off all of its accounts payable.

TABLE 9	A Schedule of Projected Cash Disbursements for Coulson Industries ($000)				
	Aug.	Sept.	Oct.	Nov.	Dec.
Purchases (0.70 × sales)	$70	$140	$280	$210	$140
Cash purchases (0.10)	$7	$14	$ 28	$ 21	$ 14
Payments of A/P:					
Lagged 1 month (0.70)		49	98	196	147
Lagged 2 months (0.20)			14	28	56
Rent payments			5	5	5
Wages and salaries			48	38	28
Tax payments					25
Fixed-asset outlays				130	
Interest payments					10
Cash dividend payments			20		
Principal payments					20
Total cash disbursements			$213	$418	$305

Lagged 1 month These figures represent purchases made in the preceding month that are paid for in the current month. Because 70% of the firm's purchases are paid for 1 month later, the payments with a 1-month lag shown for September represent 70% of the August purchases, payments for October represent 70% of September purchases, and so on.

Lagged 2 months These figures represent purchases made 2 months earlier that are paid for in the current month. Because 20% of the firm's purchases are paid for 2 months later, the payments with a 2-month lag for October represent 20% of the August purchases, and so on.

Wages and salaries These amounts were obtained by adding $8,000 to 10% of the *sales* in each month. The $8,000 represents the salary component; the rest represents wages.

The remaining items on the cash disbursements schedule are self-explanatory.

net cash flow
The mathematical difference between the firm's cash receipts and its cash disbursements in each period.

ending cash
The sum of the firm's beginning cash and its net cash flow for the period.

required total financing
Amount of funds needed by the firm if the ending cash for the period is less than the desired minimum cash balance; typically represented by notes payable.

excess cash balance
The (excess) amount available for investment by the firm if the period's ending cash is greater than the desired minimum cash balance; assumed to be invested in marketable securities.

Net Cash Flow, Ending Cash, Financing, and Excess Cash

Look back at the general-format cash budget in Table 7. We have inputs for the first two entries, and we now continue calculating the firm's cash needs. The firm's **net cash flow** is found by subtracting the cash disbursements from cash receipts in each period. Then we add beginning cash to the firm's net cash flow to determine the **ending cash** for each period.

Finally, we subtract the desired minimum cash balance from ending cash to find the **required total financing** or the **excess cash balance.** If the ending cash is less than the minimum cash balance, *financing* is required. Such financing is typically viewed as short-term and is therefore represented by notes payable. If the ending cash is greater than the minimum cash balance, *excess cash* exists. Any excess cash is assumed to be invested in a liquid, short-term, interest-paying vehicle—that is, in marketable securities.

Example

Table 10 presents Coulson Industries' cash budget, based on the data already developed. At the end of September, Coulson's cash balance was $50,000, and its notes payable and marketable securities equaled $0. The company wishes to maintain, as a reserve for unexpected needs, a minimum cash balance of $25,000.

For Coulson Industries to maintain its required $25,000 ending cash balance, it will need total borrowing of $76,000 in November and $41,000 in December. In October the firm will have an excess cash balance of $22,000, which can be held in an interest-earning marketable security. The required total financing figures in the cash budget refer to *how much will be owed at the end of the month*; they do *not* represent the monthly changes in borrowing.

The monthly changes in borrowing and in excess cash can be found by further analyzing the cash budget. In October the $50,000 beginning cash, which becomes $47,000 after the $3,000 net cash outflow, results in a $22,000 excess cash balance once the $25,000 minimum cash is deducted. In November the $76,000 of required total financing resulted from the $98,000 net cash outflow less the $22,000 of excess cash from October. The $41,000 of required total financing in December resulted from reducing November's $76,000 of required total financing by the $35,000 of net cash inflow during December. Summarizing, the *financial activities for each month* would be as follows:

October: **Invest the $22,000** excess cash balance in marketable securities.

November: Liquidate the $22,000 of marketable securities and **borrow $76,000** (notes payable).

December: **Repay $35,000** of notes payable to leave $41,000 of outstanding required total financing.

TABLE 10	A Cash Budget for Coulson Industries ($000)		
	Oct.	Nov.	Dec.
Total cash receipts[a]	$210	$320	$340
Less: Total cash disbursements[b]	213	418	305
Net cash flow	($ 3)	($ 98)	$ 35
Add: Beginning cash	50	47	(51)
Ending cash	$ 47	($ 51)	($ 16)
Less: Minimum cash balance	25	25	25
Required total financing (notes payable)[c]	—	$ 76	$ 41
Excess cash balance (marketable securities)[d]	$ 22	—	—

[a]From Table 8.

[b]From Table 9.

[c]Values are placed in this line when the ending cash is less than the desired minimum cash balance. These amounts are typically financed short-term and therefore are represented by notes payable.

[d]Values are placed in this line when the ending cash is greater than the desired minimum cash balance. These amounts are typically assumed to be invested short-term and therefore are represented by marketable securities.

Evaluating the Cash Budget

The cash budget indicates whether a cash shortage or surplus is expected in each of the months covered by the forecast. Each month's figure is based on the internally imposed requirement of a minimum cash balance and *represents the total balance at the end of the month*.

At the end of each of the 3 months, Coulson expects the following balances in cash, marketable securities, and notes payable:

Account	End-of-month balance ($000)		
	Oct.	Nov.	Dec.
Cash	$25	$25	$25
Marketable securities	22	0	0
Notes payable	0	76	41

Note that the firm is assumed first to liquidate its marketable securities to meet deficits and then to borrow with notes payable if additional financing is needed. As a result, it will not have marketable securities and notes payable on its books at the same time. Because it may be necessary to borrow up to $76,000 for the 3-month period, the financial manager should be certain that some arrangement is made to ensure the availability of these funds.

Personal Finance Example Because individuals receive only a finite amount of income (cash inflow) during a given period, they need to prepare budgets in order to make sure they can cover their expenses (cash outflows) during the period. The *personal budget* is a short-term financial planning report that helps an individual or family achieve its short-term financial goals. Personal budgets typically cover a 1-year period, broken into months.

A condensed version of a personal budget for the first quarter (3 months) is shown below. You can see a more detailed version (with breakouts of expenses) at the text's companion website.

	Jan.	Feb.	Mar.
Income			
Take-home pay	$4,775	$4,775	$4,775
Investment income			90
(1) Total income	$4,775	$4,775	$4,865
Expenses			
(2) Total expenses	$4,026	$5,291	7,396
Cash surplus or deficit [(1) − (2)]	$ 749	($ 516)	($2,531)
Cumulative cash surplus or deficit	$ 749	$ 233	($2,298)

The personal budget shows a cash surplus of $749 in January followed by monthly deficits in February and March of $516 and $2,531, resulting in a cumulative deficit of $2,298 through March. Clearly, to cover the deficit, some action—such as increasing income, reducing expenses, drawing down savings, or borrowing—will be necessary to bring the budget into balance. Borrowing by using credit can offset a deficit in the short term but can lead to financial trouble if done repeatedly.

Coping with Uncertainty in the Cash Budget

Aside from careful estimation of cash budget inputs, there are two ways of coping with uncertainty in the cash budget.[7] One is to prepare several cash budgets—based on pessimistic, most likely, and optimistic forecasts. From this range of cash flows, the financial manager can determine the amount of financing necessary to cover the most adverse situation. The use of several cash budgets, based on differing scenarios, also should give the financial manager a sense of the riskiness of the various alternatives. This *scenario analysis,* or "what if" approach, is often used to analyze cash flows under a variety of circumstances. Clearly, the use of electronic spreadsheets simplifies the process of performing scenario analysis.

Example

Table 11 presents the summary of Coulson Industries' cash budget prepared for each month of concern using pessimistic, most likely, and optimistic estimates of total cash receipts and disbursements. The most likely estimate is based on the expected outcomes presented earlier.

TABLE 11	A Scenario Analysis of Coulson Industries' Cash Budget ($000)								
	October			November			December		
	Pessi-mistic	Most likely	Opti-mistic	Pessi-mistic	Most likely	Opti-mistic	Pessi-mistic	Most likely	Opti-mistic
Total cash receipts	$160	$210	$285	$210	$320	$410	$275	$340	$422
Less: Total cash disbursements	200	213	248	380	418	467	280	305	320
Net cash flow	($ 40)	($ 3)	$ 37	($170)	($ 98)	($ 57)	($ 5)	$ 35	$102
Add: Beginning cash	50	50	50	10	47	87	(160)	(51)	30
Ending cash	$ 10	$ 47	$ 87	($160)	($ 51)	$ 30	($165)	($ 16)	$132
Less: Minimum cash balance	25	25	25	25	25	25	25	25	25
Required total financing	$ 15	—	—	$185	$ 76	—	$190	$ 41	—
Excess cash balance	—	$ 22	$ 62	—	—	$ 5	—	—	$107

---

7. The term *uncertainty* is used here to refer to the variability of the cash flow outcomes that may actually occur.

During October, Coulson will, at worst, need a maximum of $15,000 of financing and, at best, will have a $62,000 excess cash balance. During November, its financing requirement will be between $0 and $185,000, or it could experience an excess cash balance of $5,000. The December projections show maximum borrowing of $190,000 with a possible excess cash balance of $107,000. By considering the extreme values in the pessimistic and optimistic outcomes, Coulson Industries should be better able to plan its cash requirements. For the 3-month period, the peak borrowing requirement under the worst circumstances would be $190,000, which happens to be considerably greater than the most likely estimate of $76,000 for this period.

A second and much more sophisticated way of coping with uncertainty in the cash budget is *simulation*. By simulating the occurrence of sales and other uncertain events, the firm can develop a probability distribution of its ending cash flows for each month. The financial decision maker can then use the probability distribution to determine the amount of financing needed to protect the firm adequately against a cash shortage.

REVIEW QUESTIONS

10 What is the purpose of the *cash budget?* What role does the sales forecast play in its preparation?

11 Briefly describe the basic format of the cash budget.

12 How can the two "bottom lines" of the cash budget be used to determine the firm's short-term borrowing and investment requirements?

13 What is the cause of uncertainty in the cash budget, and what two techniques can be used to cope with this uncertainty?

---

4 | **Profit Planning: Pro Forma Statements**

pro forma statements
Projected, or forecast, income statements and balance sheets.

Hint A key point in understanding pro forma statements is that they reflect the goals and objectives of the firm for the planning period. For these goals and objectives to be achieved, operational plans will have to be developed. Financial plans can be realized only if the correct actions are implemented.

Whereas cash planning focuses on forecasting cash flows, *profit planning* relies on accrual concepts to project the firm's profit and overall financial position. Shareholders, creditors, and the firm's management pay close attention to the **pro forma statements**, which are projected, or forecast, income statements and balance sheets. The basic steps in the short-term financial planning process were shown in the flow diagram of Figure 2. The approaches for estimating the pro forma statements are all based on the belief that the financial relationships reflected in the firm's past financial statements will not change in the coming period. The commonly used simplified approaches are presented in subsequent discussions.

Two inputs are required for preparing pro forma statements: (1) financial statements for the preceding year and (2) the sales forecast for the coming year. A variety of assumptions must also be made. The company that we will use to illustrate the simplified approaches to pro forma preparation is Vectra Manufacturing, which manufactures and sells one product. It has two basic product models—X and Y—which are produced by the same process but require different amounts of raw material and labor.

Preceding Year's Financial Statements

The income statement for the firm's 2009 operations is given in Table 12. It indicates that Vectra had sales of $100,000, total cost of goods sold of $80,000, net profits before taxes of $9,000, and net profits after taxes of $7,650. The firm paid $4,000 in cash dividends, leaving $3,650 to be transferred to retained earnings. The firm's balance sheet for 2009 is given in Table 13.

TABLE 12	Vectra Manufacturing's Income Statement for the Year Ended December 31, 2009		
Sales revenue			
Model X (1,000 units at $20/unit)		$20,000	
Model Y (2,000 units at $40/unit)		80,000	
Total sales			$100,000
Less: Cost of goods sold			
Labor		$28,500	
Material A		8,000	
Material B		5,500	
Overhead		38,000	
Total cost of goods sold			80,000
Gross profits			$ 20,000
Less: Operating expenses			10,000
Operating profits			$ 10,000
Less: Interest expense			1,000
Net profits before taxes			$ 9,000
Less: Taxes (0.15 × $9,000)			1,350
Net profits after taxes			$ 7,650
Less: Common stock dividends			4,000
To retained earnings			$ 3,650

TABLE 13	Vectra Manufacturing's Balance Sheet, December 31, 2009		
Assets		**Liabilities and Stockholders' Equity**	
Cash	$ 6,000	Accounts payable	$ 7,000
Marketable securities	4,000	Taxes payable	300
Accounts receivable	13,000	Notes payable	8,300
Inventories	16,000	Other current liabilities	3,400
Total current assets	$39,000	Total current liabilities	$19,000
Net fixed assets	$51,000	Long-term debt	$18,000
Total assets	$90,000	Stockholders' equity	
		Common stock	$30,000
		Retained earnings	$23,000
		Total liabilities and stockholders' equity	$90,000

TABLE 14	2010 Sales Forecast for Vectra Manufacturing
Unit sales	
Model X	1,500
Model Y	1,950
Dollar sales	
Model X ($25/unit)	$ 37,500
Model Y ($50/unit)	97,500
Total	$135,000

Sales Forecast

Just as for the cash budget, the key input for pro forma statements is the sales forecast. Vectra Manufacturing's sales forecast for the coming year (2010), based on both external and internal data, is presented in Table 14. The unit sale prices of the products reflect an increase from $20 to $25 for model X and from $40 to $50 for model Y. These increases are necessary to cover anticipated increases in costs.

REVIEW QUESTION

14 What is the purpose of *pro forma statements?* What inputs are required for preparing them using the simplified approaches?

5 | Preparing the Pro Forma Income Statement

percent-of-sales method
A simple method for developing the pro forma income statement; it forecasts sales and then expresses the various income statement items as percentages of projected sales.

A simple method for developing a pro forma income statement is the **percent-of-sales method.** It forecasts sales and then expresses the various income statement items as percentages of projected sales. The percentages used are likely to be the percentages of sales for those items in the previous year. By using dollar values taken from Vectra's 2009 income statement (Table 12), we find that these percentages are

$$\frac{\text{Cost of goods sold}}{\text{Sales}} = \frac{\$80,000}{\$100,000} = 80.0\%$$

$$\frac{\text{Operating expenses}}{\text{Sales}} = \frac{\$10,000}{\$100,000} = 10.0\%$$

$$\frac{\text{Interest expense}}{\text{Sales}} = \frac{\$1,000}{\$100,000} = 1.0\%$$

Applying these percentages to the firm's forecast sales of $135,000 (developed in Table 14), we get the 2010 pro forma income statement shown in Table 15. We

TABLE 15	A Pro Forma Income Statement, Using the Percent-of-Sales Method, for Vectra Manufacturing for the Year Ended December 31, 2010
Sales revenue	$135,000
Less: Cost of goods sold (0.80)	108,000
Gross profits	$ 27,000
Less: Operating expenses (0.10)	13,500
Operating profits	$ 13,500
Less: Interest expense (0.01)	1,350
Net profits before taxes	$ 12,150
Less: Taxes (0.15 × $12,150)	1,823
Net profits after taxes	$ 10,327
Less: Common stock dividends	4,000
To retained earnings	$ 6,327

have assumed that Vectra will pay $4,000 in common stock dividends, so the expected contribution to retained earnings is $6,327. This represents a considerable increase over $3,650 in the preceding year (see Table 12).

Considering Types of Costs and Expenses

The technique that is used to prepare the pro forma income statement in Table 15 assumes that all the firm's costs and expenses are *variable*. That is, for a given percentage increase in sales, the same percentage increase in cost of goods sold, operating expenses, and interest expense would result. For example, as Vectra's sales increased by 35 percent, we assumed that its costs of goods sold also increased by 35 percent. On the basis of this assumption, the firm's net profits before taxes also increased by 35 percent.

This approach implies that the firm will not receive the benefits that result from fixed costs when sales are increasing.[8] Clearly, though, if the firm has fixed costs, these costs do not change when sales increase; the result is increased profits. But by remaining unchanged when sales decline, these costs tend to lower profits. Therefore, the use of past cost and expense ratios generally *tends to understate profits when sales are increasing.* (Likewise, it *tends to overstate profits when sales are decreasing.*) The best way to adjust for the presence of fixed costs when preparing a pro forma income statement is to break the firm's historical costs and expenses into *fixed* and *variable* components.

Example

Vectra Manufacturing's 2009 actual and 2010 pro forma income statements, broken into fixed and variable cost and expense components, are shown in the following table:

---

8. The key point to recognize here is that when the firm's revenue is *increasing,* fixed costs can magnify returns.

Vectra Manufacturing Income Statements		
	2009 Actual	2010 Pro forma
Sales revenue	$100,000	$135,000
Less: Cost of good sold		
Fixed cost	40,000	40,000
Variable cost (0.40 × sales)	40,000	54,000
Gross profits	$ 20,000	$ 41,000
Less: Operating expenses		
Fixed expense	5,000	5,000
Variable expense (0.05 × sales)	5,000	6,750
Operating profits	$ 10,000	$ 29,250
Less: Interest expense (all fixed)	1,000	1,000
Net profits before taxes	$ 9,000	$ 28,250
Less: Taxes (0.15 × net profits before taxes)	1,350	4,238
Net profits after taxes	$ 7,650	$ 24,012

Breaking Vectra's costs and expenses into fixed and variable components provides a more accurate projection of its pro forma profit. By assuming that *all* costs are variable (as shown in Table 15), we find that projected net profits before taxes would continue to equal 9% of sales (in 2009, $9,000 net profits before taxes ÷ $100,000 sales). Therefore, the 2010 net profits before taxes would have been $12,150 (0.09 × $135,000 projected sales) instead of the $28,250 obtained by using the firm's fixed-cost–variable-cost breakdown.

Clearly, when using a simplified approach to prepare a pro forma income statement, we should break down costs and expenses into fixed and variable components.

REVIEW QUESTIONS

15   How is the *percent-of-sales method* used to prepare pro forma income statements?

16   Why does the presence of fixed costs cause the percent-of-sales method of pro forma income statement preparation to fail? What is a better method?

6   Preparing the Pro Forma Balance Sheet

A number of simplified approaches are available for preparing the pro forma balance sheet. One involves estimating all balance sheet accounts as a strict percentage of sales. A better and more popular approach is the **judgmental**

judgmental approach
A simplified approach for preparing the pro forma balance sheet under which the firm estimates the values of certain balance sheet accounts and uses its external financing as a balancing, or "plug," figure.

Hint Forty-five days expressed fractionally is about one-eighth of a year: 45/365 ? 1/8.

external financing required ("plug" figure)
Under the judgmental approach for developing a pro forma balance sheet, the amount of external financing needed to bring the statement into balance. It can be either a positive or a negative value.

approach,[9] under which the firm estimates the values of certain balance sheet accounts and uses its external financing as a balancing, or "plug," figure.

To apply the judgmental approach to prepare Vectra Manufacturing's 2010 pro forma balance sheet, a number of assumptions must be made about levels of various balance sheet accounts:

1. A minimum cash balance of $6,000 is desired.
2. Marketable securities will remain unchanged from their current level of $4,000.
3. Accounts receivable on average represent about 45 days of sales. Because Vectra's annual sales are projected to be $135,000, accounts receivable should average $16,875 (1/8 × $135,000).
4. The ending inventory should remain at a level of about $16,000, of which 25 percent (approximately $4,000) should be raw materials and the remaining 75 percent (approximately $12,000) should consist of finished goods.
5. A new machine costing $20,000 will be purchased. Total depreciation for the year is $8,000. Adding the $20,000 acquisition to the existing net fixed assets of $51,000 and subtracting the depreciation of $8,000 yields net fixed assets of $63,000.
6. Purchases will represent approximately 30 percent of annual sales, which in this case is approximately $40,500 (0.30 × $135,000). The firm estimates that it can take 73 days on average to satisfy its accounts payable. Thus accounts payable should equal one-fifth (73 days ÷ 365 days) of the firm's purchases, or $8,100 (1/5 × $40,500).
7. Taxes payable will equal one-fourth of the current year's tax liability, which equals $455 (one-fourth of the tax liability of $1,823 shown in the pro forma income statement in Table 15).
8. Notes payable will remain unchanged from their current level of $8,300.
9. No change in other current liabilities is expected. They remain at the level of the previous year: $3,400.
10. The firm's long-term debt and its common stock will remain unchanged at $18,000 and $30,000, respectively; no issues, retirements, or repurchases of bonds or stocks are planned.
11. Retained earnings will increase from the beginning level of $23,000 (from the balance sheet dated December 31, 2009, in Table 13) to $29,327. The increase of $6,327 represents the amount of retained earnings calculated in the year-end 2010 pro forma income statement in Table 15.

A 2010 pro forma balance sheet for Vectra Manufacturing based on these assumptions is presented in Table 16. A **"plug" figure**—called the **external financing required**—of $8,293 is needed to bring the statement into balance. This means that the firm will have to obtain about $8,300 of additional external financing to support the increased sales level of $135,000 for 2010.

A *positive* value for "external financing required," like that shown in Table 16, means that, based on its plans, the firm will not generate enough internal financing to support its forecast growth in assets. To support the forecast level of operation, the firm must raise funds externally by using debt and/or equity financing or by reducing dividends. Once the form of financing is determined, the

9. The judgmental approach represents an improved version of the *percent-of-sales approach* to pro forma balance sheet preparation. Because the judgmental approach requires only slightly more information and should yield better estimates than the somewhat naive percent-of-sales approach, it is presented here.

TABLE 16	A Pro Forma Balance Sheet, Using the Judgmental Approach, for Vectra Manufacturing (December 31, 2010)				

Assets			Liabilities and Stockholders' Equity		
Cash		$ 6,000	Accounts payable		$ 8,100
Marketable securities		4,000	Taxes payable		455
Accounts receivable		16,875	Notes payable		8,300
Inventories			Other current liabilities		3,400
Raw materials	$ 4,000		Total current liabilities		$ 20,255
Finished goods	12,000		Long-term debt		$ 18,000
Total inventory		16,000	Stockholders' equity		
Total current assets		$ 42,875	Common stock		$ 30,000
Net fixed assets		$ 63,000	Retained earnings		$ 29,327
Total assets		$105,875	Total		$ 97,582
			External financing required[a]		$ 8,293
			Total liabilities and stockholders' equity		$105,875

[a]The amount of external financing needed to force the firm's balance sheet to balance. Because of the nature of the judgmental approach, the balance sheet is not expected to balance without some type of adjustment.

pro forma balance sheet is modified to replace "external financing required" with the planned increases in the debt and/or equity accounts.

A *negative* value for "external financing required" indicates that, based on its plans, the firm will generate more financing internally than it needs to support its forecast growth in assets. In this case, funds are available for use in repaying debt, repurchasing stock, or increasing dividends. Once the specific actions are determined, "external financing required" is replaced in the pro forma balance sheet with the planned reductions in the debt and/or equity accounts. Obviously, besides being used to prepare the pro forma balance sheet, the judgmental approach is frequently used specifically to estimate the firm's financing requirements.

REVIEW QUESTIONS

17 Describe the *judgmental approach* for simplified preparation of the pro forma balance sheet.

18 What is the significance of the "plug" figure, *external financing required?* Differentiate between strategies associated with positive values and with negative values for external financing required.

7 | Evaluation of Pro Forma Statements

It is difficult to forecast the many variables involved in preparing pro forma statements. As a result, investors, lenders, and managers frequently use the techniques presented in this chapter to make rough estimates of pro forma financial statements. Yet, it is important to recognize the basic weaknesses of these simplified approaches. The weaknesses lie in two assumptions: (1) that the firm's past financial condition is an accurate indicator of its future, and (2) that certain variables (such as cash, accounts receivable, and inventories) can be forced to take on certain "desired" values. These assumptions cannot be justified solely on the basis of their ability to simplify the calculations involved. However, despite their weaknesses, the simplified approaches to pro forma statement preparation are likely to remain popular because of their relative simplicity. The widespread use of spreadsheets certainly helps to streamline the financial planning process.

However pro forma statements are prepared, analysts must understand how to use them to make financial decisions. Both financial managers and lenders can use pro forma statements to analyze the firm's inflows and outflows of cash, as well as its liquidity, activity, debt, profitability, and market value. Various ratios can be calculated from the pro forma income statement and balance sheet to evaluate performance. Cash inflows and outflows can be evaluated by preparing a pro forma statement of cash flows. After analyzing the pro forma statements, the financial manager can take steps to adjust planned operations to achieve short-term financial goals. For example, if projected profits on the pro forma income statement are too low, a variety of pricing and/or cost-cutting actions might be initiated. If the projected level of accounts receivable on the pro forma balance sheet is too high, changes in credit or collection policy may be called for. Pro forma statements are therefore of great importance in solidifying the firm's financial plans for the coming year.

REVIEW QUESTIONS

19 What are the two basic weaknesses of the simplified approaches to preparing pro forma statements?

20 What is the financial manager's objective in evaluating pro forma statements?

Summary

Focus on Value

Cash flow, the lifeblood of the firm, is a key determinant of the value of the firm. The financial manager must plan and manage the firm's cash flow. The goal is to ensure the firm's solvency and to generate positive cash flow for the firm's owners. Both the magnitude and the risk of the cash flows generated on behalf of the owners determine the firm's value.

To carry out the responsibility **to create value for owners,** the financial manager uses tools such as cash budgets and pro forma financial statements as part of the process of generating positive cash flow. Good financial plans should result in large free cash flows. Clearly, the financial manager must deliberately and carefully plan and manage the firm's cash flows to achieve the firm's goal of maximizing share price.

Review of Learning Goals

LG 1 **Understand tax depreciation procedures and the effect of depreciation on the firm's cash flows.** Depreciation is an important factor affecting a firm's cash flow. An asset's depreciable value and depreciable life are determined by using the MACRS standards in the federal tax code. MACRS groups assets (excluding real estate) into six property classes based on length of recovery period.

LG 2 **Discuss the firm's statement of cash flows, operating cash flow, and free cash flow.** The statement of cash flows is divided into operating, investment, and financing flows. It reconciles changes in the firm's cash flows with changes in cash and marketable securities for the period. Interpreting the statement of cash flows involves both the major categories of cash flow and the individual items of cash inflow and outflow. From a strict financial point of view, a firm's operating cash flow is defined to exclude interest; the simpler accounting view does not make this exclusion. Of greater importance is a firm's free cash flow, which is the amount of cash flow available to creditors and owners.

LG 3 **Understand the financial planning process, including long-term (strategic) financial plans and short-term (operating) financial plans.** The two key aspects of the financial planning process are cash planning and profit planning. Cash planning involves the cash budget or cash forecast. Profit planning relies on the pro forma income statement and balance sheet. Long-term (strategic) financial plans act as a guide for preparing short-term (operating) financial plans. Long-term plans tend to cover periods ranging from 2 to 10 years; short-term plans most often cover a 1- to 2-year period.

LG 4 **Discuss the cash-planning process and the preparation, evaluation, and use of the cash budget.** The cash-planning process uses the cash budget, based on a sales forecast, to estimate short-term cash surpluses and shortages. The cash budget is typically prepared for a 1-year period divided into months. It nets cash receipts and disbursements for each period to calculate net cash flow. Ending cash is estimated by adding beginning cash to the net cash flow. By subtracting the desired minimum cash balance from the ending cash, the firm can determine required total financing or the excess cash balance. To cope with uncertainty in the cash budget, scenario analysis or simulation can be used. A firm must also consider its pattern of daily cash receipts and cash disbursements.

LG 5 **Explain the simplified procedures used to prepare and evaluate the pro forma income statement and the pro forma balance sheet.** A pro forma income statement can be developed by calculating past percentage relationships between certain cost and expense items and the firm's sales and then applying these percentages to forecasts. Because this approach implies that all costs and expenses are variable, it tends to understate profits when sales are increasing and to overstate profits when sales are decreasing. This problem can be avoided by breaking down costs and expenses into fixed and variable components. In this case, the fixed components remain unchanged from the most recent year, and the variable costs and expenses are forecast on a percent-of-sales basis.

Under the judgmental approach, the values of certain balance sheet accounts are estimated and the firm's external financing is used as a balancing, or "plug," figure. A positive value for "external financing required" means that the firm will not generate enough internal financing to support its forecast growth in assets and will have to raise funds externally or reduce dividends. A negative value for "external financing required" indicates that the firm will generate more financing internally than it needs to support its forecast growth in assets and funds will be available for use in repaying debt, repurchasing stock, or increasing dividends.

LG 6 **Evaluate the simplified approaches to pro forma financial statement preparation and the common uses of pro forma statements.** Simplified approaches for preparing pro forma statements assume that the firm's past financial condition is an accurate indicator of the future. Pro forma statements are commonly used to forecast and analyze the firm's level of profitability and overall financial performance so that adjustments can be made to planned operations to achieve short-term financial goals.

Self-Test Problems

  ST3–1 **Depreciation and cash flow** A firm expects to have earnings before interest and taxes (EBIT) of $160,000 in each of the next 6 years. It pays annual interest of $15,000. The firm is considering the purchase of an asset that costs $140,000, requires $10,000 in installation cost, and has a recovery period of 5 years. It will be the firm's only asset, and the asset's depreciation is already reflected in its EBIT estimates.
a. Calculate the annual depreciation for the asset purchase using the MACRS depreciation percentages in Table 2.
b. Calculate the annual operating cash flows for each of the 6 years, using both the accounting and the finance definitions of *operating cash flow*. Assume that the firm is subject to a 40% ordinary tax rate.
c. Suppose the firm's net fixed assets, current assets, accounts payable, and accruals had the following values at the start and end of the final year (year 6). Calculate the firm's free cash flow (FCF) for that year.

Account	Year 6 start	Year 6 end
Net fixed assets	$ 7,500	$ 0
Current assets	90,000	110,000
Accounts payable	40,000	45,000
Accruals	8,000	7,000

d. Compare and discuss the significance of each value calculated in parts **b** and **c**.

ST3–2 **Cash budget and pro forma balance sheet inputs** Jane McDonald, a financial analyst for Carroll Company, has prepared the following sales and cash disbursement estimates for the period February–June of the current year.

Month	Sales	Cash disbursements
February	$500	$400
March	600	300
April	400	600
May	200	500
June	200	200

McDonald notes that historically, 30% of sales have been for cash. Of *credit sales*, 70% are collected 1 month after the sale, and the remaining 30% are collected 2 months after the sale. The firm wishes to maintain a minimum ending balance in its cash account of $25. Balances above this amount would be invested in short-term government securities (marketable securities), whereas any deficits would be financed through short-term bank borrowing (notes payable). The beginning cash balance at April 1 is $115.

a. Prepare a cash budget for April, May, and June.

b. How much financing, if any, at a maximum would Carroll Company require to meet its obligations during this 3-month period?

c. A pro forma balance sheet dated at the end of June is to be prepared from the information presented. Give the size of each of the following: cash, notes payable, marketable securities, and accounts receivable.

ST3–3 **Pro forma income statement** Euro Designs, Inc., expects sales during 2010 to rise from the 2009 level of $3.5 million to $3.9 million. Because of a scheduled large loan payment, the interest expense in 2010 is expected to drop to $325,000. The firm plans to increase its cash dividend payments during 2010 to $320,000. The company's year-end 2009 income statement is below.

Euro Designs, Inc. Income Statement for the Year Ended December 31, 2009	
Sales revenue	$3,500,000
Less: Cost of goods sold	1,925,000
Gross profits	$1,575,000
Less: Operating expenses	420,000
Operating profits	$1,155,000
Less: Interest expense	400,000
Net profits before taxes	$ 755,000
Less: Taxes (rate = 40%)	302,000
Net profits after taxes	$ 453,000
Less: Cash dividends	250,000
To retained earnings	$ 203,000

a. Use the *percent-of-sales method* to prepare a 2010 pro forma income statement for Euro Designs, Inc.
b. Explain why the statement may underestimate the company's actual 2010 pro forma income.

Warm-Up Exercises

A blue box (■) indicates exercises available in .

E3-1 The installed cost of a new computerized controller was $65,000. Calculate the depreciation schedule by year assuming a recovery period of 5 years and using the appropriate MACRS depreciation percentages given in Table 2.

E3-2 Classify the following changes in each of the accounts as either an *inflow* or an *outflow* of cash. During the year (a) marketable securities increased, (b) land and buildings decreased, (c) accounts payable increased, (d) vehicles decreased, (e) accounts receivable increased, and (f) dividends were paid.

E3-3 Determine the *operating cash flow (OCF)* for Kleczka, Inc., based on the following data. (All values are in thousands of dollars.) During the year the firm had sales of $2,500, cost of goods sold totaled $1,800, operating expenses totaled $300, and depreciation expenses were $200. The firm is in the 35% tax bracket.

E3-4 During the year, Xero, Inc., experienced an increase in net fixed assets of $300,000 and had depreciation of $200,000. It also experienced an increase in current assets of $150,000 and an increase in accounts payable and accruals of $75,000. If operating cash flow (OCF) for the year was $700,000, calculate the firm's *free cash flow (FCF)* for the year.

E3-5 Rimier Corp. forecasts sales of $650,000 for 2010. Assume the firm has fixed costs of $250,000 and variable costs amounting to 35% of sales. Operating expenses are estimated to include fixed costs of $28,000 and a variable portion equal to 7.5% of sales. Interest expenses for the coming year are estimated to be $20,000. Estimate Rimier's net profits before taxes for 2010.

Problems

A blue box (■) indicates problems available in 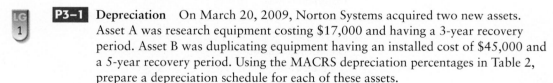.

P3-1 **Depreciation** On March 20, 2009, Norton Systems acquired two new assets. Asset A was research equipment costing $17,000 and having a 3-year recovery period. Asset B was duplicating equipment having an installed cost of $45,000 and a 5-year recovery period. Using the MACRS depreciation percentages in Table 2, prepare a depreciation schedule for each of these assets.

P3-2 **Accounting cash flow** A firm had earnings after taxes of $50,000 in 2009. Depreciation charges were $28,000, and a $2,000 charge for amortization of a bond discount was incurred. What was the firm's accounting *cash flow from operations* (see Equation 1) during 2009?

P3-3 **Depreciation and accounting cash flow**   A firm in the third year of depreciating its only asset, which originally cost $180,000 and has a 5-year MACRS recovery period, has gathered the following data relative to the current year's operations.

Accruals	$ 15,000
Current assets	120,000
Interest expense	15,000
Sales revenue	400,000
Inventory	70,000
Total costs before depreciation, interest, and taxes	290,000
Tax rate on ordinary income	40%

    a. Use the *relevant data* to determine the accounting *cash flow from operations* (see Equation 1) for the current year.

    b. Explain the impact that depreciation, as well as any other noncash charges, has on a firm's cash flows.

 P3-4 **Classifying inflows and outflows of cash**   Classify each of the following items as an inflow (I) or an outflow (O) of cash, or as neither (N).

Item	Change ($)
Cash	+100
Accounts payable	−1,000
Notes payable	+500
Long-term debt	−2,000
Inventory	+200
Fixed assets	+400
Accounts receivable	−700
Net profits	+600
Depreciation	+100
Repurchase of stock	+600
Cash dividends	+800
Sale of stock	+1,000

 P3-5 **Finding operating and free cash flows**   Consider the balance sheets and selected data from the income statement of Keith Corporation that follow.

    a. Calculate the firm's accounting *cash flow from operations* for the year ended December 31, 2009, using Equation 1.

    b. Calculate the firm's *net operating profit after taxes (NOPAT)* for the year ended December 31, 2009, using Equation 2.

    c. Calculate the firm's *operating cash flow (OCF)* for the year ended December 31, 2009, using Equation 3.

    d. Calculate the firm's *free cash flow (FCF)* for the year ended December 31, 2009, using Equation 5.

    e. Interpret, compare, and contrast your cash flow estimates in parts **a, c,** and **d.**

Keith Corporation Balance Sheets		
	December 31	
Assets	2009	2008
Cash	$ 1,500	$ 1,000
Marketable securities	1,800	1,200
Accounts receivable	2,000	1,800
Inventories	2,900	2,800
Total current assets	$ 8,200	$ 6,800
Gross fixed assets	$29,500	$28,100
Less: Accumulated depreciation	14,700	13,100
Net fixed assets	$14,800	$15,000
Total assets	$23,000	$21,800
Liabilities and Stockholders' Equity		
Accounts payable	$ 1,600	$ 1,500
Notes payable	2,800	2,200
Accruals	200	300
Total current liabilities	$ 4,600	$ 4,000
Long-term debt	$ 5,000	$ 5,000
Common stock	$10,000	$10,000
Retained earnings	3,400	2,800
Total stockholders' equity	$13,400	$12,800
Total liabilities and stockholders' equity	$23,000	$21,800
Income Statement Data (2009)		
Depreciation expense	$1,600	
Earnings before interest and taxes (EBIT)	2,700	
Interest expense	367	
Net profits after taxes	1,400	
Tax rate	40%	

P3–6 Cash receipts A firm has actual sales of $65,000 in April and $60,000 in May. It expects sales of $70,000 in June and $100,000 in July and in August. Assuming that sales are the only source of cash inflows and that half of them are for cash and the remainder are collected evenly over the following 2 months, what are the firm's expected cash receipts for June, July, and August?

P3–7 Cash disbursements schedule Maris Brothers, Inc., needs a cash disbursement schedule for the months of April, May, and June. Use the format of Table 9 and the following information in its preparation.

Sales: February = $500,000; March = $500,000; April = $560,000; May = $610,000; June = $650,000; July = $650,000

Purchases: Purchases are calculated as 60% of the next month's sales, 10% of purchases are made in cash, 50% of purchases are paid for 1 month after purchase, and the remaining 40% of purchases are paid for 2 months after purchase.

Rent: The firm pays rent of $8,000 per month.

Wages and salaries: Base wage and salary costs are fixed at $6,000 per month plus a variable cost of 7% of the current month's sales.

Taxes: A tax payment of $54,500 is due in June.

Fixed asset outlays: New equipment costing $75,000 will be bought and paid for in April.

Interest payments: An interest payment of $30,000 is due in June.

Cash dividends: Dividends of $12,500 will be paid in April.

Principal repayments and retirements: No principal repayments or retirements are due during these months.

P3-8 **Cash budget—Basic**   Grenoble Enterprises had sales of $50,000 in March and $60,000 in April. Forecast sales for May, June, and July are $70,000, $80,000, and $100,000, respectively. The firm has a cash balance of $5,000 on May 1 and wishes to maintain a minimum cash balance of $5,000. Given the following data, prepare and interpret a cash budget for the months of May, June, and July.
(1) The firm makes 20% of sales for cash, 60% are collected in the next month, and the remaining 20% are collected in the second month following sale.
(2) The firm receives other income of $2,000 per month.
(3) The firm's actual or expected purchases, all made for cash, are $50,000, $70,000, and $80,000 for the months of May through July, respectively.
(4) Rent is $3,000 per month.
(5) Wages and salaries are 10% of the previous month's sales.
(6) Cash dividends of $3,000 will be paid in June.
(7) Payment of principal and interest of $4,000 is due in June.
(8) A cash purchase of equipment costing $6,000 is scheduled in July.
(9) Taxes of $6,000 are due in June.

PERSONAL FINANCE EXAMPLE

P3-9 **Preparation of cash budget**   Sam and Suzy Sizeman need to prepare a cash budget for the last quarter of 2010 in order to make sure they can cover their expenditures during the period. Sam and Suzy have been preparing budgets for the past several years and have been able to establish specific percentages for most of their cash outflows. These percentages are based on their take-home pay (i.e., monthly utilities normally run 5% of monthly take-home pay). The information on the next page can be used to create their fourth-quarter budget for 2010.
a. Prepare a quarterly cash budget for Sam and Suzy covering the months October through December 2010.
b. Are there are individual months that incur a deficit?
c. What is the cumulative cash surplus or deficit by the end of December 2010?

Income	
Monthly take-home pay	$4,900
Expenses	
Housing	30%
Utilities	5%
Food	10%
Transportation	7%
Medical/dental	.5%
Clothing for Oct. & Nov.	3%
Clothing for Dec.	$440
Property taxes (Nov. only)	11.5%
Appliances	1%
Personal care	2%
Entertainment for Oct. & Nov.	6%
Entertainment for Dec.	$1,500
Savings	7.5%
Other	5%
Excess cash	4.5%

P3–10 **Cash budget—Advanced** The actual sales and purchases for Xenocore, Inc., for September and October 2009, along with its forecast sales and purchases for the period November 2009 through April 2010, follow.

Year	Month	Sales	Purchases
2009	September	$210,000	$120,000
2009	October	250,000	150,000
2009	November	170,000	140,000
2009	December	160,000	100,000
2010	January	140,000	80,000
2010	February	180,000	110,000
2010	March	200,000	100,000
2010	April	250,000	90,000

The firm makes 20% of all sales for cash and collects on 40% of its sales in each of the 2 months following the sale. Other cash inflows are expected to be $12,000 in September and April, $15,000 in January and March, and $27,000 in February. The firm pays cash for 10% of its purchases. It pays for 50% of its purchases in the following month and for 40% of its purchases 2 months later.

Wages and salaries amount to 20% of the preceding month's sales. Rent of $20,000 per month must be paid. Interest payments of $10,000 are due in January and April. A principal payment of $30,000 is also due in April. The firm expects to pay cash dividends of $20,000 in January and April. Taxes of $80,000 are due in April. The firm also intends to make a $25,000 cash purchase of fixed assets in December.

a. Assuming that the firm has a cash balance of $22,000 at the beginning of November, determine the end-of-month cash balances for each month, November through April.

b. Assuming that the firm wishes to maintain a $15,000 minimum cash balance, determine the required total financing or excess cash balance for each month, November through April.

c. If the firm were requesting a line of credit to cover needed financing for the period November to April, how large would this line have to be? Explain your answer.

P3–11 **Cash flow concepts**   The following represent financial transactions that Johnsfield & Co. will be undertaking in the next planning period. For each transaction, check the statement or statements that will be affected immediately.

	Statement		
Transaction	Cash budget	Pro forma income statement	Pro forma balance sheet
Cash sale			
Credit sale			
Accounts receivable are collected			
Asset with 5-year life is purchased			
Depreciation is taken			
Amortization of goodwill is taken			
Sale of common stock			
Retirement of outstanding bonds			
Fire insurance premium is paid for the next 3 years			

P3–12 **Multiple cash budgets—Scenario analysis**   Brownstein, Inc., expects sales of $100,000 during each of the next 3 months. It will make monthly purchases of $60,000 during this time. Wages and salaries are $10,000 per month plus 5% of sales. Brownstein expects to make a tax payment of $20,000 in the next month and a $15,000 purchase of fixed assets in the second month and to receive $8,000 in cash from the sale of an asset in the third month. All sales and purchases are for cash. Beginning cash and the minimum cash balance are assumed to be zero.

a. Construct a cash budget for the next 3 months.

b. Brownstein is unsure of the sales levels, but all other figures are certain. If the most pessimistic sales figure is $80,000 per month and the most optimistic is $120,000 per month, what are the monthly minimum and maximum ending cash balances that the firm can expect for each of the 1-month periods?

c. Briefly discuss how the financial manager can use the data in parts a and b to plan for financing needs.

P3–13 **Pro forma income statement**   The marketing department of Metroline Manufacturing estimates that its sales in 2010 will be $1.5 million. Interest expense is expected to remain unchanged at $35,000, and the firm plans to pay $70,000 in cash dividends during 2010. Metroline Manufacturing's income statement for the year ended December 31, 2009, is given below, along with a breakdown of the firm's cost of goods sold and operating expenses into their fixed and variable components.

Metroline Manufacturing Income Statement for the Year Ended December 31, 2009	
Sales revenue	$1,400,000
Less: Cost of goods sold	910,000
Gross profits	$ 490,000
Less: Operating expenses	120,000
Operating profits	$ 370,000
Less: Interest expense	35,000
Net profits before taxes	$ 335,000
Less: Taxes (rate = 40%)	134,000
Net profits after taxes	$ 201,000
Less: Cash dividends	66,000
To retained earnings	$ 135,000

Metroline Manufacturing Breakdown of Costs and Expenses into Fixed and Variable Components for the Year Ended December 31, 2009	
Cost of goods sold	
Fixed cost	$210,000
Variable cost	700,000
Total cost	$910,000
Operating expenses	
Fixed expenses	$ 36,000
Variable expenses	84,000
Total expenses	$120,000

a. Use the *percent-of-sales method* to prepare a pro forma income statement for the year ended December 31, 2010.
b. Use *fixed and variable cost data* to develop a pro forma income statement for the year ended December 31, 2010.
c. Compare and contrast the statements developed in parts **a** and **b**. Which statement probably provides the better estimate of 2010 income? Explain why.

P3–14 **Pro forma balance sheet—Basic**   Leonard Industries wishes to prepare a pro forma balance sheet for December 31, 2010. The firm expects 2010 sales to total $3,000,000. The following information has been gathered.
(1) A minimum cash balance of $50,000 is desired.
(2) Marketable securities are expected to remain unchanged.
(3) Accounts receivable represent 10% of sales.
(4) Inventories represent 12% of sales.
(5) A new machine costing $90,000 will be acquired during 2010. Total depreciation for the year will be $32,000.
(6) Accounts payable represent 14% of sales.
(7) Accruals, other current liabilities, long-term debt, and common stock are expected to remain unchanged.
(8) The firm's net profit margin is 4%, and it expects to pay out $70,000 in cash dividends during 2010.

(9) The December 31, 2009, balance sheet follows.

Leonard Industries Balance Sheet December 31, 2009			
Assets		**Liabilities and Stockholders' Equity**	
Cash	$ 45,000	Accounts payable	$ 395,000
Marketable securities	15,000	Accruals	60,000
Accounts receivable	255,000	Other current liabilities	30,000
Inventories	340,000	Total current liabilities	$ 485,000
Total current assets	$ 655,000	Long-term debt	$ 350,000
Net fixed assets	$ 600,000	Common stock	$ 200,000
Total assets	$1,255,000	Retained earnings	$ 220,000
		Total liabilities and stockholders' equity	$1,255,000

a. Use the *judgmental approach* to prepare a pro forma balance sheet dated December 31, 2010, for Leonard Industries.

b. How much, if any, additional financing will Leonard Industries require in 2010? Discuss.

c. Could Leonard Industries adjust its planned 2010 dividend to avoid the situation described in part **b?** Explain how.

P3–15 **Pro forma balance sheet** Peabody & Peabody has 2009 sales of $10 million. It wishes to analyze expected performance and financing needs for 2011—2 years ahead. Given the following information, respond to parts **a** and **b.**

(1) The percents of sales for items that vary directly with sales are as follows:
Accounts receivable, 12%
Inventory, 18%
Accounts payable, 14%
Net profit margin, 3%

(2) Marketable securities and other current liabilities are expected to remain unchanged.

(3) A minimum cash balance of $480,000 is desired.

(4) A new machine costing $650,000 will be acquired in 2010, and equipment costing $850,000 will be purchased in 2011. Total depreciation in 2010 is forecast as $290,000, and in 2011 $390,000 of depreciation will be taken.

(5) Accruals are expected to rise to $500,000 by the end of 2011.

(6) No sale or retirement of long-term debt is expected.

(7) No sale or repurchase of common stock is expected.

(8) The dividend payout of 50% of net profits is expected to continue.

(9) Sales are expected to be $11 million in 2010 and $12 million in 2011.

(10) The December 31, 2009, balance sheet is on next page.

a. Prepare a pro forma balance sheet dated December 31, 2011.

b. Discuss the financing changes suggested by the statement prepared in part **a.**

Peabody & Peabody Balance Sheet December 31, 2009 ($000)			
Assets		**Liabilities and Stockholders' Equity**	
Cash	$ 400	Accounts payable	$1,400
Marketable securities	200	Accruals	400
Accounts receivable	1,200	Other current liabilities	80
Inventories	1,800	Total current liabilities	$1,880
Total current assets	$3,600	Long-term debt	$2,000
Net fixed assets	$4,000	Common equity	$3,720
Total assets	$7,600	Total liabilities and stockholders' equity	$7,600

P3–16 **Integrative—Pro forma statements** Red Queen Restaurants wishes to prepare financial plans. Use the financial statements and the other information provided in what follows to prepare the financial plans.

Red Queen Restaurants Income Statement for the Year Ended December 31, 2009	
Sales revenue	$800,000
Less: Cost of goods sold	600,000
Gross profits	$200,000
Less: Operating expenses	100,000
Net profits before taxes	$100,000
Less: Taxes (rate = 40%)	40,000
Net profits after taxes	$ 60,000
Less: Cash dividends	20,000
To retained earnings	$ 40,000

Red Queen Restaurants Balance Sheet December 31, 2009			
Assets		**Liabilities and Stockholders' Equity**	
Cash	$ 32,000	Accounts payable	$100,000
Marketable securities	18,000	Taxes payable	20,000
Accounts receivable	150,000	Other current liabilities	5,000
Inventories	100,000	Total current liabilities	$125,000
Total current assets	$300,000	Long-term debt	$200,000
Net fixed assets	$350,000	Common stock	$150,000
Total assets	$650,000	Retained earnings	$175,000
		Total liabilities and stockholders' equity	$650,000

The following financial data are also available:
(1) The firm has estimated that its sales for 2010 will be $900,000.
(2) The firm expects to pay $35,000 in cash dividends in 2010.
(3) The firm wishes to maintain a minimum cash balance of $30,000.
(4) Accounts receivable represent approximately 18% of annual sales.
(5) The firm's ending inventory will change directly with changes in sales in 2010.
(6) A new machine costing $42,000 will be purchased in 2010. Total depreciation for 2010 will be $17,000.
(7) Accounts payable will change directly in response to changes in sales in 2010.
(8) Taxes payable will equal one-fourth of the tax liability on the pro forma income statement.
(9) Marketable securities, other current liabilities, long-term debt, and common stock will remain unchanged.

a. Prepare a pro forma income statement for the year ended December 31, 2010, using the *percent-of-sales method*.

b. Prepare a pro forma balance sheet dated December 31, 2010, using the *judgmental approach*.

c. Analyze these statements, and discuss the resulting *external financing required*.

P3–17 ETHICS PROBLEM   The SEC is trying to get companies to notify the investment community more quickly when a "material change" will affect their forthcoming financial results. In what sense might a financial manager be seen as "more ethical" if he or she follows this directive and issues a press release indicating that sales will not be as high as previously anticipated?

Chapter Case

Preparing Martin Manufacturing's 2010 Pro Forma Financial Statements

To improve its competitive position, Martin Manufacturing is planning to implement a major equipment modernization program. Included will be replacement and modernization of key manufacturing equipment at a cost of $400,000 in 2010. The planned program is expected to lower the variable cost per unit of finished product. Terri Spiro, an experienced budget analyst, has been charged with preparing a forecast of the firm's 2010 financial position, assuming replacement and modernization of manufacturing equipment. She plans to use the 2009 financial statements presented and the key projected financial data summarized in the following tables.

Martin Manufacturing Company Income Statement for the Year Ended December 31, 2009		
Sales revenue		$5,075,000
Less: Cost of goods sold		3,704,000
Gross profits		$1,371,000
Less: Operating expenses		
Selling expense	$650,000	
General and administrative expenses	416,000	
Depreciation expense	152,000	
Total operating expense		1,218,000
Operating profits		$ 153,000
Less: Interest expense		93,000
Net profits before taxes		$ 60,000
Less: Taxes (rate = 40%)		24,000
Net profits after taxes		$ 36,000
Less: Preferred stock dividends		3,000
Earnings available for common stockholders		$ 33,000
Earnings per share (EPS)		$0.33

Martin Manufacturing Company Balance Sheets		
	December 31	
Assets	2009	2008
Current assets		
Cash	$ 25,000	$ 24,100
Accounts receivable	805,556	763,900
Inventories	700,625	763,445
Total current assets	$1,531,181	$1,551,445
Gross fixed assets (at cost)	$2,093,819	$1,691,707
Less: Accumulated depreciation	500,000	348,000
Net fixed assets	$1,593,819	$1,343,707
Total assets	$3,125,000	$2,895,152
Liabilities and Stockholders' Equity		
Current liabilities		
Accounts payable	$ 230,000	$ 400,500
Notes payable	311,000	370,000
Accruals	75,000	100,902
Total current liabilities	$ 616,000	$ 871,402
Long-term debt	$1,165,250	$ 700,000
Total liabilities	$1,781,250	$1,571,402
Stockholders' equity		
Preferred stock (2,500 shares, $1.20 dividend)	$ 50,000	$ 50,000
Common stock (100,000 shares at $4 par)[a]	400,000	400,000
Paid-in capital in excess of par value	593,750	593,750
Retained earnings	300,000	280,000
Total stockholders' equity	$1,343,750	$1,323,750
Total liabilities and stockholders' equity	$3,125,000	$2,895,152

[a]The firm's 100,000 outstanding shares of common stock closed 2009 at a price of $11.38 per share.

Martin Manufacturing Company Key Projected Financial Data (2010)	
Data item	**Value**
Sales revenue	$6,500,000
Minimum cash balance	$25,000
Inventory turnover (times)	7.0
Average collection period	50 days
Fixed-asset purchases	$400,000
Total dividend payments (preferred and common)	$20,000
Depreciation expense	$185,000
Interest expense	$97,000
Accounts payable increase	20%
Accruals and long-term debt	Unchanged
Notes payable, preferred and common stock	Unchanged

To Do

a. Use the historical and projected financial data provided to prepare a pro forma income statement for the year ended December 31, 2010. (*Hint:* Use the *percent-of-sales method* to estimate all values *except* depreciation expense and interest expense, which have been estimated by management and included in the table.)

b. Use the projected financial data along with relevant data from the pro forma income statement prepared in part **a** to prepare the pro forma balance sheet at December 31, 2010. (*Hint:* Use the *judgmental approach*.)

c. Will Martin Manufacturing Company need to obtain *external financing* to fund the proposed equipment modernization program? Explain.

Spreadsheet Exercise

You have been assigned the task of putting together a statement for the ACME Company that shows its expected inflows and outflows of cash over the months of July 2010 through December 2010.

You have been given the following data for ACME Company:

1. Expected gross sales for May through December, respectively, are $300,000, $290,000, $425,000, $500,000, $600,000, $625,000, $650,000, and $700,000.

2. 12% of the sales in any given month are collected during that month. However, the firm has a credit policy of 3/10 net 30, so factor a 3% discount into the current month's sales collection.

3. 75% of the sales in any given month are collected during the following month after the sale.

4. 13% of the sales in any given month are collected during the second month following the sale.

5. The expected purchases of raw materials in any given month are based on 60% of the expected sales during the following month.

6. The firm pays 100% of its current month's raw materials purchases in the following month.

7. Wages and salaries are paid on a monthly basis and are based on 6% of the current month's expected sales.

8. Monthly lease payments are 2% of the current month's expected sales.

9. The monthly advertising expense amounts to 3% of sales.

10. R&D expenditures are expected to be allocated to August, September, and October at the rate of 12% of sales in those months.

11. During December a prepayment of insurance for the following year will be made in the amount of $24,000.

12. During the months of July through December, the firm expects to have miscellaneous expenditures of $15,000, $20,000, $25,000, $30,000, $35,000, and $40,000, respectively.

13. Taxes will be paid in September in the amount of $40,000 and in December in the amount of $45,000.

14. The beginning cash balance in July is $15,000.

15. The target cash balance is $15,000.

16. The firm can invest its surplus cash to earn a 6% annual return.

To Do

a. Prepare a cash budget for July 2010 through December 2010 by creating a combined spreadsheet that incorporates spreadsheets similar to those in Tables 8, 9, and 10. Divide your spreadsheet into three sections:
   (1) Collections from sales and payments to purchase inventory
   (2) Operating expenditures over the time period
   (3) Cash budget covering the period of July through December

   The cash budget should reflect the following:
   (1) Beginning and ending monthly cash balances
   (2) The month(s) in which there will be a cash deficit
   (3) The month(s) which there will be a cash surplus
   (4) The cumulative cash deficit and/or cash surplus

b. Based on your analysis, briefly describe the outlook for this company over the next 6 months. Discuss its specific obligations and the funds available to meet them. What could the firm do in the case of a cash deficit? (Where could it get the money?) What should the firm do if it has a cash surplus?

Web Exercise

Go to the text's companion website at **www.prenhall.com/gitman** to find the Web Exercise for this chapter.

> Remember to check the text's website at **www.prenhall.com/gitman** to find additional resources, including Web Exercises and a Web Case.

Solutions to Self-Test Problems

ST3–1 **a.** Depreciation Schedule

Year	Cost[a] (1)	Percentages (from Table 3.2) (2)	Depreciation [(1) × (2)] (3)
1	$150,000	20%	$ 30,000
2	150,000	32	48,000
3	150,000	19	28,500
4	150,000	12	18,000
5	150,000	12	18,000
6	150,000	5	7,500
	Totals	100%	$150,000

[a]$140,000 asset cost + $10,000 installation cost.

b. Accounting definition:

Year	EBIT (1)	Interest (2)	Net profits before taxes [(1) − (2)] (3)	Taxes [0.40 × (3)] (4)	Net profits after taxes [(3) − (4)] (5)	Depreciation (from part a, col. 3) (6)	Cash flows from operations [(5) + (6)] (7)
1	$160,000	$15,000	$145,000	$58,000	$87,000	$30,000	$117,000
2	160,000	15,000	145,000	58,000	87,000	48,000	135,000
3	160,000	15,000	145,500	58,000	87,000	28,500	115,500
4	160,000	15,000	145,000	58,000	87,000	18,000	105,000
5	160,000	15,000	145,000	58,000	87,000	18,000	105,000
6	160,000	15,000	145,500	58,000	87,000	7,500	94,500

Financial definition:

Year	EBIT (1)	NOPAT [(1) × (1 − 0.40)] (2)	Depreciation (3)	Operating cash flows [(2) + (3)] (4)
1	$160,000	$96,000	$30,000	$126,000
2	160,000	96,000	48,000	144,000
3	160,000	96,000	28,500	124,500
4	160,000	96,000	18,000	114,000
5	160,000	96,000	18,000	114,000
6	160,000	96,000	7,500	103,500

c. Change in net fixed assets in year 6 = $0 − $7,500 = −$7,500

NFAI in year 6 = −$7,500 + $7,500 = $0

Change in current assets in year 6 = $110,000 − $90,000 = $20,000

Change in (Accounts payable + Accruals) in year 6 = ($45,000 + $7,000) − ($40,000 + $8,000) = $52,000 − $48,000 = $4,000

NCAI in year 6 = $20,000 − $4,000 = $16,000

For year 6

FCF = OCF − NFAI − NCAI

= $103,500* − $0 − $16,000 = $87,500

*From part **b** financial definition, column 4 value for year 6.

d. In part **b** we can see that in each of the six years, the operating cash flow is greater when viewed from a financial perspective than when viewed from a strict accounting point of view. This difference results from the fact that the accounting definition includes interest as an operating flow, whereas the financial definition excludes it. This causes (in this case) each year's accounting flow to be $9,000 below the financial flow; $9,000 is equal to the after-tax cost of the $15,000 annual interest, $15,000 × (1 − 0.40). The free cash flow (FCF) calculated in part **c** for year 6 represents the cash flow available to investors—providers of debt and equity—after covering all operating needs and paying for net fixed asset investment (NFAI) and net current asset investment (NCAI) that occurred during the year.

ST3–2 a.

	Caroll Company Cash Budget April–June					Accounts receivable at end of June	
	February	March	April	May	June	July	August
Forecast sales	$500	$600	$400	$200	$200		
Cash sales (0.30)	$150	$180	$120	$ 60	$ 60		
Collections of A/R							
Lagged 1 month [(0.7 × 0.7) = 0.49]		245	294	196	98	$ 98	
Lagged 2 months [(0.3 × 0.7) = 0.21]			105	126	84	42	$42
						$140 + $42 = $182	
Total cash receipts			$519	$382	$242		
Less: Total cash disbursements			600	500	200		
Net cash flow			($ 81)	($118)	$ 42		
Add: Beginning cash			115	34	(84)		
Ending cash			$ 34	($ 84)	($ 42)		
Less: Minimum cash balance			25	25	25		
Required total financing (notes payable)			—	$109	$ 67		
Excess cash balance (marketable securities)			$ 9	—	—		

b. Caroll Company would need a maximum of $109 in financing over the 3-month period.

c.

Account	Amount	Source of amount
Cash	$ 25	Minimum cash balance—June
Notes payable	67	Required total financing—June
Marketable securities	0	Excess cash balance—June
Accounts receivable	182	Calculation at right of cash budget statement

ST3–3 a.

Euro Designs, Inc.,
Pro Forma Income Statement
for the Year Ended December 31, 2010

Sales revenue (given)	$3,900,000
Less: Cost of goods sold (0.55)[a]	2,145,000
Gross profits	$1,755,000
Less: Operating expenses (0.12)[b]	468,000
Operating profits	$1,287,000
Less: Interest expense (given)	325,000
Net profits before taxes	$ 962,000
Less: Taxes (0.40 × $962,000)	384,800
Net profits after taxes	$ 577,200
Less: Cash dividends (given)	320,000
To retained earnings	$ 257,200

[a]From 2009: CGS/Sales = $1,925,000/$3,500,000 = 0.55.
[b]From 2009: Oper. Exp./Sales = $420,000/$3,500,000 = 0.12.

b. The percent-of-sales method may underestimate actual 2010 pro forma income by assuming that all costs are variable. If the firm has fixed costs, which by definition would not increase with increasing sales, the 2010 pro forma income would probably be underestimated.

Answers to Selected End-of-Chapter Problems

3–5 **b.** $1,620
c. $13,367

3–7

	April	May
	($000)	
Cash 1 month delay	168	183
Cash 2 months delay	120	134.4
Total disbursements	465.3	413.1

3–9 **c.** Cumulative cash surplus at end of October 2010: $907

3–13 **a.** To retained earnings: $146,600
b. To retained earnings: $157,400

3–14 **a.** Total assets: $1,383,000
Total current liabilities: $510,000
External funds required: $53,000

3–16 **a.** To retained earnings: $32,500
c. $11,250

Chapter 11

Chapter 1

Capital Budgeting
Cash Flows

From Chapter 8 of *Principles of Managerial Finance*, Brief 5th Edition. Lawrence J. Gitman. Copyright © 2009 by Pearson Prentice Hall. All rights reserved.

Capital Budgeting Cash Flows

LEARNING GOALS

LG 1 Understand the key motives for capital expenditure and the steps in the capital budgeting process.

LG 2 Define basic capital budgeting terminology.

LG 3 Discuss relevant cash flows, expansion versus replacement decisions, sunk costs and opportunity costs, and international capital budgeting.

LG 4 Calculate the initial investment associated with a proposed capital expenditure.

LG 5 Find the relevant operating cash inflows associated with a proposed capital expenditure.

LG 6 Determine the terminal cash flow associated with a proposed capital expenditure.

Before committing resources to expand, replace, or renew fixed assets or to undertake other types of long-term investments, firms carefully estimate and analyze the expected costs and benefits associated with these expenditures. This evaluation and selection process is called capital budgeting. This chapter describes important aspects of the steps in the capital budgeting decision process and explains how the key cash flows that are inputs to it are developed.

1 | Capital Budgeting Decision Process

Long-term investments represent sizable outlays of funds that commit a firm to some course of action. Consequently, the firm needs procedures to analyze and properly select its long-term investments. It must be able to measure cash flows and apply appropriate decision techniques. As time passes, fixed assets may become obsolete or may require an overhaul; at these points, too, financial decisions may be required. **Capital budgeting** is the process of evaluating and selecting long-term investments that are consistent with the firm's goal of maximizing owner wealth. Firms typically make a variety of long-term investments, but the most common for the manufacturing firm is in *fixed assets,* which include property (land), plant, and equipment. These assets, often referred to as *earning assets,* generally provide the basis for the firm's earning power and value.

Because firms treat capital budgeting (investment) and financing decisions *separately,* this chapter will concentrate on fixed-asset acquisition without regard to the specific method of financing used. We begin by discussing the motives for capital expenditure.

Motives for Capital Expenditure

A **capital expenditure** is an outlay of funds by the firm that is expected to produce benefits over a period of time *greater than* 1 year. An **operating expenditure** is an outlay resulting in benefits received *within* 1 year. Fixed-asset outlays are capital expenditures, but not all capital expenditures are classified as fixed assets. A $60,000 outlay for a new machine with a usable life of 15 years is a capital expenditure that would appear as a fixed asset on the firm's balance sheet. A $60,000 outlay for an advertising campaign that is expected to produce benefits over a long period is also a capital expenditure, but would rarely be shown as a fixed asset.

Companies make capital expenditures for many reasons. The basic motives for capital expenditures are to expand operations, replace or renew fixed assets, or to obtain some other, less tangible benefit over a long period. Table 1 briefly describes the key motives for making capital expenditures.

Steps in the Process

The **capital budgeting process** consists of five distinct but interrelated steps.

1. *Proposal generation.* Proposals are made at all levels within a business organization and are reviewed by finance personnel. Proposals that require large outlays are more carefully scrutinized than less costly ones.

---

capital budgeting
The process of evaluating and selecting long-term investments that are consistent with the firm's goal of maximizing owner wealth.

capital expenditure
An outlay of funds by the firm that is expected to produce benefits over a period of time *greater than* 1 year.

operating expenditure
An outlay of funds by the firm resulting in benefits received *within* 1 year.

capital budgeting process
Five distinct but interrelated steps: *proposal generation, review and analysis, decision making, implementation,* and *follow-up.*

423

TABLE 1	Key Motives for Making Capital Expenditures
Motive	Description
Expansion	The most common motive for a capital expenditure is to expand the level of operations—usually through acquisition of fixed assets. A growing firm often needs to acquire new fixed assets rapidly, as in the purchase of property and plant facilities.
Replacement or renewal	As a firm's growth slows and it reaches maturity, most capital expenditures will be made to increase efficiency by replacing or renewing obsolete or worn-out assets. Renewal may involve rebuilding, over-hauling, or retrofitting an existing fixed asset. Each time a machine requires a major repair, the outlay for the repair should be compared to the outlay to replace the machine and the benefits of replacement.
Other purposes	Some capital expenditures do not result in the acquisition or transformation of tangible fixed assets. Instead, they involve a long-term commitment of funds in expectation of a future return. These expenditures include outlays for advertising campaigns, research and development, management consulting, and new products.

2. *Review and analysis.* Formal review and analysis is performed to assess the appropriateness of proposals and evaluate their economic viability. Once the analysis is complete, a summary report is submitted to decision makers.
3. *Decision making.* Firms typically delegate capital expenditure decision making on the basis of dollar limits. Generally, the board of directors must authorize expenditures beyond a certain amount. Often plant managers are given authority to make decisions necessary to keep the production line moving.
4. *Implementation.* Following approval, expenditures are made and projects implemented. Expenditures for a large project often occur in phases.
5. *Follow-up.* Results are monitored, and actual costs and benefits are compared with those that were expected. Action may be required if actual outcomes differ from projected ones.

Each step in the process is important. Review and analysis and decision making (Steps 2 and 3) consume the majority of time and effort, however. Follow-up (Step 5) is an important but often ignored step aimed at allowing the firm to improve the accuracy of its cash flow estimates continuously. Because of their fundamental importance, this and the following chapters give primary consideration to review and analysis and to decision making.

Personal Finance Example Individuals can approach the acquisition of major assets much as do corporations. Using the five-step process:

1. A personal financial plan or a special situation initiates the proposed asset purchase. For example, your personal financial plan specifies a new car purchase in 2010.
2. Review and analyze the proposed asset purchase to isolate attractive alternatives in terms of features and costs. For the car purchase, you would shop for cars with the desired features and costs that are consistent with the budgeted amount.
3. Compare the features and costs of the alternative assets and choose the preferred alternative. That is, you would decide which car you are going to buy.
4. Make the purchase. This would involve arranging financing/payment for the car, possibly negotiating a trade-in price, closing the transaction, and taking delivery of the new car.

5. Compare the actual asset performance to its expected performance. You would assess how well the new car meets your expectations. If the actual performance fails to meet expectations, you might consider new alternatives (e.g., trade in the car).

Basic Terminology

Before we develop the concepts, techniques, and practices related to the capital budgeting process, we need to explain some basic terminology. In addition, we will present some key assumptions that are used to simplify the discussion in the remainder of this chapter.

Independent versus Mutually Exclusive Projects

independent projects
Projects whose cash flows are unrelated or independent of one another; the acceptance of one *does not eliminate* the others from further consideration.

mutually exclusive projects
Projects that compete with one another, so that the acceptance of one *eliminates* from further consideration all other projects that serve a similar function.

The two most common types of projects are (1) independent projects and (2) mutually exclusive projects. **Independent projects** are those whose cash flows are unrelated or independent of one another; the acceptance of one *does not eliminate* the others from further consideration. **Mutually exclusive projects** are those that have the same function and therefore compete with one another. The acceptance of one *eliminates* from further consideration all other projects that serve a similar function. For example, a firm in need of increased production capacity could obtain it by (1) expanding its plant, (2) acquiring another company, or (3) contracting with another company for production. Clearly, accepting any one option eliminates the need for either of the others.

Unlimited Funds versus Capital Rationing

unlimited funds
The financial situation in which a firm is able to accept all independent projects that provide an acceptable return.

capital rationing
The financial situation in which a firm has only a fixed number of dollars available for capital expenditures, and numerous projects compete for these dollars.

The availability of funds for capital expenditures affects the firm's decisions. If a firm has **unlimited funds** for investment, making capital budgeting decisions is quite simple: All independent projects that will provide an acceptable return can be accepted. Typically, though, firms operate under **capital rationing** instead. This means that they have only a fixed number of dollars available for capital expenditures and that numerous projects will compete for these dollars. The discussions that follow here assume unlimited funds.

Accept–Reject versus Ranking Approaches

accept–reject approach
The evaluation of capital expenditure proposals to determine whether they meet the firm's minimum acceptance criterion.

ranking approach
The ranking of capital expenditure projects on the basis of some predetermined measure, such as the rate of return.

Two basic approaches to capital budgeting decisions are available. The **accept–reject approach** involves evaluating capital expenditure proposals to determine whether they meet the firm's minimum acceptance criterion. This approach can be used when the firm has unlimited funds, as a preliminary step when evaluating mutually exclusive projects, or in a situation in which capital must be rationed. In these cases, only acceptable projects should be considered.

The second method, the **ranking approach**, involves ranking projects on the basis of some predetermined measure, such as the rate of return. The project with the highest return is ranked first, and the project with the lowest return is ranked last. Only acceptable projects should be ranked. Ranking is useful in selecting the "best" of a group of mutually exclusive projects and in evaluating projects with a view to capital rationing.

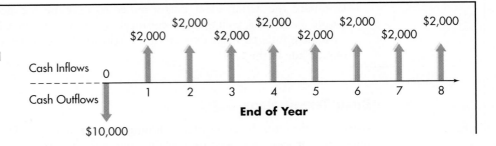

FIGURE 1

Conventional Cash Flow
Time line for a conventional
cash flow pattern

Conventional versus Nonconventional Cash Flow Patterns

Cash flow patterns associated with capital investment projects can be classified as *conventional* or *nonconventional*. A **conventional cash flow pattern** consists of an initial outflow followed only by a series of inflows. For example, a firm may spend $10,000 today and as a result expect to receive equal annual cash inflows (an annuity) of $2,000 each year for the next 8 years, as depicted on the timeline in Figure 1.[1] A conventional cash flow pattern that provides a mixed stream of cash inflows is depicted in Figure 3.

conventional cash flow pattern
An initial outflow followed only by a series of inflows.

A **nonconventional cash flow pattern** is one in which an initial outflow is followed by a series of inflows *and* outflows. For example, the purchase of a machine may require an initial cash outflow of $20,000 and may generate cash inflows of $5,000 each year for 4 years. In the fifth year after purchase, an outflow of $8,000 may be required to overhaul the machine, after which it generates inflows of $5,000 each year for 5 more years. This nonconventional pattern is illustrated on the time line in Figure 2.

nonconventional cash flow pattern
An initial outflow followed by a series of inflows *and* outflows.

Difficulties often arise in evaluating projects with nonconventional patterns of cash flow. *The discussions in the remainder of this chapter are therefore limited to the evaluation of conventional cash flow patterns.*

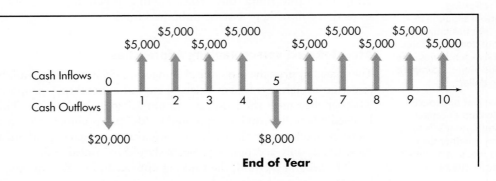

FIGURE 2

Nonconventional Cash Flow
Time line for a nonconventional cash flow pattern

---

1. Arrows rather than plus or minus signs are frequently used on time lines to distinguish between cash inflows and cash outflows. Upward-pointing arrows represent cash inflows (positive cash flows), and downward-pointing arrows represent cash outflows (negative cash flows).

REVIEW QUESTIONS

1 What is *capital budgeting?* Do all capital expenditures involve fixed assets? Explain.

2 What are the key motives for making capital expenditures? Discuss, compare, and contrast them.

3 What are the five steps involved in the capital budgeting process?

4 Differentiate between the members of each of the following pairs of capital budgeting terms: (**a**) independent versus mutually exclusive projects; (**b**) unlimited funds versus capital rationing; (**c**) accept–reject versus ranking approaches; and (**d**) conventional versus nonconventional cash flow patterns.

---

 2 | # Relevant Cash Flows

relevant cash flows
The *incremental cash outflow (investment) and resulting subsequent inflows* associated with a proposed capital expenditure.

incremental cash flows
The *additional* cash flows—outflows or inflows—expected to result from a proposed capital expenditure.

To evaluate capital expenditure alternatives, the firm must determine the **relevant cash flows.** These are the *incremental cash outflow (investment) and resulting subsequent inflows.* The **incremental cash flows** represent the *additional* cash flows—outflows or inflows—expected to result from a proposed capital expenditure. Cash flows rather than accounting figures are used, because cash flows directly affect the firm's ability to pay bills and purchase assets.

The remainder of this chapter is devoted to the procedures for measuring the relevant cash flows associated with proposed capital expenditures.

Major Cash Flow Components

The cash flows of any project having the *conventional pattern* can include three basic components: (1) an initial investment, (2) operating cash inflows, and (3) terminal cash flow. All projects—whether for expansion, replacement or renewal, or some other purpose—have the first two components. Some, however, lack the final component, terminal cash flow.

initial investment
The relevant cash outflow for a proposed project at time zero.

Figure 3 depicts on a time line the cash flows for a project. The **initial investment** for the proposed project is $50,000. This is the relevant cash outflow at time

---

FIGURE 3

Cash Flow Components
Time line for major cash flow components

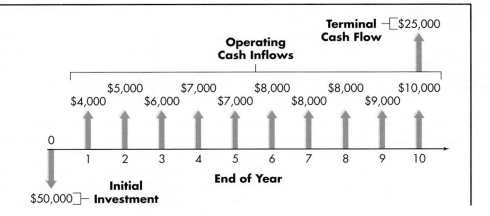

---

operating cash inflows
The incremental after-tax cash inflows resulting from implementation of a project during its life.

terminal cash flow
The after-tax nonoperating cash flow occurring in the final year of a project. It is usually attributable to liquidation of the project.

zero. The **operating cash inflows**, which are the incremental after-tax cash inflows resulting from implementation of the project during its life, gradually increase from $4,000 in its first year to $10,000 in its tenth and final year. The **terminal cash flow** is the after-tax nonoperating cash flow occurring in the final year of the project. It is usually attributable to liquidation of the project. In this case it is $25,000, received at the end of the project's 10-year life. Note that the terminal cash flow does *not* include the $10,000 operating cash inflow for year 10.

Expansion versus Replacement Decisions

Developing relevant cash flow estimates is most straightforward in the case of *expansion decisions*. In this case, the initial investment, operating cash inflows, and terminal cash flow are merely the after-tax cash outflow and inflows associated with the proposed capital expenditure.

Identifying relevant cash flows for *replacement decisions* is more complicated, because the firm must identify the *incremental* cash outflow and inflows that would result from the proposed replacement. The initial investment in the case of replacement is the difference between the initial investment needed to acquire the new asset and any after-tax cash inflows expected from liquidation of the old asset. The operating cash inflows are the difference between the operating cash inflows from the new asset and those from the old asset. The terminal cash flow is the difference between the after-tax cash flows expected upon termination of the new and the old assets. These relationships are shown in Figure 4.

Actually, all capital budgeting decisions can be viewed as replacement decisions. *Expansion decisions are merely replacement decisions in which all cash flows from the old asset are zero.* In light of this fact, this chapter focuses primarily on replacement decisions.

Sunk Costs and Opportunity Costs

When estimating the relevant cash flows associated with a proposed capital expenditure, the firm must recognize any sunk costs and opportunity costs. These costs are easy to mishandle or ignore, particularly when determining a project's incremental cash flows. **Sunk costs** are cash outlays that have already been made (past outlays) and therefore have no effect on the cash flows relevant to the current decision. As a result, *sunk costs should not be included in a project's incremental cash flows.*

Opportunity costs are cash flows that could be realized from the best alternative use of an owned asset. They therefore represent cash flows that *will not be realized* as a result of employing that asset in the proposed project. Because of this, any *opportunity costs should be included as cash outflows when one is determining a project's incremental cash flows.*

sunk costs
Cash outlays that have already been made (past outlays) and therefore have no effect on the cash flows relevant to a current decision.

opportunity costs
Cash flows that could be realized from the best alternative use of an owned asset.

Example

Jankow Equipment is considering renewing its drill press X12, which it purchased 3 years earlier for $237,000, by retrofitting it with the computerized control system from an obsolete piece of equipment it owns. The obsolete equipment could be sold today for a high bid of $42,000, but without its computerized control system, it would be worth nothing. Jankow is in the process of estimating the

FIGURE 4

Relevant Cash Flows for Replacement Decisions
Calculation of the three components of relevant cash flow for a replacement decision

| Initial investment | = | Initial investment needed to acquire new asset | − | After-tax cash inflows from liquidation of old asset |

| Operating cash inflows | = | Operating cash inflows from new asset | − | Operating cash inflows from old asset |

| Terminal cash flow | = | After-tax cash flows from termination of new asset | − | After-tax cash flows from termination of old asset |

Hint Sunk costs and opportunity costs are concepts you must fully understand. Funds already spent are irrelevant to future decisions, but the returns given up so that an existing asset can be used in a given project *are* considered a relevant cost.

labor and materials costs of retrofitting the system to drill press X12 and the benefits expected from the retrofit. The $237,000 cost of drill press X12 is a *sunk cost* because it represents an earlier cash outlay. It *would not be included* as a cash outflow when determining the cash flows relevant to the retrofit decision. Although Jankow owns the obsolete piece of equipment, the proposed use of its computerized control system represents an *opportunity cost* of $42,000—the highest price at which it could be sold today. This opportunity cost *would be included* as a cash outflow associated with using the computerized control system.

International Capital Budgeting and Long-Term Investments

Although the same basic capital budgeting principles are used for domestic and international projects, several additional factors must be addressed in evaluating foreign investment opportunities. International capital budgeting differs from the domestic version because (1) cash outflows and inflows occur in a foreign currency, and (2) foreign investments entail potentially significant political risk. Both of these risks can be minimized through careful planning.

Companies face both long-term and short-term *currency risks* related to both the invested capital and the cash flows resulting from it. Long-term currency risk can be minimized by financing the foreign investment at least partly in the local capital markets. This step ensures that the project's revenues, operating costs, and financing costs will be in the local currency. Likewise, the dollar value of short-term, local-currency cash flows can be protected by using special securities and strategies such as futures, forwards, and options market instruments.

Political risks can be minimized by using both operating and financial strategies. For example, by structuring the investment as a joint venture and selecting a well-connected local partner, the U.S. company can minimize the risk of its operations being seized or harassed. Companies also can protect themselves from having their investment returns blocked by local governments by structuring the

Focus on Practice — Changes May Influence Future Investments in China

Foreign direct investment in China soared in 2006. Not including banks, insurance, and securities, foreign direct investment amounted to $63.02 billion. China's economy has surged more than tenfold since 1980, the first year it allowed foreign investments and money began pouring into factories on China's east coast.

As its exports surged, China's trade surplus swelled 74 percent in 2006 to a record $177.5 billion. With a strong foreign exchange surplus, China is no longer desperate for capital from overseas, but is now primarily interested in foreign skills and technologies. Prime Minister Wen Jiabao wants to steer investments toward the manufacturing of higher-value products and toward less-developed regions. Wen is giving tax breaks and promising speedy approvals for investments away from areas in the east, such as Shanghai and the Pearl River Delta.

Typical of foreign investors in China is Intel Capital, a subsidiary of **Intel Corporation.** In late 2005, it invested $200 million into three Chinese companies: Chipsbrand Microelectronics Co., Ltd., a semiconductor design company; Onewave Technologies, Inc., a broadband entertainment-technology solutions provider; and Versilicon Holdings Co., Ltd., an integrated-circuit design foundry. Intel Capital is no beginner at foreign investment; it has invested more than $4 billion in more than 1,000 companies around the world.

China allows three types of foreign investments: a *wholly foreign-owned enterprise* (WFOE) in which the firm is entirely funded with foreign capital; a *joint venture* in which the foreign partner must provide at least 25 percent of initial capital; and a *representative office* (RO), the most common and easily established entity, which cannot perform business activities that directly result in profits. Generally an RO is the first step in establishing a China presence and includes mechanisms for upgrading to a WFOE or joint venture.

Like any foreign investment, investing in China is not without risk. One potential risk facing foreign investors in China is the likelihood of a future tax increase. Currently, domestic (Chinese) enterprises have heavy tax burdens, while foreign investment enterprises enjoy a lower tax rate. The difference is about 13 percent and it is one reason why foreign investors favor China. A new "unified tax" proposal is expected to be enacted in 2008, and this will result in a higher tax rate for foreign investors. In addition, higher production costs due to stricter requirements on environmental protection and higher salaries for Chinese employees will also pressure foreign investors.

■ *The Chinese government has encouraged foreign investments through favorable tax treatment. Can you think of similar situations in your own country?*

financing of such investments as debt rather than as equity. Debt-service payments are legally enforceable claims, whereas equity returns (such as dividends) are not. Even if local courts do not support the claims of the U.S. company, the company can threaten to pursue its case in U.S. courts.

foreign direct investment
The transfer of capital, managerial, and technical assets to a foreign country.

In spite of the preceding difficulties, **foreign direct investment,** which involves the transfer of capital, managerial, and technical assets to a foreign country, has surged in recent years. This is evident in the growing market values of foreign assets owned by U.S.-based companies and of foreign direct investment in the United States, particularly by British, Canadian, Dutch, German, and Japanese companies. Furthermore, foreign direct investment by U.S. companies seems to be accelerating. See the *Focus on Practice* box above for a discussion of recent foreign direct investment in China.

REVIEW QUESTIONS

5 Why is it important to evaluate capital budgeting projects on the basis of *incremental cash flows?*

6 What three components of cash flow may exist for a given project? How can expansion decisions be treated as replacement decisions? Explain.

7 What effect do *sunk costs* and *opportunity costs* have on a project's incremental cash flows?

8 How can *currency risk* and *political risk* be minimized when one is making *foreign direct investment?*

---

3 | Finding the Initial Investment

The term *initial investment* as used here refers to the relevant cash outflows to be considered when evaluating a prospective capital expenditure. Because our discussion of capital budgeting is concerned only with investments that exhibit conventional cash flows, the initial investment occurs at *time zero*—the time at which the expenditure is made. The initial investment is calculated by subtracting all cash inflows occurring at time zero from all cash outflows occurring at time zero.

The basic format for determining the initial investment is given in Table 2. The cash flows that must be considered when determining the initial investment associated with a capital expenditure are the installed cost of the new asset, the after-tax proceeds (if any) from the sale of an old asset, and the change (if any) in net working capital. Note that if there are no installation costs and the firm is not replacing an existing asset, then the cost (purchase price) of the new asset, adjusted for any change in net working capital, is equal to the initial investment.

cost of new asset
The net outflow necessary to acquire a new asset.

installation costs
Any added costs that are necessary to place an asset into operation.

Installed Cost of New Asset

As shown in Table 2, the installed cost of the new asset is found by adding the cost of the new asset to its installation costs. The **cost of new asset** is the net outflow that its acquisition requires. Usually, we are concerned with the acquisition of a fixed asset for which a definite purchase price is paid. **Installation costs** are

TABLE 2	The Basic Format for Determining Initial Investment

Installed cost of new asset =
    Cost of new asset
    + Installation costs
− After-tax proceeds from sale of old asset =
    Proceeds from sale of old asset
    ∓ Tax on sale of old asset
± Change in net working capital
Initial investment

installed cost of new asset
The *cost of new asset* plus its *installation costs;* equals the asset's depreciable value.

after-tax proceeds from sale of old asset
The difference between the old asset's sale proceeds and any applicable taxes or tax refunds related to its sale.

proceeds from sale of old asset
The cash inflows, net of any *removal* or *cleanup costs,* resulting from the sale of an existing asset.

tax on sale of old asset
Tax that depends on the relationship between the old asset's sale price and *book value,* and on existing government tax rules.

book value
The strict accounting value of an asset, calculated by subtracting its accumulated depreciation from its installed cost.

any added costs that are necessary to place an asset into operation. The Internal Revenue Service (IRS) requires the firm to add installation costs to the purchase price of an asset to determine its depreciable value, which is expensed over a period of years. The **installed cost of new asset,** calculated by adding the *cost of new asset* to its *installation costs,* equals its depreciable value.

After-Tax Proceeds from Sale of Old Asset

Table 2 shows that the **after-tax proceeds from sale of old asset** decrease the firm's initial investment in the new asset. These proceeds are the difference between the old asset's sale proceeds and any applicable taxes or tax refunds related to its sale. The **proceeds from sale of old asset** are the net cash inflows it provides. This amount is net of any costs incurred in the process of removing the asset. Included in these *removal costs* are *cleanup costs,* such as those related to removal and disposal of chemical and nuclear wastes. These costs may not be trivial.

The proceeds from the sale of an old asset are normally subject to some type of tax.[2] This **tax on sale of old asset** depends on the relationship between its sale price and *book value,* and on existing government tax rules.

Book Value

The **book value** of an asset is its strict accounting value. It can be calculated by using the following equation:

$$\text{Book value} = \text{Installed cost of asset} - \text{Accumulated depreciation} \tag{1}$$

Example

Hudson Industries, a small electronics company, 2 years ago acquired a machine tool with an installed cost of $100,000. The asset was being depreciated under MACRS using a 5-year recovery period.[3] Under MACRS for a 5-year recovery period, 20% and 32% of the installed cost would be depreciated in years 1 and 2, respectively. In other words, 52% (20% + 32%) of the $100,000 cost, or $52,000 (0.52 × $100,000), would represent the accumulated depreciation at the end of year 2. Substituting into Equation 1, we get

$$\text{Book value} = \$100,000 - \$52,000 = \underline{\$48,000}$$

The book value of Hudson's asset at the end of year 2 is therefore $48,000.

Basic Tax Rules

Three potential tax situations can occur when a firm sells an asset. These situations depend on the relationship between the asset's sale price and its book value. The two key forms of taxable income and their associated tax treatments are

---

2. Because corporate capital gains and ordinary income are taxed at the same rate, for convenience, we do not differ between them in the following discussions.

3. Under current tax law, most manufacturing equipment has a 7-year recovery period. Using this recovery period results in 8 years of depreciation, which unnecessarily complicates examples and problems. To simplify, *manufacturing equipment is treated as a 5-year asset in this chapter.*

TABLE 3	Tax Treatment on Sales of Assets		
Form of taxable income	Definition	Tax treatment	Assumed tax rate
Gain on sale of asset	Portion of the sale price that is *greater than* book value.	All gains above book value are taxed as ordinary income.	40%
Loss on sale of asset	Amount by which sale price is *less than* book value.	If the asset is depreciable and used in business, loss is deducted from ordinary income.	40% of loss is a tax savings
		If the asset is *not* depreciable or is *not* used in business, loss is deductible only against capital gains.	40% of loss is a tax savings

defined and summarized in Table 3. The assumed tax rates used throughout this text are noted in the final column. There are three possible tax situations. The asset may be sold (1) for more than its book value, (2) for its book value, or (3) for less than its book value. An example will illustrate.

Example

The old asset purchased 2 years ago for $100,000 by Hudson Industries has a current book value of $48,000. What will happen if the firm now decides to sell the asset and replace it? The tax consequences depend on the sale price. Figure 5 depicts the taxable income resulting from four possible sale prices in light of the asset's initial purchase price of $100,000 and its current book value of $48,000. The taxable consequences of each of these sale prices are described below.

The sale of the asset for more than its book value If Hudson sells the old asset for $110,000, it realizes a gain of $62,000 ($110,000 − $48,000). Technically this gain is made up of two parts—a capital gain and **recaptured depreciation,** which is the portion of the sale price that is above book value and below the initial purchase price. For Hudson, the capital gain is $10,000 ($110,000 sale price − $100,000 initial purchase price); recaptured depreciation is $52,000 (the $100,000 initial purchase price − $48,000 book value).[4]

Both the $10,000 capital gain and the $52,000 recaptured depreciation are shown under the $110,000 sale price in Figure 5. The total gain above book value of $62,000 is taxed as ordinary income at the 40% rate, resulting in taxes of $24,800 (0.40 × $62,000). These taxes should be used in calculating the initial investment in the new asset, using the format in Table 2. In effect, the taxes raise the amount of the firm's initial investment in the new asset by reducing the proceeds from the sale of the old asset.

If Hudson instead sells the old asset for $70,000, it experiences a gain above book value (in the form of *recaptured depreciation*) of $22,000 ($70,000 − $48,000), as shown under the $70,000 sale price in Figure 5. This gain is taxed as ordinary income. Because the firm is assumed to be in the 40% tax bracket, the

recaptured depreciation The portion of an asset's sale price that is above its book value and below its initial purchase price.

4. Although the current tax law requires corporate capital gains to be treated as ordinary income, the structure for corporate capital gains is retained under the law to facilitate a rate differential in the likely event of future tax revisions. For clarity and convenience, this distinction is *not* made throughout the text discussions.

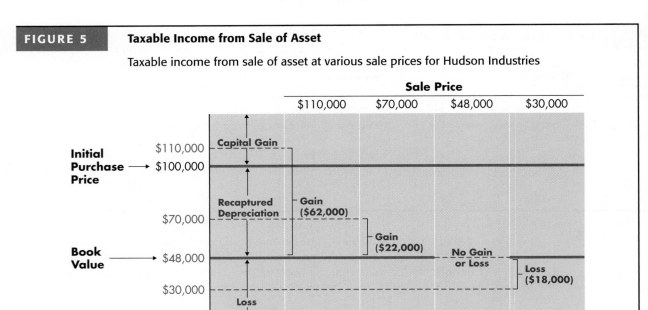

FIGURE 5   **Taxable Income from Sale of Asset**

Taxable income from sale of asset at various sale prices for Hudson Industries

taxes on the $22,000 gain are $8,800 (0.40 × $22,000). This amount in taxes should be used in calculating the initial investment in the new asset.

The sale of the asset for its book value   If the asset is sold for $48,000, its book value, the firm breaks even. There is no gain or loss, as shown under the $48,000 sale price in Figure 5. Because *no tax results from selling an asset for its book value,* there is no tax effect on the initial investment in the new asset.

The sale of the asset for less than its book value   If Hudson sells the asset for $30,000, it experiences a loss of $18,000 ($48,000 − $30,000), as shown under the $30,000 sale price in Figure 5. If this is a depreciable asset used in the business, the firm may use the loss to offset ordinary operating income. If the asset is *not* depreciable or is *not* used in the business, the firm can use the loss only to offset capital gains. In either case, the loss will save the firm $7,200 (0.40 × $18,000) in taxes. And, if current operating earnings or capital gains are not sufficient to offset the loss, the firm may be able to apply these losses to prior or future years' taxes.[5]

Change in Net Working Capital

net working capital
The amount by which a firm's current assets exceed its current liabilities.

Net working capital is the amount by which a firm's current assets exceed its current liabilities. At this point it is important to note that changes in net working capital often accompany capital expenditure decisions. If a firm acquires new

---

5. The tax law provides detailed procedures for using *tax loss carrybacks/carryforwards*. Application of such procedures to capital budgeting is beyond the scope of this text, and they are therefore ignored in subsequent discussions.

machinery to expand its level of operations, it will experience an increase in levels of cash, accounts receiv-able, inventories, accounts payable, and accruals. These increases result from the need for more cash to support expanded operations, more accounts receivable and inventories to support increased sales, and more accounts payable and accruals to support increased outlays made to meet expanded product demand. Increases in cash, accounts receivable, and invento-ries are *outflows of cash,* whereas increases in accounts payable and accruals are *inflows of cash.*

The difference between the change in current assets and the change in current liabilities is the **change in net working capital.** Generally, current assets increase by more than current liabilities, resulting in an increased investment in net working capital. This increased investment is treated as an initial outflow. If the change in net working capital were negative, it would be shown as an initial inflow. The change in net working capital—regardless of whether it is an increase or a decrease—*is not taxable* because it merely involves a net buildup or net reduction of current accounts.

change in net working capital
The difference between a change in current assets and a change in current liabilities.

Example

Danson Company, a metal products manufacturer, is contemplating expanding its operations. Financial analysts expect that the changes in current accounts summarized in Table 4 will occur and will be maintained over the life of the expansion. Current assets are expected to increase by $22,000, and current lia-bilities are expected to increase by $9,000, resulting in a $13,000 increase in net working capital. In this case, the change will represent an increased net working capital investment and will be treated as a cash outflow in calculating the initial investment.

Calculating the Initial Investment

A variety of tax and other considerations enter into the initial investment calcula-tion. The following example illustrates calculation of the initial investment according to the format in Table 2.

TABLE 4	Calculation of Change in Net Working Capital for Danson Company	
Current account	Change in balance	
Cash	+ $ 4,000	
Accounts receivable	+ 10,000	
Inventories	+ 8,000	
(1) Current assets		+$22,000
Accounts payable	+$ 7,000	
Accruals	+ 2,000	
(2) Current liabilities		+ 9,000
Change in net working capital [(1) − (2)]		+$13,000

Example

Powell Corporation, a large, diversified manufacturer of aircraft components, is trying to determine the initial investment required to replace an old machine with a new, more sophisticated model. The proposed machine's purchase price is $380,000, and an additional $20,000 will be necessary to install it. It will be depreciated under MACRS using a 5-year recovery period. The present (old) machine was purchased 3 years ago at a cost of $240,000 and was being depreciated under MACRS using a 5-year recovery period. The firm has found a buyer willing to pay $280,000 for the present machine and to remove it at the buyer's expense. The firm expects that a $35,000 increase in current assets and an $18,000 increase in current liabilities will accompany the replacement; these changes will result in a $17,000 ($35,000 − $18,000) *increase* in net working capital. The firm pays taxes at a rate of 40%.

The only component of the initial investment calculation that is difficult to obtain is taxes. The book value of the present machine can be found by using the depreciation percentages of 20%, 32%, and 19% for years 1, 2, and 3, respectively. The resulting *book value is $69,600 ($240,000 − [(0.20 + 0.32 + 0.19) ×* $240,000])*. A *gain* of $210,400 ($280,000 − $69,600) is realized on the sale. The total taxes on the gain are $84,160 (0.40 × $210,400). These taxes must be subtracted from the $280,000 sale price of the present machine to calculate the after-tax proceeds from its sale.

Substituting the relevant amounts into the format in Table 2 results in an initial investment of $221,160, which represents the net cash outflow required at time zero.

Installed cost of proposed machine		
Cost of proposed machine	$380,000	
+ Installation costs	20,000	
Total installed cost—proposed (depreciable value)		$400,000
− **After-tax proceeds from sale of present machine**		
Proceeds from sale of present machine	$280,000	
− Tax on sale of present machine	84,160	
Total after-tax proceeds—present		195,840
+ **Change in net working capital**		17,000
Initial investment		$221,160

REVIEW QUESTIONS

9 Explain how each of the following inputs is used to calculate the *initial investment:* (a) cost of new asset, (b) installation costs, (c) proceeds from sale of old asset, (d) tax on sale of old asset, and (e) change in net working capital.

10 How is the *book value* of an asset calculated? What are the two key forms of taxable income?

11 What three tax situations may result from the sale of an asset that is being replaced?

12 Referring to the basic format for calculating initial investment, explain how a firm would determine the *depreciable value* of the new asset.

4 | Finding the Operating Cash Inflows

The benefits expected from a capital expenditure or "project" are embodied in its *operating cash inflows,* which are *incremental after-tax cash inflows.* In this section we use the income statement format to develop clear definitions of the terms *after-tax, cash inflows,* and *incremental.*

Interpreting the Term After-Tax

Benefits expected to result from proposed capital expenditures must be measured on an *after-tax basis,* because the firm will not have the use of any benefits until it has satisfied the government's tax claims. These claims depend on the firm's taxable income, so deducting taxes *before* making comparisons between proposed investments is necessary for consistency when evaluating capital expenditure alternatives.

Interpreting the Term Cash Inflows

All benefits expected from a proposed project must be measured on a *cash flow basis.* Cash inflows represent dollars that can be spent, not merely "accounting profits." A simple accounting technique for converting after-tax net profits into operating cash inflows is: cash flow from operations = Net profits after taxes + Depreciation and other noncash charges. The basic calculation requires adding depreciation and any other *noncash charges* (amortization and depletion) deducted as expenses on the firm's income statement back to net profits after taxes. Because depreciation is commonly found on income statements, it is the only noncash charge we consider.

Example

Powell Corporation's estimates of its revenue and expenses (excluding depreciation and interest), with and without the proposed new machine described in the preceding example, are given in Table 5. Note that both the expected usable life of the proposed machine and the remaining usable life of the present machine are 5 years. The amount to be depreciated with the proposed machine is calculated by summing the purchase price of $380,000 and the installation costs of $20,000.

TABLE 5	Powell Corporation's Revenue and Expenses (Excluding Depreciation and Interest) for Proposed and Present Machines					
	With proposed machine			With present machine		
Year	Revenue (1)	Expenses (excl. depr. and int.) (2)		Year	Revenue (1)	Expenses (excl. depr. and int.) (2)
1	$2,520,000	$2,300,000		1	$2,200,000	$1,990,000
2	2,520,000	2,300,000		2	2,300,000	2,110,000
3	2,520,000	2,300,000		3	2,400,000	2,230,000
4	2,520,000	2,300,000		4	2,400,000	2,250,000
5	2,520,000	2,300,000		5	2,250,000	2,120,000

TABLE 6	Depreciation Expense for Proposed and Present Machines for Powell Corporation		
Year	Cost (1)	Applicable MACRS depreciation percentages (2)	Depreciation [(1) × (2)] (3)
With proposed machine			
1	$400,000	20%	$ 80,000
2	400,000	32	128,000
3	400,000	19	76,000
4	400,000	12	48,000
5	400,000	12	48,000
6	400,000	5	20,000
Totals		100%	$400,000
With present machine			
1	$240,000	12% (year-4 depreciation)	$28,800
2	240,000	12 (year-5 depreciation)	28,800
3	240,000	5 (year-6 depreciation)	12,000
4	Because the present machine is at the end of the third year of its cost recovery at the time the analysis is performed, it has only the final 3 years of depreciation (as noted above) still applicable.		0
5			0
6			0
Total			$69,600[a]

[a]The total $69,600 represents the book value of the present machine at the end of the third year, as calculated in the preceding example.

The proposed machine is to be depreciated under MACRS using a 5-year recovery period.[6] The resulting depreciation on this machine for each of the 6 years, as well as the remaining 3 years of depreciation (years 4, 5, and 6) on the present machine, are calculated in Table 6.[7]

The *operating cash inflows* each year can be calculated by using the income statement format shown in Table 7. Note that we exclude interest because we are focusing purely on the "investment decision." The interest is relevant to the "financing decision," which is separately considered. Because we exclude interest expense, "earnings before interest and taxes (EBIT)" is equivalent to "net profits before taxes," and the calculation of "operating cash inflow" in Table 7 is equivalent to "operating cash flow (OCF)" (OCF = [EBIT × (1 − T)] + Depreciation. Simply stated, the income statement format calculates OCF.

Substituting the data from Tables 5 and 6 into this format and assuming a 40% tax rate, we get Table 8. It demonstrates the calculation of operating cash

6. It takes $n + 1$ years to depreciate an n-year class asset under current tax law. Therefore, MACRS percentages are given for each of 6 years for use in depreciating an asset with a 5-year recovery period.

7. It is important to recognize that although both machines will provide 5 years of use, the proposed new machine will be depreciated over the 6-year period, whereas the present machine, as noted in the preceding example, has been depreciated over 3 years and therefore has remaining only its final 3 years (years 4, 5, and 6) of depreciation (12%, 12%, and 5%, respectively, under MACRS).

TABLE 7	Calculation of Operating Cash Inflows Using the Income Statement Format

Revenue
− Expenses (excluding depreciation and interest)
Earnings before depreciation, interest, and taxes (EBDIT)
− Depreciation
Earnings before interest and taxes (EBIT)
− Taxes (rate = T)
Net operating profit after taxes [NOPAT = EBIT × (1 − T)]
+ Depreciation
Operating cash inflows

TABLE 8	Calculation of Operating Cash Inflows for Powell Corporation's Proposed and Present Machines					
	Year 1	Year 2	Year 3	Year 4	Year 5	Year 6
With proposed machine						
Revenue[a]	$2,520,000	$2,520,000	$2,520,000	$2,520,000	$2,520,000	$ 0
− Expenses (excl. depr. and int.)[b]	2,300,000	2,300,000	2,300,000	2,300,000	2,300,000	0
Earnings before depr., int., and taxes	$ 220,000	$ 220,000	$ 220,000	$ 220,000	$ 220,000	$ 0
− Depreciation[c]	80,000	128,000	76,000	48,000	48,000	20,000
Earnings before interest and taxes	$ 140,000	$ 92,000	$ 144,000	$ 172,000	$ 172,000	−$20,000
− Taxes (rate, T = 40%)	56,000	36,800	57,600	68,800	68,800	− 8,000
Net operating profit after taxes	$ 84,000	$ 55,200	$ 86,400	$ 103,200	$ 103,200	−$12,000
+ Depreciation[c]	80,000	128,000	76,000	48,000	48,000	20,000
Operating cash inflows	$ 164,000	$ 183,200	$ 162,400	$ 151,200	$ 151,200	$ 8,000
With present machine						
Revenue[a]	$2,200,000	$2,300,000	$2,400,000	$2,400,000	$2,250,000	$ 0
− Expenses (excl. depr. and int.)[b]	1,990,000	2,110,000	2,230,000	2,250,000	2,120,000	0
Earnings before depr., int., and taxes	$ 210,000	$ 190,000	$ 170,000	$ 150,000	$ 130,000	$ 0
− Depreciation[c]	28,800	28,800	12,000	0	0	0
Earnings before interest and taxes	$ 181,200	$ 161,200	$ 158,000	$ 150,000	$ 130,000	$ 0
− Taxes (rate, T = 40%)	72,480	64,480	63,200	60,000	52,000	0
Net operating profit after taxes	$ 108,720	$ 96,720	$ 94,800	$ 90,000	$ 78,000	$ 0
+ Depreciation[c]	28,800	28,800	12,000	0	0	0
Operating cash inflows	$ 137,520	$ 125,520	$ 106,800	$ 90,000	$ 78,000	$ 0

[a]From column 1 of Table 5.
[b]From column 2 of Table 5.
[c]From column 3 of Table 6.

inflows for each year for both the proposed and the present machine. Because the proposed machine is depreciated over 6 years, the analysis must be performed over the 6-year period to capture fully the tax effect of its year-6 depreciation. The resulting operating cash inflows are shown in the final row of Table 8 for each machine. The $8,000 year-6 operating cash inflow for the proposed machine results solely from the tax benefit of its year-6 depreciation deduction.

Interpreting the Term Incremental

The final step in estimating the operating cash inflows for a proposed replacement project is to calculate the *incremental (relevant)* cash inflows. Incremental operating cash inflows are needed, because our concern is *only* with the change in operating cash inflows that result from the proposed project. Clearly, if this were an expansion project, the project's cash flows would be the incremental cash flows.

Example   Table 9 demonstrates the calculation of Powell Corporation's *incremental (relevant) operating cash inflows* for each year. The estimates of operating cash inflows developed in Table 8 appear in columns 1 and 2. Column 2 values represent the amount of operating cash inflows that Powell Corporation will receive if it does not replace the present machine. If the proposed machine replaces the present machine, the firm's operating cash inflows for each year will be those shown in column 1. Subtracting the present machine's operating cash inflows from the proposed machine's operating cash inflows, we get the incremental operating cash inflows for each year, shown in column 3. These cash flows represent the amounts by which each respective year's cash inflows will increase as a result of the replacement. For example, in year 1, Powell Corporation's cash inflows would increase by $26,480 if the proposed project were undertaken. Clearly, these are the relevant inflows to be considered when evaluating the benefits of making a capital expenditure for the proposed machine.

TABLE 9	Incremental (Relevant) Operating Cash Inflows for Powell Corporation		
		Operating cash inflows	
Year	Proposed machine[a] (1)	Present machine[a] (2)	Incremental (relevant) [(1) − (2)] (3)
1	$164,000	$137,520	$26,480
2	183,200	125,520	57,680
3	162,400	106,800	55,600
4	151,200	90,000	61,200
5	151,200	78,000	73,200
6	8,000	0	8,000

[a]From final row for respective machine in Table 8.

REVIEW QUESTIONS

13 How does depreciation enter into the calculation of operating cash inflows? How does the income statement format in Table 7 relate to the equation for finding operating cash flow (OCF)?

14 How are the *incremental (relevant) operating cash inflows* that are associated with a replacement decision calculated?

5 | Finding the Terminal Cash Flow

Terminal cash flow is the cash flow resulting from termination and liquidation of a project at the end of its economic life. It represents the after-tax cash flow, exclusive of operating cash inflows, that occurs in the final year of the project. When it applies, this flow can significantly affect the capital expenditure decision. Terminal cash flow can be calculated for replacement projects by using the basic format presented in Table 10.

Proceeds from Sale of Assets

The proceeds from sale of the new and the old asset, often called "salvage value," represent the amount *net of any removal or cleanup costs* expected upon termination of the project. For replacement projects, proceeds from both the new asset and the old asset must be considered. For expansion and renewal types of capital expenditures, the proceeds from the old asset are zero. Of course, it is not unusual for the value of an asset to be zero at the termination of a project.

Taxes on Sale of Assets

Earlier we calculated the tax on sale of old asset (as part of finding the initial investment). Similarly, taxes must be considered on the terminal sale of both the new and the old asset for replacement projects and on only the new asset in other

TABLE 10	The Basic Format for Determining Terminal Cash Flow
	After-tax proceeds from sale of new asset =
	Proceeds from sale of new asset
	∓ Tax on sale of new asset
−	After-tax proceeds from sale of old asset =
	Proceeds from sale of old asset
	∓ Tax on sale of old asset
±	Change in net working capital
	Terminal cash flow

cases. The tax calculations apply whenever an asset is sold for a value different from its book value. If the net proceeds from the sale are expected to exceed book value, a tax payment shown as an *outflow* (deduction from sale proceeds) will occur. When the net proceeds from the sale are less than book value, a tax rebate shown as a cash *inflow* (addition to sale proceeds) will result. For assets sold to net exactly book value, no taxes will be due.

Change in Net Working Capital

When we calculated the initial investment, we took into account any change in net working capital that is attributable to the new asset. Now, when we calculate the terminal cash flow, the change in net working capital represents the reversion of any initial net working capital investment. Most often, this will show up as a cash inflow due to the reduction in net working capital; with termination of the project, the need for the increased net working capital investment is assumed to end. Because the net working capital investment is in no way consumed, the amount recovered at termination will equal the amount shown in the calculation of the initial investment. Tax considerations are not involved.

Calculating the terminal cash flow involves the same procedures as those used to find the initial investment. In the following example, the terminal cash flow is calculated for a replacement decision.

Example

Continuing with the Powell Corporation example, assume that the firm expects to be able to liquidate the new machine at the end of its 5-year usable life to net $50,000 after paying removal and cleanup costs. The old machine can be liquidated at the end of the 5 years to net $10,000. The firm expects to recover its $17,000 net working capital investment upon termination of the project. The firm pays taxes at a rate of 40%.

From the analysis of the operating cash inflows presented earlier, we can see that the proposed (new) machine will have a book value of $20,000 (equal to the year-6 depreciation) at the end of 5 years. The present (old) machine will be fully depreciated and therefore have a book value of zero at the end of the 5 years. Because the sale price of $50,000 for the proposed (new) machine is below its initial installed cost of $400,000 but greater than its book value of $20,000, taxes will have to be paid only on the recaptured depreciation of $30,000 ($50,000 sale proceeds − $20,000 book value). Applying the ordinary tax rate of 40% to this $30,000 results in a tax of $12,000 ($0.40 × $30,000) on the sale of the proposed machine. Its after-tax sale proceeds would therefore equal $38,000 ($50,000 sale proceeds − $12,000 taxes). Because the present machine would net $10,000 at termination, which is less than its original purchase price of $240,000 and above its book value of zero, it would experience a taxable gain of $10,000 ($10,000 sale price − $0 book value). Applying the 40% tax rate to the $10,000 gain, the firm will have to pay a tax of $4,000 ($0.40 × $10,000) on the sale of the present machine at the end of year 5. Its after-tax sale proceeds from the present machine would therefore equal $6,000 ($10,000 sale price − $4,000 taxes). Substituting the appropriate values into the format in Table 10 results in the terminal cash inflow of $49,000.

After-tax proceeds from sale of proposed machine

Proceeds from sale of proposed machine	$50,000	
− Tax on sale of proposed machine	12,000	
Total after-tax proceeds—proposed		$38,000
− **After-tax proceeds from sale of present machine**		
Proceeds from sale of present machine	$10,000	
− Tax on sale of present machine	4,000	
Total after-tax proceeds—present		6,000
+ **Change in net working capital**		17,000
Terminal cash flow		$49,000

REVIEW QUESTION

15 Explain how the *terminal cash flow* is calculated for replacement projects.

 6 | # Summarizing the Relevant Cash Flows

Hint Capital expenditures are critical to a firm's success, and these funds are usually limited. Because of this, the process of determining cash flows should be finely tuned so that it is both objective and realistic.

The initial investment, operating cash inflows, and terminal cash flow together represent a project's *relevant cash flows*. These cash flows can be viewed as the incremental after-tax cash flows attributable to the proposed project. They represent, in a cash flow sense, how much better or worse off the firm will be if it chooses to implement the proposal.

Example

The relevant cash flows for Powell Corporation's proposed replacement expenditure can be shown graphically, on a time line. *Note that because the new asset is assumed to be sold at the end of its 5-year usable life, the year-6 incremental operating cash inflow calculated in Table 9 has no relevance; the terminal cash flow effectively replaces this value in the analysis.* As the following time line shows, the relevant cash flows follow a *conventional cash flow pattern*.

Time line for Powell Corporation's relevant cash flows with the proposed machine

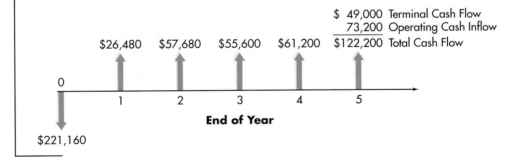

Personal Finance Example

After receiving a sizable bonus from her employer, Tina Talor is contemplating the purchase of a new car. She feels that by estimating and analyzing its cash flows she could make a more rational decision about whether to make this large purchase. Tina's cash flow estimates for the car purchase are as follows.

Negotiated price of new car	$23,500
Taxes and fees on new car purchase	$1,650
Proceeds from trade-in of old car	$9,750
Estimated value of new car in 3 years	$10,500
Estimated value of old car in 3 years	$5,700
Estimated annual repair costs on new car	0 (in warranty)
Estimated annual repair costs on old car	$400

Using the cash flow estimates, Tina calculates the initial investment, operating cash inflows, terminal cash flow, and a summary of all cash flows for the car purchase.

Initial Investment

Total cost of new car		
Cost of car	$23,500	
+ Taxes and fees	1,650	$25,150
− Proceeds from sale of old car		9,750
Initial investment		$15,400

Operating Cash Inflows	**Year 1**	**Year 2**	**Year 3**
Cost of repairs on new car	$ 0	$ 0	$ 0
− Cost of repairs on old car	400	400	400
Operating cash inflows (savings)	$400	$400	$400

Terminal Cash Flow—End of Year 3

Proceeds from sale of new car	$10,500
− Proceeds from sale of old car	5,700
Terminal cash flow	$ 4,800

Summary of Cash Flows

End of Year	Cash Flow	
0	−$15,400	
1	+ 400	
2	+ 400	
3	+ 5,200	($400 + $4,800)

The cash flows associated with Tina's car purchase decision reflect her net costs of the new car over the assumed 3-year ownership period, but they ignore the many intangible benefits of owning a car. Whereas the fuel cost and basic transportation service provided are assumed to be the same with the new car as with the old car, Tina will have to decide if the cost of moving up to a new car can be justified in terms of intangibles, such as luxury and prestige.

16   Diagram and describe the three components of the relevant cash flows for
      a capital budgeting project.

Summary

Focus on Value

A key responsibility of financial managers is to review and analyze proposed
investment decisions to make sure that the firm undertakes only those that contribute positively to the value of the firm. Utilizing a variety of tools and techniques, financial managers estimate the cash flows that a proposed investment
will generate and then apply decision techniques to assess the investment's
impact on the firm's value. The most difficult and important aspect of this capital budgeting process is developing good estimates of the relevant cash flows.

   The relevant cash flows are the incremental after-tax cash flows resulting
from a proposed investment. These estimates represent the cash flow benefits
that are likely to accrue to the firm as a result of implementing the investment.
By applying to the cash flows decision techniques that capture the time value of
money and risk factors, the financial manager can estimate how the investment
will affect the firm's share price. Consistent application of capital budgeting
procedures to proposed long-term investments should therefore allow the firm
to **maximize its stock price.**

Review of Learning Goals

LG 1 **Understand the key motives for capital expenditure and the steps in the
capital budgeting process.** Capital budgeting is the process used to evaluate
and select capital expenditures. Capital expenditures are long-term investments made to expand operations, replace or renew fixed assets, or to obtain
some other, less tangible benefit over a long period. The capital budgeting
process includes five distinct but interrelated steps: proposal generation, review
and analysis, decision making, implementation, and follow-up.

LG 2 **Define basic capital budgeting terminology.** Capital expenditure proposals
may be independent or mutually exclusive. Typically, firms have only
limited funds for capital investments and must ration them among projects.
Two basic capital budgeting approaches are the accept–reject approach and the
ranking approach. Conventional cash flow patterns consist of an initial outflow
followed by a series of inflows; any other pattern is nonconventional.

LG 3 **Discuss relevant cash flows, expansion versus replacement decisions, sunk
costs and opportunity costs, and international capital budgeting.** The relevant cash flows for capital budgeting decisions are the initial investment,
the operating cash inflows, and the terminal cash flow. For replacement decisions, these flows are the difference between the cash flows of the new asset and

the old asset. Expansion decisions are viewed as replacement decisions in which all cash flows from the old asset are zero. When estimating relevant cash flows, ignore sunk costs and include opportunity costs as cash outflows. In international capital budgeting, currency risks and political risks can be minimized through careful planning.

LG 4 **Calculate the initial investment associated with a proposed capital expenditure.** The initial investment is the initial outflow required, taking into account the installed cost of the new asset, the after-tax proceeds from the sale of the old asset, and any change in net working capital. The initial investment is reduced by finding the after-tax proceeds from sale of the old asset. The book value of an asset is used to determine the taxes owed as a result of its sale. Either of two forms of taxable income—a gain or a loss—can result from sale of an asset, depending on whether the asset is sold for (1) more than book value, (2) book value, or (3) less than book value. The change in net working capital is the difference between the change in current assets and the change in current liabilities expected to accompany a given capital expenditure.

LG 5 **Find the relevant operating cash inflows associated with a proposed capital expenditure.** The operating cash inflows are the incremental after-tax cash inflows expected to result from a project. The income statement format involves adding depreciation back to net operating profit after taxes and gives the operating cash inflows, which are the same as operating cash flows (OCF), associated with the proposed and present projects. The relevant (incremental) cash inflows for a replacement project are the difference between the operating cash inflows of the proposed project and those of the present project.

LG 6 **Determine the terminal cash flow associated with a proposed capital expenditure.** The terminal cash flow represents the after-tax cash flow (exclusive of operating cash inflows) that is expected from liquidation of a project. It is calculated for replacement projects by finding the difference between the after-tax proceeds from sale of the new and the old asset at termination and then adjusting this difference for any change in net working capital. Sale price and depreciation data are used to find the taxes and the after-tax sale proceeds on the new and old assets. The change in net working capital typically represents the reversion of any initial net working capital investment.

Use the following table for problems involving MACRS depreciation.

Rounded Depreciation Percentages by Recovery Year Using MACRS for First Four Property Classes

Recovery year	Percentage by recovery year[a]			
	3 years	5 years	7 years	10 years
1	33%	20%	14%	10%
2	45	32	25	18
3	15	19	18	14
4	7	12	12	12
5		12	9	9
6		5	9	8
7			9	7
8			4	6
9				6
10				6
11				4
Totals	100%	100%	100%	100%

[a]These percentages have been rounded to the nearest whole percent to simplify calculations while retaining realism. To calculate the *actual* depreciation for tax purposes, be sure to apply the actual unrounded percentages or directly apply double-declining balance (200%) depreciation using the half-year convention.

Self-Test Problems

ST8–1 **Book value, taxes, and initial investment**   Irvin Enterprises is considering the purchase of a new piece of equipment to replace the current equipment. The new equipment costs $75,000 and requires $5,000 in installation costs. It will be depreciated under MACRS using a 5-year recovery period. The old piece of equipment was purchased 4 years ago for an installed cost of $50,000; it was being depreciated under MACRS using a 5-year recovery period. The old equipment can be sold today for $55,000 net of any removal or cleanup costs. As a result of the proposed replacement, the firm's investment in net working capital is expected to increase by $15,000. The firm pays taxes at a rate of 40%. (See table preceding this section.)
a. Calculate the book value of the old piece of equipment.
b. Determine the taxes, if any, attributable to the sale of the old equipment.
c. Find the *initial investment* associated with the proposed equipment replacement.

ST8–2 Determining relevant cash flows A machine currently in use was originally purchased 2 years ago for $40,000. The machine is being depreciated under MACRS using a 5-year recovery period; it has 3 years of usable life remaining. The current machine can be sold today to net $42,000 after removal and cleanup costs. A new machine, using a 3-year MACRS recovery period, can be purchased at a price of $140,000. It requires $10,000 to install and has a 3-year usable life. If the new machine is acquired, the investment in accounts receivable will be expected to rise by $10,000, the inventory investment will increase by $25,000, and accounts payable will increase by $15,000. *Earnings before depreciation, interest, and taxes* are expected to be $70,000 for each of the next 3 years with the old machine and to be $120,000 in the first year and $130,000 in the second and third years with the new machine. At the end of 3 years, the market value of the old machine will equal zero, but the new machine could be sold to net $35,000 before taxes. The firm is subject to a 40% tax rate. (See table preceding this section.)

a. Determine the *initial investment* associated with the proposed replacement decision.

b. Calculate the *incremental operating cash inflows* for years 1 to 4 associated with the proposed replacement. (*Note:* Only depreciation cash flows must be considered in year 4.)

c. Calculate the *terminal cash flow* associated with the proposed replacement decision. (*Note:* This is at the end of year 3.)

d. Depict on a time line the relevant cash flows found in parts **a, b,** and **c** that are associated with the proposed replacement decision, assuming that it is terminated at the end of year 3.

Warm-Up Exercises

A blue box (■) indicates exercises available in .

 E8–1 If Halley Industries reimburses employees who earn master's degrees and who agree to remain with the firm for an additional 3 years, should the expense of the tuition reimbursement be categorized as a *capital expenditure* or an *operating expenditure?*

 E8–2 Canvas Reproductions, Inc., is considering two mutually exclusive investments. Project A requires an initial outlay of $20,000 and has expected cash inflows of $5,000 for each of the next 5 years. Project B requires an initial outlay of $25,000 and has expected cash inflows of $6,500 for each of the following 5 years. Use a simple rate of return measure to determine which project the company should choose.

 E8–3 Iridium Corp. has spent $3.5 billion over the past decade developing a satellite-based telecommunication system. It is currently trying to decide whether to spend an additional $350 million on the project. The firm expects that this outlay will finish the project and will generate cash flow of $15 million per year over the next 5 years. A competitor has offered $450 million for the satellites already in orbit. Classify the firm's outlays as *sunk costs* or *opportunity costs*, and specify the *relevant cash flows*.

E8–4 A few years ago, Largo Industries implemented an inventory auditing system at an installed cost of $175,000. Since then, it has taken depreciation deductions totalling $124,250. What is the system's current *book value*? If Largo sold the system for $110,000, how much *recaptured depreciation* would result?

 E8–5 Bryson Sciences is planning to purchase a high-powered microscopy machine for $55,000 and incur an additional $7,500 in installation expenses. It is replacing similar microscopy equipment that can be sold to net $35,000, resulting in taxes from a gain on the sale of $11,250. Because of this transaction, current assets will increase by $6,000 and current liabilities will increase by $4,000. Calculate the *initial investment* in the high-powered microscopy machine.

Problems

A blue box (■) indicates problems available in myfinancelab.

 P8–1 **Classification of expenditures** Given the following list of outlays, indicate whether each is normally considered a *capital expenditure* or an *operating expenditure*. Explain your answers.

a. An initial lease payment of $5,000 for electronic point-of-sale cash register systems.
b. An outlay of $20,000 to purchase patent rights from an inventor.
c. An outlay of $80,000 for a major research and development program.
d. An $80,000 investment in a portfolio of marketable securities.
e. A $300 outlay for an office machine.
f. An outlay of $2,000 for a new machine tool.
g. An outlay of $240,000 for a new building.
h. An outlay of $1,000 for a marketing research report.

 P8–2 **Basic terminology** A firm is considering the following three separate situations.

Situation A Build either a small office building or a convenience store on a parcel of land located in a high-traffic area. Adequate funding is available, and both projects are known to be acceptable. The office building requires an initial investment of $620,000 and is expected to provide operating cash inflows of $40,000 per year for 20 years. The convenience store is expected to cost $500,000 and to provide a growing stream of operating cash inflows over its 20-year life. The initial operating cash inflow is $20,000, and it will increase by 5% each year.

Situation B Replace a machine with a new one that requires a $60,000 initial investment and will provide operating cash inflows of $10,000 per year for the first 5 years. At the end of year 5, a machine overhaul costing $20,000 will be required. After it is completed, expected operating cash inflows will be $10,000 in year 6; $7,000 in year 7; $4,000 in year 8; and $1,000 in year 9, at the end of which the machine will be scrapped.

Situation C Invest in any or all of the four machines whose relevant cash flows are given in the following table. The firm has $500,000 budgeted to fund these machines, all of which are known to be acceptable. The initial investment for each machine is $250,000.

Year	Operating cash inflows			
	Machine 1	Machine 2	Machine 3	Machine 4
1	$ 50,000	$70,000	$65,000	$90,000
2	70,000	70,000	65,000	80,000
3	90,000	70,000	80,000	70,000
4	− 30,000	70,000	80,000	60,000
5	100,000	70,000	− 20,000	50,000

For each situation, indicate:
a. Whether the projects involved are independent or mutually exclusive.
b. Whether the availability of funds is unlimited or capital rationing exists.
c. Whether accept–reject or ranking decisions are required.
d. Whether each project's cash flows are conventional or nonconventional.

P8–3 **Relevant cash flow pattern fundamentals** For each of the following projects, determine the *relevant cash flows*, classify the cash flow pattern, and depict the cash flows on a time line.
a. A project that requires an initial investment of $120,000 and will generate annual operating cash inflows of $25,000 for the next 18 years. In each of the 18 years, maintenance of the project will require a $5,000 cash outflow.
b. A new machine with an installed cost of $85,000. Sale of the old machine will yield $30,000 after taxes. Operating cash inflows generated by the replacement will exceed the operating cash inflows of the old machine by $20,000 in each year of a 6-year period. At the end of year 6, liquidation of the new machine will yield $20,000 after taxes, which is $10,000 greater than the after-tax proceeds expected from the old machine had it been retained and liquidated at the end of year 6.
c. An asset that requires an initial investment of $2 million and will yield annual operating cash inflows of $300,000 for each of the next 10 years. Operating cash outlays will be $20,000 for each year except year 6, when an overhaul requiring an additional cash outlay of $500,000 will be required. The asset's liquidation value at the end of year 10 is expected to be zero.

P8–4 **Expansion versus replacement cash flows** Edison Systems has estimated the cash flows over the 5-year lives for two projects, A and B. These cash flows are summarized in the following table.
a. If project A were actually a *replacement* for project B and if the $12,000 initial investment shown for project B were the after-tax cash inflow expected from liquidating it, what would be the *relevant cash flows* for this replacement decision?
b. How can an *expansion decision* such as project A be viewed as a special form of a replacement decision? Explain.

Capital Budgeting Cash Flows

	Project A	Project B
Initial investment	$40,000	$12,000[a]
Year	Operating cash inflows	
1	$10,000	$ 6,000
2	12,000	6,000
3	14,000	6,000
4	16,000	6,000
5	10,000	6,000

[a]After-tax cash inflow expected from liquidation.

 P8–5 **Sunk costs and opportunity costs**   Covol Industries is developing the relevant cash flows associated with the proposed replacement of an existing machine tool with a new, technologically advanced one. Given the following costs related to the proposed project, explain whether each would be treated as a *sunk cost* or an *opportunity cost* in developing the relevant cash flows associated with the proposed replacement decision.
a. Covol would be able to use the same tooling, which had a book value of $40,000, on the new machine tool as it had used on the old one.
b. Covol would be able to use its existing computer system to develop programs for operating the new machine tool. The old machine tool did not require these programs. Although the firm's computer has excess capacity available, the capacity could be leased to another firm for an annual fee of $17,000.
c. Covol would have to obtain additional floor space to accommodate the larger new machine tool. The space that would be used is currently being leased to another company for $10,000 per year.
d. Covol would use a small storage facility to store the increased output of the new machine tool. The storage facility was built by Covol 3 years earlier at a cost of $120,000. Because of its unique configuration and location, it is currently of no use to either Covol or any other firm.
e. Covol would retain an existing overhead crane, which it had planned to sell for its $180,000 market value. Although the crane was not needed with the old machine tool, it would be used to position raw materials on the new machine tool.

PERSONAL FINANCE PROBLEM

 P8–6 **Sunk and opportunity cash flows**   Dave and Ann Stone have been living at their present home for the past 6 years. During that time, they have replaced the water heater for $375, replaced the dishwasher for $599, and have had to make miscellaneous repair and maintenance expenditures of approximately $1,500. They have decided to move out and rent the house for $975 per month. Newspaper advertising will cost $75. Dave and Ann intend to paint the interior of the home and power-wash the exterior. They estimate that that will run about $900.
   The house should be ready to rent after that. In reviewing the financial situation, Dave views all the expenditures as being relevant, and so he plans to net out the estimated expenditures discussed above from the rental income.
a. Do Dave and Ann understand the difference between *sunk costs* and *opportunity costs?* Explain the two concepts to them.

451

b. Which of the expenditures should be classified as sunk cash flows and which should be viewed as opportunity cash flows?

P8–7 **Book value** Find the book value for each of the assets shown in the following table, assuming that MACRS depreciation is being used. (See the table preceding the exercises or Table 3.2 in myfinancelab.)

Asset	Installed cost	Recovery period (years)	Elapsed time since purchase (years)
A	$ 950,000	5	3
B	40,000	3	1
C	96,000	5	4
D	350,000	5	1
E	1,500,000	7	5

P8–8 **Book value and taxes on sale of assets** Troy Industries purchased a new machine 3 years ago for $80,000. It is being depreciated under MACRS with a 5-year recovery period using the percentages given in the table preceding the exercises (or Table 3.2 in myfinancelab). Assume a 40% tax rate.
a. What is the *book value* of the machine?
b. Calculate the firm's tax liability if it sold the machine for each of the following amounts: $100,000; $56,000; $23,200; and $15,000.

P8–9 **Tax calculations** For each of the following cases, determine the total taxes resulting from the transaction. Assume a 40% tax rate. The asset was purchased 2 years ago for $200,000 and is being depreciated under MACRS using a 5-year recovery period. (See the table preceding the exercises or Table 3.2 in myfinancelab.)
a. The asset is sold for $220,000.
b. The asset is sold for $150,000.
c. The asset is sold for $96,000.
d. The asset is sold for $80,000.

P8–10 **Change in net working capital calculation** Samuels Manufacturing is considering the purchase of a new machine to replace one it believes is obsolete. The firm has total current assets of $920,000 and total current liabilities of $640,000. As a result of the proposed replacement, the following *changes* are anticipated in the levels of the current asset and current liability accounts noted.

Account	Change
Accruals	+ $ 40,000
Marketable securities	0
Inventories	− 10,000
Accounts payable	+ 90,000
Notes payable	0
Accounts receivable	+ 150,000
Cash	+ 15,000

a. Using the information given, calculate any *change in net working capital* that is expected to result from the proposed replacement action.

b. Explain why a change in these current accounts would be relevant in determining the *initial investment* for the proposed capital expenditure.

c. Would the change in net working capital enter into any of the other cash flow components that make up the relevant cash flows? Explain.

 P8–11 **Calculating initial investment** Vastine Medical, Inc., is considering replacing its existing computer system, which was purchased 2 years ago at a cost of $325,000. The system can be sold today for $200,000. It is being depreciated using MACRS and a 5-year recovery period. (See the table preceding the exercises or Table 3.2 in myfinancelab.) A new computer system will cost $500,000 to purchase and install. Replacement of the computer system would not involve any change in net working capital. Assume a 40% tax rate.

a. Calculate the *book value* of the existing computer system.

b. Calculate the after-tax proceeds of its sale for $200,000.

c. Calculate the *initial investment* associated with the replacement project.

 P8–12 **Initial investment—Basic calculation** Cushing Corporation is considering the purchase of a new grading machine to replace the existing one. The existing machine was purchased 3 years ago at an installed cost of $20,000; it was being depreciated under MACRS using a 5-year recovery period. (See the table preceding the exercises or Table 3.2 in myfinancelab.) The existing machine is expected to have a usable life of at least 5 more years. The new machine costs $35,000 and requires $5,000 in installation costs; it will be depreciated using a 5-year recovery period under MACRS. The existing machine can currently be sold for $25,000 without incurring any removal or cleanup costs. The firm is subject to a 40% tax rate. Calculate the *initial investment* associated with the proposed purchase of a new grading machine.

 P8–13 **Initial investment at various sale prices** Edwards Manufacturing Company (EMC) is considering replacing one machine with another. The old machine was purchased 3 years ago for an installed cost of $10,000. The firm is depreciating the machine under MACRS, using a 5-year recovery period. (See the table preceding the exercises or Table 3.2 in myfinancelab.) The new machine costs $24,000 and requires $2,000 in installation costs. The firm is subject to a 40% tax rate. In each of the following cases, calculate the *initial investment* for the replacement.

a. EMC sells the old machine for $11,000.

b. EMC sells the old machine for $7,000.

c. EMC sells the old machine for $2,900.

d. EMC sells the old machine for $1,500.

 P8–14 **Depreciation** A firm is evaluating the acquisition of an asset that costs $64,000 and requires $4,000 in installation costs. If the firm depreciates the asset under MACRS, using a 5-year recovery period. (See the table preceding the exercises or Table 3.2 in myfinancelab.) determine the depreciation charge for each year.

 P8–15 **Incremental operating cash inflows** A firm is considering renewing its equipment to meet increased demand for its product. The cost of equipment modifications is $1.9 million plus $100,000 in installation costs. The firm will depreciate the equipment modifications under MACRS, using a 5-year recovery period. (See the table preceding the exercises or Table 3.2 in myfinancelab.) Additional sales revenue from the renewal should amount to $1.2 million per year, and additional operating expenses and other costs (excluding depreciation and interest) will amount to 40% of the additional sales. The firm is subject to a tax rate of 40%. (*Note:* Answer the following questions for each of the next 6 *years.*)

a. What incremental earnings before depreciation, interest, and taxes will result from the renewal?

b. What incremental net operating profits after taxes will result from the renewal?

c. What *incremental operating cash inflows* will result from the renewal?

PERSONAL FINANCE PROBLEM

P8–16 **Incremental operating cash flows**   Richard and Linda Thomson operate a local lawn maintenance service for commercial and residential property. They have been using a John Deere riding mower for the past several years and feel it is time to buy a new one. They would like to know the incremental (relevant) cash flows associated with the replacement of the old riding mower. The following data are available.

> There are 5 years of remaining useful life on the old mower.
>
> The old mower has a zero book value.
>
> The new mower is expected to last 5 years.
>
> The Thomsons will follow a 5-year MACRS recovery period for the new mower.
>
> Depreciable value of the new law mower is $1,800.
>
> They are subject to a 40% tax rate.
>
> The new mower is expected to be more fuel-efficient, maneuverable, and durable than previous models and can result in reduced operating expenses of $500 per year.
>
> The Thomsons will buy a maintenance contract that calls for annual payments of $120.

Create and *incremental operating cash flow* statement for the replacement of Richard and Linda's John Deere riding mower. Show the incremental operating cash flow for the next 6 years.

P8–17 **Incremental operating cash inflows—Expense reduction**   Miller Corporation is considering replacing a machine. The replacement will reduce operating expenses (that is, increase earnings before depreciation, interest, and taxes) by $16,000 per year for each of the 5 years the new machine is expected to last. Although the old machine has zero book value, it can be used for 5 more years. The depreciable value of the new machine is $48,000. The firm will depreciate the machine under MACRS using a 5-year recovery period (See the table preceding the exercises or Table 3.2 in myfinancelab.) and is subject to a 40% tax rate. Estimate the *incremental operating cash inflows* generated by the replacement. (*Note:* Be sure to consider the depreciation in year 6.)

P8–18 **Incremental operating cash inflows**   Strong Tool Company has been considering purchasing a new lathe to replace a fully depreciated lathe that will last 5 more years. The new lathe is expected to have a 5-year life and depreciation charges of $2,000 in year 1; $3,200 in year 2; $1,900 in year 3; $1,200 in both year 4 and year 5; and $500 in year 6. The firm estimates the revenues and expenses (excluding depreciation and interest) for the new and the old lathes to be as shown in the following table. The firm is subject to a 40% tax rate.

	New lathe		Old lathe	
Year	Revenue	Expenses (excl. depr. and int.)	Revenue	Expenses (excl. depr. and int.)
1	$40,000	$30,000	$35,000	$25,000
2	41,000	30,000	35,000	25,000
3	42,000	30,000	35,000	25,000
4	43,000	30,000	35,000	25,000
5	44,000	30,000	35,000	25,000

a. Calculate the *operating cash inflows* associated with each lathe. (*Note:* Be sure to consider the depreciation in year 6.)
b. Calculate the *incremental (relevant) operating cash inflows* resulting from the proposed lathe replacement.
c. Depict on a time line the incremental operating cash inflows calculated in part **b**.

P8–19 Terminal cash flow—Various lives and sale prices Looner Industries is currently analyzing the purchase of a new machine that costs $160,000 and requires $20,000 in installation costs. Purchase of this machine is expected to result in an increase in net working capital of $30,000 to support the expanded level of operations. The firm plans to depreciate the machine under MACRS using a 5-year recovery period (See the table preceding the exercises or Table 3.2 in myfinancelab.) and expects to sell the machine to net $10,000 before taxes at the end of its usable life. The firm is subject to a 40% tax rate.
a. Calculate the *terminal cash flow* for a usable life of (1) 3 years, (2) 5 years, and (3) 7 years.
b. Discuss the effect of usable life on terminal cash flows using your findings in part **a**.
c. Assuming a 5-year usable life, calculate the terminal cash flow if the machine were sold to net (1) $9,000 or (2) $170,000 (before taxes) at the end of 5 years.
d. Discuss the effect of sale price on terminal cash flow using your findings in part **c**.

P8–20 Terminal cash flow—Replacement decision Russell Industries is considering replacing a fully depreciated machine that has a remaining useful life of 10 years with a newer, more sophisticated machine. The new machine will cost $200,000 and will require $30,000 in installation costs. It will be depreciated under MACRS using a 5-year recovery period. (See the table preceding the exercises or Table 3.2 in myfinancelab.) A $25,000 increase in net working capital will be required to support the new machine. The firm's managers plan to evaluate the potential replacement over a 4-year period. They estimate that the old machine could be sold at the end of 4 years to net $15,000 before taxes; the new machine at the end of 4 years will be worth $75,000 before taxes. Calculate the *terminal cash flow* at the end of year 4 that is relevant to the proposed purchase of the new machine. The firm is subject to a 40% tax rate.

P8–21 **Relevant cash flows for a marketing campaign**   Marcus Tube, a manufacturer of high-quality aluminum tubing, has maintained stable sales and profits over the past 10 years. Although the market for aluminum tubing has been expanding by 3% per year, Marcus has been unsuccessful in sharing this growth. To increase its sales, the firm is considering an aggressive marketing campaign that centers on regularly running ads in all relevant trade journals and exhibiting products at all major regional and national trade shows. The campaign is expected to require an *annual* tax-deductible expenditure of $150,000 over the next 5 years. Sales revenue, as shown in the income statement for 2009 below, totaled $20,000,000. If the proposed marketing campaign is not initiated, sales are expected to remain at this level in each of the next 5 years, 2010–2014. With the marketing campaign, sales are expected to rise to the levels shown in the accompanying table for each of the next 5 years; cost of goods sold is expected to remain at 80% of sales; general and administrative expense (exclusive of any marketing campaign outlays) is expected to remain at 10% of sales; and annual depreciation expense is expected to remain at $500,000. Assuming a 40% tax rate, find the *relevant cash flows* over the next 5 years associated with the proposed marketing campaign.

Marcus Tube Income Statement for the Year Ended December 31, 2009		
Sales revenue		$20,000,000
Less: Cost of goods sold (80%)		16,000,000
Gross profits		$ 4,000,000
Less: Operating expenses		
General and administrative expense (10%)	$2,000,000	
Depreciation expense	500,000	
Total operating expense		2,500,000
Earnings before interest and taxes		$ 1,500,000
Less: Taxes (rate = 40%)		600,000
Net operating profit after taxes		$ 900,000

Marcus Tube Sales Forecast	
Year	Sales revenue
2010	$20,500,000
2011	21,000,000
2012	21,500,000
2013	22,500,000
2014	23,500,000

P8–22 **Relevant cash flows—No terminal value**   Central Laundry and Cleaners is considering replacing an existing piece of machinery with a more sophisticated machine. The old machine was purchased 3 years ago at a cost of $50,000, and this amount was being depreciated under MACRS using a 5-year recovery period. The machine has 5 years of usable life remaining. The new machine that is being considered costs $76,000 and requires $4,000 in installation costs. The new machine would be depreciated under MACRS using a 5-year recovery period. The firm can currently sell the old machine for $55,000 without incurring any removal or cleanup costs. The firm is subject to a tax rate of 40%. The revenues and expenses (excluding depreciation and interest) associated with the new and the old machines for the next 5 years are given in the table below. (See the table preceding the exercises or Table 3.2 in myfinancelab.)

	New machine		Old machine	
Year	Revenue	Expenses (excl. depr. and int.)	Revenue	Expenses (excl. depr. and int.)
1	$750,000	$720,000	$674,000	$660,000
2	750,000	720,000	676,000	660,000
3	750,000	720,000	680,000	660,000
4	750,000	720,000	678,000	660,000
5	750,000	720,000	674,000	660,000

a. Calculate the *initial investment* associated with replacement of the old machine by the new one.

b. Determine the *incremental operating cash inflows* associated with the proposed replacement. (*Note:* Be sure to consider the depreciation in year 6.)

c. Depict on a time line the *relevant cash flows* found in parts a and b associated with the proposed replacement decision.

    Integrative—Determining relevant cash flows Lombard Company is contemplating the purchase of a new high-speed widget grinder to replace the existing grinder. The existing grinder was purchased 2 years ago at an installed cost of $60,000; it was being depreciated under MACRS using a 5-year recovery period. The existing grinder is expected to have a usable life of 5 more years. The new grinder costs $105,000 and requires $5,000 in installation costs; it has a 5-year usable life and would be depreciated under MACRS using a 5-year recovery period. Lombard can currently sell the existing grinder for $70,000 without incurring any removal or cleanup costs. To support the increased business resulting from purchase of the new grinder, accounts receivable would increase by $40,000, inventories by $30,000, and accounts payable by $58,000. At the end of 5 years, the existing grinder is expected to have a market value of zero; the new grinder would be sold to net $29,000 after removal and cleanup costs and before taxes. The firm is subject a 40% tax rate. The estimated *earnings before depreciation, interest, and taxes* over the 5 years for both the new and the existing grinder are shown in the following table. (See the table preceding the exercises or Table 3.2 in myfinancelab.)

	Earnings before depreciation, interest, and taxes	
Year	New grinder	Existing grinder
1	$43,000	$26,000
2	43,000	24,000
3	43,000	22,000
4	43,000	20,000
5	43,000	18,000

a. Calculate the *initial investment* associated with the replacement of the existing grinder by the new one.

b. Determine the *incremental operating cash inflows* associated with the proposed grinder replacement. (*Note:* Be sure to consider the depreciation in year 6.)

c. Determine the *terminal cash flow* expected at the end of year 5 from the proposed grinder replacement.

d. Depict on a time line the *relevant cash flows* associated with the proposed grinder replacement decision.

PERSONAL FINANCE PROBLEM

 Determining relevant cash flows for a new boat   Jan and Deana have been dreaming about owning a boat for some time and have decided that estimating its cash flows will help them in their decision process. They expect to have a disposable annual income of $24,000. Their cash flow estimates for the boat purchase are as follows:

Negotiated price of the new boat	$70,000
Sales tax rate (applicable to purchase price)	6.5%
Boat trade-in	0
Estimated value of new boat in 4 years	$40,000
Estimated monthly repair and maintenance	$800
Estimated monthly docking fee	$500

Using these cash flow estimates, calculate the following:

a. The initial investment
b. Operating cash flow
c. Terminal cash flow
d. Summary of annual cash flow
e. Based on their disposable annual income, what advice would you give Jan and Deana regarding the proposed boat purchase?

 P8–25   **ETHICS PROBLEM**   According to academic research, capital budgeting cash flow projections are used rarely in practice by small firms, which often use accounting projections instead. What is the most likely explanation of this behavior?

Chapter Case

Developing Relevant Cash Flows for Clark Upholstery Company's Machine Renewal or Replacement Decision

Bo Humphries, chief financial officer of Clark Upholstery Company, expects the firm's *net operating profit after taxes* for the next 5 years to be as shown in the following table.

Year	Net operating profit after taxes
1	$100,000
2	150,000
3	200,000
4	250,000
5	320,000

Bo is beginning to develop the relevant cash flows needed to analyze whether to renew or replace Clark's *only* depreciable asset, a machine that originally cost $30,000, has a current book value of zero, and can now be sold for $20,000. (*Note:* Because the firm's only depreciable asset is fully depreciated—its book value is zero—its expected operating cash inflows equal its net operating profit after taxes.) He estimates that at the end of 5 years, the existing machine can be sold to net $2,000 before taxes. Bo plans to use the following information to develop the relevant cash flows for each of the alternatives.

Alternative 1   Renew the existing machine at a total depreciable cost of $90,000. The renewed machine would have a 5-year usable life and would be depreciated under MACRS using a 5-year recovery period. Renewing the machine would result in the following projected revenues and expenses (excluding depreciation and interest):

Year	Revenue	Expenses (excl. depr. and int.)
1	$1,000,000	$801,500
2	1,175,000	884,200
3	1,300,000	918,100
4	1,425,000	943,100
5	1,550,000	968,100

The renewed machine would result in an increased investment in net working capital of $15,000. At the end of 5 years, the machine could be sold to net $8,000 before taxes.

Alternative 2   Replace the existing machine with a new machine that costs $100,000 and requires installation costs of $10,000. The new machine would have a 5-year usable life and would be depreciated under MACRS using a 5-year recovery period. The firm's projected revenues and expenses (excluding depreciation and interest), if it acquires the machine, would be as follows:

Year	Revenue	Expenses (excl. depr. and int.)
1	$1,000,000	$764,500
2	1,175,000	839,800
3	1,300,000	914,900
4	1,425,000	989,900
5	1,550,000	998,900

The new machine would result in an increased investment in net working capital of $22,000. At the end of 5 years, the new machine could be sold to net $25,000 before taxes.

The firm is subject to a 40% tax rate. As noted, the company uses MACRS depreciation. (See the table preceding the exercises or Table 3.2 in myfinancelab.)

To Do

a. Calculate the *initial investment* associated with each of Clark Upholstery's alternatives.

b. Calculate the *incremental operating cash inflows* associated with each of Clark's alternatives. (*Note:* Be sure to consider the depreciation in year 6.)

c. Calculate the *terminal cash flow* at the end of year 5 associated with each of Clark's alternatives.

d. Use your findings in parts **a, b,** and **c** to depict on a time line the *relevant cash flows* associated with each of Clark Upholstery's alternatives.

e. Solely on the basis of your comparison of their relevant cash flows, which alternative appears to be better? Why?

Spreadsheet Exercise

Damon Corporation, a sports equipment manufacturer, has a machine currently in use that was originally purchased 3 years ago for $120,000. The firm depreciates the machine under MACRS using a 5-year recovery period. Once removal and cleanup costs are taken into consideration, the expected net selling price for the present machine will be $70,000.

Damon can buy a new machine for a net price of $160,000 (including installation costs of $15,000). The proposed machine will be depreciated under MACRS using a 5-year recovery period. If the firm acquires the new machine, its working capital needs will change—accounts receivable will increase $15,000, inventory will increase $19,000, and accounts payable will increase $16,000.

Earnings before depreciation, interest, and taxes (EBDIT) for the present machine are expected to be $95,000 for each of the successive 5 years. For the proposed machine, the expected EBDIT for each of the next 5 years are $105,000, $110,000, $120,000, $120,000, and $120,000, respectively. The corporate tax rate (T) for the firm is 40%. (See the table preceding the exercises or Table 3.2 in myfinancelab.)

Damon expects to be able to liquidate the proposed machine at the end of its 5-year usable life for $24,000 (after paying removal and cleanup costs). The present machine is expected to net $8,000 upon liquidation at the end of the same period. Damon expects to recover its net working capital investment upon termination of the project. The firm is subject to a tax rate of 40%.

To Do

Create a spreadsheet similar to Tables 2, 6, 8, and 10 (or the spreadsheets that can be viewed at **www.prenhall.com/gitman** as Tables 8.2, 8.6, 8.8, and 8.10) to answer the following:

a. Create a spreadsheet to calculate the *initial investment*.
b. Create a spreadsheet to prepare a *depreciation schedule* for both the proposed and the present machine. Both machines are depreciated under MACRS using a 5-year recovery period. Remember, the present machine has only 3 years of depreciation remaining.
c. Create a spreadsheet to calculate the *operating cash inflows* for Damon Corporation for both the proposed and the present machine.
d. Create a spreadsheet to calculate the *terminal cash flow* associated with the project.

Web Exercise

Go to the text's companion website at **www.prenhall.com/gitman** to find the Web Exercise for this chapter.

Remember to check the text's website at **www.prenhall.com/gitman** to find additional resources, including Web Exercises and a Web Case.

Solutions to Self-Test Problems

ST8–1 **a.** Book value = Installed cost − Accumulated depreciation
Installed cost = $50,000
Accumulated depreciation = $50,000 × (0.20 + 0.32 + 0.19 + 0.12)
= $50,000 × 0.83 = $41,500
Book value = $50,000 − $41,500 = $8,500

b. Taxes on sale of old equipment:
Gain on sale = Sale price − Book value
= $55,000 − $8,500 = $46,500
Taxes = 0.40 × $46,500 = $18,600

c. Initial investment:

Installed cost of new equipment		
Cost of new equipment	$75,000	
+ Installation costs	5,000	
Total installed cost—new		$80,000
− After-tax proceeds from sale of old equipment		
Proceeds from sale of old equipment	$55,000	
− Taxes on sale of old equipment	18,600	
Total after-tax proceeds—old		36,400
+ Change in net working capital		15,000
Initial investment		$58,600

ST8–2 **a.** Initial investment:

Installed cost of new machine		
Cost of new machine	$140,000	
+ Installation costs	10,000	
Total installed cost—new (depreciable value)		$150,000
− After-tax proceeds from sale of old machine		
Proceeds from sale of old machine	$ 42,000	
− Taxes on sale of old machine[1]	9,120	
Total after-tax proceeds—old		32,880
+ Change in net working capital[2]		20,000
Initial investment		$137,120

[1]Book value of old machine = $40,000 − [(0.20 + 0.32) × $40,000]
= $40,000 − (0.52 × $40,000)
= $40,000 − $20,800 = $19,200
Gain on sale = $42,000 − $19,200 = $22,800
Taxes = .40 × $22,800 = $9,120

[2]Change in net working capital = +$10,000 + $25,000 − $15,000
= $35,000 − $15,000 = $20,000

b. Incremental operating cash inflows:

Calculation of Depreciation Expense

Year	Cost (1)	Applicable MACRS depreciation percentages (from Table 3.2) (2)		Depreciation [(1) × (2)] (3)
With new machine				
1	$150,000	33%		$ 49,500
2	150,000	45		67,500
3	150,000	15		22,500
4	150,000	7		10,500
		Totals 100%		$150,000
With old machine				
2	$ 40,000	19%	(year-3 depreciation)	$ 7,600
2	40,000	12	(year-4 depreciation)	4,800
3	40,000	12	(year-5 depreciation)	4,800
4	40,000	5	(year-6 depreciation)	2,000
			Total	$19,200[a]

[a]The total of $19,200 represents the book value of the old machine at the end of the second year, which was calculated in part **a.**

Calculation of Operating Cash Inflows

	Year			
	1	2	3	4
With new machine				
Earnings before depr., int., and taxes[a]	$120,000	$130,000	$130,000	$ 0
− Depreciation[b]	49,500	67,500	22,500	10,500
Earnings before int. and taxes	$ 70,500	$ 62,500	$107,500	−$10,500
− Taxes (rate, $T = 40\%$)	28,200	25,000	43,000	− 4,200
Net operating profit after taxes	$ 42,300	$ 37,500	$ 64,500	−$ 6,300
+ Depreciation[b]	49,500	67,500	22,500	10,500
Operating cash inflows	$ 91,800	$105,000	$ 87,000	$ 4,200
With old machine				
Earnings before depr., int., and taxes[a]	$ 70,000	$ 70,000	$ 70,000	$ 0
− Depreciation[c]	7,600	4,800	4,800	2,000
Earnings before int. and taxes	$ 62,400	$ 65,200	$ 65,200	−$ 2,000
− Taxes (rate, $T = 40\%$)	24,960	26,080	26,080	− 800
Net operating profit after taxes	$ 37,440	$ 39,120	$ 39,120	−$ 1,200
+ Depreciation	7,600	4,800	4,800	2,000
Operating cash inflows	$ 45,040	$ 43,920	$ 43,920	$ 800

[a]Given in the problem.
[b]From column 3 of the preceding table, top.
[c]From column 3 of the preceding table, bottom.

| | Calculation of Incremental Operating Cash Inflows | | |
| | Operating cash inflows | | |
Year	New machine[a] (1)	Old machine[a] (2)	Incremental (relevant) [(1) − (2)] (3)
1	$ 91,800	$45,040	$46,760
2	105,000	43,920	61,080
3	87,000	43,920	43,080
4	4,200	800	3,400

[a]From the final row for the respective machine in the preceding table.

c. Terminal cash flow (end of year 3):

After-tax proceeds from sale of new machine			
Proceeds from sale of new machine	$35,000		
Total after-tax proceeds—new[1]	9,800		
Total after-tax proceeds—new		$25,200	
− After-tax proceeds from sale of old machine			
Proceeds from sale of old machine	$ 0		
− Tax on sale of old machine[2]	− 800		
Total after-tax proceeds—old		800	
+ Change in net working capital		20,000	
Terminal cash flow		$44,400	

---

[1]Book value of new machine at end of year 3
$$= \$150,000 - [(0.33 + 0.45 + 0.15) \times \$150,000] = \$150,000 - (0.93 \times \$150,000)$$
$$= \$15,000 - \$139,500 = \$10,500$$
Tax on sale $= 0.40 \times (\$35,000$ sale price $- \$10,500$ book value$)$
$$= 0.40 \times \$24,500 = \underline{\$9,800}$$

[2]Book value of old machine at end of year 3
$$= \$40,000 - [(0.20 + 0.32 + 0.19 + 0.12 + 0.12) \times \$40,000] = \$40,000 - (0.95 \times \$40,000)$$
$$= \$40,000 - \$38,000 = \$2,000$$
Tax on sale $= 0.40 \times (\$0$ sale price $- \$2,000$ book value$)$
$$= 0.40 \times (-\$2,500 = -\underline{\$800} \text{ (i.e., } \$800 \text{ tax saving)}$$

d.

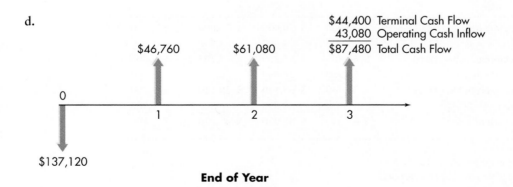

$44,400 Terminal Cash Flow
43,080 Operating Cash Inflow
$87,480 Total Cash Flow

$46,760 $61,080 $87,480

0   1   2   3

$137,120

End of Year

Note: The year-4 incremental operating cash inflow of $3,400 is not directly included; it is instead reflected in the book values used to calculate the taxes on sale of the machines at the end of year 3 and is therefore part of the terminal cash flow.

Solutions to Self-Test Problems

8–1	**a.**	Operating expenditure
	d.	Operating expenditure
	f.	Capital expenditure

8–4	*Year*	*Relevant cash flow*
	1	$4,000
	2	$6,000
	4	$10,000

8–7 A: $275,500
    B: $26,800

8–8 **a.** $23,200
    b. @$100,000: $30,720
        @$56,000: $13,120

8–9 **a.** Total tax: $49,600
    d. Total tax: ($6,400)

8–12 Initial investment $22,680

8–13 **a.** Initial investment: $18,240
    c. Initial investment: $23,100

8–15 **c.** Cash inflow, Year 3: $584,000

8–16 Incremental operating cash flow, Year 2: $458

8–18 **b.** Incremental cash flow, Year 3: $1,960

8–20 Terminal cash flow: $76,640

8–24 **b.** Operating cash flow, Year 1: ($15,600)

Chapter 12

Chapter 2

Capital Budgeting Techniques: Certainty and Risk

WHY THIS CHAPTER MATTERS TO YOU

(In Your Professional Life)

Accounting: You need to understand capital budgeting techniques to determine relevant cash flows associated with proposed capital expenditures and to appreciate how risk may affect the variability of cash flows.

Information systems: You need to understand capital budgeting techniques, including how to measure risk in those techniques, to design decision modules that help analyze proposed capital expenditures.

Management: You need to understand capital budgeting techniques, along with real options, capital rationing, and techniques for dealing with project risk, to analyze the relevant cash flows of proposed projects and decide whether to accept them.

Marketing: You need to understand capital budgeting techniques to grasp how proposals for new marketing programs, new products, and expansion of existing product lines will be evaluated by the firm's decision makers and how risk of proposed products is treated in capital budgeting.

Operations: You need to understand capital budgeting techniques to know how proposals for the acquisition of new equipment and plants will be evaluated by the firm's decision makers, especially when capital must be rationed.

(In Your Personal Life)

You can use capital budgeting techniques, such as the IRR technique, to measure both actual and forecast returns on investments in securities, real estate, the true cost of credit card debt, consumer loans, and leases. You also should consider risk when making personal-finance decisions.

LEARNING GOALS

LG 1 Calculate, interpret, and evaluate the payback period.

LG 2 Apply net present value (NPV) and internal rate of return (IRR) to relevant cash flows to choose acceptable capital expenditures.

LG 3 Use net present value profiles to compare the NPV and IRR techniques in light of conflicting rankings.

LG 4 Discuss two additional considerations in capital budgeting—recognizing real options and choosing projects under capital rationing.

LG 5 Recognize sensitivity analysis and scenario analysis, decision trees, and simulation as behavioral approaches for dealing with project risk, and the unique risks that multinational companies face.

LG 6 Understand the calculation and practical aspects of risk-adjusted discount rates (RADRs).

From Chapter 9 of *Principles of Managerial Finance*, Brief 5th Edition. Lawrence J. Gitman. Copyright © 2009 by Pearson Prentice Hall. All rights reserved.

469

F irms use the relevant cash flows to make decisions about proposed capital expenditures. These decisions can be expressed in the form of project acceptance or rejection or of project rankings. A number of techniques are used in such decision making, some more sophisticated than others. These techniques are the topic of this chapter, wherein we describe the assumptions on which capital budgeting techniques are based, show how they are used in both certain and risky situations, and evaluate their strengths and weaknesses.

1 | Capital Budgeting Techniques

When firms have developed relevant cash flows, they analyze them to assess whether a project is acceptable or to rank projects. A number of techniques are available for performing such analyses. The preferred approaches integrate time value procedures, risk and return considerations, and valuation concepts to select capital expenditures that are consistent with the firm's goal of maximizing owners' wealth. This section and the next one focus on the use of these techniques in an environment of certainty. In subsequent sections, we will look at capital budgeting under uncertain circumstances.

Bennett Company's Relevant Cash Flows

We will use one basic problem to illustrate the capital budgeting techniques. The problem concerns Bennett Company, a medium-sized metal fabricator that is currently contemplating two projects: Project A requires an initial investment of $42,000; project B requires an initial investment of $45,000. The projected relevant cash flows for the two projects are presented in Table 1 and depicted on the time lines in Figure 1.[1] The projects exhibit *conventional cash flow patterns,*

Hint Remember that the initial investment is an *outflow* occurring at time zero.

TABLE 1	Capital Expenditure Data for Bennett Company	
	Project A	Project B
Initial investment	$42,000	$45,000
Year	Operating cash inflows	
1	$14,000	$28,000
2	14,000	12,000
3	14,000	10,000
4	14,000	10,000
5	14,000	10,000

---

1. For simplification, these 5-year-lived projects with 5 years of cash inflows are used throughout this chapter. Projects with usable lives equal to the number of years of cash inflows are also included in the end-of-chapter problems. Under current tax law, MACRS depreciation results in $n + 1$ years of depreciation for an n-year class asset. This means that projects will commonly have at least 1 year of cash flow beyond their recovery period. In actual practice, the usable lives of projects (and the associated cash inflows) may differ significantly from their depreciable lives. Generally, under MACRS, usable lives are longer than depreciable lives.

FIGURE 1

Bennett Company's Projects A and B
Time lines depicting the conventional cash flows of projects A and B

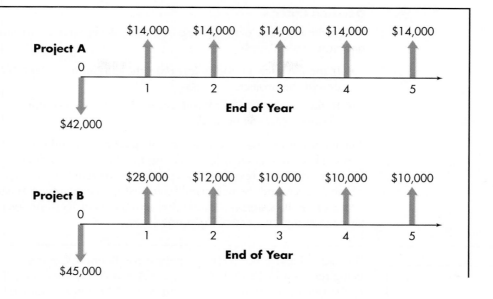

which are assumed throughout the text. In addition, we initially assume that all projects' cash flows have the same level of risk, that projects being compared have equal usable lives, and that the firm has unlimited funds. Because very few are actually made under such conditions, later in the chapter we relax some of these simplifying instructions.

We begin with a look at the three most popular capital budgeting techniques: payback period, net present value, and internal rate of return.[2]

Payback Period

payback period
The amount of time required for a firm to recover its initial investment in a project, as calculated from *cash inflows.*

Payback periods are commonly used to evaluate proposed investments. The **payback period** is the amount of time required for the firm to recover its initial investment in a project, as calculated from *cash inflows.* In the case of an *annuity,* the payback period can be found by dividing the initial investment by the annual cash inflow. For a *mixed stream* of cash inflows, the yearly cash inflows must be accumulated until the initial investment is recovered. Although popular, the payback period is generally viewed as an *unsophisticated capital budgeting technique,* because it does not *explicitly* consider the time value of money.

---

2. Two other, closely related techniques that are sometimes used to evaluate capital budgeting projects are the *average (or accounting) rate of return (ARR)* and the *profitability index (PI).* The ARR is an unsophisticated technique that is calculated by dividing a project's average profits after taxes by its average investment. Because it fails to consider cash flows and the time value of money, it is ignored here. The PI, sometimes called the *benefit–cost ratio,* is calculated by dividing the present value of cash inflows by the initial investment. This technique, which does consider the time value of money, is sometimes used as a starting point in the selection of projects under *capital rationing;* the more popular NPV and IRR methods are discussed here.

Decision Criteria

When the payback period is used to make accept–reject decisions, the following decision criteria apply.

- If the payback period is *less than* the maximum acceptable payback period, *accept* the project.
- If the payback period is *greater than* the maximum acceptable payback period, *reject* the project.

The length of the maximum acceptable payback period is determined by management. This value is set *subjectively* on the basis of a number of factors, including the type of project (expansion, replacement or renewal, other), the perceived risk of the project, and the perceived relationship between the payback period and the share value. It is simply a value that management feels, on average, will result in value-creating investment decisions.

Example

We can calculate the payback period for Bennett Company's projects A and B using the data in Table 1. *For project A, which is an annuity, the payback period is 3.0 years ($42,000 initial investment ÷ $14,000 annual cash inflow).* Because project B generates a mixed stream of cash inflows, the calculation of its payback period is not as clear-cut. In year 1, the firm will recover $28,000 of its $45,000 initial investment. By the end of year 2, $40,000 ($28,000 from year 1 + $12,000 from year 2) will have been recovered. At the end of year 3, $50,000 will have been recovered. Only 50% of the year-3 cash inflow of $10,000 is needed to complete the payback of the initial $45,000. *The payback period for project B is therefore 2.5 years (2 years + 50% of year 3).*

If Bennett's maximum acceptable payback period were 2.75 years, project A would be rejected and project B would be accepted. If the maximum payback were 2.25 years, both projects would be rejected. If the projects were being ranked, B would be preferred over A, because it has a shorter payback period.

Pros and Cons of Payback Periods

Hint In *all three* of the decision methods presented in this text, the relevant data are *after-tax cash flows.* Accounting profit is used only to help determine the after-tax cash flow.

Hint The payback period indicates to firms taking on projects of high risk how quickly they can recover their investment. In addition, it tells firms with limited sources of capital how quickly the funds invested in a given project will become available for future projects.

Large firms usually use the payback period to evaluate small projects, and small firms use it to evaluate most projects. Its popularity results from its computational simplicity and intuitive appeal. It is also appealing in that it considers cash flows rather than accounting profits. By measuring how quickly the firm recovers its initial investment, the payback period also gives *implicit* consideration to the timing of cash flows and therefore to the time value of money. Because it can be viewed as a measure of *risk exposure,* many firms use the payback period as a decision criterion or as a supplement to other decision techniques. The longer the firm must wait to recover its invested funds, the greater the possibility of a calamity. Therefore, the shorter the payback period, the lower the firm's exposure to such risk.

The major weakness of the payback period is that the appropriate payback period is merely a subjectively determined number. It cannot be specified in light of the wealth maximization goal because it is not based on discounting cash flows to determine whether they add to the firm's value. Instead, the appropriate payback period is simply the maximum acceptable period of time over which management decides that a project's cash flows must break even (that is, just equal the initial investment).

Personal Finance Example   Seema Mehdi is considering investing $20,000 in a 5% interest in a rental property. Her good friend and real estate agent, Akbar Ahmed, put the deal together, and he conservatively estimates that Seema should receive between $4,000 and $6,000 per year in cash from her 5% interest in the property. The deal is structured in a way that forces all investors to maintain their investment in the property for at least 10 years. Seema expects to remain in the 25% income-tax bracket for quite a while. In order to be acceptable, Seema requires the investment to pay itself back in terms of after-tax cash flows in less than 7 years.

Seema's calculation of the payback period on this deal begins with calculation of the range of annual after-tax cash flow:

$$\text{After-tax cash flow} = (1 - \text{tax rate}) \times \text{Pre-tax cash flow}$$
$$= (1 - 0.25) \times \$4,000 = \$3,000$$
$$= (1 - 0.25) \times \$6,000 = \$4,500$$

The after-tax cash flow ranges from $3,000 to $4,500. Dividing the $20,000 initial investment by each of the estimated after-tax cash flows, we get the payback period:

$$\text{Payback period} = \text{Initial investment} \div \text{After-tax cash flow}$$
$$= \$20,000 \div \$3,000 = 6.67 \text{ years}$$
$$= \$20,000 \div \$4,500 = 4.44 \text{ years}$$

Because Seema's proposed rental property investment will pay itself back between 4.44 and 6.67 years, which is a range below her maximum payback of 7 years, the investment is acceptable.

A second weakness is that this approach fails to take *fully* into account the time factor in the value of money.[3] This weakness can be illustrated by an example.

Example   DeYarman Enterprises, a small medical appliance manufacturer, is considering two mutually exclusive projects, which it has named projects Gold and Silver. The firm uses only the payback period to choose projects. The relevant cash flows and payback period for each project are given in Table 2. Both projects have 3-year payback periods, which would suggest that they are equally desirable. But comparison of the pattern of cash inflows over the first 3 years shows that more of the $50,000 initial investment in project Silver is recovered sooner than is recovered for project Gold. For example, in year 1, $40,000 of the $50,000 invested in project Silver is recovered, whereas only $5,000 of the $50,000 investment in project Gold is recovered. Given the time value of money, project Silver would clearly be preferred over project Gold, in spite of the fact that both have identical 3-year payback periods. The payback approach does not fully account for the time value of money, which, if recognized, would cause project Silver to be preferred over project Gold.

---

3. To consider differences in timing explicitly in applying the payback method, the *discounted payback period* is sometimes used. It is found by first calculating the present value of the cash inflows at the appropriate discount rate and then finding the payback period by using the present value of the cash inflows.

TABLE 2	Relevant Cash Flows and Payback Periods for DeYarman Enterprises' Projects	
	Project Gold	Project Silver
Initial investment	$50,000	$50,000
Year	Operating cash inflows	
1	$ 5,000	$40,000
2	5,000	2,000
3	40,000	8,000
4	10,000	10,000
5	10,000	10,000
Payback period	3 years	3 years

A third weakness of payback is its failure to recognize cash flows that occur *after* the payback period.

Example

Rashid Company, a software developer, has two investment opportunities, X and Y. Data for X and Y are given in Table 3. The payback period for project X is 2 years; for project Y it is 3 years. Strict adherence to the payback approach suggests that project X is preferable to project Y. However, if we look beyond the payback period, we see that project X returns only an additional $1,200 ($1,000 in year 3 + $100 in year 4 + $100 in year 5), whereas project Y returns an additional $7,000 ($4,000 in year 4 + $3,000 in year 5). On the basis of this information, project Y appears preferable to X. The payback approach ignored the cash inflows occurring after the end of the payback period.[4]

TABLE 3	Calculation of the Payback Period for Rashid Company's Two Alternative Investment Projects	
	Project X	Project Y
Initial investment	$10,000	$10,000
Year	Operating cash inflows	
1	$5,000	$3,000
2	5,000	4,000
3	1,000	3,000
4	100	4,000
5	100	3,000
Payback period	2 years	3 years

---

4. To get around this weakness, some analysts add a desired dollar return to the initial investment and then calculate the payback period for the increased amount. For example, if the analyst wished to pay back the initial investment plus 20% for projects X and Y in Table 3, the amount to be recovered would be $12,000 [$10,000 + (0.20 × $10,000)]. For project X, the payback period would be infinite because the $12,000 would never be recovered; for project Y, the payback period would be 3.5 years [3 years + ($2,000 ÷ $4,000) years]. Clearly, project Y would be preferred.

Net Present Value (NPV)

Because *net present value (NPV)* gives explicit consideration to the time value of money, it is considered a *sophisticated capital budgeting technique.* All such techniques in one way or another discount the firm's cash flows at a specified rate. This rate—often called the *discount rate, required return, cost of capital,* or *opportunity cost*—is the minimum return that must be earned on a project to leave the firm's market value unchanged. In this chapter, we take this rate as a "given."

net present value (NPV)
A sophisticated capital budgeting technique; found by subtracting a project's initial investment from the present value of its cash inflows discounted at a rate equal to the firm's cost of capital.

The **net present value (NPV)** is found by subtracting a project's initial investment (CF_0) from the present value of its cash inflows (CF_t) discounted at a rate equal to the firm's cost of capital (r).

$$\text{NPV} = \text{Present value of cash inflows} - \text{Initial investment}$$

$$\text{NPV} = \sum_{t=1}^{n} \frac{CF_t}{(1 + r)^t} - CF_0 \tag{1}$$

$$= \sum_{t=1}^{n} (CF_t \times PVIF_{r,t}) - CF_0 \tag{1a}$$

When NPV is used, both inflows and outflows are measured in terms of present dollars. Because we are dealing only with investments that have *conventional cash flow patterns,* the initial investment is automatically stated in terms of today's dollars. If it were not, the present value of a project would be found by subtracting the present value of outflows from the present value of inflows.

Decision Criteria

When NPV is used to make accept–reject decisions, the decision criteria are as follows:

- If the NPV is *greater than* $0, *accept* the project.
- If the NPV is *less than* $0, *reject* the project.

If the NPV is greater than $0, the firm will earn a return greater than its cost of capital. Such action should increase the market value of the firm, and therefore the wealth of its owners by an amount equal to the NPV.

Example

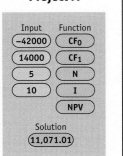

Project A

Input	Function
−42000	CF₀
14000	CF₁
5	N
10	I
	NPV

Solution

11,071.01

We can illustrate the net present value (NPV) approach by using the Bennett Company data presented in Table 1. If the firm has a 10% cost of capital, the net present values for projects A (an annuity) and B (a mixed stream) can be calculated as shown on the time lines in Figure 2. These calculations result in net present values for projects A and B of $11,071 and $10,924, respectively. Both projects are acceptable, because the net present value of each is greater than $0. If the projects were being ranked, however, project A would be considered superior to B, because it has a higher net present value than that of B ($11,071 versus $10,924).

Calculator Use The preprogrammed NPV function in a financial calculator can be used to simplify the NPV calculation. The keystrokes for project A—the annuity—typically are as shown at left. Note that because project A is an annuity, only its first cash inflow, $CF_1 = 14000$, is input, followed by its frequency, $N = 5$.

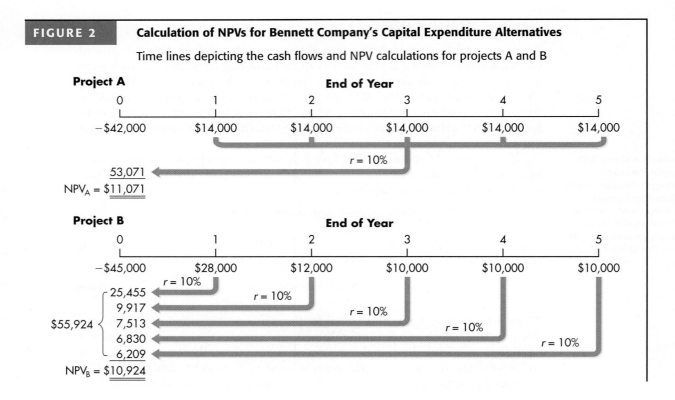

FIGURE 2 Calculation of NPVs for Bennett Company's Capital Expenditure Alternatives

Time lines depicting the cash flows and NPV calculations for projects A and B

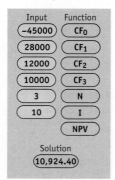

Project B

Input	Function
−45000	CF_0
28000	CF_1
12000	CF_2
10000	CF_3
3	N
10	I
	NPV

Solution
10,924.40

The keystrokes for project B—the mixed stream—are as shown at left. Because the last three cash inflows for project B are the same ($CF_3 = CF_4 = CF_5 = 10000$), after inputting the first of these cash inflows, CF_3, we merely input its frequency, $N = 3$.

The calculated NPVs for projects A and B of $11,071 and $10,924, respectively, agree with the NPVs cited above.

Spreadsheet Use The NPVs can be calculated as shown on the following Excel spreadsheet.

	A	B	C
1	DETERMINING THE NET PRESENT VALUE		
2	Firm's cost of capital		10%
3		Year-End Cash Flow	
4	Year	Project A	Project B
5	0	$ (42,000)	$ (45,000)
6	1	$ 14,000	$ 28,000
7	2	$ 14,000	$ 12,000
8	3	$ 14,000	$ 10,000
9	4	$ 14,000	$ 10,000
10	5	$ 14,000	$ 10,000
11	NPV	$ 11,071	$ 10,924
12	Choice of project		Project A

Entry in Cell B11 is
=NPV(C2,B6:B10)+B5
Copy the entry in Cell B11 to Cell C11.
Entry in Cell C12 is =IF(B11>C11,B4,C4).

Internal Rate of Return (IRR)

internal rate of return (IRR)
A sophisticated capital budgeting technique; the discount rate that equates the NPV of an investment opportunity with $0 (because the present value of cash inflows equals the initial investment); it is the compound annual rate of return that the firm will earn if it invests in the project and receives the given cash inflows.

The *internal rate of return (IRR)* is probably the most widely used *sophisticated capital budgeting technique*. However, it is considerably more difficult than NPV to calculate by hand. The **internal rate of return** (**IRR**) is the discount rate that equates the NPV of an investment opportunity with $0 (because the present value of cash inflows equals the initial investment). It is the compound annual rate of return that the firm will earn if it invests in the project and receives the given cash inflows. Mathematically, the IRR is the value of r in Equation 1 that causes NPV to equal $0.

$$\$0 = \sum_{t=1}^{n} \frac{CF_t}{(1 + IRR)^t} - CF_0 \tag{2}$$

$$\sum_{t=1}^{n} \frac{CF_t}{(1 + IRR)^t} = CF_0 \tag{2a}$$

Decision Criteria

When IRR is used to make accept–reject decisions, the decision criteria are as follows:

- If the IRR is *greater than* the cost of capital, *accept* the project.
- If the IRR is *less than* the cost of capital, *reject* the project.

These criteria guarantee that the firm will earn at least its required return. Such an outcome should increase the market value of the firm and therefore the wealth of its owners.

Calculating the IRR

The actual calculation by hand of the IRR from Equation 2a is no easy chore. It involves a complex trial-and-error search technique that logically tries different discount rates until one is found that causes the project's present value of cash inflows to just equal its initial investment (or NPV to equal $0). Details of this technique are described and demonstrated on this text's website: **www.prenhall .com/gitman**. Fortunately, many financial calculators have a preprogrammed IRR function that can be used to simplify the IRR calculation. With these calculators, you merely punch in all cash flows just as if to calculate NPV and then depress IRR to find the internal rate of return. Computer software, including spreadsheets, is also available for simplifying these calculations. All NPV and IRR values presented in this chapter are obtained by using these functions on a popular financial calculator.

Example

We can demonstrate the internal rate of return (IRR) approach by using the Bennett Company data presented in Table 1. Figure 3 uses time lines to depict the framework for finding the IRRs for Bennett's projects A and B, both of which have conventional cash flow patterns. We can see in the figure that the IRR is the unknown discount rate that causes the NPV just to equal $0.

Calculator Use   To find the IRR using the preprogrammed function in a financial calculator, the keystrokes for each project are the same as those shown on pagse 000 and 000 for the NPV calculation, except that the last two NPV keystrokes (punching **I** and then **NPV**) are replaced by a single **IRR** keystroke.

Comparing the IRRs of projects A and B given in Figure 3 to Bennett Company's 10% cost of capital, we can see that both projects are acceptable because

$$IRR_A = 19.9\% > 10.0\% \text{ cost of capital}$$
$$IRR_B = 21.7\% > 10.0\% \text{ cost of capital}$$

Comparing the two projects' IRRs, we would prefer project B over project A because $IRR_B = 21.7\% > IRR_A = 19.9\%$. If these projects are mutually exclusive, the IRR decision technique would recommend project B.

Spreadsheet Use   The internal rate of return also can be calculated as shown on the following Excel spreadsheet.

	A	B	C
1		DETERMINING THE INTERNAL RATE OF RETURN	
2		Year-End Cash Flow	
3	Year	Project A	Project B
4	0	$ (42,000)	$ (45,000)
5	1	$ 14,000	$ 28,000
6	2	$ 14,000	$ 12,000
7	3	$ 14,000	$ 10,000
8	4	$ 14,000	$ 10,000
9	5	$ 14,000	$ 10,000
10	IRR	19.9%	21.7%
11	Choice of project		Project B

Entry in Cell B10 is =IRR(B4:B9).
Copy the entry in Cell B10 to Cell C10.
Entry in Cell C11 is =IF(B10>C10,B3,C3).

It is interesting to note in the preceding example that the IRR suggests that project B, which has an IRR of 21.7%, is preferable to project A, which has an IRR of 19.9%. This conflicts with the NPV rankings obtained in an earlier example. Such conflicts are not unusual. *There is no guarantee that NPV and IRR will rank projects in the same order. However, both methods should reach the same conclusion about the acceptability or nonacceptability of projects.*

Personal Finance Example   Tony DiLorenzo is evaluating an investment opportunity. He is comfortable with the investment's level of risk. Based on competing investment opportunities, he feels that this investment must earn a minimum compound annual after-tax return of 9% in order to be acceptable. Tony's initial investment would be $7,500, and he expects to receive annual after-tax cash flows of $500 per year in each of the first 4 years, followed by $700 per year at the end of years 5 through 8. He plans to sell the investment at the end of year 8 and net $9,000, after taxes.

To calculate the investment's IRR (compound annual return), Tony first summarizes the after-tax cash flows as shown in the following table:

Year	Cash flow (− or +)
0	−$7,500 (Initial investment)
1	+ 500
2	+ 500
3	+ 500
4	+ 500
5	+ 700
6	+ 700
7	+ 700

Substituting the after-tax cash flows for years 0 through 8 into a financial calculator or spreadsheet, he finds the investment's IRR of 9.54%. Given that the expected IRR of 9.54% exceeds Tony's required minimum IRR of 9%, the investment is acceptable.

REVIEW QUESTIONS

1   What is the *payback period?* How is it calculated? What weaknesses are commonly associated with the use of the payback period to evaluate a proposed investment?

FIGURE 3   **Calculation of IRRs for Bennett Company's Capital Expenditure Alternatives**

Time lines depicting the cash flows and IRR calculations for projects A and B

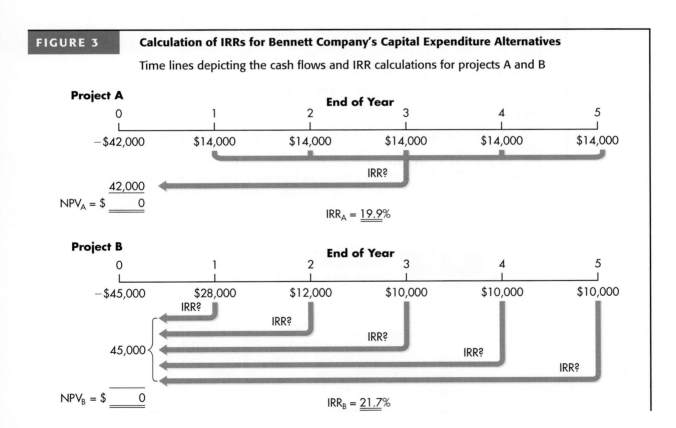

2   How is the *net present value (NPV)* calculated for a project with a *conventional cash flow pattern*? What are the acceptance criteria for NPV?

3   What is the *internal rate of return (IRR)* on an investment? How is it determined? What are the acceptance criteria for IRR?

 2 | # Comparing NPV and IRR Techniques

To understand the differences between the NPV and IRR techniques and decision makers' preferences in their use, we need to look at net present value profiles, conflicting rankings, and the question of which approach is better.

Net Present Value Profiles

net present value profile
Graph that depicts a project's NPVs for various discount rates.

Projects can be compared graphically by constructing **net present value profiles** that depict the project's NPVs for various discount rates. These profiles are useful in evaluating and comparing projects, especially when conflicting rankings exist. They are best demonstrated via an example.

Example

To prepare net present value profiles for Bennett Company's two projects, A and B, the first step is to develop a number of "discount rate–net present value" coordinates. Three coordinates can be easily obtained for each project; they are at discount rates of 0%, 10% (the cost of capital, r), and the IRR. The net present value at a 0% discount rate is found by merely adding all the cash inflows and subtracting the initial investment. Using the data in Table 1 and Figure 1, we get

For project A:

($14,000 + $14,000 + $14,000 + $14,000 + $14,000) − $42,000 = $28,000

For project B:

($28,000 + $12,000 + $10,000 + $10,000 + $10,000) − $45,000 = $25,000

The net present values for projects A and B at the 10% cost of capital are $11,071 and $10,924, respectively (from Figure 2). Because the IRR is the discount rate for which net present value equals zero, the IRRs (from Figure 3) of 19.9% for project A and 21.7% for project B result in $0 NPVs. The three sets of coordinates for each of the projects are summarized in Table 4.

TABLE 4	Discount Rate–NPV Coordinates for Projects A and B	
	Net present value	
Discount rate	Project A	Project B
0 %	$28,000	$25,000
10	11,071	10,924
19.9	0	—
21.7	—	0

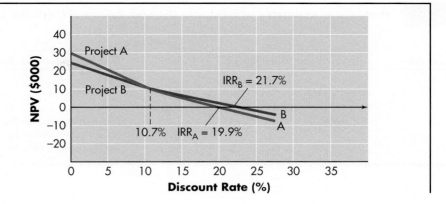

FIGURE 4

NPV Profiles
Net present value profiles for Bennett Company's projects A and B

Plotting the data from Table 4 results in the net present value profiles for projects A and B shown in Figure 4. The figure indicates that for any discount rate less than approximately 10.7%, the NPV for project A is greater than the NPV for project B. Beyond this point, the NPV for project B is greater. Because the net present value profiles for projects A and B cross at a positive NPV that occurs at a discount rate (10.7%), which is higher than the firm's cost of capital (10.0%), the IRRs for the projects result in conflicting rankings with their NPVs.

Conflicting Rankings

conflicting rankings
Conflicts in the ranking given a project by NPV and IRR, resulting from *differences in the magnitude and timing of cash flows.*

intermediate cash inflows
Cash inflows received prior to the termination of a project.

Ranking is an important consideration when projects are mutually exclusive or when capital rationing is necessary. When projects are mutually exclusive, ranking enables the firm to determine which project is best from a financial standpoint. When capital rationing is necessary, ranking projects will provide a logical starting point for determining which group of projects to accept. As we'll see, **conflicting rankings** using NPV and IRR result from *differences in the magnitude and timing of cash flows.*

The underlying cause of conflicting rankings is different implicit assumptions about the *reinvestment* of **intermediate cash inflows**—cash inflows received prior to the termination of a project. NPV assumes that intermediate cash inflows are reinvested at the cost of capital, whereas IRR assumes that intermediate cash inflows are reinvested at a rate equal to the project's IRR.[5]

In general, projects with similar-size investments and lower cash inflows in the early years tend to be preferred at lower discount rates. Projects that have

---

5. To eliminate the reinvestment rate assumption of the IRR, some practitioners calculate the *modified internal rate of return (MIRR).* The MIRR is found by converting each operating cash inflow to its future value measured at the end of the project's life and then summing the future values of all inflows to get the project's *terminal value.* Each future value is found by using the cost of capital, thereby eliminating the reinvestment rate criticism of the traditional IRR. The MIRR represents the discount rate that causes the terminal value just to equal the initial investment. Because it uses the cost of capital as the reinvestment rate, the MIRR is generally viewed as a better measure of a project's true profitability than the IRR. Although this technique is frequently used in commercial real estate valuation and is a preprogrammed function on some financial calculators, its failure to resolve the issue of conflicting rankings and its theoretical inferiority to NPV have resulted in the MIRR receiving only limited attention and acceptance in the financial literature. For a thorough analysis of the arguments surrounding IRR and MIRR, see D. Anthony Plath and William F. Kennedy, "Teaching Return-Based Measures of Project Evaluation," *Financial Practice and Education* (Spring/Summer 1994), pp. 77–86.

TABLE 5	Preferences Associated with Extreme Discount Rates and Dissimilar Cash Inflow Patterns	
	Cash inflow pattern	
Discount rate	Lower early-year cash inflows	Higher early-year cash inflows
Low	Preferred, because higher late-year cash inflows are not greatly reduced and therefore dominate in terms of present value.	Not preferred
High	Not preferred	Preferred, because the higher early-year cash inflows are not greatly reduced and therefore dominate in terms of present value.

higher cash inflows in the early years tend to be preferred at higher discount rates. Why? Because at high discount rates, later-year cash inflows tend to be severely penalized in present value terms. For example, at a high discount rate, say 20 percent, the present value of $1 received at the end of 5 years is about 40 cents, whereas for $1 received at the end of 15 years it is less than 7 cents. Clearly, at high discount rates a project's early-year cash inflows count most in terms of its NPV. Table 5 summarizes the preferences associated with extreme discount rates and dissimilar cash inflow patterns.

Example

Bennett Company's projects A and B were found to have conflicting rankings at the firm's 10% cost of capital (as depicted in Figure 4). If we review each project's cash inflow pattern as presented in Table 1 and Figure 1, we see that although the projects require similar initial investments, they have dissimilar cash inflow patterns. Table 5 indicates that project B, which has higher early-year cash inflows than project A, would be preferred over project A at higher discount rates. Figure 4 shows that this is in fact the case. At any discount rate in excess of 10.7%, project B's NPV surpasses that of project A. Clearly, the magnitude and timing of the projects' cash inflows do affect their rankings.

Which Approach Is Better?

Many companies use both the NPV and IRR techniques because current technology makes them easy to calculate. But it is difficult to choose one approach over the other, because the theoretical and practical strengths of the approaches differ. Clearly, it is wise to evaluate NPV and IRR techniques from both theoretical and practical points of view.

Theoretical View

On a purely theoretical basis, NPV is the better approach to capital budgeting as a result of several factors. Most important, the use of NPV implicitly assumes that any intermediate cash inflows generated by an investment are *reinvested at the firm's cost of capital.* The use of IRR assumes *reinvestment at the often high rate specified by the IRR.* Because the cost of capital tends to be a reasonable estimate of the rate at which the firm could *actually reinvest* intermediate cash inflows, the use of NPV, with its more conservative and realistic reinvestment rate, is in theory preferable.

multiple IRRs
More than one IRR resulting from a capital budgeting project with a *nonconventional cash flow pattern;* the maximum number of IRRs for a project is equal to the number of sign changes in its cash flows.

In addition, certain mathematical properties may cause a project with a *nonconventional cash flow pattern* to have **multiple IRRs**—more than one IRR. Mathematically, the maximum number of *real* roots to an equation is equal to its number of sign changes. Take an equation like $x^2 - 5x + 6 = 0$, which has two sign changes in its coefficients—from positive $(+x^2)$ to negative $(-5x)$ and then from negative $(-5x)$ to positive $(+6)$. If we factor the equation (remember factoring from high school math?), we get $(x - 2) \times (x - 3)$, which means that x can equal either 2 or 3—there are two correct values for x. Substitute them back into the equation, and you'll see that both values work.

This same outcome can occur when finding the IRR for projects with nonconventional cash flows, because they have more than one sign change. Clearly, when multiple IRRs occur for nonconventional cash flows, the analyst faces the time-consuming need to interpret their meanings so as to evaluate the project. The fact that such a challenge does not exist when using NPV enhances its theoretical superiority.

Practical View

Evidence suggests that in spite of the theoretical superiority of NPV, *financial managers prefer to use IRR.*[6] The preference for IRR is due to the general disposition of businesspeople toward *rates of return* rather than actual *dollar returns.* Because interest rates, profitability, and so on are most often expressed as annual rates of return, the use of IRR makes sense to financial decision makers. They tend to find NPV less intuitive because it does not measure benefits *relative to the amount invested.* Because a variety of techniques are available for avoiding the pitfalls of the IRR, its widespread use does not imply a lack of sophistication on the part of financial decision makers. Clearly, corporate financial analysts are responsible for identifying and resolving problems with the IRR before the decision makers use it as a decision technique.

REVIEW QUESTIONS

4   Do the net present value (NPV) and internal rate of return (IRR) always agree with respect to accept–reject decisions? With respect to ranking decisions? Explain.

5   How is a *net present value profile* used to compare projects? What causes conflicts in the ranking of projects via net present value and internal rate of return?

6   Does the assumption concerning the reinvestment of intermediate cash inflow tend to favor NPV or IRR? In practice, which technique is preferred and why?

6. For example, see John R. Graham and Campbell R. Harvey, "The Theory and Practice of Corporate Finance: Evidence from the Field," *Journal of Financial Economics* (May/June 2001,) pp. 187–243; Harold Bierman, Jr., "Capital Budgeting in 1992: A Survey," *Financial Management* (Autumn 1993), p. 24; and Lawrence J. Gitman and Charles E. Maxwell, "A Longitudinal Comparison of Capital Budgeting Techniques Used by Major U.S. Firms: 1986 versus 1976," *Journal of Applied Business Research* (Fall 1987), pp. 41–50, for discussions of evidence with respect to capital budgeting decision-making practices in major U.S. firms.

3 | Additional Considerations: Real Options and Capital Rationing

Two important issues that often confront the financial manager when making capital budgeting decisions are (1) the potential real options embedded in capital projects, and (2) the availability of only limited funding for acceptable projects. Here we briefly consider each of these situations.

Recognizing Real Options

real options
Opportunities that are embedded in capital projects that enable managers to alter their cash flows and risk in a way that affects project acceptability (NPV). Also called *strategic options*.

The procedures described thus far suggest that to make capital budgeting decisions, we must (1) estimate relevant cash flows, (2) apply an appropriate decision technique such as NPV or IRR to those cash flows, and (3) recognize and adjust the decision technique for project risk. Although this traditional procedure is believed to yield good decisions, a more *strategic approach* to these decisions has emerged in recent years. This more modern view considers any **real options**— opportunities that are embedded in capital projects ("real," rather than financial, asset investments) that enable managers to alter their cash flows and risk in a way that affects project acceptability (NPV). Because these opportunities are more likely to exist in, and be more important to, large "strategic" capital budgeting projects, they are sometimes called *strategic options*.

Table 6 briefly describes some of the more common types of real options— abandonment, flexibility, growth, and timing. It should be clear from their

TABLE 6	Major Types of Real Options
Option type	**Description**
Abandonment option	The option to abandon or terminate a project prior to the end of its planned life. This option allows management to avoid or minimize losses on projects that turn bad. Explicitly recognizing the abandonment option when evaluating a project often increases its NPV.
Flexibility option	The option to incorporate flexibility into the firm's operations, particularly production. It generally includes the opportunity to design the production process to accept multiple inputs, use flexible production technology to create a variety of outputs by reconfiguring the same plant and equipment, and purchase and retain excess capacity in capital-intensive industries subject to wide swings in output demand and long lead time in building new capacity from scratch. Recognition of this option embedded in a capital expenditure should increase the NPV of the project.
Growth option	The option to develop follow-on projects, expand markets, expand or retool plants, and so on, that would not be possible without implementation of the project that is being evaluated. If a project being considered has the measurable potential to open new doors if successful, then recognition of the cash flows from such opportunities should be included in the initial decision process. Growth opportunities embedded in a project often increase the NPV of the project in which they are embedded.
Timing option	The option to determine when various actions with respect to a given project are taken. This option recognizes the firm's opportunity to delay acceptance of a project for one or more periods, to accelerate or slow the process of implementing a project in response to new information, or to shut down a project temporarily in response to changing product market conditions or competition. As in the case of the other types of options, the explicit recognition of timing opportunities can improve the NPV of a project that fails to recognize this option in an investment decision.

descriptions that each of these types of options could be embedded in a capital budgeting decision and that explicit recognition of them would probably alter the cash flow and risk of a project and change its NPV.

By explicitly recognizing these options when making capital budgeting decisions, managers can make improved, more strategic decisions that consider in advance the economic impact of certain contingent actions on project cash flow and risk. The explicit recognition of real options embedded in capital budgeting projects will cause the project's *strategic NPV* to differ from its *traditional NPV* as indicated by Equation 3.

$$NPV_{strategic} = NPV_{traditional} + \text{Value of real options} \qquad (3)$$

Application of this relationship is illustrated in the following example.

Example

Assume that a strategic analysis of Bennett Company's projects A and B finds no real options embedded in project A and two real options embedded in project B. The two real options in project B are as follows: (1) The project would have, during the first 2 years, some downtime that would result in unused production capacity that could be used to perform contract manufacturing for another firm, and (2) the project's computerized control system could, with some modification, control two other machines, thereby reducing labor cost, without affecting operation of the new project.

Bennett's management estimated the NPV of the contract manufacturing over the 2 years following implementation of project B to be $1,500 and the NPV of the computer control sharing to be $2,000. Management felt there was a 60% chance that the contract manufacturing option would be exercised and only a 30% chance that the computer control sharing option would be exercised. The combined value of these two real options would be the sum of their expected values.

$$\text{Value of real options for project B} = (0.60 \times \$1,500) + (0.30 \times \$2,000)$$
$$= \$900 + \$600 = \$1,500$$

Substituting the $1,500 real options value along with the traditional NPV of $10,924 for project B (from Table 2) into Equation 3, we get the strategic NPV for project B.

$$NPV_{strategic} = \$10,924 + \$1,500 = \underline{\underline{\$12,424}}$$

Bennett Company's project B therefore has a strategic NPV of $12,424, which is above its traditional NPV and now exceeds project A's NPV of $11,071. Clearly, recognition of project B's real options improved its NPV (from $10,924 to $12,424) and causes it to be preferred over project A (NPV of $12,424 for B > NPV of $11,071 for A), which has no real options embedded in it.

It is important to realize that the recognition of attractive real options when determining NPV could cause an otherwise unacceptable project ($NPV_{traditional} < \$0$) to become acceptable ($NPV_{strategic} > \$0$). The failure to recognize the value of real options could therefore cause management to reject projects that are acceptable. Although doing so requires more strategic thinking and analysis, it is important for the financial manager to identify and incorporate real options in the NPV process. The procedures for doing this efficiently are emerging, and the use of the strategic NPV that incorporates real options is expected to become more commonplace in the future.

Choosing Projects under Capital Rationing

Hint Because everyone in the firm knows that long-term funds are rationed and they want a portion of them, there is *intense competition* for those funds. This competition increases the need for the firm to be objective and proficient in its analysis. Knowing how to use the techniques discussed in this chapter to justify your needs will help you get your share of the available long-term funds.

internal rate of return approach
An approach to capital rationing that involves graphing project IRRs in descending order against the total dollar investment to determine the group of acceptable projects.

investment opportunities schedule (IOS)
The graph that plots project IRRs in descending order against the total dollar investment.

Firms commonly operate under *capital rationing*—they have more acceptable independent projects than they can fund. In theory, capital rationing should not exist. Firms should accept all projects that have positive NPVs (or IRRs > the cost of capital). However, in practice, most firms operate under capital rationing. Generally, firms attempt to isolate and select the best acceptable projects subject to a capital expenditure budget set by management. Research has found that management internally imposes capital expenditure constraints to avoid what it deems to be "excessive" levels of new financing, particularly debt. Although failing to fund all acceptable independent projects is theoretically inconsistent with the goal of maximizing owner wealth, here we will discuss capital rationing procedures because they are widely used in practice.

The objective of *capital rationing* is to select the group of projects that provides the *highest overall net present value* and does not require more dollars than are budgeted. As a prerequisite to capital rationing, the best of any mutually exclusive projects must be chosen and placed in the group of independent projects. Two basic approaches to project selection under capital rationing are discussed here.

Internal Rate of Return Approach

The **internal rate of return approach** involves graphing project IRRs in descending order against the total dollar investment. This graph is called the **investment opportunities schedule (IOS)**. By drawing the cost-of-capital line and then imposing a budget constraint, the financial manager can determine the group of acceptable projects. The problem with this technique is that it does not guarantee the maximum dollar return to the firm. It merely provides a satisfactory solution to capital-rationing problems.

Example

Tate Company, a fast-growing plastics company, is confronted with six projects competing for its fixed budget of $250,000. The initial investment and IRR for each project are as follows:

Project	Initial investment	IRR
A	$ 80,000	12%
B	70,000	20
C	100,000	16
D	40,000	8
E	60,000	15
F	110,000	11

The firm has a cost of capital of 10%. Figure 5 presents the IOS that results from ranking the six projects in descending order on the basis of their IRRs. According

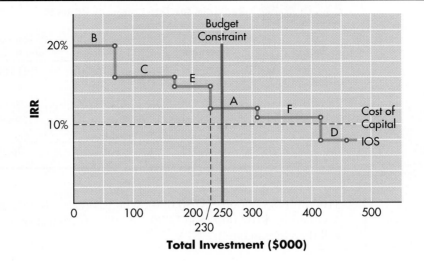

FIGURE 5

Investment Opportunities Schedule
Investment opportunities schedule (IOS) for Tate Company projects

to the schedule, only projects B, C, and E should be accepted. Together they will absorb $230,000 of the $250,000 budget. Projects A and F are acceptable but cannot be chosen because of the budget constraint. Project D is not worthy of consideration; its IRR is less than the firm's 10% cost of capital.

The drawback of this approach is that there is no guarantee that the acceptance of projects B, C, and E will maximize *total dollar returns* and therefore owners' wealth.

Net Present Value Approach

net present value approach
An approach to capital rationing that is based on the use of present values to determine the group of projects that will maximize owners' wealth.

The **net present value approach** is based on the use of present values to determine the group of projects that will maximize owners' wealth. It is implemented by ranking projects on the basis of IRRs and then evaluating the present value of the benefits from each potential project to determine *the combination of projects with the highest overall present value.* This is the same as maximizing net present value, because the entire budget is viewed as the total initial investment. Any portion of the firm's budget that is not used does not increase the firm's value. At best, the unused money can be invested in marketable securities or returned to the owners in the form of cash dividends. In either case, the wealth of the owners is not likely to be enhanced.

Example

The projects described in the preceding example are ranked in Table 7 on the basis of IRRs. The present value of the cash inflows associated with the projects is also included in the table. Projects B, C, and E, which together require $230,000, yield a present value of $336,000. However, if projects B, C, and A were implemented, the total budget of $250,000 would be used, and the present value of the cash inflows would be $357,000. This is greater than the return expected from selecting the projects on the basis of the highest IRRs. Implementing B, C, and A is preferable, because they maximize the present value for the given budget. *The firm's objective is to use its budget to generate the highest present value of inflows.* Assuming that any unused portion of the budget does not gain or lose money, the total NPV for projects B, C, and E would be

Project	Initial investment	IRR	Present value of inflows at 10%	
B	$ 70,000	20%	$112,000	
C	100,000	16	145,000	
E	60,000	15	79,000	
A	80,000	12	100,000	
F	110,000	11	126,500	Cutoff point
D	40,000	8	36,000	(IRR < 10%)

TABLE 7   Rankings for Tate Company Projects

$106,000 ($336,000 − $230,000), whereas the total NPV for projects B, C, and A would be $107,000 ($357,000 − $250,000). Selection of projects B, C, and A will therefore maximize NPV.

REVIEW QUESTIONS

7   What are *real options?* What are some major types of real options?

8   What is the difference between the *strategic NPV* and the *traditional NPV?* Do they always result in the same accept–reject decisions?

9   What is *capital rationing?* In theory, should capital rationing exist? Why does it frequently occur in practice?

10 Compare and contrast the *internal rate of return approach* and the *net present value approach* to capital rationing. Which is better? Why?

4 Behavioral Approaches for Dealing with Risk

risk (in capital budgeting)
The chance that a project will prove unacceptable or, more formally, the degree of variability of cash flows.

In the context of capital budgeting, the term **risk** refers to the chance that a project will prove unacceptable—that is, NPV < $0 or IRR < cost of capital. More formally, risk in capital budgeting is the degree of variability of cash flows. Projects with a small chance of acceptability and a broad range of expected cash flows are more risky than projects that have a high chance of acceptability and a narrow range of expected cash flows.

In the conventional capital budgeting projects assumed here, risk stems almost entirely from *cash inflows,* because the initial investment is generally known with relative certainty. These inflows, of course, derive from a number of variables related to revenues, expenditures, and taxes. Examples include the level of sales, the cost of raw materials, labor rates, utility costs, and tax rates. We will concentrate on the risk in the cash inflows, but remember that this risk actually results from the interaction of these underlying variables.

Behavioral approaches can be used to get a "feel" for the level of project risk, whereas other approaches explicitly recognize project risk. Here we present a few behavioral approaches for dealing with risk in capital budgeting: risk and cash inflows, scenario analysis, and simulation. In a later section, we consider a popular approach that explicitly recognizes risk.

Scenario Analysis

Scenario analysis can be used to deal with project risk to capture the variability of cash inflows and NPVs. *Scenario analysis* is a behavioral approach that uses several possible alternative outcomes (scenarios), such as cash inflows, to obtain a sense of the variability among returns, measured here by NPV. This technique is often useful in getting a feel for the variability of return in response to changes in a key outcome. In capital budgeting, one of the most common scenario approaches is to estimate the NPVs associated with pessimistic (worst), most likely (expected), and optimistic (best) estimates of cash inflow. The *range* can be determined by subtracting the pessimistic-outcome NPV from the optimistic-outcome NPV.

Example

Treadwell Tire Company, a tire retailer with a 10% cost of capital, is considering investing in either of two mutually exclusive projects, A and B. Each requires a $10,000 initial investment, and both are expected to provide equal annual cash inflows over their 15-year lives. The firm's financial manager created three cash inflow outcome scenarios for each project: pessimistic, most likely, and optimistic. The cash inflow outcomes and resulting NPVs in each case are summarized in Table 8. Comparing the ranges of cash inflows ($1,000 for project A and $4,000 for B) and, more important, the ranges of NPVs ($7,606 for project A and $30,424 for B) makes it clear that project A is less risky than project B. Given that both projects have the same most likely NPV of $5,212, the assumed risk-averse decision maker will take project A because it has less risk (smaller NPV range) and no possibility of loss (all NPVs > $0).

TABLE 8	Scenario Analysis of Treadwell's Projects A and B	
	Project A	Project B
Initial investment	$10,000	$10,000
	Annual cash inflows	
Outcome		
Pessimistic	$1,500	$ 0
Most likely	2,000	2,000
Optimistic	2,500	4,000
Range	$1,000	$ 4,000
	Net present values[a]	
Outcome		
Pessimistic	$1,409	−$10,000
Most likely	5,212	5,212
Optimistic	9,015	20,424
Range	$7,606	$30,424

[a]These values were calculated by using the corresponding annual cash inflows. A 10% cost of capital and a 15-year life for the annual cash inflows were used.

The widespread availability of computers and spreadsheets has greatly enhanced the use of scenario analysis.

Decision Trees

decision trees
A behavioral approach that uses diagrams to map the various investment decision alternatives and payoffs, along with their probabilities of occurrence.

Decision trees are a behavioral approach that uses diagrams to map the various investment decision alternatives and payoffs, along with their probabilities of occurrence Their name derives from their resemblance to the branches of a tree (see Figure 6). Decision trees rely on estimates of the probabilities associated with the outcomes (payoffs) of competing courses of action. The payoffs of each course of action are weighted by the associated probability; the weighted payoffs are summed; and the expected value of each course of action is then determined. The alternative that provides the highest expected value is preferred.

> **Example**
>
> Convoy, Inc., a manufacturer of picture frames, wishes to choose between two equally risky projects, I and J. To make this decision, Convoy's management has gathered the necessary data, which are depicted in the decision tree in Figure 6. Project I requires an initial investment of $120,000; a resulting expected present value of cash inflows of $130,000 is shown in column 4. Project I's expected net present value, which is calculated below the decision tree, is therefore $10,000. The expected net present value of project J is determined in a similar fashion. Project J is preferred because it offers a higher NPV—$15,000.

FIGURE 6

Decision Tree for NPV
Decision Tree for Convoy, Inc.'s choice between projects I and J

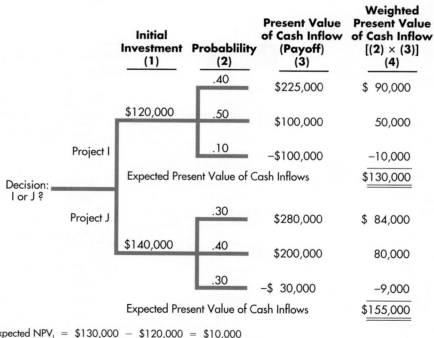

Expected NPV$_I$ = $130,000 − $120,000 = $10,000
Expected NPV$_J$ = $155,000 − $140,000 = $15,000
Because Expected NPV$_J$ > Expected NPV$_I$, Choose J.

Simulation

Simulation is a statistics-based behavioral approach that applies predetermined probability distributions and random numbers to estimate risky outcomes. By tying the various cash flow components together in a mathematical model and repeating the process numerous times, the financial manager can develop a probability distribution of project returns.

Figure 7 presents a flowchart of the simulation of the net present value of a project. The process of generating random numbers and using the probability distributions for cash inflows and cash outflows enables the financial manager to determine values for each of these variables. Substituting these values into the mathematical model results in an NPV. By repeating this process perhaps a thousand times, managers can create a probability distribution of net present values.

Although Figure 7 simulates only gross cash inflows and cash outflows, more sophisticated simulations using individual inflow and outflow components, such as sales volume, sale price, raw material cost, labor cost, or maintenance expense, are quite common. From the distribution of returns, the decision maker can determine not only the expected value of the return but also the probability of achieving or surpassing a given return. The use of computers has made the simulation approach feasible.

The output of simulation provides an excellent basis for decision making, because it enables the decision maker to view a continuum of risk–return trade-offs rather than a single-point estimate.

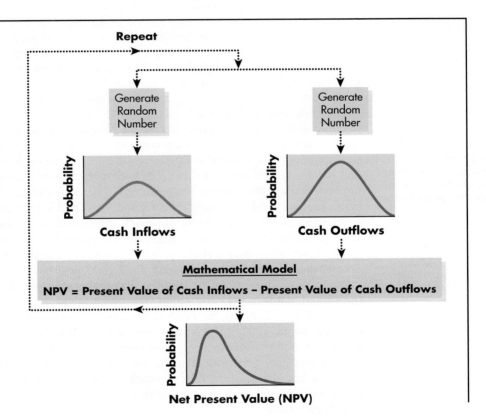

FIGURE 7

NPV Simulation
Flowchart of a net present value simulation

International Risk Considerations

exchange rate risk
The danger that an unexpected change in the exchange rate between the dollar and the currency in which a project's cash flows are denominated will reduce the market value of that project's cash flow.

Although the basic techniques of capital budgeting are the same for multinational companies (MNCs) as for purely domestic firms, firms that operate in several countries face risks that are unique to the international arena. Two types of risk are particularly important: exchange rate risk and political risk.

Exchange rate risk reflects the danger that an unexpected change in the exchange rate between the dollar and the currency in which a project's cash flows are denominated will reduce the market value of that project's cash flow. The dollar value of future cash inflows can be dramatically altered if the local currency depreciates against the dollar. In the short term, specific cash flows can be hedged by using financial instruments such as currency futures and options. Long-term exchange rate risk can best be minimized by financing the project, in whole or in part, in local currency.

Political risk is much harder to protect against. Once a foreign project is accepted, the foreign government can block the return of profits, seize the firm's assets, or otherwise interfere with a project's operation. The inability to manage political risk after the fact makes it even more important that managers account for political risks *before* making an investment. They can do so either by adjusting a project's expected cash inflows to account for the probability of political interference or by using *risk-adjusted discount rates* (discussed later in this chapter) in capital budgeting formulas. In general, it is much better to adjust individual project cash flows for political risk subjectively than to use a blanket adjustment for all projects.

In addition to unique risks that MNCs must face, several other special issues are relevant only for international capital budgeting. One of these special issues is *taxes*. Because only after-tax cash flows are relevant for capital budgeting, financial managers must carefully account for taxes paid to foreign governments on profits earned within their borders. They must also assess the impact of these tax payments on the parent company's U.S. tax liability.

Another special issue in international capital budgeting is *transfer pricing*. Much of the international trade involving MNCs is, in reality, simply the shipment of goods and services from one of a parent company's subsidiaries to another subsidiary located abroad. The parent company therefore has great discretion in setting **transfer prices,** the prices that subsidiaries charge each other for the goods and services traded between them. The widespread use of transfer pricing in international trade makes capital budgeting in MNCs very difficult unless the transfer prices that are used accurately reflect actual costs and incremental cash flows.

transfer prices
Prices that subsidiaries charge each other for the goods and services traded between them.

Finally, MNCs often must approach international capital projects from a *strategic point of view,* rather than from a strictly financial perspective. For example, an MNC may feel compelled to invest in a country to ensure continued access, even if the project itself may not have a positive net present value. This motivation was important for Japanese automakers that set up assembly plants in the United States in the early 1980s. For much the same reason, U.S. investment in Europe surged during the years before the market integration of the European Community in 1992. MNCs often invest in production facilities in the home country of major rivals to deny these competitors an uncontested home market. MNCs also may feel compelled to invest in certain industries or countries to achieve a broad corporate objective such as completing a product line or diversifying raw material sources, even when the project's cash flows may not be sufficiently profitable.

REVIEW QUESTIONS

11   Define *risk* in terms of the cash inflows from a capital budgeting project. How can determination of the *breakeven cash inflow* be used to gauge project risk? Briefly describe how each of the following behavioral approaches can be used to deal with project risk: (**a**) scenario analysis, (**b**) decision trees, and (**c**) simulation.

12   Briefly explain how the following items affect the capital budgeting decisions of multinational companies: (**a**) exchange rate risk; (**b**) political risk; (**c**) tax law differences; (**d**) transfer pricing; and (**e**) a strategic rather than a strict financial viewpoint.

---

5 | Risk-Adjusted Discount Rates

The approaches for dealing with risk that have been presented so far enable the financial manager to get a "feel" for project risk. Unfortunately, they do not explicitly recognize project risk. We will now illustrate the most popular risk-adjustment technique that employs the net present value (NPV) decision method.[7] The NPV decision rule of accepting only those projects with NPVs > \$0 will continue to hold. Close examination of the basic equation for NPV, Equation 1, should make it clear that because the initial investment (CF_0) is known with certainty, a project's risk is embodied in the present value of its cash inflows:

$$\sum_{t=1}^{n} \frac{CF_t}{(1 + r)^t}$$

Two opportunities to adjust the present value of cash inflows for risk exist: (1) The cash inflows (CF_t) can be adjusted, or (2) the discount rate (r) can be adjusted. Adjusting the cash inflows is highly subjective, so here we describe the more popular process of adjusting the discount rate. In addition, we consider the portfolio effects of project analysis as well as the practical aspects of the risk-adjusted discount rate.

Determining Risk-Adjusted Discount Rates (RADRs)

A popular approach for risk adjustment involves the use of risk-adjusted discount rates (RADRs). This approach uses Equation 1 but employs a risk-adjusted discount rate, as noted in the following expression:

$$\text{NPV} = \sum_{t=1}^{n} \frac{CF_t}{(1 + RADR)^t} - CF_0 \qquad (4)$$

risk-adjusted discount rate (RADR)
The rate of return that must be earned on a given project to compensate the firm's owners adequately—that is, to maintain or improve the firm's share price.

The **risk-adjusted discount rate (RADR)** is the rate of return that must be earned on a given project to compensate the firm's owners adequately—that is, to maintain or improve the firm's share price. The higher the risk of a project, the higher the RADR, and therefore the lower the net present value for a given stream of cash inflows.

---

7. The IRR could just as well have been used, but because NPV is theoretically preferable, it is used instead.

Personal Finance Example Talor Namtig is considering investing $1,000 in either of two stocks—A or B. She plans to hold the stock for exactly 5 years and expects both stocks to pay $80 in annual end-of-year cash dividends. At the end of the year 5 she estimates that stock A can be sold to net $1,200 and stock B can be sold to net $1,500. Talor has carefully researched the two stocks and feels that although stock A has average risk, stock B is considerably riskier. Her research indicates that she should earn an annual return on an average risk stock of 11%. Because stock B is considerably riskier, she will require a 14% return from it. Talor makes the following calculations to find the risk-adjusted net present values (NPVs) for the two stocks:

$$NPV_A = [\$80 \times (PVIFA_{11\%,5yrs})] + [\$1,200 \times (PVIF_{11\%,5yrs})] - \$1,000$$

Using a financial calculator, she gets:
$$NPV_A = \$1,007.81 - \$1,000 = \underline{\$7.81}$$

$$NPV_B = [\$80 \times (PVIFA_{14\%,5yrs})] + [\$1,500 \times (PVIF_{14\%,5yrs})] - \$1,000$$

Using a financial calculator, she gets:
$$NPV_B = \$1,053.70 - \$1,000 = \underline{\$53.70}$$

Although Talor's calculations indicate that both stock investments are acceptable (NPVs > $0), on a risk-adjusted basis, she should invest in Stock B because it has a higher NPV.

 The logic underlying the use of RADRs is closely linked to the capital asset pricing model (CAPM). For a brief review of the CAPM and further explanation of using the CAPM to find RADRs, see the text's website.

Applying RADRs

Because the CAPM is based on an assumed efficient market, which does *not* exist for real corporate (nonfinancial) assets such as plant and equipment, the CAPM is not directly applicable in making capital budgeting decisions. Financial managers therefore assess the *total risk* of a project and use it to determine the risk-adjusted discount rate (RADR), which can be used in Equation 4 to find the NPV.

To avoid damaging its market value, the firm must use the correct discount rate to evaluate a project. The *Focus on Ethics* box describes real examples of companies that failed to recognize (or that ignored) certain risks associated with their business operations. As a result, their firms experienced monetary sanctions. If a firm fails to incorporate all relevant risks in its decision-making process, it may discount a risky project's cash inflows at too low a rate and accept the project. The firm's market price may drop later as investors recognize that the firm itself has become more risky. Conversely, if the firm discounts a project's cash inflows at too high a rate, it will reject acceptable projects. Eventually the firm's market price may drop, because investors who believe that the firm is being overly conservative will sell their stock, putting downward pressure on the firm's market value.

Unfortunately, there is no formal mechanism for linking *total project risk* to the level of required return. As a result, most firms subjectively determine the RADR by adjusting their existing required return. They adjust it up or down depending on whether the proposed project is more or less risky, respectively,

Focus on Ethics — Environmental Compliance: Honesty Is the Best Policy

IN PRACTICE

It doesn't matter whether you manufacture specialty chemicals or household cleansers, operate a paint shop, sell turf products, or dispose of complex products such as aircraft engines, regulators want you to account for the effect your operations have on the environment, consumer health, and employee safety.

Not only do today's firms need to find a way to track the product as well as the environmental and exposure specifications associated with environmental regulations, they also have to manage their manufacturing processes to ensure that their storage and distribution facilities, equipment, personnel, processes, and products conform. This goes well beyond finished-product quality testing against regulated specifications. Firms have to manage the level of emissions and waste created throughout the entire lifecycle of their products and facilities, from R&D through transportation to customers—and increasingly to disposal.

The Environmental Protection Agency (EPA) has the authority to levy significant fines on companies that violate environmental regulations. In May 2007, the EPA announced that a settlement had been reached with **Kerr-McGee** after the EPA discovered violations of the Clean Air Act at several of Kerr-McGee's natural gas compressor stations near Vernal, Utah. The agreement requires Kerr-McGee to pay a $200,000 penalty and spend $250,000 on environmental projects to benefit the area in which the violations occurred. In addition, Kerr-McGee announced that it would spend $18 million on pollution controls that will reduce harmful emissions and conserve natural gas at its production facilities. The EPA also announced a $2.9 million penalty assessed against **Total Petrochemical USA Inc.** for alleged violations of the Clean Air Act. According to Granta Nakayama, EPA's assistant administrator for Enforcement and Compliance Assurance, "With today's settlement,

86 refineries in 25 states across the nation have agreed to address environmental problems and invest more than $4.5 billion in new pollution control technologies."

Companies that self-disclose violations of federal environmental regulations are fined, but they face a smaller penalty than they otherwise would if the EPA discovered the violations first. On May 9, 2007, the EPA announced that **Kmart** would pay a $102,422 fine to settle self-disclosed violations of clean water, hazardous waste, and emergency planning and preparedness regulations. If the EPA had discovered Kmart's violations through an inspection, the company would have faced a fine of more than $1.6 million. Although still economically painful, when it comes to reporting environmental violations, honesty is the best policy.

■ *What are some factors to consider when prioritizing and budgeting environmental compliance initiatives?*

---

than the average risk of the firm. This CAPM-type of approach provides a "rough estimate" of the project risk and required return because both the project risk measure and the linkage between risk and required return are estimates.

Example

Bennett Company wishes to use the risk-adjusted discount rate approach to determine, according to NPV, whether to implement project A or project B. In addition to the data presented earlier, Bennett's management after much analysis subjectively assigned "risk indexes" of 1.6 to project A and 1.0 to project B. The risk index is merely a numerical scale used to classify project risk: Higher index values are assigned to higher-risk projects, and vice versa. The CAPM-type relationship used by the firm to link risk (measured by the risk index) and the required return (RADR) is shown in the following table. Management developed this relationship after analyzing CAPM and the risk–return relationships of the projects that they considered and implemented during the past few years.

	Risk index	Required return (RADR)
	0.0	6% (risk-free rate, R_F)
	0.2	7
	0.4	8
	0.6	9
	0.8	10
Project B →	1.0	11
	1.2	12
	1.4	13
Project A →	1.6	14
	1.8	16
	2.0	18

Because project A is riskier than project B, its RADR of 14% is greater than project B's 11%. The net present value of each project, calculated using its RADR, is found as shown on the time lines in Figure 8. The results clearly show

---

FIGURE 8   **Calculation of NPVs for Bennett Company's Capital Expenditure Alternatives Using RADRs**

Time lines depicting the cash flows and NPV calculations using RADRs for projects A and B

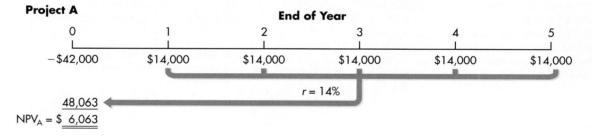

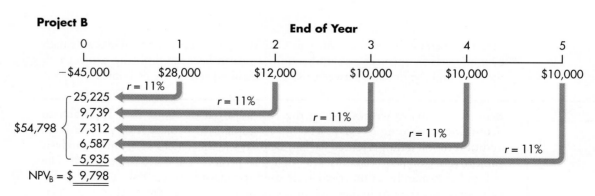

Note: When we use the risk indexes of 1.6 and 1.0 for projects A and B, respectively, along with the table above, a risk-adjusted discount rate (RADR) of 14% results for project A and a RADR of 11% results for project B.

Project A

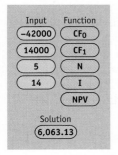

that project B is preferable, because its risk-adjusted NPV of $9,798 is greater than the $6,063 risk-adjusted NPV for project A. As reflected by the NPVs in Figure 2, if the discount rates were not adjusted for risk, project A would be preferred to project B.

Calculator Use We can again use the preprogrammed NPV function in a financial calculator to simplify the NPV calculation. The keystrokes for project A—the annuity—typically are as shown at the left. The keystrokes for project B—the mixed stream—are also shown at the left. The calculated NPVs for projects A and B of $6,063 and $9,798, respectively, agree with those shown in Figure 8.

Spreadsheet Use Analysis of projects using risk-adjusted discount rates (RADRs) also can be performed as shown on the following Excel spreadsheet.

Project B

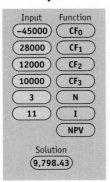

	A	B	C	D
1	ANALYSIS OF PROJECTS USING RISK-ADJUSTED DISCOUNT RATES			
2	Year	Cash Inflow	Present Value	Formulas for Calculated Values in Column C
3		Project A		
4	1-5	$ 14,000	$48,063	–PV(C7,5,B4,0)
5	Initial Investment		$42,000	
6	Net Present Value		$ 6,063	C4–C5
7	Required Return (RADAR)		14%	
8		Project B		
9	1	$ 28,000	$25,225	–PV(C17,A9,0,B9,0)
10	2	12,000	9,739	–PV(C17,A10,0,B10,0)
11	3	10,000	7,312	–PV(C17,A11,0,B11,0)
12	4	10,000	6,587	–PV(C17,A12,0,B12,0)
13	5	10,000	5,935	–PV(C17,A13,0,B13,0)
14	Present value		$54,798	SUM(C9:C13) or NPV(C17,B9:B13)
15	Initial Investment		$45,000	
16	Net Present Value		$ 9,798	C14–C15
17	Required Return (RADAR)		11%	
18	Choice of project		B	IF(C6>=C16,"A","B")

The minus signs appear before the entries in Cells D4 and D9:D13 to convert the results to positive values.

The usefulness of risk-adjusted discount rates should now be clear. The real difficulty lies in estimating project risk and linking it to the required return (RADR).

RADRs in Practice

In spite of the appeal of total risk, *RADRs are often used in practice.* Their popularity stems from two facts: (1) They are consistent with the general disposition of financial decision makers toward rates of return, and (2) they are easily estimated and applied. The first reason is clearly a matter of personal preference, but the second is based on the computational convenience and well-developed procedures involved in the use of RADRs.

In practice, firms often establish a number of *risk classes,* with an RADR assigned to each. Like the CAPM-type risk–return relationship described earlier,

Hint The use of risk classes is consistent with the concept that risk-averse investors require a greater return for greater risks. To increase shareholders' wealth—and hence warrant acceptance— risky projects must earn greater returns.

management develops the risk classes and RADRs based on both CAPM and the risk–return behaviors of past projects. Each new project is then subjectively placed in the appropriate risk class, and the corresponding RADR is used to evaluate it. This is sometimes done on a division-by-division basis, in which case each division has its own set of risk classes and associated RADRs, similar to those for Bennett Company in Table 9. The use of *divisional costs of capital* and associated risk classes enables a large multidivisional firm to incorporate differing levels of divisional risk into the capital budgeting process and still recognize differences in the levels of individual project risk.

Example

Assume that the management of Bennett Company decided to use risk classes to analyze projects and so placed each project in one of four risk classes according to its perceived risk. The classes ranged from I for the lowest-risk projects to IV for the highest-risk projects. Associated with each class was an RADR appropriate to the level of risk of projects in the class, as given in Table 9. Bennett classified as lower-risk those projects that tend to involve routine replacement or renewal activities; higher-risk projects involve expansion, often into new or unfamiliar activities.

The financial manager of Bennett has assigned project A to class III and project B to class II. The cash flows for project A would be evaluated using a 14% RADR, and project B's would be evaluated using a 10% RADR.[8] The NPV of project A at 14% was calculated in Figure 8 to be $6,063, and the NPV for project B at a 10% RADR was shown in Figure 2 to be $10,924. Clearly, with RADRs based on the use of risk classes, project B is preferred over project A. As noted earlier, this result is contrary to the preferences shown in Figure 2, where differing risks of projects A and B were not taken into account.

TABLE 9	Bennett Company's Risk Classes and RADRs	
Risk class	Description	Risk-adjusted discount rate, RADR
I	*Below-average risk:* Projects with low risk. Typically involve routine replacement without renewal of existing activities.	8%
II	*Average risk:* Projects similar to those currently implemented. Typically involve replacement or renewal of existing activities.	10%[a]
III	*Above-average risk:* Projects with higher than normal, but not excessive, risk. Typically involve expansion of existing or similar activities.	14%
IV	*Highest risk:* Projects with very high risk. Typically involve expansion into new or unfamiliar activities.	20%

[a]This RADR is actually the firm's cost of capital. It represents the firm's required return on its existing portfolio of projects, which is assumed to be unchanged with acceptance of the "average risk" project.

---

8. Note that the 10% RADR for project B using the risk classes in Table 9 differs from the 11% RADR used in the preceding example for project B. This difference is attributable to the less precise nature of the use of risk classes.

REVIEW QUESTIONS

13 Describe the basic procedures involved in using *risk-adjusted discount rates (RADRs)*. How is this approach related to the *capital asset pricing model (CAPM)?*

14 How are *risk classes* often used to apply RADRs?

Summary

Focus on Value

After estimating the relevant cash flows, the financial manager must apply appropriate decision techniques to assess whether the project creates value. Net present value (NPV) and internal rate of return (IRR) are the generally preferred capital budgeting techniques. Both use the cost of capital as the required return. Both indicate whether a proposed investment creates or destroys shareholder value. NPV is the theoretically preferred approach, but IRR is preferred in practice because of its intuitive appeal.

Procedures for explicitly recognizing real options embedded in capital projects and procedures for selecting projects under capital rationing enable the financial manager to refine the capital budgeting process further. Not all capital budgeting projects have the same level of risk as the firm's existing portfolio of projects. The financial manager must adjust projects for differences in risk when evaluating their acceptability. Risk-adjusted discount rates (RADRs) provide a mechanism for adjusting the discount rate so that it is consistent with the risk–return preferences of market participants. These techniques should enable the financial manager to make capital budgeting decisions that are consistent with the firm's goal of **maximizing stock price.**

Review of Learning Goals

Key formulas and decision criteria for this chapter are summarized in Table 10.

LG 1 **Calculate, interpret, and evaluate the payback period.** The payback period is the amount of time required for the firm to recover its initial investment, as calculated from cash inflows. Shorter payback periods are preferred. The payback period is relatively easy to calculate, has simple intuitive appeal, considers cash flows, and measures risk exposure. Its weaknesses include lack of linkage to the wealth maximization goal, failure to consider time value explicitly, and the fact that it ignores cash flows that occur after the payback period.

LG 2 **Apply net present value (NPV) and internal rate of return (IRR) to relevant cash flows to choose acceptable capital expenditures.** Sophisticated capital budgeting techniques use the cost of capital to consider the time factor in the value of money. NPV measures the amount of value created by a given project; only positive NPV projects are acceptable. IRR is the compound annual

TABLE 10	Summary of Key Formulas/Definitions and Decision Criteria for Capital Budgeting Techniques	
Technique	Formula/definition	Decision criteria
Payback period[a]	*For annuity:* $$\frac{\text{Initial investment}}{\text{Annual cash inflow}}$$ *For mixed stream:* Calculate cumulative cash inflows on year-to-year basis until the initial investment is recovered.	*Accept* if < maximum acceptable payback period. *Reject* if > maximum acceptable payback period.
Net present value (NPV)[b]	Present value of cash inflows − Initial investment.	*Accept* if > \$0. *Reject* if < \$0.
Internal rate of return (IRR)[b]	The discount rate that causes $NPV = \$0$ (present value of cash inflows equals the initial investment).	*Accept* if > the cost of capital. *Reject* if < the cost of capital.

[a]Unsophisticated technique, because it does not give explicit consideration to the time value of money.

[b]Sophisticated technique, because it gives explicit consideration to the time value of money.

rate of return that the firm will earn by investing in a project and receiving the given cash inflows. Both NPV and IRR yield the same accept–reject decisions, but they often provide conflicting rankings.

Use net present value profiles to compare NPV and IRR techniques in the light of conflicting rankings. A net present value profile graph projects' NPVs for various discount rates. NPV profiles are useful for comparing projets, especially when NPV and IRR rankings conflict. On a purely theoretical basis, NPV is preferred over IRR because NPV assumes the more conservative reinvestment rate and does not exhibit the mathematical problem of multiple IRRs that often occurs when IRRs are calculated for nonconventional cash flows. In practice, the IRR is more commonly used because it is consistent with the general preference of businesspeople for rates of return.

Discuss two additional considerations in capital budgeting—recognizing real options and choosing projects under capital rationing. By explicitly recognizing real options—opportunities that are embedded in capital projects and that allow managers to alter their cash flow and risk in a way that affects project acceptability (NPV)—the financial manager can find a project's strategic NPV. Some of the more common types of real options are abandonment, flexibility, growth, and timing options. The strategic NPV improves the quality of the capital budgeting decision.

Capital rationing exists when firms have more acceptable independent projects than they can fund. Capital rationing commonly occurs in practice. Its objective is to select from all acceptable projects the group that provides the highest overall net present value and does not require more dollars than are budgeted. The two basic approaches for choosing projects under capital rationing are the internal rate of return approach and the net present value approach. The NPV approach better achieves the objective of using the budget to generate the highest present value of inflows.

 Recognize sensitivity analysis and scenario analysis, decision trees, and simulation as behavioral approaches for dealing with project risk, and the unique risks that multinational companies face. Risk in capital budgeting is concerned with either the chance that a project will prove unacceptable or, more formally, the degree of variability of cash flows. Sensitivity analysis and scenario analysis are two behavioral approaches for capturing the variability of cash inflows and NPVs. A decision tree is a behavioral approach for dealing with risk that relies on estimates of probabilities associated with the outcomes of competing courses of action to determine the expected values used to select a preferred action. Simulation is a statistics-based approach that results in a probability distribution of project returns.

Although the basic capital budgeting techniques are the same for multinational and purely domestic companies, firms that operate in several countries must also deal with exchange rate and political risks, tax law differences, transfer pricing, and strategic issues.

Understand the calculation and practical aspects of risk-adjusted discount rates (RADRs). The risk-adjusted discount rate (RADR) uses a market-based adjustment of the discount rate to calculate NPV. The RADR is closely linked to CAPM, but because real corporate assets are generally not traded in an efficient market, the CAPM cannot be applied directly to capital budgeting. RADRs are commonly used in practice, because decision makers find rates of return easy to estimate and apply.

Self-Test Problems

ST9–1 All techniques with NPV profile—Mutually exclusive projects Fitch Industries is in the process of choosing the better of two equal-risk, mutually exclusive capital expenditure projects—M and N. The relevant cash flows for each project are shown in the following table. The firm's cost of capital is 14%.

	Project M	Project N
Initial investment (CF_0)	$28,500	$27,000
Year (t)	Cash inflows (CF_t)	
1	$10,000	$11,000
2	10,000	10,000
3	10,000	9,000
4	10,000	8,000

a. Calculate each project's *payback period.*
b. Calculate the *net present value (NPV)* for each project.

c. Calculate the *internal rate of return (IRR)* for each project.

d. Summarize the preferences dictated by each measure you calculated, and indicate which project you would recommend. Explain why.

e. Draw the *net present value profiles* for these projects on the same set of axes, and explain the circumstances under which a conflict in rankings might exist.

ST9–2 **Risk-adjusted discount rates** CBA Company is considering two mutually exclusive projects, A and B. The following table shows the CAPM-type relationship between a risk index and the required return (RADR) applicable to CBA Company.

Risk index	Required return (RADR)
0.0	7.0% (risk-free rate, R_F)
0.2	8.0
0.4	9.0
0.6	10.0
0.8	11.0
1.0	12.0
1.2	13.0
1.4	14.0
1.6	15.0
1.8	16.0
2.0	17.0

Project data are shown as follows:

	Project A	Project B
Initial investment (CF_0)	$15,000	$20,000
Project life	3 years	3 years
Annual cash inflow (CF)	$7,000	$10,000
Risk index	0.4	1.8

a. Ignoring any differences in risk and assuming that the firm's cost of capital is 10%, calculate the *net present value (NPV)* of each project.

b. Use NPV to evaluate the projects, using *risk-adjusted discount rates (RADRs)* to account for risk.

c. Compare, contrast, and explain your findings in parts **a** and **b**.

Warm-Up Exercises

A blue box (■) indicates exercises available in .

E9–1 Elysian Fields, Inc., uses a maximum payback period of 6 years, and currently must choose between two mutually exclusive projects. Project Hydrogen requires an initial outlay of $25,000; project Helium requires an initial outlay of $35,000. Using the expected cash inflows given for each project in the following table, calculate each project's *payback period*. Which project meets Elysian's standards?

| | Expected cash inflows | |
Year	Hydrogen	Helium
1	$6,000	$7,000
2	6,000	7,000
3	8,000	8,000
4	4,000	5,000
5	3,500	5,000
6	2,000	4,000

 E9–2 Herky Foods is considering acquisition of a new wrapping machine. The initial investment is estimated at $1.25 million, and the machine will have a 5-year life with no salvage value. Using a 6% discount rate, determine the *net present value (NPV)* of the machine given its expected operating cash inflows shown in the following table. Based on the project's NPV, should Herky make this investment?

Year	Cash inflow
1	$400,000
2	375,000
3	300,000
4	350,000
5	200,000

  E9–3 Billabong Tech uses the *internal rate of return (IRR)* to select projects. Calculate the IRR for each of the following projects and recommend the best project based on this measure. Project T-Shirt requires an initial investment of $15,000 and generates cash inflows of $8,000 per year for 4 years. Project Board Shorts requires an initial investment of $25,000 and produces cash inflows of $12,000 per year for 5 years.

 E9–4 Cooper Electronics uses *NPV profiles* to visually evaluate competing projects. Key data for the two projects under consideration is given in the following table. Using these data, graph, on the same set of axes, the NPV profiles for each project using discount rates of 0%, 8%, and the IRR.

	Terra	Firma
Initial investment	$30,000	$25,000
Year	Operating cash inflows	
1	$ 7,000	$ 6,000
2	10,000	9,000
3	12,000	9,000
4	10,000	8,000

E9–5 Longchamps Electric is faced with a capital budget of $150,000 for the coming year. It is considering six investment projects and has a cost of capital of 7%. The six projects are listed in the follwing table, along with their initial investments and their IRRs. Using the data given, prepare an *investment opportunities schedule (IOS)*. Which projects does the IOS suggest should be funded? Does this group of projects maximize NPV? Explain.

Project	Initial investment	IRR
1	$75,000	8%
2	40,000	10
3	35,000	7
4	50,000	11
5	45,000	9
6	20,000	6

E9–6 Like most firms in its industry, Yeastime Bakeries uses a subjective risk assessment tool of its own design. The tool is a simple index by which projects are ranked by level of perceived risk on a scale of 0–10. The scale is recreated below.

Risk	Required Return
0	4.0% (current risk-free rate)
1	4.5
2	5.0
3	5.5
4	6.0
5	6.5 (current IRR)
6	7.0
7	7.5
8	8.0
9	8.5
10	9.0

The firm is analyzing two projects based on their RADRs. Project Sourdough requires an initial investment of $12,500 and is assigned a risk index of 6. Project Greek Salad requires an initial investment of $7,500 and is assigned a risk index of 8. The two projects have 7-year lives. Sourdough is projected to generate cash inflows of $5,500 per year. Greek Salad is projected to generate cash inflows of $4,000 per year. Use each project's RADR to select the better project.

Problems

A blue box (■) indicates problems available in .

P9–1 **Payback period** Jordan Enterprises is considering a capital expenditure that requires an initial investment of $42,000 and returns after-tax cash inflows of $7,000 per year for 10 years. The firm has a maximum acceptable payback period of 8 years.

a. Determine the *payback period* for this project.
b. Should the company accept the project? Why or why not?

 P9-2 **Payback comparisons** Nova Products has a 5-year maximum acceptable payback period. The firm is considering the purchase of a new machine and must choose between two alternative ones. The first machine requires an initial investment of $14,000 and generates annual after-tax cash inflows of $3,000 for each of the next 7 years. The second machine requires an initial investment of $21,000 and provides an annual cash inflow after taxes of $4,000 for 20 years.
a. Determine the *payback period* for each machine.
b. Comment on the acceptability of the machines, assuming that they are independent projects.
c. Which machine should the firm accept? Why?
d. Do the machines in this problem illustrate any of the weaknesses of using payback? Discuss.

PERSONAL FINANCE PROBLEM

 P9-3 **Long-term investment decision, payback method** Bill Williams has the opportunity to invest in project A that costs $9,000 today and promises to pay annual end-of-year payments of $2,200, $2,500, $2,500, $2,000, and $1,800 over the next 5 years. Or, Bill can invest $9,000 in project B that promises to pay annual end-of-year payments of $1,500, $1,500, $1,500, $3,500, and $4,000 over the next 5 years.
a. How long will it take for Bill to recoup his initial investment in project A?
b. How long will it take for Bill to recoup his initial investment in project B?
c. Using the *payback period*, which project should Bill choose?
d. Do you see any problems with his choice?

 P9-4 **NPV** Calculate the *net present value (NPV)* for the following 20-year projects. Comment on the acceptability of each. Assume that the firm has an opportunity cost of 14%.
a. Initial investment is $10,000; cash inflows are $2,000 per year.
b. Initial investment is $25,000; cash inflows are $3,000 per year.
c. Initial investment is $30,000; cash inflows are $5,000 per year.

 P9-5 **NPV for varying costs of capital** Dane Cosmetics is evaluating a new fragrance-mixing machine. The machine requires an initial investment of $24,000 and will generate after-tax cash inflows of $5,000 per year for 8 years. For each of the costs of capital listed, (1) calculate the *net present value (NPV)*, (2) indicate whether to accept or reject the machine, and (3) explain your decision.
a. The cost of capital is 10%.
b. The cost of capital is 12%.
c. The cost of capital is 14%.

 P9-6 **Net present value—Independent projects** Using a 14% cost of capital, calculate the *net present value* for each of the independent projects shown in the following table, and indicate whether each is acceptable.

	Project A	Project B	Project C	Project D	Project E
Initial investment (CF_0)	$26,000	$500,000	$170,000	$950,000	$80,000
Year (t)			Cash inflows (CF_t)		
1	$4,000	$100,000	$20,000	$230,000	$ 0
2	4,000	120,000	19,000	230,000	0
3	4,000	140,000	18,000	230,000	0
4	4,000	160,000	17,000	230,000	20,000
5	4,000	180,000	16,000	230,000	30,000
6	4,000	200,000	15,000	230,000	0
7	4,000		14,000	230,000	50,000
8	4,000		13,000	230,000	60,000
9	4,000		12,000		70,000
10	4,000		11,000		

P9–7 **NPV and maximum return** A firm can purchase a fixed asset for a $13,000 initial investment. The asset generates an annual after-tax cash inflow of $4,000 for 4 years.
a. Determine the *net present value (NPV)* of the asset, assuming that the firm has a 10% cost of capital. Is the project acceptable?
b. Determine the maximum required rate of return (closest whole-percentage rate) that the firm can have and still accept the asset. Discuss this finding in light of your response in part **a**.

P9–8 **NPV—Mutually exclusive projects** Hook Industries is considering the replacement of one of its old drill presses. Three alternative replacement presses are under consideration. The relevant cash flows associated with each are shown in the following table. The firm's cost of capital is 15%.

	Press A	Press B	Press C
Initial investment (CF_0)	$85,000	$60,000	$130,000
Year (t)		Cash inflows (CF_t)	
1	$18,000	$12,000	$50,000
2	18,000	14,000	30,000
3	18,000	16,000	20,000
4	18,000	18,000	20,000
5	18,000	20,000	20,000
6	18,000	25,000	30,000
7	18,000	—	40,000
8	18,000	—	50,000

a. Calculate the *net present value (NPV)* of each press.
b. Using NPV, evaluate the acceptability of each press.
c. Rank the presses from best to worst using NPV.

Capital Budgeting Techniques: Certainty and Risk

PERSONAL FINANCE PROBLEM

P9–9 **Long-term investment decision, NPV method**   Jenny Jenks has researched the financial pros and cons of entering into an elite MBA program at her state university. The tuition and needed books for a master's program will have an upfront cost of $100,000. On average, a person with an MBA degree earns an extra $20,000 per year over a business career of 40 years. Jenny feels that her opportunity cost of capital is 6%. Given her estimates, find the *net present value (NPV)* of entering this MBA program. Are the benefits of further education worth the associated costs?

P9–10 **Payback and NPV**   Neil Corporation has three projects under consideration. The cash flows for each project are shown in the following table. The firm has a 16% cost of capital.

	Project A	Project B	Project C
Initial investment (CF_0)	$40,000	$40,000	$40,000
Year (t)	Cash inflows (CF_t)		
1	$13,000	$ 7,000	$19,000
2	13,000	10,000	16,000
3	13,000	13,000	13,000
4	13,000	16,000	10,000
5	13,000	19,000	7,000

a. Calculate each project's *payback period*. Which project is preferred according to this method?
b. Calculate each project's *net present value (NPV)*. Which project is preferred according to this method?
c. Comment on your findings in parts **a** and **b,** and recommend the best project. Explain your recommendation.

P9–11 **Internal rate of return**   For each of the projects shown in the following table, calculate the *internal rate of return (IRR)*. Then indicate, for each project, the maximum cost of capital that the firm could have and still find the IRR acceptable.

	Project A	Project B	Project C	Project D
Initial investment (CF_0)	$90,000	$490,000	$20,000	$240,000
Year (t)	Cash inflows (CF_t)			
1	$20,000	$150,000	$7,500	$120,000
2	25,000	150,000	7,500	100,000
3	30,000	150,000	7,500	80,000
4	35,000	150,000	7,500	60,000
5	40,000	—	7,500	—

P9–12 **IRR—Mutually exclusive projects**   Bell Manufacturing is attempting to choose the better of two mutually exclusive projects for expanding the firm's warehouse capacity. The relevant cash flows for the projects are shown in the following table. The firm's cost of capital is 15%.

	Project X	Project Y
Initial investment (CF_0)	$500,000	$325,000
Year (t)	Cash inflows (CF_t)	
1	$100,000	$140,000
2	120,000	120,000
3	150,000	95,000
4	190,000	70,000
5	250,000	50,000

a. Calculate the *IRR* to the nearest whole percent for each of the projects.
b. Assess the acceptability of each project on the basis of the IRRs found in part **a.**
c. Which project, on this basis, is preferred?

PERSONAL FINANCE PROBLEM

P9–13 **Long-term investment decision, IRR method**   Billy and Mandy Jones have $25,000 to invest. On average, they do not make any investment that will not return at least 7.5% per year. They have been approached with an investment opportunity that requires $25,000 upfront and has a payout of $6,000 at the end of each of the next 5 years. Using the *internal rate of return (IRR)* method and their requirements, determine whether Billy and Mandy should undertake the investment.

P9–14 **IRR, investment life, and cash inflows**   Oak Enterprises accepts projects earning more than the firm's 15% cost of capital. Oak is currently considering a 10-year project that provides annual cash inflows of $10,000 and requires an initial investment of $61,450. (*Note:* All amounts are after taxes.)
a. Determine the *IRR* of this project. Is it acceptable?
b. Assuming that the cash inflows continue to be $10,000 per year, how many *additional years* would the flows have to continue to make the project acceptable (that is, to make it have an IRR of 15%)?
c. With the given life, initial investment, and cost of capital, what is the minimum annual cash inflow that the firm should accept?

P9–15 **NPV and IRR**   Benson Designs has prepared the following estimates for a long-term project it is considering. The initial investment is $18,250, and the project is expected to yield after-tax cash inflows of $4,000 per year for 7 years. The firm has a 10% cost of capital.
a. Determine the *net present value (NPV)* for the project.
b. Determine the *internal rate of return (IRR)* for the project.
c. Would you recommend that the firm accept or reject the project? Explain your answer.

P9–16 Payback, NPV, and IRR Rieger International is attempting to evaluate the feasibility of investing $95,000 in a piece of equipment that has a 5-year life. The firm has estimated the *cash inflows* associated with the proposal as shown in the following table. The firm has a 12% cost of capital.

Year (t)	Cash inflows (CF_t)
1	$20,000
2	25,000
3	30,000
4	35,000
5	40,000

a. Calculate the *payback period* for the proposed investment.
b. Calculate the *net present value (NPV)* for the proposed investment.
c. Calculate the *internal rate of return (IRR)*, rounded to the nearest whole percent, for the proposed investment.
d. Evaluate the acceptability of the proposed investment using NPV and IRR. What recommendation would you make relative to implementation of the project? Why?

P9–17 NPV, IRR, and NPV profiles Thomas Company is considering two mutually exclusive projects. The firm, which has a 12% cost of capital, has estimated its cash flows as shown in the following table.

	Project A	Project B
Initial investment (CF_0)	$130,000	$85,000
Year (t)	Cash inflows (CF_t)	
1	$25,000	$40,000
2	35,000	35,000
3	45,000	30,000
4	50,000	10,000
5	55,000	5,000

a. Calculate the *NPV* of each project, and assess its acceptability.
b. Calculate the *IRR* for each project, and assess its acceptability.
c. Draw the *NPV profiles* for both projects on the same set of axes.
d. Evaluate and discuss the rankings of the two projects on the basis of your findings in parts **a, b,** and **c.**
e. Explain your findings in part **d** in light of the pattern of cash inflows associated with each project.

P9–18 All techniques—Decision among mutually exclusive investments Pound Industries is attempting to select the best of three mutually exclusive projects. The initial investment and after-tax cash inflows associated with these projects are shown in the following table.

Cash flows	Project A	Project B	Project C
Initial investment (CF_0)	$60,000	$100,000	$110,000
Cash inflows (CF_t), $t = 1$ to 5	$20,000	$31,500	$32,500

a. Calculate the *payback period* for each project.

b. Calculate the *net present value (NPV)* of each project, assuming that the firm has a cost of capital equal to 13%.

c. Calculate the *internal rate of return (IRR)* for each project.

d. Draw the *net present value profiles* for both projects on the same set of axes, and discuss any conflict in ranking that may exist between NPV and IRR.

e. Summarize the preferences dictated by each measure, and indicate which project you would recommend. Explain why.

P9–19 **All techniques with NPV profile—Mutually exclusive projects** Projects A and B, of equal risk, are alternatives for expanding Rosa Company's capacity. The firm's cost of capital is 13%. The cash flows for each project are shown in the following table.

	Project A	Project B
Initial investment (CF_0)	$80,000	$50,000
Year (t)	Cash inflows (CF_t)	
1	$15,000	$15,000
2	20,000	15,000
3	25,000	15,000
4	30,000	15,000
5	35,000	15,000

a. Calculate each project's *payback period*.

b. Calculate the *net present value (NPV)* for each project.

c. Calculate the *internal rate of return (IRR)* for each project.

d. Draw the *net present value profiles* for both projects on the same set of axes, and discuss any conflict in ranking that may exist between NPV and IRR.

e. Summarize the preferences dictated by each measure, and indicate which project you would recommend. Explain why.

P9–20 **Integrative—Complete investment decision** Wells Printing is considering the purchase of a new printing press. The total installed cost of the press is $2.2 million. This outlay would be partially offset by the sale of an existing press. The old press has zero book value, cost $1 million 10 years ago, and can be sold currently for $1.2 million before taxes. As a result of acquisition of the new press, sales in each of the next 5 years are expected to be $1.6 million higher than with the existing press, but product costs (excluding depreciation) will represent 50% of sales. The new press will not affect the firm's net working capital requirements. The new press will be depreciated under MACRS using a 5-year recovery period (see table on the following page). The firm is subject to a 40% tax rate. Wells Printing's cost of capital is 11%. (*Note:* Assume that both the old and the new press will have terminal values of $0 at the end of year 6.)

	Percentage by recovery year[a]			
Recovery year	3 years	5 years	7 years	10 years
1	33%	20%	14%	10%
2	45	32	25	18
3	15	19	18	14
4	7	12	12	12
5		12	9	9
6		5	9	8
7			9	7
8			4	6
9				6
10				6
11				4
Totals	100%	100%	100%	100%

Rounded Depreciation Percentages by Recovery Year Using MACRS for First Four Property Classes

[a]These percentages have been rounded to the nearest whole percent to simplify calculations while retaining realism. To calculate the *actual* depreciation for tax purposes, be sure to apply the actual unrounded percentages or directly apply double-declining balance (200%) depreciation using the half-year convention.

a. Determine the *initial investment* required by the new press.
b. Determine the *operating cash inflows* attributable to the new press.
   (*Note:* Be sure to consider the depreciation in year 6.)
c. Determine the *payback period*.
d. Determine the *net present value (NPV)* and the *internal rate of return (IRR)* related to the proposed new press.
e. Make a recommendation to accept or reject the new press, and justify your answer.

P9–21 **Integrative—Investment decision** Holliday Manufacturing is considering the replacement of an existing machine. The new machine costs $1.2 million and requires installation costs of $150,000. The existing machine can be sold currently for $185,000 before taxes. It is 2 years old, cost $800,000 new, and has a $384,000 book value and a remaining useful life of 5 years. It was being depreciated under MACRS using a 5-year recovery period (see table from Problem P9-20) and therefore has the final 4 years of depreciation remaining. If it is held for 5 more years, the machine's market value at the end of year 5 will be $0. Over its 5-year life, the new machine should reduce operating costs by $350,000 per year. The new machine will be depreciated under MACRS using a 5-year recovery period (see table from Problem P9-20). The new machine can be sold for $200,000 net of removal and cleanup costs at the end of 5 years. An increased investment in net working capital of $25,000 will be needed to support operations if the new machine is acquired.

Assume that the firm has adequate operating income against which to deduct any loss experienced on the sale of the existing machine. The firm has a 9% cost of capital and is subject to a 40% tax rate.

a. Develop the *relevant cash flows* needed to analyze the proposed replacement.

b. Determine the *net present value (NPV)* of the proposal.

c. Determine the *internal rate of return (IRR)* of the proposal.

d. Make a recommendation to accept or reject the replacement proposal, and justify your answer.

e. What is the highest cost of capital that the firm could have and still accept the proposal? Explain.

 P9–22 **Real options and the strategic NPV**   Jenny Rene, the CFO of Asor Products, Inc., has just completed an evaluation of a proposed capital expenditure for equipment that would expand the firm's manufacturing capacity. Using the traditional NPV methodology, she found the project unacceptable because

$$\text{NPV}_{\text{traditional}} = -\$1{,}700 < \$0$$

Before recommending rejection of the proposed project, she has decided to assess whether there might be real options embedded in the firm's cash flows. Her evaluation uncovered three options:

> *Option 1: Abandonment*—The project could be abandoned at the end of 3 years, resulting in an addition to NPV of $1,200.

> *Option 2: Growth*—If the projected outcomes occurred, an opportunity to expand the firm's product offerings further would become available at the end of 4 years. Exercise of this option is estimated to add $3,000 to the project's NPV.

> *Option 3: Timing*—Certain phases of the proposed project could be delayed if market and competitive conditions caused the firm's forecast revenues to develop more slowly than planned. Such a delay in implementation at that point has a NPV of $10,000.

Jenny estimated that there was a 25% chance that the abandonment option would need to be exercised, a 30% chance that the growth option would be exercised, and only a 10% chance that the implementation of certain phases of the project would affect timing.

a. Use the information provided to calculate the *strategic NPV*, $\text{NPV}_{\text{strategic}}$, for Asor Products' proposed equipment expenditure.

b. Judging on the basis of your findings in part **a**, what action should Jenny recommend to management with regard to the proposed equipment expenditure?

c. In general, how does this problem demonstrate the importance of considering real options when making capital budgeting decisions?

 P9–23 **Capital rationing—IRR and NPV approaches**   Valley Corporation is attempting to select the best of a group of independent projects competing for the firm's fixed capital budget of $4.5 million. The firm recognizes that any unused portion of this budget will earn less than its 15% cost of capital, thereby resulting in a present value of inflows that is less than the initial investment. The firm has summarized, in the following table, the key data to be used in selecting the best group of projects.

Project	Initial investment	IRR	Present value of inflows at 15%
A	$5,000,000	17%	$5,400,000
B	800,000	18	1,100,000
C	2,000,000	19	2,300,000
D	1,500,000	16	1,600,000
E	800,000	22	900,000
F	2,500,000	23	3,000,000
G	1,200,000	20	1,300,000

a. Use the *internal rate of return (IRR) approach* to select the best group of projects.
b. Use the *net present value (NPV) approach* to select the best group of projects.
c. Compare, contrast, and discuss your findings in parts **a** and **b**.
d. Which projects should the firm implement? Why?

P9–24 **Capital rationing—NPV approach** A firm with a 13% cost of capital must select the optimal group of projects from those shown in the following table, given its capital budget of $1 million.

Project	Initial investment	NPV at 13% cost of capital
A	$300,000	$ 84,000
B	200,000	10,000
C	100,000	25,000
D	900,000	90,000
E	500,000	70,000
F	100,000	50,000
G	800,000	160,000

a. Calculate the *present value of cash inflows* associated with each project.
b. Select the optimal group of projects, keeping in mind that unused funds are costly.

P9–25 **Basic scenario analysis** Murdock Paints is in the process of evaluating two mutually exclusive additions to its processing capacity. The firm's financial analysts have developed pessimistic, most likely, and optimistic estimates of the annual cash inflows associated with each project. These estimates are shown in the following table.

	Project A	Project B
Initial investment (CF_0)	$8,000	$8,000
Outcome	Annual cash inflows (CF)	
Pessimistic	$ 200	$ 900
Most likely	1,000	1,000
Optimistic	1,800	1,100

a. Determine the *range* of annual cash inflows for each of the two projects.
b. Assume that the firm's cost of capital is 10% and that both projects have 20-year lives. Construct a table similar to this for the NPVs for each project. Include the *range* of NPVs for each project.
c. Do parts **a** and **b** provide consistent views of the two projects? Explain.
d. Which project do you recommend? Why?

P9–26 **Scenario analysis** James Secretarial Services is considering the purchase of one of two new personal computers, P and Q. The company expects both to provide benefits over a 10-year period, and each has a required investment of $3,000. The firm uses a 10% cost of capital. Management has constructed the following table of estimates of annual cash inflows for pessimistic, most likely, and optimistic results.

	Computer P	Computer Q
Initial investment (CF_0)	$3,000	$3,000
Outcome	Annual cash inflows (CF)	
Pessimistic	$ 500	$ 400
Most likely	750	750
Optimistic	1,000	1,200

a. Determine the *range* of annual cash inflows for each of the two computers.
b. Construct a table similar to this for the NPVs associated with each outcome for both computers.
c. Find the *range* of NPVs, and subjectively compare the risks associated with purchasing these computers.

P9–27 **Decision trees** The Ouija Board-Games Company can bring out one of two new games this season. The *Signs Away* game has a higher initial cost but also a higher expected return. *Monopolistic Competition*, the alternative, has a slightly lower initial cost but also a lower expected return. The present values and probabilities associated with each game are listed in the table below.

Games	Initial investment	Present value of cash inflows	Probabilities
Signs Away	$140,000		1.00
		$320,000	.30
		220,000	.50
		− 80,000	.20
Monopolistic Competition	$120,000		1.00
		$260,000	.20
		$200,000	.45
		− 50,000	.35

a. Construct a *decision tree* to analyze the games.
b. Which game do you recommend (following a decision-tree analysis)?

c. Has your analysis captured the differences in the risks associated with these games? Explain.

P9–28 **Simulation** Ogden Corporation has compiled the following information on a capital expenditure proposal:

(1) The projected cash *inflows* are normally distributed with a mean of $36,000 and a standard deviation of $9,000.

(2) The projected cash *outflows* are normally distributed with a mean of $30,000 and a standard deviation of $6,000.

(3) The firm has an 11% cost of capital.

(4) The probability distributions of cash inflows and cash outflows are not expected to change over the project's 10-year life.

a. Describe how the foregoing data can be used to develop a simulation model for finding the net present value of the project.

b. Discuss the advantages of using a simulation to evaluate the proposed project.

P9–29 **Risk-adjusted discount rates—Basic** Country Wallpapers is considering investing in one of three mutually exclusive projects, E, F, and G. The firm's cost of capital, r, is 15%, and the risk-free rate, R_F, is 10%. The firm has gathered the following basic cash flow and risk index data for each project.

	Project (j)		
	E	F	G
Initial investment (CF_0)	$15,000	$11,000	$19,000
Year (t)	Cash inflows (CF_t)		
1	$ 6,000	$ 6,000	$ 4,000
2	6,000	4,000	6,000
3	6,000	5,000	8,000
4	6,000	2,000	12,000
Risk index (RI_j)	1.80	1.00	0.60

a. Find the *net present value (NPV)* of each project using the firm's cost of capital. Which project is preferred in this situation?

b. The firm uses the following equation to determine the risk-adjusted discount rate, $RADR_j$, for each project j:

$$RADR_j = R_F + [RI_j \times (r - R_F)]$$

where

R_F = risk-free rate of return

RI_j = risk index for project j

r = cost of capital

Substitute each project's risk index into this equation to determine its RADR.

c. Use the RADR for each project to determine its *risk-adjusted NPV*. Which project is preferable in this situation?

d. Compare and discuss your findings in parts **a** and **c**. Which project do you recommend that the firm accept?

P9–30 **Risk-adjusted discount rates—Tabular**   After a careful evaluation of investment alternatives and opportunities, Masters School Supplies has developed a CAPM-type relationship linking a risk index to the required return (RADR), as shown in the following table.

Risk index	Required return (RADR)
0.0	7.0% (risk-free rate, R_F)
0.2	8.0
0.4	9.0
0.6	10.0
0.8	11.0
1.0	12.0
1.2	13.0
1.4	14.0
1.6	15.0
1.8	16.0
2.0	17.0

The firm is considering two mutually exclusive projects, A and B. Following are the data the firm has been able to gather about the projects.

	Project A	Project B
Initial investment (CF_0)	$20,000	$30,000
Project life	5 years	5 years
Annual cash inflow (CF)	$7,000	$10,000
Risk index	0.2	1.4

All the firm's cash inflows have already been adjusted for taxes.
a. Evaluate the projects using *risk-adjusted discount rates.*
b. Discuss your findings in part **a,** and recommend the preferred project.

PERSONAL FINANCE PROBLEM

P9–31 **Mutually exclusive investments and risk**   Lara Fredericks is interested in two mutually exclusive investments. Both investments cover the same time horizon of 6 years. The cost of the first investment is $10,000, and Lara expects equal and consecutive year-end payments of $3,000. The second investment promises equal and consecutive payments of $3,800 with an initial outlay of $12,000 required. The current required return on the first investment is 8.5%, and the second carries a required return of 10.5%.
a. What is the *net present value* of the first investment?
b. What is the *net present value* of the second investment?
c. Being mutually exclusive, which investment should Lara choose? Explain.
d. Which investment was relatively more risky? Explain.

P9–32 **Risk classes and RADR**   Moses Manufacturing is attempting to select the best of three mutually exclusive projects, X, Y, and Z. Although all the projects have 5-year lives, they possess differing degrees of risk. Project X is in class V, the highest-risk class; project Y is in class II, the below-average-risk class; and project Z is in class III, the average-risk class. The basic cash flow data for each project and the risk classes and risk-adjusted discount rates (RADRs) used by the firm are shown in the following tables.

	Project X	Project Y	Project Z
Initial investment (CF_0)	$180,000	$235,000	$310,000
Year (t)	Cash inflows (CF_t)		
1	$80,000	$50,000	$90,000
2	70,000	60,000	90,000
3	60,000	70,000	90,000
4	60,000	80,000	90,000
5	60,000	90,000	90,000

Risk Classes and RADRs		
Risk Class	Description	Risk-adjusted discount rate (RADR)
I	Lowest risk	10%
II	Below-average risk	13
III	Average risk	15
IV	Above-average risk	19
V	Highest risk	22

a. Find the *risk-adjusted* NPV for each project.

b. Which project, if any, would you recommend that the firm undertake?

 P9–33 **ETHICS PROBLEM** One way to avoid the EPA penalties (see *Focus on Ethics*) for excessive air pollution is to use carbon credits. Carbon credits are a tradable permit scheme that allows businesses that cannot meet their greenhouse-gas-emissions limits to purchase carbon credits from businesses that are below their quota. By allowing credits to be bought and sold, a business for which reducing its emissions would be expensive or prohibitive can pay another business to make the reduction for it. Do you agree with this arrangement? How would you feel as an investor in a company that utilizes carbon credits to legally exceed its pollution limits?

Chapter Case

Making Norwich Tool's Lathe Investment Decision

Norwich Tool, a large machine shop, is considering replacing one of its lathes with either of two new lathes—lathe A or lathe B. Lathe A is a highly automated, computer-controlled lathe; lathe B is a less expensive lathe that uses standard technology. To analyze these alternatives, Mario Jackson, a financial analyst, prepared estimates of the initial investment and incremental (relevant) cash inflows associated with each lathe. These are shown in the following table.

	Lathe A	Lathe B
Initial investment (CF_0)	$660,000	$360,000
Year (t)	Cash inflows (CF_t)	
1	$128,000	$ 88,000
2	182,000	120,000
3	166,000	96,000
4	168,000	86,000
5	450,000	207,000

Note that Mario plans to analyze both lathes over a 5-year period. At the end of that time, the lathes would be sold, thus accounting for the large fifth-year cash inflows.

Mario believes that the two lathes are equally risky and that the acceptance of either of them will not change the firm's overall risk. He therefore decides to apply the firm's 13% cost of capital when analyzing the lathes. Norwich Tool requires all projects to have a maximum payback period of 4.0 years.

To Do

a. Use the *payback period* to assess the acceptability and relative ranking of each lathe.
b. Assuming equal risk, use the following sophisticated capital budgeting techniques to assess the acceptability and relative ranking of each lathe:
   (1) *Net present value (NPV).*
   (2) *Internal rate of return (IRR).*
c. Summarize the preferences indicated by the techniques used in parts **a** and **b**, and indicate which lathe you recommend, if either, (1) if the firm has unlimited funds and (2) if the firm has capital rationing.
d. Repeat part **b** assuming that Mario decides that because of its greater risk, lathe A's cash inflows should be evaluated by using a 15% cost of capital.
e. What effect, if any, does recognition of lathe A's greater risk in part **d** have on your recommendation in part **c**?

Spreadsheet Exercise

The Drillago Company is involved in searching for locations in which to drill for oil. The firm's current project requires an initial investment of $15 million and has an estimated life of 10 years. The expected future cash inflows for the project are as follows:

Year	Cash inflows
1	$ 600,000
2	1,000,000
3	1,000,000
4	2,000,000
5	3,000,000
6	3,500,000
7	4,000,000
8	6,000,000
9	8,000,000
10	12,000,000

The firm's current cost of capital is 13%.

To Do

Create a spreadsheet to answer the following:

a. Calculate the project's *net present value (NPV)*. Is the project acceptable under the NPV technique? Explain.

b. Calculate the project's *internal rate of return (IRR)*. Is the project acceptable under the IRR technique? Explain.

c. In this case, did the two methods produce the same results? Generally, is there a preference between the NPV and IRR techniques? Explain.

d. Calculate the *payback period* for the project. If the firm usually accepts projects that have payback periods between 1 and 7 years, is this project acceptable?

Web Exercise

Go to the text's companion website at **www.prenhall.com/gitman** to find the Web Exercise for this chapter.

Remember to check the text's website at **www.prenhall.com/gitman** to find additional resources, including Web Exercises and a Web Case.

Solutions to Self-Test Problems

ST9–1 a. Payback period:

Project M: $\dfrac{\$28,500}{\$10,000} = \underline{\underline{2.85}}$ years

Project N:

Year (t)	Cash inflows (CF_t)	Cumulative cash inflows
1	$11,000	$11,000
2	10,000	21,000 ←
3	9,000	30,000
4	8,000	38,000

$2 + \dfrac{\$27,000 - \$21,000}{\$9,000}$ years

$2 + \dfrac{\$6,000}{\$9,000}$ years $= \underline{\underline{2.67}}$ years

b. Net present value (NPV):

Project M:
$$\begin{aligned}
\text{NPV} &= (\$10,000 \times PVIFA_{14\%,\,4\text{yrs}}) - \$28,500 \\
&= (\$10,000 \times 2.914) - \$28,500 \\
&= \$29,140 - \$28,500 = \underline{\underline{\$640}}
\end{aligned}$$

(Calculator solution = $637.12)

Project N:

Year (t)	Cash inflows (CF_t) (1)	$PVIF_{14\%,\,t}$ (2)	Present value at 14% [(1) ÷ (2)] (3)
1	$11,000	0.877	$ 9,647
2	10,000	0.769	7,690
3	9,000	0.675	6,075
4	8,000	0.592	4,736
	Present value of cash inflows		$28,148
	− Initial investment		27,000
	Net present value (NPV)		$ 1,148

(Calculator solution = $1,155.18)

c. Internal rate of return (IRR):

Project M: $\dfrac{\$28,500}{\$10,000} = 2.850$

$PVIFA_{IRR,4yrs} = 2.850$

From Table A–4:

$PVIFA_{15\%,4yrs} = 2.855$

$PVIFA_{16\%,4yrs} = 2.798$

IRR = $\underline{\underline{15\%}}$ (2.850 is closest to 2.855)

(Calculator solution = 15.09%)

Project N:

Average annual cash inflow $= \dfrac{\$11,000 + \$10,000 + \$9,000 + \$8,000}{4}$

$$= \dfrac{\$38,000}{4} = \$9,500$$

$PVIFA_{r,4yrs} = \dfrac{\$27,000}{\$9,500} = 2.842$

$r \approx 15\%$

Try 16%, because there are more cash inflows in early years.

Year (t)	CF_t (1)	$PVIF_{16\%,t}$ (2)	Present value at 16% [(1) × (2)] (3)	$PVIF_{17\%,t}$ (4)	Present value at 17% [(1) × (4)] (5)
1	$11,000	0.862	$ 9,482	0.855	$ 9,405
2	10,000	0.743	7,430	0.731	7,310
3	9,000	0.641	5,769	0.624	5,616
4	8,000	0.552	4,416	0.534	4,272
	Present value of cash inflows		$27,097		$26,603
	− Initial investment		27,000		27,000
	NPV		$ 97		−$ 397

IRR = $\underline{\underline{16\%}}$ (rounding to nearest whole percent)

(Calculator solution = 16.19%)

d.

	Project	
	M	N
Payback period	2.85 years	2.67 years[a]
NPV	$640	$1,148[a]
IRR	15%	16%[a]

[a]Preferred project.

Project N is recommended, because it has the shorter payback period and the higher NPV, which is greater than zero, and the larger IRR, which is greater than the 14% cost of capital.

e. Net present value profiles:

	Data	
	NPV	
Discount rate	Project M	Project N
0%	$11,500[a]	$11,000[b]
14	640	1,148
15	0	—
16	—	0

[a]($10,000 + $10,000 + $10,000 + $10,000) − $28,500
  = $40,000 − $28,500
  = $11,500

[b]($11,000 + $10,000 + $9,000 + $8,000) − $27,000
  = $38,000 − $27,000
  = $11,000

From the NPV profile that follows, it can be seen that if the firm has a cost of capital below approximately 6% (exact value is 5.75%), conflicting rankings of the projects would exist using the NPV and IRR decision techniques. Because the firm's cost of capital is 14%, it can be seen in part **d** that no conflict exists.

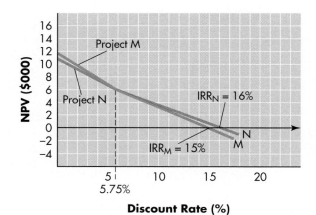

ST9–2   a. $NPV_A = (\$7,000 \times PVIFA_{10\%,3yrs}) - \$15,000$
            $= (\$7,000 \times 2.487) - \$15,000$
            $= \$17,409 - \$15,000 = \underline{\$2,409}$

(Calculator solution = $2,407.96)

$NPV_B = (\$10,000 \times PVIFA_{10\%,3yrs}) - \$20,000$
            $= (\$10,000 - 2.487) - \$20,000$
            $= \$24,870 - \$20,000 = \underline{\$4,870}*$

(Calculator solution = $4,868.52)

*Preferred project, because higher NPV.

b. From the CAPM-type relationship, the risk-adjusted discount rate ($RADR$) for project A, which has a risk index of 0.4, is 9%; for project B, with a risk index of 1.8, the $RADR$ is 16%.

$$NPV_A = (\$7,000 \times PVIFA_{9\%,3yrs}) - \$15,000$$
$$= (\$7,000 \times 2.531) - \$15,000$$
$$= \$17,717 - \$15,000 = \underline{\$2,717}^*$$

(Calculator solution = $2,719.06)

$$NPV_B = (\$10,000 \times PVIFA_{16\%,3yrs}) - \$20,000$$
$$= (\$10,000 \times 2.246) - \$20,000$$
$$= \$22,460 - \$20,000 = \underline{\$2,460}$$

(Calculator solution = $2,458.90)

*Preferred project, because higher NPV.

c. When the differences in risk were ignored in part **a**, project B was preferred over project A; but when the higher risk of project B is incorporated into the analysis using risk-adjusted discount rates in part **b**, *project A is preferred over project B.* Clearly, project A should be implemented.

Solutions to Self-Test Problems

9–2   **a.** Machine 1: 4 years, 8 months
           Machine 2: 5 years, 3 months
9–3   **a.** Project A payback: 3.9 years
9–4   **a.** $3,246 Accept
       b. −$5,131 Reject
9–5   **a.** $2,675 Accept
       c. −$805 Reject
9–10   **a.** Project A: 3.08 years
           Project C: 2.38 years
       b. Project C: NPV $5,451
9–11   **a.** Project A: 17%
           Project D: 21%
9–15   **a.** NPV = $1,222
       b. IRR = 12%
       c. Accept
9–20   **a.** Initial Investment: $1,480,000
       b.

Year	Cash Flow
1	$656,000
2	761,600
3	647,200
4	585,600
5	585,600
6	44,000

       c. 2.1 years
       d. NPV = $959,289
            IRR = 35%

9–22   **a.** Value of real options: $2,200
           $NPV_{strategic}$: $500
9–25   **a.** Range A: $1,600
           Range B: $200
9–26   **b.** Project A:
           Pessimistic: $73
           Most likely: $1,609
           Optimistic: $3,145
9–29   **a.** Project E: $2,130; Project F: $1,678
       c. Project E: $834; Project F: $1,678
9–31   **b.** $2,223
9–32   **a.** Project X: NPV = $14,960
           Project Y: NPV = $2,650

Chapter 13

Chapter 13

Determining the Cost of Capital

- Understand the drivers of the firm's overall cost of capital.

- Measure the costs of debt, preferred stock, and common stock.

- Compute a firm's overall, or weighted average, cost of capital.

- Apply the weighted average cost of capital to value projects.

- Adjust the cost of capital for the risk associated with the project.

- Account for the direct costs of raising external capital.

notation

$D\%$	fraction of the firm financed with debt	r_D	required return (cost of capital) for debt
Div_1	dividend due in one year	r_E	required return (cost of capital) of levered equity
Div_{pfd}	dividend on preferred stock		
$E\%$	fraction of the firm financed with equity	r_{pfd}	required return (cost of capital) for preferred stock
FCF_t	incremental free cash flow in year t	r_U	required return (cost of capital) of unlevered equity
g	expected growth rate for dividends		
$P\%$	fraction of the firm financed with preferred stock	r_{wacc}	weighted average cost of capital
P_E	price of common stock	T_c	marginal corporate tax rate
P_{pfd}	price of preferred stock	V_0^L	initial levered value

From Chapter 12 of *Fundamentals of Corporate Finance*, 1/e. Jonathan Berk, Peter DeMarzo, Jarrad Harford. Copyright © 2009 by Pearson Prentice Hall. All rights reserved.

INTERVIEW WITH Priscilla Srbu, Qualcomm's Strategic Finance Group

Cornell University, 2007

"Whenever you assess a project, whether it's a marketing campaign, an operations initiative, or a new market segment, you must evaluate the benefits and costs of doing the project."

As a staff financial analyst in Qualcomm's Strategic Finance group, Priscilla Srbu is responsible for valuation analysis for mergers and acquisitions, internal business units, and internal strategic initiatives. She received her MBA from Cornell University in 2007 and her BS from New York University in 2000.

Qualcomm, a world leader in digital wireless communications technology products and services, uses the weighted average cost of capital (WACC) as one of several tools to value an investment. When Priscilla analyzes a new line of business or an acquisition candidate, she uses the WACC as the discount rate for future cash flows in calculating the net present value of a potential investment. "The WACC represents the minimum rate of return at which an investment or project produces value for investors," Priscilla explains. "It also serves as a hurdle rate against which Qualcomm assesses return on invested capital and plays a key role in determining economic value added. For example, assume that a project produces a return of 25 percent and a company's WACC is 15 percent. Every $1 the company invests in this project creates 10 cents of value. If the company's return is less than the WACC, however, it is destroying economic value, indicating that the company should invest in other projects."

WACC appears easier to calculate than it really is, Priscilla cautions. "Two individuals may interpret the pieces used to calculate WACC very differently and derive different WACC numbers. Also, the methodologies behind the calculations may differ. Therefore companies like Qualcomm establish guidelines and methodologies for calculating WACC."

WACC has relevance for people in non-financial positions as well. "Whenever you assess a project, whether it's a marketing campaign, an operations initiative, or a new market segment, you must evaluate the benefits and costs of doing the project. The WACC allows you to ascribe a certain level of risk to the future cash flows associated with these projects. If the NPV is positive, the project's benefits cover, at a minimum, its cost and create value for shareholders—the number one concern for management."

In reality, most firms are financed with a combination of equity, debt, and other securities such as preferred stock. As a result, financial managers must determine their firm's overall cost of capital based on all sources of financing. This overall cost of capital is a critical input into the capital budgeting process. The Valuation Principle tells us that the value of a project is the present value of its benefits net of the present value of its costs. In capital budgeting, we implement this important concept with net present value (NPV). To calculate a project's NPV, we need a cost of capital to use as a discount rate.

In this chapter, we will learn how to calculate and use the firm's overall cost of capital, which is typically referred to as its weighted average cost of capital (WACC). We will see that the WACC is a weighted average of the costs of capital from each of the firm's different financing sources. After we have learned how to estimate the WACC, we will apply it in capital budgeting. As part of that discussion, we will learn the conditions under which we can use the firm's overall cost of capital as a discount rate and identify those situations in which we will instead need to determine a cost of capital specific to a project or division of the firm.

A First Look at the Weighted Average Cost of Capital

Most firms draw on some combination of equity, debt, and other securities to raise the funds they need for investment. In this section, we examine the role of financing sources in determining the firm's overall cost of capital. We begin by stepping back to assess these financing sources in the context of the firm's balance sheet.

The Firm's Capital Structure

capital A firm's sources of financing—debt, equity, and other securities that it has outstanding.

A firm's sources of financing, which usually consist of debt and equity, represent its **capital**. The typical firm raises funds to invest by selling shares to stockholders (its equity) and borrowing from lenders (its debt). Recall the most basic form of the balance sheet, as represented in Figure 1. The left side of the balance sheet lists the firm's assets, and the right side describes the firm's capital.

FIGURE 1

A Basic Balance Sheet

This figure provides a very basic balance sheet for reference. The two sides of the balance sheet must equal each other: Assets = Liabilities + Equity. The right side represents the way the assets are financed. In this chapter, we will focus on the required returns for the different forms of financing found on the right side of the balance sheet.

Assets	Liabilities and Equity
Current Assets Long-Term Assets	Debt Preferred Stock Equity

FIGURE 2

Two Capital Structures

This figure shows the capital structures of two real firms. Apple is financed 100% with common equity, shown in blue, while Anheuser Busch is financed 82% with common equity and 18% with debt, shaded in yellow.

Source: Authors' calculations based on publicly available data in 2007.

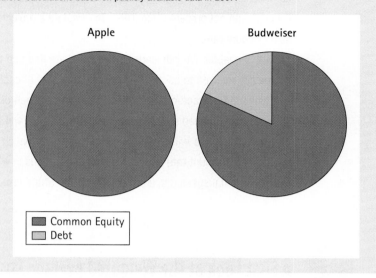

capital structure The relative proportions of debt, equity, and other securities that a firm has outstanding.

The relative proportions of debt, equity, and other securities that a firm has outstanding constitute its **capital structure**. When corporations raise funds from outside investors, they must choose which type of security to issue. The most common choices are financing through equity alone and financing through a combination of debt and equity. Figure 2 shows the capital structures of Apple and Anheuser Busch. Capital structures vary widely across firms.

Opportunity Cost and the Overall Cost of Capital

Financial managers take into account each component of the firm's capital structure when determining the firm's overall cost of capital. Throughout the discussion that follows, keep in mind the intuition behind the term "cost of capital." When investors buy the stock or bonds of a company, they forgo the opportunity to invest that money elsewhere. The expected return from those alternative investments constitutes an opportunity cost to them. Thus, to attract their investments as capital to the firm, the firm must offer potential investors an expected return equal to what they could expect to earn elsewhere for assuming the same level of risk. Providing this return is the cost a company bears in exchange for obtaining capital from investors.

Weighted Averages and the Overall Cost of Capital

weighted average cost of capital (WACC) The average of a firm's equity and debt costs of capital, weighted by the fractions of the firm's value that correspond to equity and debt, respectively.

Intuitively, the firm's overall cost of capital should be a blend of the costs of the different sources of capital. In fact, we calculate the firm's overall cost of capital as a weighted average of its equity and debt costs of capital, known as the firm's **weighted average cost of capital (WACC).**

But what should the weights be? Imagine you owned all of the stock and all of the debt of the firm. If that was all you had in your portfolio, the return on your portfolio would be the total return of the firm. A portfolio return is the weighted average of the returns of the securities in the portfolio. In this case, the return on your portfolio—the total return of the firm—is a weighted average of the return you earn holding all the stock of the firm and the return you earn holding all of the debt. Since you hold all of each, your portfolio weights are just the relative amount of debt and equity issued by the firm. Thus the weights we use in the WACC are the proportions of debt and equity used in the firm's capital structure. For example, if the firm is financed 30% by debt and 70% by equity, then the weights used in its WACC would be 30% on the debt cost of capital and 70% on the equity cost of capital.

This example suggests that you can determine the weights by looking at the right side of the firm's balance sheet. That assumption is correct, with one important modification: You must use the *market values* of the debt and equity to determine the proportions, not the accounting-based *book values* listed on the balance sheet. Book values reflect historical costs, but market values are forward-looking, based on what the assets are expected to produce in the future. Holders of the firm's financial claims—equity and, if the firm has it, debt—assess the firm based on the market value of its assets, not the book value.

market-value balance sheet Similar to an accounting balance sheet, but all values are current market values rather than historical costs.

In fact, it is useful to think about the **market-value balance sheet**, where the assets, debt, and equity are all listed in terms of their market values, instead of their book values. Of course, the market-value balance sheet must still balance:

$$\text{Market Value of Equity} + \text{Market Value of Debt} = \text{Market Value of Assets} \qquad (1)$$

Equation 1 states that the total market value of all the claims (equity and debt) issued by the firm must be equal to the total market value of all its assets. This equality drives home the point that the equity and debt issued by the firm derive their value from the underlying assets they claim. The risk, and hence the required return, of the debt and equity of the firm are determined by the risk of the firm's assets. This point will be useful as we derive the firm's WACC.

Weighted Average Cost of Capital Calculations

In this section, we will develop the intuition behind the use of market-value weights as well as the link between the risk of the assets and the risk of the debt and equity claims on those assets.

unlevered A firm that does not have debt outstanding.

levered A firm that has debt outstanding.

leverage The relative amount of debt on a firm's balance sheet.

We begin with the straightforward case of the firm that does not issue debt—the **unlevered** firm that pays out all of the free cash flows generated by its assets to its equity holders. When some of a firm's financing comes from debt, we say the firm is **levered**. Just as a lever allows you to lift a heavy object by exerting relatively little force, so borrowing money through debt allows equity holders to control highly valued assets with relatively little investment of their own money. We refer to the relative amount of debt on the balance sheet as the firm's **leverage**.

The Weighted Average Cost of Capital: Unlevered Firm. If a firm is unlevered, so that it has no debt, all of the free cash flows generated by its assets are ultimately paid out to its equity holders. Because the free cash flows to the equity holders are the same as the free cash flows from the assets, the Valuation Principle tells us that the market value, risk, and cost of capital for the firm's equity are equal to the corresponding amounts for its assets. Given this relationship, we can estimate the firm's equity cost of capital using the Capital Asset Pricing Model (CAPM). The resulting estimate is the cost of capital for the firm as a whole. For example, both Cisco and Apple do not issue debt, so the cost of capital for Cisco's or Apple's assets is the same as the firms' costs of equity.

The Weighted Average Cost of Capital: Levered Firm. But what if the firm has debt? How should we incorporate the cost of this debt to determine the cost of capital for the firm's assets as a whole? The market-value balance sheet provides the answer. We can interpret the equality in Eq. 1 in terms of a portfolio: By holding a portfolio of the firm's equity and debt, we can get the same cash flows as if we held the assets directly. Because the return of a portfolio is equal to the weighted average of the returns of the securities in it, this equality implies the following relationship between the required returns (costs) of equity, debt, and assets:

Weighted Average Cost of Capital (Pre-tax)

$$r_{wacc} \equiv \left(\begin{array}{c}\text{Fraction of Firm Value}\\\text{Financed by Equity}\end{array}\right)\left(\begin{array}{c}\text{Equity}\\\text{Cost of Capital}\end{array}\right)$$

$$+ \left(\begin{array}{c}\text{Fraction of Firm Value}\\\text{Financed by Debt}\end{array}\right)\left(\begin{array}{c}\text{Debt}\\\text{Cost of Capital}\end{array}\right)$$

$$= \left(\begin{array}{c}\text{Asset}\\\text{Cost of Capital}\end{array}\right) \tag{2}$$

We now have the justification for our intuition that the overall cost of capital for a firm should be a weighted average of its equity and debt costs of capital. Eq. 2 shows that we can calculate the cost of capital of the firm's assets by computing the weighted average of the firm's equity and debt cost of capital. In the next section, we explore how to estimate the firm's costs of equity and debt capital.

EXAMPLE 1

Calculating the Weights in the WACC

Problem

Suppose Sony Corporation has debt with a market value of $12 billion outstanding, and common stock with a market value of $49 billion and a book value of $30 billion. Which weights should Sony use in calculating its WACC?

Solution

▶ **Plan**

Equation 2 tells us that the weights are the fractions of Sony financed with debt and financed with equity. Furthermore, these weights should be based on market values because the cost of capital is based on investors' current assessment of the value of the firm, not their assessment of accounting-based book values. As a consequence, we can ignore the book value of equity.

▶ **Execute**

Given its $12 billion in debt and $49 billion in equity, the total value of the firm is $61 billion. The weights are

$$\frac{\$12\,\text{billion}}{\$61\,\text{billion}} = 19.7\% \text{ for debt} \quad \text{and} \quad \frac{\$49\,\text{billion}}{\$61\,\text{billion}} = 80.3\% \text{ for equity.}$$

▶ **Evaluate**

When calculating its overall cost of capital, Sony will use a weighted average of the cost of its debt capital and the cost of its equity capital, giving a weight of 19.7% to its cost of debt and a weight of 80.3% to its cost of equity.

Concept Check

1. Why does a firm's capital have a cost?

2. Why do we use market value weights in the weighted average cost of capital?

The Firm's Costs of Debt and Equity Capital

Section 1 made it clear that to measure the firm's overall cost of capital, we need to start by determining the cost of each type of capital a firm might use. We now turn to how a company measures the costs of its debt, preferred stock, and common stock. We will use Alcoa, Inc., a global aluminum producer, as an example.

Cost of Debt Capital

We will start at the top of the right side of the balance sheet with the cost of the firm's debt. A firm's cost of debt is the interest rate it would have to pay to refinance its existing debt, such as through new bond issues. This rate differs from the coupon rate on the firm's existing debt, which reflects the interest rate the firm had to offer at the time the debt was issued.

Yield to Maturity and the Cost of Debt. Existing debt trades in the marketplace, so its price fluctuates to reflect both changes in the overall credit environment and changes in the risk specifically associated with the firm. The market price of the firm's existing debt implies a yield to maturity, which is the return that current purchasers of the debt would earn if they held the debt to maturity and received all of the payments as promised. So, we can use the yield to maturity to estimate the firm's current cost of debt: It is the yield that investors demand to hold the firm's debt (new or existing).[1]

Suppose Alcoa has debt due in 2017 with a coupon rate of 5.55% priced at $961.85 per $1000 face value. Because the market price of the debt is below its face value, investors in debt earn a yield that exceeds the 5.55% coupon rate. In fact, we can calculate that this price implies a yield to maturity of 6.09%, which is Alcoa's current cost of debt. In reality, you would not need to actually compute the yield to maturity yourself because prices and their implied yields to maturity are always quoted together in the bond market.[2]

Taxes and the Cost of Debt. In the case of debt, the return paid to the debt holders is not the same as the cost to the firm. How could this be? The difference arises because interest paid on debt is a tax-deductible expense. When a firm uses debt financing, the cost of the interest it must pay is offset to some extent by the tax savings from the tax deduction.

For example, suppose a firm with a 35% tax rate borrows $100,000 at 10% interest per year. Then its net cost at the end of the year is calculated as follows:

		Year-End
Interest expense	$r_D \times \$100,000 =$	10,000
Tax savings	$-\text{Tax Rate} \times r_D \times \$100,000 =$	−3,500
Effective after-tax interest expense	$r_D \times (1 - \text{Tax Rate}) \times \$100,000 =$	$6,500

---

[1]In fact, the yield to maturity is the *most* the firm will pay because there is some risk the firm may not repay its debt.

[2]Find current prices and yields to maturity for corporate bonds online using the Web site http://cxa.marketwatch.com/finra/BondCenter/Default.aspx.

Common Mistake — Using the Coupon Rate as the Cost of Debt

A common mistake in estimating a company's overall cost of capital is to use the coupon rate on its existing debt as its debt cost of capital. The company's cost of capital is forward-looking and based on current conditions. By contrast, the coupon rate on existing debt is historical and set under potentially very different conditions. A better estimate of the firm's debt cost of capital is the yield to maturity of its existing debt, which is the promised return its lenders currently demand.

Consider Ford Motor Company as an example. Ford has bonds that were originally issued in 1998 and are due in 2018; these bonds have a coupon rate of 6.5%. In recent years, however, Ford's performance has suffered

and the risk that it might not be able to meet all of its debt obligations has increased. By the end of 2007, those 6.5% coupon bonds were trading at a yield to maturity of 10.2%. Thus the market was saying that to be willing to take a creditor position in Ford, investors must be offered a yield to maturity of 10.2%.

So, which is a better estimate of the cost of debt capital for Ford in 2007: the 6.5% coupon or the 10.2% yield to maturity? Ford should use 10.2% as its cost of debt capital. The 6.5% rate, which was set under different circumstances, is not a relevant measure of Ford's debt holders' required return in 2007, so it should not enter into the WACC calculation.

effective cost of the debt
A firm's net cost of interest on its debt after accounting for the interest tax deduction.

The **effective cost of the debt**—the firm's net cost of interest on the debt after taxes—is only $6500/$100{,}000 = 6.50\%$ of the loan amount, rather than the full 10% interest. Thus the tax deductibility of interest lowers the effective cost of debt financing for the firm. More generally, with tax-deductible interest and denoting the corporate tax rate as T_C, the effective after-tax borrowing rate is

$$r_D(1 - T_C) \qquad (3)$$

EXAMPLE 2
Effective Cost of Debt

Problem

By using the yield to maturity on Alcoa's debt, we found that its pre-tax cost of debt is 6.09%. If Alcoa's tax rate is 35%, what is its effective cost of debt?

Solution

▶ **Plan**

We can use Eq. 3 to calculate Alcoa's effective cost of debt: $r_D(1 - T_C)$.

$$r_D = 6.09\% \text{ (pre-tax cost of debt)}$$
$$T_C = 35\% \text{ (corporate tax rate)}$$

▶ **Execute**

Alcoa's effective cost of debt is $0.0609(1 - 0.35) = 0.039585 = 3.9585\%$.

▶ **Evaluate**

For every $1000 it borrows, Alcoa pays its bondholders $0.0609(\$1000) = \$60.90$ in interest every year. Because it can deduct that $60.90 in interest from its income, every dollar in interest saves Alcoa 35 cents in taxes, so the interest tax deduction reduces the firm's tax payment to the government by $0.35(\$60.90) = \$21.315$. Thus Alcoa's net cost of debt is the $60.90 it pays minus the $21.315 in reduced tax payments, which is $39.9585 per $1000 or 3.9585%.

Cost of Preferred Stock Capital

Firms may also raise capital by issuing preferred stock. Typically, holders of the preferred stock are promised a fixed dividend, which must be paid "in preference to" (i.e., before) any dividends can be paid to common stockholders.

If the preferred dividend is known and fixed, we can estimate the preferred stock's cost of capital using the following equation,

$$r_{\mathrm{E}} = \frac{Div_1}{P_0} + g$$

where the growth rate $g = 0$. Thus,

$$\text{Cost of Preferred Stock Capital} = \frac{\text{Preferred Dividend}}{\text{Preferred Stock Price}} = \frac{Div_{pfd}}{P_{pfd}} \qquad (4)$$

For example, Alcoa's preferred stock has a price of \$54.50 and an annual dividend of \$3.75. Its cost of preferred stock, therefore, is 3.75/54.50 = 6.88%.

Cost of Common Stock Capital

A company cannot directly observe its cost of common stock (equity), but must instead estimate it. We now present and compare the two major methods for doing so.

Capital Asset Pricing Model. The most common approach is to use the CAPM. To summarize that approach:

1. Estimate the firm's beta of equity, typically by regressing 60 months of the company's returns against 60 months of returns for a market proxy such as the S&P 500.
2. Determine the risk-free rate, typically by using the yield on Treasury bills or bonds.
3. Estimate the market risk premium, typically by comparing historical returns on a market proxy to contemporaneous risk-free rates.
4. Apply the CAPM:

   Cost of Equity = Risk-Free Rate + Equity Beta × Market Risk Premium

For example, suppose the equity beta of Alcoa is 2.05, the yield on 10-year Treasury notes is 4.5%, and you estimate the market risk premium to be 5%. Alcoa's cost of equity is 4.5% + 2.05 × 5% = 14.75%.

Constant Dividend Growth Model. Another way to estimate a company's cost of equity comes from the Constant Dividend Growth Model (CDGM):

$$\text{Cost of Equity} = \frac{\text{Dividend (in one year)}}{\text{Current Price}} + \text{Dividend Growth Rate} = \frac{Div_1}{P_E} + g \qquad (5)$$

Thus, to estimate the cost of equity, we need the current price of the stock, the expected dividend in one year, and an estimate of the dividend growth rate. The current price of the stock is easy to obtain online. We may even have a reasonable estimate of next year's dividend. Estimating the future dividend growth rate can be very difficult. For example, Alcoa's dividend was 60 cents per share per year from 2001 to 2006 and then increased to 68 cents in 2007. Perhaps it is reasonable to assume that 2008's dividend would be 68 cents per year, but what about the dividend's long-term growth rate? Should we assume that it will increase by about 8/60 (13.3%) every six years?

Rather than looking backward at historical growth, one common approach is to use estimates produced by stock analysts, as these estimates are forward-looking. If Alcoa keeps its dividend payout rate constant, then the long-run growth in dividends will equal

TABLE 1		Capital Asset Pricing Model	Constant Dividend Growth Model
Estimating the Cost of Equity	**Inputs**	Equity beta Risk-free rate Market risk premium	Current stock price Expected dividend next year Future dividend growth rate
	Major Assumptions	Estimated beta is correct Market risk premium is accurate CAPM is the correct model	Dividend estimate is correct Growth rate matches market expectations Future dividend growth is constant

the long-run growth in earnings. In late 2007, the average forecast for Alcoa's long-run earnings growth rate was 11%. Thus, with an expected dividend in one year of $0.68, a price of $39.35, and long-run dividend growth of 11%, the CDGM estimates Alcoa's cost of equity as follows (using Eq. 5) as:

$$\text{Cost of Equity} = \frac{Div_1}{P_E} + g = \frac{\$0.68}{\$39.35} + 0.11 = 0.127, \text{ or } 12.7\%$$

We should not be surprised that the two estimates of Alcoa's cost of equity (14.75% and 12.7%) do not match, because each was based on different assumptions. Further, even given an estimate of future growth of dividends, Eq. 5 makes an assumption that future dividend growth will continue at a constant rate. This assumption is unlikely to be valid for most firms. Looking again at Alcoa, prior to the six-year run of 60 cents per share per year dividends, the firm paid 50 cents per share for one year. Finally, many young, growing firms do not pay a dividend and have no plans to do so in the near future.

We could use any model relating a firm's stock price to its future cash flows to estimate its cost of equity—the CDGM is just one of the possible models.

CAPM and CDGM Comparison. Because of the difficulties with the CDGM, the CAPM is the most popular approach for estimating the cost of equity. Table 1 compares the two approaches.

EXAMPLE 3

Estimating the Cost of Equity

Problem

The equity beta for Weyerhaeuser (ticker: WY) is 1.2. The yield on 10-year treasuries is 4.5%, and you estimate the market risk premium to be 5%. Further, Weyerhaeuser issues an annual dividend of $2. Its current stock price is $71, and you expect dividends to increase at a constant rate of 4% per year. Estimate Weyerhaeuser's cost of equity in two ways.

Solution

▶ **Plan**

The two ways to estimate Weyerhaeuser's cost of equity are to use the CAPM and the CDGM.

1. The CAPM requires the risk-free rate, an estimate of the equity's beta, and an estimate of the market risk premium. We can use the yield on 10-year Treasury bills as the risk-free rate.
2. The CDGM requires the current stock price, the expected dividend next year, and an estimate of the constant future growth rate for the dividend:

Risk-free rate: 4.5%	Current price: $71
Equity beta: 1.2	Expected dividend: $2
Market risk premium: 5%	Estimated future dividend growth rate: 4%

We can use the CAPM to estimate the cost of equity using the CAPM approach and Eq. 5 to estimate it using the CDGM approach.

▶ **Execute**

1. The CAPM says that

Cost of Equity = Risk-Free Rate + Equity Beta × Market Risk Premium

For Weyerhaeuser, this implies that its cost of equity is 4.5% + 1.2 × 5% = 10.5%.

2. The CDGM says

$$\text{Cost of Equity} = \frac{\text{Dividend (in one year)}}{\text{Current Price}} + \text{Dividend Growth Rate} = \frac{\$2}{\$71} + 4\% = 6.8\%$$

▶ **Evaluate**

According to the CAPM, the cost of equity capital is 10.5%; the CDGM produces a result of 6.8%. Because of the different assumptions we make when using each method, the two methods do not have to produce the same answer—in fact, it would be highly unlikely that they would. When the two approaches produce different answers, we must examine the assumptions we made for each approach and decide which set of assumptions is more realistic.

We can also see what assumption about future dividend growth would be necessary to make the answers converge. By rearranging the CDGM and using the cost of equity we estimated from the CAPM, we have

$$\text{Dividend Growth Rate} = \text{Cost of Equity} - \frac{\text{Dividend (in one year)}}{\text{Current Price}} = 10.5\% - 2.8\% = 7.7\%$$

Thus, if we believe that Weyerhaeuser's dividends will grow at a rate of 7.7% per year, the two approaches would produce the same cost of equity estimate.

Concept Check

3. How can you measure a firm's cost of debt ?
4. What are the major tradeoffs in using the CAPM versus the CDGM to estimate the cost of equity?

3 A Second Look at the Weighted Average Cost of Capital

Now that we have estimated the costs of Alcoa's different sources of capital, we are ready to calculate the firm's overall WACC. The weights are the percentage of firm value financed by equity, preferred stock, and debt. We can represent these as $E\%$, $P\%$, and $D\%$, respectively, and note that they must sum to 100% (i.e., we must account for all the sources of financing).

WACC Equation

Formally, denoting the cost of equity, preferred and debt capital as r_E, r_{pfd}, and r_D, and the corporate tax rate as T_C, the WACC is

Weighted Average Cost of Capital

$$r_{wacc} = r_E E\% + r_{pfd} P\% + r_D(1 - T_C)D\% \tag{6}$$

For a company that does not have preferred stock, the WACC condenses to

$$r_{wacc} = r_E E\% + r_D(1 - T_C)D\% \tag{7}$$

For example, in late 2007, the market values of Alcoa's common stock, preferred stock, and debt were \$31,420 million, \$40 million, and \$7397 million, respectively. Its total value was, therefore, \$31,420 million + \$40 million + \$7397 million = \$38,857 million. Given the costs of common stock, preferred stock, and debt we have already computed, Alcoa's WACC in late 2007 was

$$WACC = r_E E\% + r_{pfd} P\% + (1 - T_C) r_D D\%$$

$$WACC = 14.75\% \left(\frac{31{,}420}{38{,}857}\right) + 6.88\% \left(\frac{40}{38{,}857}\right) + (1 - 0.35)6.09\% \left(\frac{7397}{38{,}857}\right)$$

$$WACC = 12.69\%$$

EXAMPLE 4

Computing the WACC

Problem

The expected return on Target's equity is 11.5%, and the firm has a yield to maturity on its debt of 6%. Debt accounts for 18% and equity for 82% of Target's total market value. If its tax rate is 35%, what is this firm's WACC?

Solution

▶ **Plan**

We can compute the WACC using Eq. 7. To do so, we need to know the costs of equity and debt, their proportions in Target's capital structure, and the firm's tax rate. We have all that information, so we are ready to proceed.

▶ **Execute**

$$r_{wacc} = r_E E\% + r_D(1 - T_C)D\% = (0.115)(0.82) + (0.06)(1 - 0.35)(0.18) = 0.101, \text{ or } 10.1\%$$

▶ **Evaluate**

Even though we cannot observe the expected return of Target's investments directly, we can use the expected return on its equity and debt and the WACC formula to estimate it, adjusting for the tax advantage of debt. Target needs to earn at least a 10.1% return on its investment in current and new stores to satisfy both its debt and equity holders.

Weighted Average Cost of Capital in Practice

The WACC is driven by the risk of a company's line of business and, because of the tax effect of interest, its leverage. As a result, WACCs vary widely across industries and companies. Figure 3 presents the WACC for several real companies to provide a sense of the degree to which the cost of capital can vary. Some lines of business are clearly riskier than others. For example, selling beer is a fairly low-risk proposition, but selling high-end electronics (as Apple and TiVo do) is much riskier.

Methods in Practice

We now turn to some issues that arise for financial managers when they are estimating the WACC in practice.

net debt Total debt outstanding minus any cash balances.

Net Debt. When calculating the weights for the WACC, it is increasingly common practice to make an adjustment to the debt. Many practitioners now use **net debt**, the total debt outstanding minus any cash balances:

$$\text{Net Debt} = \text{Debt} - \text{Cash and Risk-Free Securities} \tag{8}$$

Why subtract a company's cash from its debt? The assets on a firm's balance sheet include any holdings of cash or risk-free securities. If a firm holds $1 in cash and has $1 of risk-free debt, then the interest earned on the cash will equal the interest paid on the debt. The cash flows from each source cancel each other, just as if the firm held no cash and no debt. In fact, we can view cash as being equivalent to negative debt. Significant

FIGURE 3

WACCs for Real Companies

The cost of equity is computed using the company's equity beta, a risk-free rate of 4.5%, and a market risk premium of 5%. The cost of debt is taken from the company's debt. The percent equity and percent debt are determined from the company's market capitalization and balance sheet. The WACC is computed using Eq. 7 with a 35% tax rate and is shown in the accompanying bar graph. "N/A" means that the cost of debt is not applicable and refers to companies that have no debt.

Source: Authors' calculations based on publicly available information in 2007.

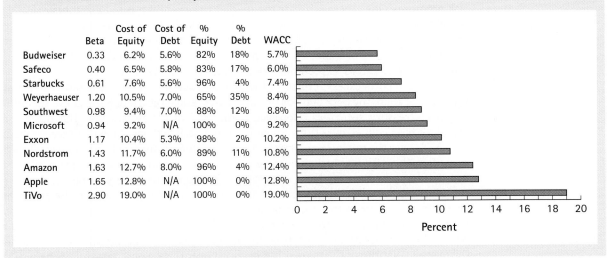

	Beta	Cost of Equity	Cost of Debt	% Equity	% Debt	WACC
Budweiser	0.33	6.2%	5.6%	82%	18%	5.7%
Safeco	0.40	6.5%	5.8%	83%	17%	6.0%
Starbucks	0.61	7.6%	5.6%	96%	4%	7.4%
Weyerhaeuser	1.20	10.5%	7.0%	65%	35%	8.4%
Southwest	0.98	9.4%	7.0%	88%	12%	8.8%
Microsoft	0.94	9.2%	N/A	100%	0%	9.2%
Exxon	1.17	10.4%	5.3%	98%	2%	10.2%
Nordstrom	1.43	11.7%	6.0%	89%	11%	10.8%
Amazon	1.63	12.7%	8.0%	96%	4%	12.4%
Apple	1.65	12.8%	N/A	100%	0%	12.8%
TiVo	2.90	19.0%	N/A	100%	0%	19.0%

excess cash on a firm's balance sheet can complicate the assessment of the risk (and hence the cost of capital) of the assets the firm actually uses in the course of business. Thus, when trying to evaluate a firm's business assets separate from any cash holdings, practitioners often measure the leverage of the firm in terms of its net debt and measure the market value of a firm's business assets using its enterprise value.

Using this approach, the weights in the WACC would then be

$$\left(\frac{\text{Market Value of Equity}}{\text{Enterprise Value}} \right) \quad \text{and} \quad \left(\frac{\text{Net Debt}}{\text{Enterprise Value}} \right)$$

For firms with substantial excess cash reserves, this adjustment could be important. For firms with relatively low levels of cash, it will not have a large effect on the overall WACC estimate.

The Risk-Free Interest Rate. Estimating the equity cost of capital using the CAPM requires the risk-free interest rate. The risk-free interest rate is generally determined using the yields of U.S. Treasury securities, which are free from default risk. But which horizon should we choose? The CAPM states that we should use the risk-free interest corresponding to the investment horizon of the firm's investors. When surveyed, the vast majority of large firms and financial analysts report using the yields of long-term (10- to 30-year) bonds to determine the risk-free rate.[3]

---

[3]See Robert Bruner, et al., "Best Practices in Estimating the Cost of Capital: Survey and Synthesis," *Financial Practice and Education* 8 (1998): 13–28.

TABLE 2

Historical Excess Returns of the S&P 500 Compared to One-Year Treasury Bills and Ten-Year Treasury Notes

Risk-Free Security	Period	S&P 500 Excess Return
One-year Treasury security	1926–2005	8.0%
	1955–2005	5.7%
Ten-year Treasury security*	1955–2005	4.5%

*Based on a comparison of compounded returns over a ten-year holding period.

The Market Risk Premium.   Using the CAPM also requires an estimate of the market risk premium. One way to estimate the market risk premium is to look at historical data. Because we are interested in the *future* market risk premium, we face a tradeoff in terms of the amount of data we use. It takes many years of data to produce even moderately accurate estimates of expected returns—yet data that are very old may have little relevance for investors' expectations of the market risk premium today.

Table 2 reports excess returns of the S&P 500 versus one-year and ten-year Treasury rates. Since 1926, the S&P 500 has produced an average return of 8.0% above the rate for one-year Treasury securities. However, some evidence indicates that the market risk premium has declined over time. Since 1955, the S&P 500 has shown an excess return of only 5.7% over the rate for one-year Treasury securities. Compared with ten-year Treasury securities, the S&P 500 had an average excess return of only 4.5% (due primarily to the fact that ten-year Treasury bond rates tend to be higher than one-year rates).

How can we explain this decline? One reason may be that as more investors have begun to participate in the stock market and the costs of constructing a diversified portfolio have declined, investors have tended to hold less risky portfolios. As a result, the return they require as compensation for taking on that risk has diminished. In addition, the overall volatility of the market has declined over time. Some researchers believe that the future expected returns for the market are likely to be even lower than these historical numbers, in a range of 3% to 5% over Treasury bills.[4] Consequently, many financial managers currently use market risk premiums closer to 5%, rather than 8%.

Concept Check

5. Why do different companies have different WACCs?

6. What are the tradeoffs in estimating the market risk premium?

Using the WACC to Value a Project

A project's cost of capital depends on its risk. When the market risk of the project is similar to the average market risk of the firm's investments, then its cost of capital is equivalent to the cost of capital for a portfolio of all the firm's securities. In other words, the project's cost of capital is equal to the firm's WACC. As shown in Eq. 6, the WACC incorporates the benefit of the interest tax deduction by using the firm's *after-tax* cost of capital for debt.

Because the WACC incorporates the tax savings from debt, we can compute the value of an investment including the benefit of the interest tax deduction given the

[4]See Ivo Welch, "The Equity Premium Consensus Forecast Revisited," Cowles Foundation Discussion Paper 1325 (2001), and John Graham and Campbell Harvey, "The Long-Run Equity Risk Premium," SSRN working paper (2005).

levered value The value of an investment, including the benefit of the interest tax deduction, given the firm's leverage policy.

WACC method Discounting future incremental free cash flows using the firm's WACC. This method produces the levered value of a project.

firm's leverage policy, sometimes called the investment's **levered value**. To do so, we discount the firm's future incremental free cash flow using the WACC, a process we refer to as the **WACC method**. Specifically, if FCF_t is the expected incremental free cash flow of an investment at the end of year t, then the Valuation Principle tells us that the investment's levered value, V_0^L, is

$$V_0^L = \frac{FCF_1}{1 + r_{wacc}} + \frac{FCF_2}{(1 + r_{wacc})^2} + \frac{FCF_3}{(1 + r_{wacc})^3} + \cdots \tag{9}$$

The intuition for the WACC method is that the firm's WACC represents the average return the firm must pay to its investors (both debt and equity holders) on an after-tax basis. Thus, to have a positive NPV, a project with the same risk as the average risk for the firm's projects should generate an expected return of at least the firm's WACC.

EXAMPLE 5

The WACC Method

Problem

Suppose Anheuser Busch is considering introducing a new ultra-light beer with zero calories to be called BudZero. The firm believes that the beer's flavor and appeal to calorie-conscious drinkers will make it a success. The cost of bringing the beer to market is $200 million, but Anheuser Busch expects first-year incremental free cash flows from BudZero to be $100 million and to grow at 3% per year thereafter. Should Anheuser Busch go ahead with the project?

Solution

▶ **Plan**

We can use the WACC method shown in Eq. 9 to value BudZero and then subtract the upfront cost of $200 million. We will need Anheuser Busch's WACC, which was estimated in Figure 3 as 5.7%.

▶ **Execute**

The cash flows for BudZero are a growing perpetuity. Applying the growing perpetuity formula with the WACC method, we have

$$V_0^L = FCF_0 + \frac{FCF_1}{r_{wacc} - g} = -200 + \frac{\$100 \text{ million}}{0.057 - 0.03} = \$3{,}503.7 \text{ million } (\$3.5 \text{ billion})$$

▶ **Evaluate**

The BudZero project has a positive NPV because it is expected to generate a return on the $200 million far in excess of Anheuser Busch's WACC of 5.7%. Taking positive-NPV projects adds value to the firm. Here, we can see that the value is created by exceeding the required return of the firm's investors.

Key Assumptions

While it is common practice to use the WACC as the discount rate in capital budgeting, it is important to be aware of the underlying assumptions. We examine the critical assumptions here and then explore these assumptions further in the context of an application.

Assumption 1: Average Risk. We assume initially that the market risk of the project is equivalent to the average market risk of the firm's investments. In that case, we assess the project's cost of capital based on the risk of the firm.

Assumption 2: Constant Debt-Equity Ratio. We assume that the firm adjusts its leverage continuously to maintain a constant ratio of the market value of debt to the market

debt-equity ratio A ratio of the market value of debt to the market value of equity.

value of equity—a relationship referred to as the **debt-equity ratio**. This policy determines the amount of debt the firm will take on when it accepts a new project. It also implies that the risk of the firm's equity and debt, and therefore its WACC, will not fluctuate owing to leverage changes.

Assumption 3: Limited Leverage Effects. We assume initially that the main effect of leverage on valuation follows from the interest tax deduction. We assume that any other factors (such as possible financial distress) are not significant at the level of debt chosen.

Assumptions in Practice. These assumptions are reasonable for many projects and firms. The first assumption is likely to fit typical projects of firms with investments concentrated in a single industry. In that case, the market risk of both the project and the firm will primarily depend on the sensitivity of the industry to the overall economy. The second assumption, while unlikely to hold exactly, reflects the fact that firms tend to increase their levels of debt as they grow larger; some may even have an explicit target for their debt-equity ratio.[5] Finally, for firms without very high levels of debt, the interest tax deduction is likely to be the most important factor affecting the capital budgeting decision. Hence, the third assumption is a reasonable starting point to begin our analysis.

Of course, while these three assumptions may be a reasonable approximation in many situations, there are certainly projects and firms for which they do not apply. In the following section, we apply the WACC method under all three assumptions. Next, we relax the first assumption, which states that the project has average risk. (We will relax the other two assumptions in later chapters.)

WACC Method Application: Extending the Life of an Alcoa Mine

Let's apply the WACC method to value a project. Suppose Alcoa is considering an investment that would extend the life of one of its aluminum mines for four years. The project would require upfront costs of $6.67 million plus a $24 million investment in equipment. The equipment will be obsolete in four years and will be depreciated via the straight-line method over that period. During the next four years, however, Alcoa expects annual sales of $60 million per year from this mine. Mining costs and operating expenses are expected to total $25 million and $9 million, respectively, per year. Finally, Alcoa expects no net working capital requirements for the project, and it pays a corporate tax rate of 35%.

Using this information, the spreadsheet in Table 3 forecasts the project's expected free cash flow. The market risk of the project of extending the life of the mine is the same as that for the Alcoa's business of aluminum mining. As a consequence, we can use Alcoa's WACC to compute the NPV of the project.

We can determine the value of the project, including the present value of the interest tax deduction from the debt, by calculating the present value of its future free cash flows, V_0^L, using the WACC method and Alcoa's WACC of 12.69%, which we computed in Section 3:

$$V_0^L = \frac{19}{1.1269} + \frac{19}{1.1269^2} + \frac{19}{1.1269^3} + \frac{19}{1.1269^4} = \$56.88 \text{ million}$$

Because the upfront cost of launching the product line is only $28 million, this project is a good idea. Taking the project results in an NPV of $56.88 million – $28.34 million = $28.54 million for the firm.

---

[5]There is a tradeoff between debt and equity and the concept of a target debt-equity ratio.

TABLE 3

Expected Free Cash Flow from Alcoa's Mining Project

1	Year	0	1	2	3	4
2	**Incremental Earnings Forecast ($million)**					
3	Sales	—	60.00	60.00	60.00	60.00
4	Cost of Goods Sold	—	−25.00	−25.00	−25.00	−25.00
5	**Gross Profit**	—	35.00	35.00	35.00	35.00
6	Operating Expenses	−6.67	−9.00	−9.00	−9.00	−9.00
7	Depreciation	—	−6.00	−6.00	−6.00	−6.00
8	**EBIT**	−6.67	20.00	20.00	20.00	20.00
9	Income Tax at 35%	2.33	−7.00	−7.00	−7.00	−7.00
10	**Unlevered Net Income**	−4.43	13.00	13.00	13.00	13.00
11	**Incremental Free Cash Flow ($ million)**					
12	Plus: Depreciation	—	6.00	6.00	6.00	6.00
13	Less: Capital Expenditures	−24.00	—	—	—	—
14	Less: Increases in NWC	—	—	—	—	—
15	**Incremental Free Cash Flow**	−28.34	19.00	19.00	19.00	19.00

Summary of the WACC Method

To summarize, the key steps in the WACC valuation method are as follows:

1. Determine the incremental free cash flow of the investment.
2. Compute the weighted average cost of capital using Eq. 6.
3. Compute the value of the investment, including the tax benefit of leverage, by discounting the incremental free cash flow of the investment using the WACC.

In many firms, the corporate treasurer performs the second step, calculating the firm's WACC. This rate can then be used throughout the firm as the companywide cost of capital for new investments *that are of comparable risk to the rest of the firm and that will not alter the firm's debt-equity ratio.* Employing the WACC method in this way is very simple and straightforward. As a result, this method is the most commonly used in practice for capital budgeting purposes.

Concept Check

7. What are the main assumptions you make when you use the WACC method?
8. What inputs do you need to be ready to apply the WACC method?

5 Project-Based Costs of Capital

Up to this point we have assumed that both the risk and the leverage of the project under consideration matched those characteristics for the firm as a whole. This assumption allowed us, in turn, to assume that the cost of capital for a project matched the firm's cost of capital.

In reality, specific projects often differ from the average investment made by the firm. Consider General Electric Company, a large firm with many divisions that operate in completely different lines of business. Projects in GE's health care division are likely to have different market risk than projects in its air transportation equipment division or at NBC Universal. Projects may also vary in terms of the amount of leverage they will support—for example, acquisitions of real estate or capital equipment are often highly levered, while investments in intellectual property are not. In this section, we show how to calculate the cost of capital for the project's cash flows when a project's risk differs from the firm's overall risk.

Cost of Capital for a New Acquisition

We begin by explaining how to calculate the cost of capital of a project with market risk that is different from the risk for the rest of the firm. Suppose Alcoa wants to enter the forest products business. To do so, it is considering acquiring Weyerhaeuser, a company that is focused on timber, paper, and other forest products. Weyerhaeuser faces different market risks than Alcoa does in its mining business. What cost of capital should Alcoa use to value a possible acquisition of Weyerhaeuser?

Because the risks are different, Alcoa's WACC would be inappropriate for valuing Weyerhaeuser. Instead, Alcoa should calculate and use Weyerhaeuser's WACC when assessing the acquisition. In Figure 3, we find the following information for Weyerhaeuser:

	Beta	Cost of Equity	Cost of Cost	% Equity	% Debt	WACC
Weyerhaeuser	1.20	10.5%	7.0%	65%	35%	8.4%

Assuming that Alcoa will find it appropriate to continue to finance Weyerhaeuser with the same mix of debt and equity after it buys Weyerhaeuser, we can use Weyerhaeuser's WACC as the cost of capital for acquiring it. Thus Alcoa would use a cost of capital of 8.4% to value Weyerhaeuser for purchase.

Divisional Costs of Capital

Now assume Alcoa makes a different decision: It decides to create a forest products division internally, rather than buying Weyerhaeuser. What should the cost of capital for the new division be? If Alcoa plans to finance the division with the same proportion of debt as is used by Weyerhaeuser, then Alcoa would use Weyerhaeuser's WACC as the WACC for its new division. Because Weyerhaeuser's WACC is the right cost of capital given the risks of forest products and 35% debt financing, it has to be the right cost of capital for an internally created forest products division that is financed 35% with debt.

In reality, firms with more than one division rarely use a single companywide WACC to evaluate projects. More typically, they perform analyses similar to Alcoa's analysis of Weyerhaeuser. Multidivisional firms benchmark their own divisions off of companies that compete with their division and are focused in that single line of business. By performing the same analysis as we did in Figure 3, the multidivisional firm can estimate the WACCs of its divisions' competitors—adjusting for different financing if necessary—to estimate the cost of capital for each division.

EXAMPLE 6

A Project in a New Line of Business

Problem

You are working for Cisco evaluating the possibility of selling digital video recorders (DVRs). Cisco's WACC is 13.3%. DVRs would be a new line of business for Cisco, however, so the systematic risk of this business would likely differ from the systematic risk of Cisco's current business. As a result, the assets of this new business should have a different cost of capital. You need to find the cost of capital for the DVR business. Assuming that the risk-free rate is 4.5% and the market risk premium is 5%, how would you estimate the cost of capital for this type of investment?

Solution

▶ **Plan**

The first step is to identify a company operating in Cisco's targeted line of business. TiVo, Inc., is a well-known marketer of DVRs. In fact, that is all TiVo does. Thus the cost of capital for TiVo would be a good estimate of the cost of capital for Cisco's proposed DVR business. Many Web sites are available that provide betas for traded stocks, including http://finance.yahoo.com. Suppose you visit that site and find that the beta of TiVo stock is 2.9. With this beta, the risk-free rate, and the market risk premium, you can use the CAPM to estimate the cost of equity for TiVo. Fortunately for us, TiVo has no debt, so its cost of equity is the same as its cost of capital for its assets.

▶ **Execute**

Using the CAPM, we have

TiVo's Cost of Equity = Risk-Free Rate + TiVo's Equity Beta × Market Risk Premium
$$= 4.5\% + 2.9 \times 5\% = 19\%$$

Because TiVo has no debt, its WACC is equivalent to its cost of equity.

▶ **Evaluate**

The correct cost of capital for evaluating a DVR investment opportunity is 19%. If we had used the 13.3% cost of capital that is associated with Cisco's *existing* business, we would have mistakenly used too low of a cost of capital. That could lead us to go ahead with the investment, even though it truly had a negative NPV.

Concept Check

9. When evaluating a project in a new line of business, which assumption about the WACC method are most likely to be violated?

10. How can you estimate the WACC to be used in a new line of business?

6 When Raising External Capital Is Costly

So far, we have assumed that there are no important factors to consider in seeking capital other than taxes. Among other things, this implies that we can raise external capital without any extra costs associated with the capital-raising transaction. As a consequence, we have no reason to treat a project financed with new external funds any differently than a project financed with internal funds (retained earnings).

In reality, issuing new equity or bonds carries a number of costs. These costs include the costs of filing and registering with the Securities and Exchange Commission and the fees charged by investment bankers to place the securities. We will discuss the process for issuing equity and bonds in detail in the next two chapters. Here, we mention it briefly in the context of the cost of capital.

Determining the Cost of Capital

Because of these issuing costs, a project that can be financed from internal funds will be less costly overall than the same project if it were financed with external funds. One approach would be to adjust the costs of equity and debt capital in the WACC to incorporate the issuing costs. A better and far more direct route is to simply treat the issuing costs as what they are—cash outflows that are necessary to the project. We can then incorporate this additional cost as a negative cash flow in the NPV analysis.

EXAMPLE 7

Evaluating an Acquisition with Costly External Financing

Problem

You are analyzing Alcoa's potential acquisition of Weyerhaeuser. Alcoa plans to offer $23 billion as the purchase price for Weyerhaeuser, and it will need to issue additional debt and equity to finance such a large acquisition. You estimate that the issuance costs will be $800 million and will be paid as soon as the transaction closes. You estimate the incremental free cash flows from the acquisition will be $1.4 billion in the first year and will grow at 3% per year thereafter. What is the NPV of the proposed acquisition?

Solution

▶ **Plan**

We know from Section 5 that the correct cost of capital for this acquisition is Weyerhaeuser's WACC. We can value the incremental free cash flows as a growing perpetuity:

$$PV = FCF_1/(r - g)$$

where

$FCF_1 = $1.4 billion
r = Weyerhaeuser's WACC = 8.4%
g = 3%

The NPV of the transaction, including the costly external financing, is the present value of this growing perpetuity net of both the purchase cost and the transaction costs of using external financing.

▶ **Execute**

Noting that $800 million is $0.8 billion,

$$NPV = -\$23 - 0.8 + \frac{1.4}{0.084 - 0.03} = \$2.126 \text{ billion}$$

▶ **Evaluate**

It is not necessary to try to adjust Weyerhaeuser's WACC for the issuance costs of debt and equity. Instead, we can subtract the issuance costs from the NPV of the acquisition to confirm that the acquisition remains a positive-NPV project even if it must be financed externally.

In this chapter, we learned what a firm's cost of capital is, where it comes from, and how it is used in capital budgeting. The role of capital budgeting is to identify positive-NPV projects that allow a firm to cover the costs of its various types of capital. Now we turn to another aspect of capital financing—where the firm gets that capital. In the next three chapters, we explore how a firm raises equity and debt capital and how it decides the proportion of each to have in its capital structure.

11. What types of additional costs does a firm incur when accessing external capital?

12. What is the best way to incorporate these additional costs into capital budgeting?

Here is what you should know after reading this chapter. MyFinanceLab will help you identify what you know, and where to go when you need to practice.

Key Points and Equations	Terms	Online Practice Opportunities

1 A First Look at the Weighted Average Cost of Capital
▶ A firm's debt and equity represent its capital. The relative proportions of debt, equity, and other securities that a firm has outstanding constitute its capital structure.
▶ Investors of each type of capital have a required return. Providing this return is the cost a company bears to obtain capital from investors.
▶ We calculate the firm's overall cost of capital as a weighted average of its equity and debt costs of capital, referred to as the firm's weighted average cost of capital.
▶ The weights in the WACC must be based on the market values of each of the firm's debt and equity, not the book values.
	capital
	capital structure
	leverage
	levered
	market-value
	  balance sheet
	unlevered
	weighted average
	  cost of capital (WACC)
		MyFinanceLab
		Study Plan 12.1

2 The Firm's Costs of Debt and Equity Capital
▶ To estimate the cost of capital for a company as a whole, we usually start by estimating the cost of each of the company's sources of capital.
▶ The cost of debt is the interest a firm would need to pay on *new* debt. It will generally differ from the coupon rate on existing debt, but can be estimated from the yield to maturity on existing debt.
▶ The cost of preferred stock is straightforward to estimate because of its constant and known dividend:
 	
$$\text{Cost of Preferred Stock Capital} = \frac{Div_{pfd}}{P_{pfd}} \quad (4)$$
 	
▶ The Capital Asset Pricing Model (CAPM) is the most common approach for estimating the cost of equity capital. To apply the CAPM, we need an estimate of the firm's equity beta, the market risk premium, and the risk-free rate:
 	
Cost of Equity = Risk-Free Rate + Equity Beta
      × Market Risk Premium
	effective cost
	  of debt
		MyFinanceLab
		Study Plan 12.2

▶ Another approach to estimating the cost of equity is to use the Constant Dividend Growth Model (CDGM). To apply this model, we need the current stock price, the expected future dividend, and an estimate of the dividend's constant growth rate:

$$\text{Cost of Equity} = \frac{Div_1}{P_E} + g \qquad (5)$$

3 A Second Look at the Weighted Average Cost of Capital

▶ The WACC equation is

$$r_{wacc} = r_E E\% + r_{pfd} P\% + r_D (1 - T_C) D\% \qquad (6)$$

net debt

MyFinanceLab
Study Plan 12.3

▶ For a company that does not have preferred stock, the WACC equation condenses to

$$r_{wacc} = r_E E\% + r_D (1 - T_C) D\% \qquad (7)$$

▶ The WACC is driven by the risk of a company's line of business and, because of the tax effect of interest, its leverage. As a result, WACCs vary widely across industries and companies.

4 Using the WACC to Value a Project

▶ Assuming a project has average risk for the firm, that the firm will maintain its current leverage ratio, and that a firm's leverage affects its value only through taxes, the WACC can be used to value the cash flows from a new project.

debt-equity ratio
levered value
WACC method

MyFinanceLab
Study Plan 12.4

Spreadsheet
Table 12.3

5 Project-Based Costs of Capital

▶ If the project's risk differs from the average risk for the firm, the WACC will not be the appropriate discount rate for the project. Instead, you must estimate the WACC from the WACC of other firms operating in the same line of business as the new project.

MyFinanceLab
Study Plan 12.5

6 When Raising External Capital Is Costly

▶ The WACC is calculated without accounting for the direct costs of raising external financing. Rather than adjusting the WACC, the correct way to account for these costs is to subtract their present value from the NPV of the project.

MyFinanceLab
Study Plan 12.6

Review Questions

1. What does the WACC measure?

2. Why are market-based weights important?

3. Why is the coupon rate of existing debt irrelevant for finding the cost of debt capital?

4. Why is it easier to determine the costs of preferred stock and of debt than it is to determine the cost of common equity?

5. Describe the steps involved in the CAPM approach to estimating the cost of equity.

6. Under what assumptions can the WACC be used to value a project?

7. What are some possible problems that might be associated with the assumptions used in applying the WACC method?

8. How should you value a project in a line of business with risk that is different than the average risk of your firm's projects?

9. What is the right way to adjust for the costs of raising external financing?

Problems

All problems in this chapter are available in MyFinanceLab.

A First Look at the Weighted Average Cost of Capital

1. MV Corporation has debt with market value of $100 million, common equity with a book value of $100 million, and preferred stock worth $20 million outstanding. Its common equity trades at $50 per share, and the firm has 6 million shares outstanding. What weights should MV Corporation use in its WACC?

2. Andyco, Inc., has the following balance sheet and an equity market-to-book ratio of 1.5. Assuming the market value of debt equals its book value, what weights should it use for its WACC calculation?

Assets	Liabilities and Equity	
1000	Debt	400
	Equity	600

3. Consider a simple firm that has the following market-value balance sheet:

Assets	Liabilities and Equity	
1000	Debt	400
	Equity	600

Next year, there are two possible values for its assets, each equally likely: $1200 and $960. Its debt will be due with 5% interest. Because all of the cash flows from the assets must go to either the debt or the equity, if you hold a portfolio of the debt and equity in the same proportions as the firm's capital structure, your portfolio should earn exactly the expected return on the firm's assets. Show that a portfolio invested 40% in the firm's debt and 60% in its equity will have the same expected return as the assets of the firm. That is, show that the firm's pre-tax WACC is the same as the expected return on its assets.

The Firm's Costs of Debt and Equity Capital

4. Avicorp has a $10 million debt issue outstanding, with a 6% coupon rate. The debt has semi-annual coupons, the next coupon is due in six months, and the debt matures in five years. It is currently priced at 95% of par value.
    a. What is Avicorp's pre-tax cost of debt?
    b. If Avicorp faces a 40% tax rate, what is its after-tax cost of debt?

5. Laurel, Inc., has debt outstanding with a coupon rate of 6% and a yield to maturity of 7%. Its tax rate is 35%. What is Laurel's effective (after-tax) cost of debt?

6. Dewyco has preferred stock trading at $50 per share. The next preferred dividend of $4 is due in one year. What is Dewyco's cost of capital for preferred stock?

7. Steady Company's stock has a beta of 0.20. If the risk-free rate is 6% and the market risk premium is 7%, what is an estimate of Steady Company's cost of equity?

8. Wild Swings, Inc.'s stock has a beta of 2.5. Given the information in Problem 7, what is an estimate of Wild Swings' cost of equity?

9. HighGrowth Company has a stock price of $20. The firm will pay a dividend next year of $1, and its dividend is expected to grow at a rate of 4% per year thereafter. What is your estimate of HighGrowth's cost of equity capital?

10. Slow 'n Steady, Inc., has a stock price of $30, will pay a dividend next year of $3, and has expected dividend growth of 1% per year. What is your estimate of Slow 'n Steady's cost of equity capital?

11. Mackenzie Company has a price of $36 and will issue a dividend of $2 next year. It has a beta of 1.2, the risk-free rate is 5.5% and it estimates the market risk premium to be 5%.
    a. Estimate the equity cost of capital for Mackenzie.
    b. Under the CGDM, at what rate do you need to expect Mackenzie's dividends to grow to get the same equity cost of capital as in part (a)?

A Second Look at the Weighted Average Cost of Capital

12. CoffeeCarts has a cost of equity of 15%, has an effective cost of debt of 4%, and is financed 70% with equity and 30% with debt. What is this firm's WACC?

13. Pfd Company has debt with a yield to maturity of 7%, a cost of equity of 13%, and a cost of preferred stock of 9%. The market values of its debt, preferred stock, and equity are $10 million, $3 million and $15 million, respectively, and its tax rate is 40%. What is this firm's WACC?

14. Growth Company's current share price is $20 and it is expected to pay a $1 dividend per share next year. After that, the firm's dividends are expected to grow at a rate of 4% per year.
    a. What is an estimate of Growth Company's cost of equity?
    b. Growth Company also has preferred stock outstanding that pays a $2 per share fixed dividend. If this stock is currently priced at $28, what is Growth Company's cost of preferred stock?

c. Growth Company has existing debt issued 3 years ago with a coupon rate of 6%. The firm just issued new debt at par with a coupon rate of 6.5%. What is Growth Company's pre-tax cost of debt?

d. Growth Company has 5 million common shares outstanding and 1 million preferred shares outstanding, and its equity has a total book value of $50 million. Its liabilities have a market value of $20 million. If Growth Company's common and preferred shares are priced as in parts (a) and (b), what is the market value of Growth Company's assets?

e. Growth Company faces a 35% tax rate. Given the information in parts (a)–(d), and your answers to those problems, what is Growth Company's WACC?

Using the WACC to Value a Project

15. RiverRocks, Inc., is considering a project with the following projected free cash flows:

0	1	2	3	4
–50	10	20	20	15

The firm believes that, given the risk of this project, the WACC method is the appropriate approach to valuing the project. RiverRocks' WACC is 12%. Should it take on this project? Why or why not?

Project-Based Costs of Capital

16. RiverRocks (whose WACC is 12%) is considering an acquisition of Raft Adventures (whose WACC is 15%0). What is the appropriate discount rate for RiverRocks to use to evaluate the acquisition? Why?

17. RiverRocks' purchase of Raft Adventures (from Problem 16) will cost $100 million, but will generate cash flows that start at $15 million in one year and then grow at 4% per year forever. What is the NPV of the acquisition?

18. Starbucks primarily sells coffee. It recently introduced a premium coffee-flavored liquor. Suppose the firm faces a tax rate of 35% and collects the following information. If it plans to finance 11% of the new liquor-focused division with debt and the rest with equity, what WACC should it use for its liquor division? Assume a risk-free rate of 55% and a risk premium of 5%.

	Beta	% Equity	% Debt
Starbucks	0.61	96%	4%
Brown-Forman Liquors	0.26	89%	11%

19. Your company has two divisions: One division sells software and the other division sells computers through a direct sales channel, primarily taking orders over the Internet. You have decided that Dell Computer is very similar to your computer division, in terms of both risk and financing. You go online and find the following information: Dell's beta is 1.21, the risk-free rate is 4.5%, its market value of equity is $67 billion, and it has $700 million worth of debt with a yield to maturity of 6%. Your tax rate is 35% and you use a market risk premium of 5% in your WACC estimates.

a. What is an estimate of the WACC for your computer sales division?

b. If your overall company WACC is 12% and the computer sales division represents 40% of the value of your firm, what is an estimate of the WACC for your software division?

When Raising External Capital Is Costly

20. RiverRocks realizes that it will have to raise the financing for the acquisition of Raft Adventures (described in Problem 17) by issuing new debt and equity. The firm estimates that the direct issuing costs will come to $7 million. How should it account for these costs in evaluating the project? Should RiverRocks go ahead with the project?

Data Case

You work in Walt Disney Company's corporate finance and treasury department and have just been assigned to the team estimating Disney's WACC. You must estimate this WACC in preparation for a team meeting later today. You quickly realize that the information you need is readily available online.

1. Go to http://finance.yahoo.com. Under "Market Summary," you will find the yield to maturity for ten-year Treasury bonds listed as "10 Yr Bond(%)." Collect this number as your risk-free rate.

2. In the box next to the "Get Quotes" button, type Walt Disney's ticker symbol (DIS) and press enter. Once you see the basic information for Disney, find and click "Key Statistics" on the left side of the screen. From the key statistics, collect Disney's market capitalization (its market value of equity), enterprise value (market-value equity + net debt), cash, and beta.

3. To get Disney's cost of debt and the market value of its long-term debt, you will need the price and yield to maturity on the firm's existing long-term bonds. Go to http://cxa.marketwatch.com/finra/BondCenter/Default.aspx. Under "Quick Bond Search," click "Corporate" and type Disney's ticker symbol. A list of Disney's outstanding bond issues will appear. Assume that Disney's policy is to use the yield to maturity on non-callable ten-year obligations as its cost of debt. Find the non-callable bond issue that is as close to ten years from maturity as possible. (*Hint:* You will see a column titled "Callable"; make sure the issue you choose has "No" in this column.) Find the yield to maturity for your chosen bond issue (it is in the column titled "Yield"). Hold the mouse over the table of Disney's bonds and right-click. Select "Export to Microsoft Excel." An Excel spreadsheet with all of the data in the table will appear.

4. You now have the price for each bond issue, but you need to know the size of the issue. Returning to the Web page, click "Walt Disney Company" in the first row. This brings up a Web page with all of the information about the bond issue. Scroll down until you find "Amount Outstanding" on the right side. Noting that this amount is quoted in thousands of dollars (e.g., $60,000 means $60 million = $60,000,000), record the issue amount in the appropriate row of your spreadsheet. Repeat this step for all of the bond issues.

5. The price for each bond issue in your spreadsheet is reported as a percentage of the bond's par value. For example, 104.50 means that the bond issue is trading at 104.5% of its par value. You can calculate the market value of each bond issue by multiplying the amount outstanding by (Price ÷ 100). Do so for each issue and then calculate the total of all the bond issues. This is the market value of Disney's debt.

6. Compute the weights for Disney's equity and debt based on the market value of equity and Disney's market value of debt, computed in step 6.

7. Calculate Disney's cost of equity capital using the CAPM, the risk-free rate you collected in step 1, and a market risk premium of 5%.

8. Assuming that Disney has a tax rate of 35%, calculate its effective cost of debt capital.

9. Calculate Disney's WACC.

10. Calculate Disney's net debt by subtracting its cash (collected in step 2) from its debt. Recalculate the weights for the WACC using the market value of equity, net debt, and enterprise value. Recalculate Disney's WACC using the weights based on the net debt. How much does it change?

11. How confident are you of your estimate? Which implicit assumptions did you make during your data collection efforts?

Appendix

Financial Tables

TABLE A–1 Future Value Interest Factors for One Dollar Compounded at i Percent for n Periods:

$$FVIF_{i,n} = (1 + i)^n$$

TABLE A–2 Present Value Interest Factors for One Dollar Discounted at i Percent for n Periods:

$$PVIF_{i,n} = \frac{1}{(1 + i)^n}$$

TABLE A–3 Future Value Interest Factors for a One-Dollar Ordinary Annuity Compounded at i Percent for n Periods:

$$FVIFA_{i,n} = \sum_{t=1}^{n} (1 + i)^{t-1}$$

TABLE A–4 Present Value Interest Factors for a One-Dollar Annuity Discounted at i Percent for n Periods:

$$PVIFA_{i,n} = \sum_{t=1}^{n} \frac{1}{(1 + i)^t}$$

From the Appendix of *Principles of Managerial Finance*, Brief 5th Edition. Lawrence J. Gitman. Copyright © 2009 by Pearson Prentice Hall. All rights reserved.

TABLE A–1 — Future Value Interest Factors for One Dollar Compounded at *i* Percent for *n* Periods: $FVIF_{i,n} = (1+i)^n$

Period	1%	2%	3%	4%	5%	6%	7%	8%	9%	10%	11%	12%	13%	14%	15%	16%	17%	18%	19%	20%
1	1.010	1.020	1.030	1.040	1.050	1.060	1.070	1.080	1.090	1.100	1.110	1.120	1.130	1.140	1.150	1.160	1.170	1.180	1.190	1.200
2	1.020	1.040	1.061	1.082	1.102	1.124	1.145	1.166	1.188	1.210	1.232	1.254	1.277	1.300	1.322	1.346	1.369	1.392	1.416	1.440
3	1.030	1.061	1.093	1.125	1.158	1.191	1.225	1.260	1.295	1.331	1.368	1.405	1.443	1.482	1.521	1.561	1.602	1.643	1.685	1.728
4	1.041	1.082	1.126	1.170	1.216	1.262	1.311	1.360	1.412	1.464	1.518	1.574	1.630	1.689	1.749	1.811	1.874	1.939	2.005	2.074
5	1.051	1.104	1.159	1.217	1.276	1.338	1.403	1.469	1.539	1.611	1.685	1.762	1.842	1.925	2.011	2.100	2.192	2.288	2.386	2.488
6	1.062	1.126	1.194	1.265	1.340	1.419	1.501	1.587	1.677	1.772	1.870	1.974	2.082	2.195	2.313	2.436	2.565	2.700	2.840	2.986
7	1.072	1.149	1.230	1.316	1.407	1.504	1.606	1.714	1.828	1.949	2.076	2.211	2.353	2.502	2.660	2.826	3.001	3.185	3.379	3.583
8	1.083	1.172	1.267	1.369	1.477	1.594	1.718	1.851	1.993	2.144	2.305	2.476	2.658	2.853	3.059	3.278	3.511	3.759	4.021	4.300
9	1.094	1.195	1.305	1.423	1.551	1.689	1.838	1.999	2.172	2.358	2.558	2.773	3.004	3.252	3.518	3.803	4.108	4.435	4.785	5.160
10	1.105	1.219	1.344	1.480	1.629	1.791	1.967	2.159	2.367	2.594	2.839	3.106	3.395	3.707	4.046	4.411	4.807	5.234	5.695	6.192
11	1.116	1.243	1.384	1.539	1.710	1.898	2.105	2.332	2.580	2.853	3.152	3.479	3.836	4.226	4.652	5.117	5.624	6.176	6.777	7.430
12	1.127	1.268	1.426	1.601	1.796	2.012	2.252	2.518	2.813	3.138	3.498	3.896	4.334	4.818	5.350	5.936	6.580	7.288	8.064	8.916
13	1.138	1.294	1.469	1.665	1.886	2.133	2.410	2.720	3.066	3.452	3.883	4.363	4.898	5.492	6.153	6.886	7.699	8.599	9.596	10.699
14	1.149	1.319	1.513	1.732	1.980	2.261	2.579	2.937	3.342	3.797	4.310	4.887	5.535	6.261	7.076	7.987	9.007	10.147	11.420	12.839
15	1.161	1.346	1.558	1.801	2.079	2.397	2.759	3.172	3.642	4.177	4.785	5.474	6.254	7.138	8.137	9.265	10.539	11.974	13.589	15.407
16	1.173	1.373	1.605	1.873	2.183	2.540	2.952	3.426	3.970	4.595	5.311	6.130	7.067	8.137	9.358	10.748	12.330	14.129	16.171	18.488
17	1.184	1.400	1.653	1.948	2.292	2.693	3.159	3.700	4.328	5.054	5.895	6.866	7.986	9.276	10.761	12.468	14.426	16.672	19.244	22.186
18	1.196	1.428	1.702	2.026	2.407	2.854	3.380	3.996	4.717	5.560	6.543	7.690	9.024	10.575	12.375	14.462	16.879	19.673	22.900	26.623
19	1.208	1.457	1.753	2.107	2.527	3.026	3.616	4.316	5.142	6.116	7.263	8.613	10.197	12.055	14.232	16.776	19.748	23.214	27.251	31.948
20	1.220	1.486	1.806	2.191	2.653	3.207	3.870	4.661	5.604	6.727	8.062	9.646	11.523	13.743	16.366	19.461	23.105	27.393	32.429	38.337
21	1.232	1.516	1.860	2.279	2.786	3.399	4.140	5.034	6.109	7.400	8.949	10.804	13.021	15.667	18.821	22.574	27.033	32.323	38.591	46.005
22	1.245	1.546	1.916	2.370	2.925	3.603	4.430	5.436	6.658	8.140	9.933	12.100	14.713	17.861	21.644	26.186	31.629	38.141	45.923	55.205
23	1.257	1.577	1.974	2.465	3.071	3.820	4.740	5.871	7.258	8.954	11.026	13.552	16.626	20.361	24.891	30.376	37.005	45.007	54.648	66.247
24	1.270	1.608	2.033	2.563	3.225	4.049	5.072	6.341	7.911	9.850	12.239	15.178	18.788	23.212	28.625	35.236	43.296	53.108	65.031	79.496
25	1.282	1.641	2.094	2.666	3.386	4.292	5.427	6.848	8.623	10.834	13.585	17.000	21.230	26.461	32.918	40.874	50.656	62.667	77.387	95.395
30	1.348	1.811	2.427	3.243	4.322	5.743	7.612	10.062	13.267	17.449	22.892	29.960	39.115	50.949	66.210	85.849	111.061	143.367	184.672	237.373
35	1.417	2.000	2.814	3.946	5.516	7.686	10.676	14.785	20.413	28.102	38.574	52.799	72.066	98.097	133.172	180.311	243.495	327.988	440.691	590.657
40	1.489	2.208	3.262	4.801	7.040	10.285	14.974	21.724	31.408	45.258	64.999	93.049	132.776	188.876	267.856	378.715	533.846	750.353	1051.642	1469.740
45	1.565	2.438	3.781	5.841	8.985	13.764	21.002	31.920	48.325	72.888	109.527	163.985	244.629	363.662	538.752	795.429	1170.425	1716.619	2509.583	3657.176
50	1.645	2.691	4.384	7.106	11.467	18.419	29.456	46.900	74.354	117.386	184.559	288.996	450.711	700.197	1083.619	1670.669	2566.080	3927.189	5988.730	9100.191

Using the Calculator to Compute the Future Value of a Single Amount

Before you begin, make sure to clear the memory, ensure that you are in the *end mode* and that your calculator is set for *one payment per year*, and set the number of decimal places that you want (usually two for dollar-related accuracy).

Sample Problem

You place $800 in a savings account at 6% compounded annually. What is your account balance at the end of 5 years?

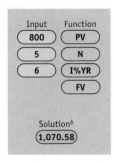

Hewlett-Packard HP 12C, 17 BII, and 19 BII[a]

Input	Function
800	PV
5	N
6	I%YR
	FV

Solution[b]
1,070.58

---

[a]For the 12C, you would use the (n) key instead of the (N) key and use the (i) key instead of the (I%YR) key.

[b]The minus sign that precedes the solution should be ignored.

TABLE A–1 (Continued)

Period	21%	22%	23%	24%	25%	26%	27%	28%	29%	30%	31%	32%	33%	34%	35%	40%	45%	50%
1	1.210	1.220	1.230	1.240	1.250	1.260	1.270	1.280	1.290	1.300	1.310	1.320	1.330	1.340	1.350	1.400	1.450	1.500
2	1.464	1.488	1.513	1.538	1.562	1.588	1.613	1.638	1.664	1.690	1.716	1.742	1.769	1.796	1.822	1.960	2.102	2.250
3	1.772	1.816	1.861	1.907	1.953	2.000	2.048	2.097	2.147	2.197	2.248	2.300	2.353	2.406	2.460	2.744	3.049	3.375
4	2.144	2.215	2.289	2.364	2.441	2.520	2.601	2.684	2.769	2.856	2.945	3.036	3.129	3.224	3.321	3.842	4.421	5.063
5	2.594	2.703	2.815	2.932	3.052	3.176	3.304	3.436	3.572	3.713	3.858	4.007	4.162	4.320	4.484	5.378	6.410	7.594
6	3.138	3.297	3.463	3.635	3.815	4.001	4.196	4.398	4.608	4.827	5.054	5.290	5.535	5.789	6.053	7.530	9.294	11.391
7	3.797	4.023	4.259	4.508	4.768	5.042	5.329	5.629	5.945	6.275	6.621	6.983	7.361	7.758	8.172	10.541	13.476	17.086
8	4.595	4.908	5.239	5.589	5.960	6.353	6.767	7.206	7.669	8.157	8.673	9.217	9.791	10.395	11.032	14.758	19.541	25.629
9	5.560	5.987	6.444	6.931	7.451	8.004	8.595	9.223	9.893	10.604	11.362	12.166	13.022	13.930	14.894	20.661	28.334	38.443
10	6.727	7.305	7.926	8.594	9.313	10.086	10.915	11.806	12.761	13.786	14.884	16.060	17.319	18.666	20.106	28.925	41.085	57.665
11	8.140	8.912	9.749	10.657	11.642	12.708	13.862	15.112	16.462	17.921	19.498	21.199	23.034	25.012	27.144	40.495	59.573	86.498
12	9.850	10.872	11.991	13.215	14.552	16.012	17.605	19.343	21.236	23.298	25.542	27.982	30.635	33.516	36.644	56.694	86.380	129.746
13	11.918	13.264	14.749	16.386	18.190	20.175	22.359	24.759	27.395	30.287	33.460	36.937	40.745	44.912	49.469	79.371	125.251	194.620
14	14.421	16.182	18.141	20.319	22.737	25.420	28.395	31.691	35.339	39.373	43.832	48.756	54.190	60.181	66.784	111.119	181.614	291.929
15	17.449	19.742	22.314	25.195	28.422	32.030	36.062	40.565	45.587	51.185	57.420	64.358	72.073	80.643	90.158	155.567	263.341	437.894
16	21.113	24.085	27.446	31.242	35.527	40.357	45.799	51.923	58.808	66.541	75.220	84.953	95.857	108.061	121.713	217.793	381.844	656.841
17	25.547	29.384	33.758	38.740	44.409	50.850	58.165	66.461	75.862	86.503	98.539	112.138	127.490	144.802	164.312	304.911	553.674	985.261
18	30.912	35.848	41.523	48.038	55.511	64.071	73.869	85.070	97.862	112.454	129.086	148.022	169.561	194.035	221.822	426.875	802.826	1477.892
19	37.404	43.735	51.073	59.567	69.389	80.730	93.813	108.890	126.242	146.190	169.102	195.389	225.517	260.006	299.459	597.625	1164.098	2216.838
20	45.258	53.357	62.820	73.863	86.736	101.720	119.143	139.379	162.852	190.047	221.523	257.913	299.937	348.408	404.270	836.674	1687.942	3325.257
21	54.762	65.095	77.268	91.591	108.420	128.167	151.312	178.405	210.079	247.061	290.196	340.446	398.916	466.867	545.764	1171.343	2447.515	4987.883
22	66.262	79.416	95.040	113.572	135.525	161.490	192.165	228.358	271.002	321.178	380.156	449.388	530.558	625.601	736.781	1639.878	3548.896	7481.824
23	80.178	96.887	116.899	140.829	169.407	203.477	244.050	292.298	349.592	417.531	498.004	593.192	705.642	838.305	994.653	2295.829	5145.898	11222.738
24	97.015	118.203	143.786	174.628	211.758	256.381	309.943	374.141	450.974	542.791	652.385	783.013	938.504	1123.328	1342.781	3214.158	7461.547	16834.109
25	117.388	144.207	176.857	216.539	264.698	323.040	393.628	478.901	581.756	705.627	854.623	1033.577	1248.210	1505.258	1812.754	4499.816	10819.242	25251.164
30	304.471	389.748	497.904	634.810	807.793	1025.904	1300.477	1645.488	2078.208	2619.936	3297.081	4142.008	5194.516	6503.285	8128.426	24201.043	69348.375	191751.000
35	789.716	1053.370	1401.749	1861.020	2465.189	3258.053	4296.547	5653.840	7423.988	9727.598	12719.918	16598.906	21617.363	28096.695	36448.051	130158.687	*	*
40	2048.309	2846.941	3946.340	5455.797	7523.156	10346.879	14195.051	19426.418	26520.723	36117.754	49072.621	66519.313	89962.188	121388.437	163433.875	700022.688	*	*
45	5312.758	7694.418	11110.121	15994.316	22958.844	32859.457	46897.973	66748.500	94739.937	134102.187	*	*	*	*	*	*	*	*
50	13779.844	20795.680	31278.301	46889.207	70064.812	104354.562	154942.687	229345.875	338440.000	497910.125	*	*	*	*	*	*	*	*

*Not shown because of space limitations.

**Texas Instruments,
BA-35, BAII,
and BAII Plus[c]**

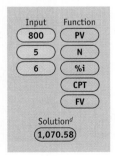

Input	Function
800	PV
5	N
6	%i
	CPT
	FV

Solution[d]
1,070.58

[c]For the Texas Instruments BAII, you would use the ⟨2nd⟩ key instead of the ⟨CPT⟩ key; for the Texas Instruments BAII Plus, you would use the ⟨I/Y⟩ key instead of the ⟨%i⟩ key.

[d]If a minus sign precedes the solution, it should be ignored.

TABLE A–2 | **Present Value Interest Factors for One Dollar Discounted at *i* Percent**

for *n* Periods: $PVIF_{i,n} = \dfrac{1}{(1 + i)^n}$

Period	1%	2%	3%	4%	5%	6%	7%	8%	9%	10%	11%	12%	13%	14%	15%	16%	17%	18%	19%	20%
1	.990	.980	.971	.962	.952	.943	.935	.926	.917	.909	.901	.893	.885	.877	.870	.862	.855	.847	.840	.833
2	.980	.961	.943	.925	.907	.890	.873	.857	.842	.826	.812	.797	.783	.769	.756	.743	.731	.718	.706	.694
3	.971	.942	.915	.889	.864	.840	.816	.794	.772	.751	.731	.712	.693	.675	.658	.641	.624	.609	.593	.579
4	.961	.924	.888	.855	.823	.792	.763	.735	.708	.683	.659	.636	.613	.592	.572	.552	.534	.516	.499	.482
5	.951	.906	.863	.822	.784	.747	.713	.681	.650	.621	.593	.567	.543	.519	.497	.476	.456	.437	.419	.402
6	.942	.888	.837	.790	.746	.705	.666	.630	.596	.564	.535	.507	.480	.456	.432	.410	.390	.370	.352	.335
7	.933	.871	.813	.760	.711	.665	.623	.583	.547	.513	.482	.452	.425	.400	.376	.354	.333	.314	.296	.279
8	.923	.853	.789	.731	.677	.627	.582	.540	.502	.467	.434	.404	.376	.351	.327	.305	.285	.266	.249	.233
9	.914	.837	.766	.703	.645	.592	.544	.500	.460	.424	.391	.361	.333	.308	.284	.263	.243	.225	.209	.194
10	.905	.820	.744	.676	.614	.558	.508	.463	.422	.386	.352	.322	.295	.270	.247	.227	.208	.191	.176	.162
11	.896	.804	.722	.650	.585	.527	.475	.429	.388	.350	.317	.287	.261	.237	.215	.195	.178	.162	.148	.135
12	.887	.789	.701	.625	.557	.497	.444	.397	.356	.319	.286	.257	.231	.208	.187	.168	.152	.137	.124	.112
13	.879	.773	.681	.601	.530	.469	.415	.368	.326	.290	.258	.229	.204	.182	.163	.145	.130	.116	.104	.093
14	.870	.758	.661	.577	.505	.442	.388	.340	.299	.263	.232	.205	.181	.160	.141	.125	.111	.099	.088	.078
15	.861	.743	.642	.555	.481	.417	.362	.315	.275	.239	.209	.183	.160	.140	.123	.108	.095	.084	.074	.065
16	.853	.728	.623	.534	.458	.394	.339	.292	.252	.218	.188	.163	.141	.123	.107	.093	.081	.071	.062	.054
17	.844	.714	.605	.513	.436	.371	.317	.270	.231	.198	.170	.146	.125	.108	.093	.080	.069	.060	.052	.045
18	.836	.700	.587	.494	.416	.350	.296	.250	.212	.180	.153	.130	.111	.095	.081	.069	.059	.051	.044	.038
19	.828	.686	.570	.475	.396	.331	.277	.232	.194	.164	.138	.116	.098	.083	.070	.060	.051	.043	.037	.031
20	.820	.673	.554	.456	.377	.312	.258	.215	.178	.149	.124	.104	.087	.073	.061	.051	.043	.037	.031	.026
21	.811	.660	.538	.439	.359	.294	.242	.199	.164	.135	.112	.093	.077	.064	.053	.044	.037	.031	.026	.022
22	.803	.647	.522	.422	.342	.278	.226	.184	.150	.123	.101	.083	.068	.056	.046	.038	.032	.026	.022	.018
23	.795	.634	.507	.406	.326	.262	.211	.170	.138	.112	.091	.074	.060	.049	.040	.033	.027	.022	.018	.015
24	.788	.622	.492	.390	.310	.247	.197	.158	.126	.102	.082	.066	.053	.043	.035	.028	.023	.019	.015	.013
25	.780	.610	.478	.375	.295	.233	.184	.146	.116	.092	.074	.059	.047	.038	.030	.024	.020	.016	.013	.010
30	.742	.552	.412	.308	.231	.174	.131	.099	.075	.057	.044	.033	.026	.020	.015	.012	.009	.007	.005	.004
35	.706	.500	.355	.253	.181	.130	.094	.068	.049	.036	.026	.019	.014	.010	.008	.006	.004	.003	.002	.002
40	.672	.453	.307	.208	.142	.097	.067	.046	.032	.022	.015	.011	.008	.005	.004	.003	.002	.001	.001	.001
45	.639	.410	.264	.171	.111	.073	.048	.031	.021	.014	.009	.006	.004	.003	.002	.001	.001	.001	*	*
50	.608	.372	.228	.141	.087	.054	.034	.021	.013	.009	.005	.003	.002	.001	.001	.001	*	*	*	*

*PVIF is zero to three decimal places.

Using the Calculator to Compute the Present Value of a Single Amount

Before you begin, make sure to clear the memory, ensure that you are in the *end mode* and that your calculator is set for *one payment per year,* and set the number of decimal places that you want (usually two for dollar-related accuracy).

Sample Problem

You want to know the present value of $1,700 to be received at the end of 8 years, assuming an 8% discount rate.

Hewlett-Packard HP 12C, 17 BII, and 19 BII[a]

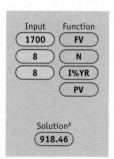

---

[a]For the 12C, you would use the n key instead of the N key and use the i key instead of the I%YR key.

[b]The minus sign that precedes the solution should be ignored.

TABLE A-2 (Continued)

Period	21%	22%	23%	24%	25%	26%	27%	28%	29%	30%	31%	32%	33%	34%	35%	40%	45%	50%
1	.826	.820	.813	.806	.800	.794	.787	.781	.775	.769	.763	.758	.752	.746	.741	.714	.690	.667
2	.683	.672	.661	.650	.640	.630	.620	.610	.601	.592	.583	.574	.565	.557	.549	.510	.476	.444
3	.564	.551	.537	.524	.512	.500	.488	.477	.466	.455	.445	.435	.425	.416	.406	.364	.328	.296
4	.467	.451	.437	.423	.410	.397	.384	.373	.361	.350	.340	.329	.320	.310	.301	.260	.226	.198
5	.386	.370	.355	.341	.328	.315	.303	.291	.280	.269	.259	.250	.240	.231	.223	.186	.156	.132
6	.319	.303	.289	.275	.262	.250	.238	.227	.217	.207	.198	.189	.181	.173	.165	.133	.108	.088
7	.263	.249	.235	.222	.210	.198	.188	.178	.168	.159	.151	.143	.136	.129	.122	.095	.074	.059
8	.218	.204	.191	.179	.168	.157	.148	.139	.130	.123	.115	.108	.102	.096	.091	.068	.051	.039
9	.180	.167	.155	.144	.134	.125	.116	.108	.101	.094	.088	.082	.077	.072	.067	.048	.035	.026
10	.149	.137	.126	.116	.107	.099	.092	.085	.078	.073	.067	.062	.058	.054	.050	.035	.024	.017
11	.123	.112	.103	.094	.086	.079	.072	.066	.061	.056	.051	.047	.043	.040	.037	.025	.017	.012
12	.102	.092	.083	.076	.069	.062	.057	.052	.047	.043	.039	.036	.033	.030	.027	.018	.012	.008
13	.084	.075	.068	.061	.055	.050	.045	.040	.037	.033	.030	.027	.025	.022	.020	.013	.008	.005
14	.069	.062	.055	.049	.044	.039	.035	.032	.028	.025	.023	.021	.018	.017	.015	.009	.006	.003
15	.057	.051	.045	.040	.035	.031	.028	.025	.022	.020	.017	.016	.014	.012	.011	.006	.004	.002
16	.047	.042	.036	.032	.028	.025	.022	.019	.017	.015	.013	.012	.010	.009	.008	.005	.003	.002
17	.039	.034	.030	.026	.023	.020	.017	.015	.013	.012	.010	.009	.008	.007	.006	.003	.002	.001
18	.032	.028	.024	.021	.018	.016	.014	.012	.010	.009	.008	.007	.006	.005	.005	.002	.001	.001
19	.027	.023	.020	.017	.014	.012	.011	.009	.008	.007	.006	.005	.004	.004	.003	.002	.001	*
20	.022	.019	.016	.014	.012	.010	.008	.007	.006	.005	.005	.004	.003	.003	.002	.001	.001	*
21	.018	.015	.013	.011	.009	.008	.007	.006	.005	.004	.003	.003	.003	.002	.002	.001	*	*
22	.015	.013	.011	.009	.007	.006	.005	.004	.004	.003	.003	.002	.002	.002	.001	.001	*	*
23	.012	.010	.009	.007	.006	.005	.004	.003	.003	.002	.002	.002	.001	.001	.001	*	*	*
24	.010	.008	.007	.006	.005	.004	.003	.003	.002	.002	.002	.001	.001	.001	.001	*	*	*
25	.009	.007	.006	.005	.004	.003	.003	.002	.002	.001	.001	.001	.001	.001	.001	*	*	*
30	.003	.003	.002	.002	.001	.001	.001	.001	*	*	*	*	*	*	*	*	*	*
35	.001	.001	.001	.001	*	*	*	*	*	*	*	*	*	*	*	*	*	*
40	*	*	*	*	*	*	*	*	*	*	*	*	*	*	*	*	*	*
45	*	*	*	*	*	*	*	*	*	*	*	*	*	*	*	*	*	*
50	*	*	*	*	*	*	*	*	*	*	*	*	*	*	*	*	*	*

*$PVIF$ is zero to three decimal places.

**Texas Instruments,
BA-35, BAII,
and BAII Plus[c]**

Input	Function
1700	FV
8	N
8	%i
	CPT
	FV

Solution[d]
918.46

[c]For the Texas Instruments BAII, you would use the (2nd) key instead of the (CPT) key; for the Texas Instruments BAII Plus, you would use the (I/Y) key instead of the (%i) key.

[d]If a minus sign precedes the solution, it should be ignored.

TABLE A–3 Future Value Interest Factors for a One-Dollar Ordinary Annuity

Compounded at i Percent for n Periods: $FVIFA_{i,n} = \sum_{t=1}^{n} (1 + i)^{t-1}$

Period	1%	2%	3%	4%	5%	6%	7%	8%	9%	10%	11%	12%	13%	14%	15%	16%	17%	18%	19%	20%
1	1.000	1.000	1.000	1.000	1.000	1.000	1.000	1.000	1.000	1.000	1.000	1.000	1.000	1.000	1.000	1.000	1.000	1.000	1.000	1.000
2	2.010	2.020	2.030	2.040	2.050	2.060	2.070	2.080	2.090	2.100	2.110	2.120	2.130	2.140	2.150	2.160	2.170	2.180	2.190	2.200
3	3.030	3.060	3.091	3.122	3.152	3.184	3.215	3.246	3.278	3.310	3.342	3.374	3.407	3.440	3.472	3.506	3.539	3.572	3.606	3.640
4	4.060	4.122	4.184	4.246	4.310	4.375	4.440	4.506	4.573	4.641	4.710	4.779	4.850	4.921	4.993	5.066	5.141	5.215	5.291	5.368
5	5.101	5.204	5.309	5.416	5.526	5.637	5.751	5.867	5.985	6.105	6.228	6.353	6.480	6.610	6.742	6.877	7.014	7.154	7.297	7.442
6	6.152	6.308	6.468	6.633	6.802	6.975	7.153	7.336	7.523	7.716	7.913	8.115	8.323	8.535	8.754	8.977	9.207	9.442	9.683	9.930
7	7.214	7.434	7.662	7.898	8.142	8.394	8.654	8.923	9.200	9.487	9.783	10.089	10.405	10.730	11.067	11.414	11.772	12.141	12.523	12.916
8	8.286	8.583	8.892	9.214	9.549	9.897	10.260	10.637	11.028	11.436	11.859	12.300	12.757	13.233	13.727	14.240	14.773	15.327	15.902	16.499
9	9.368	9.755	10.159	10.583	11.027	11.491	11.978	12.488	13.021	13.579	14.164	14.776	15.416	16.085	16.786	17.518	18.285	19.086	19.923	20.799
10	10.462	10.950	11.464	12.006	12.578	13.181	13.816	14.487	15.193	15.937	16.722	17.549	18.420	19.337	20.304	21.321	22.393	23.521	24.709	25.959
11	11.567	12.169	12.808	13.486	14.207	14.972	15.784	16.645	17.560	18.531	19.561	20.655	21.814	23.044	24.349	25.733	27.200	28.755	30.403	32.150
12	12.682	13.412	14.192	15.026	15.917	16.870	17.888	18.977	20.141	21.384	22.713	24.133	25.650	27.271	29.001	30.850	32.824	34.931	37.180	39.580
13	13.809	14.680	15.618	16.627	17.713	18.882	20.141	21.495	22.953	24.523	26.211	28.029	29.984	32.088	34.352	36.786	39.404	42.218	45.244	48.496
14	14.947	15.974	17.086	18.292	19.598	21.015	22.550	24.215	26.019	27.975	30.095	32.392	34.882	37.581	40.504	43.672	47.102	50.818	54.841	59.196
15	16.097	17.293	18.599	20.023	21.578	23.276	25.129	27.152	29.361	31.772	34.405	37.280	40.417	43.842	47.580	51.659	56.109	60.965	66.260	72.035
16	17.258	18.639	20.157	21.824	23.657	25.672	27.888	30.324	33.003	35.949	39.190	42.753	46.671	50.980	55.717	60.925	66.648	72.938	79.850	87.442
17	18.430	20.012	21.761	23.697	25.840	28.213	30.840	33.750	36.973	40.544	44.500	48.883	53.738	59.117	65.075	71.673	78.978	87.067	96.021	105.930
18	19.614	21.412	23.414	25.645	28.132	30.905	33.999	37.450	41.301	45.599	50.396	55.749	61.724	68.393	75.836	84.140	93.404	103.739	115.265	128.116
19	20.811	22.840	25.117	27.671	30.539	33.760	37.379	41.446	46.018	51.158	56.939	63.439	70.748	78.968	88.211	98.603	110.283	123.412	138.165	154.739
20	22.019	24.297	26.870	29.778	33.066	36.785	40.995	45.762	51.159	57.274	64.202	72.052	80.946	91.024	102.443	115.379	130.031	146.626	165.417	186.687
21	23.239	25.783	28.676	31.969	35.719	39.992	44.865	50.422	56.764	64.002	72.264	81.698	92.468	104.767	118.809	134.840	153.136	174.019	197.846	225.024
22	24.471	27.299	30.536	34.248	38.505	43.392	49.005	55.456	62.872	71.402	81.213	92.502	105.489	120.434	137.630	157.414	180.169	206.342	236.436	271.028
23	25.716	28.845	32.452	36.618	41.430	46.995	53.435	60.893	69.531	79.542	91.147	104.602	120.203	138.295	159.274	183.600	211.798	244.483	282.359	326.234
24	26.973	30.421	34.426	39.082	44.501	50.815	58.176	66.764	76.789	88.496	102.173	118.154	136.829	158.656	184.166	213.976	248.803	289.490	337.007	392.480
25	28.243	32.030	36.459	41.645	47.726	54.864	63.248	73.105	84.699	98.346	114.412	133.333	155.616	181.867	212.790	249.212	292.099	342.598	402.038	471.976
30	34.784	40.567	47.575	56.084	66.438	79.057	94.459	113.282	136.305	164.491	199.018	241.330	293.192	356.778	434.738	530.306	647.423	790.932	966.698	1181.865
35	41.659	49.994	60.461	73.651	90.318	111.432	138.234	172.314	215.705	271.018	341.583	431.658	546.663	693.552	881.152	1120.699	1426.448	1816.607	2314.173	2948.294
40	48.885	60.401	75.400	95.024	120.797	154.758	199.630	259.052	337.872	442.580	581.812	767.080	1013.667	1341.979	1779.048	2360.724	3134.412	4163.094	5529.711	7343.715
45	56.479	71.891	92.718	121.027	159.695	212.737	285.741	386.497	525.840	718.881	986.613	1358.208	1874.086	2590.464	3585.031	4965.191	6879.008	9531.258	13203.105	18280.914
50	64.461	84.577	112.794	152.664	209.341	290.325	406.516	573.756	815.051	1163.865	1668.723	2399.975	3459.344	4994.301	7217.488	10435.449	15088.805	21812.273	31514.492	45496.094

Using the Calculator to Compute the Future Value of an Ordinary Annuity

Hewlett-Packard HP 12C, 17 BII, and 19 BII[a]

Before you begin, make sure to clear the memory, ensure that you are in the *end mode* and that your calculator is set for *one payment per year,* and set the number of decimal places that you want (usually two for dollar-related accuracy).

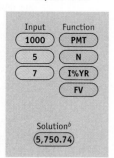

Sample Problem

You want to know what the future value will be at the end of 5 years if you place five end-of-year deposits of $1,000 in an account paying 7% annually. What is your account balance at the end of 5 years?

---

[a]For the 12C, you would use the ⬭n⬭ key instead of the ⬭N⬭ key and use the ⬭i⬭ key instead of the ⬭I%YR⬭ key.
[b]The minus sign that precedes the solution should be ignored.

TABLE A–3 (Continued)

Period	21%	22%	23%	24%	25%	26%	27%	28%	29%	30%	31%	32%	33%	34%	35%	40%	45%	50%
1	1.000	1.000	1.000	1.000	1.000	1.000	1.000	1.000	1.000	1.000	1.000	1.000	1.000	1.000	1.000	1.000	1.000	1.000
2	2.210	2.220	2.230	2.240	2.250	2.260	2.270	2.280	2.290	2.300	2.310	2.320	2.330	2.340	2.350	2.400	2.450	2.500
3	3.674	3.708	3.743	3.778	3.813	3.848	3.883	3.918	3.954	3.990	4.026	4.062	4.099	4.136	4.172	4.360	4.552	4.750
4	5.446	5.524	5.604	5.684	5.766	5.848	5.931	6.016	6.101	6.187	6.274	6.362	6.452	6.542	6.633	7.104	7.601	8.125
5	7.589	7.740	7.893	8.048	8.207	8.368	8.533	8.700	8.870	9.043	9.219	9.398	9.581	9.766	9.954	10.946	12.022	13.188
6	10.183	10.442	10.708	10.980	11.259	11.544	11.837	12.136	12.442	12.756	13.077	13.406	13.742	14.086	14.438	16.324	18.431	20.781
7	13.321	13.740	14.171	14.615	15.073	15.546	16.032	16.534	17.051	17.583	18.131	18.696	19.277	19.876	20.492	23.853	27.725	32.172
8	17.119	17.762	18.430	19.123	19.842	20.588	21.361	22.163	22.995	23.858	24.752	25.678	26.638	27.633	28.664	34.395	41.202	49.258
9	21.714	22.670	23.669	24.712	25.802	26.940	28.129	29.369	30.664	32.015	33.425	34.895	36.429	38.028	39.696	49.152	60.743	74.887
10	27.274	28.657	30.113	31.643	33.253	34.945	36.723	38.592	40.556	42.619	44.786	47.062	49.451	51.958	54.590	69.813	89.077	113.330
11	34.001	35.962	38.039	40.238	42.566	45.030	47.639	50.398	53.318	56.405	59.670	63.121	66.769	70.624	74.696	98.739	130.161	170.995
12	42.141	44.873	47.787	50.895	54.208	57.738	61.501	65.510	69.780	74.326	79.167	84.320	89.803	95.636	101.840	139.234	189.734	257.493
13	51.991	55.745	59.778	64.109	68.760	73.750	79.106	84.853	91.016	97.624	104.709	112.302	120.438	129.152	138.484	195.928	276.114	387.239
14	63.909	69.009	74.528	80.496	86.949	93.925	101.465	109.611	118.411	127.912	138.169	149.239	161.183	174.063	187.953	275.299	401.365	581.858
15	78.330	85.191	92.669	100.815	109.687	119.346	129.860	141.302	153.750	167.285	182.001	197.996	215.373	234.245	254.737	386.418	582.980	873.788
16	95.779	104.933	114.983	126.010	138.109	151.375	165.922	181.867	199.337	218.470	239.421	262.354	287.446	314.888	344.895	541.985	846.321	1311.681
17	116.892	129.019	142.428	157.252	173.636	191.733	211.721	233.790	258.145	285.011	314.642	347.307	383.303	422.949	466.608	759.778	1228.165	1968.522
18	142.439	158.403	176.187	195.993	218.045	242.583	269.885	300.250	334.006	371.514	413.180	459.445	510.792	567.751	630.920	1064.689	1781.838	2953.783
19	173.351	194.251	217.710	244.031	273.556	306.654	343.754	385.321	431.868	483.968	542.266	607.467	680.354	761.786	852.741	1491.563	2584.665	4431.672
20	210.755	237.986	268.783	303.598	342.945	387.384	437.568	494.210	558.110	630.157	711.368	802.856	905.870	1021.792	1152.200	2089.188	3748.763	6648.508
21	256.013	291.343	331.603	377.461	429.681	489.104	556.710	633.589	720.962	820.204	932.891	1060.769	1205.807	1370.201	1556.470	2925.862	5436.703	9973.762
22	310.775	356.438	408.871	469.052	538.101	617.270	708.022	811.993	931.040	1067.265	1223.087	1401.215	1604.724	1837.068	2102.234	4097.203	7884.215	14961.645
23	377.038	435.854	503.911	582.624	673.626	778.760	900.187	1040.351	1202.042	1388.443	1603.243	1850.603	2135.282	2462.669	2839.014	5737.078	11433.109	22443.469
24	457.215	532.741	620.810	723.453	843.032	982.237	1144.237	1332.649	1551.634	1805.975	2101.247	2443.795	2840.924	3300.974	3833.667	8032.906	16579.008	33666.207
25	554.230	650.944	764.596	898.082	1054.791	1238.617	1454.180	1706.790	2002.608	2348.765	2753.631	3226.808	3779.428	4424.301	5176.445	11247.062	24040.555	50500.316
30	1445.111	1767.044	2160.459	2640.881	3227.172	3941.953	4812.891	5873.172	7162.785	8729.805	10632.543	12940.672	15737.945	19124.434	23221.258	60500.207	154105.313	383500.000
35	3755.814	4783.520	6090.227	7750.094	9856.746	12527.160	15909.480	20188.742	25596.512	32422.090	41028.887	51868.563	65504.199	82634.625	104134.500	325394.688	*	*
40	9749.141	12936.141	17153.691	22728.367	30088.621	39791.957	52570.707	69376.562	91447.375	120389.375	*	*	*	*	*	*	*	*
45	25294.223	34970.230	48300.660	66638.937	91831.312	126378.937	173692.875	238384.312	326686.375	447005.062	*	*	*	*	*	*	*	*

*Not shown because of space limitations.

**Texas Instruments,
BA-35, BAII,
and BAII Plus[c]**

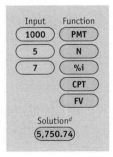

Solution[d]
5,750.74

[c]For the Texas Instruments BAII, you would use the 2nd key instead of the CPT key; for the Texas Instruments BAII Plus, you would use the I/Y key instead of the %i key.

[d]If a minus sign precedes the solution, it should be ignored.

TABLE A–4 Present Value Interest Factors for a One-Dollar Annuity Discounted at *i* Percent for *n* Periods: $PVIFA_{i,n} = \sum_{t=1}^{n} \dfrac{1}{(1+i)^t}$

Period	1%	2%	3%	4%	5%	6%	7%	8%	9%	10%	11%	12%	13%	14%	15%	16%	17%	18%	19%	20%
1	.990	.980	.971	.962	.952	.943	.935	.926	.917	.909	.901	.893	.885	.877	.870	.862	.855	.847	.840	.833
2	1.970	1.942	1.913	1.886	1.859	1.833	1.808	1.783	1.759	1.736	1.713	1.690	1.668	1.647	1.626	1.605	1.585	1.566	1.547	1.528
3	2.941	2.884	2.829	2.775	2.723	2.673	2.624	2.577	2.531	2.487	2.444	2.402	2.361	2.322	2.283	2.246	2.210	2.174	2.140	2.106
4	3.902	3.808	3.717	3.630	3.546	3.465	3.387	3.312	3.240	3.170	3.102	3.037	2.974	2.914	2.855	2.798	2.743	2.690	2.639	2.589
5	4.853	4.713	4.580	4.452	4.329	4.212	4.100	3.993	3.890	3.791	3.696	3.605	3.517	3.433	3.352	3.274	3.199	3.127	3.058	2.991
6	5.795	5.601	5.417	5.242	5.076	4.917	4.767	4.623	4.486	4.355	4.231	4.111	3.998	3.889	3.784	3.685	3.589	3.498	3.410	3.326
7	6.728	6.472	6.230	6.002	5.786	5.582	5.389	5.206	5.033	4.868	4.712	4.564	4.423	4.288	4.160	4.039	3.922	3.812	3.706	3.605
8	7.652	7.326	7.020	6.733	6.463	6.210	5.971	5.747	5.535	5.335	5.146	4.968	4.799	4.639	4.487	4.344	4.207	4.078	3.954	3.837
9	8.566	8.162	7.786	7.435	7.108	6.802	6.515	6.247	5.995	5.759	5.537	5.328	5.132	4.946	4.772	4.607	4.451	4.303	4.163	4.031
10	9.471	8.983	8.530	8.111	7.722	7.360	7.024	6.710	6.418	6.145	5.889	5.650	5.426	5.216	5.019	4.833	4.659	4.494	4.339	4.192
11	10.368	9.787	9.253	8.760	8.306	7.887	7.499	7.139	6.805	6.495	6.207	5.938	5.687	5.453	5.234	5.029	4.836	4.656	4.486	4.327
12	11.255	10.575	9.954	9.385	8.863	8.384	7.943	7.536	7.161	6.814	6.492	6.194	5.918	5.660	5.421	5.197	4.988	4.793	4.611	4.439
13	12.134	11.348	10.635	9.986	9.394	8.853	8.358	7.904	7.487	7.013	6.750	6.424	6.122	5.842	5.583	5.342	5.118	4.910	4.715	4.533
14	13.004	12.106	11.296	10.563	9.899	9.295	8.745	8.244	7.786	7.367	6.982	6.628	6.302	6.002	5.724	5.468	5.229	5.008	4.802	4.611
15	13.865	12.849	11.938	11.118	10.380	9.712	9.108	8.560	8.061	7.606	7.191	6.811	6.462	6.142	5.847	5.575	5.324	5.092	4.876	4.675
16	14.718	13.578	12.561	11.652	10.838	10.106	9.447	8.851	8.313	7.824	7.379	6.974	6.604	6.265	5.954	5.668	5.405	5.162	4.938	4.730
17	15.562	14.292	13.166	12.166	11.274	10.477	9.763	9.122	8.544	8.022	7.549	7.120	6.729	6.373	6.047	5.749	5.475	5.222	4.990	4.775
18	16.398	14.992	13.754	12.659	11.690	10.828	10.059	9.372	8.756	8.201	7.702	7.250	6.840	6.467	6.128	5.818	5.534	5.273	5.033	4.812
19	17.226	15.679	14.324	13.134	12.085	11.158	10.336	9.604	8.950	8.365	7.839	7.366	6.938	6.550	6.198	5.877	5.584	5.316	5.070	4.843
20	18.046	16.352	14.878	13.590	12.462	11.470	10.594	9.818	9.129	8.514	7.963	7.469	7.025	6.623	6.259	5.929	5.628	5.353	5.101	4.870
21	18.857	17.011	15.415	14.029	12.821	11.764	10.836	10.017	9.292	8.649	8.075	7.562	7.102	6.687	6.312	5.973	5.665	5.384	5.127	4.891
22	19.661	17.658	15.937	14.451	13.163	12.042	11.061	10.201	9.442	8.772	8.176	7.645	7.170	6.743	6.359	6.011	5.696	5.410	5.149	4.909
23	20.456	18.292	16.444	14.857	13.489	12.303	11.272	10.371	9.580	8.883	8.266	7.718	7.230	6.792	6.399	6.044	5.723	5.432	5.167	4.925
24	21.244	18.914	16.936	15.247	13.799	12.550	11.469	10.529	9.707	8.985	8.348	7.784	7.283	6.835	6.434	6.073	5.746	5.451	5.182	4.937
25	22.023	19.524	17.413	15.622	14.094	12.783	11.654	10.675	9.823	9.077	8.422	7.843	7.330	6.873	6.464	6.097	5.766	5.467	5.195	4.948
30	25.808	22.396	19.601	17.292	15.373	13.765	12.409	11.258	10.274	9.427	8.694	8.055	7.496	7.003	6.566	6.177	5.829	5.517	5.235	4.979
35	29.409	24.999	21.487	18.665	16.374	14.498	12.948	11.655	10.567	9.644	8.855	8.176	7.586	7.070	6.617	6.215	5.858	5.539	5.251	4.992
40	32.835	27.356	23.115	19.793	17.159	15.046	13.332	11.925	10.757	9.779	8.951	8.244	7.634	7.105	6.642	6.233	5.871	5.548	5.258	4.997
45	36.095	29.490	24.519	20.720	17.774	15.456	13.606	12.108	10.881	9.863	9.008	8.283	7.661	7.123	6.654	6.242	5.877	5.552	5.261	4.999
50	39.196	31.424	25.730	21.482	18.256	15.762	13.801	12.233	10.962	9.915	9.042	8.304	7.675	7.133	6.661	6.246	5.880	5.554	5.262	4.999

Using the Calculator to Compute the Present Value of an Annuity

Hewlett-Packard HP 12C, 17 BII, and 19 BII[a]

Before you begin, make sure to clear the memory, ensure that you are in the *end mode* and that your calculator is set for *one payment per year,* and set the number of decimal places that you want (usually two for dollar-related accuracy).

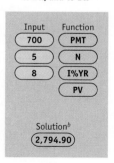

Sample Problem

You want to know what the present value of an annuity of $700 received at the end of each year for 5 years, given a discount rate of 8%.

---

[a]For the 12C, you would use the ⬚n⬚ key instead of the ⬚N⬚ key and use the ⬚i⬚ key instead of the ⬚I%YR⬚ key.
[b]The minus sign that precedes the solution should be ignored.

TABLE A–4 (Continued)

Period	21%	22%	23%	24%	25%	26%	27%	28%	29%	30%	31%	32%	33%	34%	35%	40%	45%	50%
1	.826	.820	.813	.806	.800	.794	.787	.781	.775	.769	.763	.758	.752	.746	.741	.714	.690	.667
2	1.509	1.492	1.474	1.457	1.440	1.424	1.407	1.392	1.376	1.361	1.346	1.331	1.317	1.303	1.289	1.224	1.165	1.111
3	2.074	2.042	2.011	1.981	1.952	1.923	1.896	1.868	1.842	1.816	1.791	1.766	1.742	1.719	1.696	1.589	1.493	1.407
4	2.540	2.494	2.448	2.404	2.362	2.320	2.280	2.241	2.203	2.166	2.130	2.096	2.062	2.029	1.997	1.849	1.720	1.605
5	2.926	2.864	2.803	2.745	2.689	2.635	2.583	2.532	2.483	2.436	2.390	2.345	2.302	2.260	2.220	2.035	1.876	1.737
6	3.245	3.167	3.092	3.020	2.951	2.885	2.821	2.759	2.700	2.643	2.588	2.534	2.483	2.433	2.385	2.168	1.983	1.824
7	3.508	3.416	3.327	3.242	3.161	3.083	3.009	2.937	2.868	2.802	2.739	2.677	2.619	2.562	2.508	2.263	2.057	1.883
8	3.726	3.619	3.518	3.421	3.329	3.241	3.156	3.076	2.999	2.925	2.854	2.786	2.721	2.658	2.598	2.331	2.109	1.922
9	3.905	3.786	3.673	3.566	3.463	3.366	3.273	3.184	3.100	3.019	2.942	2.868	2.798	2.730	2.665	2.379	2.144	1.948
10	4.054	3.923	3.799	3.682	3.570	3.465	3.364	3.269	3.178	3.092	3.009	2.930	2.855	2.784	2.715	2.414	2.168	1.965
11	4.177	4.035	3.902	3.776	3.656	3.544	3.437	3.335	3.239	3.147	3.060	2.978	2.899	2.824	2.752	2.438	2.185	1.977
12	4.278	4.127	3.985	3.851	3.725	3.606	3.493	3.387	3.286	3.190	3.100	3.013	2.931	2.853	2.779	2.456	2.196	1.985
13	4.362	4.203	4.053	3.912	3.780	3.656	3.538	3.427	3.322	3.223	3.129	3.040	2.956	2.876	2.799	2.469	2.204	1.990
14	4.432	4.265	4.108	3.962	3.824	3.695	3.573	3.459	3.351	3.249	3.152	3.061	2.974	2.892	2.814	2.478	2.210	1.993
15	4.489	4.315	4.153	4.001	3.859	3.726	3.601	3.483	3.373	3.268	3.170	3.076	2.988	2.905	2.825	2.484	2.214	1.995
16	4.536	4.357	4.189	4.033	3.887	3.751	3.623	3.503	3.390	3.283	3.183	3.088	2.999	2.914	2.834	2.489	2.216	1.997
17	4.576	4.391	4.219	4.059	3.910	3.771	3.640	3.518	3.403	3.295	3.193	3.097	3.007	2.921	2.840	2.492	2.218	1.998
18	4.608	4.419	4.243	4.080	3.928	3.786	3.654	3.529	3.413	3.304	3.201	3.104	3.012	2.926	2.844	2.494	2.219	1.999
19	4.635	4.442	4.263	4.097	3.942	3.799	3.664	3.539	3.421	3.311	3.207	3.109	3.017	2.930	2.848	2.496	2.220	1.999
20	4.657	4.460	4.279	4.110	3.954	3.808	3.673	3.546	3.427	3.316	3.211	3.113	3.020	2.933	2.850	2.497	2.221	1.999
21	4.675	4.476	4.292	4.121	3.963	3.816	3.679	3.551	3.432	3.320	3.215	3.116	3.023	2.935	2.852	2.498	2.221	2.000
22	4.690	4.488	4.302	4.130	3.970	3.822	3.684	3.556	3.436	3.323	3.217	3.118	3.025	2.936	2.853	2.498	2.222	2.000
23	4.703	4.499	4.311	4.137	3.976	3.827	3.689	3.559	3.438	3.325	3.219	3.120	3.026	2.938	2.854	2.499	2.222	2.000
24	4.713	4.507	4.318	4.143	3.981	3.831	3.692	3.562	3.441	3.327	3.221	3.121	3.027	2.939	2.855	2.499	2.222	2.000
25	4.721	4.514	4.323	4.147	3.985	3.834	3.694	3.564	3.442	3.329	3.222	3.122	3.028	2.939	2.856	2.499	2.222	2.000
30	4.746	4.534	4.339	4.160	3.995	3.842	3.701	3.569	3.447	3.332	3.225	3.124	3.030	2.941	2.857	2.500	2.222	2.000
35	4.756	4.541	4.345	4.164	3.998	3.845	3.703	3.571	3.448	3.333	3.226	3.125	3.030	2.941	2.857	2.500	2.222	2.000
40	4.760	4.544	4.347	4.166	3.999	3.846	3.703	3.571	3.448	3.333	3.226	3.125	3.030	2.941	2.857	2.500	2.222	2.000
45	4.761	4.545	4.347	4.166	4.000	3.846	3.704	3.571	3.448	3.333	3.226	3.125	3.030	2.941	2.857	2.500	2.222	2.000
50	4.762	4.545	4.348	4.167	4.000	3.846	3.704	3.571	3.448	3.333	3.226	3.125	3.030	2.941	2.857	2.500	2.222	2.000

**Texas Instruments,
BA-35, BAII,
and BAII Plus[c]**

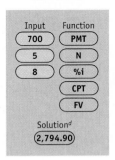

Input	Function
700	PMT
5	N
8	%i
	CPT
	FV

Solution[d]
2,794.90

[c]For the Texas Instruments BAII, you would use the **2nd** key instead of the **CPT** key; for the Texas Instruments BAII Plus, you would use the **I/Y** key instead of the **%i** key.

[d]If a minus sign precedes the solution, it should be ignored.

Appendix: Alternative Models of Systematic Risk

From Chapter 11 of *Fundamentals of Corporate Finance*, 1/e. Jonathan Berk, Peter DeMarzo, Jarrad Harford. Copyright © 2009 by Pearson Prentice Hall. All rights reserved.

Alternative Models of Systematic Risk

While the CAPM is the most widely used model for estimating the cost of capital in practice, recently some practitioners have tried to improve on the CAPM.

Problems with the CAPM in Practice

Researchers have found that using only the S&P 500, or some other simple proxy for the true market portfolio, has led to consistent pricing errors from the CAPM. That is, some stocks and portfolios of stocks earn consistently higher or lower returns than the CAPM would predict. For example, researchers have found that small stocks, stocks with high ratios of book to market value of equity, and stocks that have recently performed very well have consistently earned higher returns than the CAPM would predict using a simple stock market proxy for the market portfolio.

Multi-Factor Models

risk factors Different components of systematic risk (used in a multi-factor model).

multi-factor model A model that uses more than one portfolio to capture systematic risk. Each portfolio can be thought of as either the risk factor itself or a portfolio of stocks correlated with an unobservable risk factor.

These findings have led researchers to add new portfolios to the CAPM pricing equation in an attempt to construct a better proxy for the true market portfolio that captures the components of systematic risk that just using the S&P 500 alone misses. Although we might not be able to identify a perfect proxy for the true market portfolio, the market portfolio can be constructed from other portfolios. This observation implies that so long as the market portfolio can be constructed from a collection of portfolios, the collection itself can be used to measure risk. *Thus, it is not actually necessary to identify the market portfolio itself.* All that is required is to identify a collection of portfolios from which it can be constructed.

Thus, we can use a collection of portfolios to capture the components of systematic risk, referred to as **risk factors**. A model with more than one portfolio to capture risk is known as a **multi-factor model**. Each portfolio can be thought of as either the risk factor itself or a portfolio of stocks correlated with an unobservable risk factor. This particular form of the multi-factor model was originally developed by Professor Stephen Ross but Professor Robert Merton developed an alternative multifactor model earlier.[6] The model is also referred to as the **Arbitrage Pricing Theory (APT)**.

Fama-French-Carhart Factor Specification

Arbitrage Pricing Theory (APT) One of the earliest multifactor models, relying on the absence of arbitrage to price securities.

Practitioners have added portfolios specifically to address the CAPM pricing errors. Thus, the first portfolio is one that is constructed by buying small firms and selling large firms. This portfolio is widely known as the small-minus-big (SMB) portfolio. The second portfolio buys high book-to-market firms and sells low book-to-market firms, and we call it the high-minus-low (HML) portfolio. Finally, the third portfolio buys stocks that have recently done extremely well and sells those that have done extremely poorly. Since this portfolio addresses the problem that this extremely good and bad performance continues in the short run, it is called the prior 1-year momentum (PR1YR) portfolio.

The collection of these four portfolios–the stock market (Mkt), SMB, HML, and PR1YR—is the most popular collection of portfolios used as an alternative model to the

---

[6]See Stephen A. Ross, "The Arbitrage Theory of Capital Asset Pricing." *Journal of Economic Theory* 3 (December 1976): 343–62 and Robert C. Merton "An Intertemporal Capital Asset Pricing Model." *Econometrica* 41(1973): 867–887.

	Average Monthly Return (%)
Mkt$-r_f$	0.64
SMB	0.17
HML	0.53
PR1YR	0.76

TABLE 5

FFC Portfolio Average Monthly Returns (1926–2005)

Source: Professor Kenneth French's personal Web site.

CAPM and is one example of a multi-factor model. Using this collection, the expected return of security i is given by:

$$E[R_i] = r_f + \beta_i^{Mkt}(E[R_{Mkt}] - r_f) + \beta_i^{SMB}E[R_{SMB}] + \beta_i^{HML}E[R_{HML}]$$
$$+ \beta_i^{PR1YR}E[R_{PR1YR}] \tag{8}$$

Fama-French-Carhart factor specification (FFC) A multi-factor model of risk and return in which the factor portfolios are the market, small-minus-big, high-minus-low, and PR1YR portfolios identified by Fama, French, and Carhart.

where β_i^{Mkt}, β_i^{SMB}, β_i^{HML} and β_i^{PR1YR} are the factor betas of stock i and measure the sensitivity of the stock to each portfolio. Because the collection of portfolios in Eq. 8 (Mkt, SMB, HML, and PR1YR) were identified by Professors Eugene Fama, Kenneth French, and Mark Carhart, we refer to this collection of portfolios as the **Fama-French-Carhart factor specification (FFC)**.

The average monthly returns for each of the four portfolios in the FFC are given in Table 5.

EXAMPLE 8

Using the FFC Factor Specification to Calculate the Cost of Capital

Problem

You are currently considering making an investment in a project in the Food and Beverages industry. You determine the project has the same riskiness as investing in Coca-Cola. You use data over the past five years to estimate the factor betas of Coca-Cola (Ticker: KO). Specifically, you regress the monthly excess return (the realized return in each month minus the risk-free rate) of Coca-Cola's stock on the return of each of the four-factor portfolios. You determine that the factor betas for KO are:

$$\beta_{KO}^{Mkt} = 0.158$$
$$\beta_{KO}^{SMB} = 0.302$$
$$\beta_{KO}^{HML} = 0.497$$
$$\beta_{KO}^{PR1YR} = -0.276$$

The current risk-free monthly rate is 5%/12 = 0.42%. Determine the cost of capital by using the FFC factor specification.

Solution

▶ **Plan**

First, gather the information you have. Combining the information in the problem with the data in Table 5, you have:

	Average Monthly Return (%)	**KO's β with Factor**
Mkt$-r_f$	0.64	0.158
SMB	0.17	0.302
HML	0.53	0.497
PR1YR	0.76	-0.276

Using the information you have collected along with the monthly risk-free rate of 0.42%, you can use Eq. 8 to calculate the monthly expected return for investing in Coca-Cola. From there, you can multiply by 12 to get the annual expected return, represented as an APR.

▶ **Execute**

Using Eq. 8, the monthly expected return of investing in Coca-Cola is:

$$E[R_{KO}] = r_f + \beta_{KO}^{Mkt}(E[R_{Mkt}] - r_f) + \beta_{KO}^{SMB}E[R_{SMB}] + \beta_{KO}^{HML}E[R_{HML}] + \beta_{KO}^{PR1YR}E[R_{PR1YR}]$$

$$= 0.42 + 0.158 \times 0.64 + 0.302 \times 0.17 + 0.497 \times 0.53 - 0.276 \times 0.76$$

$$= 0.626\%$$

The annual expected return is $0.626 \times 12 = 7.5\%$.

▶ **Evaluate**

By gathering all of the inputs and applying the FFC specification in the same way we would apply the CAPM, we can calculate this alternative estimate of the cost of capital for Coca-Cola. According to this approach, we would conclude that the annual cost of capital of the investment opportunity is about 7.5%.

Appendix: Using Excel to Build a Dividend-Discount Model

From Chapter 9 of *Fundamentals of Corporate Finance*, 1/e. Jonathan Berk, Peter DeMarzo, Jarrad Harford. Copyright © 2009 by Pearson Prentice Hall. All rights reserved.

Using Excel to Build a Dividend-Discount Model

In this appendix, we show how to build a flexible model in Excel that computes the current price and year-by-year expected price for a stock based on the dividend-discount model. The model we will build allows you to vary the expected growth rate in earnings and the dividend payout rate year-by-year up until the sixth year. It also gives you the flexibility to see how changes in your assumption about the equity cost of capital change your computed stock prices. The numerical values in the spreadsheet are based on Example 5.

Compute Future Earnings

To make the spreadsheet as flexible as possible, we enter the past year's earnings and expected growth rates and let it compute future earnings. That way, we have to change only the past earnings or any of the future growth rates as our assumptions change; the spreadsheet will automatically update the future expected earnings. In the screenshot below, we enter the numbers in blue; the formulas in black instruct Excel how to compute the cell contents. For example, cell F4 is next year's expected EPS and is computed using this past year's EPS ($2, found in cell E4) and the expected growth rate (20%, or 0.2, found in cell F3). We proceed through year 6 in the same way—each year's earnings are computed as the previous year's earnings multiplied by 1 plus the growth rate.

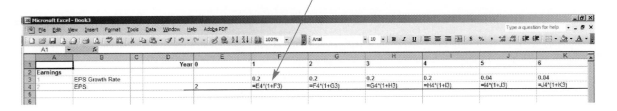

Calculate Expected Dividends

Next, we translate these projected EPS numbers into dividends to apply the dividend-discount model. We do so by adding a line determining the dividend payout ratio each year. Here, we assume that the company will not pay any dividends in years 1–3, and will then pay 60% of its earnings as dividends thereafter. Finally, we compute the expected dividends as the EPS in row 4 multiplied by the dividend payout ratio in row 6.

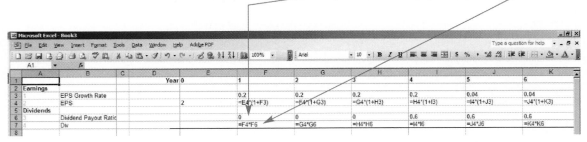

After we complete this step, the entered and calculated values are as follows:

Determine the Stock Price

Now we are ready for the final step, which is to compute the stock price. To do so, we need an equity cost of capital, which we enter into cell F9. We also need to make an assumption about dividends from year 6 onward. We decide to apply the constant growth model, so that the value of the stock in year 5 is equal to the dividend in year 6 divided by the equity cost of capital minus the dividend growth rate, which in this case is equal to the EPS growth rate. Once we have the year 5 price, we can compute the year 4 price as the one-year discounted value of the dividend in year 5 (cell J7) plus the price of the stock in year 5 (cell J10). As a discount rate, we use the equity cost of capital (cell F9). We continue this way until we get to the year 0 (current) price.

The final spreadsheet will look like the screenshot below. Because we built it with flexibility in mind, we can change any of the numbers in blue and immediately see the effect on the current and future stock prices.

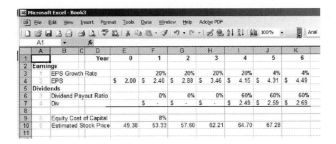

571

Appendix: Using Excel for Capital Budgeting

From Chapter 8 of *Fundamentals of Corporate Finance*, 1/e. Jonathan Berk, Peter DeMarzo, Jarrad Harford. Copyright © 2009 by Pearson Prentice Hall. All rights reserved.

Using Excel for Capital Budgeting

In this appendix, we illustrate how to build a pro forma statement and perform a sensitivity analysis in Excel.

Building a Pro Forma Statement

The key to frustration-free capital budgeting is to base your analysis on a spreadsheet containing a flexible model of the project's pro forma free cash flows.

List Assumptions

Start by creating a box in the spreadsheet with all of your assumptions, shown here shaded in gray:

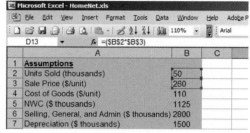

Although this step will take you a little more time upfront, it has two advantages. First, you are forced to present all of your major assumptions clearly, so you can see the drivers of your analysis. Second, setting them apart this way makes it far easier to change your assumptions later and quickly see the impact on the incremental free cash flows.

Base Cell Formulas on Assumptions

Once you have listed all of your assumptions, it is time to build the pro forma statement by dynamically referring back to the cells containing your assumptions. Here, we will show how to build the first year's pro forma cash flows. For example, rather than entering $13,000 into the Sales line of Year 1, you will enter the formula shown in the screen shot.

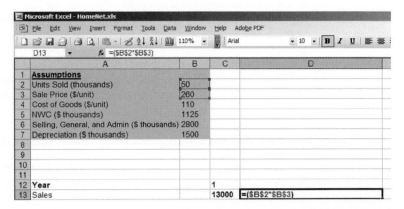

This formula is simply the cell-referenced version of our calculation from Example 1: Unit Sold × Price per unit = 50 × $260 = $13,000. As you can see from the screen shot, we have referred back to our Assumptions box for each of these inputs (units sold and price per unit). Later, if we want to change the assumption for price per unit, we can change it in our Assumptions box and it will automatically change the calculation for Sales in Year 1.

To complete the pro forma statement for year 1, we continue down the column. Each time we need to draw on an assumed number, we refer back to our Assumptions box. For calculations such as Gross Profit, we simply refer to the cells in the column: summing Sales and the negative Cost of Goods Sold.

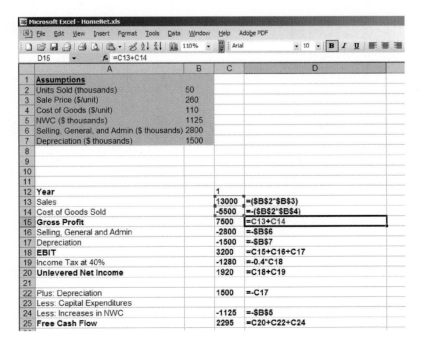

As you can imagine, building a pro forma statement like this greatly eases our analysis of the effects of changes in our assumptions. In the next section, we will show how to use a spreadsheet similar to the one we just constructed to perform sensitivity analysis.

Performing Sensitivity Analysis

Rather than recalculating HomeNet's NPV for each possible number of units sold, we can use Excel's Data Table tool. A data table shows us how the outcome of a formula (such as the NPV of HomeNet) changes when we change one of the cells in the spreadsheet (such as the number of units sold). In the previous Using Excel box, we showed how to build a pro forma statement of HomeNet that would make it easy to change our assumptions later. That is exactly what we do in sensitivity analysis: change our assumptions and see how the NPV changes. This screen shot shows a completed Excel pro forma statement of the incremental free cash flows of the HomeNet project. It also shows the NPV calculation and a data table (outlined in red) for our assumption on Units Sold:

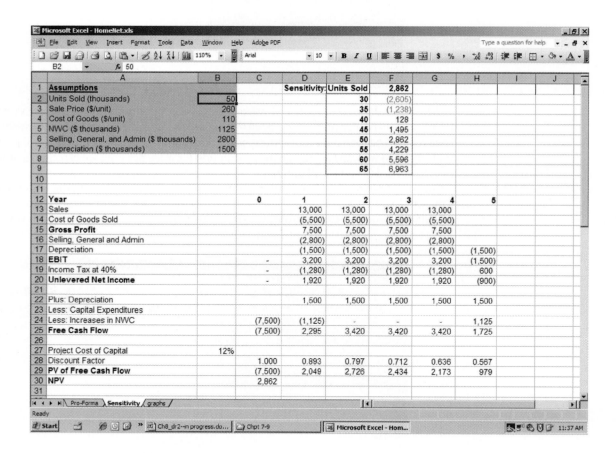

To set up the data table, we first create a cell that simply repeats the NPV. In this case, cell F1 is set to equal cell C30 to create a new NPV column. Next, we create the column that will contain the different assumptions of Units Sold. This column must be directly to the left of the NPV cell (F1). Finally, we highlight the Units Sold and NPV columns, and select Table from the Data menu.

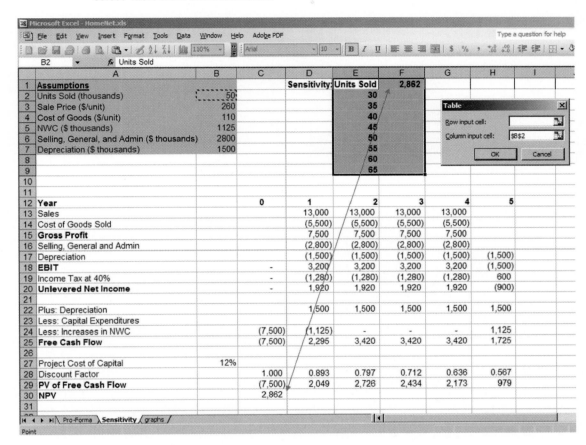

As the screen shot shows, the Table input box will appear. Since our Units Sold assumptions are in a column, we enter, into the column input cell (not the row input cell), the cell in our spreadsheet containing the base case Units Sold assumption (B2). Once we do this and hit Enter, Excel will create the sensitivity table shown in the first screen shot.

The U.S. tax code allows for accelerated depreciation of most assets. The depreciation method that you use for any particular asset is determined by the tax rules in effect at the time you place the asset into service. (Congress has changed the depreciation rules many times over the years, so many firms that have held property for a long time may have to use several depreciation methods simultaneously.)

For most business property placed in service after 1986, the IRS allows firms to depreciate the asset using the MACRS (Modified Accelerated Cost Recovery System) method. Under this method, you categorize each business asset into a recovery class that determines the time period over which you can write off the cost of the asset. The most commonly used items are classified as shown below:

- *3-year property:* Tractor units, racehorses over 2 years old, and horses over 12 years old.

- *5-year property:* Automobiles, buses, trucks, computers and peripheral equipment, office machinery, and any property used in research and experimentation. Also includes breeding and dairy cattle.

- *7-year property:* Office furniture and fixtures, and any property that has not been designated as belonging to another class.

- *10-year property:* Water transportation equipment, single-purpose agricultural or horticultural structures, and trees or vines bearing fruit or nuts.

- *15-year property:* Depreciable improvements to land such as fences, roads, and bridges.

- *20-year property:* Farm buildings that are not agricultural or horticultural structures.

- *27.5-year property:* Residential rental property.

- *39-year property:* Nonresidential real estate, including home offices. (Note that the value of land may not be depreciated.)

Generally speaking, residential and nonresidential real estate is depreciated via the straight-line method, but other classes can be depreciated more rapidly in early years. Table 4 shows the standard depreciation rates for assets in the other recovery classes; refinements of this table can be applied depending on the month that the asset was placed into service (consult IRS guidelines). The table indicates the percentage of the asset's cost that may be depreciated each year, with year 1 indicating the year the asset was first put into use. Generally, year 1 is the acquisition year and the table contains the "half-year" convention, allowing for a half year of depreciation in the acquisition year itself. This is why the first year's depreciation percentage is smaller than the second year's.

From Chapter 8 of *Fundamentals of Corporate Finance*, 1/e. Jonathan Berk, Peter DeMarzo, Jarrad Harford. Copyright © 2009 by Pearson Prentice Hall. All rights reserved.

TABLE 4

MACRS Depreciation Table Showing the Percentage of the Asset's Cost That May Be Depreciated Each Year Based on Its Recovery Period

	Depreciation Rate for Recovery Period					
Year	3 Years	5 Years	7 Years	10 Years	15 Years	20 Years
1	33.33	20.00	14.29	10.00	5.00	3.750
2	44.45	32.00	24.49	18.00	9.50	7.219
3	14.81	19.20	17.49	14.40	8.55	6.677
4	7.41	11.52	12.49	11.52	7.70	6.177
5		11.52	8.93	9.22	6.93	5.713
6		5.76	8.92	7.37	6.23	5.285
7			8.93	6.55	5.90	4.888
8			4.46	6.55	5.90	4.522
9				6.56	5.91	4.462
10				6.55	5.90	4.461
11				3.28	5.91	4.462
12					5.90	4.461
13					5.91	4.462
14					5.90	4.461
15					5.91	4.462
16					2.95	4.461
17						4.462
18						4.461
19						4.462
20						4.461
21						2.231

Appendix: Using Excel to Make an NPV Profile

From Chapter 7 of *Fundamentals of Corporate Finance*, 1/e. Jonathan Berk, Peter DeMarzo, Jarrad Harford. Copyright © 2009 by Pearson Prentice Hall. All rights reserved.

Using Excel to Make an NPV Profile

Constructing an NPV profile of a project is a very useful way to really *see* the project's IRR(s) and how the NPV of the project changes with the discount rate. Take Fredrick's fertilizer project from Section 1. In the Excel screen shot below, the cash flows from that project are in black in cells D2 to H2. Cell B5 shows the NPV, taking the contents of cell B1 as the discount rate. The formula for doing this is shown just to the left of cell B2. Note that in order to make the NPV a dynamic function of whatever discount rate is entered into cell B1, you enter "B1" instead of "10%" where the formula takes this discount rate. For reference, we also compute the IRR in cell B3 and the formula for doing so is given just to the left of B3.

With the cash flows set up and the NPV entered in cell B5 as a dynamic function of the discount rate, we are ready to use the Data Table function of Excel to calculate the NPV for a range of different discount rates. A data table shows us how the outcome of a formula (such as NPV) changes when we change one of the cells in the spreadsheet (such as the discount rate). To do this:

1. Enter the range of discount rates down a column, as shown below in cells A6 to A30. The placement of these rates is important. They must start in the cell below and to the left of the cell with the NPV. (Cell A6 is immediately below and to the left of cell B5.)

2. Highlight the area containing your range of discount rates and the NPV cell, as shown in the screen shot (cells A5 to B30).

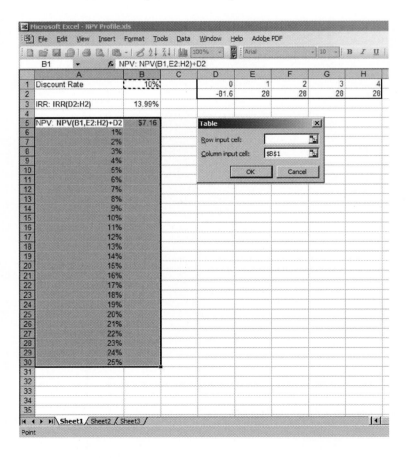

3. From the Data pull-down menu, select Table.

4. Since our discount rates are in a column, we are using a "Column input cell" instead of a "Row input cell." In the Column input cell box, enter B1 or click on the B1 cell. By doing this, you are telling Excel to recalculate the NPV by substituting the numbers running down the column into cell B1, which contains the discount rate.

5. Click OK.

After clicking OK, the cells next to the range of discount rates will fill with the NPVs corresponding to each of the discount rates, as shown in the screen shot below. To create an NPV profile graphing these NPVs as a function of the discount rates:

1. Highlight the discount rates and NPVs: cells A6 to B30.

2. Click on the Chart icon or select Chart from the Insert pull-down menu.

3. Choose XY(Scatter) as your Chart type and click on the Chart sub-type shown below in the screen shot.

4. Click Next to customize your chart further or click Finish to display the chart.

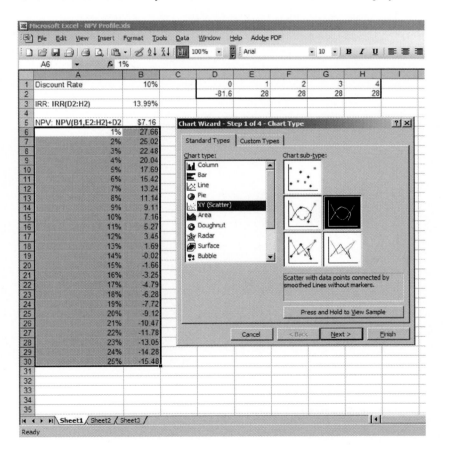

Appendix: The Yield Curve and the Law of One Price

From Chapter 6 of *Fundamentals of Corporate Finance*, 1/e. Jonathan Berk, Peter DeMarzo, Jarrad Harford. Copyright © 2009 by Pearson Prentice Hall. All rights reserved.

The Yield Curve and the Law of One Price

Thus far, we have focused on the relationship between the price of an individual bond and its yield to maturity. In this section, we explore the relationship between the prices and yields of different bonds. Using the Law of One Price, we show that given the spot interest rates, which are the yields of default-free zero-coupon bonds, we can determine the price and yield of any other default-free bond. As a result, the yield curve provides sufficient information to evaluate all such bonds.

Valuing a Coupon Bond with Zero-Coupon Prices

We begin with the observation that it is possible to replicate the cash flows of a coupon bond using zero-coupon bonds. Therefore, we can use the Valuation Principle's Law of One Price to compute the price of a coupon bond from the prices of zero-coupon bonds. For example, we can replicate a three-year, $1000 bond that pays 10% annual coupons using three zero-coupon bonds as follows:

	0	1	2	3
Coupon bond:		$100	$100	$1100
1-year zero:		$100		
2-year zero:			$100	
3-year zero:				$1100
Zero-coupon Bond portfolio:		$100	$100	$1100

We match each coupon payment to a zero-coupon bond with a face value equal to the coupon payment and a term equal to the time remaining to the coupon date. Similarly, we match the final bond payment (final coupon plus return of face value) in three years to a three-year, zero-coupon bond with a corresponding face value of $1100. Because the coupon bond cash flows are identical to the cash flows of the portfolio of zero-coupon bonds, the Law of One Price states that the price of the portfolio of zero-coupon bonds must be the same as the price of the coupon bond.

To illustrate, assume that current zero-coupon bond yields and prices are as shown in Table 7 (they are the same as in Example 1).

We can calculate the cost of the zero-coupon bond portfolio that replicates the three-year coupon bond as follows:

Zero-Coupon Bond	Face Value Required	Cost
1 Year	100	96.62
2 Years	100	92.46
3 Years	1100	$11 \times 87.63 = 963.93$
		Total Cost: $1153.00

By the Law of One Price, the three-year coupon bond must trade for a price of $1153. If the price of the coupon bond were higher, you could earn an arbitrage profit by selling

Maturity	1 Year	2 Years	3 Years	4 Years
YTM	3.50%	4.00%	4.50%	4.75%
Price	$96.62	$92.46	$87.63	$83.06

TABLE 7

Yields and Prices (per $100 Face Value) for Zero-Coupon Bonds

the coupon bond and buying the zero-coupon bond portfolio. If the price of the coupon bond were lower, you could earn an arbitrage profit by buying the coupon bond and selling the zero-coupon bonds.

Valuing a Coupon Bond Using Zero-Coupon Yields

To this point, we have used the zero-coupon bond *prices* to derive the price of the coupon bond. Alternatively, we can use the zero-coupon bond *yields*. Recall that the yield to maturity of a zero-coupon bond is the competitive market interest rate for a risk-free investment with a term equal to the term of the zero-coupon bond. Since the cash flows of the bond are its coupon payments and face value repayment, the price of a coupon bond must equal the present value of its coupon payments and face value discounted at the competitive market interest rates:

Price of a Coupon Bond

$$P = PV(\text{Bond Cash Flows})$$
$$= \frac{CPN}{1 + YTM_1} + \frac{CPN}{(1 + YTM_2)^2} + \cdots + \frac{CPN + FV}{(1 + YTM_n)^n} \tag{4}$$

where CPN is the bond coupon payment, YTM_n is the yield to maturity of a *zero-coupon* bond that matures at the same time as the nth coupon payment, and FV is the face value of the bond. For the three-year, $1000 bond with 10% annual coupons considered earlier, we can use Eq. 4 to calculate its price using the zero-coupon yields in Table 7:

$$P = \frac{100}{1.035} + \frac{100}{1.04^2} + \frac{100 + 1000}{1.045^3} = \$1153$$

This price is identical to the price we computed earlier by replicating the bond. Thus, we can determine the no-arbitrage price of a coupon bond by discounting its cash flows using the zero-coupon yields. In other words, the information in the zero-coupon yield curve is sufficient to price all other risk-free bonds.

Coupon Bond Yields

Given the yields for zero-coupon bonds, we can use Eq. 4 to price a coupon bond. You have learned how to compute the yield to maturity of a coupon bond from its price. Combining these results, we can determine the relationship between the yields of zero-coupon bonds and coupon-paying bonds.

Consider again the three-year, $1000 bond with 10% annual coupons. Given the zero-coupon yields in Table 7, we calculate a price for this bond of $1153. From Eq. 3, the yield to maturity of this bond is the rate y that satisfies:

$$P = 1153 = \frac{100}{(1 + y)} + \frac{100}{(1 + y)^2} + \frac{100 + 1000}{(1 + y)^3}$$

We can solve for the yield by using a financial calculator:

	N	I/Y	PV	PMT	FV
Given:	3		−1153	100	1000
Solve for:		4.44			
	Excel Formula: =RATE(NPER,PMT,PV,FV)=RATE(3,100,−1153,1000)				

Therefore, the yield to maturity of the bond is 4.44%. We can check this result directly as follows:

$$P = \frac{100}{1.0444} + \frac{100}{1.0444^2} + \frac{100 + 1000}{1.0444^3} = \$1153$$

Because the coupon bond provides cash flows at different points in time, the yield to maturity of a coupon bond is a weighted average of the yields of the zero-coupon bonds of equal and shorter maturities. The weights depend (in a complex way) on the magnitude of the cash flows each period. In this example, the zero-coupon bonds yields were 3.5%, 4.0%, and 4.5%. For this coupon bond, most of the value in the present value calculation comes from the present value of the third cash flow because it includes the principal, so the yield is closest to the three-year, zero-coupon yield of 4.5%.

EXAMPLE 11
Yields on Bonds with the Same Maturity

Problem

Given the following zero-coupon yields, compare the yield to maturity for a three-year, zero-coupon bond; a three-year, coupon bond with 4% annual coupons; and a three-year coupon bond with 10% annual coupons. All of these bonds are default free.

Solution

▶ **Plan**

Maturity	1 Year	2 Years	3 Years	4 Years
Zero-coupon YTM	3.50%	4.00%	4.50%	4.75%

From the information provided, the yield to maturity of the three-year, zero-coupon bond is 4.50%. Also, because the yields match those in Table 7, we already calculated the yield to maturity for the 10% coupon bond as 4.44%. To compute the yield for the 4% coupon bond, we first need to calculate its price, which we can do using Eq. 4. Since the coupons are 4%, paid annually, they are $40 per year for 3 years. The $1000 face value will be repaid at that time. Once we have the price, we can use Eq. 3 to compute the yield to maturity.

▶ **Execute**
Using Eq. 4, we have:

$$P = \frac{40}{1.035} + \frac{40}{1.04^2} + \frac{40 + 1000}{1.045^3} = \$986.98$$

The price of the bond with a 4% coupon is $986.98. From Eq. 4:

$$\$986.98 = \frac{40}{(1 + y)} + \frac{40}{(1 + y)^2} + \frac{40 + 1000}{(1 + y)^3}$$

We can calculate the yield to maturity using a financial calculator or spreadsheet:

	N	I/Y	PV	PMT	FV
Given:	3		−986.98	40	1000
Solve for:		4.47			

Excel Formula: =RATE(NPER,PMT,PV,FV)=RATE(3,40,−986.98,1000)

To summarize, for the three-year bonds considered:

Coupon Rate	0%	4%	10%
YTM	4.50%	4.47%	4.44%

▶ **Evaluate**

Note that even though the bonds all have the same maturity, they have different yields. In fact, holding constant the maturity, the yield decreases as the coupon rate increases. We discuss why below.

Example 11 shows that coupon bonds with the same maturity can have different yields depending on their coupon rates. The yield to maturity of a coupon bond is a weighted average of the yields on the zero-coupon bonds. As the coupon increases, earlier cash flows become relatively more important than later cash flows in the calculation of the present value. The shape of the yield curve keys us in on trends with the yield to maturity:

1. If the yield curve is upward sloping (as it is for the yields in Example 11), the resulting yield to maturity decreases with the coupon rate of the bond.

2. When the zero-coupon yield curve is downward sloping, the yield to maturity will increase with the coupon rate.

3. With a flat yield curve, all zero-coupon and coupon-paying bonds will have the same yield, independent of their maturities and coupon rates.

Treasury Yield Curves

As we have shown in this section, we can use the zero-coupon yield curve to determine the price and yield to maturity of other risk-free bonds. The plot of the yields of coupon bonds of different maturities is called the coupon-paying yield curve. When U.S. bond traders refer to "the yield curve," they are often referring to the coupon-paying Treasury yield curve. As we showed in Example 11, two coupon-paying bonds with the same maturity may have different yields. By convention, practitioners always plot the yield of the most recently issued bonds, termed the on-the-run bonds. Using similar methods to those employed in this section, we can apply the Law of One Price to determine the zero-coupon bond yields using the coupon-paying yield curve. Thus, either type of yield curve provides enough information to value all other risk-free bonds.

Solving for the Yield to Maturity of a Bond Using a Financial Calculator

You are looking to purchase a 3-year, $1000 par, 10% annual coupon bond. Payments begin one year from now in November 2008. The price of the bond is $1074.51 per $1000 par value. What is the yield to maturity of the bond? [answer: 7.15%]?

HP-10BII

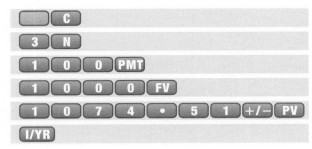

Press [Orange Shift] and then the [C] button to clear all previous entries.

Enter the Number of periods.

Enter the payment amount per period.

Enter the par value of the bond you will receive in year 3.

Enter present value or price of the bond you solved for earlier.

Solves for the yield to maturity.

TI-BAII Plus Professional

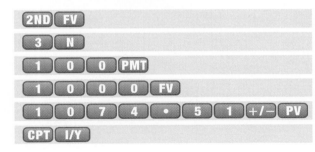

Press [2ND] and then the [FV] button to clear all previous entries.

Enter the Number of periods.

Enter the payment amount per period.

Enter the par value of the bond you will receive in year 3.

Enter present value or price of the bond you solved for earlier.

Solves for the yield to maturity.

From Chapter 6 of *Fundamentals of Corporate Finance*, 1/e. Jonathan Berk, Peter DeMarzo, Jarrad Harford. Copyright © 2009 by Pearson Prentice Hall. All rights reserved.

Using a Financial Calculator

Specifying Decimal Places

Make sure you have plenty of decimal places displayed!

HP-10BII

TI BAII Plus Professional

Toggling Between the Beginning and End of a Period

You should always make sure that your calculator is in *end-of-period* mode.

HP-10BII

TI BAII Plus Professional

Set the Number of Periods per Year

You will avoid a lot of confusion later if you always set your periods per year "P/Y" to 1:

HP-10BII

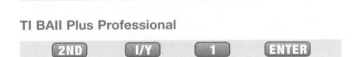

TI BAII Plus Professional

General TVM Buttons

HP-10BII

TI BAII Plus Professional

From Chapter 4 of *Fundamentals of Corporate Finance*, 1/e. Jonathan Berk, Peter DeMarzo, Jarrad Harford. Copyright © 2009 by Pearson Prentice Hall. All rights reserved.

Solving for the Present Value of a Single Future Cash Flow

You are considering investing in a savings bond that will pay $15,000 in ten years. If the competitive market interest rate is fixed at 6% per year, what is the bond worth today? [Answer: 8375.92]

HP-10BII

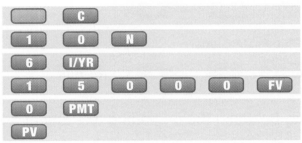

Press [Orange Shift] and then the [C] button to clear all previous entries.

Enter the Number of periods.

Enter the market annual interest rate.

Enter the Value you will recieve in 10 periods.

Indicate that there are no payments.

Solve for the Present Value.

TI-BAII Plus Professional

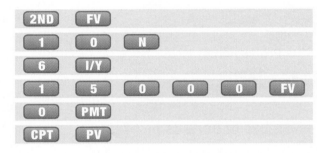

Press [2ND] and then the [FV] button to clear all previous entries.

Enter the Number of periods.

Enter the market annual interest rate.

Enter the Value you will recieve in 10 periods.

Indicate that there are no payments.

Solve for the Present Value.

Solving for the Future Value of an Annuity

Ellen is 35 years old, and she has decided it is time to plan seriously for her retirement. At the end of each year until she is 65, she will save $10,000 in a retirement account. If the account earns 10% per year, how much will Ellen have saved at age 65? [Answer: 1,644,940]

HP-10BII

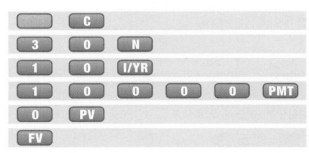

Press [Orange Shift] and then the [C] button to clear all previous entries.

Enter the Number of periods.

Enter the market annual interest rate.

Enter the Payment amount per period.

Indicate that there is no initial amount in the retirement account.

Solve for the Future Value.

TI-BAII Plus Professional

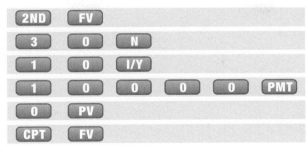

[2ND] [FV]	Press [2ND] and then the [FV] button to clear all previous entries.
[3] [0] [N]	Enter the Number of periods.
[1] [0] [I/Y]	Enter the market annual interest rate.
[1] [0] [0] [0] [0] [PMT]	Enter the payment amount per period.
[0] [PV]	Indicate that there is no initial amount in the retirement account.
[CPT] [FV]	Solve for the Future Value.

Solving for the Internal Rate of Return

If you have an initial cash outflow of $2000 and one cash inflow per year for the following four years of $1000, $400, $400, and $800, what is the internal rate of return on the project per year? [Answer: 12.12%]

HP-10BII

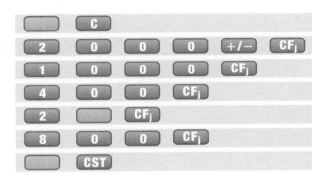

[ ] [C]	Press [Orange Shift] and then the [C] button to clear all previous entries.
[2] [0] [0] [0] [+/-] [CFj]	Enter the initial cash outflow.
[1] [0] [0] [0] [CFj]	Enter the first cash inflow.
[4] [0] [0] [CFj]	Enter the second cash inflow.
[2] [ ] [CFj]	Enter the number of consecutive periods the second cash inflow occurs.
[8] [0] [0] [CFj]	Enter the fourth cash inflow.
[ ] [CST]	Press [Orange Shift] and then the [CST] button to calculate the IRR/year.

TI-BAII Plus Professional

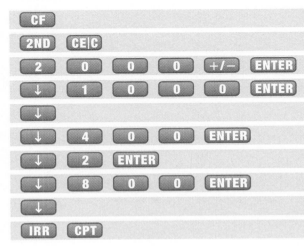

[CF]	Access Cash Flow Worksheet.
[2ND] [CE|C]	Press [2ND] and then the [CE/C] button to clear all previous entries.
[2] [0] [0] [0] [+/-] [ENTER]	Enter the initial cash outflow.
[↓] [1] [0] [0] [0] [ENTER]	Enter the first cash inflow.
[↓]	Leave the frequency of the initial cash inflow at 1 (Default Setting).
[↓] [4] [0] [0] [ENTER]	Enter the second cash inflow.
[↓] [2] [ENTER]	Enter the frequency of the second cash inflow as 2.
[↓] [8] [0] [0] [ENTER]	Enter the fourth cash inflow.
[↓]	Leave the frequency of the fourth cash inflow at 1 (Default Setting).
[IRR] [CPT]	Solve for the IRR.

When a firm fails to make a required payment to debt holders, it is in default. Debt holders can then take legal action against the firm to collect payment by seizing the firm's assets. Because most firms have multiple creditors, coordination is required to guarantee that each creditor will be treated fairly. Moreover, because the assets of the firm might be more valuable if kept together, creditors seizing assets in a piecemeal fashion might destroy much of the remaining value of the firm.

The U.S. bankruptcy code was created to organize this process so that creditors are treated fairly and the value of the assets is not needlessly destroyed. According to the provisions of the 1978 Bankruptcy Reform Act, U.S. firms can file for two forms of bankruptcy protection: Chapter 7 or Chapter 11.

In Chapter 7 liquidation, a trustee is appointed to oversee the liquidation of the firm's assets through an auction. The proceeds from the liquidation are used to pay the firm's creditors, and the firm ceases to exist.

In the more common form of bankruptcy for large corporations, Chapter 11 reorganization, all pending collection attempts are automatically suspended, and the firm's existing management is given the opportunity to propose a reorganization plan. While developing the plan, management continues to operate the business. The reorganization plan specifies the treatment of each creditor of the firm. In addition to cash payment, creditors may receive new debt or equity securities of the firm. The value of cash and securities is generally less than the amount each creditor is owed, but more than the creditors would receive if the firm were shut down immediately and liquidated. The creditors must vote to accept the plan, and it must be approved by the bankruptcy court.[4] If an acceptable plan is not put forth, the court may ultimately force a Chapter 7 liquidation of the firm.

---

[4]Specifically, management holds the exclusive right to propose a reorganization plan for the first 120 days, and this period may be extended indefinitely by the bankruptcy court. Thereafter, any interested party may propose a plan. Creditors who will receive full payment or have their claims fully reinstated under the plan are deemed unimpaired, and do not vote on the reorganization plan. All impaired creditors are grouped according to the nature of their claims. If the plan is approved by creditors holding two-thirds of the claim amount in each group and a majority in the number of the claims in each group, the court will confirm the plan. Even if all groups do not approve the plan, the court may still impose the plan (in a process commonly known as a "cram down") if it deems the plan fair and equitable with respect to each group that objected.

Appendix: The Balance Sheet and Statement of Cash Flows

From Chapter 17 of *Fundamentals of Corporate Finance*, 1/e. Jonathan Berk, Peter DeMarzo, Jarrad Harford.

The Balance Sheet and Statement of Cash Flows

The information we have calculated so far can be used to project KMS's balance sheet and statement of cash flows through 2012. While these statements are not critical for our valuation of the expansion, they often prove helpful in providing a more complete picture of how a firm will grow during the forecast period. These statements for KMS are shown in the spreadsheets in Table 17 and Table 18.

The balance sheet (Table 17) continues the work we started in Table 10. Current assets and liabilities come from the net working capital spreadsheet (Table 9). The inventory entry on the balance sheet includes both raw materials and finished goods. Property, plant, and equipment information comes from the forecasted capital expenditure spreadsheet (Table 6), and the debt comes from Table 7.

TABLE 17

Pro Forma Balance
Sheet for KMS,
2007–2012

1	Year	2007	2008	2009	2010	2011	2012
2	**Balance Sheets ($000s)**						
3	**Assets**						
4	Cash and Cash Equivalents	11,982	14,139	16,520	19,167	22,107	25,367
5	Accounts Receivable	14,229	16,790	19,617	22,761	26,252	30,124
6	Inventories	14,978	17,674	20,649	23,959	27,633	31,709
7	**Total Current Assets**	41,189	48,603	56,786	65,886	75,992	87,201
8	Property, Plant, and Equipment	49,427	66,984	67,486	67,937	68,344	68,709
9	**Total Assets**	90,616	115,587	124,272	133,823	144,335	155,910
10							
11	**Liabilities**						
12	Accounts Payable	11,982	14,139	16,520	19,167	22,107	25,367
13	Debt	4,500	24,500	24,500	24,500	24,500	24,500
14	**Total Liabilities**	16,482	38,639	41,020	43,667	46,607	49,867
15							
16	**Stockholders' Equity**						
17	Starting Stockholders' Equity	69,275	74,134	76,948	83,252	90,156	97,729
18	Net Income	6,940	7,600	8,807	11,141	13,739	16,627
19	Dividends	−2,082	−4,786	−2,503	−4,237	−6,167	−8,313
20	**Stockholders' Equity**	74,134	76,948	83,252	90,156	97,729	106,042
21	**Total Liabilities and Equity**	90,616	115,587	124,272	133,823	144,335	155,910

TABLE 18

Pro Forma Statement
of Cash Flows for
KMS, 2008–2012

1	Year	2007	2008	2009	2010	2011	2012
2	**Statement of Cash Flows ($000s)**						
3	**Net Income**		7,600	8,807	11,141	13,739	16,627
4	Depreciation		7,443	7,498	7,549	7,594	7,634
5	**Changes in Working Capital**						
6	Accounts Receivable		−2,561	−2,827	−3,144	−3,491	−3,872
7	Inventory		−2,696	−2,976	−3,309	−3,675	−4,076
8	Accounts Payable		2,157	2,381	2,647	2,940	3,261
9	**Cash from Operating Activities**		11,942	12,884	14,884	17,107	19,574
10	Capital Expenditures		−25,000	−8,000	−8,000	−8,000	−8,000
11	Other Investment		—	—	—	—	—
12	**Cash from Investing Activities**		−25,000	−8,000	−8,000	−8,000	−8,000
13	Net Borrowing		20,000	—	—	—	—
14	Dividends		−4,786	−2,503	−4,237	−6,167	−8,313
15	**Cash from Financing Activities**		15,214	−2,503	−4,237	−6,167	−8,313
16							
17	**Change in Cash (9+12+15)**		**2,157**	**2,381**	**2,647**	**2,940**	**3,261**

KMS's book value of equity will steadily grow as it expands and remains profitable, only paying out a portion of its net income each year. Its debt will jump from $4500 to $24,500 in 2008 when it finances its expansion. KMS's other liabilities—accounts payable—will grow steadily with sales. KMS's book debt-equity ratio will jump from $4500/74{,}134 = 6\%$ in 2007 to $24{,}500/76{,}948 = 32\%$ in 2008, and then will steadily decline to 23% by 2012.

The statement of cash flows in Table 18 starts with net income. Cash from operating activities includes depreciation as well as *changes* to working capital items (other than cash) from Table 9. Cash from investing activities includes the capital expenditures in Table 6. Cash from financing activities includes net borrowing from Table 7, and dividends are equal to free cash flows to equity because we assume KMS pays out all excess cash. We can compute FCF to equity from Table 12 using the following equation:

$$\text{FCF to Equity} = \text{FCF of the Firm} + \text{Net Borrowing} - \text{After-tax Interest Expense} \tag{12}$$

KMS is not planning to raise any additional equity financing, so there are no capital contributions on the cash flow statement. As a final check on the calculations, note that the change in the minimum cash balance shown on the balance sheet (Table 17). For example, in 2008, the change in cash and cash equivalents is 2157, which is the amount by which 2008 cash exceeds 2007 cash on the balance sheet.

Appendix: Using a Financial Calculator to Calculate Yield to Call

From Chapter 14 of *Fundamentals of Corporate Finance*, 1/e. Jonathan Berk, Peter DeMarzo, Jarrad Harford. Copyright © 2009 by Pearson Prentice Hall. All rights reserved.

APPENDIX — Using a Financial Calculator to Calculate Yield to Call

Calculate the yield to call of the bond from Example 1. In the example, the bond is called at year one; however, this can be generalized and solved for longer periods than one year.|

HP-10BII

Keys	Description
[ ] [C]	Press [Orange Shift] and then the [C] button to clear all previous entries.
[1] [N]	Enter the Number of periods.
[8] [PMT]	Enter the Payment amount per period.
[1] [0] [0] [FV]	Enter the price you would receive when it is called.
[1] [0] [3] [+/−] [PV]	Enter the present value or price of the bond.
[I/YR]	Solve for yield to call.

TI-BAII Plus Professional

Keys	Description
[2ND] [FV]	Press [2nd] and then the [FV] button to clear all previous entries.
[1] [N]	Enter the Number of periods.
[8] [PMT]	Enter the Payment amount per period.
[1] [0] [0] [FV]	Enter the price you would receive when it is called.
[1] [0] [3] [+/−] [PV]	Enter the present value or price of the bond.
[CPT] [I/Y]	Solve for yield to call.

If the bond was called after two years, you would simply use 2 instead of 1 for the number of periods.

Glossary

ABC inventory system Inventory management technique that divides inventory into three groups—A, B, and C, in descending order of importance and level of monitoring, on the basis of the dollar investment in each.

ability to service debts The ability of a firm to make the payments required on a scheduled basis over the life of a debt.

accept–reject approach The evaluation of capital expenditure proposals to determine whether they meet the firm's minimum acceptance criterion.

accounts payable management Management by the firm of the time that elapses between its purchase of raw materials and its mailing payment to the supplier.

accrual basis In preparation of financial statements, recognizes revenue at the time of sale and recognizes expenses when they are incurred.

accruals Liabilities for services received for which payment has yet to be made.

ACH (automated clearinghouse) transfer Preauthorized electronic withdrawal from the payer's account and deposit into the payee's account via a settlement among banks by the *automated clearinghouse*, or *ACH*.

activity ratios Measure the speed with which various accounts are converted into sales or cash—inflows or outflows.

after-tax proceeds from sale of old asset The difference between the old asset's sale proceeds and any applicable taxes or tax refunds related to its sale.

agency costs The costs borne by stockholders to maintain a *governance structure* that minimizes agency problems and contributes to the maximization of owner wealth.

agency problem The likelihood that managers may place personal goals ahead of corporate goals.

aggressive funding strategy A funding strategy under which the firm funds its seasonal requirements with short-term debt and its permanent requirements with long-term debt.

aging schedule A credit-monitoring technique that breaks down accounts receivable into groups on the basis of their time of origin; it shows the percentages of the total accounts receivable balance that have been outstanding for specified periods of time.

American depositary receipts (ADRs) Claims issued by U.S. banks representing ownership of shares of a foreign company's stock held on deposit by the U.S. bank in the foreign market and issued in dollars to U.S. investors.

American depositary shares (ADSs) Securities backed by *American depositary receipts (ADRs)* that permit U.S. investors to hold shares of non-U.S. companies and trade them in U.S. markets.

angel capitalists (angels) Wealthy individual investors who do not operate as a business but invest in promising early-stage companies in exchange for a portion of the firm's equity.

annual cleanup The requirement that for a certain number of days during the year borrowers under a line of credit carry a zero loan balance (that is, owe the bank nothing).

annual percentage rate (APR) The *nominal annual rate* of interest, found by multiplying the periodic rate by the number of periods in 1 year, that must be disclosed to consumers on credit cards and loans as a result of "truth-in-lending laws."

annual percentage yield (APY) The *effective annual rate* of interest that must be disclosed to consumers by banks on their savings products as a result of "truth-in-savings laws."

annuity A stream of equal periodic cash flows, over a specified time period. These cash flows can be *inflows* of returns earned on investments or *outflows* of funds invested to earn future returns.

annuity due An annuity for which the cash flow occurs at the *beginning* of each period.

articles of partnership The written contract used to formally establish a business partnership.

ask price The lowest price at which a security is offered for sale.

asymmetric information The situation in which managers of a firm have more information about operations and future prospects than do investors.

authorized shares The number of shares of common stock that a firm's corporate charter allows it to issue.

average age of inventory Average number of days' sales in inventory.

average collection period The average amount of time needed to collect accounts receivable.

average payment period The average amount of time needed to pay accounts payable.

average tax rate A firm's taxes divided by its taxable income.

balance sheet Summary statement of the firm's financial position at a given point in time.

bar chart The simplest type of probability distribution; shows only a limited number of outcomes and associated probabilities for a given event.

behavioral finance A growing body of research that focuses on investor behavior and its impact on investment decisions and stock prices. Advocates are commonly referred to as "behaviorists."

benchmarking A type of *cross-sectional analysis* in which the firm's ratio values are compared to those of a key competitor or group of competitors that it wishes to emulate.

beta coefficient (*b*) A relative measure of nondiversifiable risk. An *index* of the degree of movement of an asset's return in response to a change in the *market return*.

bid price The highest price offered to purchase a security.

bird-in-the-hand argument The belief, in support of *dividend relevance theory*, that investors see current dividends as less risky than future dividends or capital gains.

board of directors Group elected by the firm's stockholders and typically responsible for developing strategic goals and plans, setting general policy, guiding corporate affairs, approving major expenditures, and hiring/firing, compensating, and monitoring key officers and executives.

bond Long-term debt instrument used by business and government to raise large sums of money, generally from a diverse group of lenders.

bond indenture A legal document that specifies both the rights of the bondholders and the duties of the issuing corporation.

book value The strict accounting value of an asset, calculated by subtracting its accumulated depreciation from its installed cost.

book value per share The amount per share of common stock that would be received if all of the firm's assets were *sold for their exact book (accounting) value* and the proceeds remaining after paying all liabilities (including preferred stock) were divided among the common stockholders.

book value weights Weights that use accounting values to measure the proportion of each type of capital in the firm's financial structure.

breakeven analysis Indicates the level of operations necessary to cover all operating costs and the profitability associated with various levels of sales.

break point The level of *total* new financing at which the cost of one of the financing components rises, thereby causing an upward shift in the *weighted marginal cost of capital (WMCC)*.

broker market The securities exchanges on which the two sides of a transaction, the buyer and seller, are brought together to trade securities.

business ethics Standard of conduct or moral judgment that applies to persons engaged in commerce.

business risk The risk to the firm of being unable to cover operating costs.

call feature A feature included in nearly all corporate bond issues that gives the issuer the opportunity to repurchase bonds at a stated *call price* prior to maturity.

call premium The amount by which a bond's *call price* exceeds its par value.

call price The stated price at which a bond may be repurchased, by use of a *call feature*, prior to maturity.

capital The long-term funds of a firm; all items on the right-hand side of the firm's balance sheet, *excluding current liabilities*.

capital asset pricing model (CAPM) The basic theory that links risk and return for all assets; describes the relationship between the required return, r_s, and the nondiversifiable risk of the firm as measured by the beta coefficient, *b*.

capital budgeting The process of evaluating and selecting long-term investments that are consistent with the firm's goal of maximizing owner wealth.

capital budgeting process Five distinct but interrelated steps: *proposal generation, review and analysis, decision making, implementation,* and *follow-up*.

capital expenditure An outlay of funds by the firm that is expected to produce benefits over a period of time *greater than* 1 year.

capital gain The amount by which the sale price of an asset exceeds the asset's initial purchase price.

capital market A market that enables suppliers and demanders of *long-term funds* to make transactions.

capital rationing The financial situation in which a firm has only a fixed number of dollars available for capital expenditures, and numerous projects compete for these dollars.

capital structure   The mix of long-term debt and equity maintained by the firm.

carrying costs   The variable costs per unit of holding an item in inventory for a specific period of time.

cash basis   Recognizes revenues and expenses only with respect to actual inflows and outflows of cash.

cash bonuses   Cash paid to management for achieving certain performance goals.

cash budget (cash forecast)   A statement of the firm's planned inflows and outflows of cash that is used to estimate its short-term cash requirements.

cash concentration   The process used by the firm to bring lockbox and other deposits together into one bank, often called the *concentration bank*.

cash conversion cycle (CCC)   The amount of time a firm's resources are tied up; calculated by subtracting the average payment period from the *operating cycle*.

cash disbursements   All outlays of cash by the firm during a given financial period.

cash discount   A percentage deduction from the purchase price; available to the credit customer who pays its account within a specified time.

cash discount period   The number of days after the beginning of the credit period during which the cash discount is available.

cash receipts   All of a firm's inflows of cash in a given financial period.

change in net working capital   The difference between a change in current assets and a change in current liabilities.

clearing float   The time between deposit of a payment and when spendable funds become available to the firm.

clientele effect   The argument that a firm attracts shareholders whose preferences for the payment and stability of dividends correspond to the payment pattern and stability of the firm itself.

closely owned (stock)   All common stock of a firm owned by a small group of investors (such as a family).

coefficient of variation (CV)   A measure of relative dispersion that is useful in comparing the risks of assets with differing expected returns.

collateral trust bonds   Secured by stock and (or) bonds that are owned by the issuer. Collateral value is generally 25% to 35% greater than bond value.

commercial finance companies   Lending institutions that make *only* secured loans—both short-term and long-term—to businesses.

commercial paper   A form of financing consisting of short-term, unsecured promissory notes issued by firms with a high credit standing.

commitment fee   The fee that is normally charged on a *revolving credit agreement;* it often applies to the average unused balance of the borrower's credit line.

common stock   The purest and most basic form of corporate ownership.

common-size income statement   An income statement in which each item is expressed as a percentage of sales.

compensating balance   A required checking account balance equal to a certain percentage of the amount borrowed from a bank under a line-of-credit or revolving credit agreement.

compound interest   Interest that is earned on a given deposit and has become part of the principal at the end of a specified period.

conflicting rankings   Conflicts in the ranking given a project by NPV and IRR, resulting from *differences in the magnitude and timing of cash flows.*

conservative funding strategy   A funding strategy under which the firm funds both its seasonal and its permanent requirements with long-term debt.

constant-growth model   A widely cited dividend valuation approach that assumes that dividends will grow at a constant rate, but a rate that is less than the required return.

constant-growth valuation (Gordon) model   Assumes that the value of a share of stock equals the present value of all future dividends (assumed to grow at a constant rate) that it is expected to provide over an infinite time horizon.

constant-payout-ratio dividend policy   A dividend policy based on the payment of a certain percentage of earnings to owners in each dividend period.

continuous compounding   Compounding of interest an infinite number of times per year at intervals of microseconds.

continuous probability distribution   A probability distribution showing all the possible outcomes and associated probabilities for a given event.

controlled disbursing   The strategic use of mailing points and bank accounts to lengthen mail float and clearing float, respectively.

controller   The firm's chief accountant, who is responsible for the firm's accounting activities, such as corporate accounting, tax management, financial accounting, and cost accounting.

conventional cash flow pattern   An initial outflow followed only by a series of inflows.

conversion feature An option that is included as part of a bond or a preferred stock issue and allows its holder to change the security into a stated number of shares of common stock.

conversion feature (preferred stock) A feature of *convertible preferred stock* that allows holders to change each share into a stated number of shares of common stock.

corporate bond A long-term debt instrument indicating that a corporation has borrowed a certain amount of money and promises to repay it in the future under clearly defined terms.

corporate governance The system used to direct and control a corporation. Defines the rights and responsibilities of key corporate participants, decision-making procedures, and the way in which the firm will set, achieve, and monitor objectives.

corporation An artificial being created by law (often called a "legal entity").

correlation A statistical measure of the relationship between any two series of numbers representing data of any kind.

correlation coefficient A measure of the degree of correlation between two series.

cost of capital The rate of return that a firm must earn on the projects in which it invests to maintain its market value and attract funds.

cost of common stock equity, r_s The rate at which investors discount the expected dividends of the firm to determine its share value.

cost of giving up a cash discount The implied rate of interest paid to delay payment of an account payable for an additional number of days.

cost of long-term debt, r_i The after-tax cost today of raising long-term funds through borrowing.

cost of new asset The net outflow necessary to acquire a new asset.

cost of a new issue of common stock, r_n The cost of common stock, net of underpricing and associated flotation costs.

cost of preferred stock, r_p The ratio of the preferred stock dividend to the firm's net proceeds from the sale of preferred stock; calculated by dividing the annual dividend, D_p, by the net proceeds from the sale of the preferred stock, N_p.

cost of retained earnings, r_r The same as the cost of an *equivalent fully subscribed issue of additional common stock*, which is equal to the cost of common stock equity, r_s.

coupon interest rate The percentage of a bond's par value that will be paid annually, typically in two equal semiannual payments, as interest.

coverage ratios Ratios that measure the firm's ability to pay certain fixed charges.

credit monitoring The ongoing review of a firm's accounts receivable to determine whether customers are paying according to the stated credit terms.

credit period The number of days after the beginning of the credit period until full payment of the account is due.

credit scoring A credit selection method commonly used with high-volume/small-dollar credit requests; relies on a credit score determined by applying statistically derived weights to a credit applicant's scores on key financial and credit characteristics.

credit standards The firm's minimum requirements for extending credit to a customer.

credit terms The terms of sale for customers who have been extended credit by the firm.

cross-sectional analysis Comparison of different firms' financial ratios at the same point in time; involves comparing the firm's ratios to those of other firms in its industry or to industry averages.

cumulative preferred stock Preferred stock for which all passed (unpaid) dividends in arrears, along with the current dividend, must be paid before dividends can be paid to common stockholders.

current assets Short-term assets, expected to be converted into cash within 1 year or less.

current liabilities Short-term liabilities, expected to be paid within 1 year or less.

current rate (translation) method Technique used by U.S.-based companies to translate their foreign-currency-denominated assets and liabilities into dollars, for consolidation with the parent company's financial statements, using the exchange rate prevailing at the fiscal year ending date (the current rate).

current ratio A measure of liquidity calculated by dividing the firm's current assets by its current liabilities.

current yield A measure of a bond's cash return for the year; calculated by dividing the bond's annual interest payment by its current price.

date of record (dividends) Set by the firm's directors, the date on which all persons whose names are recorded as stockholders receive a declared dividend at a specified future time.

dealer market The market in which the buyer and seller are not brought together directly but instead have their orders executed by securities dealers that "make markets" in the given security.

debentures   Unsecured bonds that only creditworthy firms can issue. Convertible bonds are normally debentures.

debt capital   All long-term borrowing incurred by a firm, including bonds.

debt ratio   Measures the proportion of total assets financed by the firm's creditors.

decision trees   A behavioral approach that uses diagrams to map the various investment decision alternatives and payoffs, along with their probabilities of occurrence.

degree of financial leverage (DFL)   The numerical measure of the firm's financial leverage.

degree of indebtedness   Measures the amount of debt relative to other significant balance sheet amounts.

degree of operating leverage (DOL)   The numerical measure of the firm's operating leverage.

degree of total leverage (DTL)   The numerical measure of the firm's total leverage.

depository transfer check (DTC)   An unsigned check drawn on one of a firm's bank accounts and deposited in another.

depreciable life   Time period over which an asset is depreciated.

depreciation   The systematic charging of a portion of the costs of fixed assets against annual revenues over time.

dilution of ownership   Occurs when a new stock issue results in each present shareholder having a claim on a *smaller* part of the firm's earnings than previously.

discount   The amount by which a bond sells at a value that is less than its par value.

discount loans   Loans on which interest is paid in advance by being deducted from the amount borrowed.

discounting cash flows   The process of finding present values; the inverse of compounding interest.

diversifiable risk   The portion of an asset's risk that is attributable to firm-specific, random causes; can be eliminated through diversification. Also called *unsystematic risk*.

dividend irrelevance theory   Miller and Modigliani's theory that in a perfect world, the firm's value is determined solely by the earning power and risk of its assets (investments) and that the manner in which it splits its earnings stream between dividends and internally retained (and reinvested) funds does not affect this value.

dividend payout ratio   Indicates the percentage of each dollar earned that is distributed to the owners in the form of cash. It is calculated by dividing the firm's cash dividend per share by its earnings per share.

dividend per share (DPS)   The dollar amount of cash distributed during the period on behalf of each outstanding share of common stock.

dividend policy   The firm's plan of action to be followed whenever a dividend decision is made.

dividend reinvestment plans (DRIPs)   Plans that enable stockholders to use dividends received on the firm's stock to acquire additional shares—even fractional shares—at little or no transaction cost.

dividend relevance theory   The theory, advanced by Gordon and Lintner, that there is a direct relationship between a firm's dividend policy and its market value.

dividends   Periodic distributions of earnings to the stockholders of a firm.

double taxation   Occurs when the already once-taxed earnings of a corporation are distributed as cash dividends to stockholders, who must pay taxes of up to a maximum rate of 15 percent on them.

DuPont formula   Multiplies the firm's *net profit margin* by its *total asset turnover* to calculate the firm's *return on total assets (ROA)*.

DuPont system of analysis   System used to dissect the firm's financial statements and to assess its financial condition.

earnings per share (EPS)   The amount earned during the period on behalf of each outstanding share of common stock, calculated by dividing the period's total earnings available for the firm's common stockholders by the number of shares of common stock outstanding.

EBIT–EPS approach   An approach for selecting the capital structure that maximizes earnings per share (EPS) over the expected range of earnings before interest and taxes (EBIT).

economic order quantity (EOQ) model   Inventory management technique for determining an item's optimal order size, which is the size that minimizes the total of its *order costs* and *carrying costs*.

economic value added (EVA®)   A popular measure used by many firms to determine whether an investment contributes positively to the owners' wealth; calculated as the difference between an investment's *net operating profit after taxes (NOPAT)* and the cost of funds used to finance the investment which is found by multiplying the dollar amount of funds used to finance the investment by the firm's weighted average cost of capital (WACC).

effective (true) annual rate (EAR)   The annual rate of interest actually paid or earned.

efficient market A market that allocates funds to their most productive uses as a result of competition among wealth-maximizing investors that determines and publicizes prices that are believed to be close to their true value; a market with the following characteristics: many small investors, all having the same information and expectations with respect to securities; no restrictions on investment, no taxes, and no transaction costs; and rational investors, who view securities similarly and are risk-averse, preferring higher returns and lower risk.

efficient-market hypothesis Theory describing the behavior of an assumed "perfect" market in which (1) securities are typically in equilibrium, (2) security prices fully reflect all public information available and react swiftly to new information, and, (3) because stocks are fully and fairly priced, investors need not waste time looking for mispriced securities.

efficient portfolio A portfolio that maximizes return for a given level of risk or minimizes risk for a given level of return.

ending cash The sum of the firm's beginning cash and its net cash flow for the period.

enterprise resource planning (ERP) A computerized system that electronically integrates external information about the firm's suppliers and customers with the firm's departmental data so that information on all available resources—human and material—can be instantly obtained in a fashion that eliminates production delays and controls costs.

equipment trust certificates Used to finance "rolling stock"—airplanes, trucks, boats, railroad cars. A trustee buys the asset with funds raised through the sale of trust certificates and then leases it to the firm; after making the final scheduled lease payment, the firm receives title to the asset. A type of leasing.

equity capital The long-term funds provided by the firm's owners, the stockholders.

Eurobond An *international bond* that is sold primarily in countries other than the country of the currency in which the issue is denominated.

Eurobond market The market in which corporations and governments typically issue bonds denominated in dollars and sell them to investors located outside the United States.

Eurocurrency market International equivalent of the domestic money market.

ex dividend Period, beginning 2 *business days* prior to the date of record, during which a stock is sold without the right to receive the current dividend.

excess cash balance The (excess) amount available for investment by the firm if the period's ending cash is greater than the desired minimum cash balance; assumed to be invested in marketable securities.

excess earnings accumulation tax The tax the IRS levies on retained earnings above $250,000 when it determines that the firm has accumulated an excess of earnings to allow owners to delay paying ordinary income taxes on dividends received.

exchange rate risk The danger that an unexpected change in the exchange rate between the dollar and the currency in which a project's cash flows are denominated will reduce the market value of that project's cash flow; the risk caused by varying exchange rates between two currencies.

expectations theory The theory that the yield curve reflects investor expectations about future interest rates; an increasing inflation expectation results in an upward-sloping yield curve, and a decreasing inflation expectation results in a downward-sloping yield curve.

expected value of a return ($\bar{r}$) The most likely return on a given asset.

extendible notes Short maturities, typically 1 to 5 years, that can be renewed for a similar period at the option of holders. Similar to a floating-rate bond. An issue might be a series of 3-year renewable notes over a period of 15 years; every 3 years, the notes could be extended for another 3 years, at a new rate competitive with market interest rates at the time of renewal.

external financing required ("plug" figure) Under the judgmental approach for developing a pro forma balance sheet, the amount of external financing needed to bring the statement into balance. It can be either a positive or a negative value.

external forecast A sales forecast based on the relationships observed between the firm's sales and certain key external economic indicators.

extra dividend An additional dividend optionally paid by the firm if earnings are higher than normal in a given period.

factor A financial institution that specializes in purchasing accounts receivable from businesses.

factoring accounts receivable The outright sale of accounts receivable at a discount to a *factor* or other financial institution.

finance The art and science of managing money.

Financial Accounting Standards Board (FASB) Standard No. 52 Mandates that U.S.-based companies translate their foreign-currency-denominated assets and liabilities into dollars, for consolidation with the parent company's financial statements. This is done by using the *current rate (translation method)*.

Financial Accounting Standards Board (FASB) The accounting profession's rule-setting body, which authorizes *generally accepted accounting principles (GAAP)*.

financial breakeven point The level of EBIT necessary to just cover all *fixed financial costs;* the level of EBIT for which EPS = $0.

financial institution An intermediary that channels the savings of individuals, businesses, and governments into loans or investments.

financial leverage multiplier (FLM) The ratio of the firm's total assets to its common stock equity.

financial leverage The potential use of *fixed financial costs* to magnify the effects of changes in earnings before interest and taxes on the firm's earnings per share.

financial manager Actively manages the financial affairs of any type of business, whether financial or nonfinancial, private or public, large or small, profit-seeking or not-for-profit.

financial markets Forums in which suppliers of funds and demanders of funds can transact business directly.

financial planning process Planning that begins with long-term, or *strategic,* financial plans that in turn guide the formulation of short-term, or *operating,* plans and budgets.

financial risk The risk to the firm of being unable to cover required financial obligations (interest, lease payments, preferred stock dividends).

financial services The part of finance concerned with the design and delivery of advice and financial products to individuals, business, and government.

financing flows Cash flows that result from debt and equity financing transactions; includes incurrence and repayment of debt, cash inflow from the sale of stock, and cash outflows to pay cash dividends or repurchase stock.

five C's of credit The five key dimensions—character, capacity, capital, collateral, and conditions—used by credit analysts to provide a framework for in-depth credit analysis.

fixed-payment coverage ratio Measures the firm's ability to meet all fixed-payment obligations.

fixed-rate loan A loan with a rate of interest that is determined at a set increment above the prime rate and at which it remains fixed until maturity.

flat yield curve A yield curve that reflects relatively similar borrowing costs for both short- and longer-term loans.

float Funds that have been sent by the payer but are not yet usable funds to the payee.

floating inventory lien A secured short-term loan against inventory under which the lender's claim is on the borrower's inventory in general.

floating-rate bonds Stated interest rate is adjusted periodically within stated limits in response to changes in specified money market or capital market rates. Popular when future inflation and interest rates are uncertain. Tend to sell at close to par because of the automatic adjustment to changing market conditions. Some issues provide for annual redemption at par at the option of the bondholder.

floating-rate loan A loan with a rate of interest initially set at an increment above the prime rate and allowed to "float," or vary, above prime *as the prime rate varies* until maturity.

flotation costs The total costs of issuing and selling a security.

foreign bond Bond that is issued by a foreign corporation or government and is denominated in the investor's home currency and sold in the investor's home market.

foreign direct investment (FDI) The transfer by a multinational firm of capital, managerial, and technical assets from its home country to a host country.

foreign exchange manager The manager responsible for monitoring and managing the firm's exposure to loss from currency fluctuations.

free cash flow (FCF) The amount of cash flow available to investors (creditors and owners) after the firm has met all operating needs and paid for investments in net fixed assets and net current assets.

free cash flow valuation model A model that determines the value of an entire company as the present value of its expected free cash flows discounted at the firm's *weighted average cost of capital,* which is its expected average future cost of funds over the long run.

future value The value at a given future date of a present amount placed on deposit today and earning interest at a specified rate. Found by applying *compound interest* over a specified period of time.

future value interest factor The multiplier used to calculate, at a specified interest rate, the future value of a present amount as of a given time.

future value interest factor for an ordinary annuity The multiplier used to calculate the future value of an *ordinary annuity* at a specified interest rate over a given period of time.

generally accepted accounting principles (GAAP) The practice and procedure guidelines used to prepare and maintain financial records and reports; authorized by the *Financial Accounting Standards Board (FASB).*

Gordon model A common name for the *constant-growth model* that is widely cited in dividend valuation.

gross profit margin Measures the percentage of each sales dollar remaining after the firm has paid for its goods.

historical weights Either book or market value weights based on *actual* capital structure proportions.

incentive plans Management compensation plans that tend to tie management compensation to share price; most popular incentive plan involves the grant of *stock options*.

income bonds Payment of interest is required only when earnings are available. Commonly issued in reorganization of a failing firm.

income statement Provides a financial summary of the firm's operating results during a specified period.

incremental cash flows The *additional* cash flows—outflows or inflows—expected to result from a proposed capital expenditure.

independent projects Projects whose cash flows are unrelated or independent of one another; the acceptance of one *does not eliminate* the others from further consideration.

individual investors Investors who buy relatively small quantities of shares in order to meet personal investment goals.

informational content The information provided by the dividends of a firm with respect to future earnings, which causes owners to bid up or down the price of the firm's stock.

initial investment The relevant cash outflow for a proposed project at time zero.

initial public offering (IPO) The first public sale of a firm's stock.

installation costs Any added costs that are necessary to place an asset into operation.

installed cost of new asset The cost of *a new asset* plus its *installation costs;* equals the asset's depreciable value.

institutional investors Investment professionals, such as insurance companies, mutual funds, and pension funds, that are paid to manage other people's money and that trade large quantities of securities.

interest rate The compensation paid by the borrower of funds to the lender; from the borrower's point of view, the cost of borrowing funds.

interest rate risk The chance that interest rates will change and thereby change the required return and bond value. Rising rates, which result in decreasing bond values, are of greatest concern.

intermediate cash inflows Cash inflows received prior to the termination of a project.

internal forecast A sales forecast based on a buildup, or consensus, of sales forecasts through the firm's own sales channels.

internal rate of return (IRR) A sophisticated capital budgeting technique; the discount rate that equates the NPV of an investment opportunity with $0 (because the present value of cash inflows equals the initial investment); it is the compound annual rate of return that the firm will earn if it invests in the project and receives the given cash inflows.

internal rate of return approach An approach to capital rationing that involves graphing project IRRs in descending order against the total dollar investment to determine the group of acceptable projects.

international equity market A market that allows corporations to sell blocks of shares to investors in a number of different countries simultaneously.

inventory turnover Measures the activity, or liquidity, of a firm's inventory.

inverted yield curve A *downward-sloping* yield curve that indicates generally cheaper long-term borrowing costs than short-term borrowing costs.

investment bankers Financial intermediaries who, in addition to their role in selling new security issues, can be hired by acquirers in mergers to find suitable target companies and assist in negotiations.

investment flows Cash flows associated with purchase and sale of both fixed assets and equity investments in other firms.

investment opportunities schedule (IOS) A ranking of investment possibilities from best (highest return) to worst (lowest return); the graph that plots project IRRs in descending order against the total dollar investment.

issued shares The number of shares of common stock that have been put into circulation; the sum of outstanding shares and treasury stock.

judgmental approach A simplified approach for preparing the pro forma balance sheet under which the values of certain balance sheet accounts are estimated, some as a percentage of sales and others by management assumption, and the firm's external financing is used as a balancing, or "plug," figure.

junk bonds Debt rated Ba or lower by Moody's or BB or lower by Standard & Poor's. Commonly used by rapidly growing firms to obtain growth capital, most often as a way to finance mergers and takeovers. High-risk bonds with high yields—often yielding 2% to 3% more than the best-quality corporate debt.

just-in-time (JIT) system Inventory management technique that minimizes inventory investment by having materials arrive at exactly the time they are needed for production.

letter of credit A letter written by a company's bank to the company's foreign supplier, stating that the bank guarantees payment of an invoiced amount if all the underlying agreements are met.

letter to stockholders Typically, the first element of the annual stockholders' report and the primary communication from management.

leverage Results from the use of fixed-cost assets or funds to magnify returns to the firm's owners.

lien A publicly disclosed legal claim on collateral.

limited liability corporation (LLC) Permitted in most states, the LLC gives its owners, like those of S corps, limited liability and taxation as a partnership. But unlike an S corp, the LLC can own more than 80% of another corporation, and corporations, partnerships, or non-U.S. residents can own LLC shares. LLCs work well for corporate joint ventures or projects developed through a subsidiary.

limited liability partnership (LLP) A partnership permitted in many states; governing statutes vary by state. All LLP partners have limited liability. They are liable for their own acts of malpractice, but not for those of other partners. The LLP is taxed as a partnership. LLPs are frequently used by legal and accounting professionals.

limited partnership (LP) A partnership in which one or more partners have limited liability as long as at least *one* partner (the general partner) has unlimited liablity. The *limited partners* cannot take an active role in the firm's management; they are passive investors.

line of credit An agreement between a commercial bank and a business specifying the amount of unsecured short-term borrowing the bank will make available to the firm over a given period of time.

liquidation value per share The *actual amount* per share of common stock that would be received if all of the firm's assets were *sold for their market value,* liabilities (including preferred stock) were paid, and any remaining money were divided among the common stockholders.

liquidity A firm's ability to satisfy its short-term obligations *as they come due.*

liquidity preferences General preferences of investors for shorter-term securities.

liquidity preference theory Theory suggesting that for any given issuer, long-term interest rates tend to be higher than short-term rates because (1) lower liq-

uidity and higher responsiveness to general interest rate movements of longer-term securities exists and (2) borrower willingness to pay a higher rate for long-term financing causes the yield curve to be upward-sloping.

loan amortization The determination of the equal periodic loan payments necessary to provide a lender with a specified interest return and to repay the loan principal over a specified period.

loan amortization schedule A schedule of equal payments to repay a loan. It shows the allocation of each loan payment to interest and principal.

lockbox system A collection procedure in which customers mail payments to a post office box that is emptied regularly by the firm's bank, who processes the payments and deposits them in the firm's account. This system speeds up collection time by reducing processing time as well as mail and clearing time.

long-term debt Debts for which payment is not due in the current year.

long-term (strategic) financial plans Lay out a company's planned financial actions and the anticipated impact of those actions over periods ranging from 2 to 10 years.

low-regular-and-extra dividend policy A dividend policy based on paying a low regular dividend, supplemented by an additional dividend when earnings are higher than normal in a given period.

mail float The time delay between when payment is placed in the mail and when it is received.

managerial finance Concerns the duties of the financial manager in the business firm.

manufacturing resource planning II (MRP II) A sophisticated computerized system that integrates data from numerous areas such as finance, accounting, marketing, engineering, and manufacturing and generates production plans as well as numerous financial and management reports.

marginal cost-benefit analysis Economic principle that states that financial decisions should be made and actions taken only when the added benefits exceed the added costs.

marginal tax rate The rate at which *additional income* is taxed.

market/book (M/B) ratio Provides an assessment of how investors view the firm's performance. Firms expected to earn high returns relative to their risk typically sell at higher M/B multiples.

market makers Securities dealers who "make markets" by offering to buy or sell certain securities at stated prices.

market ratios   Relate a firm's market value, as measured by its current share price, to certain accounting values.

market return   The return on the market portfolio of all traded securities.

market segmentation theory   Theory suggesting that the market for loans is segmented on the basis of maturity and that the supply of and demand for loans within each segment determine its prevailing interest rate; the slope of the yield curve is determined by the general relationship between the prevailing rates in each segment.

market value weights   Weights that use market values to measure the proportion of each type of capital in the firm's financial structure.

marketable securities   Short-term debt instruments, such as U.S. Treasury bills, commercial paper, and negotiable certificates of deposit issued by government, business, and financial institutions, respectively.

materials requirement planning (MRP) system   Applies EOQ concepts to determine what materials to order and when to order them; simulates each product's bill of materials, inventory status, and manufacturing process.

mixed stream   A stream of unequal periodic cash flows that reflect no particular pattern.

modified accelerated cost recovery system (MACRS)   System used to determine the depreciation of assets for tax purposes.

modified DuPont formula   Relates the firm's *return on total assets (ROA)* to its *return on common equity (ROE)* using the *financial leverage multiplier (FLM)*.

money market   A financial relationship created between suppliers and demanders of *short-term funds*.

mortgage bonds   Secured by real estate or buildings.

multiple IRRs   More than one IRR resulting from a capital budgeting project with a *nonconventional cash flow pattern*; the maximum number of IRRs for a project is equal to the number of sign changes in its cash flows.

mutually exclusive projects   Projects that compete with one another, so that the acceptance of one *eliminates* from further consideration all other projects that serve a similar function.

Nasdaq market   An all-electronic trading platform used to execute securities trades.

negatively correlated   Describes two series that move in opposite directions.

net cash flow   The mathematical difference between the firm's cash receipts and its cash disbursements in each period.

net operating profits after taxes (NOPAT)   A firm's earnings before interest and after taxes, $EBIT \times (1 - T)$.

net present value (NPV)   A sophisticated capital budgeting technique; found by subtracting a project's initial investment from the present value of its cash inflows discounted at a rate equal to the firm's cost of capital.

net present value approach   An approach to capital rationing that is based on the use of present values to determine the group of projects that will maximize owners' wealth.

net present value profile   Graph that depicts a project's NPV for various discount rates.

net proceeds   Funds actually received from the sale of a security.

net profit margin   Measures the percentage of each sales dollar remaining after all costs and expenses, *including* interest, taxes, and preferred stock dividends, have been deducted.

net working capital   The amount by which a firm's current assets exceed its current liabilities; can be *positive* or *negative*.

nominal (stated) annual rate   Contractual annual rate of interest charged by a lender or promised by a borrower.

noncash charge   An expense that is deducted on the income statement but does not involve the actual outlay of cash during the period; includes depreciation, amortization, and depletion.

nonconventional cash flow pattern   An initial outflow followed by a series of inflows *and* outflows.

noncumulative preferred stock   Preferred stock for which passed (unpaid) dividends do not accumulate.

nondiversifiable risk   The relevant portion of an asset's risk attributable to market factors that affect all firms; cannot be eliminated through diversification. Also called *systematic risk*.

nonnotification basis   The basis on which a borrower, having pledged an account receivable, continues to collect the account payments without notifying the account customer.

nonrecourse basis   The basis on which accounts receivable are sold to a factor with the understanding that the factor accepts all credit risks on the purchased accounts.

nonvoting common stock   Common stock that carries no voting rights; issued when the firm wishes to raise capital through the sale of common stock but does not want to give up its voting control.

no-par preferred stock   Preferred stock with no stated face value but with a stated annual dollar dividend.

normal yield curve   An *upward-sloping* yield curve that indicates generally cheaper short-term borrowing costs than long-term borrowing costs.

notes to the financial statements   Footnotes detailing information on the accounting policies, procedures, calculations, and transactions underlying entries in the financial statements.

notification basis The basis on which an account customer whose account has been pledged (or factored) is notified to remit payment directly to the lender (or factor).

operating breakeven point The level of sales necessary to cover all *operating costs;* the point at which EBIT = $0.

operating cash flow (OCF) The cash flow a firm generates from its normal operations; calculated as EBIT − taxes + depreciation.

operating cash inflows The incremental after-tax cash inflows resulting from implementation of a project during its life.

operating cycle (OC) The time from the beginning of the production process to the collection of cash from the sale of the finished product.

operating expenditure An outlay of funds by the firm resulting in benefits received *within* 1 year.

operating flows Cash flows directly related to sale and production of the firm's products and services.

operating leverage The potential use of *fixed operating costs* to magnify the effects of changes in sales on the firm's earnings before interest and taxes.

operating profit margin Measures the percentage of each sales dollar remaining after all costs and expenses *other than* interest, taxes, and preferred stock dividends are deducted; the "pure profits" earned on each sales dollar.

operating-change restrictions Contractual restrictions that a bank may impose on a firm's financial condition or operations as part of a line-of-credit agreement.

opportunity costs Cash flows that could be realized from the best alternative use of an owned asset.

optimal capital structure The capital structure at which the weighted average cost of capital is minimized, thereby maximizing the firm's value.

order costs The fixed clerical costs of placing and receiving an inventory order.

ordinary annuity An annuity for which the cash flow occurs at the *end* of each period.

ordinary income Income earned through the sale of a firm's goods or services.

outstanding shares The number of shares of common stock held by the public.

over-the-counter (OTC) market Market where smaller, unlisted securities are traded.

paid-in capital in excess of par The amount of proceeds in excess of the par value received from the original sale of common stock.

partnership A business owned by two or more people and operated for profit.

par value (stock) A relatively useless value for a stock established for legal purposes in the firm's corporate charter.

par-value preferred stock Preferred stock with a stated face value that is used with the specified dividend percentage to determine the annual dollar dividend.

payback period The amount of time required for a firm to recover its initial investment in a project, as calculated from *cash inflows.*

payment date Set by the firm's directors, the actual date on which the firm mails the dividend payment to the holders of record.

pecking order A hierarchy of financing that begins with retained earnings, which is followed by debt financing and finally external equity financing.

percentage advance The percent of the book value of the collateral that constitutes the principal of a secured loan.

percent-of-sales method A simple method for developing the pro forma income statement; it forecasts sales and then expresses the various income statement items as percentages of projected sales.

perfectly negatively correlated Describes two *negatively correlated* series that have a *correlation coefficient* of −1.

perfectly positively correlated Describes two *positively correlated* series that have a *correlation coefficient* of +1.

performance plans Plans that tie management compensation to measures such as EPS, growth in EPS, and other ratios of return. *Performance shares* and/or *cash bonuses* are used as compensation under these plans.

performance shares Shares of stock given to management for meeting stated performance goals.

permanent funding requirement A constant investment in operating assets resulting from constant sales over time.

perpetuity An annuity with an infinite life, providing continual annual cash flow.

pledge of accounts receivable The use of a firm's accounts receivable as security, or collateral, to obtain a short-term loan.

political risk Risk that arises from the possibility that a host government will take actions harmful to foreign investors or that political turmoil in a country will endanger investments there.

portfolio A collection, or group, of assets.

positively correlated Describes two series that move in the same direction.

preemptive right Allows common stockholders to maintain their *proportionate* ownership in the corporation when new shares are issued.

preferred stock A special form of ownership having a fixed periodic dividend that must be paid prior to payment of any common stock dividends.

premium The amount by which a bond sells at a value that is greater than its par value.

present value The current dollar value of a future amount—the amount of money that would have to be invested today at a given interest rate over a specified period to equal the future amount.

present value interest factor The multiplier used to calculate, at a specified discount rate, the present value of an amount to be received in a future period.

present value interest factor for an ordinary annuity The multiplier used to calculate the present value of an *ordinary annuity* at a specified discount rate over a given period of time.

president or chief executive officer (CEO) Corporate official responsible for managing the firm's day-to-day operations and carrying out the policies established by the board of directors.

price/earnings multiple approach A popular technique used to estimate the firm's share value; calculated by multiplying the firm's expected earnings per share (EPS) by the average price/earnings (P/E) ratio for the industry.

price/earnings (P/E) ratio Measures the amount that investors are willing to pay for each dollar of a firm's earnings; the higher the P/E ratio, the greater is investor confidence.

primary market Financial market in which securities are initially issued; the only market in which the issuer is directly involved in the transaction.

prime rate of interest (prime rate) The lowest rate of interest charged by leading banks on business loans to their most important business borrowers.

principal The amount of money on which interest is paid.

private placement The sale of a new security issue, typically bonds or preferred stock, directly to an investor or group of investors.

privately owned (stock) All common stock of a firm owned by a single individual.

pro forma statements Projected, or forecast, income statements and balance sheets.

probability The *chance* that a given outcome will occur.

probability distribution A model that relates probabilities to the associated outcomes.

proceeds from sale of old asset The cash inflows, net of any *removal* or *cleanup costs*, resulting from the sale of an existing asset.

processing float The time between receipt of a payment and its deposit into the firm's account.

profitability The relationship between revenues and costs generated by using the firm's assets—both current and fixed—in productive activities.

prospectus A portion of a security registration statement that describes the key aspects of the issue, the issuer, and its management and financial position.

proxy battle The attempt by a nonmanagement group to gain control of the management of a firm by soliciting a sufficient number of proxy votes.

proxy statement A statement giving the votes of a stockholder to another party.

Public Company Accounting Oversight Board (PCAOB) A not-for-profit corporation established by the *Sarbanes-Oxley Act of 2002* to protect the interests of investors and further the public interest in the preparation of informative, fair, and independent audit reports.

public offering The nonexclusive sale of either bonds or stocks to the general public.

publicly owned (stock) Common stock of a firm owned by a broad group of unrelated individual or institutional investors.

putable bonds Bonds that can be redeemed at par (typically, $1,000) at the option of their holder either at specific dates after the date of issue and every 1 to 5 years thereafter or when and if the firm takes specified actions, such as being acquired, acquiring another company, or issuing a large amount of additional debt. In return for its conferring the right to "put the bond" at specified times or when the firm takes certain actions, the bond's yield is lower than that on a nonputable bond.

quarterly compounding Compounding of interest over four periods within the year.

quick (acid-test) ratio A measure of liquidity calculated by dividing the firm's current assets minus inventory by its current liabilities.

range A measure of an asset's risk, which is found by subtracting the pessimistic (worst) outcome from the optimistic (best) outcome.

ranking approach The ranking of capital expenditure projects on the basis of some predetermined measure, such as the rate of return.

ratio analysis Involves methods of calculating and interpreting financial ratios to analyze and monitor the firm's performance.

real options Opportunities that are embedded in capital projects that enable managers to alter their cash flows and risk in a way that affects project acceptability (NPV). Also called *strategic options*.

real rate of interest The rate that creates an equilibrium between the supply of savings and the demand for investment funds in a perfect world, without inflation, where funds suppliers and demanders are indifferent to the term of loans or investments and have no liquidity preference, and where all outcomes are certain.

recaptured depreciation The portion of an asset's sale price that is above its book value and below its initial purchase price.

recovery period The appropriate depreciable life of a particular asset as determined by MACRS.

red herring A preliminary prospectus made available to prospective investors during the waiting period between the registration statement's filing with the SEC and its approval.

regular dividend policy A dividend policy based on the payment of a fixed-dollar dividend in each period.

relevant cash flows The *incremental cash outflow (investment) and resulting subsequent inflows* associated with a proposed capital expenditure.

reorder point The point at which to reorder inventory, expressed as days of lead time × daily usage.

required return The cost of funds obtained by selling an ownership interest; it reflects the funds supplier's level of expected return.

required total financing Amount of funds needed by the firm if the ending cash for the period is less than the desired minimum cash balance; typically represented by notes payable.

residual theory of dividends A school of thought that suggests that the dividend paid by a firm should be viewed as a *residual*—the amount left over after all acceptable investment opportunities have been undertaken.

restrictive covenants Provisions in a *bond indenture* that place operating and financial constraints on the borrower.

retained earnings The cumulative total of all earnings, net of dividends, that have been retained and reinvested in the firm since its inception; earnings not distributed to owners as dividends—a form of *internal* financing.

return The total gain or loss experienced on an investment over a given period of time; calculated by dividing the asset's cash distributions during the period, plus change in value, by its beginning-of-period investment value.

return on common equity (ROE) Measures the return earned on the common stockholders' investment in the firm.

return on total assets (ROA) Measures the overall effectiveness of management in generating profits with its available assets; also called the *return on investment (ROI)*.

reverse stock split A method used to raise the market price of a firm's stock by exchanging a certain number of outstanding shares for one new share.

revolving credit agreement A line of credit *guaranteed* to a borrower by a commercial bank regardless of the scarcity of money.

rights Financial instruments that permit stockholders to purchase additional shares at a price below the market price, in direct proportion to their number of owned shares.

risk The chance of financial loss or, more formally, the *variability of returns associated with a given asset*.

risk (in capital budgeting) The chance that a project will prove unacceptable or, more formally, the degree of variability of cash flows.

risk (of technical insolvency) The probability that a firm will be unable to pay its bills as they come due.

risk premium The amount by which the interest rate or required return on a security exceeds the risk-free rate of interest R_F; it varies with specific issuer and issue characteristics.

risk-adjusted discount rate (RADR) The rate of return that must be earned on a given project to compensate the firm's owners adequately—that is, to maintain or improve the firm's share price.

risk-averse The attitude toward risk in which an increased return would be required for an increase in risk.

risk-free rate of interest, R_F The required return on a risk-free asset, typically a 3-month *U.S. Treasury bill (T-bill)*.

risk-free rate of return, R_F The required return on a *risk-free asset*, typically a 3-month *U.S. Treasury bill*.

S corporation (S corp) A tax-reporting entity that (under Subchapter S of the Internal Revenue Code) allows certain corporations with 100 or fewer stockholders to choose to be taxed as partnerships. Its stockholders receive the organizational benefits of a corporation and the tax advantages of a partnership. But S corps lose certain tax advantages related to pension plans.

safety stock Extra inventory that is held to prevent stockouts of important items.

sales forecast The prediction of the firm's sales over a given period, based on external and/or internal data; used as the key input to the short-term financial planning process.

Sarbanes-Oxley Act of 2002 (SOX) An act aimed at eliminating corporate disclosure and conflict of interest. Contains provisions about corporate financial disclosures and the relationships among corporations, analysts, auditors, attorneys, directors, officers, and shareholders.

scenario analysis A behavioral approach that evaluates the impact on the firm's return of simultaneous changes in a number of variables.

seasonal funding requirement An investment in operating assets that varies over time as a result of cyclic sales.

secondary market Financial market in which preowned securities (those that are not new issues) are traded.

secured short-term financing Short-term financing (loan) that has specific assets pledged as collateral.

Securities and Exchange Commission (SEC) The federal regulatory body that governs the sale and listing of securities.

securities exchanges Organizations that provide the marketplace in which firms can raise funds through the sale of new securities and purchasers can resell securities.

security agreement The agreement between the borrower and the lender that specifies the collateral held against a secured loan.

security market line (SML) The depiction of the *capital asset pricing model* (*CAPM*) as a graph that reflects the required return in the marketplace for each level of nondiversifiable risk (beta).

selling group A large number of brokerage firms that join the originating investment banker(s); each accepts responsibility for selling a certain portion of a new security issue on a commission basis.

semiannual compounding Compounding of interest over two periods within the year.

short-term (operating) financial plans Specify short-term financial actions and the anticipated impact of those actions.

short-term financial management Management of current assets and current liabilities.

short-term, self-liquidating loan An unsecured short-term loan in which the use to which the borrowed money is put provides the mechanism through which the loan is repaid.

signal A financing action by management that is believed to reflect its view of the firm's stock value; generally, debt financing is viewed as a *positive signal* that management believes the stock is "undervalued," and

a stock issue is viewed as a *negative signal* that management believes the stock is "overvalued."

simulation A statistics-based behavioral approach that applies predetermined probability distributions and random numbers to estimate risky outcomes.

single-payment note A short-term, one-time loan made to a borrower who needs funds for a specific purpose for a short period.

sinking-fund requirement A restrictive provision often included in a bond indenture, providing for the systematic retirement of bonds prior to their maturity.

small (ordinary) stock dividend A stock dividend representing less than 20 to 25 percent of the common stock outstanding when the dividend is declared.

sole proprietorship A business owned by one person and operated for his or her own profit.

spontaneous liabilities Financing that arises from the normal course of business; the two major short-term sources of such liabilities are accounts payable and accruals.

stakeholders Groups such as employees, customers, suppliers, creditors, owners, and others who have a direct economic link to the firm.

standard debt provisions Provisions in a *bond indenture* specifying certain record-keeping and general business practices that the bond issuer must follow; normally, they do not place a burden on a financially sound business.

standard deviation (σ_r) The most common statistical indicator of an asset's risk; it measures the dispersion around the *expected value.*

statement of cash flows Provides a summary of the firm's operating, investment, and financing cash flows and reconciles them with changes in its cash and marketable securities during the period.

statement of retained earnings Reconciles the net income earned during a given year, and any cash dividends paid, with the change in retained earnings between the start and the end of that year. An abbreviated form of the *statement of stockholders' equity.*

statement of stockholders' equity Shows all equity account transactions that occur during a given year.

stock dividend The payment, to existing owners, of a dividend in the form of stock.

stock options An incentive allowing managers to purchase stock at the market price set at the time of the grant.

stock purchase warrants Instruments that give their holders the right to purchase a certain number of shares of the issuer's common stock at a specified price over a certain period of time.

stock repurchase   The repurchase by the firm of outstanding common stock in the marketplace; desired effects of stock repurchases are that they either enhance shareholder value or help to discourage an unfriendly takeover.

stock split   A method commonly used to lower the market price of a firm's stock by increasing the number of shares belonging to each shareholder.

stockholders   The owners of a corporation, whose ownership, or *equity,* is evidenced by either common stock or preferred stock.

stockholders' report   Annual report that publicly owned corporations must provide to stockholders; it summarizes and documents the firm's financial activities during the past year.

stretching accounts payable   Paying bills as late as possible without damaging the firm's credit rating.

subordinated debentures   Claims are not satisfied until those of the creditors holding certain (senior) debts have been fully satisfied.

subordination   In a bond indenture, the stipulation that subsequent creditors agree to wait until all claims of the *senior debt* are satisfied.

sunk costs   Cash outlays that have already been made (past outlays) and therefore have no effect on the cash flows relevant to a current decision.

supervoting shares   Stock that carries with it multiple votes per share rather than the single vote per share typically given on regular shares of common stock.

target capital structure   The desired optimal mix of debt and equity financing that most firms attempt to maintain.

target dividend-payout ratio   A dividend policy under which the firm attempts to pay out a certain *percentage* of earnings as a stated dollar dividend and adjusts that dividend toward a target payout as proven earnings increases occur.

target weights   Either book or market value weights based on *desired* capital structure proportions.

tax on sale of old asset   Tax that depends on the relationship among the old asset's sale price, initial purchase price, and *book value,* and on existing government tax rules.

technically insolvent   Describes a firm that is unable to pay its bills as they come due.

tender offer   A formal offer to purchase a given number of shares of a firm's stock at a specified price.

term structure of interest rates   The relationship between the interest rate or rate of return and the time to maturity.

terminal cash flow   The after-tax nonoperating cash flow occurring in the final year of a project. It is usually attributable to liquidation of the project.

time line   A horizontal line on which time zero appears at the leftmost end and future periods are marked from left to right; can be used to depict investment cash flows.

times interest earned ratio   Measures the firm's ability to make contractual interest payments; sometimes called the *interest coverage ratio.*

time-series analysis   Evaluation of the firm's financial performance over time using financial ratio analysis.

total asset turnover   Indicates the efficiency with which the firm uses its assets to generate sales.

total cost of inventory   The sum of order costs and carrying costs of inventory.

total leverage   The potential use of *fixed costs, both operating and financial,* to magnify the effect of changes in sales on the firm's earnings per share.

total risk   The combination of a security's *nondiversifiable* and *diversifiable risk.*

transfer prices   Prices that subsidiaries charge each other for the goods and services traded between them.

treasurer   The firm's chief financial manager, who is responsible for the firm's financial activities, such as financial planning and fund raising, making capital expenditure decisions, and managing cash, credit, the pension fund, and foreign exchange.

treasury stock   The number of shares of outstanding stock that have been repurchased by the firm.

trust receipt inventory loan   A secured short-term loan against inventory under which the lender advances 80 to 100 percent of the cost of the borrower's relatively expensive inventory items in exchange for the borrower's promise to repay the lender, with accrued interest, immediately after the sale of each item of collateral.

trustee   A paid individual, corporation, or commercial bank trust department that acts as the third party to a bond indenture and can take specified actions on behalf of the bondholders if the terms of the indenture are violated.

two-bin method   Unsophisticated inventory-monitoring technique that is typically applied to C group items and involves reordering inventory when one of two bins is empty.

uncorrelated   Describes two series that lack any interaction and therefore have a correlation coefficient close to zero.

U.S. Treasury bills (T-bills)   Short-term IOUs issued by the U.S. Treasury; considered the *risk-free asset.*

underpriced Stock sold at a price below its current market price, P_0.

underwriting The role of the *investment banker* in bearing the risk of reselling, at a profit, the securities purchased from an issuing corporation at an agreed-on price.

underwriting syndicate A group formed by an investment banker to share the financial risk associated with *underwriting* new securities.

unlimited funds The financial situation in which a firm is able to accept all independent projects that provide an acceptable return.

unlimited liability The condition of a sole proprietorship (or general partnership) allowing the owner's total wealth to be taken to satisfy creditors.

unsecured short-term financing Short-term financing obtained without pledging specific assets as collateral.

valuation The process that links risk and return to determine the worth of an asset.

variable-growth model A dividend valuation approach that allows for a change in the dividend growth rate.

venture capital Privately raised external equity capital used to fund early-stage firms with attractive growth prospects.

venture capitalists (VCs) Providers of venture capital; typically, formal businesses that maintain strong oversight over the firms they invest in and that have clearly defined exit strategies.

warehouse receipt loan A secured short-term loan against inventory under which the lender receives control of the pledged inventory collateral, which is stored by a designated warehousing company on the lender's behalf.

weighted average cost of capital (WACC), r_a Reflects the expected average future cost of funds over the long run; found by weighting the cost of each specific type of capital by its proportion in the firm's capital structure.

weighted marginal cost of capital (WMCC) The firm's weighted average cost of capital (WACC) associated with its *next dollar* of total new financing.

weighted marginal cost of capital (WMCC) schedule Graph that relates the firm's weighted average cost of capital to the level of total new financing.

wire transfer An electronic communication that, via bookkeeping entries, removes funds from the payer's bank and deposits them in the payee's bank.

working capital Current assets, which represent the portion of investment that circulates from one form to another in the ordinary conduct of business.

yield curve A graph of the relationship between the debt's remaining time to maturity (x axis) and its yield to maturity (y axis); it shows the yield to maturity for debts of equal quality and different maturities. Graphically depicts the *term structure of interest rates*.

yield to maturity Compound annual rate of return earned on a debt security purchased on a given day and held to maturity.

zero- (or low-) coupon bonds Issued with no (zero) or a very low coupon (stated interest) rate and sold at a large discount from par. A significant portion (or all) of the investor's return comes from gain in value (i.e., par value minus purchase price). Generally callable at par value. Because the issuer can annually deduct the current year's interest accrual without having to pay the interest until the bond matures (or is called), its cash flow each year is increased by the amount of the tax shield provided by the interest deduction.

zero-balance account (ZBA) A disbursement account that always has an end-of-day balance of zero because the firm deposits money to cover checks drawn on the account only as they are presented for payment each day.

zero-growth model An approach to dividend valuation that assumes a constant, nongrowing dividend stream.

Index